S0-AEY-480

THE CHRISTIANIZATION OF ICELAND

THE CHRISTIANIZATION OF ICELAND

PRIESTS, POWER, AND SOCIAL CHANGE 1000–1300

Orri Vésteinsson

BR
994
.V47
2000

OXFORD
UNIVERSITY PRESS

Great Clarendon Street, Oxford OX2 6DP
Oxford University Press is a department of the University of Oxford.
It furthers the University's objective of excellence in research, scholarship,
and education by publishing worldwide in

Oxford New York

Athens Auckland Bangkok Bogotá Buenos Aires Calcutta
Cape Town Chennai Dar es Salaam Delhi Florence Hong Kong Istanbul
Karachi Kuala Lumpur Madrid Melbourne Mexico City Mumbai
Nairobi Paris São Paulo Singapore Taipei Tokyo Toronto Warsaw

and associated companies in Berlin Ibadan

Oxford is a registered trade mark of Oxford University Press
in the UK and certain other countries

Published in the United States
by Oxford University Press Inc., New York

© Orri Vésteinsson 2000

The moral rights of the author have been asserted
Database right Oxford University Press (maker)

First published 2000

All rights reserved. No part of this publication may be reproduced,
stored in a retrieval system, or transmitted, in any form or by any means,
without the prior permission in writing of Oxford University Press,
or as expressly permitted by law, or under terms agreed with the appropriate
reprographics rights organizations. Enquiries concerning reproduction
outside the scope of the above should be sent to the Rights Department,
Oxford University Press, at the address above

You must not circulate this book in any other binding or cover
and you must impose the same condition on any acquirer

British Library Cataloguing in Publication Data
Data available

Library of Congress Cataloging in Publication Data
Vésteinsson, Orri.
The Christianization of Iceland: priests, power, and
social change, 1000–1300/Orri Vésteinsson
Based on the author's thesis (Ph.D.)—University of London, 1996.
Includes bibliographical references (p.) and index.
1. Iceland—Church history. 2. Social structure—Iceland—History–To 1500.
I. Title.
BR994,V47 2000
274.912′04–dc21 99-048333

ISBN 0–19–820799–9

1 3 5 7 9 10 8 6 4 2

Typeset by J&L Composition Ltd, Filey, North Yorkshire
Printed in Great Britain
on acid-free paper by
T.J. International Ltd,
Padstow, Cornwall

This book is dedicated to the memory of my grandmother Helga Jónsdóttir Proppé who introduced me to history

PREFACE

This book is based on my Ph.D. thesis which I defended at the University of London in 1996. Although I did resist the urge to rewrite it completely, the text has seen some reshuffling and considerable revision. The revisions owe much to my examiners David d'Avray and Gunnar Karlsson who identified many faults which I have been able to put right. In particular I am indebted to Gunnar Karlsson who gave me a long list of comments and suggestions which has been an invaluable help in the revision process.

In revising the text I have omitted much of the technical discussion of the thesis in order to make the text more readable. Instead a list of terms has been inserted after the Bibliography where Icelandic terms and other concepts relating to medieval Iceland which are used in the text are explained, and short descriptions are given of the main sources used.

Most of the conventions used are self-explanatory. Names of medieval Icelanders are spelt in standardized Old Icelandic. Icelandic place-names are spelt in modern Icelandic. All place-names are followed by an indicator of the region they are in, and can be found in the maps at the end of the book. The majority of names given to individual families in the twelfth and thirteenth centuries are modern constructs (Karlsson 1994). The names used here are based on the genealogical tables in *SturlR* ii.

Since I finished my studies in London in 1995 I have, as Head of Research and Training at the Institute of Archaeology, Iceland, been fortunate to be able to continue my research into medieval Iceland. This research has, however, mainly been into other aspects of Icelandic society—I have hardly ever had occasion to refer to the sagas of the Sturlunga compilation or the sagas of the bishops—and as a result my thinking on the subjects dealt with in this book has not developed much. Aided by an award from the Gjöf Jóns Sigurðssonar I was able to take time off in the first months of 1999 to work on the manuscript of this book. As it is in essence the same work as my thesis it is in order to mention some of the people on whom I was able to rely for assistance and advice during the course of my original research. My greatest debt is to my supervisor, Wendy Davies, an inspiring teacher and a relentless rectifier of sloppy thought. I have benefited greatly from the unwaveringly constructive critique of my good friend and colleague, Agnes S. Arnórsdóttir. As if the occasional pint with Peter Foote was not enough intellectual luck, the text, and many a translation, has been greatly improved by his suggestions. I am also grateful to Svanhildur Óskarsdóttir, Richard Perkins, and Þorsteinn Vilhjálmsson for their many comments and suggestions. Needless to say, I alone am responsible for the mistakes.

I am indebted to Mjöll Snæsdóttir, who taught me most of what I know about archaeology, for profitable discussions and help. I have for a long time attempted to lead a kind of double existence as an archaeologist as well as a historian and I am deeply thankful to Adolf Friðriksson for dragging me into the field every summer. This book would have a very different shape if it were not for those experiences and the consistently fruitful discussions with Adolf.

I would also like to thank my parents for their support and my love, María Reyndal, for being in my life.

CONTENTS

LIST OF FIGURES

In the genealogical tables names in italic indicate a priest and names in bold lettering a chieftain.

LIST OF TABLES

LIST OF MAPS

ABBREVIATIONS

A	Austurland (see Map 4).
Aarbøger	*Aarbøger for nordisk oldkyndighed og historie* (Copenhagen, 1866–).
Adam	*Magistri Adam Bremensis Gesta Hammaburgensis ecclesiae pontificum*, ed. B. Schmeidler, 3rd edn. (Monumenta Germaniae historica, Scriptores rerum Germanicorum; Hanover, 1917).
AÍ	*Alfræði íslenzk: Islandsk encyklopædisk litteratur*, i. *Cod. mbr. AM. 194, 8vo*, ed. K. Kaalund (SUGNL 37; Copenhagen, 1908); ii. *Rímtol*, ed. N. Beckman and K. Kaalund (SUGNL 41; Copenhagen, 1914–16); iii. *Landalýsingar m. fl.*, ed. K. Kaalund (SUGNL 45; Copenhagen, 1917–18).
AM	Arnamagnean collection of manuscripts.
ANF	*Arkiv for nordisk filologi* (Christiania/Lund, 1883–).
ASB	*Altnordische Saga-Bibliothek*, i–xviii (Halle, 1892–1929).
ÁB	*Árna saga biskups*, ed. Þ. Hauksson (*RSÁ* 2; Reykjavík, 1972).
Árbók	*Árbók hins íslenzka fornleifafélags* (Reykjavík, 1881–).
BA	*Bibliotheca Arnamagnæana* (Copenhagen, 1941–).
Bsk	*Biskupa sögur gefnar út af Hinu íslenzka bókmenntafélagi*, i–ii, ed. G. Vigfússon (Copenhagen, 1858–78).
Bysp	*Byskupa sogur*, 1. hefte udgivet af Det kongelige nordiske oldskriftselskab, ed. J. Helgason (Copenhagen, 1938); 2. hefte (EAA 13), ed. Jón Helgason (Copenhagen, 1978).
CCI	*Corpus codicum Islandicorum medii aevi*, i–xx (Copenhagen, 1930–56).
CIC	*Corpus iuris canonici*, i–ii, ed. E. R. Richter, rev. E. Friedberg (Leipzig, 1879).
D	Dalir (see Map 2).
DD	*Diplomatarium Danicum*, 1st series, i–vii (Copenhagen, 1963–90).
DI	*Diplomatarium Islandicum, Íslenzkt fornbréfasafn 834–1600*, i–xvi (Copenhagen and Reykjavík, 1857–1972).
DMA	*Dictionary of the Middle Ages*, i–xiii (New York, 1982–9).
DN	*Diplomatarium Norvegicum*, i–xxi (Christiania and Oslo, 1847–1976).
EAA	Editiones Arnamagnæanæ Series A (Copenhagen, 1958–).
EAB	Editiones Arnamagnæanæ Series B (Copenhagen, 1960–).
EIM	*Early Icelandic Manuscripts in Facsimile* (Copenhagen, 1958–).
En tale	*En tale mot biskopene: En sproglig-historisk undersøkelse* (Skrifter Utgitt av Det Norske Videnskabs-Akademi i Oslo II. Hist.-Filos. Klasse 1930. No. 9), ed. A. Holtsmark (Oslo, 1931).
Flat	*Flateyjarbok: En samling af norske konge-sager*, i–iii, ed. C. Unger and G. Vigfússon (Christiania, 1860–8).
FM	*Fornmannasögur*, i–xii (Copenhagen, 1825–37).
Grg 1a–b	*Grágás: Elzta lögbók Íslendinga. Útgefin eptir skinnbókinni í bókasafni konungs*, 2 vols., ed. V. Finsen (Copenhagen, 1852; repr. with an introduction, Reykjavík, 1945).
Grg II	*Grágás efter det Arnamagnæanske Haandskrift Nr. 334 fol., Stadarhólsbók* (Copenhagen, 1879).

Grg III — *Grágás. Stykker, som findes i det Arnamagnæanske Haandskrift Nr. 351 fol., Skálholtsbók og en Række andre Haandskrifter* (Copenhagen, 1883).

GSB — *Guðmundar sögur biskups*, i. *Ævi Guðmundar biskups. Guðmundarsaga A* (EAB 6), ed. S. Karlsson (Copenhagen, 1983).

H — *Hauksbók.*

HakAM81 — *Hakonar saga Hakonarsonar in Det Arnamagnæanske håndskrift 81A Fol (Skálholtsbók yngsta)*, ed. A. Kjær and L. Holm-Olsen (Christiania and Oslo, 1910–86).

Hauksbók — *Hauksbók udgiven efter de Arnamagnæanske håndskrifter No. 371, 544 og 675, 4° samt forskellige papirshåndskrifter*, ed. E. Jónsson and F. Jónsson (Copenhagen, 1892–6).

HE — Finni Johannæi, *Historia ecclesiastica Islandiæ*, i–iv (Havniæ, 1772–8).

HMS — *Heilagramanna søgur: Fortællinger og legender om hællige mænd og kvinder*, i–ii, ed. C. R. Unger (Christiania, 1877).

HT — *Historisk tidskrift utgitt av den norske historiske forening* (Christiania and Oslo, 1871–).

IA — *Islandske Annaler indtil 1578*, ed. G. Storm (Christiania, 1888).

Icel. Sagas — *Icelandic Sagas and Other Historical Documents relating to the Settlements and Descents of the Northmen on the British Isles*, i–ii, ed. G. Vigfússon (London, 1887).

ÍBS — *Íslensk bókmenntasaga*, i–ii, ed. V. Ólason (Reykjavík, 1992–3).

ÍF — *Íslenzk fornrit* (Reykjavík, 1933–).

ÍÞ — *Íslensk þjóðmenning*, i, v–vii (Reykjavík, 1987–90).

JÁM — *Jarðabók Árna Magnússonar og Páls Vidalíns*, i–xi (Copenhagen, 1913–43), xii–xiii (Reykjavík, 1990).

JJ — *Jarðatal á Íslandi með brauðalýsingum, fólkstölu í hreppum og prestaköllum, ágripi af búnaðartöflum 1835–1845, og skýrslum um sölu þjóðjarða á landinu*, ed. J. Johnsen (Copenhagen, 1847).

KHL — *Kulturhistorisk leksikon for nordisk middelalder*, i–xxii (Reykjavík, 1956–78).

KLN — *Kirke leksikon for Norden*, i–iv, ed. F. Nielsen and J. O. Andersen (Copenhagen, 1900–29).

KVHAA — Kungliga vitterhets historie och antikvitets akademien, Stockholm.

Lat.dok — *Latinske dokumenter til norsk historie*, ed. E. Vandvik (Oslo, 1952).

LEI — *Laws of Early Iceland: Grágás*, i. *The Codex Regius of Grágás with Material from Other Manuscripts*, trans. A. Dennis, P. Foote, and R. Perkins (University of Manitoba Icelandic Studies, 3; Winnipeg, 1980).

Messk — *Messuskýringar: Liturgisk symbolik frå den norsk-islandske kyrkja i millomalderen*, part 1, O. Kolsrud (Oslo, 1952).

MHN — *Monumenta historica Norwegiæ: Latinske kildeskrifter til Norges historie i middelalderen*, ed. G. Storm (Christiania, 1880).

Mork — *Morkinskinna*, ed. F. Jónsson (SUGNL 53; Copenhagen, 1932).

MS — *Medieval Scandinavia*, 1–11 (Odense, 1968–82).

N — Norðurland (see Map 5).

NBL — *Norsk biografisk leksikon*, i–xxviii (Oslo, 1923–77).

NgL — *Norges gamle love indtil 1387*, i–v (Christiania, 1846–95).

NID — E. H. Lind, *Norsk-Isländska dopnamn ock fingerade namn från medeltiden* (Uppsala, 1905–15).

NIDs E. H. Lind, *Norsk-Isländska dopnamn ock fingerade namn från medeltiden, Supplementband* (Oslo, 1931).

No.Dipl. *Norske diplomer til og med år 1300* (Corpus codicum norvegicorum medii aevi, folio serie 2), ed. F. Hødnebø (Oslo, 1960).

Ob.Isl. *Íslenzkar ártíðaskrár eða Obituaria Islandica*, ed. J. Þorkelsson (Copenhagen, 1893–6).

OGNS Johan Fristzner, *Ordbog over det gamle norske sprog*, i–iii (Christiania, 1886–96).

OGNS IV *Ordbog over det gamle norske sprog: Rettelser og tillegg*, ed. F. Hødnebø (Oslo, 1972).

ONPR *Ordbog over det norrøne prosasprog. Registre: A Dictionary of Old Norse Prose. Indices* (Copenhagen, 1989).

ÓSHS *Saga Óláfs konungs hins helga: Den store saga om Olav den hellige*, ed. O. A. Johnsen and J. Helgason (Oslo, 1941).

ÓST *Óláfs saga Tryggvasonar en mesta*, i–ii, ed. Ó. Halldórsson (EAA 1–2; Copenhagen, 1958–61).

PP Sveinn Níelsson, *Prestatal og prófasta*, 2nd edn. (Reykjavík, 1950).

RGA *Reallexikon der germanischen Altertumskunde. 2. völlig neu bearbeitete und stark erweiterte Auflage* (Berlin, 1973–).

RHÍ *Rit Handritastofnunar Íslands* (Reykjavík, 1958–69).

RSÁ *Rit Stofnunar Árna Magnússonar á Íslandi* (Reykjavík, 1972–).

S Suðurland (see Map 3).

SI *Studia Islandica* (Reykjavík, 1937–).

Skjald *Den norsk-islandske skjaldedigtning*, A. *Tekst efter handskriftene*, i–ii, ed. F. Jónsson (Copenhagen, 1912–15).

SÓT *Saga Óláfs Tryggvasonar af Oddr Snorrason munk*, ed. F. Jónsson (Copenhagen, 1932).

SS *Scandinavian Studies* (Lawrence, Kan., 1911–).

StSÍ *Safn til sögu Íslands og íslenzkra bókmennta*, i–vi (Copenhagen and Reykjavík, 1856–1939).

Sturl *Sturlunga saga. Árna saga biskups. Hrafns saga Sveinbjarnarsonar hin sérstaka*, ed. Ö. Thorsson (Reykjavík, 1988).

SturlK *Sturlunga saga*, i–ii. *Efter membranen Króksfjarðarbók. Udfyldt efter Reykjafjarðarbók*, ed. K. Kaalund (Copenhagen, 1906–11).

SturlR *Sturlunga saga*, i–ii, ed. J. Jóhannesson, M. Finnbogason, and K. Eldjárn (Reykjavík, 1946).

SUGNL Samfund til udgivelse af gammel nordisk litteratur, Copenhagen.

Sv *Sverris saga etter Cod. AM 327 4º*, ed. G. Indrebø (Christiania, 1920).

THÍB *Tímarit hins íslenzka bókmenntafélags*, 1–24 (Reykjavík, 1880–1904).

TMM *Tímarit Máls og menningar* (Reykjavík, 1938–).

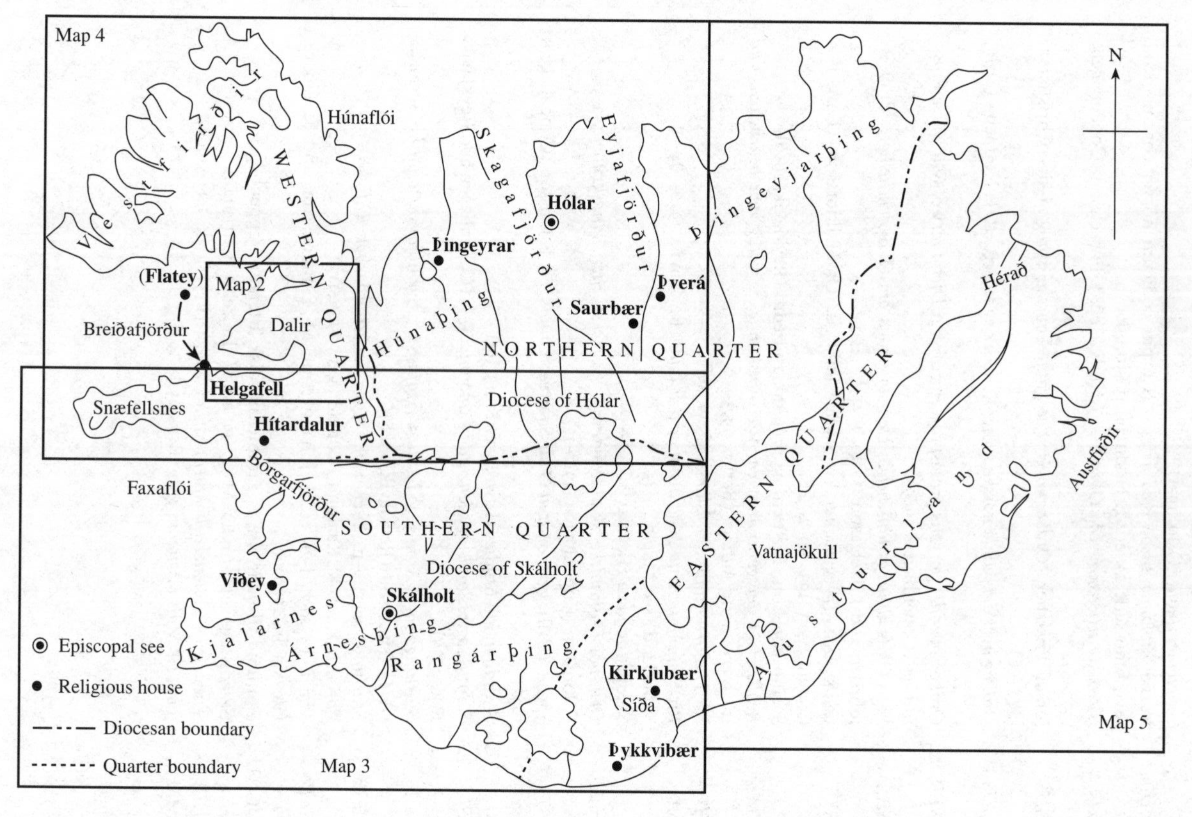

MAP 1. *Iceland: showing quarters and regions*

Introduction

Any student of late medieval Europe would have little difficulty in recognizing the administration and judicial system of fourteenth-century Icelandic society. Apart from the economic base, which was sedentary-pastoral rather than agrarian, Icelandic society was structured much like any other poor, remote, and isolated part of a European kingdom. It was governed by a distant king who appointed sheriffs and tax-collectors but who had otherwise little influence, or interest for that matter. Real political power lay in the hands of a landed gentry, a small group of church magnates, and another small group of royal administrators. The Church was by far the largest landowner but secular land was to a large extent in the hands of no more than a dozen families. This was a poor and apparently simple society; there were no great resources to fight over or hostile neighbours to be wary of. The documents this society produced about itself were of the dull sort; deeds of property transfer, church-charters, marriage contracts, and wills. Together with the annals, the writing of which was waning in the fourteenth century, these documents are the principal sources for Icelandic society in the late middle ages. They differed from comparable documents from the same period in Europe only in that they were written in the vernacular.

This is a society which most students of the slightly earlier period, the high medieval society of the Icelandic Sagas, would be hard put to recognize. The saga literature describes a completely different society; a society with no administration, no centralized authority or executive power and a church dominated by secular interests. The rules governing conflict were very different and power structures were at best unstable and usually completely chaotic. The sagas, both those describing Iceland's heroic past and those describing contemporary or near-contemporary events, were for the most part written in the thirteenth century. It is clear from these sagas that Icelandic society was undergoing fundamental changes in the twelfth and thirteenth centuries.

It is with these changes this book is concerned. The objective is to identify and describe the mechanisms which made Icelandic society change. The simplest way to approach this is to study the formation of the institutions of this society which in turn is best examined in the context of the Church. The Church was the dominating power in late medieval Iceland and its introduction must have affected the structure of the simple society which had been established in Iceland by the eleventh century. The Church is also the most obvious channel through which ideas were transmitted to Iceland and all the sources for Icelandic society were produced directly or indirectly in association with the

Church. It is therefore in every aspect natural to attempt to describe the development of Icelandic society from the eleventh to the end of the thirteenth century by examining the development and growth of the Church.

There is another dimension to this approach. It is the question of what defines a Christian society, a question most students of Christian missions and conversions must sooner or later grapple with. It is obvious that a mass-conversion like the one which took place in Iceland in AD 1000 did not change the nature of society overnight. It is through examining the growth of ecclesiastical institutions and their interaction with society, and its power structures in particular, that we can get an idea of how Christian societies came into being and how the Church affected the societies in which it became established.

In Scandinavian history writing of the high middle ages it is conventional to contrast Church and State as diametrically opposed entities with different agendas, the friction between which dominated high-level political conflict in the twelfth and thirteenth centuries. This view presupposes that the State had an identity of its own and that the Church also was a corporate entity, and that both were aware of the different interests and aims of each other. This view is of course perfectly applicable when the two were in conflict, as in Norway in the late twelfth century when King Sverrir and Archbishop Eiríkr struggled over the limits of the Church's sphere of power or in Iceland in the late thirteenth century when control over church property became a bone of contention between Bishop Árni Þorláksson and leaders of the secular aristocracy.

While different in detail these disputes all follow the same general pattern and all in the end were resolved in favour of the Church. Furthermore, all broke out in periods when royal power was consolidating in the respective countries, and although the issues were always settled in favour of the Church it is also true to say that royal authority emerged stronger as a consequence. The conflict between *regnum et sacerdotium* therefore resulted in two fairly well defined institutions each with its own identity and agenda. This of course conforms well with the government of other European countries in the high and late middle ages, but it begs the question of how this came about. What was government like before the dual hegemony of Church and King became established?

The classical view is that royal authority always existed, at least from the beginning of the Viking age onwards, and that it simply became more effective/burdensome/visible according to which school of thought one belongs, in the course of the twelfth and thirteenth centuries. The Church is normally seen as a most important agent in this development. It furnished the kings with a royal ideology and to begin with it supported them against the autonomous chieftains or barons who formerly had held real power. In this context the Church is almost always seen as having a corporate identity, capable of having uniform and long-term interests and following them through. Those who take a negative view of its influence would see it as a parasite imported from abroad, which although frail in the beginning steadily grew in influence until it became equal to its host in size and power. Those who take a more positive view also see the

Church as a foreign import which gradually grew as society learnt to appreciate its offerings: its humanizing influence on government and legislation and the stability and order that eventually permeated society through its efforts. Most modern scholars take up their positions somewhere in-between these two extremes and most try to avoid such subjective reasoning. It remains that the Church is always seen as an independent and imported agent which has a clear identity and agenda of its own from the outset.

In Icelandic historiography it is usually assumed that from the beginning the men of the Church were quite conscious of their separate identity and that there was a fairly well-defined division between the secular and ecclesiastical spheres. Representing the traditional stance is Magnús Stefánsson who thinks that in the eleventh and twelfth centuries ecclesiastical institutions like the *staðir* (major land-owning churches—for this and other Icelandic terms used see the list of terms at the end of the main text) were established by a self-conscious clergy, whereas in the thirteenth century the *staðir* came under the influence of laymen who began to treat them as their private property. This view is clearly coloured by the sources which view the late eleventh and early twelfth century as the golden age of Icelandic Christianity (see Ch. 2, s. 1) but it also stresses the particular Icelandicness of the Church in the twelfth century. Bishops Ísleifr (1056–80) and Gizurr (1082–1118), St Jón (1106–21), and the priest Sæmundr *fróði* (d. 1133) are seen to have imported Christian institutions and quite consciously adjusted them to Icelandic circumstances. The differences between these institutions and what is seen as established practice elsewhere are seen as conscious choices of Icelanders committed to developing their own national church (Stefánsson 1975: 69, 72, 97, 98, 111–18).

This view has its roots in nationalistic historiography and although it was developed as late as the 1970s it probably does not have many adherents now. The opposition has been slow in pointing out the weaknesses in the traditional view. It is most clearly represented by Sveinbjörn Rafnsson (1975: 220; also 1982*a*: 94–101; 1979*b*) whose emphasis and arguments are analogous with the diffusionist view of the origins of Icelandic medieval literature (B. Einarsson 1961; L. Lönnroth 1965; T. M. Andersson 1964, 1967; Clover 1982; Tómasson 1988*a*). According to this view Icelandic medieval literature owes less to the circumstances of Icelandic society than to the supra-national Christian culture of medieval Europe. Similarly Sveinbjörn Rafnsson stresses that the Church in Iceland was primarily a vehicle for influence from abroad; that there was nothing national about it and that real Icelandic churchmen like St Þorlákr (bishop of Skálholt, 1178–93) and Guðmundr Arason (bishop of Hólar, 1203–37) strove to free the Church from secular influence much in the same way as the reforming church was trying elsewhere in Europe in the eleventh and twelfth centuries.

In-between these extremes is the view of Helgi Þorláksson (1982*a*) who still sees the Church and the chieftains in conflict but denies the notion of a 'national church' and stresses the eagerness of the Icelandic chieftains to co-operate with the Church for much of the thirteenth century. All these views assume that the Church had a corporate identity at least from around 1100, that there was a body of men conscious of their special role as men of the Church, and that this role was seen as separate from the interests of secular society.

The principal aim of this book is to challenge this view and show that it took a long time for the Nordic church to gain an identity of its own, and that before it did, the Church was simply one aspect of life—an aspect which grew in importance because of its intrinsic need to organize itself and conditions around it. The emphasis on uniformity and constancy in the interpretation of the scriptures and celebration of the rites which is inherent to the Christian religion makes it necessary for it to establish organization and hierarchies where there were none before. Those who established the first Christian institutions, the first bishops and the first abbots, did not foresee that the end product of their labours—one or two centuries later—would be an autonomous institution with its own jurisdiction, its own property, and an institutionalized influence over the governance of the State. Their objectives were much more humble and in no way can they be seen as hostile to the existing societal structure. There were of course aspects of society, notably those associated with heathen practices, which the early church struggled against, but in general it is safe to say that the first generations of indigenous churchmen viewed their society as a unitary phenomenon and they viewed their task as one of adding to the cohesion and quality of this society. It was the fruit of their labours, the institutional structures which they created, which allowed secular rulers to begin to extend their influence. The development of institutional structures is an issue of particular relevance in relatively poor and under-populated countries like Scandinavia where surplus wealth was insufficient and not concentrated enough for complex secular structures to develop on their own. It was only after secular rulers began to use ecclesiastical structures as leverage to increase the sway and permanence of their powers, or, which was equally or more often the case, churchmen began to be able to use ecclesiastical structures to increase their temporal influence, that there arose a friction between the two. From that point onwards there was still a long way to go before the Church developed a corporate identity and an ideology matching it.

Historical inquiry into high-medieval Iceland is traditionally concerned mainly with its constitution and its constitutional development. For non-Icelandic students of the Commonwealth from Maurer to Miller the fascination has been with the constitution/societal structure as described in the sagas and the laws, while Icelandic historians have been more concerned to explain the development of this society and the changes which led to the union with Norway in 1262–4. Although it can hardly be classified as a state, high-medieval Icelandic society was clearly a constitutional entity and there is widespread agreement that this entity came into being within a century of the first Norsemen settling on the island. The date given by the twelfth-century chronicler

Ari *fróði* for the establishment of an assembly for the whole country, the Alþing at Þingvellir (S), was 930 (*ÍF* i. 8–9). According to Ari the country was divided into jurisdictions in a constitutional reform around 965 (*ÍF* i. 11–12). With the conversion in 999/1000 and the establishment of the fifth court, a court of final instance, in 1004–30 (*ÍF* i. 19; *Grg 1a*, 77–83) it is usually assumed that the Icelandic constitution had acquired the shape it would stay in until it began to disintegrate in the twelfth century. The union with Norway in 1262–4 which had been preceded by a phase of extremely violent conflict, the *Sturlungaöld* or Age of the Sturlungs 1220–62, is then seen as the final collapse of the indigenous constitutional order which had been established more than three centuries earlier.

Within Icelandic historiography the emphasis has been squarely on identifying the factors which contributed to the disintegration and demise of this order. This debate has revolved around the concepts of independence and subjection and has at its roots the concerns of the generations of historians who lived through the struggle for independence from 1830 to 1944. Enough time has, however, lapsed from the proclamation of the republic in 1944 for a redefinition of interests to be in order.

To the present author it is far from clear what it was the Icelanders lost in 1262–4; losing independence in the sense that they acknowledged a Norwegian king is a rather subtle constitutional point which was far more meaningful in the nineteenth century than the thirteenth. On the other hand it is obvious what they obtained: a king, executive power, a new judicial system, and a revised and updated law code. In other words they obtained the raw material of statehood and the means to keep peace. It is clear that Icelandic society was changing in the course of the twelfth and thirteenth centuries, but instead of seeing these changes as a disintegration of an established order the view is taken here that the upheavals of the twelfth and thirteenth centuries were rather symptoms of a society in the process of establishing more permanent structures of government.

Except for Ari *fróði*'s chronicle *Íslendingabók*, which was written in 1122–33, all our sources for the history of high-medieval Icelandic society, both legal and narrative, were produced in the thirteenth century or later. The beginnings of writing and bookkeeping in the vernacular are usually traced back to around 1100. By this time a cathedral school had been established in Skálholt (S) and instruction of priests was taking place at major *staðir* like Oddi (S) and Haukadalur (S). Another cathedral school was established in the new bishopric at Hólar (N) in 1106. Literacy was therefore on the increase and with it arose both the need to have things in writing and a market for books, and, just as importantly, an audience which could be influenced more easily than before. In 1117–18 a project was initiated the aim of which was to codify the law. In that year the Treatment of Homicide section was committed to parchment and it is usually assumed that the rest of the laws were written down in the following years. A Christian law section was composed by Bishops Þorlákr of Skálholt (1118–33) and Ketill of Hólar (1122–45) with the advice of Archbishop Özurr of Lund. The law of the Commonwealth, *Grágás*, survives however only in late thirteenth-century versions. Apart from *Íslendingabók*, Ari *fróði* (d. 1148) is also associated with a list of high-born Icelandic priests from 1143 and may have written a Life of Snorri *goði*, an early eleventh-century chieftain, both of which survive. Furthermore, he is thought to have compiled a first version of *Landnámabók* or *Book of Settlements* but after his day interest in Icelandic history seems to have waned. Instead there followed the writing of sagas of Norwegian kings and it was not until the beginning of the thirteenth century that works on Icelandic matters re-emerge. Among the first of these were the Latin Lives of the two indigenous saints, St Þorlákr and St Jón. Both were later translated into the vernacular. Ecclesiastical enthusiasm in the opening years of the thirteenth century is also witnessed by *Hungrvaka*, a chronicle of the bishops of Skálholt and a saga of Bishop Páll (1195–1211). To this period belong also the earliest Contemporary Sagas, *Sturlu saga* and *Guðmundar saga dýra*, which both deal with political struggle in the second half of the twelfth century. Most of the Contemporary Sagas as well as the Sagas of Icelanders were written towards the middle and in the second half of the thirteenth century. By 1300 saga-writing was on the decrease while the making of administrative records was on the increase (Vésteinsson 1994). Annals in the form they are now known began to be compiled in the second half of the thirteenth century but their writing ceased before the middle of the fifteenth.[1]

As the vast majority of the available sources are from the thirteenth century our ideas of the earlier centuries are therefore to a large extent conditioned by thirteenth-century views of the past. Since society was going through drastic changes in the thirteenth century it is likely that these views of the past had to some extent been adapted to the changing conditions. It is also likely that they reflect thirteenth-century justifications of what was then perceived as established order as much as genuine traditions about the past. In particular there is reason to be wary of the sense of permanence of the judicial and legislative system suggested by the legal sources and elaborations on the theme in some of the Sagas of Icelanders. There is no independent confirmation that these systems ever existed in the form in which they are described by the law codes. While for nineteenth-century historians this meant that the arrangements described must be ancient, a more modern way of interpretation must be to accept that it is possible that they never existed at all or that they represent thirteenth-century attempts to rationalize what systems there were in place and/or a thirteenth-century bid to construct systems that someone thought should exist. The legal material has not been subject to study, from the point of view of

[1] J. Kristjánsson 1988 is the best treatment of medieval Icelandic literary evidence and deals with every type of source except the charters. Also Byock 1990: 14–50; Miller 1990: 43–76; Breisch 1994: 39–58, and the literary histories; Jónsson 1920–4; Turville-Petre 1953; de Vries 1964–7; *ÍBS* i, ii.

dating the provisions and putting them in context with social change, since the days of Konrad von Maurer (1823–1902), Vilhjálmur Finsen (1823–92), and Andreas Heusler (1865–1940); and as long as a revision of their works based on more recent ideas on medieval society has not been attempted it is unsafe to assume that the legal sources can tell us anything about pre-twelfth-century conditions.

To the mind of the present author it makes more sense—in the absence of evidence to the contrary—to assume that political, legislative, and judicial structures took some time to develop and that power structures were at first chaotic and only slowly took on permanent features. Traditionally, the tendency has been to ascribe considerable permanence and complexity to the political structures established in Iceland in the tenth century. An example can be taken of the notion that in pre-Christian times the *goðar* or chieftains based their powers partly on having religious functions like hallowing assemblies, running pagan temples, and presiding over religious ceremonies and feasts.[2] In light of the close links between chieftains and the Church in the twelfth century explored below (Ch. 5, s. 2, in particular), it is interesting to explore this idea of pagan chieftain-priests.

In high-medieval Iceland chieftains were called *goðar*, and their power *goðorð*. The term *goði* is clearly cognate with *goð* (= deity) and *guð* (= god) which suggests that the bearers of such a distinction had some kind of association with religion. While there is no reason to reject the idea that the term was originally coined because of an association with religion, it does not of course mean that the men who called themselves *goðar* in Iceland in the tenth century had any formal religious functions. However, in order to find evidence for this religious function earlier scholarship attached significance to heathen temples which are mentioned in the saga literature. Many such sites were identified in the nineteenth century (Friðriksson and Vésteinsson 1997) but a critical examination of the evidence, both literary and archaeological, has concluded that the idea of heathen temples is a high-medieval, Christian, construct and is not based on genuine knowledge of the pagan past (O. Olsen 1966). It is now generally accepted that purpose-built temples did not exist in pagan Scandinavia, but Olsen's (1966) suggestion that chieftains presided over religious feasts in their large feasting halls ('temple-farms') has however gained widespread support (e.g. Lidén 1969; G. S. Munch 1987, 1991).

It is easy to criticize this idea. Communal eating and drinking can have a social and political significance, but it does not have to have a religious connotation. The historical evidence for feasting in pre-Christian times and the large halls which have been excavated at places like Borg in Lofoten in Norway and Hofstaðir in Mývatnssveit (A) are evidence for the social significance of

[2] It is arguable that many Icelandic 13th-cent. authors subscribed to this idea. Jonae 1951: 55–9; K. v. Maurer 1874*a*: 38–45; Melsteð 1903–30 i. 291–9; Nordal 1942: 201, cf. 107; Jóhannesson 1956: 72–3; J. Benediktsson 1974*a*: 172–3; Þorsteinsson 1978: 51; Aðalsteinsson 1985; Ingvarsson 1986–7 i, 150–9; Byock 1990: 59. On *eigen-tempel* see Stutz 1948: 44–5, 1895: 89 ff.; Chaney 1970: 73–4. For an early criticism see Boden 1905.

feasting among the Germanic and Nordic peoples—and this did of course continue long into Christian times. Whether or to what extent the business of getting drunk was considered to be a religious act in pre-Christian times is however impossible to know. Large buildings with exotic objects are evidence for social stratification: such sites indicate that in the society in question there were people who exercised power over others and could command resources over large areas. It is possible that such people tried to link their political and social status to religious ideas, and it is not inconceivable that in Nordic society the chieftains were theocrats. There is, however, nothing in particular to suggest that they were. Without purpose-built temples or other clear manifestations of a religious dimension of the chieftains' power it is both unsafe and unnecesary to make assumptions about such a role.

It is easier to comprehend pagan society and the subsequent developments if we do away with the religious functions of chieftains. Religious functions imply a duality for which there is no good evidence. Instead it is reasonable to assume that people who had—or aspired to—power, tried to establish their authority over every sort of gathering of people that occurred in their area; a basic requirement of power is people over whom to exercise it. One of the effectual ways of asserting authority over gatherings of people is to have them take place at the home of, or some other place which is directly associated with, the person who wants to exercise power. That chieftains strove to do this in pre-Christian times is not only inherently likely but is also supported by the evidence of the very large long-houses. We do not need to know the nature of the gatherings that took place in the chieftains' halls to appreciate that they were one of the principal means through which power was maintained and exercised.

In this book the position is taken that the development of the Icelandic political system was not a matter of a system being founded in the tenth century, collapsing in the thirteenth and then being replaced by an alien one, but much rather a continuing process of power structures becoming increasingly complicated and effective and that the submission to the Norwegian king was but a stage in that process. Here attention will be restricted to a few simple geographical factors which can give insight into the initial rise of the powerful families we know from the twelfth and thirteenth centuries.

Commenting in 1956 on the reasons for the uneven development of petty states across Iceland, Jón Jóhannesson (1956: 280) pointed out that it was easier to form states in densely populated and physically uninterrupted areas than in sparsely populated regions intersected by mountains and fjords. More recently Helgi Þorláksson (1989*a*, cf. 1979*a*) has argued convincingly for the importance of good communications for the formation of the petty state of the Oddaverjar in Rangárþing. Central to his argument is the strategic situation of Oddi (S), the family's power base, which was not only on the high road across the southern plain but also had easy access to the surrounding countryside.

These ideas centre around the theme of the formation of petty states. The formation of petty states began country-wide in the last decade of the twelfth century at the earliest (J. V. Sigurðsson 1989). These petty states are usually regarded as the final stage in the corruption of the old order, a result of individual chieftains coming to own more than one *goðorð* and, by getting their hands on all the *goðorð* of any one area, thereby usurping the powers formerly exercised by the local assemblies (which were consequently abolished). This model of change takes it for granted that before this process began a structure existed such as that described in *Grágás* where the four quarters of the country were divided into thirteen spring-assembly areas (four in the northern quarter, three in each of the others). According to the law code there were three chieftains, *goðar*, each controlling a *goðorð*, in each spring-assembly area. In all, therefore, there were thirty-nine *goðar*. The power of the *goðar* rested on their followers, the *þingmenn*, who were free to change their allegiances as they pleased. This structure, which clearly was not in operation in the thirteenth century, has been assumed to have been established in the tenth century and to have been in operation until the twelfth. The explanation which Helgi Skúli Kjartansson (1989) has come up with for the legal provisions for the Icelandic chieftaincies, the *goðorð*, that they were not a definition of local power but only the right to representation at the Alþing, makes excellent sense and it allows us to view the chieftaincies and their development in a much less constrained way than previously. Instead of a fixed number of chieftaincies, the numbers of which decreased through power accumulation, we can assume that chieftains came in all sorts, some owned *goðorð* and some did not, and that the nature of their power varied more according to local than national conditions. The importance of the *goðorð* and their accumulation in the hands of few families can then be seen as a late development and a consequence of the formation of overlordships. The importance which thirteenth-century chieftains seem to have attached to owning or controlling *goðorð* may primarily have been a way for them to justify their claims to overlordship instead of being the root and reason for their authority.

Jón Jóhannesson's and Helgi Þorláksson's arguments do point towards this sort of scenario. As there are no reliable descriptive sources earlier than the twelfth century—when it is imagined that the political structure had already begun to disintegrate—and as the law texts are now seen as normative rather than descriptive, geography and the environment, along with archaeology, emerge as the likeliest candidates to yield material for creating ideas about Icelandic society in the tenth and eleventh centuries.

Iceland is a large country (103,000 km^2—one-third larger than Ireland), but only around a quarter of the total area (24,000 km^2) lies under 200 metres above sea level, and it is estimated that by the time of the settlement some 40,000 km^2 were covered with vegetation of some kind and the rest was barren.[3] The whole

[3] Corresponding roughly to the area of habitable land, the vast majority of which lies beneath the 200 m contour, although human habitation is known as high as 500 m above sea level. S. Friðriksson 1987: 171, 174.

centre of the island is totally uninhabitable (and therefore a major barrier to communications, although it was crossed in times of need) and habitation is restricted largely to the coastal areas. In the habitable coastal areas three main types of physical environment can be identified: a fjord environment, a valley environment, and a plain environment. All types of environment can be found in all parts of the country, but a useful generalization may be reached, based on the three main stages in the geological formation of the country's coastal areas.

The oldest parts of the island (furthest from the Atlantic ridge) comprise the whole of the eastern coast (Austfirðir) and the north-west peninsula (Vestfirðir). These regions are characterized by deep fjords cutting into the basaltic Tertiary plateau, the mountain sides plunging almost straight into the sea, with only narrow strips of land available for human habitation. Closer to the ridge is the south-west (Breiðafjörður and (northern) Faxaflói) and most of the north (Norðurland), which are slightly later basaltic Tertiary formations characterized by wide fjords or bays with long and wide glacial valleys cutting into the highland, silted up with Quaternary deposits. In stark contrast, the length of the southern coast is uninterrupted flatland made up of Quaternary deposits, both alluvial and volcanic (i.e. lava, ash, and pumice), fringing the late (Pleistocene and Holocene) dolerite and tuff formations. The southern flatland is cut in two by a mountain range representing the hub of the Atlantic ridge, governed on its southern fringe by two middle-sized glaciers (Eyjafjallajökull and Mýrdalsjökull). To the east of these, there is considerable flatland reaching up to 30 km inland but it is dominated by glacial rivers, forever shifting their course in unstable alluvial sands, thus being both a major barrier to communications and a constant threat to settlement. It is only on the western fringe of this area that there remains today a sizeable area of agricultural land, and although there is good evidence for much more widespread settlement in the middle ages, these settlements must always have been isolated from the rest of the country and internally inaccessible as well.

The western part of the southern flatland is very different, reaching much further inland—as much as 70 km—and with lava rather than alluvium as subsoil, so its rivers are stable. The southern plain and the somewhat smaller Borgarfjörður plain, with its inland valleys, are the only two sizeable regions where there are large landlocked communities. In both these areas the seaboard itself is the least habitable. In Borgarfjörður, the coastal region (Mýrar) is dominated by deep bogs, difficult to utilize and a danger to travel. In the southern plain most of the coast is unstable sand-dunes, and the immediate hinterland (Flói (S), Landeyjar (S)) is also dominated by bogs. In addition the southern coast, being sandy and unstable, has no good natural harbours. All these factors make the landlocked communities of these two plains largely independent of the sea, in terms of resources, communications, and to some extent climate.[4]

In considering the relevance of these three different types of environment for the development of social structures the factor of population has to be taken into account. In this context the size of the total population is the least important as well as being the least knowable. More important questions are how fast the whole country was fully settled and how the population was distributed. The former is an important point, because even if we want to believe Ari *fróði*'s totally unverifiable words, 'Wise men have said, that Iceland was fully settled in sixty winters, so that there has been no increase since' (*ÍF* i. 9), that only has to mean that all land had been claimed, not that all land was already utilized by 930 (Jóhannesson 1956: 49). In fact it is natural to expect the full utilization of the land to have been a long process of exploration and making of mistakes; woods had to be cleared and knowledge had to be established on how to make the most of available resources. Ari *fróði* informs us that Bishop Gizurr had assembly-tax-paying householders in each of the quarters counted, usually thought to have been preparation either for the tithe-law in 1097 or the splitting of the diocese in 1106, or both (Jóhannesson 1956: 182). Ari gives his numbers in hundreds, but as he himself uses both the (Latin) small hundred (= 100) and the (Nordic) long one (= 120), we have no way of knowing whether the total was 3,800 or 4,560 (*ÍF* i. 23). Tax-paying householders were 3,812 in 1311 (*DI* iv. 9–10) and these numbers correspond well with the number of *lögbýli* known from the eighteenth century, *c.*4,000—as opposed to homes which were 7,092 in 1703 (*Tölfræðihandbók* 1984: 34) and are likely to have always been much more numerous than independent farmsteads. As the number of independent farmsteads is an indicator of the extent to which the land as a whole was utilized, we can safely assume from Ari's numbers that, as by 1100 tax-paying householders had reached the average observable in later centuries, a balance had been reached between population and land utilization already by the late eleventh century.

Ari gives the numbers of assembly-tax-paying householders in each quarter, and from these we can get an idea of population density according to environment types. The largest of the quarters, the eastern, had the fewest householders at 700. This quarter comprises the fjord environment of the eastern coast and the glacier-dominated plain environment of the eastern part of the south coast described above. The smallest quarter is the southern one, almost entirely plain environment, and had 1,000 tax-paying householders. The northern quarter, almost entirely valley environment, was the most densely populated, with 1,200 assembly-tax-paying householders. The western quarter, with mainly fjord and some valley environment had 900 householders.

[4] This is of course true also of many other communities—the inland valleys of Húnaflói (N), Skagafjörður, Eyjafjörður, and Skjálfandi (A), the highland settlements of the north-east (Mývatnssveit (A), Fjöll (A)), and Hérað (A)—the difference being that these are much smaller.

The figure for the northern quarter strongly suggests that valley environment could support the largest numbers, and the figures for the eastern and western quarters likewise suggest that the fjord environment could support the smallest numbers. It is natural to assume that social structures would develop first in the most densely populated areas. And so they may have done. There is nothing to suggest that institutions like the spring assemblies or the *þingmaðr–goði* relationship developed earlier in the southern plain rather than the northern valleys. In fact it could be suggested that these institutions developed later in the southern plain because it was initially not as accessible as the northern valleys, owing to the forest which covered most of the area. But once this forest was cleared a fundamental difference between these two quarters with the greatest populations comes apparent, in that the population of the north is divided between four main fjord-valley regions, cut off from each other by mountain ranges, while most of the population of the southern quarter is found in the uninterrupted southern plain.[5] The point is, then, that the southern plain is the largest single area with continuous settlement and can as such be expected to have developed and sustained more complex social structures locally than any other region in the country.

In order to understand how this may have come about, we can look more closely at how the different environment types affected social interaction in different ways. The factors which can be considered are communications, distance from resources, and access to other people to communicate with. As there is nothing which suggests otherwise, it is taken for granted that the distribution of settlement had by the eleventh century reached the stage as we know it from later centuries and that subsistence patterns were not radically different from what is observable in later times.

Another important factor in this context is the way in which power is exercised. Even in the thirteenth century Icelandic society was very decentralized and lacked any kind of political entities that could wield executive powers. Among the small class of the politically free no individual or group of individuals was powerful or organized enough to be able to force their will permanently on others. In conditions like these, one of the most easily identifiable sources of power is conflict management or the ability to settle disputes. That is, when two people quarrel and cannot settle their dispute it is natural that they or their friends turn to a third party for resolution. The stronger the persuasion of this third party the more likely that the dispute will be settled. As this third party will normally gain something for his (rarely her) efforts—at least reputation—it is in his favour if he can enhance his persuasive force. The means to do that are increased economic wealth (to give gifts, display outward signs of leadership, to take on and feed dependants, to do other people favours of

[5] The southern quarter also includes the Reykjanes peninsula, which was probably not as densely populated *c.*1100 as from the 14th cent. onwards, and the southern half of the Borgarfjörður plain, which no doubt was quite densely populated.

various types), the building of a personal reputation, and the making of friends and forging of family ties with other important people. If our third party then manages to put himself in the position where he is indispensable in his role, he has gained power. And power has a tendency to breed more power—given the right circumstances. The restraining circumstances for the development of power that we can examine are those which are decided by the environment.

In a fjord environment a farmstead will normally only have had boundaries with the two farmsteads on each side of it. Lowland normally being scarce in the fjords, each farmstead will have needed a much larger area to sustain its household than in the two other types of environment, especially if the basis of the diet came primarily from agriculture and not fishing as in later centuries. Each farmstead will also have had access to the range of resources available from sea to highland: fish, home field and meadow, pasture and in many cases forest, driftwood and jetsam. Each fjord is a clearly defined geographical unit where internal communications will usually have been easy, whereas communications with neighbouring areas will have been difficult. As the average fjord is not very long, each fjord community was quite small. Considering this we can understand better why most fjord environments could not sustain chieftains as they are known from the twelfth and thirteenth centuries. The only chieftainly estates attested in a fjord environment are Vatnsfjörður in Ísafjarðardjúp, Eyri in Arnarfjörður, and Reykhólar in Breiðafjörður—all centrally placed in long and wide fjords with many smaller fjords branching off. No chieftain is known to have had his principal estate in any of the eastern fjords.

In fjord environments, then, farmsteads were few and far apart, and each farmstead normally had access to all the basic resources within its own boundaries. All this means that social interaction will have been limited, both because of the physical barriers to communications and also because the economic need for close contact with others was slight. Areas of friction will have been fewer than in the other types of environment, simply because there were fewer resources and boundaries that had to be shared and because people had fewer opportunities or needs to meet and get on each other's nerves. It is

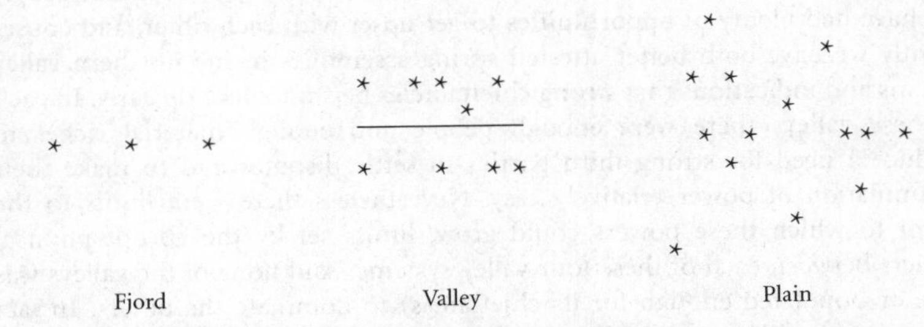

FIGURE 1. *Schematic representation of the three different settlement patterns. Each * represents one farmstead*

therefore no surprise that spring assemblies are not well attested for either the eastern or the western fjords. The basic sources of power will also have been missing to a large extent, there were too few people accessible to any one individual for his power over them to be extensive, and too long distances to other powerful people to back anyone's local power. It is therefore clear that in fjord environments strong chieftaincies could not develop—they were neither needed nor sustainable. The only major chieftaincy that developed in a fjord environment was that of the Vatnsfirðingar (N) family. That exception becomes quite understandable if the map is consulted. The family estate, Vatnsfjörður, is strategically situated, from the point of view of sea transport, in the huge fjord Ísafjarðardjúp, which is the only fjord environment where a large number of farmsteads in many small fjords are easily accessible to each other by sea. There was therefore a comparatively large population which could relatively easily have internal dealings, and no doubt did so as a consequence. No other fjord environment developed its own chieftaincy (the chieftaincy of Hrafn Sveinbjarnarson in Arnarfjörður around 1200 is notable mainly for its failure to last) and the eastern and western fjords only came to experience the rule of chieftains when chieftaincies that had developed in other environments became strong enough to hold sway over large and faraway regions.

In valley environments circumstances were more favourable to the development of social structures like spring assemblies and chieftaincies. In a valley each farmstead will have had boundaries with at least three other farmsteads, on either side and across the river. Each farmstead will have had access within its boundaries to most of the important resources except the marine ones, but the major difference between the fjord and valley environments seems to have been that density of settlement was much greater in the valleys than in the fjords or even the plains. The reason that most easily suggests itself is that the alluvial soil of the valley floors was more fertile than the (mainly aeolian) soil in the fjords, and that the more sheltered conditions in the valleys contributed to the build-up of rich humic soils. As a result many more people had much more contact with each other in the valleys than in the fjords. This is especially true of the four large fjord-valley systems of the north, each with 200–400 independent farmsteads within manageable reach of each other. In this environment people will have had plenty of opportunities to get upset with each other, and consequently we have both better attested spring assemblies in the northern valley systems and indications that strong chieftaincies began to develop early. In each of these valleys there were enough people and enough material riches to produce a need for strong third parties to settle disputes and to make their accumulation of power relatively easy. Nevertheless there were limits to the extent to which these powers could grow, limits set by the abrupt physical barriers between each of these four valley systems. And none of the valleys was large or populated enough for its chieftain(s) to dominate the others. In fact none of the northern valleys became dominated by any one chieftain or family until around and after 1200.[6] It will be suggested here that the failure of the northern chieftaincies to develop further was mainly due to their inability to create the conditions for enduring families, like the Haukdælir and to some extent the Oddaverjar managed in the southern plain.

The southern plain has its natural barriers, most notably the great rivers Hvítá/Ölfusá, Þjórsá, and Markarfljót. The density of settlement seems to have been quite uneven and only in areas like Fljótshlíð and Ölfus was it comparable to valleys like Eyjafjörður or Fljót. Nevertheless, the single outstanding feature about the settlement patterns of the southern plain is that they were not shaped by any abrupt natural barriers (save the above-named rivers) and each farmstead consequently could have boundaries with a large number of others. The conditions for agriculture are varied within the plain and access to important resources will as a result in many cases not have been possible within the boundaries of a farmstead. Access to pasture will have been particularly problematic for the farmers of the coastal areas of the plain like Flói, where access to forest will also have been difficult, whereas the settlements deeper inland will have missed out entirely on marine resources. These conditions were of course very favourable to extensive and frequent communications between farmsteads within the region. And this region is large, probably with as many as 700 independent farmsteads by 1100. There was therefore much need and favourable circumstances for the development of social structures, and plenty of opportunities for chieftains to increase their powers.

The problem of the chieftains was that their powers were personal, they were based on an individual's ability to accumulate wealth, friends, family connections, and trust. No chieftain had the means to ensure that his powers would pass on undiminished to his heirs, although in practice they were of course in the best position to take over. What was wanting was some factor, independent of life and death, which could ensure the dependence of others. Chieftaincy was an expensive job, and chieftains never seem to have managed to accumulate land or livestock to the extent that the dependants thus gained were enough to sustain enduring types of power. What was needed was some kind of inexpensive way of binding people to a place, the ruling of which secured the power of the occupant.

It will be argued in this book that, by linking their fortunes to the Church, the chieftains of the south, of which the Haukdælir seem to have been the first, managed to create power bases which were independent of the lives of individuals, and thereby could ensure the endurance of their families. Chieftains elsewhere no doubt saw the same benefits in building churches and offering services to their neighbours but the difference was that in the south there was

[6] It is accepted by most scholars that the Ásbirningar had established a supremacy over Skagafjörður already by the beginning of the 12th cent. (Jóhannesson 1956: 279; G. Karlsson 1975: 34; J. V. Sigurðsson 1989: 44, 51, 60). The evidence for this is meagre and really only amounts to the Ásbirningar being the most prominent family in Skagafjörður from at least the beginning of the 12th cent. but there is no direct evidence for their full control over the region until the 1190s.

the room to expand this power and, most importantly, maintain it. The ability to maintain power over large areas depends largely on access to enough resources to finance the institutions which make power possible. This is easiest in Árnesþing where consequently the first episcopal see was established. Ecclesiastical institutions then sprang up in one region after another; first in the largest regions with dense settlement and later in smaller regions of more scattered settlement. Of the four northern valley systems Skagafjörður had the largest area of uninterrupted settlement as well as being the central region in the quarter. This access to resources as well as geographical centrality made Skagafjörður the natural place for the second episcopal see. The first monastery at Þingeyrar was established in Húnaþing, a region with equally many farmsteads as Skagafjörður but scattered over a larger area and divided between several valleys. The second monastery at Munkaþverá was in Eyjafjörður, which also had equally many farmsteads as the other two regions but where they were firmly divided between three main valleys. The third religious house, Þykkvibær, was established in Álftaver, a plain environment with far fewer farmsteads than Árnesþing or Rangárþing, and the fourth, Flatey/Helgafell, in Breiðafjörður, a rich fjord environment. In between these and in smaller regions of dense settlement major churches with many clerics were established; Oddi in Rangárvellir and Breiðabólstaður in Fljótshlíð (S); Reykholt, Stafholt, and Hítardalur (where there was a short-lived monastery) in Borgarfjörður (S); Vellir in Svarfaðardalur and Möðruvellir in Hörgárdalur (N); Grenjaðarstaður and Múli in Aðaldalur (A); Valþjófsstaður in Fljótsdalur and Vallanes in Vellir (A).

This kind of geographical determinism is only useful as a general indicator of the reasons behind the development of ecclesiastical institutions and its effect on the process of power consolidation. There must have been other factors which influenced this equation; it could for instance have been expected that power consolidation and/or the establishment of major ecclesiastical institutions would have occurred early in the relatively densely settled region of Borgarfjörður where it did not. Conversely it should not have been expected that power consolidation would have occurred as early in the eastern quarter as it seems to have done.

This approach has great implications for our understanding of the structure of Icelandic society and its development, some of which will be explored in this book. The rest of the book is concerned with the Church and how it influenced the development of power structures in Iceland from the beginning of the eleventh century to the end of the thirteenth when the Icelandic chieftains accepted the Norwegian king as their overlord.

1
Prehistory

1. THE CONVERSION

The conversion[1] of the Icelanders is one of the really strange events in the history of Christian missions. Without much coercion or help from outside, the Icelanders decided at their annual assembly, the Alþing, to become Christian in the year 999 or 1000.

At least two missions had been sent to Iceland in the late tenth century, one apparently by Archbishop Adaldag of Hamburg-Bremen in the 980s, which seems to have had very little effect (*ÍF* i. 18; K. v. Maurer 1855–6 i. 201–26; Líndal 1974*b*: 236; Piebenga 1984), and another in 997 by the Norwegian missionary king Ólafr Tryggvason. His envoy, the priest Þangbrandr, was not a very tactful man and while he appears to have had some success he also seems to have antagonized many (*ÍF* i. 14; *MHN* 19–20; Maurer 1855–6 i. 382–410; Líndal 1974*b*: 236–8). In a change of tactics in the year 999/1000 King Ólafr took as hostages a few Icelanders who were staying in Norway, and sent two converted chieftains to Iceland with the message that he would like the Icelanders to convert. At the general assembly of that summer divisions arose among the householders and chieftains, and the two parties declared that each would have its own law and have nothing to do with the other. It was immediately felt that this would be impossibly complicated in practice, and after some deliberation the leader of the pagan party declared that they should all become Christians, but that pagan practices such as infanticide and eating horse-flesh would still be allowed, as would sacrifices to the pagan gods, as long as they were done in private (*ÍF* i. 14–17).[2]

The source for this is Ari *fróði*'s *Íslendingabók* from 1122–33. All other accounts are much later and do not seem to derive material on the conversion itself from any other source.[3] Ari's source was Teitr (d. 1110) who was a son of Iceland's first native bishop, Ísleifr Gizurarson (1056–80) and brother of the

[1] K. v. Maurer 1855–6: i. 411–43; Ólsen 1900; F. Jónsson 1901; Magnús Jónsson 1921*a*; Arnórsson 1930*b*, 1941, 1942: 105–16; Nordal 1942: 200–3; Sigfússon 1944: 43–7; J. Jóhannesson 1956: 151–66; Einarsdóttir 1964: 52–4, 1967; Líndal 1974*b*: 236–48; Strömbäck 1975; Rafnsson 1977*b*, 1979*b*; B. Þorsteinsson 1978: 66–72; Düwel 1978; Aðalsteinsson 1971, 1978; Byock 1990: 138–43; Mundal 1990; Fidjestøl 1991; Sørensen 1993: 87–9.

[2] St Ólafr is in his saga credited with having convinced the Icelanders to abandon these practices, i.e. before 1030. *ÍF* xxvii. 74, 77, 214; *ÓSHS* 105, 110–11, 325.

[3] The other accounts are: *Historia de antiquitate regum norwagensium* (*MHN* 21); *Saga Ólafs Tryggvasonar* (*SÓT* 122–30; *ÓST* ii. 188–98; *ÍF* xxvi. 347); *Kristni saga* (*ASB* xi. 36–42); and *Njáls saga* (*ÍF* xii. 269–72).

second, Gizurr Ísleifsson (1082–1118). Teitr was born in the middle of the eleventh century and had no doubt known people who remembered the conversion—his grandfather was one of the chieftains who brought King Ólafr's message to the Alþing in 999/1000. Ari's tale is therefore likely to be a credible tradition but it is clearly a well-moulded tradition and cannot be read as an accurate account of what happened. We have little choice but to accept that the Icelanders did convert around 1000, possibly under pressure from Norway, that the decision was taken by the leaders of men at the Alþing, and that this decision was effectual enough for an Icelandic bishop-elect to turn up in Bremen fifty years later (*Adam* iv. 36; *ÍF* i. 20–1). That delay does, however, also suggest that there was not in Iceland, at the time of the conversion, a Christian party ready to take political advantage of their victory.

An interesting aspect of Ari's tale is that to him the conversion was not so much a matter of salvation as political unity; the drama of the tale revolves not around the eternal well-being of Icelandic souls but about whether they were capable of taking momentous decisions like these without the fragile political system disintegrating. The account is primarily an illustration of effective crisis management where wisdom and cool-headedness conquer the forces of strife and dissension. It may be that this interest tells us more about the preoccupations of high-powered churchmen in the early twelfth century than the actual proceedings at the Alþing a good century earlier. The core of Ari's tale however remains credible; it seems that there was no great opposition to the introduction of Christianity and the matter seems to have been settled more or less peacefully.

This is the most intriguing aspect of the conversion and it has occasioned the spending of vast amounts of scholarly calories. Explanations have been put forward claiming that the Icelanders were so well acquainted with Christianity as a result of their journeys from Norway through the British Isles to Iceland, a century earlier, that the conversion was almost a formality. This explanation is contradicted by the archaeological evidence which suggests that in the tenth century burial practices at least were thoroughly heathen. Others suggest that the decision to convert was primarily a sign of political shrewdness; that the Icelanders knew that Christianity was winning through in the neighbouring countries and that, conscious of being a potential outback, they converted so as to keep abreast of developments.

All such explanations are superfluous because we cannot know what import the decision to convert had for people around 1000; the tendency is to attribute to the people at the assembly some understanding of the momentous significance of the decision whereas there is more reason to think that an official change of religion held no great significance for those involved and was probably not expected to affect people's lives greatly (Líndal 1974*b*: 248). That it did not is supported by the slow development of Christian institutions in the eleventh century.

The point on which the story of the conversion is revealing is the political organization of the Icelanders around 1000. The history of the conversion of the peoples of Northern and Eastern Europe is the history of fledgling state structures taking form through association with the Church and by overcoming organized opposition to the new religion. Religion is an excellent cause to unite around and Christianity in particular forces people to take a stance either for or against it. The clear-cut nature of the issue meant that it was an ideal issue from which ambitious chieftains, princes, and every kind of king and would-be-king could make political capital. That this did not happen in Iceland suggests that the country's political organization had not even reached the point where it began to pay to force one's will on unrelated people.

2. THE EARLY BISHOPS

The history of Icelandic Christianity well into the twelfth century is dominated by one family. Not only were the first two bishops, Ísleifr and his son Gizurr, of the Haukdælir themselves, but all the bishops until Bishop Klængr of Skálholt from 1152 and Bishop Brandr of Hólar from 1163, can be shown to have had close connections with the Haukdælir,[4] and to have owed their careers at least partly to the family's influence. Whereas the family's overpowering influence over the Church by 1100 is beyond doubt, it is largely unknown why and how it came to exert that influence. Our only indisputable fact is that in Bremen on Whit Sunday 1056 a priest called Ísleifr Gizurarson, a son of an Icelandic chieftain and a pupil of a Saxon convent, was consecrated missionary bishop to Iceland (Bekker-Nielsen 1960). Was this Ísleifr's private ambition, or had Christianity become so important to the Icelanders that one or many of the chieftains realized it was time to have their own bishop and asked Ísleifr to do the job? Was Ísleifr the only presentable churchman in the country or were there others who could have sought nomination?

The problem is not only that all our sources are written with hindsight in periods when the developing Church and the Haukdælir must have been seen as inseparable but also that the two main sources, Ari's *Íslendingabók* and the later *Hungrvaka*, were both written under the aegis of the Haukdælir. Ari's main source for the conversion story and the subsequent development of the Church was Teitr, son of Bishop Ísleifr and brother of Bishop Gizurr. *Hungrvaka's* main source for the history of the bishops of Skálholt was Gizurr Hallsson, Teitr's grandson and leader of the family. There is no special reason to think that the authors or Teitr or Gizurr were deliberately trying to hide relevant facts in order to make the Haukdælir's part in the making of the Icelandic church look larger. They did not need to. First it is only natural to expect these men to have been

[4] For the sake of clarity the whole family from the primary settler Ketilbjörn *gamli* will be called Haukdælir, although strictly speaking that term only applies to Teitr Ísleifsson (d. 1110), who was the first of the kindred to live at Haukadalur (S), and his descendants. The term for the earlier generations down to Bishop Gizurr, Teitr's brother, is Mosfellingar.

unconsciously biased towards their own family and/or patrons, and secondly the success of the Haukdælir being already established, it was that which was interesting and needed explaining. And in explaining their success it was natural for these men to direct their attentions towards the positive events which best illuminated the development. As a result we are presented with a simple sequence of causation: Bishop Ísleifr's father, Gizurr *hvíti*, is baptized by a missionary in 998. Two years later he is one of the main protagonists of conversion and soon puts his mind to reinforce Christianity and sends his son abroad to be educated. The son in due course, having shown his ability, is asked by the public to become their bishop.

Whereas this may all be true in some sense, the political and social reality behind each of these events is hidden from us. This sequence of causation is too simple for us to draw any conclusions from it regarding the nature of the early Icelandic church or how society reacted to it. We can neither assume that the Icelandic church was conceived entirely by the Haukdælir, nor that other families could have been influential in the development. As will be shown below there is some evidence which suggests that other families were actively interested in the Church but also that there are good grounds to believe that the Haukdælir were just the kind of family which could make use of an institution like the Church.

The Haukdælir and Bishop Ísleifr[5]

The Old German eleventh-century poem *Merigarto* mentions an excellent, learned, and honourable priest called Reginpreht whom the author had met in Utrecht and who had been to Iceland and profited greatly from selling grain, wine, and timber (F. Maurer 1964: 71–2, see K. v. Maurer 1855–6 i. 599; Thoroddsen 1892–1904 i. 58–9). This is the only contemporary source mentioning foreign clerics in Iceland in the eleventh century, but in addition Ari *fróði* names six missionary bishops active in Iceland in the eleventh century (*ÍF* i. 18; Kolsrud 1913*a*: 196–8).[6] *Hungrvaka* also lists these and adds information on them extracted from Adam of Bremen. The earliest date that can be attached to any of these is 1020; Bjarnharðr *bókvísi* was sent by King Ólafr to minister to the Icelanders and was in the country five years according to *Hungrvaka* (*Bysp* 1. 78). From 1030 onwards there was always at least one bishop in the country at a time, and two at least stayed for long periods. Hróðólfr (Rodulf) was in Borgarfjörður between 1030 and 1049, and is said to have left three monks at Bær (S) when he went to England to become abbot of Abingdon (d. 1052) (*Bysp* 1. 80; *ÍF* i. 65; Stevenson 1888: i. 463–4; *Adam* ii. 57, 64; Anglo-Saxon Chronicle [1050]; Joys 1948: 21–3). Bjarnharðr *saxlenski* (the Saxon) was in Iceland between

[5] Á. Guðmundsson 1943; J. Jóhannesson 1956: 167–75; Köhne: 1972, 1974, 1987; Líndal 1974*b*: 249–59.

[6] Ari also gives the names of a further five who he said claimed to be bishops—see M. M. Lárusson 1960*a*.

1048 and 1067. He lived in Vatnsdalur in the north and was praised for his blessings of churches and chimes, bridges and wells, fords and lakes, cliffs and bells. He later became the first bishop of Selja in Norway (*Bysp* 1. 80; *DI* iii. 21, 26; *Adam* iv. 34). Apart from Hróðólfr's monastic founding and Bjarnharðr's blessings, nothing is known of the activities of the missionary bishops. We do not know how many priests they had with them (if any), if they preferred to bring experienced priests with them from abroad, or if they put the emphasis on educating Icelanders to be priests. Nor have we any idea of their relations with the Icelandic chieftains, nor indeed the relations between the missionary bishops and Ísleifr after he became bishop in 1056.

What we do know is that at least some of the chieftains took an active interest in the Church. Gizurr *hvíti* who, according to his grandson Teitr Ísleifsson (quoted by Ari, *ÍF* i. 17), was one of the protagonists of the conversion, took his son, Ísleifr, to Saxony and had him educated at the convent in Herford (*Bysp* 1. 75; Líndal 1974*b*: 255).[7] According to Ari, Ísleifr was 50 when consecrated in 1056 (*ÍF* i. 21) so he must have been born around 1006 and it is therefore reasonable to assume that he went to Saxony in the 1020s (cf. Köhne 1972: 13–14).

This was a significant step. Here we have an Icelandic chieftain making a decisive career move on behalf of his son of a type until then unknown in Icelandic society. Ísleifr was Gizurr's son by his third wife, Þórdís daughter of Þóroddr *goði*, a neighbouring chieftain. We do not know enough about Gizurr's other children to appreciate Ísleifr's position regarding his chances of inheritance. Gizurr had had at least one child by each of his two earlier wives and *Hungrvaka* tells us that Gizurr and Þórdís had many children besides Ísleifr (*Bysp* 1. 75). Of these children nothing is known and there is little to suggest that Ísleifr was a youngest son with slim chances of a career. After he returned from Saxony he acquired Skálholt as his estate, which must have been a reasonable property, although it is not entirely clear whether it had been his father's main estate.[8] One source, *Ísleifs þáttr*, states that Ísleifr owned a *goðorð*, which can be assumed to have been inherited from his father (*Bysp* 1. 22). *Ísleifs þáttr* was probably composed in the thirteenth century[9] and its author may simply have assumed that Ísleifr owned a *goðorð* as his father had no doubt owned one and as his descendants did as well, but then that is a very reasonable assumption.

[7] This is not mentioned by Ari.

[8] *Hungrvaka* says that Teitr, Gizurr *hvíti*'s father, first built a farm at Skálholt, but then it must be remembered that the author of that work had set out to glorify the bishops of Skálholt and the see itself. *Bysp* 1. 75. *Kristni saga* has Gizurr *hvíti* living at Höfði, a farm adjacent to Skálholt before he moved it to Skálholt and Höfði is also mentioned as Gizurr's farm in *Landnámabók* (both H and S versions) (*ASB* xi. 45; *ÍF* i. 378). *Njáls saga* has Gizurr living at Mosfell, his grandfather's original settlement (*ÍF* xii. 119).

[9] The *þáttr* is preserved in the compilation *Flateyjarbók* made in 1387–94 as an interpolation in *Ólafs saga helga*, and as an independent piece in a defective 15th-cent. MS (AM 75e fol) (*Bysp* 1. 15–16). Koppenberg 1980 argues that *Ísleifs þáttr* is earlier than the first Icelandic revision of *Jóns saga helga*.

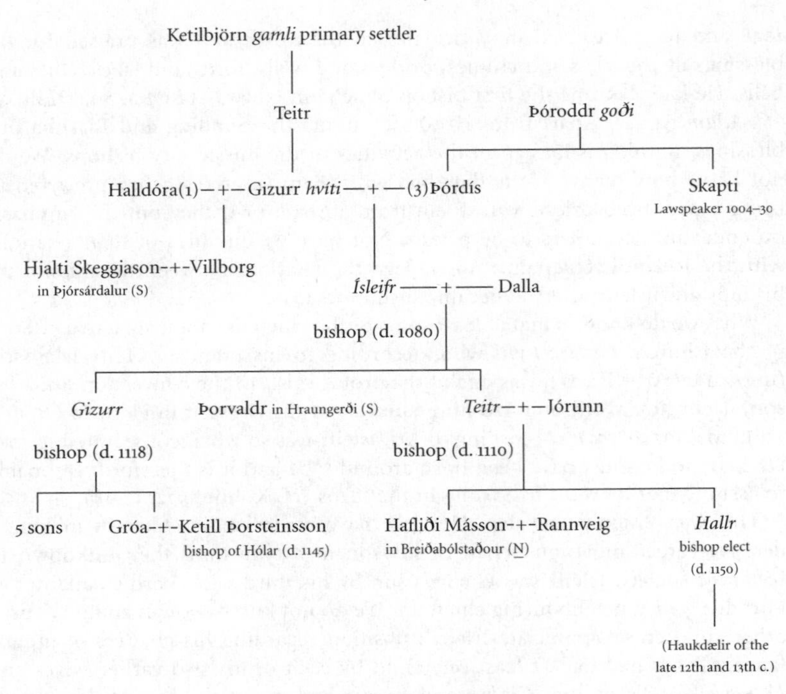

FIGURE 2. *The Haukdælir*

Ísleifr also acquired what seems to have been a respectable bride.[10] All this rather points to Ísleifr being his father's intended successor as chieftain.[11]

Although we cannot know what was in Gizurr *hvíti*'s mind when he decided to take his son to a Saxon convent, we can assume that it was something more than just making a career for a young son. If he had only been interested in making Ísleifr a priest, it would have sufficed to place him in the hands of one of the missionary bishops.[12] By going to the considerable trouble and expense of giving his son a proper education abroad, Gizurr was not only staking his bet on the Church, but he gave himself and his son a clear advantage over both foreign missionaries and other Icelandic chieftains who may have let it suffice to have their sons educated by these missionaries or not bothered at all. With his

[10] Dalla was St Ólafr's second cousin once removed according to some sources (*ÍF* i. 216, 230; *Bysp* 1. 8, 11, 22–3, 75; *ASB* xi. 45; also R. Ólafsson 1969).

[11] Ari mentions none of this, i.e. neither Ísleifr's farmstead—although he says he was buried there—nor his owning a *goðorð*, nor his bride, but then that is not the kind of information he gives and there is nothing to refute the later sources.

[12] As we do not know exactly when Ísleifr was in Herford it is possible that no missionary bishops were available at the time of Gizurr's decision, i.e. it is quite possible that Ísleifr was younger than 14 when taken to Saxony. But whether or not any missionary bishops had arrived before Ísleifr's departure, Gizurr's decision remains significant.

foreign education Ísleifr could claim to be just as good a churchman as the foreign missionaries and he had the advantage over them in family connections and an economic base to work from.

As far as we can gather Ísleifr must have preached at his church in Skálholt from his arrival in Iceland, and it is significant to note that the two missionary bishops whose places of residence are known and who seem to have been the most active, chose different regions of the country to work in.[13] Settlement patterns and population distribution are largely unknown for the eleventh century, but the geography speaks for itself: the southern plain, in which Skálholt is centrally placed, is the single largest area of continuous habitable land in the country and if all its habitable land had been occupied by the eleventh century that population represented the largest group of people in the country who were accessible without having to cross mountains or deserts. It would be natural to expect strategically minded missionaries to have chosen this region to work in; as they did not, as far as can be seen, it is tempting to assume that Ísleifr, with his powerful family connections around much of the plain, had already established himself there and meant serious business as a churchman.

How, or if, Ísleifr was elected bishop is obscure. Ari is completely silent on the issue and the later sources only say that he was chosen by the men of the country, which is what one would expect the authors to have believed; even if they had a genuine source for it, the meaning of this is difficult to assess.[14] His journey to the mainland, probably begun in 1053 or 1054, seems to have been well organized and planned: he first went to the court of the Emperor Henry III, and presented him with a polar bear and received a letter of safe conduct in return. Thence he went to Rome where he was detained some time and got a letter from the pope ordering Archbishop Adalbert of Bremen to consecrate him. He stayed with Adalbert for a while and after his consecration he spent one winter in Norway before returning home in 1057 (*Bysp* 1. 76–7; also *ÍF* i. 21 and *Adam* iv. 36). Bringing polar bears from Greenland to Germany is not a feat one would expect of penniless country-priests, but again the significance of this is

[13] *Hungrvaka* says Bishop Kolr was buried at Skálholt (*Bysp* 1. 78) which suggests that he was active in the south, but when he was there is not certain. Ari says he was only a few years in the country and mentions him between Bjarnharðr *bókvísi* whom St Ólafr sent to Iceland, probably somewhere *c.*1020, and Hróðólfr who came to Iceland in 1030. If Björn Jónsson's comment in his *Skarðsárbók* is to be taken seriously, that Kolr stayed with Hallr Þórarinsson in Haukadalur (S), it must have been after 1025 (J. Benediktsson 1958*a*: 195; *ÍF* i. 18, 21). Taken together, this rather patchy evidence suggests that he must have died around 1030, when Ísleifr was either still in Saxony or just newly arrived in Iceland. Both Björn Þorsteinsson (1953: 187; Þorsteinsson and Jónsson 1991: 57) and Jón Jóhannesson (1956: 16) think Kolr was, like Bjarnharðr, sent by St Ólafr. The author of *Víga-Glúms saga* on the other hand makes Kolr confirm Víga-Glúmr on his deathbed, which according to the saga's chronology was in 1002–3 (*ÍF* ix. 97–8; Turville-Petre 1960: pp. xlvi–xlviii).

[14] *ASB* xi. 45–6; *Bysp* 1. 23, 76; *Bsk* i. 152 (also 216), which is reminiscent of Adam of Bremen: 'On their [the Icelanders] petition, therefore, the archbishop consecrated a certain most holy man named Ísleif.' (*Adam* iv. 36). M. M. Lárusson (1967*c*: 52–5) interprets these sources as evidence for the early bishops being democratically elected, or somehow selected by the general public, but there are no grounds for that kind of understanding. Cf. Joys 1948: 70–1. On episcopal selection in Iceland see further in Ch. 4, s. 1.

difficult to assess,[15] because we cannot know whether Ísleifr planned and financed his trip himself or if he was only the protégé of more powerful chieftains, or anything between these two alternatives. It does, however, suggest indigenous interest and investment in Christianity; that is in accordance with the view that from an early stage the shaping of the Icelandic church was in the hands of the Icelandic aristocracy, and that the influence of foreign missionaries was slight. The archbishop in Bremen clearly had the power to consecrate bishops in his diocese without asking the pope so it was probably not his idea that Ísleifr travelled all the way to Rome.

3. EARLY EVIDENCE OF PRIESTS

Late summer in the year 1000 must have been a very busy time for one Þormóðr, a priest who is supposed to have been brought from Norway by the chieftains who carried King Ólafr's message of conversion to the Alþing of that summer (*ÍF* i. 15; *ASB* xi. 38; *ÍF* xxvi. 347).[16] As far as our sources can tell us, he was the only priest in the country at the time and he was faced with the task of baptizing the whole population in compliance with the decision to convert taken at the Alþing.[17]

We can only speculate on how Þormóðr fared, how and when the whole nation was baptized, or in what form Christian services were given.[18] The task must have been enormous and it must have taken a long time to establish any kind of basic Christian practices. An important problem was that of manpower. Not only was there the technical difficulty of persuading priests to make the perilous journey across the sea to an isolated and little known country, but also the political difficulty that royal support for Christianity in the North Atlantic had receded with the fall of King Ólafr Tryggvason in September 1000 and was not continued until King Ólafr Haraldsson, the saint, took power after 1015. In the mean time Norway had rulers who were at best indifferent to Christianity and often hostile to it, and this can hardly have encouraged English or German

[15] There is a possibility that this is a literary motif: there are some frightening parallels between this account and the episode *Auðunar þáttr vestfirzka* which is preserved in *Morkinskinna*. *Auðunar þáttr* tells of one Auðun, a man of inconsiderable means and humble family, who takes it into his head to present a polar bear to King Sveinn Úlfsson of Denmark (1047–74), and having accomplished that after considerable tribulations, receives a travel grant from Sveinn and goes to Rome (Mork 180–7; *ÍBS* ii. 35–6).

[16] This Þormóðr was possibly the same as one of the priests brought by King Ólafr Tryggvason from England to Norway some years previously; cf. Thermo in Theodoricus Monachus (*MHN* 21).

[17] *Kristni saga* mentions seven robed men with two crosses at the Law rock when Gizurr *hvíti* and Hjalti Skeggjason delivered their message of conversion at the Alþing of 1000 (*ASB* xi. 38). It is not entirely certain what is meant, although *skýrddur* usually refers to the clothing of a cleric (from *skrúði* = vestments). This story seems to be a part of a folk-tale about standing crosses at Skarð in Land, one representing the height of King Ólafr and the other the height of Hjalti Skeggjason (*ASB* xi. 38).

[18] *Kristni saga*'s account of the baptism of the men of the different quarters immediately after the Alþing does not have to be taken seriously (*ASB* xi. 42; *ÓST* ii. 198); and in any case it only accounts for those who had attended the assembly.

priests or bishops to go and save souls in Norway, let alone Iceland (Kolsrud 1958: 134–5). The issue of recruitment is a very important one, not only in the traditional sense of the cultural origins of influence, but even more so in the sense of numbers of priests active in the country in the first decades of Christianity and the scope of the missionary activity.

As related above, missionary bishops did make their way to Iceland, but none are known until the 1020s and of them little is known but the names. We would give much to have an idea of the conditions these missionaries worked in; were the Icelanders heathen at heart long after the conversion, so that the missionaries had to concentrate on teaching the basics to the populace? Or were the Icelanders already well acquainted with Christianity, in which case the missionaries' efforts can have been directed towards consolidating the position of the Church in society? In other words, was it difficult to convince people that they had to attend mass regularly and observe all kinds of rules and rites, and was it an uphill struggle to make chieftains and/or other men of means spend their wealth on building and endowing churches and paying priests or having their sons ordained? Or were people quite happy to attend churches and chieftains more than ready to invest in churches and priests? In the latter case the job of the missionaries will have been more to organize and bring practices into line, overseeing that things were done correctly, rather than trying to see to it that they were done at all.

We have no way of knowing which of these extremes is more true. Only five churches can with reasonable certainty be said to have been built in Iceland before 1100 (see Ch. 3, s. 1, also Ch. 1, s. 4) and only nine Icelandic priests—who can be regarded as historical personages—are mentioned as being active before that date (see s. 3 below). We cannot even read much into these small numbers because of the patchy nature of the sources. The handful of facts concerning the development of the Church in the eleventh century have all come down to us in isolation from any accompanying evidence which might have allowed us to judge their relevance. All these scraps of evidence can be made to fit either of the scenarios sketched above.

Landnáma's tale of the monks left by Bishop Hróðólfr at Bær (S), for instance, can be taken as an argument for both models (*ÍF* i. 65). On the one hand Hróðólfr may be seen to have been copying the practices of many of his more famous predecessors in the missionary profession, founding a monastery in the midst of a heathen population, as a base for further missionary activity. On the other hand it may well be argued that a monastery could hardly have been founded unless there was economic, and therefore spiritual, support for it. This could be debated indefinitely, but it would be fruitless because the cynical view can easily be taken that the story in Haukr Erlendsson's version of *Landnámabók* has no basis in reality. Haukr was writing in the first decade of the fourteenth century (Karlsson 1964), which is in itself reason enough not to take his story seriously; the story which the tale is a part of is also found in *Ólafs saga Tryggvasonar hin mesta*, but there no mention is made of Hróðólfr or the monks (*ÓST* i. 278–9), which makes Haukr's addition of them suspicious.

This is only an example of the problems we run into whenever we try to extract usable information from the few scraps of evidence left to us: it usually ends with us having to admit that we can say very little with any degree of certainty. Even Ari's account, which is on the whole credible, is so laconic that we are left totally to our own devices in giving meaning to the few scraps of evidence he does supply.

One of the events Ari relates, which is undoubtedly a significant one, is the consecration of Ísleifr Gizurarson in 1056. While the importance of this event for later developments is unquestionable, its relevance for our understanding of Icelandic society and the place of the Church within it at that time is far from clear. It is useful to remember that Ísleifr was consecrated as missionary bishop,[19] and in that sense his position was little different from that of the other missionary bishops active in the country at his time. The only difference was that his mission was specifically to Iceland (*Bsk* i. 151 (216); *Bysp* 1. 77) and that he was an Icelander himself. The question is: do we see in this a stage in the development of the native Icelandic church, which had by 1050 become strong enough and sufficiently integrated with the native power structure to have the need for, and means to produce, an Icelandic head of an Icelandic church. Or do we see in this the actions of a perceptive individual in a still half-heathen and only nominally Christian society, who saw the Church as a vehicle of power and took it upon himself to bring Christianity upon his unsuspecting countrymen, much in the same way as the two Ólafrs decided to do for the Norwegians?

On the basis of *Íslendingabók* and the few other available sources, we simply cannot discern which of these two options could be closer to reality. But we can speculate on the likeliest type of development and try to construct hypotheses which are credible in themselves and best explain both the few pieces of evidence known from the earlier times and the later situation that can be described from fuller source material. There are two principal types of evidence to consider in this context; on the one hand there is the evidence of churches, their numbers and locations and on the other the evidence of the priests who appear in the sources, their numbers, and stations in life. The churches will be dealt with in the next chapter, but let us here first look at the handful of eleventh-century priests and what can be inferred from the little surviving information about them, and then at the early twelfth-century evidence and what can be inferred from that.

Some eleventh-century priests

Eyrbyggja saga mentions four early churches, two of them built by Snorri *goði*, the central figure of that saga (*ÍF* iv. 136, 183). A related account is also found in Jón Ólafsson's retelling of the manuscript of *Heiðarvíga saga* that burnt in the

[19] It was only during the episcopacy of his son Gizurr that an episcopal see was established, as Gizurr had a law passed to that effect and gave Skálholt to the see (*ÍF* i. 23).

fire of Copenhagen in 1728 (*ÍF* iii. 230). This unusually high number is in accordance with the author's antiquarian interests evident by his various tales and anecdotes about pagan rituals and other lore about the faded past. In the light of his historical interests it is tempting to suggest that the author was not wholly comfortable with his statement about the churches built soon after the conversion by three chieftains, because he felt he had to explain: 'but priests did not hold services at the churches that were built because there were few priests in Iceland in that time' (*ÍF* iv. 136). The author either knew or realized that there could have been very few priests in Iceland in the first years after the conversion, but he still had to make his chieftains church-builders or accommodate traditions to that effect, and therefore tried to make the reader believe that churches were built with little prospect of services being given. He also explains why the chieftains should have gone to the trouble: 'And it encouraged men to build churches, that preachers promised that a man would dispose of places in heaven for as many men as could stand in the church he would build' (*ÍF* iv. 136):[20] a theology implying on the one hand that one's place in heaven was up to one's chieftain and on the other that building a church and standing in it was a satisfactory Christian observance. This may very well have been a ploy of desperate and hard-pressed missionaries hoping that this form of monumentalism would appeal to the possibly eager but definitely ignorant flock.[21]

It is almost comic to imagine the newly converted congregation, more or less ignorant of Christian practices, standing on the church floor, awed by a splendid building but slightly puzzled about what to do in it. It is of course unlikely that there were many churches when there were still few priests, particularly churches which were intended for large gatherings. The other possibility, that as soon as the majority of the population was at least nominally Christian, church structures of some sort were built to accommodate funeral services and possibly the occasional mass by an itinerant priest, will be argued for in section 4 below. What is certain is that there is no reliable evidence for Icelandic priests giving regular services at a church until after the middle of the eleventh century.

The first Icelander to be associated with clerical vows was one Guðlaugr, fourth son of Snorri *goði* and Ásdís Víga-Styrsdóttir. They were married in 983 according to the chronology of *Eyrbyggja saga* (*ÍF* iv. 75), making a likely birth date for Guðlaugr around 990. According to *Ævi Snorra goða*, Guðlaugr was a

[20] The same idea occurs in *Heiðarvíga saga* (*ÍF* iii. 230, unfortunately in the part which Jón Ólafsson wrote from memory). Jón may have been unconsciously affected by the account in *Eyrbyggja saga*, although the sagas overlap to a considerable extent and one can easily have been a source for the other on matters like these. It strengthens the case that *Heiðarvíga saga* had accounts of early church building, that it adds that one of the three early churches, the one built by Víga-Styrr at Berserkjahraun, was later burnt and that Víga-Styrr's bones were reburied at Helgafell (*ÍF* iii. 235).

[21] Cf. Gren 1989 who stresses the monumental aspect of stone church building by aristocrats in 12th-cent. Scandinavia.

monk (*ÍF* iv. 185), and that is as good a source as can be asked for, with a likely twelfth or early thirteenth century date (see s. 4 below). In the part of *Heiðarvíga saga* only preserved through Jón Ólafsson's retelling,[22] there is an account of how one morning the good-mannered and devout but mostly idle Guðlaugr met his father in the doorway of the church in Sælingsdalstunga (D) (presumably in 1008) and preferred not to accompany his father and brothers to avenge their grandfather, Víga-Styrr. Snorri said he had not asked him to work hitherto, that he should occupy himself as he pleased thereafter, and that it pleased him if Guðlaugr did not accompany them and cultivated his virtues instead. The sun was shining in Guðlaugr's face and his father was later reported to have said that he had never seen a face like Guðlaugr's that morning, red as blood, so that Snorri almost took fright. According to Jón Ólafsson, Guðlaugr went to England a few years later with his father's support and joined a monastery, lived a pious life, and was considered an excellent cleric to his dying day (*ÍF* iii. 246–7).

This story is of course mainly about Snorri's magnanimity and support for Christianity; he appreciated the value of Guðlaugr's devotion and we are possibly to understand that Guðlaugr's prayers were equally important to the family's cause as his brothers' resolve to take revenge on their grandfather's slayer. Guðlaugr's red face may be a sign of holiness, although it may also be interpreted as signifying that Guðlaugr was just as upset about his unavenged grandfather as his father and brothers. These are of course thirteenth-century sentiments,[23] but the tradition that Guðlaugr was a monk may well have been based on fact; it is at any rate entirely plausible that in the first decades after the conversion there were individuals who took more to Christianity than others and had to go abroad to follow their vocation. It is furthermore likely that Christian teaching first influenced households of powerful chieftains like Snorri *goði*, who were active supporters of Christianity. But if Guðlaugr in reality went to England to become a monk in the 1010s, that indicates that, even if Christianity had powerful supporters, ecclesiastical institutions had not yet developed in Iceland.

Later in the same chapter of *Heiðarvíga saga*, which also survives only in Jón Ólafsson's retelling, when Snorri and his sons had gone to Bær (S) and killed one Þorsteinn Gíslason and his son in revenge for Víga-Styrr, their corpses were found outside the farmstead by Þorsteinn's wife as she came back from the shieling. The wife hurried to the next farmstead, presumably Varmalækur, and found there a relative of hers, a cleric called Eldjárn. He responds quickly and gathers men to go and look at the corpses and send messages to the neighbouring farmsteads (*ÍF* iii. 250).

Of this cleric nothing more is known, and the lack of genealogical information

[22] On Jón Ólafsson's memory see *ÍF* iii. pp. cvii–cxv.

[23] *Heiðarvíga saga* has been considered to be among the earliest of the Sagas of Icelanders, if not the earliest, and written *c.*1200, but recently it has been suggested that it postdates *Laxdæla saga* and therefore has a late 13th-cent. date (*ÍF* iii. pp. cxxxiv–cxliv; *ÍBS* ii. 113).

about him in the saga suggests that either its author or Jón Ólafsson thought it fitting that a cleric should be called upon in circumstances such as these, and therefore made him up, rather than that this represents a genuine tradition about an early eleventh-century Icelandic priest.

Similar literary reasons must account for Snorri Sturluson's account of one Bárðr or Brandr, whom we meet as a young priest from Vestfirðir, on a ship owned by the Icelander Steinn Skaptason in Norway *c.*1025. In this episode Steinn is the hero; he had become irritated with King Ólafr and killed one of his men. He then fled to where his ship was moored, off the island of Gizka, which also was the home of a powerful chieftain. The chieftain was not at home, but his wife was about to give birth, and it looked as if the birth would be difficult. With that in mind people saw that a priest might be needed, but there was no priest on the island or in the vicinity. The chieftain's men at last came to Steinn's ship and asked Bárðr the priest to come with them. It is explained that he was lacking in education and he declined on account of his ignorance. Steinn then stepped in and asked Bárðr to go nevertheless, and the priest agreed on condition that Steinn came with him. The pair of them then went to the woman's chambers where she soon afterwards bore a sickly girl. Bárðr baptized her with Steinn acting as godfather, and he gave the infant a ring. The chieftain's wife was now in Steinn's debt, and with her help he eventually managed to escape King Ólafr's wrath (*ÍF* xxvii. 244–5). In this episode the priest has no other function than being the means through which Steinn could gain access to the bedside of an influential wife in order to save his skin. As with Eldjárn in *Heiðarvíga saga*, the lack of genealogical information and the usefulness of a cleric in the story-line make Bárðr an unlikely candidate for the status of a historical personage.

There are two other priests who according to *Grettis saga* had pastoral responsibilities in the 1020s. With them we enter firmly into the realm of folklore; both the nameless priest in Forsæludalur (N) and Steinn priest at Eyjardalsá in Bárðardalur (N) (*ÍF* vii. 112 (cf. 110), 209) are clearly folkloric creations and are as such probably not even intended to be historically significant (see also s. 4 below on the churches in *Grettis saga*).

Bishop Ísleifr Gizurarson (b. *c.*1005, d. 1080) is the first Icelander known to have been ordained as priest and to have had pastoral responsibilities in Iceland, and there is very little evidence of others of his generation doing the same. It is commonly stated that Sigfúss Loðmundarson, the father of Sæmundr *fróði*, was a priest, but this is based on a scribal error in the *Hauksbók* version of *Landnámabók*. Sæmundr was well known as a priest but in one case where his ancestry is related it is not he but his father who is called a priest (*ÍF* i. 363), suggesting that the scribe got mixed up. If it was intentional, this early fourteenth-century tradition is not supported by any other evidence.

According to *Ljósvetninga saga* there was in Eyjafjörður in the episcopacy of Ísleifr (1056–80) a priest called Ketill *Möðruvellingaprestr.* Ketill supervised an ordeal which took place in Laufás (N). A woman had become pregnant and claimed that the father was a man who was then abroad. The man's *fóstbróðir* and legal representative, a certain Þorkell of the Ljósvetningar, contested the woman's claim, arguing that she had slept with too many men for it to be possible to decide who was the father. The chieftain Eyjólfr *halti* Guðmundsson of the Möðruvellingar, who had taken on the case on behalf of the woman's father, offered that she would undergo an ordeal if he pledged to pay the (child's) *réttr*[24] and guaranteed paternity (the legal responsibilities of fatherhood) should she emerge clean. Þorkell refused to guarantee paternity, a precautionary measure as he might be liable to honour his pledge even if she emerged scathed, but agreed to the ordeal and pledged the *réttr* and its final due date to the priest who supervised the ordeal. This was accepted and the woman began her fast. When her bandages were removed, Ketill the priest did not give the verdict immediately and Þorkell then asked him why he was worse than his father (*verrfeðrungr*) and did not declare the woman scathed, and promptly named witnesses to his words. The priest replied: 'It's out of order for you two to pronounce the judgement and take the case out of my hands; the decision is mine to make. We shall make a second, clearer trial of the matter' (*ÍF* x. 69: transl: Andersson and Miller 1989: 209). This apparently was not heeded and the quarrel developed into a serious dispute.

This story of the ordeal is suspicious, because of the priest's demand for a retrial. The law codes do not explain what to do if a verdict in an ordeal was interfered with, or how ordeals could be declared mistrials. There is however a clause, which seems to be an amendment, allowing the bishops to repeat ordeals in paternity cases and heed the verdict from the later ordeal (*Grg 1b*, 216).[25] This indicates that by 1200 ordeals, in paternity cases at least, were considered to be under the Church's supervision and that the bishops had the privilege to have them repeated. The Church's prerogative in sexual matters can hardly have been established until the late twelfth century (see Ch. 4, s. 2). This therefore suggests that this account in *Ljósvetninga saga* is coloured by thirteenth-century legal practices and that, as priests normally supervised ordeals then, the author had to invent a priest to supervise his eleventh-century ordeal. The fact that the priest is given a name and a nickname indicates however that the author had some historical personage in mind. The nickname *Möðruvellingaprestr* (the priest of the men of Möðruvellir) suggests a connection with Möðruvellir in Eyjafjörður (N) or Möðruvellir in Hörgárdalur (N). It may either mean that he was a priest who had served the Church at either place, or that he was of the Möðruvellingar kindred from Möðruvellir in Eyjafjörður. Plot-wise that is, however, unlikely as that Möðruvellir was the seat of Eyjólfr

[24] A fixed fine of 48 ounce units, payable in fornication cases like these, as well as for libel, killing, wounding, and treachery. The fine is expressed as a person's 'right' and was the same for everyone except vagabonds. In cases of fornication the fine would be paid to the child (*Grg* iii. 661–2; Andersson and Miller 1989: 208 nn. 147, 148, 149).

[25] On ordeals see K. v. Maurer 1874*b*; M. M. Lárusson 1960*h*; Páll Sigurðsson 1971: 252–7, 277–82; Miller 1988*b*.

halti, and Þorkell is unlikely to have accepted someone to supervise the ordeal who was not completely neutral. As the ordeal took place in Laufás it seems likely that the author intended the priest to be from there; a neutral man on neutral ground. There were important churches on all three farms in the thirteenth century so that does not help us. Þorkell's insinuation that Ketill was a lesser man than his father is strange as the father's identity is not given, but it implies that the father was of some standing. If Ketill was of good family and had connections with Möðruvellir, the saga's audience will have connected him with the Möðruvellingar kindred and its more famous representative, also called Ketill, who was bishop of Hólar 1122–45. It is possible that Ketill *Möðruvellingaprestr* and Ketill the bishop were originally the same person, and that the priest and chieftain at Möðruvellir had got so completely divorced from the bishop in popular legend, that it became possible to move the former fifty years or so back in time. Alternatively Ketill *Möðruvellingaprestr* may have been the invention of the author of *Ljósvetninga saga*, and in both cases the author would then have intended the names to be meaningful to his audience, suggesting that the priest was on the Möðruvellingar side. That would add meaning to the passage; Ketill hesitated in giving his verdict, because the hand was indeed scathed, and right was on the side of the Ljósvetningar as usual. That would however make Þorkell look somewhat simple: he had no reason to place his trust in someone called Ketill *Möðruvellingaprestr* (on this case see Andersson and Miller 1989: 32–7). Whatever the identity of Ketill *Möðruvellingaprestr* there are no grounds for placing much faith in the historicity of this account, and it cannot be used to shed light on the role of priests in the eleventh century or their relationship with powerful laymen.[26]

According to one version of *Bandamanna saga*, composed in the late thirteenth or early fourteenth century (*ÍBS* ii. 121–2), there was in the middle of the eleventh century a priest in Reykholt (S) called Þórðr Sölvason. The chieftain Hermundr Illugason at Gilsbakki (S), who is one of the bad characters in the saga, became sick on his way to do some mischief and had to be taken back to Gilsbakki with all kinds of eerie portents happening on the way. At Gilsbakki he was put in bed and Þórðr the priest was sent for. When he came Hermundr could not speak so Þórðr prepared to leave; he was called in again but Hermundr could still not speak. Þórðr left again but was sent for the third time, and this time Hermundr managed to utter the words 'five in the gully, five in the gully' and then died (*ÍF* vii. 361, cf. p. lxxxi). What Hermundr was referring to is obscure, it may have something to do with what he considered to have lost out on in his and his allies' vain attempt to confiscate the property of the chieftain Oddr Ófeigsson.

This story is in both principal manuscripts of the saga, but the other version does not give the priest a name and has him living at Síðumúli (S). This story

[26] B. Guðmundsson 1953: 46–52 has suggested that the story of the ordeal is based on an almost identical case which took place in the 1150s (*Sturl* 60–2). There, however, it was the bishop who supervised the ordeal.

has all the characteristics of a well-moulded folk-tale of an unexpected but just and apparently painful death, with portents, success in the third attempt, and an obscure uttering. It is uncharacteristic for the saga, which is considered among those that are primarily literary creations. The saga's author was well versed in the laws of *Grágás*, and had sound knowledge of the principal chieftains of the mid eleventh century. There is no particular reason why the name of the priest is included in one version, an anonymous one would have done perfectly well as it does in the other, except of course that it adds a flavour of authenticity. Þórðr was a real person who is mentioned widely in genealogies (*ÍF* i. 78, 79, 157; *ÍF* xiii. 28; *Sturl* 5. 92). He was the forefather of the Reykhyltingar; his son was Magnús in Reykholt who is mentioned among the chieftains who were ordained as priests in Gizurr Ísleifsson's episcopacy (1082–1118) (*ASB* xi. 50). The Reykhyltingar owned a *goðorð* and so did their neighbours the Gilsbekkingar whose ancestor Hermundr was. It is plausible that the story about Hermundr's strange death was preserved among the Reykhyltingar, who are likely to have enjoyed telling stories at the Gilsbekkingar's expense, although outright hostilities are not recorded between them.[27] If the story originates among the Reykhyltingar, it is likely that Þórðr Sölvason being a priest was based on family tradition. It is of course equally possible that, just as he made use of other historical figures, the author of *Bandamanna saga* made Þórðr a priest because all his more famous descendants were priests. It is testimony to the author's historical awareness that in this story it is implied that there was no priest at Gilsbakki by the middle of the eleventh century—there certainly was one there, if not two, in the author's time (*DI* xii. 10; iv. 121–3)—and as it is unlikely that he knew that for sure, he must have held similar views on early church organization as the author of *Eyrbyggja saga*, assuming that there were churches but very few priests.

While there are few grounds to place much faith in this type of source, it is perfectly possible that Þórðr was a priest. If saga traditions can be trusted, the Gilsbekkingar were the dominant family in this area in the tenth and early eleventh centuries, but by the twelfth the Reykhyltingar had risen to prominence. Þórðr's son Magnús is the first of that family on record as a chieftain, and while we do not of course know how he came to that position, the temptation is to explain it in similar terms as the rise of the Haukdælir; that sometime in the early or mid-eleventh century the Reykhyltingar recognized the political advantages of holding church office, and managed through that to consolidate their position to the extent that by 1100 they had become equal to or even more prominent than the Gilsbekkingar.[28]

[27] In fact the chieftain Hermundr Koðránsson in Kalmannstunga (S) (d. 1197), Hermundr Illugason's great-grandson, supported Páll Sölvason in his dispute with Böðvarr Þórðarson and Sturla Þórðarson (*Sturl* 93, cf. 92).

[28] *Kristni saga* lists Magnús Þórðarson among the chieftains who were ordained in Bishop Gizurr's time, but Styrmir Hreinsson of the Gilsbekkingar among the greatest chieftains in Iceland at the death of Bishop Gizurr (*ASB* xi. 50, 53).

The evidence for priests of Bishop Ísleifr's generation is therefore meagre to say the least; there is only Þórðr Sölvason who can be tentatively regarded as having been a priest. The presence of foreign missionary bishops in Iceland into the 1060s suggests that down to that time native clergymen were thin on the ground, or more precisely that it was only in Ísleifr's episcopacy that an indigenous priesthood, of the type we know from later sources, emerged. For the second generation there is slightly better evidence than for the first; there are seven candidates of whom six did almost certainly exist.

Of Bishop Ísleifr's three sons two were priests: Gizurr (b. 1042, d. 1118) who succeeded him as bishop of Skálholt in 1082 and Teitr (d. 1110) in Haukadalur (S) who fostered and taught Ari *fróði* (b. 1067 d. 1148), Bishop Þorlákr Rúnólfsson (b. 1085 d. 1133), and Bishop Björn Gilsson (d. 1162) (*ÍF* i. 20; *Bsk* i. 153). As far as we know neither Gizurr nor Teitr were taught by their father; Gizurr studied in Saxony and Teitr was fostered by Hallr Þórarinsson *mildi* in Haukadalur (S) (d. 1089) (*Sturl* 192). All three sons of Bishop Ísleifr are called chieftains (*höfðingjar*) (*ÍF* i. 20; *Bsk* i. 153, 219; *Sturl* 192; *Bysp* 1. 23; *Bysp* 1. 75–6), but it was only Teitr's descendants who owned *goðorð* later on. The only thing that is known about Þorvaldr is that he lived at Hraungerði (S), and *Hungrvaka* calls him a 'great chieftain', which may indicate his seniority. With Gizurr at Skálholt and Teitr at Haukadalur the three are likely to have exercised control over much, if not all, of Árnesþing and their secure regional position is reflected in their marriages. Both Gizurr and Teitr married women from different corners of the country; Gizurr's wife was Steinunn Þorgrímsdóttir from Borgarhöfn (A) (*ÍF* i. 310). She was a widow of Þórir Skegg-Broddason from Hof in Vopnafjörður (A) (*ÍF* i. 291, 292), with whom the chieftain family of the Hofverjar came to an end,[29] and from a political point of view it was to that inheritance Gizurr was marrying. Teitr was married to Jórunn Einarsdóttir, probably from Öxnadalur (N) on her father's side, but a great-granddaughter of Síðu-Hallr on her mother's side (*ÍF* i. 259 n. 5, 318). Both Teitr and Gizurr married off their daughters to powerful chieftains in the north: Gróa Gizurardóttir was married to Ketill Þorsteinsson from Möðruvellir (N), later bishop of Hólar, and Rannveig Teitsdóttir was married to the chieftain Hafliði Másson.

These alliances are a testimony to the high societal status of these men, and to their importance in national politics. They were clearly on a level with the most powerful secular chieftains in the country, but they were also dedicated to the Church and its advancement. However inflated Bishop Gizurr's achievements may have become in later sources, it is beyond doubt that he donated his ancestral lands to the see of Skálholt, thereby putting the bishopric on a sound financial footing, and that he at least supported the introduction of the tithe and the establishment of the second see at Hólar. Teitr's contribution is apparent in his rather splendid disciples. Whether the Haukdælir came to wield

[29] Þórir's and Steinunn's son Broddi is said to have become impoverished and moved to live with his half-sister Gróa Gizurardóttir, wife of Bishop Ketill Þorsteinsson at Hólar (*ÍF* xi. 350).

political power because of their involvement with the Church, or ecclesiastical office just added to their prominence, and whether they considered ecclesiastical office primarily as a means to increase their worldly influence or their drive was principally a spiritual one, it seems certain that Gizurr and Teitr considered their fortunes to be closely linked with the advancement of the Church as an institution.

The same can be argued for the other priests of their generation, and Ari *fróði* attributes this to the example of Ísleifr: 'But when chieftains and other good men saw that Ísleifr was much more competent than other clergymen available in that country, many of them gave him their sons to be taught and had them ordained as priests. Two of them were later consecrated as bishops; Kollr who was east in the Vík [in Norway], and Jón at Hólar' (*ÍF* i. 20).

According to *Landnámabók* Kollr Þorkelsson *Víkverjabiskup* was the great-grandson of Ketilbjörn Teitsson in a direct male line and therefore Bishop Ísleifr's first cousin twice removed. Kollr's career in Norway is not mentioned in sources independent of *Íslendingabók*, and the status of his family is obscure. It seems certain that by the time Kollr was studying at Skálholt Ketilbjörn's line had been sidelined by their cousins of Gizurr *hvíti*'s line. Kollr may therefore be the first example of someone of aristocratic birth taking holy orders not to enhance his secular power but to save himself from obscurity by making a career for himself within the Church. The fact that Kollr made his career in Norway indicates that his cousins had ensured that there were no ancestral lands or powers for him in Árnesþing.

As discussed in Chapter 4, section 1, St Jón's career shows similar symptoms. He did however spend more than twenty years as a priest, and probably chieftain, at Breiðabólstaður in Fljótshlíð (S), and it may be that his becoming bishop of Hólar in 1106 was either due to his failure in establishing his power in Rangárþing or because he did not have any heirs to hand it to.

When it had been agreed to create a second diocese in the northern quarter there was according to *Jóns saga helga* prolonged bickering among the chieftains of that quarter about which of them should concede his patrimony for the establishment of the see. In the end a respectable priest, one Illugi Bjarnarson, relinquished his land at Hólar in Hjaltadalur (N), for which, *Jóns saga helga* assures us, God gave him a beautiful placement in everlasting bliss which is rightly understood as the patrimony of good men (*Bsk* i. 159, 231–2).[30] Hafliði Másson at Breiðabólstaður in Vesturhóp (N) had among his daughters one who was married to the priest Ingimundr, son of Illugi and Arna daughter of Þorkell Gellisson (*ASB* xi. 55, where she is called Árný). According to a fourteenth-century source, Illugi of Hólar moved to Breiðabólstaður after giving up Hólar

[30] It does not seem that Hólar was Illugi's patrimony because according to *Jóns saga* one Oxi Hjaltason lived there earlier in the 11th cent. (*Bsk* i. 163, 235) who was no doubt the son of Hjalti Þórðarson who lived there in 1028 according to the chronology of *Grettis saga* (*ÍF* vii. 226), grandson of Hjalti Þórðarson the primary settler in Hjaltadalur (*ÍF* i. 238; Tobíasson 1943: 17, cf. 62–3).

for the new see (*ÍF* xvii. 218) and it is reasonable to assume that he is the same as Ingimundr's father.

It makes good sense that Hafliði was influential, if not instrumental, in the establishment of the new see (J. Jóhannesson 1956: 184; M. Stefánsson 1975: 64), and the suggested familial connections between him and Illugi of Hólar may go some way to explain why Illugi felt he could relinquish his land. If Illugi was a chieftain, as his marriage with a daughter of Þorkell Gellisson would indicate, he can well have secured the marriage of his son to Hafliði's daughter long before the question of the see arose and those affinities may then have eased his generosity. It is equally possible that Hafliði and Illugi made a deal whereby Illugi gave up his land for the see but secured a very advantageous marriage for his son and comfort at Breiðabólstaður in his old age.

In Illugi Bjarnarson we have the only example of an Icelandic eleventh-century priest outside the southern quarter. The admittedly circumstantial evidence for his familial relations also suggests that like the first priests in the south he was of high status, but it seems clear that unlike the Haukdælir the chieftains of Skagafjörður lacked the interest or organization to have control over the see from the outset.

A priest called Þorkell *trandill*, 'a most respectable clergyman', is mentioned in *Jóns saga helga*, in one version (A) as having been St Jón's *fóstbróðir* (foster brother), in another (C) as his fosterer from his father's death, and in the third (B) as his *skólabróðir* (fellow student) (*Bsk* i. 172, 245).[31] There is no saying which of the three versions is closest to the original, but as A and B are closest in meaning, it can be assumed that St Jón and Þorkell *trandill* were contemporaries and friends who had known each other since boyhood. Þorkell died in Skálholt sometime in St Jón's episcopacy, probably in its latter part. The subject of the story in *Jóns saga helga* is that St Jón in Hólar dreamt of Þorkell's death in Skálholt on the night he died. If Þorkell died in Skálholt and was perhaps educated there as well, it seems likely that he served at the cathedral. In the fourteenth century the monks of Þingeyrar put Þorkell *trandill* to good use and made him the *fundator* of their monastery. While this is of course not impossible, the tradition is too late to be given much weight and it is then strange that the author of *Jóns saga*, brother Gunnlaugr of Þingeyrar, should have kept quiet about it (see Ch. 3, s. 5). That then leaves us with little to say about Þorkell *trandill* except that he probably existed and may have served the cathedral at Skálholt.

Þorkell *trandill* is an obscure figure but he is likely to have existed. That is probably not the case with the priest Guttormr Finnólfsson from Laugardalur (S) whom *Hungrvaka* mentions as being Bishop Ísleifr's preferred successor. As discussed in Chapter 4, section 1, the story is suspicious and probably the author's invention to justify Gizurr's inheritance of the episcopacy. It is of

[31] All three versions could be a translation of some Latin word like *confrater* which in turn was a translation of one of the others.

course possible that the author made use of the name of some priest he knew had lived in the eleventh century, but in that case we have nothing to go by on his status or career.

The case of St Jón's friend, neighbour, and contemporary, the priest Sæmundr *fróði* Sigfússon in Oddi in Rangárvellir (1054/6–1133) is very different from that of the saint and very similar to the Haukdælir brothers. His ancestry suggests that local power had been in the hands of his family since the tenth century (whether they owned a *goðorð* or not), although the fame of some of the Oddaverjar's ancestors must be considered in the context of their considerable cultural influence in the twelfth and thirteenth century. Judging from the marriages of Sæmundr's father and grandfather they were of considerable standing. Sæmundr's mother was the daughter of Eyjólfr *halti* of the Möðruvellingar mentioned above. Sæmundr's own marriage to a local girl, Guðrún Kolbeinsdóttir of the Vallverjar, indicates however that he was more interested in consolidating his regional powers. The important estate Vellir in Land (S) which was in the possession of the Oddaverjar in the early thirteenth century may have come to them through Sæmundr's marriage (*Sturl* 256; Arnórsson 1944–8: 236–9).[32] According to Ari *fróði* Sæmundr studied in Franconia and came back in 1076–83 (*ÍF* i. 20–1)[33] and that expedition indicates that his family had learnt from the example of the Haukdælir and were bent on comparable success. Sæmundr seems to have established himself as the learned man *par excellence* in Iceland. He is widely quoted (Ellehøj 1965: 16–25) and neither the tithe law, *Íslendingabók*, nor the original draft of the Old Christian law section could be composed without his advice. To what extent he laid the foundations of the later power of the Oddaverjar is however unclear. Neither he nor his sons are listed among the thirteen greatest chieftains in the country in 1118 (*ASB* xi. 53), and there is no good evidence for the supremacy of the Oddaverjar in Rangárþing until the times of Sæmundr's grandson Jón Loptsson (d. 1197) (Þorláksson 1989*a*: 14–19). Sæmundr's main contribution to his family's later prominence must have been the foundation of the *staðr* at Oddi, which his descendants attributed to him (*Bsk* i. 283; *ÍF* xvii. 36, 37) as well as the respect he built for his family's wisdom and erudition, which no doubt helped his grandson Jón in getting King Magnús Erlingsson to recognize their consanguinity in 1164, accepting the claim that Jón's mother Þóra was the daughter of King Magnús *berfættr* (Barelegs) (*ÍF* xxviii. 395).[34]

Although it is difficult to estimate the extent of Sæmundr's regional influence, and the Oddaverjar seem to have taken longer to consolidate power in

[32] According to modern folklore Sæmundr's wife was of much lower class than he (Tómasson 1966).

[33] M. M. Lárusson's (1967*a*: 358) explanation that Ari's *Frakkland* is Franconia and not France seems the most acceptable one. Medieval tradition located Sæmundr's place of study variously at Rome (*Bsk* i. 156 n. 2) or Paris (*IA* 471), but his studies abroad had very quickly become the stuff of myth (*Bsk* i. 227–9; B. Einarsson 1955: pp. cii–cxii; also Foote 1984*a*: 101–20).

[34] In the poem *Nóregskonungatal* Sæmundr is called *haufuds madr* | *við hluti alla* (principal in all things) *Skjald* i. 589.

their region in their own hands than the Haukdælir in theirs, there is no doubting the extent of Sæmundr's influence on church politics in his own day and that his reputation, if not concrete power, was one of the keys to his descendants' political success. Like Gizurr and Teitr, Sæmundr seems to have been committed to strengthening the Church as an institution. The evidence for these men's secular power is circumstantial, but that of their descendants is not, and there can be little doubt that their involvement with the Church, and their influence over it, was the advantage these two families had over all others, and one of the main reasons why they dominated national politics in the twelfth century, and in the case of the Haukdælir right through to the end of the Commonwealth.

The evidence for eleventh-century priests is meagre, and it is to be expected that those who were of high birth and those who had influential descendants are over-represented. After 1100 the picture gets more complex because of the increase in source material. It is however useful to remember that the writing of records began only in the first half of the twelfth century, because of the introduction of the means of writing by the Church, and that the reason why written records do not appear earlier must be that the Church was not strong or organized enough to produce them. There are neither reasons nor indications to think that a considerable number of organized clergy existed in the country until around or after 1100. The fact that men of aristocratic birth, who either were chieftains, or had aspirations in that direction, sought ordination as priests suggests strongly that there was not a large number of priests of lower status. One of the main reasons why aristocrats became priests must have been the exclusivity such a position offered. It is possible that there was a class of itinerant priests who were sufficiently few or foreign not to detract from the status value of the chieftains' ordinations, but there is no evidence for this and such a class would at any rate have disappeared when the trend for aristocrats to take orders became more marked.

4. EARLY CHURCH BUILDING

Proto-Historic Evidence

The Sagas of Icelanders, *Landnámabók* and *Kristni saga*, record traditions about thirty-five churches which were supposed to have been built in the eleventh century or earlier. Four of these are linked to tales of the conversion. Curiously enough, the four were quite insignificant or had ceased to exist when detailed sources became available: the church widely regarded as the first, Ás in Hjaltadalur (N), was still standing in 1238–46 according to *Kristni saga* (*Bsk* i. 6–7)[35] but then disappears from

[35] The building of the church in 984 is also mentioned in *Þáttr af Þorvaldi* (*ASB* xi. 72) and all the major annals (*IA* 16, 48, 104, 178, 249, 315, 463).

TABLE 1. *Churches reported as built before 1100*

Farmstead	Date	Source	Reference	Type of church
Traditions about Christian settlers				
Esjuberg (S)	*c.*900	*Landnáma*	*ÍF* i. 54, 55	?
		Kjalnesinga s.	*ÍF* xiv. 5, 43	
Bjarnastaðir (S)	*c.*925	*Landnáma*	*ÍF* i. 82	Ø
Traditions about missionary activity				
Ás in Hjaltadalur (N)	984	*Kristni s.*	*ASB* xi. 10[a]	?
Haukagil in Vatnsdalur (N)	982–6	*Þáttr af Þorvaldi*	*ASB* xi. 71	a
Holt in Ásar (N)	*c.*1000	*Þáttr af Þorvaldi*	*ASB* xi. 75–6	a
Vestmannaeyjar (S)	1000	*Kristni s.*	*ASB* xi. 37	Ø
Traditions about early church building by chieftains				
Þingvellir (S)	*c.*1000	*Ólafs s. helga*	*ÍF* xxvii. 214[b]	public
Skálholt (S)	1001	*Eyrbyggja s.*	*ÍF* iv. 141, 145	see
Hjalli in Ölfus (S)	*c.*1000	*Flóamanna s.*	*ÍF* xiii. 325–6	imp/*b*
Mosfell in Mosfellssveit (S)	*c.*1000	*Egils s.*	*ÍF* ii. 298[c]	imp/*b*
Borg in Mýrar (S)	*c.*1000	*Egils s.*	*ÍF* ii. 299	imp/*b*
		Laxdæla s.	*ÍF* v. 158	
Vellir in Hítardalur (S)	1020–4	*Bjarnar s.*	*ÍF* iii. 163, 207	Ø
Fróðá (S)	1001	*Eyrbyggja s.*	*ÍF* iv. 136	*staðr*
Berserkjahraun (S)	*aq* 1007	*Heiðarvíga s.*	*ÍF* iii. 230, 235	a
		Eyrbyggja s.	*ÍF* iv. 136	
Helgafell in Helgafellssveit (D) (1)	1000–8	*Ævi Snorra*	*ÍF* iv. 186	monastery
(2)	*c.*1020	*Ævi Snorra*	*ÍF* iv. 186	
		Laxdæla s.	*ÍF* v. 196	
Ljárskógar in Dalir (D)	*c.*1020	*Grettis s.*	*ÍF* vii. 173	Ø
Sælingsdalstunga in Dalir (D)	*aq* 1031	*Ævi Snorra*	*ÍF* iv. 186	imp/*b*
	1008	*Heiðarvíga s.*	*ÍF* iii. 246–7	
Reykhólar in Reykjanes (D)	*aq* 1030	*Fóstbr. s*	*ÍF* vi. 124	imp/*b*
Finnbogastaðir in Trékyllisvík (N)	*c.*1000	*Finnboga s.*	ÍF xiv. 324	Ø
Bjarg in Miðfjörður (N)	*c.*1020	*Grettis s.*	*ÍF* vii. 139, 270	a
Hof in Vatnsdalur (N)	*c.*1000	*Vatnsdæla s.*	*ÍF* viii. 126	b
Þórhallsstaðir in Forsæludalur (N)	*c.*1024	*Grettis s.*	*ÍF* vii. 110	Ø
Reykir in Reykjaströnd (N)	*c.*1032	*Grettis s.*	*ÍF* vii. 269	Ø
Glaumbær in Skagafjörður (N)	*pq* 1008	*Grænlendinga s.*	*ÍF* iv. 269	imp/*b*
Hólar in Hjaltadalur (N) (1)	*pq* 1028	*Jóns s. helga*	*Bsk* i. 163	see
(2)	*c.*1080	*Jóns s. helga*	*Bsk* i. 163	
Knappsstaðir in Fljót (N)	*c.*1000	*Þórhalls þ. knapps*	*ÓST* ii. 184–7	b
Bægisá in Öxnadalur (N)	*c.*1050	*Ljósvetninga s.*	*ÍF* x. 18	*staðr*
Fornhagi in Hörgárdalur (N)	*c.*1000	*Víga Glúms s.*	*ÍF* ix. 98	Ø
Þórhallsstaðir in Þorvaldsdalur (N)	*c.*1000	*Hávarðar s. Ísf.*	*ÍF* vi. 357–8	Ø
Grund in Svarfaðardalur (N)	*c.*1000	*Valla-Ljóts s.*	*ÍF* ix. 243	a
Eyjardalsá in Bárðardalur (N)	*c.*1026	*Grettis s.*	*ÍF* vii. 209–18	b
Þvottá in Álftafjörður (A)	1011	*Njáls s.*	*ÍF* xii. 459	*staðr*
Svínafell in Ingólfshöfðahverfi (A)	1011	*Njáls s.*	*ÍF* xii. 459	imp/*staðr*
Kirkjubær in Síða (S)	1011	*Njáls s.*	*ÍF* xii. 322	monastery
Traditions about late 11th-century churches				
Rauðilækur in Ingólfshöfðahverfi (A)	*pq* 1071	*Sörla þáttr*	*ÍF* x. 113	*staðr*
Hólmur in Akranes (S)	*pq* 1049	*Landnáma* (H)	*ÍF* i. 65	b

TABLE 1. *Churches reported as built before 1100 (continued)*

Farmstead	Date	Source	Reference	Type of church
Historical sources				
Breiðabólstaður in Fljótshlíð (S)	*c.*1080	*Jóns s. helga*	*Bsk.* i. 157	imp/*staðr*
Oddi in Rangárvellir (S)	*c.*1080	*Jóns s. helga*	*Bsk.* i, 157	imp/*staðr*
Haukadalur in Biskupstungur (S)	1082–1118	*Kristni s.*	*ASB* xi. 50	imp/*b*
Skálholt (S)	*pq* 1080	*Íslendingabók*	*ÍF* i. 23	see
	(*c.*1010	*Hungrvaka*	*Bysp* 1. 76)	
Þingvallakirkja (S)	*pq* 1050	*Kristni s.*	*ASB* xi. 52	public
Reykholt in Borgarfjörður (S)	1082–1118	*Kristni s.*	*ASB* xi. 50	imp/*staðr*
Bær in Borgarfjörður (S)	1082–1118	*Kristni s.*	*ASB* xi. 50	imp
	(*aq* 1049	*Landnáma* (H)	*ÍF* i. 65)	
Helgafell in Helgafellssveit (D)	*aq* 1073	*Laxdæla s.*	*ÍF* v. 229	monastery
Hjarðarholt in Laxárdalur (D)	1082–1118	*Kristni s.*	*ASB* xi. 50–51	imp/*staðr*
Reykhólar in Reykjanes (D)	1082–1118	*Kristni s.*	*ASB* xi. 51	imp/*b*
Hólar in Hjaltadalur (N)	*pq* 1106	*Jóns s.*	*Bsk.* i. 163	see
Möðruvellir in Eyjafjörður (N)	1082–1118	*Kristni s.*	*ASB* xi. 51	imp/*b*

a = annex church; *aq* = ante quem; *b* = *bændakirkja* or church which owns less than half the land it stands on; imp = residence of important chieftains in 12th or 13th cent.; *pq* = *post quem*; public = public church; *staðr* = church which owns the land which it stands on, ecclesiastical centre; Ø = no church known in later times; ? = status or fate of church uncertain

[a] Also *ASB* xi. 72–3, 79; *IA*, 16, 48, 104, 178, 249, 315, 463.
[b] Also ÓSHS, 325; *Flat* iii. 247, 344, 415; *ÍF* vii. 344; *ÍF* x. 38, 41; *ÍF* xii. 312; *ÍF* xxviii. 119; *ÍF* xxix. 261; *Mork* 170; *ASB* xi. 52.
[c] Also *Gunnlaugs saga ormstungu, ÍF* iii. 105.

records. A church has been excavated at this site, surrounded by graves dated to the eleventh century (Vésteinsson 1998*c*). The churches at Holt in Ásar (N) and Haukagil in Vatnsdalur (N), which were supposed to have been built before 1000 (*ASB* xi. 71, 75), were both annex-churches in the fourteenth and fifteenth centuries (*DI* ii. 475; v. 353, 354). The church Gizurr *hvíti* and Hjalti Skeggjason are supposed to have built on Hörgaeyri in Vestmannaeyjar (S), the day after they came ashore on their mission to make the Icelanders accept Christianity (*Bsk* i. 20; *ÓST* ii. 188),[36] is not mentioned in later records.[37] The story has clear

[36] The two texts are very similar and no doubt based on the same source—Gunnlaugr Leifsson's Latin Saga of Ólafr Tryggvason (written *c.*1200, now lost) has been suggested—Ólsen 1893: 263–349; F. Jónsson 1920–4: ii. 572–7; Aðalbjarnarson 1937: 120–4; Lönnroth 1963: 54–94; Halldórsson 1990*b*: 50.

[37] The place-name was lost in the 19th cent., but was then reidentified as the eyri (= small and flat promontory) called Klemenseyri, on the northern side of the harbour (Kaalund 1877: i. 279; Brynjólfur Jónsson 1918: 27–8). Whether this identification is correct or not—there is not much space between the steep cliffs of Heimaklettur and the sea—the location of this church on a small and inaccessible parcel of land on the far side of the settled area of the island must be considered strange. Skeletal remains have been found in the same area although not on the promontory itself and not in circumstances which allow it to be ascertained whether they were Christian burials (Brynjúlfur Jónsson 1907*a*: 11; Þórðarson 1913: 37; Sigurfinnsson 1913: 12; Brynjólfur Jónsson 1918: 27). If Klemenseyri is the same as Hörgaeyri the place-name element hörga- (*hörgr* = pagan ritual site; pile of stones, cf. *hearg* in Old English) could suggest that this was a pagan cult place and the burials therefore pagan. The identification of Klemenseyri as Hörgaeyri has led scholars to link the early church with an otherwise unknown annex-church of St Clemence mentioned in a 14th-cent. charter

dramatic qualities; the church building is a definite statement of the heroes' intentions; they waste no time in realizing their task, and it was fitting for the introducers of Christianity to build a church on a site where pagan rituals had been performed.

In addition to this *Landnámabók* preserves traditions about two very early churches, which are supposed to have been built by primary settlers, that is around 900. The one at Esjuberg (S) appears in the inventory of churches connected with Bishop Páll's counting of churches around 1200, and was still there in 1269–98 according to *Kjalnesinga saga*, but is never heard of after that (*ÍF* i. 54, 55; xiv. 5, 43; *DI* xv. 9). Local traditions have long pointed to a site in the home field of Esjuberg (Hallgrímsson 1989: ii. 141, 415–16, 440–1; Kaalund 1877: i. 54; B. Jónsson 1902: 33–5; S. Vigfússon 1881: 66), but when investigated in 1981 it turned out to be a natural pile of stones (Magnússon 1983: 193; see also A. Friðriksson 1994*a*: 100–1). The other church, at Bjarnastaðir (S) (*ÍF* i. 82), is not mentioned in any other sources. Nineteenth-century antiquarians found a site which they identified with Bjarnastaðir, badly eroded with skeletal remains scattered on the ground around a stone foundation believed to be the remains of the church (Hallgrímsson 1989: ii. 415, 440–1; Kaalund 1877: i. 337–8; B. Jónsson 1893: 75–6; Þórðarson 1909*b*: 45; see also *JÁM* iv. 259–60; A. Friðriksson 1994*a*: 97–8).

It turns out that the six churches connected with traditions about early Christianity and early missionary activity were either churches of minor significance in later times or did not exist at all. In a sense this makes it more difficult to dismiss these traditions. It is far from obvious what interests should have conspired to make up stories like these. On the other hand that matters little; even if these tales were all true and these churches actually were built, their non-existence or insignificance in more recent times suggests that they were not important for the later development. The twenty-seven churches mentioned in the Sagas of Icelanders as being built by chieftains shortly after the conversion, belong to a different kind of tradition. In thirteen sagas the hero/chieftain is said to have built a church at his farm shortly after the conversion.[38] Commonly this occurs at the end of the saga when the hero

of Kirkjubær (*DI* ii. 66—the charter is dated there to 1269, but is undoubtedly more recent. Brynjúlfur Jónsson 1907*a*: 10–11; Þórðarson 1913: 35–41; Hofmann 1994). A more mundane—and it seems the more original—explanation of this place-name is that a merchant of the Royal Danish trading company (17th and 18th cents.) called Klemens added to the promontory to secure the harbour (Sigurfinnsson 1913: 13). Identifications based on place-name evidence and tales of archaeological finds will always be doubtful, although they may indicate that the 13th-cent. authors of *Kristni saga* and *Ólafs saga Tryggvasonar hin mesta* built their story on some kind of tradition; they could have made similar connections as the 20th-cent. scholars. Whatever the sources for this tale, it is best regarded as a literary device.

[38] *Bjarnar saga Hítdælakappa*, *ÍF* iii. 163, 207; *Egils saga*, *ÍF* ii. 298, 299; *Eyrbyggja saga*, *ÍF* iv. 136, 183; *Finnboga saga ramma*, *ÍF* xiv. 324; *Flóamanna saga*, *ÍF* xiii. 325–6; *Fóstbræðra saga*, *ÍF* vi. 124; *Grænlendinga saga*, *ÍF* iv. 269; *Hávarðar saga Ísfirðings*, *ÍF* vi. 357–8; *Heiðarvíga saga*, *ÍF* iii. 235; *Laxdæla saga*, *ÍF* v. 158, 196, 229; *Vatnsdæla saga*, *ÍF* viii. 126; *Víga Glúms saga*, *ÍF* ix. 98; *Þórhalls þáttr knapps*, *ÓST* ii. 184–7.

has done all his deeds, and is put among the standard conventions of ending a saga, saying that the hero had many important descendants, etc. In the majority of these cases the hero is the righteous type who seeks nothing but peace and to be a good leader of men. These are not the fey types of heroes, the warriors, poets, outlaws, or victims of circumstance, but heroes who were the pillars of their society and to whom in many cases a great number of people could trace their ancestry. In short they were men whom thirteenth-century historical tradition knew to have been important in the late tenth and early eleventh century. The best examples are Snorri *goði*, one of the most widely mentioned early chieftains,[39] and Snorri Karlsefnisson, born in Vínland and forefather of three bishops.

These were the good guys, and their goodness was of course measured in terms of thirteenth-century ideas, which included among other things being a Christian. According to thirteenth-century attitudes, a good chieftain meant being an active supporter and upholder of things Christian. Being good, these heroes/chieftains had to be made Christian as soon as it was chronologically possible and they had to be seen to embrace the new religion and actively support it. There are therefore literary and ideological reasons behind these tales of early churches. There may also have been contemporary political reasons for such tales in that at least fourteen of the churches were later rich and important and owned by important people who may have found that it increased respectability to be able to claim seniority and connections with famous forefathers.

That these were ideals rather than traditions based on actual events is probably best seen in the more fictional sagas like *Finnboga saga ramma* and *Hávarðar saga Ísfirðings*. In both sagas the authors attempt to draw attention to otherwise little known personages. In *Finnboga saga* especially, the author tries to create an important chieftain out of a, possibly historical, figure who seems to have been remembered more for his muscular deeds than for his high position in society. At least, Finnbogi *rammi* does not occur anywhere else in a chieftain capacity.[40] It is in accordance with the author's other attempts to move his hero up the social ladder to make him build a church at his farm Finnbogastaðir (N) (*ÍF* xiv. 324). In the thirteenth century the church of that area was at Árnes, which is only a few hundred metres away from Finnbogastaðir, and there is no evidence for a church or chapel at Finnbogastaðir later when sources become more extensive. It could be suggested that Árnes was a more recent farm carved out of the land of Finnbogastaðir (although *Grettis saga*'s account would not agree with that (*ÍF* vii. 21–2, cf. *ÍF* i. 198))[41] or that the church had been moved. But if the author had thought so he would surely have mentioned

[39] Blöndal 1931 is an interesting study of the type of character Snorri *goði* represents.

[40] Cf. his negative portrayal in *Vatnsdæla saga* (*ÍF* viii. 85–94).

[41] To further compound this issue there are traditions that there was a church at Bær (between Árnes and Finnbogastaðir) before it was moved to Árnes (*PP*, 207), and in the home field of Bær an enclosure is identified as the churchyard of Finnbogi *rammi* (Georgsson 1990: 39).

it, like the author of *Egils saga* on the church at Mosfell in Mosfellssveit (S) (*ÍF* ii. 298). That he did not, suggests that his story about the church at Finnbogastaðir is pure fiction, intended to support the idea of Finnbogi's social importance. The same is even more true of the church which Hávarðr, in *Hávarðar saga Ísfirðings*, is supposed to have had built at Þórhallsstaðir in Þorvaldsdalur (N), a marginally habitable valley in the north (*ÍF* vi. 357–8). Hávarðr was not a chieftain but a respectable householder of considerable means according to his story, which is an almost comic account of how he in his old age avenged his son's death on his social superiors. In the two final chapters of the story the author is at pains to describe his hero as a man respected in his community: he has him give a splendid banquet inviting the great chieftains of his region and when he hears of King Ólafr Tryggvason converting the Norwegians he promptly sails off for Norway with his wife to be baptized and brings back wood to build a church. He dies soon afterwards but had earlier instructed his cousin Þórhallr (hence the name of the farm) to build a church at a new farm in an even more remote part of the valley, where Hávarðr was subsequently buried. This suggests that the author was in some trouble finding a credible location for his hero's church, and had to invent a remote location, or link his tale with a known place-name which happened to be in a desolate valley. In either case it is beyond reasonable doubt that the tale of Hávarðr's church is fictional and made up to emphasize his goodness. Another way of looking at this saga's rather improbable accounts of conversion and church building is to see it as a parody of older Sagas of Icelanders (H. Guðmundsson 1990), in which case we can take the account of Hávarðr's conversion and posthumous church building as confirmation that these sort of stories were seen as a standard device in medieval saga-writing.

These are all thirteenth- or fourteenth-century traditions, which alone is sufficient reason not to take them at their face value. The only text containing similar traditions which is possibly of a twelfth-century date is the so-called *Ævi Snorra goða*, a short and truncated account of the main events in the life of the chieftain Snorri Þorgrímsson (963/4–1031) with a list of his twenty-two children (*ÍF* iv. 185–6).[42]

According to this text Snorri had a church built at Helgafell (D), presumably between 1000 and 1008, and another one at Sælingsdalstunga after he moved there in 1008. 'But some say that he had a second church built at Helgafell with

[42] In his edition Einar Ólafur Sveinsson argued (*ÍF* iv, pp. xi–xiii) that *Ævi Snorra goða* is an early memorandum which was a source for *Eyrbyggja saga* and *Laxdæla saga*, and that it had probably been put together by Ari *fróði*, but a reference to him in *Laxdæla saga* agrees with a clause in Ævi *Snorra goða*, (*ÍF* v, pp. xxxvi–xxxvii, 226) and on Ari's own account Snorri's daughter Þuríðr was one of the main sources for *Íslendingabók* (*ÍF* i. 4). Einar's hypothesis has been accepted without much reservation by later scholars (*IBS* i. 294, 357) and his argument that *Ævi Snorra goða* is an independent construction put together before *Eyrbyggja saga* or *Laxdæla saga* were written is convincing, but the authorship of Ari, and therefore an early 12th-cent. date, must remain questionable. *Eyrbyggja saga* and *Laxdæla saga* are not believed to be written until the third quarter of the 13th cent. (*IBS* ii. 117, 133–4) and *Ævi Snorra goða* can only be said to predate that.

Guðrún, when the church he had had built burned' (*ÍF* iv. 186), that is sometime between 1008 and 1031 as Guðrún Ósvífursdóttir, the heroine of *Laxdæla saga*, had changed Sælingsdalstunga (D) for Helgafell in 1008. The account of *Eyrbyggja saga* to similar effect is clearly based on this authority and therefore has no independent value (*ÍF* iv. 136, 183). *Laxdæla saga*'s version is slightly different; it mentions a church Guðrún Ósvífursdóttir had built at Helgafell (*ÍF* v. 196), which may fit *Ævi Snorra goða*'s story about Snorri's involvement with the building of the second church at Helgafell. It then claims that Guðrún's son and successor at Helgafell, Gellir Þorkelsson (1008–73/4), had a magnificent church built there, and refers to a poem about Gellir by Arnórr *jarlaskáld*[43] which is not preserved (*ÍF* v. 229). Here it seems the author of *Laxdæla saga* preferred a different tradition from the one available to him or her in *Ævi Snorra goða*, although an outright contradiction is avoided. There was of course more reason to emphasize the good works of the saga's main heroine and her descendants than to give credit to a personage who was only in a supporting role in the saga.

There is no reason to discredit the traditions about early church buildings at Helgafell and Sælingsdalstunga; a poem by Arnórr *jarlaskáld* is a contemporary source for Gellir's construction work and must be taken as good evidence for what, according to *Ævi Snorra goða*, would have been the third church at Helgafell. *Ævi Snorra goða* is a slightly more problematic source but there are no particular grounds to dismiss it either. Whether it was Ari or somebody else who wrote it, the author was clearly somebody who had detailed knowledge of Snorri and his descendants at an earlier stage than most Sagas of Icelanders were written. Moreover it is simply likely that great chieftains like Snorri *goði* were the first to build churches in Iceland; it must have been they who led the decision to convert and who were in the best position to take advantage of the introduction of Christianity.

A smaller group of stories about early churches are not concerned with the swiftness of householders/chieftains in building churches immediately after the conversion. These stories function more as simple supports to a character description. An example of this is Þorsteinn Kuggason, householder at Ljárskógar (D), who we are told had had a church built at his farm. This information comes in the introduction to this personage in *Grettis saga*, where he is praised for his industriousness and construction work. The church is not mentioned again and has no bearing on the following accounts (*ÍF* vii. 173). Þorsteinn was a friend and supporter of the outlaw Grettir, and we are clearly to understand his church building as a sign of his magnanimity and social significance, if not political importance. It says something about a man that he had the drive and wealth to construct a church at his farm. Stories like these are in essence no different from the stories of chieftains building churches

[43] Arnórr Þórðarson composed poems about King Magnús Ólafsson the good and King Haraldr *harðráði* and Rögnvaldr Brúsason and Þorfinnr Sigurðarson, earls of Orkney in the middle of the 11th cent. (*ÍBS* i. 222–4; *Skjald* i. 332–54; Fidjestøl 1984).

immediately after the conversion. They differ only in that time of construction is not given or is put slightly later into the eleventh century, and that the men involved are sometimes of a lower social standing. The outcome is the same: the churches are signs of these men's goodness and greatness.

A related type of story is, for instance, as in the run-up to the dramatic high point of *Njáls saga*—the burning of Njáll and his family at Bergþórshvoll (S)—when the chieftain Flosi and his party on their way to the burning stop at Kirkjubær (S) and say their prayers at the church there (*ÍF* xii. 322). This is but one of many indications that we are given in the saga that Flosi was entirely conscious of the wrong he was about to do, and that he resented having to do it. In other words he was a good man and his prayers at Kirkjubær are among numerous signs we are given of his goodness. The difference between this type of story and those mentioned above is that here the church itself is not the focus of attention. The church at Kirkjubær was a well-known church and convent in the author's time and was on the route to Bergþórshvoll. It is therefore only a convenient prop in the narrative, with no other function than to serve as a setting for a note on the qualities of the personages involved.

Similar references to churches, where the building itself is not the focus of attention, are found in a few sagas, and normally they occur in stories with religious or spiritual connotations, where the audience/readers would have recognized well-known topoi involving churches. Examples are the ghost stories of *Grettis saga*, where we learn of the otherwise unattested church at Þórhallsstaðir in Forsæludalur (N) because the farmhand Glámr refused to attend the church and to fast before Christmas and was promptly turned into one of the saga literature's most notorious ghosts (*ÍF* vii. 110). Later in Grettir's ghost-busting career we hear of the church at Eyjardalsá in Bárðardalur (N) because a woman at a nearby farm was in the habit of going to mass at Christmas and her household began to disappear mysteriously one by one every Christmas (*ÍF* vii. 209–10, 216–17). Both stories are set in the 1020s but they are also clearly representatives of common folk-tales which have been told in different guises down to this day (A. Björnsson 1963: 139–40). *Grettis saga* is believed to have been written shortly after 1300 (*ÍBS* ii. 144) and its author naturally made use of symbols which his audience would have readily understood. When piety, or lack of it, was the issue, it was natural to make use of well-known topoi, with churches serving as symbols for piety, in order to get the meaning across. The same is even more true of topoi originating in Christian literature. Such are for instance the portent stories of *Njáls saga*, where blood falls on the surplice of the priest at Svínafell (A) and the priest at Þvottá (A) saw, besides his altar, into the depths of the sea with many terrors in it, both on Good Friday 1014, the same day as the battle of Clontarf was being fought, according to the saga (*ÍF* xii. 459).[44] In these stories the church itself,

[44] Other Icelandic medieval sources date the battle of Clontarf to 1003 (*IA* 467), 1004 (*IA* 105, 179, 248) or 1005 (*IA* 57).

who built it and when, is not the issue; it is only a setting and it is far from certain whether the authors of *Njáls saga* or *Grettis saga* had any clear idea of the chronological implications when they used a church as a prop in their narrative.

It is impossible to prove that the traditions regarding early churches are all fictitious, but as the context of these traditions shows them to be a literary device, the possibility that some of them were actually built very early can neither be argued for nor against. These traditions can therefore not be taken as indications for the nature or scope of early Christian activity. They do however suggest, and in this they are entirely consistent with other evidence, that the initiative for and patronage of Christian institutions came from individual chieftains and not groups of householders collectively nor the clergy, foreign or native.

The Archaeological Evidence

No churches have been excavated which can with certainty be dated to the earliest phase of Christianity in Iceland.[45] Burials and burial practices may however be able to tell us something of the development of church building in the eleventh century. In Iceland 304 pagan burials, all inhumations, have been found. Of these 100 are isolated graves, seventy-six are paired graves and of the rest seventy-one graves are found in eleven grave-fields with more than five graves (S. Einarsson 1994: 46). In his study of 246 pagan burials known in 1956 Kristján Eldjárn (1956: 195, see also 197–201) remarks that only in some cases can it be said to be certain that a burial was in fact isolated, and it is clear from his catalogue (Eldjárn 1956: 28–193) that in the majority of such cases reports of the circumstances of the finds are either non-existent or too vague to exclude the possibility that they were parts of grave-fields. When it can be ascertained, the grave-fields seem always to be situated just outside a farmstead's home field, normally a few hundred metres from the farmhouses (Eldjárn 1956: 201–5). The grave-fields seem therefore to have been used only by the inhabitants of a single farmstead. This makes much practical sense; there was no reason to take up valuable farmland for the dead, but there was also no reason to carry them long distances for burial.

Pagan burials disappear abruptly around 1000, if the stylistic dating of grave goods can be trusted. From the whole assemblage of grave goods found in Iceland there is only one brooch with an eleventh-century dating, of the type Rygh 656, which may in fact have gone into circulation just before 1000 (Eldjárn 1956: 428–9), so that can hardly be taken as good evidence for the continuation of pagan burial practices into the eleventh century. If people really did change their burial practices immediately or soon after the conversion, where and how

[45] The small chapels at Stöng (S) and Neðri-Ás (N) are the earliest excavated church sites—the former is from the second half of the eleventh century at the earliest and at the latter site only graves have been uncovered which can be dated to the early phase (Vilhjálmsson 1996; Vésteinsson 1998*c*).

Table 2. *Sites of chapels or annex churches where burials have come to light*

Farmstead	Type of church	Docum. date	Arch. date	References
Varmá in Mosfellssveit (S)	a		14th c.	*DI* iii. 220; iv. 112; Rafnsson 1971
Belgsholt in Melasveit (S)	chapel	13th c.	16th c.	*DI* i. 271–2, 419; iv. 192–3; Friðriksson and Vésteinsson 1992: 54–6
Indriðastaðir in Reykjadalur (S)	a	14th–17th c.		*DI* iv. 192; *JÁM* iv. 158; Vésteinsson 1996: 103
Steindórsstaðir in Reykholtsdalur (S)	Ø			Byggðir Borgarfjarðar ii. 293
Neðranes in Stafholtstungur (S)	Ø			Árnadóttir 1982
Staðarbakki in Helgafellssveit (S)	a			*PP* 153; ÍSLEIF
Ljárskógar (D)	a	saga		*ÍF* vii. 173; Vigfússon 1882: 79
Kjallaksstaðir in Fellsströnd (D)	Ø			Magnússon 1983
Kross in Skarðsströnd (D)	a	14th c.		*DI* ii. 635–6; iv. 157–9; Eldjárn 1974
Kirkjuból in Kollsvík (N)	a	16th c.		*JÁM* vi. 316; *DI* viii. 268; Þórðarson 1924: 45; *Íslenzkir annálar* iii. 544–5
Dufansdalur in Arnarfjörður (N)	chapel	trad.		*JÁM* vi. 380; Vésteinsson and Gunnarsdóttir 1997: 291
Brekka in Dýrafjörður (N)	chapel	trad.		*JÁM* vii. 45; Guðmundsson 1978: 93–94
Álfadalur in Ingjaldssandur (N)	chapel	18th c.		*JÁM* vii. 89; Davíðsson 1959: 127
Kirkjuból in Skutulsfjörður (N)	a	14th c.		Magnús Þorkelsson pers. comm.
Sæból in Aðalvík (N)	chapel	16th c.		*DI* xii. 694–8; *JÁM* vii. 288–9; Björnsson 1975: 119
Kirkjuból in Reykjafjörður (N)	chapel	trad.		*JÁM* vii. 315–16; Olavius 1964–65: i. 172–3; Lárusson 1944: 321–3; Thoroddsen 1913–15: ii. 82
Krossanes in Strandir (N)	Ø			Björnsson 1972*b*: 9
Hóll in Svartárdalur (N)	chapel	15th c.		*DI* v, 352; ÍSLEIF
Ás in Hjaltadalur (N)	a	13th c.	11th c.	*ASB* xi. 10, 72; Vésteinsson 1998*c*
Hof in Hjaltadalur (N)	Ø			Ólafsson 1984
Gunnólfsá in Ólafsfjörður (N)	chapel	trad.		*JÁM* x. 19; ÍSLEIF
Hella in Árskógsströnd (N)	a	1487		DI V, 356; Friðriksson and Vésteinsson 1989
Glerá in Kræklingahlíð (N)	a	trad.		Gestsdóttir and Vésteinsson 1998: 7–9
Gullbrekka in Eyjafjörður (N)	a	18th c.		*JÁM* x. 248; Hjálmarsson and Kristjánsson 1957: 140–1
Torfufell in Eyjafjörður (N)	chapel	trad.		*JÁM* x. 254; Hjálmarsson and Kristjánsson 1957: 110
Ytri Tjarnir in Staðarbyggð (N)	Ø			Friðriksson and Vésteinsson 1995: 37
Lómatjörn in Kjálki (N)	chapel	15th c.		*DI* v. 357; ÍSLEIF
Þverá in Fnjóskadalur (N)	a	15th c.		*DI* v. 357; ÍSLEIF

TABLE 2. *Sites of chapels or annex churches where burials have come to light (continued)*

Farmstead	Type of church	Docum. date	Arch. date	References
Steinkirkja in Fnjóskadalur (N)	Ø			Hermanns-Auðardóttir 1995: 28–31
Syðra Fjall in Aðaldalur (A)	Ø			Þorkelsson 1916
Syðri-Tunga in Tjörnes (A)	chapel	trad.		*JÁM* xi. 260; ÍSLEIF
Hóll in Tjörnes (A)	chapel	PN		ÍSLEIF
Víkingavatn in Kelduhverfi (A)	chapel	trad.		*JÁM* xi. 279; ÍSLEIF
Hallfreðarstaðir in Tunga (A)	Ø			Kristinsdóttir 1988: 95–7
Rangá in Tunga (A)	Ø			*Sveitir og jarðir* i. 360
Urriðavatn in Fell (A)	Ø			Snæsdóttir *et al.* 1991
Ekkjufell in Fell (A)	chapel	17th c.		PP 11, Zöega *et al.* 1997: 76
Víðivellir ytri in Fljótsdalur (A)	a	14th c.		*DI* iv. 213; *Sveitir og jarðir* ii. 66
Mýnes in Eiðaþinghá (A)	a	13th–16th c.		*DI* i. 249; ÍSLEIF
Svínafell in Hornafjörður (A)	chapel	14th c.		*DI* iii. 126–7, 242–3; ÍSLEIF
Sandar in Eyjafjöll (S)	chapel	14th c.		*DI* ii. 683; iii. 262–3; *JÁM* xiii. 511
Skarfanes in Land (S)	Ø			Jónsson 1907*b*: 27–8
Tröllaskógur in Rangárvellir (S)		trad.		*JÁM* i. 234, 278
Skeljastaðir in Þjórsárdalur (S)	Ø			Þórðarson 1943
Stöng in Þjórsárdalur	Ø		11th c.	Vilhjálmsson 1996

a = annex church; PN = place name indicating church; saga = church mentioned in sagas; trad. = early modern traditions about church or chapel; Ø = no documentary evidence or traditions about church or chapel

were people buried then? Even if we decide to take those sagas of Icelanders seriously which tell of church building by chieftains just after 1000, it is still difficult to believe that there were enough churches in the country in the first decades of the eleventh century to receive all the corpses in the country without people having to travel long distances. It may have been within the means of the jet-setters of the age, like Kjartan Ólafsson—whose corpse was brought to burial all the way from Hjarðarholt in Dalir (D) to Borg in Mýrar (S) (*ÍF* vi. 158)—but for ordinary people that is too much of a break with custom to consider.

There are suggestions in the archaeological literature that there was an intermediate stage in burial practices. At Jarðbrú in Svarfaðardalur (N) five inhumations in four graves have come to light during construction work this century. No grave-goods were found in any of the graves and all were aligned SSW–NNE, facing SSW. One of the skeletons lay on its side (grave II), but the others were stretched on their backs with arms straight down the sides. In one of the graves (II) traces of wood and iron were found, indicating a coffin. In grave III stones had been lined around the upper half of the corpse and a large slab put above the head. The five corpses seem to have been the only ones ever buried in this locality. Jarðbrú is the next farm to Tjörn where the parish church of the area was, and this led Kristján Eldjárn (1964) to suggest that there could hardly have been a church or chapel at Jarðbrú as well, and that the graves must therefore be from the eleventh century when people had ceased pagan burial customs, but had not yet established Christian cemeteries. See also below on similar claims for the single burial at Hallfreðarstaðir in Tunga (A).

The graves at Jarðbrú have not been dated; the absence of surface structures (i.e. church, chapel, cemetery wall) is far from certain. The graves were discovered in the course of construction work in the 1930s and 1950s and there is no way of telling what structures could have been on the surface earlier. In his report Kristján Eldjárn (1964) says he dug several trial holes to look for further graves—enough to convince himself that there were not more, but no details are given, and it is therefore impossible to verify his conclusion. Furthermore there are several examples of churches and chapels situated on adjacent farms,[46] so the proximity to Tjörn cannot be taken as an argument for the non-existence of a church or chapel at Jarðbrú. Although Kristján Eldjárn's theory cannot be refuted, and will remain a distinct possibility, it is only one among several possible explanations for the graves at Jarðbrú. While the remains have not been dated, their relevance for the discussion of eleventh-century burial practices will remain limited.[47]

A more exciting but unverifiable tale comes from Hrafnagil in Eyjafjörður (N). Hrafnagil was a parish church until 1863 and the location of the latest church is still marked by a single grave in the home field. According to a place-name inventory for this farm the farmhouses had formerly stood some 100–50 metres to the north and somewhat higher up in the slope above the present farmhouses. A hill protrudes from the slope at this location and there, in some unspecified past, several skeletons were found, judged to be Christian, apparently on account of their alignment. This would not be surprising if a horse-skull and a shield had not also come to light, if not on the same occasion then at least in the same location. According to the present farmer seven inhumations came to light in this location in 1958 in the course of construction work. All the inhumations were apparently aligned north–south but no grave-goods were found with them. The bones were reburied and the find was not investigated at the time; the exact location of the finds cannot be pinpointed on account of recent rearrangement of the landscape (Vésteinsson and Friðriksson 1994: 95). It is therefore impossible to decide what to make of this, as well as the tale of the earlier location of the farmhouses.

The idea that there was some sort of transitional stage is however appealing; if people did discontinue pagan burial practices immediately or very shortly after the conversion, some sort of solution must have been found to accommodate corpses in the period until a church had been built within a reasonable distance of every farmstead. In the present state of research we can only

[46] For instance Fell, Skálá, and Hraun in Sléttahlíð (N) (*DI* v. 355); Holtastaðir and Geitaskarð in Langidalur (N) (*DI* ii. 471–2). Árskógur, Litli Árskógur, and Brattavellir on Árskógsströnd (N) (*DI* v. 356).

[47] Cf. G. Ólafsson 1984 and criticisms in A. Friðriksson 1994*a*: 98–100, of this type of explanation in archaeology.

speculate on what form this solution took, but this is one of the fields where further investigations may produce fresh evidence. Two incentives for building a church without a realistic prospect of services being given in it regularly can be proposed. One was that building and maintaining a church increased or affirmed a man's prestige and social standing, and the other was to provide consecrated ground for the dead.

In some Sagas of Icelanders there are accounts of the relocation of churches and reburial of the bones, usually an opportunity for the author to comment on the shape and characteristics of his hero's appearance or personality (also B. Einarsson 1976; Heller 1984; Þorláksson 1992*a*: 303–5). Such tales are therefore liable to be literary clichés rather than reliable traditions, although the reburials are usually set much closer to the author's times than the saga itself, in the twelfth century as opposed to the tenth. In all the cases it seems that the churches were not moved a great distance; Grímr at Mosfell (S) built a church there soon after the conversion, we are told by the author of *Egils saga*, but in the time of the priest Skapti Þórarinsson (mentioned in 1121 and 1143) that same church was moved from a place called Hrísbrú to Mosfell (*ÍF* ii. 298–9). Hrísbrú is now a neighbouring farm to Mosfell, some 260 metres separate the farmhouses, and was most probably a part of the original estate of Mosfell. At Hjalli in Ölfus (S), the lawspeaker Skapti Þóroddsson (1004–30) is said to have built a church when his wife broke her leg while washing her linen. We are told that he built his church on the other side of the brook, but that the bones of his father and two other chieftains were later moved to the place where the church now stands (*ÍF* xiii. 325–6). It seems therefore that the church was moved from across the brook, closer to the farmhouses. No dating is given for the reburial at Hjalli, but at Sælingsdalstunga (D) the church was relocated in the lifetime of Guðný Böðvarsdóttir who died in 1221 (*ÍF* iv. 183–4; *IA* 24, 126, 326),[48] and at Reykir in Reykjaströnd (N) the church was relocated 'in the time of the Sturlungar', which probably refers to the first half of the thirteenth century (*ÍF* vii. 269).[49] It may also be that the wording in *Oddaverja þáttr* that Jón Loptsson had a church and monastic buildings built north of the brook at Keldur (S) (*c.*1190) (*Bsk* i. 293), where the farm and church still are, indicates that the church had formerly stood on the southern side of the brook.[50] A similar account is found in a version of *Ólafs saga helga*, where we are told that Björn *Hítdælakappi* was buried at Vellir in Hítardalur (S), but that when nearby Húsafell in the same valley became a *staðr*, the church at Vellir was relocated and all the bones moved to Húsafell (*ÓSHS*. 766 cf. *ÍF* iii. 134, 163, 206–7).

In an episode preserved in *Ólafs saga Tryggvasonar in mesta*, one Þórhallr

[48] Guðný had been married to Hvamm-Sturla by 1171 (*Sturl* 76) and the reference is probably to the period when she lived in Hvammssveit.

[49] On the saga author's source for this passage, see S. Nordal 1938: 16; Haraldsdóttir 1986: 50.

[50] The church at Skarð in Skarðsströnd could also be considered in this context; according to *Geirmundar þáttr heljarskinns* it was situated in a grove on Geirmundr's land (*Sturl* 5). Although it is not unambiguous the wording does not suggest close proximity to home field or farmhouses.

knappr of Knappsstaðir in Fljót (N) had a dream in the winter before the conversion. He dreamt that a regally attired man came to him, riding a white horse with a golden spear and led him to the fence surrounding his home field and told him to build a house there to the glory of the one and only true God. The man then marked the plan of the house on the ground with his spear and gave Þórhallr details of how it should be constructed, adding that he should use the timber from the temple that stood some distance from the farm (*ÓST* ii. 184–7). This fourteenth-century story is either a fabrication or a refashioning of a local tradition, but in neither case can it be without significance that the church is supposed to have been built by the home field fence. It must be either because the church at Knappsstaðir was thus situated at the time this was composed or had been in recent times, or because the author knew such locations to be more original and felt that adding this detail would add a flavour of authenticity.

In addition to these medieval traditions there are numerous tales recorded in the eighteenth and nineteenth centuries about churches originally having stood some distance from the farm and then moved for various reasons (Ó. Lárusson 1944: 341).[51] A curious set-up is found at Eyvindarmúli in Fljótshlíð (S), where in the early sixteenth century there was both a church and a chapel (*DI* ix. 648–9). The church at Eyvindarmúli was a parish church with a tithe area of only two farms. It is mentioned in Bishop Páll's inventory of churches from around 1200 and several fourteenth-century charters (*DI* xii. 6; ii. 686; iii. 216, 404; iv. 76–7). The church was abolished in 1898 but by that time the chapel had long vanished. The church was presumably situated close to the farmhouses but according to a nineteenth-century account the chapel was situated on a hill called Kapelluhóll, 'chapel-hill', in the home field of an adjacent farm which was originally a cottage from Eyvindarmúli. In other words the chapel was situated just outside the home field of Eyvindarmúli. In the same account it is noted that human burials had been found where the chapel had been situated and that there was a path 'obviously made by ancient men' between the chapel site and the farmhouses at Eyvindarmúli (Tómasson, Þ. 1983: 107–9). This is the only known example of an Icelandic farm with two churches and this may suggest that, when the church at Eyvindarmúli was relocated, the earlier church outside the home field was not torn down but maintained, presumably for the private devotion of the household at Eyvindarmúli. Eyvindarmúli was a rich farm and the residence of important families. The nineteenth-century account mentions specifically a Hólmfríður Erlendsdóttir *hin ríka*, 'the rich', who was a wealthy landowner in the early sixteenth century and lived at Eyvindarmúli (Ólason 1944: 391–2). It explains that the path between chapel and farmhouses is called Hólmfríðargata 'Hólmfríðr's path', 'and it is an old tale that mistress

[51] Also Búðardalur in Skarðsströnd (D) (*JÁM* vi. 146; Kálfafell in Fellshverfi (A) (Jón Þorkelsson 1921–3: 253); Sauðanes on Langanes (A) (S. Einarsson 1994: 300); Staður in Steingrímsfjörður (N) where the folk-tale has the earlier church far west of the present farmstead (Árnason 1954–61: iv. 36); while skeletal remains have been found on the eastern edge of the farmland (ÍSLEIF).

Hólmfríður Erlendsdóttir had this path made when she lived at Eyvindarmúli and that she was very fond of this chapel and went there to say her prayers every morning' (Tómasson, Þ. 1983: 108; also in Árnason 1954–61: iii. 71).

The fact that the word for chapel preserved in the place-name is *kapella* and not *bænhús* suggests a more private and aristocratic establishment than the chapels mentioned in charters.[52] It is of course possible that the chapel at Eyvindarmúli was a late medieval establishment, built by an aristocratic family for its private devotion. It is however equally likely that the chapel represents the original church site and that it was maintained after the church was moved closer to the farmhouses because the owners wanted to have a separate place for their prayers and their dead away from the ordinary folk who were allowed into the parish church. It may be that this can be linked with twelfth-century attitudes that a church was not only a private property but was to be used exclusively by its owners and that admitting strangers into it or into the cemetery was an intrusion into the family's privacy (Vésteinsson forthcoming-*a*). The fact that the tithe area of Eyvindarmúli was very small suggests that it was a late developer and this may reflect the owners' reluctance to take on a responsibility for a cure of souls. When the householders of Eyvindarmúli accepted the responsibility of burying people from the two nearby farms and allowed their priest to minister to them they may therefore have decided to build a new church which suited that purpose better than the old church, a new church which was possibly larger and closer to the farmhouses, but with the old church retained as a private oratory and family graveyard.

Archaeological evidence is of little help in this context; it is not unthinkable that the graves at Jarðbrú described above constitute the first Christian cemetery of Tjörn, in which case it was used only for a very short while before a church was built closer to the farmhouses at Tjörn. To argue for this possibility it must first be shown that the farm Jarðbrú was carved out of the land of Tjörn in the eleventh century or later. At Stóraborg (S) remains of secular buildings were found beneath the cemetery, suggesting that the church could have been relocated there, but the lack of dating of the material as well as the possibility that the farm itself had been relocated (in the thirteenth century?) and that the church is a late medieval foundation makes it difficult to draw firm conclusions from this evidence (Snæsdóttir 1988: 20–2; Ó. Lárusson 1944: 141–2; Páll Sigurðsson 1865).

In 1987 human remains were found in a small hill some 150–200 metres from the farmhouses at Hallfreðarstaðir in Tunga (A). The finds were made during construction work and before a controlled investigation could be made incomplete remains of a man and a horse were revealed. The investigation revealed an inhumation in a very small coffin without any grave-goods, aligned almost exactly east–west. The bones were believed to be of a child, perhaps 10–12 years

[52] *Kapella* is in Icelandic contexts almost always used of side-chapels in larger churches (M. M. Lárusson 1963*c*).

old. The corpse had originally been laid on its back with hands along the sides (Kristinsdóttir 1988: 95–7). It is suggested by the excavator that the grave might be from the earliest Christian times when grave-goods were no longer put with the deceased but before burial in sacred ground was fully established. There was no dating for this grave and there is therefore no particular reason to believe it must be ancient. There are no indications about annex-churches or chapels in the ministry of Kirkjubær and there may well have been a church or chapel at Hallfreðarstaðir, which is one of the larger farms in the ministry.

According to the Land register of 1712 a chapel was still standing at Valþjófsstaðir in Núpasveit (A) but services had not been given in it for as long as men could remember (*JÁM* xi. 327). The farmer at Valþjófsstaðir wrote in 1954 that the chapel ruin was situated outside the home field some 280 metres from the farmhouses. A doorway could be seen on the ruin's west side and there was a circular wall around it and inside the wall small hummocks which could have been graves (Halldór Stefánsson quoted in M. M. Lárusson 1967*c*: 193). Magnús Már Lárusson (1967*c*: 150–2) has made a compelling case that it was this church which burnt in 1361 according to an annal (*IA* 226), and if that is so it had presumably been demoted to a chapel sometime before the seventeenth century, although complete faith cannot of course be put in the accurate usage of these concepts. Whether this was a church or a chapel the indications are that in this case it was never relocated and always stood outside the home field.[53] Whereas we do know that all churches stood close to the farmhouses in modern times, we have very scant knowledge of the locations of the almost 1,000 chapels which existed in Iceland in the middle ages and it may very well be that many of them were never relocated.

Ólafur Lárusson has made the case that the reason for at least some of the twenty-six Kirkjuból farm names known in Iceland was that they were the original locations of churches which were later moved to more prominent farms (Ó. Lárusson 1944: 336, 340–7).[54] His prime example is that of Kirkjubólstaður in Innri Hólmur in Akranes (S), but according to *Landnámabók* and *Ólafs saga Tryggvasonar in mesta* Halldórr Illugason is supposed to have built the church at Innri-Hólmur on the site of the grave and hut of the Christian

[53] The possibility that there was a more recent chapel ruin closer to the farmhouses cannot of course be ruled out, although there is nothing in particular to suggest this.

[54] On Ólafur Lárusson's hypothesis in general it may be noted that chapels or annex-churches are known to have been at the majority of the Kirkjuból farms, but only two parish churches, which both seem to be late medieval upgrades from lesser churches. Only three of the Kirkjuból farms were relatively rich, but most were middle-sized. This pattern compares very well with the Kirbisters (ON = Kirkjubólstaðr) of Orkney which are generally not among the richest farms and did not have parish churches (Marwick 1931: 29–32). This has been interpreted as a sign of a secondary phase of settlement (Crawford 1987: 113) and it may well be that a similar explanation applies to Iceland, i.e. that many of the Kirkjuból farms were only founded after the conversion, even much later. The highest concentration of these farm names is in the north-west where there seems to have been a significant population increase from the 13th century onwards as a result of increased importance of fishing, and the Kirkjuból may either be due to new foundations or the result of established farms being subdivided, the one with the church acquiring this new name.

primary settler and hermit Ásólfr *alskikk*, and Ásólfr is said to have lived at Kirkjubólstaður (*ÍF* i. 63–5; *ÓST* i. 278–9; Ó. Lárusson 1944: 301–4). Kirkjuból(staður) and Innri-Hólmur share the same field, and have been farmed separately at least since the thirteenth century, Kirkjuból owned by the church at Hólmur (*DI* i. 416). It seems clear that at least the author of the *Hauksbók* version of this tale was describing the present location of the church: Ásólfr's 'hut was where the church is now' (*ÍF* i. 63). The *Sturlubók* version and *Ólafs saga Tryggvasonar* locate the church on Ásólfr's grave, which may of course have been close to the hut, and indicate that it was some distance from the farmhouses at Innri-Hólmur: *Sturlubók* has it by the path to the cow-shed but *Ólafs saga Tryggvasonar* by the path to the pen where cows or sheep were milked (*ÓST* i. 278). The church was clearly not situated next to the farmhouses at Hólmur, but whether it was only a stone's throw away or some greater distance, or if it was where the farmstead Kirkjuból is now located cannot be deduced from these sources. Kirkjuból may just as well have got its name because it was a part of the original estate donated to the church and farmed separately on behalf of the church.

It may be that the rather detailed regulations in the Old Christian Law section on reburial of human remains in case of a church being moved (*Grg 1a*, 12–13) were put together because of frequent moving of churches from outside the home field to the farmhouses, but it is more likely that the legislators had in mind relocation because of natural catastrophes. It is stated that churches shall only be relocated on account of landslides, floods, fire, storm, or general devastation of an area, or if the bishop gives his permission.[55]

These examples indicate that some churches at least were originally built some distance from the farmhouses, and that in the twelfth and early thirteenth centuries such churches were being moved closer to the farmhouses, probably to be situated as was customary in late medieval and modern times: a few metres in front, and towards one end of the farmhouse-row.[56] It is impossible not to connect this with the pre-Christian practice of situating grave-fields just outside the home field, a few hundred metres from the farmhouses. It does also make good sense: in the eleventh century churches were situated on the same principle as pre-Christian grave-fields, because their main function was in connection with the cemeteries. It is of course possible that there could have been consecrated cemeteries without any church structure,[57] but that does not alter the issue here, because if the cemetery preceded the church, the church's subsequent building in or adjacent to it suggests that the burial function was

[55] The evidence from Stöng supports this interpretation, see also Steffensen 1967.

[56] As at Kúabót (S) (Gestsson and Árnadóttir 1987: Teikning 2); and Stóraborg (S) (Snæsdóttir 1988: 9). From many of the references to churches in the contemporary sagas it is clear that they were situated adjacent to the farmhouses (*Sturl* 152, 175, 311, 391, 494, cf. 690–1, 554–5, 565), whereas in other cases they may have been some distance away but within the home field (*Sturl* 356, 507–8, 667–8).

[57] As may have been the case in Norway, where excavations of church floors have in several instances revealed Christian burials beneath the earliest wooden church, see Müller 1991.

still the most important, or at least that no other function was important enough to affect a change of location. This was in a period when the few available priests either travelled around or were in the service of the few chieftains who could afford them. If services were only given infrequently and irregularly at a church, when an itinerant priest happened by, its principal use for its owner and his household must have been funereal and commemorative—there is hardly any other regular use imaginable—and it is unlikely that the prestige earned by building a church depended on its exact location; the structure itself was testament enough to a man's piety and wealth. The same applies if early churches were used as places of prayer, remembering the decrees attributed to St Jón, exhorting people to say their prayers regularly at a cross or in church (only in the A version, *Bsk* i. 164; see also Ch. 2, s. 1). We have no way of knowing if such religious devotion was widespread among the populace in the eleventh century, but even if it was it is difficult to imagine that it could have been the decisive factor in the building of the high number of churches which can be accounted for by the funereal explanation.

Another possible influence on the early building of churches might have been the desire to have a sanctuary nearby, to which people might flee in times of trouble. Respect for the immunity of people who sought refuge in church seems to have been established as the norm, if not always the practice, by the thirteenth century.[58] However, neither the Old Christian Law section nor the oldest Scandinavian legislation acknowledge this (Nilsson 1989: 150–4), and lack of this respect was one of the worries Archbishop Eysteinn (1161–88) had about the religious conduct of the Icelanders (*DI* i. 291). With that sort of evidence we cannot consider the prospect of sanctuary as one of the motives for early church building. It may, however, have influenced the relocation of churches from outside the home field to the farmhouses in the early thirteenth century when conflict was escalating but respect for sanctuary was at the same time becoming established. As is evident from the many descriptions in the Sturlunga compilation of people scrambling into churches on the sudden arrival of a hostile war band, it was eminently more practical to have the church near at hand than far away outside the home field. A less compelling consideration may have been a church's capacity to serve as defence works. There are no indications that churches were deliberately built as fortifications in Iceland as in Southern and Eastern Scandinavia (Tuulse 1960, Marit Anglert 1984)—the lack of building-stone no doubt being the basic reason—but there are a number of examples of churches and cemetery walls being used in active defence and even of war

[58] There are numerous examples of people seeking refuge in church (*Sturl* 63, 152, 169, 391, 422–3, 480, 482, 507–8, 509, 555–6, 591, 634, 639–41, 646, 648, 667–8, 670, 673, 683–4, 690–1, 705, 753, 756, 762), and of property being stored there for safety (*Sturl* 175, 443, 472, 651, 718); but also of people being dragged out of church (*Sturl* 70, 256, 475, 653, 762–3, cf. 488, 510); of churches being attacked (*Sturl* 494); of battles in graveyards (*Bsk* i. 512–13; *Sturl* 266); of men being killed or maimed in church (*Sturl* 133, 229); of property being robbed from a church (*Sturl* 378, 472, 527, 643, 651; *IA* 129); and of threats to burn churches where people had sought refuge (*Sturl* 169).

bands adding wooden constructions to strengthen the defences of the pre-existing constructions (A. Friðriksson 1994*b*: 6–9). Richer householders and chieftains who played the most dangerous politics seem as a rule to have had some fortifications at or near their estates, but for others who invested less in conflicts but nevertheless might need to defend themselves a high and well-built cemetery wall near at hand may have been a basic precaution.[59]

If a large number of churches were built in the eleventh century because of the need for household-cemeteries, that goes some way to explain two features of the ministry system. One is the sheer number of churches and chapels known from late medieval times. In the fourteenth and fifteenth centuries there was a chapel or church at more than every third farmstead in the country; if the normal population was around 50,000 that means there was a church or chapel to every thirty to forty persons. There is no evidence available which can tell us whether all these chapels and churches existed in the twelfth or thirteenth centuries; we only know that chapels and lesser churches were known. On the other hand nor is there evidence suggesting that there had been a sudden increase in the building of churches or chapels just before reliable sources for the number of dependent churches and chapels become available. The only thing we do know is that by the beginning of the fourteenth century the majority of churches and chapels had already been built, and their numbers did not increase significantly after that.[60]

The other feature is the common association of skeletal remains with chapels or annex-churches. All full excavations of chapels or annex-churches in Iceland have revealed surrounding graves and there are several reports of skeletal remains coming to light in the course of construction work where annex-churches or chapels have formerly been situated.[61]

At Stöng in Þjórsárdalur (S) a re-excavation of the small structure between the farmhouse and the cow-shed which was interpreted in the 1939 excavation as a pantry (Roussel 1943) has revealed that it is built on top of a church-like structure which in turn is built on top of a smithy. The identification of the structure in the middle as a church is based mainly on surrounding graves which were dug from the same level, and later emptied. The ruin is dated to the period between the second half of the eleventh century and the middle of the twelfth (Vilhjálmsson 1996). The settlement in Þjórsárdalur ceased in the first half of the thirteenth century according to the latest theories (Vilhjálmsson 1989),[62] and there is no documentary evidence for churches either at Stöng or at Skeljastaðir, also in Þjórsárdalur (S), where a large cemetery was excavated in

[59] G. Jónsson 1919–29: 78–84, made much of the defensive capacity of circular graveyards, criticized in Olsen 1966: 200–1.

[60] Judging mainly from *Auðunarmáldagar* from 1318 compared with the inventory of churches and chapels from 1486–7.

[61] Eldjárn 1964: 66 says that every year the National Museum is informed of skeletal finds, but these seem normally not to have been investigated, and files are not available of such reports.

[62] The demise of the settlement had previously been connected with the eruption of Mt. Hekla (S) in 1104, while 18th- and 19th-cent. traditions had connected it with the eruption of 1300.

1939 (Þórðarson 1943). There is therefore no way of guessing the status of these churches, although in the case of Stöng it is difficult to believe that the church there had a large tithe area, both on account of the location of the farmstead and the size of the church structure.[63]

Considering that no systematic efforts have been made in Iceland to survey burial places and the small amount of archaeological research that has taken place, the number of church and chapel sites where burials have been found is very high, and it suggests that it was common to have cemeteries in connection with chapels and annex-churches. That would seem to contradict the interpretation of the late thirteenth- and early fourteenth-century legal texts that burial was the privilege of parish churches. The problem is that, except for Neðri Ás, Varmá, Stöng, and Skeljastaðir, no datings are available for any of the cemeteries. The single skeleton at Belgsholt datable to the sixteenth century does not preclude the possibility that the rest of the cemetery had been in use for a long time. The datings of the cemeteries at Varmá to the fourteenth century and later, and at Stöng and Skeljastaðir to the eleventh and twelfth centuries, do not allow many conclusions to be drawn, although together these datings suggest that lesser churches and chapels did have cemeteries in all periods down to the Reformation. If the annex-church at Varmá was first founded in the fourteenth century, it is equally plausible that it acquired burial rights because it was normal for annex-churches to have them and had always been so, as it may be that annex-churches only began to acquire burial rights in the fourteenth century, just as their rights to tithes, baptism, marriage, and churching of women seem to have been on the increase from the fourteenth century onwards (Vésteinsson forthcoming-*a*). The latter alternative seems slightly less likely, considering the strong emphasis in the legal texts of the same period on the privilege of parish churches in respect of burial. This emphasis would make it strange for new cemeteries to be consecrated at lesser churches. It is also worth noting the fact that foundation charters of annex-churches from the fourteenth and fifteenth centuries normally do not mention burial rights. When they do it is impossible to say if the cemetery was new or if it had been associated with the chapel which the annex-churches always seem to be upgrades of.[64]

The following can therefore be argued: in the eleventh century, before there were many priests around and before bishops can be expected to have been able to exercise their prerogative to decide the location of cemeteries in any systematic manner, people must have been buried somewhere. Pagan burial practices were clearly discontinued, and it must therefore be assumed that an alternative was found. The solution which has been suggested here is that consecrated cemeteries were located by the same principle as that governing

[63] At Kúabót in Álftaver (S) no graves were revealed in connection with the church-like structure there, but the excavation stopped short of the floor levels (Gestsson and Árnadóttir 1987).

[64] As at Engey (S) in 1379 (*DI* iii. 338–9).

the location of pagan grave-fields—outside the farmstead's home field—and that such cemeteries were common and on the whole not shared by the inhabitants of many farmsteads, but looked on as the preserve of a single household. Churches need not have been built in connection with these cemeteries, but it seems nevertheless to have been common, whether the church was built when the cemetery was first consecrated or added later.[65] At first the main practical function of these structures must have been funereal and commemorative; very little else in the way of regular religious services can be expected to have been held there. This is a point which seems to be borne out by the size of the church structure at Stöng, which has a floor-space of 4.8 × 2.8 metres. Such a small space cannot have been intended for big crowds of people attending elaborate ceremonies; it is more likely that such small buildings were intended mainly to furnish a respectable setting for funerals and remembering the dead, as well as the private prayers of the household. These proposed early funereal churches were then the ancestors of what in the twelfth century and later came to be classified as chapels and lesser churches (*bænhús, útkirkjur*, etc.), which—judging from the archaeological evidence—were a customary place of burial for at least members of the household of the estate where they stood.

[65] Cf. that in Norway, at Mære, Lom, Høre, Ringebu, and other places, the earliest churches were built in already existing Christian cemeteries (Skre 1988: 8).

2
The First Christian Institutions

1. THE IDEA OF A GOLDEN AGE, 1082–1122

Except for *Íslendingabók* all the sources which describe events in the early twelfth century were composed in the early thirteenth century or later. They agree in painting a favourable picture of this period in which all the major Christian institutions emerged. These traditions have at their roots the image of Bishop Gizurr's (1082–1118) unrivalled authority, which was evidenced on the one hand in his achievements in laying the foundations of the Icelandic church—the two sees and the tithe—and on the other in the peace that prevailed under his strong leadership. The idea of a period of peace was accentuated by the dramatic events which were seen to put an end to it and which are the subject of *Þorgils saga ok Hafliða.*

The ways in which the authors of *Hungrvaka* and *Kristni saga* describe Gizurr's episcopacy make it out to be advantageous for the whole country but they nevertheless represent a basically southern outlook. It is probably not a coincidence that when the northerners picked their saint the choice fell on their first bishop, Bishop Gizurr's friend and contemporary, Jón Ögmundarson (1106–22).[1]

St Jón

Brother Gunnlaugr Leifsson had several problems on his hands when faced with the task of writing a Life of St Jón. The main problem was that Jón's saintliness seems to have gone unnoticed until the late 1190s, more than seventy years after his death. This meant that Gunnlaugr had some convincing to do and also that very little had been recorded about St Jón and memories of him were rapidly becoming obscure. This is clearly reflected in *Jóns saga helga* as it comes to us. It appears that accounts of St Jón available to Gunnlaugr were few. This is surprising considering that, although we do not know when Gunnlaugr was born, it is quite likely that he could have known somebody who remembered St Jón himself or somebody close to him. There is evidence for this in the B version of *Jóns saga* where it says: 'All the most respectable clergymen in the Northern quarter spent some time studying at Hólar [in the time of St Jón], those who our age, says brother Gunnlaugr, could remember . . . Many of

[1] There was a pool to choose from. According to a contingent of Nordic saints who gave Rannveig, during her vision, a guided tour of heaven, all the dead bishops were saintly, but Jón and Þorlákr were most saintly and Ísleifr, Björn, and Þorlákr Rúnólfsson came next: *Bsk* i. 454.

[these] students died in our time . . .' (*Bsk* i. 240). Apart from a few miracles attributed to St Jón in his own lifetime,[2] Gunnlaugr could not come up with a single story or event concerning St Jón after he came to Hólar as bishop.

On St Jón's life before he became bishop we hear mostly about his exploits abroad. These stories contain the motif, very common in both Sagas of Icelanders and hagiographic literature, where the hero goes abroad to be recognized by foreign kings and magnates. Royal acknowledgement of St Jón is ensured when a Norwegian queen foresees his becoming a bishop while he was still a child (*Bsk* i. 152 (217–18)). Later he finds immediate favour with King Sveinn Úlfsson of Denmark and manages to soothe the anger of King Magnús Ólafsson of Norway against the Icelandic community in Niðarós (the modern town of Trondheim) (*Bsk* i. 154–7 (220–7)). St Jón stuns foreign audiences more than once with his exceptional singing voice (*Bsk* i. 155 (220–1), 160 (232)), but his most outstanding achievement—the only one recognized in other sources (*IA*. 251)—was when he tracked down Sæmundr *fróði*, who had studied himself to oblivion, somewhere in Europe and brought him home (*Bsk* i. 156 (227–9)). Remarkable exploits abroad are one of the surest ways to consolidate an Icelander's claim to fame and greatness (see Hill 1993), and in this case sainthood. Gunnlaugr made use of this in that nearly all he has to say of the fifty-four years of St Jón's life before he became bishop happens abroad. Gunnlaugr's efforts have not seemed enough though, because the story of St Jón's soothing of the anger of King Magnús has been shown to be an interpolation, probably by the translator (Louis-Jensen 1977: 113–17; cf. *ÍF* iii, pp. cxlvii–cliii).

When St Jón comes to Hólar his saga changes greatly in character. Gunnlaugr can only give a general description of the fifteen years of his episcopate. Excluding the miracles there are virtually no incidents or events to relate, not a breath on politics or St Jón's relations with the secular powers. Indeed the description is almost entirely confined to Hólar and in general terms to the diocese as far as it was affected by the church reforms St Jón is meant to have initiated. Although the factual value of Gunnlaugr's description is difficult to assess it is extremely interesting, both in what he chooses to describe and the general impression his description is meant to give.

Gunnlaugr chose to emphasize two aspects of St Jón's episcopacy. The first is St Jón's commitment to education. Not only did he initiate a proper education of priests, he also brought to the school two foreign teachers, one of whom taught grammar and the other liturgical chant (i.e. *musica* and *versificatio*) (*Bsk* i. 163–4 (235–6), 168 (239–40)). The B version gives a fuller account of the cathedral school and its students. Among them it mentions Ingunn, the young maiden who became so learned that she taught *grammaticam* and corrected Latin books which were read to her while she embroidered scenes of holy men (*Bsk* i. 241). The impression we are meant to get is further emphasized: 'There was hardly a house [at Hólar] where some useful activity did not take place; the

[2] Nine in version A, *Bsk* i. 169–75; ten in version B, *Bsk* i. 242–9.

older taught the younger and the younger wrote [books, i.e. transcribed] between their lessons' (*Bsk* i. 168; cf. 240).

The other aspect Gunnlaugr stresses even more was St Jón's effort to improve Christian practice in his diocese and increase faith in God among his flock. Gunnlaugr tells us that at the Alþing in the first summer after St Jón returned to Iceland as bishop (i.e. 1107), he and Gizurr 'discussed many useful things, and decided with other learned men, what they should command their subordinates' (*Bsk* i. 162; cf. 234). Unfortunately Gunnlaugr can give no details of these commands, which suggests that he did not know them and assumed, as is quite natural, that the bishops would have many things to discuss on St Jón's arrival as bishop.

According to Gunnlaugr, St Jón had not long been in office when he started to improve the mores of his flock. These modest reforms can be grouped in two. On the one hand he fought remnants of heathendom and other immoral habits, and on the other he sought to regulate the religious practice of his people. In the latter group, Gunnlaugr lists a few of St Jón's directives which he says had been followed since:

- People should come to offices on feast days and other stipulated days.
- Priests should repeat often what the people should know. [B: Priests were to instruct their flocks in those things needed for salvation.]

Daily habits should be those fitting to Christians, namely:

- to pray at a church or cross at the beginning and end of each day;
- to have in one's room the symbol of the holy cross and
- on waking up cross one self and sing *credo in deum* and declare one's belief in God almighty;
- never to go to sleep or eat or drink without crossing oneself beforehand.
- Everybody should know *pater noster* and *credo in deum*,
- and praise God seven times a day, and sing *credo in deum* and *pater noster* every night before falling asleep (*Bsk* i. 164–5; 236–7).

Some scholars have suggested that these are the directives agreed on by Gizurr and Jón at the Alþing of 1107 (M. Stefánsson 1975: 65; Þorsteinsson and Jónsson 1991: 67). The detailed form of this list suggests that Gunnlaugr bases it on some kind of written evidence. If that is true, that written evidence will have been known to others than Gunnlaugr, and he could hardly have omitted Gizurr's part if the document said that the two of them issued it. If the list is not based on any written evidence, it can best be interpreted as a summary of what Gunnlaugr considered to be good Christian practice and that he decided to attribute these directives to St Jón because he felt that the saint would have done the right thing in introducing them. Considering that St Jón was the first bishop of a new diocese, it seems quite natural that he would have begun his term in office by issuing directives on basic issues of this kind. Bishops issued such directives frequently, but there are no examples of the two Icelandic bishops issuing documents of this nature together. The question remains what relevance we are to attach to this list. Were these novel directives being issued for the first time or were they just a routine reiteration of generally accepted practices? If the former is true, as Gunnlaugr is claiming and most scholars have believed, this list is a major piece of evidence for the development of Icelandic Christianity and its state around 1100.

The main objection to that interpretation is that directives of this kind were issued over and over again by much later bishops.[3] The difference is that the later directives put little emphasis on personal observance and are much more concerned with church organization and the practical details of the liturgy. That Gunnlaugr does not mention any such aspects of St Jón's administration is in itself a good indication of Gunnlaugr's ideals and how he wanted to depict his hero. The important point is, of course, that in any perfectly Christian population there are always those black sheep who forget to say their prayers and do not cross themselves before eating, not to mention other more serious sins. These people need constant reminding and guidance to better their ways, and that is what a good bishop should occupy himself with, in Gunnlaugr's opinion. He no doubt knew and worried about many an errant soul and may have been critical of his own bishop's lack of concern for these matters. He at least states that, as a result of St Jón's directives, 'holy Christianity in the Northern quarter, had never, neither before nor since, flourished to the same extent as when the people were blessed with the government of this kind of bishop' (*Bsk* i. 165; cf. 237). Gunnlaugr wanted to depict St Jón as the good shepherd, a bishop whose primary concern was the salvation of his flock and the strengthening of Christianity in the spiritual sense. That is why he chose to relate exactly these directives and that is their relevance.

Gunnlaugr's St Jón was not only the good shepherd, he was also a champion in the fight against heathendom. According to Gunnlaugr he forbade all kinds of paganism, sacrifices and magic 'and fought against it with all his strength, because these [practices] had not been abolished completely while Christianity was young' (*Bsk* i. 165 (237)). He also forbade all superstitions connected with the calendar and calling the weekdays after heathen gods. A game involving men and women reciting lewd poetry was also forbidden, but although St Jón tried he did not manage to uproot love poetry. Among these achievements changing the names of the weekdays is the most remarkable. Icelandic is the only Germanic language which does not name any weekdays after heathen gods (unless sun and moon are taken as gods) and it is clear that by the late twelfth century *Týsdagr* (Tuesday), *Óðinsdagr* (Wednesday), and *Þórsdagr* (Thursday) had been replaced by *þriðjudagr* (lit. third day), *miðvikudagr* (lit. mid-week day) and *fimmtudagr* (lit. fifth day). *Frjádagr* (Friday) remained an alternative to *föstudagr* (literally, fast day) until the sixteenth century when it disappeared.

[3] Cf. similar commands in the Icelandic Book of Homilies from *c.*1200 (S. Einarsson *et al.* 1993: 163–5). The statutes of Bishop Jón Sigurðsson of 26 July 1345 are a good example of directives on personal observance, *DI* ii. 790–831.

Þriðjudagr and *fimmtudagr* are translations of the terms favoured by the Catholic Church: *Feria tertia* and *Feria quinta* respectively. *Miðvikudagr* on the other hand is clearly derived from the German *Mittwoch* (Á. Björnsson 1990: 71–4). That implies German influence which is easier to connect with Ísleifr and Gizurr, the first two bishops of Skálholt, who had both studied in Germany (cf. M. M. Lárusson, 1967*a*: 358–9). Changing the names of the weekdays may therefore have been a concern of other bishops than just St Jón. St Jón, himself a student of Ísleifr, was probably only continuing a campaign which must have taken a long time to have effect.[4] The same is no doubt true of the other remnants of heathendom he is credited with having crushed. The rather general terms Gunnlaugr uses, suggest that he did not have a very clear idea of what these remnants of heathendom actually were. He may have been relying on some document originating from St Jón, similar to the chapter in *Grágás* banning heathen practices (*Grg 1a*, 22_{22}–23_{16}). But he may just as well have assumed, as is quite reasonable, that in St Jón's time there were still visible traces of heathendom to be found, and that St Jón fought against them, which is equally reasonable. That does not of course mean that some kind of definite victory over heathen practices was accomplished under St Jón. The only thing we know is that Gunnlaugr seems confident that there were no remnants of heathendom in his own time and that he had some notion that this had been a more serious problem for the earlier bishops.

Jóns saga helga has been dealt with here at some length mainly because Gunnlaugr's image of the past has tended to be accepted too readily by scholars, hungry for information on this period about which so little else is known. There is no reason to doubt that St Jón did establish a cathedral school, that he did try to improve Christian practice in his diocese, and that he did ban heathen practices. It is the relevance and importance of these facts which must be questioned.

While there was no doubt a core based on tradition which Gunnlaugr utilized, the aspects of St Jón's episcopacy which he chose to emphasize are probably those which best reflect his own views of what a model bishop should concern himself with. Gunnlaugr's idea of a model bishop was not of a belligerent reformer who carried his ideals through in spite, or against the advice of, the other bishop or other important people—a model applicable to his own bishop, Guðmundr *góði*, whom Gunnlaugr opposed (*Sturl.* 225, *Bsk* i. 465). There is a clear message in the story that St Jón required the people of the region to come to Hólar at least once a year. As a result of this, almost 500 people massed on Hólar at major festivals, and although many brought their own provisions many had to rely on the see to be fed (*Bsk* i. 168 (239)). This

[4] The seemingly easy acceptance of the Church's message on the names of the weekdays may have an explanation. It may be that the Germanic names were not that deeply rooted. They themselves were translations of the Roman names of the weekdays, dating from the early Viking age (Á. Björnsson 1990: 72–3). If the practice replaced by the Germanic names was not yet fully forgotten that may have made the bishops' task easier.

story is mentioned in *Jóns saga* as an example of the responsibilities of St Jón's aides, but it is clearly also a memory of better days when the people of the diocese were eager to obey their bishop and flocked to him. The parallel with the era of peace and splendour initiated by St Jón's contemporary Bishop Gizurr Ísleifsson in Skálholt is clear and it is to the southern tradition we now turn.

Bishop Gizurr

According to *Hungrvaka* Bishop Ísleifr (1056–80) did not have an easy time in office. 'He had much trouble in many ways in his office as bishop because of peoples' disobedience.' As an example the author says that the lawspeaker had two wives, a mother and daughter (in succession), and that some men went on Viking raids, 'and did many other misdeeds, which would be thought to be outrageous, if they befell men now'. Ísleifr was also troubled by foreign missionary bishops who were much more lenient than him, but were favoured by evil men. We are also told that Ísleifr was hard-pressed financially (*Bysp* 1. 77–8).[5] The fact that Ísleifr did not have a reliable income, except his own inherited wealth, probably contributed to this view of his episcopacy. The author knew that tithes only began to be paid in Bishop Gizurr's time, and it was probably inconceivable to him that a bishop could execute his duties without a sound financial base. The gloom of this picture also fits the darkness of periods little or nothing is known about, and it also serves the purpose of enhancing the brightness surrounding the person of Bishop Gizurr. The concern about lenient missionary bishops possibly has some basis in reality since the Old Christian law section has a clause regulating acceptance of services from foreign bishops (*Grg* 1a, 22_{10-20}), and the author of *Hungrvaka* may have based his account on this source. It seems that very little, if anything at all, was known about Ísleifr's episcopacy, and that the author was mainly attaching meaning to this lack of information, giving his account a dramatic effect by making Ísleifr's pioneering role look difficult.

In sharp contrast Bishop Gizurr (1082–1118) 'gained rank and respect early in his episcopate, and every man wanted to do [sit and stand] as he ordered, both young and old, rich and poor, men and women, and it was right to say that he was both king and bishop of the country[6] while he lived'. His lasting achievements are then related with much praise: the bequest of the estate Skálholt to the cathedral, the introduction of the tithe, and the establishment of the second see of Hólar. In this the author follows Ari's account closely. After Gizurr's death in 1118, we are told of a series of bad weather with freak accidents, followed by deprivation in many places.

> The wisest men were of the opinion that Iceland withered after Gizurr's death as Rome after Pope Gregory's. And that Gizurr's death was a foreboding of all suffering in Iceland

[5] On the historicity of these claims see Einar Arnórsson 1944–8.

[6] Cf. Adam of Bremen on the Icelanders and Bishop Ísleifr: 'Episcopum suum habent pro rege . . .' (*Adam* iv. 36; cf. Jakobsson 1994: 33–5).

from bad times, both in shipwrecks and fatalities, and financial loss resulting therefrom, and thereafter turmoil and lawbreaking, and on top of that the highest mortality around the whole country since the country had been settled.

To set things in their right perspective the author then adds that two years later Hafliði was injured at the Alþing, and that the case was not settled that summer (*Bysp* 1. 85, 91).

The message is clear; Gizurr's episcopacy was truly a golden age. On this the author of *Hungrvaka* rests on the authority of Ari, who, although not as vividly, also mentions how Gizurr was loved by his people and remarks that it was a great sign how obedient the people were in accepting the tithe (*ÍF* i. 22). And he, being a contemporary, would hardly have said that if there had been great resistance to it. The portents following Gizurr's death are not found in *Íslendingabók*, but we do know from other sources that there was a famine in 1120 (*IA* 19, 112, 320) and Hafliði's injury is the subject of *Þorgils saga ok Hafliða*, also mentioned in the annals (*IA* 19, 59, 112, 320).

To the author of *Hungrvaka* the peace ended with Gizurr's death and the period of trouble began, which he no doubt thought of as extending to his own days. He had good grounds for his interpretation. His knowledge of Gizurr's episcopacy probably did not extend far beyond what *Íslendingabók* describes, and it is significant that Ari is, by his own terse standards, unusually laudatory of Gizurr. To the author, the peaceful acceptance of the tithe must have seemed, as it does to us, a remarkable achievement. He can only have interpreted it as conclusive evidence for Gizurr's authority and power and the peace and harmony which prevailed during his episcopate. To him it was no accident that almost immediately following Gizurr's death, dissension arose among the chieftains.

The author of *Hungrvaka* was not alone in his view of Gizurr's episcopate. Indeed this seems to have been the view of the past accepted by thirteenth-century historians. It is significant that the author of *Kristni saga* gives the same picture as *Hungrvaka*, painting it in even stronger colours. He follows *Íslendingabók* quite closely but also uses some of the material found in *Hungrvaka*.[7] His account of Bishop Ísleifr is much shorter than *Hungrvaka*'s and contains only the most basic information, with no mention of Ísleifr's troubles (*ASB* xi. 45–6). The description of Gizurr's episcopacy is much fuller, matching *Hungrvaka*'s description to a large degree, putting even more emphasis on the peace which prevailed under Bishop Gizurr and the abrupt change following his death. *Kristni saga* adds that 'Bishop Gizurr pacified the country so thoroughly, that no major conflicts occurred between chieftains, and the carrying of arms all but disappeared' (*ASB* xi. 50). The author then goes on to give a list of chieftains who were ordained as priests by Bishop Gizurr, no doubt understanding that as further evidence of the state of grace the country was in. *Kristni saga* has the same portents as recorded in *Hungrvaka*, but gives somewhat more detail and adds a killing, also mentioned in the annals (*IA*

[7] It is not clear whether the author of *Kristni saga* knew *Hungrvaka* or if he only had access to some of the material also used in *Hungrvaka*.

112, 320), to the list. Like the author of *Hungrvaka*, the author of *Kristni saga* ends with Þorgils's and Hafliði's dispute which he describes more fully. He also adds that at the Alþing when Þorgils injured Hafliði 'there was so little carrying of arms, that only a single steel helmet was then at the Alþing, even though nearly every householder rode to the assembly' (*ASB* xi. 54). The lack of arms is not the impression one gets from *Þorgils saga ok Hafliða*, but it may be that the author was just a little clumsy here, intending this to apply to Gizurr's episcopacy in general although the context suggests otherwise. Anyway it is clear that the author of *Kristni saga* was even keener than the author of *Hungrvaka* to depict Gizurr's episcopate as a golden age, by drawing the reader's attention more forcefully to the contrast between it and his own unstable times when every other man was armed and householders no longer bothered to come to the Alþing.

The dispute between Þorgils and Hafliði is the first unruliness known to us since the 1020s,[8] and if the annals are anything to go by that also seems to have been the state of knowledge in the thirteenth century. Many modern scholars have taken this quite literally to mean that no news is good news and that there was a period of peace and stability from the early eleventh century up to 1120 when Þorgils cut off Hafliði's finger at the Alþing. The affair of Hafliði's finger is then seen as the beginning of the struggles between chieftains which came to characterize Icelandic history in the twelfth and thirteenth centuries (B. Þorsteinsson 1953: 229–30; J. Jóhannesson 1956: 271; Þorsteinsson and Jónsson 1991: 80–1). As Gunnar Karlsson (1975: 38) has pointed out, the nature of the sources available to us does not allow this interpretation. The main sources, *Íslendingabók*, *Jóns saga helga*, and *Hungrvaka*, were all written by clergymen about their Church, and they cannot be expected to draw attention to secular strife or troubles relating to the Church which would have blackened its image. Nor does our understanding of Icelandic medieval society, or human nature in general, make almost a century of actual peace and stability seem very plausible. Yet it remains to be explained why other sources, particularly the annals, do not mention any unrest in this long period. The annals record struggles and killings not mentioned in any saga almost every other year in the 1120s and with increasing regularity after that (*IA*, especially 112–13, also 20, 59, 252, 320). Why then this complete silence about the pre-1120 period?

One reason may be that Gizurr's period in office simply was a relatively peaceful period, compared to what went before and what came after. The memory of this relative peace then became idealized by the early thirteenth

[8] Unless we take *Hungrvaka*'s account of the Viking raids in Bishop Ísleifr's time seriously, although it is in any case not clear whether these raids were supposed to be at home or abroad (Arnórsson 1944–8: 226–7). Ari says of Skapti Þóroddsson who was lawspeaker 1004–30 that in his days many chieftains and magnates were sentenced or made outlaws for killings or beatings because of his authority and government. (*ÍF* i. 19). Some of the disputes dealt with in the Sagas of Icelanders are also set in the middle of 11th cent., for instance *Ljósvetninga saga* and *Bandamanna saga* (*ÍF* vii. 293–363; x. 3–121). The annals also mention strife in the 1020s but not after that until 1120, *IA*.

century, reinforced by Ari's great authority, and came to be linked with Gizurr's person in the minds of pious historians like the authors of *Hungrvaka* and *Kristni saga*. This in turn then affected the annal writers. As the earliest date known to us for the recording of contemporary events is 1131, it may also be that such recording had then only recently commenced and did not include recording of earlier events. These pre-1120 events were then, as a result, rapidly forgotten, making this idealized view more easily acceptable to people around 1200. All this is plausible enough but a more specific explanation centres on the affair of Hafliði's finger.

The affair of Hafliði's finger has always been treated as a major political event in Icelandic history, not only by modern scholars but also by thirteenth-century historians. The fact that a special saga was written about it, that this saga was included in the Sturlunga compilation and the comparative thoroughness with which the affair is described in the annals suggests the significance attached to this dispute by thirteenth-century Icelanders. Yet this dispute seems to have been far less dramatic or bloody than many in the latter half of the twelfth century, not to mention the thirteenth. The dispute arose because of clashes between totally insignificant men who were dependants of the chieftains Þorgils and Hafliði. According to the saga neither chieftain did anything to settle these quarrels and both induced their dependants to step up the confrontations. In the end each chieftain had a killed dependant on his hands and each took his case to the Alþing of 1120. There neither would budge an inch and in a throng where Hafliði had first tried to dissolve Þorgils's court proceedings and then was urged to state his conditions for settlement, he raised his axe against Þorgils, but the latter managed to be first and cut off Hafliði's finger. Hafliði then had Þorgils sentenced to greater outlawry (virtual death sentence with confiscation of all property). Þorgils nevertheless went home and aided by his large following managed to stave off Hafliði's attempts to confiscate his property. In the following summer both rode to the Alþing in great numbers and a bloody showdown was only averted at the last minute, after the mediation of Bishop Þorlákr and Ketill Þorsteinsson, the bishop in waiting. Þorgils agreed to let Hafliði decide the terms of settlement, and paid the fine in full although it was outrageously high. Both honoured the settlement we are then told and remained on the same side in conflicts while both lived (*Sturl* 7–46).

The author of the saga puts the emphasis on the pride and stubbornness of the chieftains but the political significance of this affair seems to have been that the chieftains could not or did not want to settle the trivial matters of their dependants peacefully, that they came close to killing each other at the Alþing, that a chieftain was sentenced, and that both threatened to use force on a large scale even if it meant breaking the law and violating the sanctity of the Alþing. The hypothesis will be suggested here that the affair of Hafliði's finger was a political watershed, where the political struggle took on new dimensions (cf. Breisch 1994: 149–58). That the strength and organization of the chieftains had been gradually building up since the period of settlement and that the affair of

Hafliði's finger was the first sign of the chieftains having gained enough power to attempt to side-step accepted procedures and use force to further their objectives. Þorgils and Hafliði did not manage to break each other, but the attempt had been made. They had shown that chieftains were capable of mustering hundreds of men to fight for a cause which was no immediate concern of these men, and thereby they showed that chieftains had the will and the means to crush each other by force, with little or no regard for the law or the established order. If, as is suggested here, these were totally new concepts, it makes it easier to understand why so much was made of this affair and why memories of earlier conflicts were not preserved. With the emergence of these new concepts, the political parameters changed and the context of earlier conflicts will soon have become both incomprehensible and insignificant in comparison to the new political reality. As a result the earlier conflicts, although no doubt highly significant in their day, soon began to seem to have been of little consequence and were therefore not recorded.

The usefulness of this hypothesis lies not only in that it explains why the pre-1120 period is so consistently seen as a golden age. It also allows us to imagine a much weaker authority of chieftains in the tenth and eleventh centuries than hitherto believed, which in turn makes the development of the chieftains' power into the twelfth century easier to understand. That is, a gradual development from weak power in a weak economy rather than a disintegration of a stable and strong system of government.

2. THE TITHE LAW OF 1097[9]

Because of the affection [Bishop Gizurr] was held in, and because of his and Sæmundr's exhortations, with the counsel of Markús the Lawspeaker, it was made law that all men calculated and valued their property, and swore that it was correctly valued, whether it was in land or moneys, and then paid tithe on it. It is a great sign, how obedient the countrymen were to that man, that he brought about a valuation on oaths, of all the property that was in Iceland, and of the land itself so that tithe was paid on it and a law passed that so it should remain as long as Iceland was settled. (*ÍF* i. 22)

This is Ari *fróði*'s description of the passing of the tithe law in 1097 (*IA* 19, 59, 110, 251, 319).[10] Writing in 1122–33 he was no doubt justified in becoming excited

[9] J. Jóhannesson 1956: 204–9; M. M. Lárusson 1967*a*: 359–61; Skovgaard-Petersen 1960: 263–70; M. Stefánsson 1974, 1975: 60–2, 86–91.

[10] In the 14th-cent. MS of the Old Christian law section, *Belgsdalsbók*, there is an introduction to the tithe law, found in no other MS, where this event is dated to 1096: 'When MXCVJ winters had passed from the birth of our Lord Jesus Christ, in the 16th year of the episcopacy of honourable lord Gizurr bishop of Skálholt, this tithe making was proclaimed as law over the whole of Iceland by both clergy and lay people as follows.' (*Grg III*, 134_{2-6}). Although many scholars have chosen to follow this source on the dating of the tithe law instead of the annals, it is difficult to see why it should be preferred, especially as Gizurr's sixteenth year as bishop was not in 1096 but from 4 Sept. 1097 to 4 Sept. 1098, according to which the tithe law would have been passed at the Alþing (held in July) 1098. Following J. Jóhannesson 1956: 178 n. 1, the year 1097 will be preferred here.

(and this is about as excited as he gets) about Bishop Gizurr's achievement. At that time tithe was only about to be introduced in Norway and Denmark, and in Norway at least it is generally not believed to have been fully accepted until the 1150s.[11] In Denmark it had been accepted by 1135 (*DD* ii. 127) but most Danish scholars believe it had been introduced shortly after 1100 as a result of the establishment of the archdiocese of Lund, although recently arguments have been put forward that the tithe was not pushed through until around 1120 (Dahlerup 1974: 291; Breengaard 1982: 147–8). The Danish tithe was, however, at first only divided between the Church and the priest and it was not until the late twelfth century that Danish bishops got their full third of the tithe (Dahlerup 1974: 291–2; Skyum-Nielsen 1971: 24–5, 188–92; Koch 1972: ii. 121–2). In Scania disaffection with the newly introduced bishop's tithe was one of the grievances expressed in the revolt of 1180–2 (Holm 1988). In Sweden there is no evidence for the introduction of tithe until the late twelfth century (Schück 1974: 295; Nylander 1953: 205–6).

In Denmark St Knud had made an attempt to introduce tithe in his kingdom in the 1080s, and this seems to have been one of the main causes for the rebellion against him which resulted in his killing in 1086 (Breengaard 1982: 122–49; Wåhlin 1988). Apart from that very little is heard about the introduction of tithe or reactions to it in Scandinavia. In Norway and Denmark the relatively lengthy period between the first attempts to have the tithe introduced and its full acceptance suggests that there was considerable opposition to it. That is of course what we would expect; in none of the Scandinavian countries was there a tradition of regular taxation,[12] nor was royal authority and administration developed enough for the kings to be able to force the acceptance of tithe in the face of opposition.[13] In Iceland conditions were apparently even less favourable; there was no tradition of this sort of taxation and no central authority which could impose taxation on the populace and organize its collection.

It stands out clearly in Ari's description of the introduction of the tithe law, that he considered it to be a major achievement and the finest witness to Bishop Gizurr's statesmanship. His words are usually interpreted as the tithe having

[11] According to *Heimskringla* King Sigurðr *Jórsalafari* (d. 1130) vowed to introduce tithe in Norway when King Baldwin of Jerusalem gave him a piece of the Holy Cross in 1110 (*ÍF* xxviii. 250), but although the saga claims he fulfilled his vow (*ÍF* xxviii. 257) this is not supported by other sources. In a 14th-cent. MS a Símun who was bishop of Niðarós before the establishment of the archbishopric in 1152–3 is credited with having introduced the tithe (*DI* iii. 25), Símun was still bishop in 1139 (Kolsrud 1913*a*: 199). The earliest definite evidence for the tithe in Norway are King Magnús Erlingsson's privileges to the Norwegian church from 1163–70 (*Lat.dok* 63; Kolsrud 1929; Helle 1964: 41, 167; Hamre 1974: 281).

[12] It was only in the 12th cent. that the Scandinavian kings began to exact taxes annually—before that people's contribution to society took the form of manning or furnishing war parties. On *leidang* see Bolin 1934; C. A. Christensen 1965; Ekbom 1979 for Denmark; for Norway Bull 1920; Bjørkvik 1965; and for Sweden Hafström 1949*a*; 1965.

[13] On the development of royal authority in the Scandinavian countries see Bagge 1975, 1986*a*, 1986*b*, 1989*b*; A. E. Christensen 1968; Gunnes 1976*a*; Helle 1964: esp. 160–5; 1981; Jørgensen 1987; Koch 1969; E. Lönnroth 1940, 1966, 1982.

met little or no serious resistance and having at least been fully accepted by the time he wrote his account (B. Þorsteinsson 1953: 205–6; J. Jóhannesson 1956: 178; M. Stefánsson 1975: 60). That is reasonable enough; had there been serious opposition to the tithe, Ari could hardly have written so gleefully about the countrymen's obedience to Bishop Gizurr, although it is of course not impossible that he was simplifying matters somewhat. There is, however, no need to be suspicious; as all scholars who have written on this subject agree, it is easily understandable why the tithe law was introduced in Iceland without opposition (e.g. B. Þorsteinsson 1953: 205–6; J. Jóhannesson 1956: 178; M. Stefánsson 1974: 287; Karlsson 1975: 38; M. Stefánsson 1975: 60, 86–7; J. V. Sigurðsson 1989: 96; Þorsteinsson and Jónsson 1991: 65). Half of the tithe was payable to the church-owners and all churches were privately owned. It is reasonable to assume that the church-owners were among the richest and most powerful in society, they were those who controlled legislation at the Alþing. It was clearly to their advantage to let such a law be passed.

There are problems with this reasoning however. On the one hand it only explains why the tithe law could be introduced, it does not explain how or to what extent it was possible to enforce it. It is easy to understand why those who received the tithe were in favour of it, but that does not get us any closer to understanding why those who actually had to pay should have done so without a murmur. On the other hand this reasoning is a far too simplistic treatment of the tithe law and its introduction. While it emphasizes the advantages of the tithe to chieftains and rich householders and the implications of that for power consolidation in the twelfth century it does not recognize the effect of the tithe law on those who had to pay it; did they see it as a welcome rationalization of payments for essential services or as an unreasonable burden? Nor does this reasoning account for the implications of half the tithe: the bishop's quarter and the quarter which was ascribed to the maintenance of the poor.

The Tithe Law: A Re-evaluation

The Icelandic tithe was unique in that it was a 1 per cent property tax, the rationale being that as standard interest was 10 per cent, 1 per cent of property would equal 10 per cent of potential yields. As this was clearly usury, as the Norwegian envoy Loðinn *leppr* pointed out in 1281,[14] this has sometimes been

[14] 'But where you spoke of usury I believe it is truly evil, and those who are usurers should be excommunicated, but what is more clearly usury than the wrongful tithe reckoning which is in this country? You bishops claim tithe of buckles and silver-girdles, buckets and bushels and other dead objects, and it amazes me that the populace tolerates such wrong from you, that you do not take Nordic tithe as is practised in the whole world, and is the only right and legislated [tithe].' (*ÍF* xvii. 95–6). Bishop Árni, in reply claimed that 'from the words of Pope Innocent we know that this tithe reckoning is not usury and is no danger to anyone's soul.' (*ÍF* xvii. 96). Which Innocent Árni was referring to is not known nor whether this means that the pope's sanction had been sought or whether Bishop Árni was interpreting some decree or other. Magnús Stefánsson (1974, 1975: 62) has suggested that the Icelandic tithe may have been based on a model from Franconia.

interpreted as evidence for the Icelanders' independent turn of mind and their lack of respect for canon law, but it is more directly ascribed to the fact that there was little choice; Iceland's was not an agrarian economy and calculating yields from animal husbandry and hunting would have been impossibly complicated.

It is not known how the tithe was divided when it was first introduced. *Hungrvaka* claims that the fourfold division (church, priest, bishop, and the poor) was original (*Bysp* 1. 86), but it is unlikely that the author knew this for a fact. Ari does not mention how the tithe was divided, and the tithe law, in the form it is preserved from around 1200, cannot be taken as a source for the original division. If changes had been made to the tithe system we cannot expect to see traces of an earlier system in the legal material. Although there is no reason to expect that any such change took place, and we must therefore assume that the fourfold division was original, it is necessary to keep in mind that the sources for the division of the tithe and for regulations regarding its calculation and payment postdate the introduction of the tithe by more than a century.

The tithe law is preserved as a special section in *Grágás*. In the *Konungsbók* version it comes at the end of the collection (*Grg 1b*, 205–14), but in the *Staðarhólsbók* version it has been added to the Christian law section at the beginning of the collection (*Grg II*, 46–57) and the two are also found together in several fourteenth century manuscripts. Formerly it was believed that the tithe law was committed to writing already when it was passed in 1097 and as a consequence the preserved texts were thought to represent the most ancient Icelandic writing.[15] As most modern scholars recognize, there are no grounds for believing that the preserved texts represent the original legislation even if there may have been a written record of it at the time (M. Stefánsson 1974: 287; 1975, 60; J. Kristjánsson 1975: 212).

The view that the tithe law must have been written down when it was passed is based on the assumption that, as the tithe law can be seen as a church law, it is reasonable to think it was committed to writing because that was what church people did. This is however making unnecessary assumptions about the levels of literacy in Iceland in the 1090s and about contemporary perceptions of the difference between the secular and ecclesiastical spheres. It is perfectly possible that the tithe law was written down in 1097 but there is no particular evidence which points in that direction. In fact the available evidence suggests a much slower development of written legislation regarding the tithe.

Jón Jóhannesson pointed out that there are in the Old Christian law section regulations regarding tithe payments and he argued that it would have been unnecessary to write them into that section if a separate tithe law had already existed in writing in 1122–33 (J. Jóhannesson 1956: 204).

[15] Alongside the Treaty between the Icelanders and St Ólafr confirmed by Bishop Gizurr Ísleifsson in 1082–1118 (*Grg 1b*, 195–7; on the treaty see Sigfússon 1964; J. Jóhannesson 1956: 134–42; Páll Sigurðsson 1967; Líndal 1974*a*: 221–2). In this spirit the tithe law MSS were printed in *DI* under the year 1096: *DI* i. 70–162.

The regulations found in the Old Christian law section are not extensive but they do cover issues such as to which church tithes are to be paid; the bishop's duty to divide the land into tithe areas and the date, place, and tender of the payment of the priest's, church, and bishop's quarters (*Grg 1a*, 14_{12}–15_{9}, 19_{22}–20_{12}). While it is clear in the Old Christian law section that the tithe was divided in four, the paupers' quarter is not mentioned at all. Nor are there any rules on the procedure for assessing taxable property, scrutiny of accounts, or the process for litigation in case of intentionally low assessments. These issues are dealt with at length in the separate tithe law section and the simplest explanation is to see the provisions in the Old Christian law section as an earlier stage of the legislation, while the more detailed provisions in the separate tithe law section represent a more recent refinement.

It is then likely that the clauses on the tithe in the Old Christian law section represent the earliest codification of rules relating to the tithe, or at least an earlier stage in the codification than the separate tithe law. They were clearly not meant to be a full treatment of the tithe system and only cover it in so far as it had a direct bearing on the affairs of the Church. As shall be discussed in more detail below, supervision of property assessments was not in the hands of the Church but the commune, as was the distribution of the paupers' quarter. This affects our appreciation of the tithe law as it suggests that secular and non-religious interests were just as influential in its acceptance and it may suggest that the Church was not necessarily the influential body by 1100 that it is sometimes made out to be.

There is no particular reason to think that the tithe law was written down when first accepted in 1097, and much less reason to think that it was already then the comprehensive piece of legislation we know from the thirteenth century manuscripts. If this view is accepted it changes considerably our evaluation of the effects of the tithe on Icelandic society. In Icelandic historiography the passing of the tithe law is normally taken to indicate the close of the formative period of the Icelandic church organization and the establishment of a fully developed ecclesiastical structure. It will be argued here that this is a misleading and unfounded view and that, as elsewhere, the introduction of the tithe represented only one of the first steps towards any kind of established order.

Íslendingabók is largely responsible for this perception of the tithe. Ending as it does in 1120, it describes a development which ends in an established order and this has affected the views of all later onlookers. The authors of *Hungrvaka* and *Kristni saga* add to this feeling by emphasizing the achievements of Bishop Gizurr and by indicating that permanence in church organization had set in by the end of his episcopacy. These medieval views of the past coupled with the first fruits of ecclesiastical activity—the emergence of writing in the vernacular and the beginnings of clerical education in the schools at Skálholt and Haukadalur in the late eleventh century and in those at Hólar and Oddi in the early twelfth century—have combined to produce an idea of an established church which had already gone through its formative stages by the 1120s (B. Þorsteinsson 1953: 184–228; J. Jóhannesson 1956: 167–212, especially 201; see also Líndal 1974*b*: 270–1 and Þorsteinsson and Jónsson 1991: 63–81).[16] To take but one recent example, Helgi Þorláksson (1989*a*: 83), in his study of the power of the Oddaverjar, has suggested that the parish of the church at Oddi was unusually large in the late thirteenth century because Sæmundr *fróði* (d. 1133) had been in a position to secure his church a large tithe area.[17] This presupposes an episcopal structure which, following the tithe law of 1097, governed the division of the country into tithe areas. It has been suggested that the counting of *þingfararkaupsbændr* attributed to Bishop Gizurr by Ari (*ÍF* i. 23) was in preparation for this task (Ólsen 1915: 349–50). Ari, however, puts the counting in the context of preparations for the establishment of the second see at Hólar and it is difficult to see why he should have chosen to be unclear on this point.

A school of thought within the debate about the reasons behind the writing of *Landnámabók* holds that Bishop Gizurr commissioned Ari the priest to compile information on the farmsteads where churches stood and that the original *Landnámabók* was the fruit of that labour, although later revisions changed its contents (Hermannsson 1948: 22–7; Sigurjónsson 1970, 1976; Pétursson 1986).[18] This information is then supposed to have been used to divide the country into tithe areas. Arguments have not been forthcoming on how the kind of information preserved in *Landnámabók* could in practice have facilitated such a division.

All this is based on doubtful premises. First it is assumed that valuation of all land and property in the country could only be done with a standardized value-reckoning and that this could only be developed by the bishops. This is an unnecessary assumption; it is for the first part inconceivable that some kind of system for valuing property did not exist already. A farming society which does not have the means to estimate the value of land and livestock is difficult to imagine; how could property otherwise be bought, sold, or divided between heirs? For the second part there was neither need for, nor the bureaucratic means to provide, a standardized system of value-reckoning. The assessments

[16] M. Stefánsson 1975: 57–60, seems to be of the other opinion; that the Church only really began to develop as a result of the changes that were taking place in the early 12th cent.

[17] There are in fact no sources for the size of the tithe area of Oddi from medieval times, but it is clear from the absence of serviced churches in the vicinity of Oddi and early modern sources that its tithe area must have been quite large. In 1847 there were 24 *lögbýli* in the parish of Oddi, and although that is a large parish it is not exceptionally large, and the neighbouring parish of Breiðabólstaður in Fljótshlíð was equally large (*JJ* 49, 51). Also Víkingur 1970: 209. This also presupposes that there were as many serviced churches in the area at that time as later—if they were not as many Sæmundr would not have had to use his position to secure a large tithe area; it would have been large anyway. There are of course no indications on the number of churches in the vicinity of Oddi in the early 12th cent. and it is just as likely that the size of the tithe area of Oddi is due to its seniority among the churches of the region.

[18] This is a minority view. The traditional 'Quest for knowledge' view is represented by J. Jóhannesson (1941, 1954) and the 'Conspiracy of the landowners' view by B. Guðmundsson 1938 and Rafnsson 1974. See *ÍF* i. pp. cxviii–cxix; J. Benediktsson 1969*b*: 283–90; 1974*b* for a more relaxed treatment. Also Vésteinsson 1994: 633–5; Friðriksson and Vésteinsson (forthcoming).

were conducted by each commune and the different quarters of the tithe were paid on that basis. The assessments may very well have been based on slightly different premises in different regions but it is not possible to show that the bishops were in any position to realize that, or if they did, in any position to impose a system of value-reckoning of their own devising. The tithe law does not foresee that the basis of the assessments could be a problem, which suggests that the householders of each commune trusted themselves and their appointed officers to place value on their property.

The second doubtful interpretation of the tithe law is that the bishops were being ordered to divide the country into tithe areas, and that they were being given the right to organize things on a country-wide scale. This is based on clauses in the Old Christian law section and the tithe law, where it is decreed that the bishop shall decide to which church each individual is to pay his tithe and that the bishops shall divide the districts so that the inhabitants of each farmstead pay their tithes to a particular church (*Grg 1a*, 14; *Grg 1b*, 210, 214). As it is, these clauses, like the rest of *Grágás*, are not general guidelines for government but solutions for individuals concerning particular issues. They refer only to whose right it is to take these kinds of decisions when they needed to be taken, for example when church-owners disagreed about their tithe areas.

Executive power did not exist in Iceland prior to 1262–4, nor were there any kind of impersonal structures which could take unilateral decisions which were legally binding on others. In the eyes of the law the Church was not a legal person; it existed only as individuals with certain qualifications. Its existence could be expressed only as the duties invested in certain individuals on account of their ordination and as the rules governing their interrelationship (i.e. bishop–priest, priest–deacon, etc.) and their relationship with laymen. In the law text the idea that it is everybody's duty to pay tithe is not expressed; rather the emphasis is on everybody's duty to have their property valued.[19] It is then up to the individuals who received parts of the tithe to call for their share. The legal plaintiffs were the pauper or an officer of the commune for the paupers' quarter, the bishop or his appointed representative in the commune for the bishop's quarter, and the church-owner for the church and priest's quarters or—in case he showed no interest—the priest who served the church 'if he will use the monies for the benefit of the church' (*Grg 1a*, 15_{1-2}; 19_{27}–20_{2}; *Grg 1b*, 208_{16-19}; 209_{20-23}; 210_{18-23}). In cases of wrongful oaths on property the plaintiff was any other member of the commune (*Grg 1b*, 207_{23-5}).

There was therefore no single body which oversaw tithe payments. It was up to the commune and its officers to supervise the assessments, but once the paupers' quarter had been paid the commune had no further responsibility. The priests had no say in matters of the tithe except in the unlikely event that a church-owner neglected to call for his half of the tithe. The bishops had no

[19] As the opening sentence of the tithe law: 'It is spoken in laws here that all men in this country shall proclaim a legal tithe of their property' (*Grg 1b*, 205).

grounds to intervene in cases of non-payment of the paupers', priest's, or church quarters of the tithe.[20] The only influence the bishops had was in deciding to which churches half the tithe was paid and they could also direct the 'undivided tithe' or tithe which amounted to less than one ounce unit and was normally given whole to the paupers, to churches (*Grg 1b*, 214_{7-9}).[21] These were of course considerable powers but they did not allow the bishops any more influence over tithe payments. It is also well to remember that the law texts being cited here postdate the original legislation by more than a century and as episcopal authority and power were on the increase in the twelfth century they reflect what the bishops had achieved, amongst other things on the strength of the tithe, since 1097.

On the basis of this revaluation of the tithe law the following can be argued.

1. Although the tithe is a Christian idea and its acceptance in Iceland in 1097 is therefore testimony to the influence of the Church and the extent to which its teachings had affected society, the limited influence the Church is given over its reckoning and distribution shows that as an institution it was still in its infancy.
2. That said, comparison with Denmark, where the bishop's share in the tithe was accepted much later than the other parts and only after resistance, suggests that in Iceland the position of the bishops was relatively strong.
3. The fact that the property assessments were in the hands of the commune which also distributed the paupers' quarter, leads to the suggestion, expanded below, that secular interest in reforming poor relief was an important factor in the acceptance of the law in 1097.
4. The laws of *Grágás* are not normative and the tithe law cannot be interpreted as a directive to divide the country into tithe areas. It should rather be interpreted as a warrant for certain individuals to claim their share of the tithe. The law provides the legal procedure for such claims but realizing a claim was up to the claimant, like all other litigation in Icelandic society, and his success depended on his political skill and influence. It is therefore wrong to assume that the tithe law was immediately followed by a country-wide demarcation of tithe-area boundaries. It may have resulted in the defining of boundaries between tithe areas in some regions but there is reason to expect that, in others, churches with permanent ministries were still few and far between and that their owners were not able to extract tithe from people who lived far afield and did not attend the church regularly or at all.

[20] The bishops did have a right to appoint a plaintiff in cases of overfeeding or underfeeding of invalids and could rightfully be asked to arbitrate in such cases (*Grg 1b*, 178–9), but it is not clear whether this could include calling for a pauper's tithe. See below on the distinction between paupers and incapable persons.

[21] The regulations found in the manuscript AM 315 fol Litr. B, allowing the bishops to direct the whole paupers' quarter to churches (*Grg 1b*, 228), are probably more recent (13th or 14th cent.) as all the clauses on this single piece of vellum seem to be amendments (*Grg III*, pp. xlii–xliii).

Church Economics Before the Tithe

As discussed above most scholars have assumed that the tithe law was passed towards the end of the formative period of the Icelandic church organization. This would be argued by pointing out that there would hardly have been a need for such legislation if there were not plenty of churches and priests to benefit from it. In order to support this idea scholars have looked for other sources of income which could account for all these early churches and the priests who served them.

Unlike Norwegian scholarship which holds that a 'capital tithe' (Nor. *höfuð-tíund*, Lat. *decima capitales*; a large offering payable once in a lifetime) preceded the ordinary, annual tithe (K. v. Maurer 1874c: 16–51; Hamre 1974: 280–1), there is agreement that the corresponding Icelandic 'greater tithe' (*tíund in meiri*) was a secondary introduction (Finsen in *Grg III*, s.v. *tíund*; M. Stefánsson 1974: 290–1; cf. K. v. Maurer 1874c: 4–16, who was of the other opinion). Nor has anyone suggested that the tithe law of 1097 was only a rubber-stamp on already accepted practice. Instead a precursor to the tithe has been identified; Björn Þorsteinsson (1953: 200) and Jón Jóhannesson (1956: 202) believed that temple dues had been exacted in heathen times and that this had been changed into some kind of church dues after the conversion. The idea of temple dues is only found in thirteenth and fourteenth century sources and is almost certainly fiction (Olsen 1966: 43–8; J. Benediktsson 1974*a*: 172–3; 1975),[22] although some modern scholars still seem to believe in them (Byock 1990: 83).

Ísleifs þáttr mentions that, while tithes did not exist in Bishop Ísleifr's time (1056–80), dues were paid to him from all around the country (*Bysp* 1. 23), whereas *Hungrvaka* stresses the financial troubles of Bishop Ísleifr because 'the income was small but the expenses great' (*Bysp* 1. 78). It is unlikely that either author had much in the way of concrete evidence regarding the finances of Bishop Ísleifr. As discussed in Chapter 2, section 1, the author of *Hungrvaka* seems to exaggerate Bishop Ísleifr's financial and pastoral difficulties in order to emphasize Bishop Gizurr's brilliance. *Ísleifs þáttr* is a more recent source (mid or late thirteenth century, see Ch. 1, s. 2) and it is likely that its author simply could not imagine an episcopal see without some sort of income. That is of course consistent with the tendency among saga authors to envisage structural arrangements in the pre-Christian past as essentially the same as in their present.[23]

It is safe to dismiss temple dues as well as any sort of levies for Ísleifr's bishopric. Although few set much store by such ideas nowadays, earlier

[22] Temple dues are mentioned in *Landnámabók* (H) (*ÍF* i. 315) as in *Þórðar saga hreðu* (*ÍF* xiv. 231) and *Þorsteins þáttr uxafóts* (*ÍF* xiii. 343); *Kristni saga* (*ASB* xi. 10) as in *Þáttr af Þorvaldi víðförla* (*ASB* xi. 72), as in *ÓST* i. 291; *Eyrbyggja saga* (*ÍF* iv. 9, 17); *Egils saga* (*ÍF* ii. 293); *Vopnfirðinga saga* (*ÍF* xi. 33); *Þorskfirðinga saga* (*ÍF* xiii. 193) and *Kjalnesinga saga* (*ÍF* xiv. 7).

[23] 'Each man was to give dues to a temple, as they now give tithe to a church.' (*ÍF* i. 315); 'At one end of the temple there was a chamber in the same manner as there are now chancels in churches.' (*ÍF* iv. 8). On this see O. Olsen 1966: 25–34, 111–12.

scholarship built elaborate constructions on these grounds, which still influence current views even if the basic evidence has been refuted. In particular this applies to views on the nature of the power of the chieftains, the *goðar*, and to some extent pre-Christian social organization and the origins of territorial divisions.

Many scholars still have no scruples in attributing religious functions to Viking-age chieftains (Aðalsteinsson 1985; G. S. Munch 1991: 328; Gräslund 1992: 132), and such ideas still influence current thought on the origins and nature of power in medieval Scandinavia. As already discussed in the Introduction, there are neither sources nor reasons to attribute religious functions to pre-Christian chieftains or to suppose that they presided over any sort of communal gatherings. There is no need to look any further than the Sagas of Icelanders and contemporary sagas for indications about the nature of the power of the *goðar* (Sørensen 1977, 1992, 1993; Miller 1990) and in no way do these sources suggest that the *goðar*'s power had a base in communal responsibilities. On the contrary, it is evident that the *goðar* had particular difficulty in translating their powers as leaders of men into lordships over territories and that this only happened from the twelfth century onwards.

This is an important consideration for the present inquiry because the extent of religious involvement of the chieftains in the eleventh century greatly affects our estimates of the development of religious institutions before the introduction of the tithe. Here it will be maintained that at the beginning of the eleventh century the chieftains had no sort of territorial powers and were not regarded by their neighbours as having any religious responsibilities. It is however likely that the chieftains were already then aspiring to more consolidated powers and strove to increase their authority and influence by building churches and paying for priests to give services.

The missionary bishops, at least those like Hróðólfr in Borgarfjörður and Bjarnharðr in Húnaþing who stayed for considerable periods of time, must have found patrons to support them in their task. It is reasonable to assume that effective patronage could only be provided by chieftains or wealthy farmers of influence. Itinerant priests like the good Reginpreht, whether they were trading or preaching or both, were probably also in need of the patronage of chieftains.[24] In Iceland there were no bases independent of the indigenous society from which the missionaries could operate, like the monasteries from which much of Central and Eastern Europe was christianized. Nor was there any royal authority which could sustain and protect the missionaries as there was in the Scandinavian kingdoms.

It is therefore difficult to imagine how the earliest missionaries could have even travelled to Iceland, let alone stayed there for protracted periods of time, without the active support and involvement of those who exercised authority and had command over enough resources to maintain them.

[24] See Þorláksson 1991*b*: 153–77 for the importance chieftains attached to lodging foreign merchants.

Without going any further into the realms of speculation we can surmise that the first missionaries were to all intents and purposes entirely dependent on chieftains for support and protection, as well as for the building of churches and procurement of wine and other materials needed. The material requirements of the missionaries may not have been great but there are certain materials which a Christian ministry cannot be without in the long run, especially after the first phase when nominal conversion has been achieved and the building of organized Christian life has begun.

It is reasonable to imagine that there was a slow increase in the number of clergy in Iceland from the 1020s onwards, as a result of the labours of the missionaries. It is of course also possible that there were more foreign priests of Reginpreht's ilk although we have no way of assessing that. Eleventh century priests fall into two distinct groups; on the one hand there are the Icelanders of aristocratic birth like Sæmundr *fróði* and St Jón who owned their own estates, and on the other itinerant priests who had no landed property on which they could base their income. There is no direct evidence for the existence of the latter class of priests; it is postulated here because it is difficult to see how the mission could have been achieved without any foot soldiers and because it is unlikely that all chieftains could be bothered to become priests themselves. We cannot of course know how numerous or influential such itinerant priests were. It does not seem that they were important for the later developments.

Like the missionaries it is difficult to see how itinerant priests could survive and operate without the active support of the chieftains. Procuring the basic necessities of life was one problem which faced such priests, but a larger problem was no doubt that, judging from attitudes in *Grágás*, people with uncertain income or people who based their livelihood on something other than farming were barely tolerated in Icelandic society. If itinerant priests were to operate successfully they can only have done so under the protection of the chieftains.

There were most likely economic limits to how many priests could be supported in this way. Adam of Bremen complains about the iniquitous ways of the clergy in Denmark and Norway who extracted fees for baptism and confirmation as did the bishops for consecrating altars and ordaining clergy (*Adam* iv. 31). This most likely was also the practice in Iceland; throughout the middle ages special fees were paid to priests in Iceland for reciting funeral rites (*Grg 1a*, 9_{7-8}, cf. *NgL* v. 30_{22-29}).[25] Fees paid for individual services can, however, hardly have been the basis for permanent ministries or have acted as an attraction for young men to seek ordination.

As was argued in Chapter 1, section 2, at least some leading families identified their fortunes with those of the Church from an early stage. It was this

[25] In the late 13th cent. there is also mention of a fee for extreme unction (*DI* ii. 12, 14, 16–19; iii. 59–60, 129–30, 257). Bishops also received special fees for consecrating churches and chapels but they were required to give it back to the church or chapel in question (*Grg 1a*, 19_{14-18}). This practice may originate in the bishops taking a fee for such services for themselves.

aristocratic involvement which no doubt made it possible for the missionaries to work in Iceland, and it was because of this interest that the first Icelanders were sent abroad to become priests. It is likely that the missionary bishops educated and ordained Icelandic men as priests, and that these men were, like the pupils of Bishop Ísleifr, from the higher echelons of society. Towards the end of the century we meet aristocratic priests like Sæmundr *fróði* in Oddi (S), Jón Ögmundarson in Breiðabólstaður (S), and Teitr Ísleifsson in Haukadalur (S), who owned their respective farmsteads and probably had established an effective cure of souls in their respective areas by the time the tithe was introduced.

Kristni saga's list of chieftains who were ordained during Gizurr's episcopacy and the list of high-born priests from 1143 indicate that, in the first half of the twelfth century, chieftains considered it worthwhile and beneficial for their influence over others to be priests. It is unlikely that they would have sought ordination in such numbers if the priesthood was swelled by men of humbler rank. In the late eleventh and early twelfth century chieftains became priests in great numbers (Ch. 5, s. 2) and this suggests that at the time there were few priests about; by performing priestly services the chieftains increased their influence among their neighbours and followers. That in turn would indicate that, by the last quarter of the eleventh century at least, there had developed among the populace a need for religious services on a regular basis.

In Chapter 1, section 4 we saw that there are strong indications that shortly after the conversion Christian graveyards were established outside the home field of most or all farmsteads in the country. We cannot know when churches or chapels began to be built in these graveyards although the mid-eleventh-century date for the church structure excavated at Stöng suggests that it was already in that century. If that was the case in general it does attest to an interest in Christianity and a willingness to invest in the necessary trappings.

The conclusion is, therefore, that by 1097 there must have been a significant number of priests operating in the country; significant in the sense that their labours had produced conditions where many more priests were seen to be needed. It has been argued here that the barrier to an increase in the number of priests was primarily an economic one; there were too few men of enough wealth to be able to maintain a priest or finance study trips abroad for themselves and demanding fees for individual services was probably not a viable mechanism for maintaining priests or their services in the long run. Living off fees alone was probably not to the benefit of the priests; they may not always have been in a strong position to claim their fees from householders and the householders are likely to have resented fees that were too high.

With these preconditions in mind we can appreciate why different layers of society should have supported, or at least not opposed, the introduction of the tithe.

1. The chieftains who owned churches and those who were priests themselves or employed priests naturally supported the tithe law as it made their running

of a ministry cheaper and more reliable. They no doubt also welcomed the opportunity to be able to claim money from their neighbours.

2. Chieftains who, because of financial constraints, were not already maintaining priests and had not already built churches, as well as others with aspirations to power, must have welcomed the opportunity to found ministries and thereby join the already successful class of priest-chieftains. In other words the tithe offered a much larger portion of the better off an opportunity to establish their own ministries or at least to get their own tithe areas for the maintenance of their churches.

3. It is argued here that householders at large viewed the tithe law as a rationalization of an inadequate system, that the services of a priest were already seen to have become a necessity[26] and that paying fees for individual services did not ensure this in a satisfactory manner.

The last point does of course hinge on the 4,000 or so householders in the country having full control and authority over the rest of the populace, and while this may not have been entirely so, it is likely that a sufficient part of the new tithe payers identified their fortunes with that of the head of the household to which they belonged.

Another consideration is that people who were not householders or did not own land were not likely to own very much at all; those who owned less than 10 ounce units worth apart from their everyday clothes did not pay any tithe, nor did those who owned more than 10 ounce units but had to maintain incapable persons. The tithe of those who owned between 10 and 100 ounce units was exclusively apportioned to poor relief (*Grg 1b*, 205_1–206_{10}, 208_{3-4}, 214_{7-9}).[27] In other words only those who owned more than 100 ounce units, which equals at least five cows or three to four years wages of a farmhand around the year 1200 (Þorláksson 1981: 54) and is more than the maximum annual wages of a priest (*Grg 1a*, 21_{1-2}), paid *skiptitíund* or enough tithe to be divided in four: so tithe to the bishops and church-owners only came from those who were relatively well off. Those who owned less than 100 ounce units paid only for poor relief and it is understandable that there was not widespread dissatisfaction with that arrangement as those who owned least property were most likely to hit hard times and therefore stood to benefit from the new system.

In the late middle ages the amount of tithe returned to churches in individual ministries corresponded roughly to 0.25 per cent of the total value of land in the ministry in question.[28] That means that tithe was not paid on much property apart from land and if the same holds for the late eleventh century it indicates

[26] Adam of Bremen maintains that in Norway people are not considered Christian who do not listen to mass every day and give alms (*Adam* iv. 31), which if even half-true might also hold for Iceland.

[27] The right given to the bishops to direct the tithe allocated to paupers to churches may be a more recent amendment (cf. *Grg 1b*, 228_{9-20}; Jóhannesson 1956: 208).

[28] Based on calculations of tithe returns for eight parish churches in Dalir in the 14th and 15th cents. See Table 3.

TABLE 3. *Expected and observed annual tithe returns of the churches in Dalir (ells)*

Church	Expected tithe return, 1703–5	Observed tithe returns	
		1350–1400	1450–1500
Snóksdalur	130		85.7
Sauðafell	115		120
Kvennabrekka	85		49.1
Vatnshorn	100	63	102.8
Hjarðarholt	155		112.5
Sælingsdalstunga	55		46.5
Staðarfell	145		120
Hvoll	75		82.5

Source: *DI* iv. 164; v. 101, 494–5, 596; vi. 165–6; vii. 67, 69, 71; *JÁM* i.
Note: Values in ells. Expected tithe returns are calculated as total land value of farms in each parish in 1703–5 converted into ells (× 120) and divided by 100 to find the total tithe value, which is then divided by four to find the church's quarter. In some of the parishes one or more annex-churches may have taken the tithe payable on the farm where it stood, but this could not be taken into account because this type of information is not available for all the parishes or known half-churches and is usually more recent than the 14th cent. Nor is any attempt made here to evaluate the value of the glebes and other church lands which were exempt from tithe payment. As a result the expected tithe value should be read as a maximum.

that it was primarily landowners who paid *skiptitíund* while those householders who were tenants were considered to be likely to be unable to pay any tithe, as the paupers' quarter of the tithe was to be given to householders who could not pay tithe.[29] If there was a considerable body of householders who could not afford to pay any tithe that suggests that, on the whole, servants and the like could not pay much either.

Tithe seems therefore primarily to have been paid by the better off in society. This does not reflect any particular sense of justice or egalitarianism. The Icelandic economy was simply poor and a large part of the population could not do much better than sustain themselves and their dependants. Most of the wealth in society was in the hands of a small group of landowning householders in whose interest it was to stop impoverished householders from becoming destitute. If they became destitute they could not of course pay rent any more and, a more visible fear, their dependants became the responsibility of other and better off people.

Maintenance of Paupers: The Tithe System and the Commune[30]

The Icelandic tithe law is unique in that it makes supervision of tithe assessments the responsibility of the communes and gives the Church no part in

[29] No research has been done into the information tithe reckonings can give on the economic structure of Icelandic society. The indications are that it was from the outset extremely unequal, originally with few very large households where no one owned much except the householder, and that householders of new farms being created in the 11th cent. and later were mostly tenants who were not much better off property-wise than servants of rich householders (Vésteinsson 1998*b*.)

[30] Nordal 1942: 295; J. Jóhannesson 1956: 103–9; M. M. Lárusson 1962*a*; L. B. Björnsson 1972*a*: 34–50; Miller 1990: 147–54.

handing out alms. This of course reflects the limited extent to which the Church had become an institution around 1100, but it also suggests that reform of poor relief was a secular interest which was one of the factors which made the tithe law acceptable in 1097.

One of the principal chapters of *Grágás*, the *Ómagabálkr*, is devoted to poor relief (*Grg 1b*, 1–28; *Grg II*, 103–51). It is an extremely detailed and sophisticated piece of legislation which has few parallels (Rindal 1975)[31] and bears witness to a deep-rooted sense that people who cannot sustain themselves are a menace to society.

The *Ómagabálkr* deals with incapable persons, that is, people who because of their age or health cannot sustain themselves whether they own money or not, and regulates whose responsibility it is to maintain them. That responsibility rests firmly with next of kin, but failing that the incapable person's maintenance had to be apportioned between householders in the commune, the quarter, or the whole country (*Grg 1b*, 178_{17-21}). Incapable persons were of two kinds. First were those who had close kin who could support them, such people were a part of the household which maintained them. The other type did not belong to any particular household, normally because they had no or only distant kin, and were itinerant, staying at a prearranged number of households for short periods of time. This was in no way a humane system; it divided society into two, those who could provide for themselves and those who could not. The latter were defined as a burden and the aim of the law is to apportion their maintenance as fairly as possible. Those who did not qualify for maintenance[32] had no rights whatsoever; aiding vagabonds was punishable and flogging or castrating them was recommended (*Grg 1a*, 139_{25}–140_{9}; *Grg 1b*, 14_{8-27}; 173_{23-5}; 178_{21-23}; 179_{12-25}; *Grg II*, 151_{5-7}).

It is clear that maintenance of incapable persons was not seen in terms of charity. Except for meals given to the poor designated by the commune on certain feast days (*Grg 1a*, 25_{11-19}, $_{28}$–26_{3}, 31_{4-10}, 32_{6-7}, 34_{18-22}; *Grg 1b*, 171_{10-13}, 206_{12-14}) the only instance of the compilers of *Grágás* foreseeing a charitable act, that I have come across, is a clause dealing with a man who sustains an incapable person 'for the sake of God'. Even if he was not supposed to maintain the incapable person and the incapable person died, such a benefactor was to inherit the estate of the incapable person while the legal heirs of the incapable person got nothing (*Grg 1a*, 229_{11-14}). This is of course a warning to potential

[31] See Tierney 1959 for canonical thinking on poor relief and its practice in England; Pirinen 1959 for poor law in Scandinavia. Also Dahlerup 1958*b*; Hamre 1958*b*; Suvanto 1961: 1–2; Skyum-Nielsen 1961: 6–7; Bjørkvik 1961: 11–13; Kealey 1985.

[32] It is not clear whether people could be *dis*qualified from maintenance; the law tries to cover every eventuality and the aim seems to be that everyone has a claim on someone to be fed and accommodated. Those who stood outside the system probably did so because they chose to. The legislators seem to envisage that vagabonds are primarily healthy people who because of indolence chose to become beggars. On begging and vagrants also Þ. Jóhannesson 1933: 177–89; Rindal 1974.

heirs of incapable persons not to let some virtuous people deprive them of their inheritance and is not an appeal for charity.[33]

The law suggests that the maintenance of paupers could become a matter of disputes, and this is borne out by the Contemporary Sagas (*Sturl* 233–4, 552). That of course tells us that the laws to some extent represent real conditions (Miller 1990: 147–54) and that in reality it was not socially acceptable to let incapable persons starve or freeze. The attitude of the legislators is clear: it was imperative that everyone who was unable to support him/herself was put in charge of somebody else who could sustain him or her. The law of incapable persons also attempts equality in that a householder should only be made to sustain so many incapable persons as would not endanger the economic viability of the household. If there were more incapable persons than a householder could sustain they were to be sustained by more distant relatives or by the commune, or, in other words, householders who were either wealthier or less burdened by the maintenance of incapable persons.

The thought behind the *Ómagabálkr* seems to be that the poor and destitute are dangerous to society; either directly because they might steal or kill to get food, or indirectly, which is a more likely consideration, because their maintenance might become too much of a burden for some households, which would then potentially be dissolved and become even more of a burden for someone else.

This explains why the, presumably aristocratic, legislators were at such pains to secure the maintenance of everyone. Iceland was a relatively poor country. It was poor in the sense that the economy was unable to translate its produce into permanent goods, which meant that even if there was plenty of food in normal years and good years, the occasional bad year could have disastrous effects. Most people eked out a living at subsistence level and those who were better off were not so much better off that they could not also be in danger of being swamped by hungry relatives or becoming destitute themselves in bad years. There is a clear sense that keeping society afloat was a delicate balance which must not be upset. It was in a householder's interest to keep his neighbour's household from dissolution; if one household was dissolved it might have a domino effect. The first defence was the kin group, and the second the commune.

A commune was an association of twenty or more *þingfararkaupsbændr* who appointed up to five officials to oversee its business. The officials were normally landowners, that is, the most affluent householders in each commune, although tenants were acceptable if no member objected (*Grg 1b*, $171_{3-4,\ 12-17}$). Each commune had its assembly which met at least twice a year, where communal

[33] The heirs of an incapable person had a right to his or her estate and the benefactor's chance of profiting from his good deed was remote—reaping rewards in heaven is not among the motivations the compilers of *Grágás* reckon with; there is a hint of scorn in the phrase 'God's gratitude to the other for his toil' (*Grg 1a*, 17_{14}), in a case when a tenant has been so presumptuous as to repair a church without asking the church-owner first and a jury bears witness that services could still have been given in the church without repairs.

matters were solved and inter-communal disputes could be settled. The commune was therefore the smallest judicial unit and the only administrative unit which existed in Iceland before 1262–4. Although the communes had several other tasks, among them insurance of property and management of pasture (*Grg 1b*, 171–9; M. M. Lárusson 1962*a*; Björnsson 1972*a*: 33–46), it seems that poor relief was their principal business and the main reason behind their development. If the tithe law preserves the arrangement decided on in 1097—and there is no reason to suspect it does not—it means that the communes were already in existence then, and that they were sufficiently widespread and uniformly organized to take on the administration of the paupers' quarter of the tithe.

This suggests that, while maintenance of incapable persons was originally and principally the responsibility of the family or kin group, it had by the end of the eleventh century come to be seen as a matter of concern for the community. It also suggests that the communes had already by then taken on the burden of sustaining incapable persons who had no relatives who could support them. The system of poor relief as represented in the *Ómagabálkr*, while clearly displaying the perceived need to keep one's neighbours afloat, does not allow for preventative measures to be taken to ensure they were not dissolved. The will to do this is apparent in the attempts to distribute the burden of maintaining incapable persons and linking maintenance liability with wealth, but this was obviously a cumbersome system which could not be used to avert the dissolution of households in times of crisis.

This problem was solved by the tithe law; it put money in the hands of the commune, money which was not intended for the maintenance of incapable persons, but a new category of poor people, *þurfamenn* or paupers. Paupers were householders who owned so little property that they did not pay any tithe or had more incapable persons in their charge than they could sustain (*Grg 1b*, 206_{8-9}, 208_{4-6}), and were as a consequence always at risk of becoming destitute. It paid for the community to maintain poor households rather than letting them dissolve and having to sustain its members as incapable persons. This is sound economics; it is cheaper to subsidize poor households, so that they nevertheless sustain themselves to some extent, than to allow them to become unproductive as incapable persons or less productive as servants in other households.[34]

Although the paupers' quarter was primarily intended for the support of poor householders it seems that the commune's officials could distribute it in whatever way they saw fit, the law even envisages that they might want to support other communes (*Grg 1b*, 208_{7-9}). It was, however, the primary aim of the paupers' quarter to keep poor households from dissolution and to help householders who were burdened by many incapable persons to maintain

[34] Note for instance that paupers (men who had to support incapable persons) were allowed to demand more than the otherwise fixed maximum wages for freelance work (*Grg 1a*, 129_{24-26}).

them, the effect being that more affluent householders were less likely to become burdened by the maintenance of their neighbours' dependants.

It is therefore arguable that it was the more affluent householders who benefited most from the tithe law. It is likely that their direct contribution decreased while the middle-income householders who previously had contributed little or nothing had to increase their share in the burden of maintaining the poor. Poor households benefited in the sense that they were less likely to be dissolved, but accepting aid meant that the commune gained power over their affairs; the number and stability of impoverished households may have increased as a result of the tithe but so did their political dependence on their more affluent neighbours. The tithe law therefore contributed on a small, but fundamental scale, to increased social differentiation and the formation of extra-familial bonds of dependency. It is likely that this was an important influence on early power consolidation; the first requirement for a potential chieftain was to have control over his immediate neighbours and having command of poor relief was surely a very practical way to serve that aim.

It has been argued here that in Iceland fear of poverty and the poor resulted in an emphasis on a universal right to basic sustenance. This meant that apportioning responsibility for maintenance of the poor became a matter of the greatest concern, and while the family or kin group was originally responsible for its poor, this responsibility was increasingly falling to the community by the end of the eleventh century. There were therefore clear and practical reasons for more affluent householders to support the introduction of the tithe; it put money in their hands which allowed them to manage the affairs of their less affluent neighbours; it lessened the risk of affluent householders having to take on other householders' dependants, and increased their chances of establishing direct authority over their neighbours.

The individual poor may have benefited from the tithe in the sense that it enabled householders who otherwise would have gone bust to keep going but as a class they became more distinct and more dependent on affluent householders. It is unlikely that the introduction of the tithe meant an increase in resources directed towards poor relief, the money was just collected and distributed in a different way than previously. In this way the Church did contribute to increased social differentiation and the development of territorialized authority; it provided the institutional structures around which power could be consolidated.

This is also an example of how the apparent weakness of the early church in Iceland—its inability to administer poor relief with its own agents—meant that Christian institutions were run and fostered by laymen until the Church was strong enough to claim its own identity and control of its institutions. While the Church never gained control over the administration of poor relief from the communes, the means it provided to invest in pensions and poor relief may have been one of the reasons behind the endowment of churches in the twelfth century.

Political and Economic Effects of the Tithe

The close ties between chieftains and Church in the twelfth century have long been recognized as one of the main characteristics of that century and an important stage in the development of secular power in Iceland. Sigurður Nordal (1942: 296) coined the term *goðakirkja* (chieftains' church) and applied it to the Icelandic church in the eleventh and twelfth centuries but Björn Þorsteinsson (1953: 207, 229–92; 1966: 88, 207–24; 1978: 100–12) developed the theme further and called the chieftains of the twelfth century *kirkjugoðar* (church-chieftains) and named the period between Bishop Gizurr's death in 1118 and 1230 when the Age of the Sturlungs (*Sturlungaöld*) started, *kirkjugoðaveldi* (supremacy of the church-chieftains).

Alongside Jón Jóhannesson, Björn Þorsteinsson is undoubtedly the most influential historian of medieval Iceland in the second half of the twentieth century and his sharp exposition and lucid style, as well as his penchant for sweeping theories on long-term historical developments, will ensure that his influence will be felt for some time to come. While Björn Þorsteinsson's own particular brand of nationalistic Marxism[35] is no longer a strong influence in Icelandic historiography, his view that the roots of the political changes which took place in the thirteenth century are to be found in social and economic changes in the eleventh and twelfth century has been adopted by virtually everyone writing on the subject, and his assertion that the tithe was the principal factor behind power consolidation in the twelfth century is still a powerful notion (M. Stefánsson 1975 and J. V. Sigurðsson 1989: 96–7 and to some extent Byock 1990: 91–5; also G. Karlsson 1975: 38–9; 1980*a*: 9–11, 24, 30).

Like Jón Jóhannesson, Björn Þorsteinsson was of the opinion that the Church was a crucial influence on the development of Icelandic society in the high middle ages. The difference was that Björn Þorsteinsson (1953: 205–6, 229; 1966: 171) ascribed to it a largely destabilizing role, and the means by which the Church effected this instability was through the tithe. In his view of medieval Iceland the tithe was imposed on a largely egalitarian agrarian society which had developed in Iceland since the tenth century. In this rather rosy wonderland all, however, was not well because already the first bishops were determined to establish feudal structures (Þorsteinsson 1966: 191), and the means to do that was to empower the hitherto largely powerless chieftains by ordaining them and giving them churches which they could profit from.

It was Sigurður Nordal (1942: 296) who pointed out the mechanism whereby the tithe was supposed to lead directly to an increase in the wealth and power of church-owners.[36] He pointed out that churches were privately owned, that their owners received half the tithe, and that church property was exempt from tithe

[35] On Björn Þorsteinsson's historical views and their development see Þorláksson 1988*a*.

[36] Ólafur Lárusson pointed out as early as 1929 that there must have been a relationship between the tithe and chieftains owning churches (Lárusson 1944: 38–9). See also Gíslason 1944: 72–88 for a thorough overview of the sources.

payments. It then followed that it became profitable for chieftains to be ordained and bequeath their estate and/or other holdings to their church. In this way they did not have to pay any tithe themselves or pay for the upkeep of a priest but could stand to profit from the tithe payable to them from their neighbours. To Björn Þorsteinsson this meant that the chieftains suddenly received vastly increased amounts of wealth which they promptly invested in land, so that by the beginning of the thirteenth century a manorial aristocracy had arisen balanced at the other end by an expanding class of tenants. The tithe therefore contributed to power consolidation and social differentiation and Björn Þorsteinsson (1966: 124–5; 1978: 34–6, 108–9; 1986) attributed particular importance to its influence on the development of the *aðalból* (*höfuðból* in *Jónsbók*; Norwegian: *óðal*, inalienable and undividable core holding of a family which was always inherited by the eldest son), which he interpreted as a 'feudal' institution.[37]

Björn Þorsteinsson saw in this reconstructed increase in social and economic differentiation an explanation for the political unrest of the thirteenth century and the eventual unification with Norway in 1262–4. His view was that the constitution of the Commonwealth as preserved in *Grágás* had developed and acquired its final form in a society of more or less equal householders. Once the economic balance had been tipped it was natural that social and political unrest and reorganization should follow. This hypothesis was put forward in opposition to earlier views which ascribed the strife of the thirteenth century to a lack of moral fibre and a decline in Nordic values.[38] As such it was a vast improvement in the quality of historical debate but it was unfortunately not supported by research or indeed anything but inference from the tithe law.

Jón Viðar Sigurðsson (1989: 96–107) who is strongly influenced by Björn Þorsteinsson's scholarship, has tried to stop this research gap and in a recent work has assembled evidence showing that in the thirteenth century the chieftains were running large estates with big households, that some of them owned more than one farmstead, and that many impoverished people are mentioned. He also argues that tenancy was on the increase. To him these were recent developments in the thirteenth century; the supposed increase in the number of impoverished people was a direct result of the growth in ecclesiastical and aristocratic land-holding and he is unsure whether descriptions of large estates in the tenth century indicate that there was an early phase with large estates,

[37] On the debate concerning *aðalból* see Magerøy 1965: 24–8; M. M. Lárusson, 1967*e*; 1970; Rafnsson 1974: 142–51 cf. Benediktsson 1974*b*; Gurevich 1977, 1987; Arnórsdóttir 1995: 78–104. For *óðal* in Norway see Helle 1964: 110–15; Andersen 1977: 84–91.

[38] Although Björn Þorsteinsson was himself not above using such explanations in his earlier works: 'The principal reason why the Icelanders accepted the rule of the King of Norway, was the treason of the Icelandic ruling class. [It] lacked the mettle and ambition to form an indigenous state structure and sought foreign assistance to establish such a structure. In that way [the ruling class] humiliated itself and signalled the demise of its powers and prestige and forsook the nation, because it is not possible to sell oneself without loss' (Þorsteinsson 1953: 319). On these and other more poetic kinds of explanations see Haraldsson 1988: 29–48.

followed by a more egalitarian period in the eleventh and twelfth centuries, or whether these sources are simply describing thirteenth-century conditions (Sigurðsson 1989: 100 n. 113; 103 n. 123).

It is of course unacceptable to assume that thirteenth-century conditions must be recent developments when no comparable evidence is available for the previous periods. There is no direct evidence for the system of land ownership in Iceland before the final decades of the twelfth century and there is therefore no reason to suppose that it was characterized by a free landowning peasantry rather than some other system closer to the actual conditions we know from the thirteenth century (cf. Vésteinsson 1998*a*). The reason why scholars have always readily assumed a period of free peasantry in equilibrium is that that is what has traditionally been expected of pre- or proto-historic Germanic peoples (for complex and no really good reasons) and because that sort of setting seemed to explain the apparently independent householders of *Grágás* and the Sagas of Icelanders in a way which appealed to the nineteenth- and early twentieth-century audience. While such assumptions served their purpose in an earlier age when nationality and democracy topped the list of historians' interests, they are only assumptions and the necessary research remains to be done before we can assess the relationship between land ownership and political change in Iceland in the twelfth and thirteenth centuries.

That said, it is reasonable to expect that the tithe did contribute to the changes Icelandic society was undergoing in the twelfth and thirteenth centuries. Great weight must be attached to the significance of a universal tax being imposed on a society which previously had not experienced this sort of regular taxation. The impact of the first generation's experience of taxation is difficult to assess; it is likely that, while annual assessments soon became established, it did take some time before all three claimants had established an effective collection of their shares.

The communes were in the best position to collect their shares and these are likely to have been paid from an early stage. It was to the benefit of all the householders of a commune that the paupers' tithe was paid, and if one or two tried to evade payment the rest were in a strong position to compel them to pay or else drive them out of the commune.

The collection of the bishop's quarter required a more complex and substantial organization. The law envisages that the bishops appoint a collector in every district (*Grg 1a*, 19_{22}–20_{13}; *Grg 1b*, 209_{20}–210_{8}), and they probably chose men with political clout who could influence or control proceedings at assemblies and force payments if necessary. Failing that, the bishops were in a good position to pursue reluctant payers through the judicial system and to bestow political favours on those who carried out the eventual confiscations if it came to that. Collecting the bishop's quarter was therefore manageable, even if the bishops only had the most rudimentary administrative structures in place. It is likely that the organization needed to collect the bishop's tithe and bring the goods to the sees took many years to develop and become effective. It can only, however, have been a question of time, and developing a system of tithe collections must have been the principal impetus behind the development of episcopal administration, as well as being an effective means to increase and consolidate episcopal authority.

While the commune had the advantage of proximity and peer pressure and the bishops that of political influence, contacts, and control of assemblies, the position of church-owners to realize their claims must have varied considerably. Their relationship with their neighbours might influence their chances of effective tithe collection, as would the stability and permanence of the services they could provide and the tithe payers' perception of the usefulness of these. The effective and enduring collection of the church's and priest's portions may have been based on coercion where the church-owners had effective political authority, but it is more likely that it was based on some sort of contractual arrangement whereby those who attended a church on a regular basis agreed to pay their tithe there. This reciprocal relationship was probably symbolized by the feast of the church's dedication (*dies ecclesiae*) hosted by the church-owner for the congregation (*Grg 1a*, 14_{9-16}). The effectiveness of this must have depended on three factors.

First is religious inclination. We are not in a position to evaluate the extent to which people in general had become accustomed to attend church as a matter of routine by 1100. The social/religious need to attend church should probably not be underestimated. The tithe law itself is good evidence that by 1100 there was a perceived lack of permanence and stability in pastoral care and this feeling must have been based on generally accepted attitudes. That however does not preclude the possibility that there was a sizeable part of the population which did not share the majority's view that attending church was desirable and beneficial. Before there were structures in place to compel people to attend church there must always have been those who could find reasons not to.

Second there is the number of effective ministries and the distances people had to travel to attend church. Even if people may have been interested in attending church on a regular basis this may not always have been workable because of long distances to the nearest church where services were given. Again the tithe law itself is evidence that a sufficient number of ministries in sufficiently many regions had been established by 1100 for it to be conceivable to introduce such legislation. There are still likely to have been many areas, especially where settlements were widely separated, where attending church more than occasionally was not an option. It is difficult to see why people who never or seldom attended a church should have consented to pay the same amount to the church-owner as he collected from more regular attendants. The capacity to compel infrequent attendants to pay is something which can only have evolved after the coercive and territorial powers of chieftains and the effectiveness of the bishops' supervisory powers had become more established than they seem to have been around 1100.

Thirdly and perhaps most importantly there is the political significance of paying and being paid. If the traditional view of a society of reasonably equal property-owning householders running relatively small farmsteads more or less independently of each other is to be taken seriously, it follows that a great number of such householders and their retainers must have agreed to pay tithe to a smaller group of church-owning householders who probably already had an economic and political edge over the others. However, as all householders, church-owners or not, are supposed to have had equal political rights, it seems unlikely that all those who did not own churches were from the outset happy to place themselves in a subordinate relationship with neighbours whom they had previously regarded as equals. Anyone with ambitions to authority, however modest, must have been suspicious of entering a relationship which added to somebody else's status while reducing the other's social standing to that of a tithe payer. If there was a large body of politically and economically independent householders who disadvantaged their social and political standing as a result of becoming tithe payers we should expect that establishing full and universal payment of the priest's and church's portions of the tithe was a long and complicated process.

Although it is the accepted model, there is no good evidence for all these equal property-owning householders.[39] Serious research remains to be done in this field and the alternatives need therefore to be kept in mind. A contrary model can be proposed whereby only a small number of householders were politically and economically independent and that it was those who built churches while everybody else was dependent on them in one way or another. The prospective tithe payers were therefore already in a subordinate position when the tithe was introduced. If this was the case, the effects of the introduction of the tithe will have been quite different from in the other model. Collecting tithes will then have been relatively simple and based on pre-existing patterns of authority; the tithe will have cemented those patterns and made them less contingent on personal relationships while increasing the importance of territorial relationships.

Which of these two models is closer to reality greatly affects our assessment of the effects of the tithe on Icelandic society and, indeed, its development in general, but in the present state of research we are only allowed to conclude that, despite Ari *fróði*'s sanguine version, it is possible and even likely that the collection of at least half the tithe was undeveloped in places for a long time after the ratification of the tithe law. It is possible that in a few places payment of the church's and priest's quarters had not been instituted as late as the

[39] The classical exposition of settlement patterns and household sizes is Ólafur Lárusson 1944: 9–58. Also J. Jóhannesson 1956: 410–15; B. Þorsteinsson 1953: 142–7; 1966: 119–25; and 1978: 32–7; Byock 1990: 55–7; Teitsson and Stefánsson 1972; Thoroddsen 1908–22: iii. 5–30; Miller 1990: 111–37; Vésteinsson 1998*a*, 1998*b*. The debate on the extent and significance of slavery is also important in this context: Foote 1975, 1977*c*; B. Þorsteinsson 1978: 38–41; Agnarsdóttir and Árnason 1983 and more generally Karras 1988.

mid-thirteenth century, as reflected in the adjustments of the tithe areas of Stóriás (S) in 1258 and Akrar (S) in 1238–68, (*DI* i. 594, 596) and in some regions of scattered settlements even as late as the beginning of the fourteenth century, as reflected in the formation of the new ministries of Eyri in Bitra (D) in 1317 and Kaldaðarnes (N) in 1304–20 (*DI* ii. 407, 409–10), but on the whole it seems likely that tithe payments had become firmly rooted by the end of the twelfth century.

Irrespective of which of the two economic patterns prevailed in Iceland the tithe helped to shape a new type of association of dependency: the relationship between congregation and church-owner. Whatever forces united neighbours before the institution of the tithe, it contributed to the development of a new social unit which was based on territorial rather than personal, familial, economic, or political ties. Before the institution of the tithe the possession of a specific farmstead did not necessarily put the householder into any particular type of relationship with anyone, but after tithe areas had been established, the location of the same farmstead began to predetermine a series of social and economic conditions. In buying or renting a farmstead in the 1050s the prospective householder had to consider the size and quality of the land and he might also have taken account of the neighbours' personalities and whether or not they were domineering or aggressive, although he had no guarantee that these factors would stay unchanged. The prospective householder of the late twelfth century entered into very different and much more concrete relationships with his neighbours. He became part of a congregation, a group of people defined only by residence and who, irrespective of personalities, had quite a lot to do with each other. The presence of a consecrated church with a designated tithe area on the farmstead then defined whether our householder became a tithe payer or tithe receiver; in other words possession of a certain piece of land with certain qualities had become a factor in defining the social position of the householder.

This, it will be argued at more length in Chapter 6, is the principal and basic reason behind the power consolidation of the twelfth and thirteenth centuries. The possession of a church and the influence gained by offering a service and making neighbours dependent on it no doubt began this process in the eleventh century but it was only after the ties between church and congregation had become institutionalized through tithe payments that it became possible to accumulate power and to define its extent in terms of territory.

By the beginning of the thirteenth century the possession of *staðir* and other rich churches had become a basic precondition for taking part in power games. The players' eventual success might depend on their personality, political skill, and contacts but many an inept and untactical man was allowed a bid for power and sometimes protracted involvement in politics through the accident of possessing a rich and/or tactically placed church.[40] The overriding political

[40] The sons of Þorvaldr *Vatnsfirðingr* and Magnús Pálsson in Reykholt are examples of such characters.

advantage of possessing a church did not come from access to disposable wealth as many have imagined but from the access to predefined and fixed ties of dependency between congregation and church-owner. Such ties did not in themselves determine political allegiance but where the church-owners had taken care to use their favourable position to nurture and strengthen the ties with their congregations, such groups must have been fairly unwavering and dependable, if only not to stir up trouble in a chieftain's backyard.

The reason why some churches had become immensely rich by the beginning of the thirteenth century was not, as Björn Þorsteinsson thought, because church-owners converted tithes into land which they subsequently donated to their churches in order not to have to pay tithes themselves. Although the tithe did of course contribute to the development of the *staðir* and other churches, endowment of churches in the twelfth century is a more complex issue which will be examined in detail in the following chapters.

While the tithe did contribute to power consolidation, it did not do so by putting cash in the hands of chieftains but by creating social units which could be manipulated for political ends.[41] The effect of the tithe on the power structures in the country was also not a simple linear development. On the contrary it seems likely that in the first instance the tithe contributed to an increase in the number of men with claims to authority. This is because, while a large number of householders had built churches by the end of the eleventh century (Ch. 1, s. 4), it seems that only a few of them had been able to afford the permanent services of a priest. The tithe made it possible for a much larger group of ambitious householders to hire priests and this will have made them potential contenders for authority or at the very least better equipped to withstand or turn to their advantage the encroachments of more powerful chieftains. In short the tithe effected a fundamental change in the nature of politics; it was of course only one of several factors influencing the development, but it was the gaming board itself which became changed as a result of its introduction. Instead of having to spend their energy on forging personal ties with individual householders, chieftains could begin to secure authority over sizeable groups of people. In overcoming this hurdle the stakes were raised and the way carved out for the wide-ranging territorial powers which chieftains were beginning to exercise by the mid-thirteenth century.

Here we have considered the wider, political implications of the tithe; its influence on church ownership, pastoral care, and episcopal administration in the twelfth century will be considered in the following chapters. It remains that the lasting and most deep-seated effects of the tithe were on the conditions of rural life in Iceland. The tithe contributed to the cohesion of the probably pre-existing communes and made poor relief the prerequisite of these secular associations of householders which were to become the basic units in the

[41] Cf. Þorláksson (1982*b*: 88–90; 1983: 276) who is emphatic that *stórbændr* cannot have benefited financially from the possession of churches while he concedes that the *goðar* may have.

country's judicial system with the introduction of *Jónsbók* in 1281. The tithe created a new territorial division, the tithe area, which in turn defined the congregation, a new social group uniting neighbouring households. The tithe also contributed to the formation of territorially defined ministries which had by the end of the thirteenth century become the basic divisions of ecclesiastical administration or parishes.

3

Churches and Property

According to *Páls saga*, Bishop Páll of Skálholt (1195–1211) had the churches and priests in his diocese counted because he wanted to give his priests leave to go abroad only if there were sufficient numbers left to uphold all the services. There were found to be 290 priests and 220 churches. It is clear from the text that annex-churches were not included but only 'churches that by obligation, priests were needed for', in other words churches that had ministries attached to them and which would later be classified as parish churches (*Bsk* i. 136).[1] An inventory of churches from the same diocese survives in several manuscripts from the seventeenth century, listing 242 churches, but giving the total as 220 (Rafnsson 1993: 68–79, 90–105). It includes several churches that are known to have been moved, deserted, or abolished in the fourteenth and fifteenth centuries, long before some of the churches also listed in the inventory were established. On this evidence Jón Þorkelsson the editor of volume xii of the *Diplomatarium Islandicum* suggested that the inventory had its origins in Bishop Páll's counting of churches around 1200, and that new churches had been added to it subsequently, while churches were not erased from it even if they had been abolished (*DI* xii. 1–3).[2] It is possible to identify the twenty-two churches which were established later and as nothing has been put forward to contradict Jón Þorkelsson's analysis it is reasonable to assume that the locations of the 220 churches around 1200 are known to us, although some margin of error has to be allowed for because of the irregular transmission of this document.

Even if the locations of the 220 churches were not known, the number itself is significant. It means that by 1200 the number of ministries had reached the level it would stay at throughout the middle ages (i.e. around 220–30 in the southern diocese and 90–100 in the northern, based on fourteenth–sixteenth-century charter collections). It therefore gives us a *terminus ante quem* for the process of establishment of ministries around the country. This evidence does not allow us to speculate on the actual number of churches in the country. The high number of churches without ministries in the fourteenth century makes it unsafe to assume anything about the proportion of churches with ministries in the earlier centuries. The building of a church and the establishment of a

[1] The number of priests is not the actual number of ordained priests resident in the diocese but the sum of ministries attached to churches as laid down in their charters. The number of priests is not the same in all the MSS, e.g. 190 in *Bysp* 2. 421 and 240 in the list of churches printed in Rafnsson 1993, 104, but judging by the late-medieval ratio between the number of churches and the number of priests 290 is about right for 220 churches.

[2] See also Ó. Lárusson 1944: 123–45; Víkingur 1970: 152–70; Rafnsson 1993: 79–82.

ministry are two separate issues, and Bishop Páll's inventory only allows us to pursue the latter one. In this chapter we will examine the different types of evidence for early churches and church building, with emphasis on changing ideas regarding ownership of ecclesiastical property.

1. CHURCHES IN NARRATIVE SOURCES

Not many early churches are mentioned directly in the narrative sources. In the southern diocese only thirty-nine churches are referred to explicitly before 1200. Of this number several may be doubted, for example those mentioned in *Þorgils saga ok Hafliða* which was written in the early thirteenth century and to which the same principles may apply as to the Sagas of Icelanders. The majority, however, are from more reliable sources. There is good correlation between a priest living at a farm and that farm having a church, even if the church itself is not mentioned until later. There are 226 priests and deacons of the southern diocese mentioned in sources before 1300 whose residence is known; in all cases but two a church can be shown to have been at the farm. Of these 226 all but five lived at farms mentioned in the church inventory connected with Bishop Páll's counting of churches from around 1200. Two lived at farmsteads not known to have had churches, two at farmsteads known to have had annex-churches and one deacon is said to have lived at a farmstead but served a church at another. In the northern diocese all the 103 priests whose residence is known lived at farmsteads which are known to have had churches in the fourteenth century. This strongly suggests that it is possible to assume that there was a church at a given farmstead at the time a priest is mentioned as living there, even if the church is not mentioned until much later. Accordingly it is possible to name sixty-seven churches in the southern diocese built before 1200 and thirty-two in the northern diocese. More than half of these are mentioned only in the last quarter of the twelfth century.

There are only five churches which can with reasonable certainty be said to have been built before 1100. These are the cathedral at Skálholt (S) and the public church at Þingvellir (S) which the Kings Ólafr Haraldsson and later Haraldr *harðráði* paid for (*ÍF* xxvii. 214; *Flat* iii. 344; *ÍF* xxviii. 119; *ASB* xi. 52), the churches at Oddi (S) and Breiðabólstaður í Fljótshlíð (S) which are connected with two early priests who came from abroad around 1080, Sæmundr *fróði* and St Jón Ögmundarson respectively (*Bsk* i. 157), and the church Gellir Þorkelsson (d. 1073/4) built at Helgafell (D) mentioned above. To this list ten more churches can be added which almost certainly were built before or around 1100. The church at Hólar (N) is not mentioned before 1106, but there is every reason to believe that it was long established by that date (*ÍF* i. 25; *Bsk* i. 159, 232, 163, 235). The other nine candidates are based on conjecture from *Kristni saga*'s list of chieftains who were ordained in Bishop Gizurr's episcopacy (1082–1118) (*ASB* xi. 50–1), considering that it is likely that these chieftains had churches on their farms. The list has ten chieftains, one of them Sæmundr *fróði* at Oddi already attested, but the farms of three of the others are unknown, although informed guesses can be made regarding two of them. Ari *fróði* probably lived at Staðarstaður in Snæfellsnes (S): his son lived there, Ari's family was from the region, and Staðarstaður was early an important church (*Sturl* 211; *ÍF* i. 20, 28, 122, 142; *DI* ii. 114). Ketill Guðmundsson (d. 1158) possibly lived at Holt in Fljót (N): he was called Fljóta-Ketill which suggests the region he was from and he was probably the father of a Jón Ketilsson who was priest at Holt and owned the *goðorð* in the area later in the century (d. 1192) (*Sturl* 129–30; Ingvarsson 1986–7 iii. 525–6).

To these fourteen churches several more can be added with ever diminishing degrees of certainty. For instance it could be suggested that there was a church at Hof in Vopnafjörður (A) when Gizurr Ísleifsson lived there before becoming bishop (*Bysp* 1. 83), or at Laugardalur (S) where the bishop-elect in 1080 Guttormr Finnólfsson lived (*Bysp* 1. 78). Other major churches known from the first years of the twelfth century, like Grenjaðarstaður in Aðaldalur (A) or Hofteigur in Jökuldalur (A) (*Bsk* i. 242; *Sturl* 25), could also be suggested. Similarly it could be argued that *Sörla þáttr*'s information about the burial of Kolbeinn Flosason (lawspeaker 1066–71) at the church at Rauðilækur in Ingólfshöfðahverfi (A) is so quaint and out of place that it must be true (*ÍF* x. 113).[3]

Interpreting these scraps of information leads in two opposite directions. On the one hand it is obvious that the source material is far from complete and one would expect to hear first of the richest and most important churches, because they are connected with the richest and most important people whose names and deeds were preserved by their rich and important descendants. On the other hand it could be argued that the oldest churches were the most likely to become rich and important and that, as there is no direct evidence to suggest that churches were more numerous, it is not possible to suggest that they were.

Although there is reason not to dismiss the latter alternative it cannot be overlooked that the patchiness of the sources is demonstrable. More than half of the sixty-seven churches in the southern diocese attested before 1200 are mentioned in the context of events occurring in the last decades of the century, that is shortly before Bishop Páll had the churches counted. That the sources fail to mention nearly three-quarters of churches can only tell us that they are not a useful indicator of the number of churches in any period. Sources like the miracles of St Þorlákr, *Sturlu saga*, *Guðmundar saga dýra* and *Prestssaga Guðmundar Arasonar*—which are all believed to have been written very shortly after 1200 (*ÍBS* i. 315–16, 474)—give the impression that in the second half of the twelfth century the density of churches and number of priests was not substantially lower than in the fourteenth century. Chapels and dependent

[3] Kolbeinn does not figure at all in this short *þáttr*, and is not connected with its subject in any other way than being the husband of a great-niece of Sörli, whose bid for a wife the *þáttr* relates.

TABLE 4. *Churches referred to explicitly before 1200*

Farmstead	Source	Reference	Date
Diocese of Skálholt			
Valþjófsstaður in Fljótsdalur (A)	*HSS*	*Sturl* 889	1190s
Hallormsstaður (A)	*ÞSO*	*Bsk* i. 282	1179
Þvottá in Álftafjörður (A)	*ÞSO*	*Bsk* i. 282	1179
Rauðilækur (A)	(*Sörla þáttr*); *ÞSO*	(*ÍF* x. 113); *Bsk* i. 281	*c.*1070; 1179
Svínafell (A)	*ÞSO*; Annal	*Bsk* i. 280–1; *IA* 119	1179; 1185
Höfðabrekka (2 churches) (S)	*ÞSO*	*Bsk* i. 282–3	1179
Arnarbæli in Eyjafjallasveit (S)	*MSÞ*	*Bsk* i. 348–9	1190s
Holt in Eyjafjallasveit (S)	*Landnámabók* (H)	*ÍF* i. 63	*c.*1170
Breiðabólstaður in Fljótshlíð (S)	*JSA*, *PSG*	*Bsk* i. 157; *Sturl* 172	*c.*1080, 1185
Hof in Rangárvellir (S)	*MSÞ*	*Bsk* i. 334 (+316)	1198
Keldur in Rangárvellir (S)*	*ÞSO*	*Bsk* i. 293	1190s
Oddi in Rangárvellir (S)*	*JSA*; *ÞSO*	*Bsk* i. 157, 320	*c.*1080
Skarð in Land (S)	*ÞSO*	*Bsk* i. 291	1185
Vellir in Land (S)	*ÞSO*	*Bsk* i. 290	1185
Skálholt (S)	*Hungrvaka*	*Bysp* 1. 76, 78, 85–6	
Haukadalur in Biskupstungur (S)*	*ÞSH*	*Sturl* 34	1121
Skálmholt in Flói (annex) (S)	*JSA*	*Bsk* i. 195	*c.*1200
Þingvellir (S)	*Kristni s.*, *MSÞ*	*ASB* xi 52; *Bsk* i. 352	1118; 1199
Mosfell in Mosfellssveit (S)*	*Egils s.*	*ÍF* i. 298–9	*c.*1140
Viðey (S)	*MSÞ*	*Bsk* i. 350	1190s
Hólmur in Akranes (S)	*Landnámabók* (H)	*ÍF* i. 65	*c.*1050
Melar in Melasveit (S)	charter	*DI* i. 419	*c.*1180
Bær in Borgarfjörður (S)*	*ÞSO*	*Bsk* i, 284–87	1178–93
Reykholt in Reykholtsdalur (S)*	charter	*DI* i. 279–80	1180s
Húsafell (S)*	charter; *Ceciliu s.*	*DI* vii. 1–2; *HMS* 294–7	*c.*1170
Stafholt in Stafholtstungur (S)	charter	*DI* i. 179–80	*c.*1140
Staðarhraun (S)	charter	*DI* i. 174	*c.*1120
Helgafell (D)*	*Laxdæla*; *PSG*; Annals	*ÍF* v. 229; *Bsk* i. 425; *IA* 118, 180	*c.*1060; 1181
Sælingsdalstunga (D)*	*Eyrbyggja s.*	*ÍF* iv. 183–4	*c.*1175–1221
Hvammur in Hvammssveit (D)*	*Sturlu s.*	*Sturl* 63, 75–6	1160; 1171
Skarfsstaðir (chapel) (D)	*Sturlu s.*	*Sturl* 75	1171
Fagridalur (annex) (D)	*Sturlu s.*	*Sturl* 70	1169
Hvoll in Saurbær (D)*	*Sturlu s.*	*Sturl* 68	1160s
Staðarhóll in Saurbær (D)*	*ÞSH*	*Sturl* 24, 25	1119
Flatey (N)	Annal	*IA* 61	1192
Saurbær in Rauðisandur (N)	*HSS*	*Sturl* 889–90	1190s
Hvalsker (chapel) (N)	*HSS*	*Sturl* 890	1190s
Vatnsfjörður in Ísafjarðardjúp (N)*	*ÁSB*	*ÍF* xvii. 38–9	*aq* 1150
Kálfanes (annex) (N)	*PSG*	*Bsk* i. 425	1182
Diocese of Hólar			
Breiðabólstaður in Vesturhóp (N)	*Kristni s.*	*ASB* xi. 57	1150
Þingeyrar (N)	*JSA*	*Bsk* i. 171, cf. *IA* 320	1112
Hólar in Hjaltadalur (N)	*JSA*	*Bsk* i. 163	*c.*1050; 1106–10
Marbæli in Óslandshlíð (annex) (N)	*PSG*	*Sturl* 122	1187–9
Holt in Fljót (N)*	*JSA*	*Bsk* i. 197–8	1198
Tjörn in Svarfaðardalur (N)	*GSD*	*Sturl* 136	1191
Hofsá in Svarfaðardalur (annex) (N)	*PSG*	*Bsk* i. 440	1190–6
Árskógur in Árskógsströnd (N)*	*GSD*	*Sturl* 133	*aq* 1191
Auðbrekka in Hörgárdalur (N)	*GSD*	*Sturl* 169	1199

TABLE 4. *Churches referred to explicitly before 1200 (continued)*

Farmstead	Source	Reference	Date
Langahlíð in Hörgárdalur (N)	*GSD*	*Sturl* 152	1197
Öxnhóll in Hörgárdalur (N)*	*GSD*	*Sturl* 136	1191
Bægisá in Öxnadalur (N)	*GSD*	*Sturl* 168	1199
Hrafnagil in Eyjafjörður (N)*	*PSG*	*Bsk* i. 456	1198
Saurbær in Eyjafjörður (N)	*PSG*	*Bsk* i. 460	1200
Laufás (N)*	Annals; *PSG*	*IA* 117, 322; *Bsk* i. 417	1167/9
Flatey in Skjálfandi (N)	*MSÞ*	*Bsk* i. 366	1190s

ÁSB = *Árna saga biskups*; *GSD* = *Guðmundar saga dýra*; *HSS* = the separate version of *Hrafns saga Sveinbjarnarsonar*; *JSA* = *Jóns saga*, A version; *JSB* = *Jóns saga*, B version; *PSG* = *Prestssaga Guðmundar Arasonar*; *MSÞ* = *Miracles of St Þorlákr*; *ÞSH* = *Þorgils saga ok Hafliða*; *ÞSO* = *Oddaverja þáttr* in *Þorláks saga* B and C; * = evidence that a priest lived at the farmstead.

churches appear to be common, and in areas like Dalir and around Tröllaskagi, where events are described in detail, a very high proportion of the later parish churches are mentioned. This really only confirms the evidence of Bishop Páll's inventory that by 1200 a tight network of ministries had been established in Iceland. It does not allow us to attach any earlier dates to the end of that process. The narrative sources cannot be used to discern whether the formation of ministries was long complete before the second half of the twelfth century, whether that process was in its final stages then, or even if it had only recently got under way. What the narrative sources do add to the evidence of Bishop Páll's inventory is that the system of dependent churches and chapels served by priests attached to principal churches was already in existence in the late twelfth century.

Apart from incidental references to chapels and churches which according to more recent sources were dependent, there are a few stories from the late twelfth century which clearly indicate that the system of dependency was in place. According to *Prestssaga Guðmundar Arasonar*, when Guðmundr was a priest at Miklibær in Óslandshlíð (N) in 1187–9 'he had annex-service to a farm called Marbæli; he sang [mass] there one feast day' (*Bsk* i. 435).[4] Later, in 1190–6 when Guðmundr was a priest at Vellir in Svarfaðardalur (N) he sang mass at a church at nearby Hofsá (*Bsk* i. 440). That the ties of dependency were formal and fixed is witnessed by a dispute arising from a ruined chapel at Hvalsker in Patreksfjörður (N) in the 1190s:

> At the farm where Ingi lived [i.e. Hvalsker] there was a chapel. It was subject to the church in Rauðisandur [i.e. Saurbær]. But it was the command of the holy bishop Þorlákr [1178–93] that where chapels had been built they should nowhere become derelict, and if a chapel was in disrepair or fell in ruins then six ounce units should be paid from the site to the burial-church which the chapel was subject to. At the farm where Ingi lived the chapel fell in ruins but Ingi did not repair it and refused to pay for

[4] *Brottsöngr* is here translated as annex-service; it means literally 'away-song', *að eiga brottsöng til* is used of a priest who is duty-bound to sing mass at a dependent church at regular intervals.

TABLE 5. *Farms where there is Indirect evidence for churches before 1200*

Farmstead	Source	Reference	Date
Diocese of Skálholt			
Hofteigur in Jökuldalur (A)*	*ÞSH*	*Sturl* 25	*c.*1120–45
Kirkjubær in Síða (S)*	*ÞSA*	*Bsk* i. 94–5	1160s
Gunnarsholt in Rangárvellir (S)*	*GSD*, Annal	*SturlR* i. 161; *IA* 119	*aq* 1186
Skarð in Rangárvellir (S)*	*GSD*	*Sturl* 161–2	1198
Fellsmúli in Land (annex) (S)†	*ÞSO*	*Bsk* i. 290	*c.*1185
Leirubakki in Land (S)†	*ÞSO*	*Bsk* i. 290	*c.*1185
Vestmannaeyjar (S)†	*MSÞ*	*Bsk* i. 351	1190s
Hruni in Hrunamannahreppur (S)†	Annals *GSD*; *Haukdæla þ*	*IA* 120, 180; *Sturl* 155–6, 193, 288	1190s
Bræðratunga in Biskupstungur (S)*	*Íslendinga s.*	*Sturl* 186	1197
Gaulverjabær in Flói (S)*	charter	*DI* i. 404	1178–93
Arnarbæli in Ölfus (S) or Eyjafjallasveit (S)†	*MSÞ*	*Bsk* i. 339	*c.*1200
Reykir in Ölfus (S)†	*MSÞ*	*Bsk* i. 339	*c.*1200
Reynivellir in Kjós (S)†	*MSÞ*	*Bsk* i. 340	*c.*1200
Saurbær in Kjalarnes (S)*	*PSG*; Annals	*Bsk* i. 418; *IA* 118, 323, 476	*aq* 1175
Lundur in Lundarreykjadalur (S)*	*Íslendinga s.*	*Sturl* 184	1195
Deildartunga (annex) (S)*	*Sturlu s.*	*Sturl* 90–1	*c.*1165–74
Borg in Mýrar (S)*	*Íslendinga s.*	*Sturl* 210	*aq* 1202
Staðarstaður in Snæfellsnes (S)*	*Íslendinga s.*	*Sturl* 211	*c.*1140–70
Hjarðarholt in Laxárdalur (D)*	*Kristni s.*, *Hungrvaka*	*Bsk* i. 29, 79; *Sturl* 8, 186	*c.*1120–97
Ásgarður in Hvammssveit (D)*	*Sturlu s.*	*Sturl* 67, 69–70, 82	*c.*1160–72
Skarð in Skarðsströnd (D)*	Sturlu s.; *Íslendinga s.*	*Sturl* 54, 68, 182, 187	1148–1201
Reykhólar in Reykjanes (D)*	*Kristni s.*, *PSG*	*Bsk* i. 29, 424	*c.*1120; 1181
Staður in Reykjanes (D)*	*PSG*	*Bsk* i. 457 cf. 464	1199
Hagi in Barðaströnd (N)*	*HSS*	*Sturl* 893, 920, 923	1197–1212
Eyri in Arnarfjörður (N)*	*HSS*	*Sturl* 884	*c.*1190
Mýrar in Dýrafjörður (N)*	*HSS*	*Sturl* 897	*c.*1195
Staður in Steingrímsfjörður (N)*	*PSG*; *HSS*	*Bsk* i. 424; *Sturl* 893	*aq* 1181–97
Diocese of Hólar			
Staður in Reynines (N)*	*PSG*	*Bsk* i. 455	1198–9
Víðimýri (N)*	*PSG*	*Bsk* i. 457	1199
Silfrastaðir in Blönduhlíð (N)*	*GSD*	*Sturl* 133	*c.*1190
Miklibær in Blönduhlíð (N)*	*PSG*	*Bsk* i. 435	1187–9
Viðvík in Viðvíkursveit (N)*	*PSG*	*Bsk* i. 436	1189–90
Hof in Höfðaströnd (N)*	*PSG*	*Bsk* i. 430	1185–7
Fell in Sléttahlíð (N)*	*GSD*	*Sturl* 133	*c.*1190
Knappsstaðir in Fljót (N)*	*JSB*	*Bsk* i. 248	1121
Ufsir in Ufsaströnd (N)*	PSG	*Bsk* i. 450	1196–8
Vellir in Svarfaðardalur (N)*	*PSG*; *GSD*	*Bsk* i. 437; *Sturl* 135	1190–6
Urðir in Svarfaðardalur (N)*	*GSD*	*Sturl* 157	1198
Grund in Eyjafjörður (N)*	*PSG*	*Bsk* i. 418	*aq* 1173
Laugaland in Hörgárdalur (N)*	*GSD*	*Sturl* 136	1191
Möðruvellir in Eyjafjörður (N)*	*Kristni s.*; *GSD*	*Bsk* i. 29; *Sturl* 130	*c.*1120; 1188
Grenjaðarstaður (A)*	*JSB*; *PSG*; *GSD*	*Bsk* i. 242; *Bsk* i. 472; *Sturl* 123	1106–21; *pq* 1185
Helgastaðir in Reykjadalur (A)†	GSD	*Sturl* 124	1186

ÞSA = *Þorláks saga*, A version; * = record of priest living at the farm; † = record of bishop visiting a farm.

the site. Markús [church-owner at Saurbær] claimed the money from Ingi but he did not pay it. From thereon animosity grew between Markús and Ingi. (*Sturl* 890)

It is clear from the context that burial-church refers to a main church to which chapels (and possibly other churches) can be subject. That disrepair of a chapel incurred fines to the church it was subject to suggests that the main church normally received an income from a chapel, presumably in return for services. The source here is the separate version of *Hrafns saga Sveinbjarnarsonar* which is believed to have been written *c.*1230–60 (*ÍBS* i. 315) and may therefore reflect mid thirteenth-century conditions. There is however little reason to be suspicious of the association between the command and St Þorlákr; if chapels were as numerous in the thirteenth century as later it is likely that the command and its instigator were well known to the saga's audience. That St Þorlákr had decreed that chapels should not become derelict and that the owners had a responsibility to keep them in repair, or else be fined, is also in accordance with the argument put forward in section 4 below about the introduction of *ius patronatus* in Iceland in the late twelfth century.

The most famous passage on church organization in the late twelfth century is in a much more difficult source: the *Oddaverja þáttr* in the B and C versions of *Þorláks saga helga*, which has been suggested to be a translation of a part of an original Latin Vita from *c.*1200 or else a work of propaganda from the second round of *Staðamál* after 1270 (*ÍBS* i. 476–7). It is naturally of great importance for the understanding of this source which hypothesis is accepted. As will be discussed in section 4 there are more grounds for accepting the latter alternative and that of course calls for caution in the interpretation of *Oddaverja þáttr*. According to this source St Þorlákr visited the eastern quarter in his first summer as bishop of Skálholt in 1179, successfully gaining control over the majority of the privately owned churches there. On his way back to Skálholt in the autumn he met the chieftain Jón Loptsson at Höfðabrekka in Mýrdalur (S). Jón (d. 1197) was the most powerful chieftain in the country in the last decades of the twelfth century and had recently extended his power sphere to the east by acquiring Höfðabrekka, 'which was reckoned among the best [estates] before Höfðá [river] damaged it' (*Bsk* i. 282). We are told that a storm had ruined two churches 'but Jón had then had a new church built, a very well appointed construction; the holy Bishop Þorlákr was to sojourn there that autumn . . . It was planned that he would consecrate the church there' (*Bsk* i. 282). In the morning before the consecration was to take place Jón and St Þorlákr discussed the conditions of the church's charter, resulting in a famous exchange of words where Jón flatly refused to relinquish the control of his church even after St Þorlákr had threatened to excommunicate him. But there was another matter of contention between them:

arising from floods in the river Höfðá, because it had destroyed many farms, which were subject to [Höfðabrekka] and two where there were churches. That resulted in less tithe and fewer houses [= churches, chapels] to sing at. Because of this Jón wanted there to be no more than one priest and a deacon at the church; but earlier there had been two priests and two deacons. This was granted by the honourable bishop on these same grounds. (*Bsk* i. 283)

The author may have been confusing traditions in having two churches broken by storm and two that perished in floods; it seems one too many natural catastrophes to befall a small area in a short time. It is, however, not unthinkable, and the author seems to indicate that Höfðabrekka itself was one of the churches which was broken by the storm but that both of those which were destroyed by the flood were annexes. In the fourteenth century there was one priest and a deacon at Höfðabrekka and three farms in the ministry, two of which had annex-churches.[5] That is a very small parish to have a deacon and this may suggest that the ministry had previously included more farms.

Höfðabrekka is situated on the eastern edge of the Mýrdalur mountain range (S), overlooking what is now a coastal desert called Mýrdalssandur which is dominated by glacial rivers. Apart from *Oddaverja þáttr* there are indications that this area was habitable and densely settled before the thirteenth century and further to the east the communities in Álftaver and Meðalland (S) are still being gradually reduced by land erosion from sand and glacial waters. It seems that the settlements in Mýrdalssandur had to a large extent disappeared by the fourteenth century and it may even be that they had long since been devastated or greatly reduced when *Oddaverja þáttr* was written.[6] Höfðabrekka itself was situated on the lowlands and was only moved to its present location in the hills after a flood in 1660; another farm remained on the lowlands until a flood in 1721 forced its relocation into the hills (Þórarinsson 1974: 79). The extent of the devastation by the twelfth- or thirteenth-century flood in Höfðá river (now Múlakvísl) is unclear but the farms and churches which were supposed to have perished must have been situated on the lowlands which subsequently became desert, so that only four farms remained in the ministry of Höfðabrekka. If that was so it is likely that the author based his story about the clash between St Þorlákr and Jón Loptsson around folkloric explanations about the devastation of the settlements in Mýrdalssandur. Such folklore is common in Iceland; tales of flourishing communities perishing as a result of floods, lava, or plague have long been a source of horror and fascination, and the common theme in these stories is that the abandonment of the settlements is always the result of a single catastrophic event. Archaeological and historical research has shown that this is only rarely the case; the causes for farm abandonment are usually complex and the abandonment of whole communities is normally a drawn out process (Gissel *et al.* 1981; V. Ö. Vilhjálmsson 1989; Rafnsson 1990*a*: 93–100; Sveinbjarnardóttir

[5] At Kerlingadalur and Hjörleifshöfði, the third farm was Fagridalur (*DI* ii. 741; iii. 293; ix. 88, 189; Sveinsson 1947: 201–2).

[6] Sveinsson 1947 has collected all the documentary evidence for the settlements in Mýrdalssandur, and for this part of it—the so-called Lágeyjarhverfi—his conclusions are that they must have been fragile from the outset, although Lágey—where tradition has it that there was a church—may have been occupied into the 14th cent. See also Þórarinsson 1974: 76–9.

1992: 171–7). While *Oddaverja þáttr* does not claim that the whole community in Mýrdalssandur was abandoned, it clearly indicates that the abandonment of many farms was permanent and was the result of a single recent natural catastrophe. It is safest to interpret this as a folkloric theme, which indicates that the author was somewhat removed in time from the events he was describing, strengthening the case for the late thirteenth-century time of writing. It also indicates that the information contained in these passages about the structure of the ministry may not be taken at face value; it is more likely that the tale about the former importance of the farm and church at Höfðabrekka, its numerous staff, and dependent churches was preserved in connection with the tale about the vanished settlements in Mýrdalssandur, and that the author worked out the details in accordance with accepted practices and conditions in his own time. That means that a bishop's say in the staffing of churches may not have been established in the late twelfth century, while *Oddaverja þáttr* is naturally a good source for it being firmly established in the second half of the thirteenth century; not even the rebellious Jón Loptsson is meant to have questioned that. It also means that we cannot say if tithe areas were as firmly and formally fixed in the late twelfth century as *Oddaverja þáttr* indicates that they were in the late thirteenth, and that we cannot use this source to show that the terms of charters were a matter of agreement between bishop and church-owner before the thirteenth century. Of course this does not mean that these features could not have been in place in the late twelfth century; they may have been, but there are no reliable sources to confirm it.

To sum up, the narrative sources cannot on their own be made to throw any light on the nature and development of church building and parish formation in the first two centuries of Christianity in Iceland. *Prestssaga Guðmundar Arasonar* and *Hrafns saga Sveinbjarnarsonar* do suggest that already before 1200 a sort of a ministry structure was in place, at least regarding ties of dependency between a main church with a priest or priests attached and lesser churches and chapels. This was the most conspicuous feature of the Icelandic parish system when more detailed sources become available in the fourteenth century and later, and it governed payments of the tithe and the priest's fee, as well as the distribution and number of masses and hours given in different churches. How fixed in geographical terms and formal in legal terms this structure had become in the late twelfth century we cannot say on the basis of the narrative sources. Nor do they allow us to speculate on the extent of episcopal authority over tithe arrangements, staffing of churches, or the distribution of services between churches within a ministry.

2. THE CHARTER EVIDENCE

There were two principal types of charter in the twelfth century (Vésteinsson forthcoming-*b*). On the one hand there were records of the property belonging to a church (e.g. *DI* i. 279–80, 470–2, 394–5) and on the other there were documents recording the conditions under which a church was held by its caretaker. It is primarily with the latter type that we will be concerned here. Excluding the suspicious charters of Stafholt and Staðarhraun (Vésteinsson forthcoming-*b*) the charter of Húsafell (S) is the earliest datable example of this type. It is principally a record of the establishment of a *staðr* at Húsafell and deals with the extent and arrangements of the functions of this institution. To the church-owner the most important clause must have been the one where control of the church property is secured for him and his descendants:

Brandr Þórarinsson shall have charge of this church property for as long as he wants to, and then his sons for as long as they want to. They shall appoint a caretaker if they want to depart but if they have no heirs that can [have] control, then a man from their family shall be appointed to have charge of the church property, a man whom the bishop who rules in Skálholt thinks is suitable. (*DI* i. 217–18).

Although it is not explicitly stated, it is likely that the charter represents the terms of agreement reached between church-owner and bishop when the *staðr* was established, or when the church was consecrated if the two events did not coincide. Similar documents are preserved from Hítarnes (S) and the monastery at Helgafell (D), the latter with a likely dating of 1184–8.

[Hítarnes:] Jörundr shall have charge of this church property and his heirs, if the bishop thinks they are suitable, but otherwise someone who the bishop wishes from the kindred of Þórhallr or Steinunn. (*DI* i. 275–6)

[Helgafell:] We have decided this arrangement, that Guðmundr and Ólafr and Eyjólfr shall take over the *staðr* here at Helgafell and be in charge of a community of Canons [regular] . . . as large as it will be, while I live, but hold the *staðr* for as long as they want to and if they have health, and that one of them who lives longer, if he has health. Now I want either Guðmundr or Ólafr to take this seat after me . . . but if that will not be so, then I want them to have control over the finances and take an abbot, if that may transpire; I would prefer that he was from our kin group, if that is possible with the bishop's supervision. (*DI* i. 282)[7]

Most of the charters dated to the twelfth and thirteenth century in *DI* are not dated securely enough to be useful sources but three can be mentioned which are relevant to the discussion about twelfth-century church landscape. A charter of Melar in Melasveit (S) from 1199–1226 states that the church there owns 'the whole land at Melar with all the goods which Þorlákr bought and Magnús has since donated' (*DI* i. 419).[8] Magnús Þorláksson is mentioned in 1179 (*Sturl* 92), was probably more than middle-aged by then, and may have lived a few years into the thirteenth century. The charter refers to him in the present tense and

[7] 'We' is probably Ögmundr Kálfsson the first abbot of Helgafell (1184–8) but the others are unknown—the second abbot is usually considered to be one Þorfinnr Þorgeirsson (d. 1216) (J. Jóhannesson 1941: 155).

[8] The charter of Melar dated to [1181] in *DI* i. 272 is a 15th-cent. copy of the *Vilchinsbók* copy of the first charter.

has the church dedicated to St Þorlákr who was canonized at the Alþing in 1199 (*IA* 22, 62, 121, 181, 324; *Bsk* i. 134, 456). The donation could have been made long before the charter was drawn up. The charter is of the Húsafell type although its style is closer to the mainstream pre-1300 charters and it does not have a clause on control over the property. We know however that control over the *staðr* at Melar remained in the hands of Magnús's descendants throughout the thirteenth century.[9]

In an early or mid thirteenth-century charter of Gaulverjabær in Flói (S) there is this message at the end: 'Eyjólfr upheld this charter [= agreement] when he lived at Bær and rendered then what the holy bishop Þorlákr and Gunnarr priest had agreed on' (*DI* i. 404). This seems to mean that in 1178–93 St Þorlákr and the priest Gunnarr, who presumably owned Gaulverjabær, made an agreement where Gunnarr promised to donate something to the church. *Að halda upp máldaga* probably means that Eyjólfr (Gunnarr's heir?) had declared the agreement formally at an assembly,[10] rather than that he only honoured its terms, although that possibility cannot be ruled out. What is clear is that it was left to Eyjólfr to pay up whatever it was that Gunnarr had promised, which does suggest that the bishops of Skálholt had some kind of overview over what had been promised to their predecessors and did try to see that such promises were kept.

In *DI* a charter of Álftamýri in Arnarfjörður (N) is dated to 1211, based mainly on a questionable identification of one of the donors mentioned in the charter (*DI* i. 371–2). This charter is definitely earlier than the charters of Álftamýri in the fourteenth-century charter collections *Hítardalsbók* and *Vilchinsbók* (*DI* iii. 776; iv. 147),[11] and its features are so unusual—some are unique—that it must be considered unlikely that it was made later than the mid-thirteenth century when conventions had developed in episcopal charter-making. It is of course possible that church-owners continued to have their own charters drawn up and have them declared in the law court—like this one was—but there is no evidence to support that. In this case that hardly applies as the charter's main interest is in the running of the church and no mention is made of who is to be in control. It is more likely that this charter is among the oldest, written at a time when traditions on the basic shape and content of charters were still developing, and long before charters were routinely drawn up by the bishops. The time-frame for this charter is therefore *c*.1100–*c*.1250, probably earlier rather than later in this period. The name Cecilia among the church's benefactors may suggest a tighter time frame of the second half of the twelfth century, when the name was in vogue as a result of the saint's popularity (*Sturl* 109; *NID* 189; *NIDs* 195).

[9] Magnús's great-grandson the lawman Snorri Markússon lived at Melar and died in 1313 (*IA* 343).

[10] Cf. *Grg 1b*, 185_{17}, where *halda upp* refers to a declaration at an assembly. *Að halda upp kirkju* on the other hand means to be answerable for a church (*Grg 1a*, 17_{16}) the core meaning in both usages apparently being 'to hold up in full view.'

[11] The charter in *DI* iv. 12–13 is probably more recent than *Vilchinsbók*, which was assembled in and after 1397.

The most unusual features of this charter are first that the church's share of property on Álftamýri is expressed as the total value of the farm, and not the proportion of the land owned by the church and number of livestock as is otherwise the convention. Secondly, the 12 ells which are to be given to the needy every autumn are to be divided with other tithe. The payment of a specific sum to the poor is unusual, although not unknown (*DI* ii. 396, 778–80; iii. 115; iv. 180–3, 214–15), but this is the only instance where it is specified that the money is to go into the pool which the commune had at its disposal for the maintenance of paupers. Normally it was at the priest's or church-owner's discretion to whom such support was given.

Thirdly, masses are to be sung in the period when the Alþing was in session, but such detail is unusual, the only comparable cases being permission to give fewer masses or none at all in the Alþing time (*DI* i. 303, 416, 419; ii. 480–1). The priest at Álftamýri was clearly not to attend any synod or ecclesiastical courts, whereas the possibility is mentioned that he might have reason to leave his *þing* (ministry), at other times presumably, in which case mass had not to be sung three days every week. Relaxing services because the priest might not be at home is only mentioned in one other charter (from Hof in Gnúpverjahreppur (S): *DI* i. 303), and they must both belong to some other period than the fourteenth century when episcopal statutes are adamant that priests should never leave their cure of souls (*DI* ii. 512, 519, 539, 805, 817). The fourth feature is unique: 'The priest shall mention, in every mass which he sings at the church of St Mary, all those men who have donated their riches to that church, in particular [he should] name Steingrímr, Þuríðr, Kárr, Yngvildr, Högni the priest, and Cecilia, and turn his mind to all those men who have given their alms to it' (*DI* i. 371–2).

This is the only indication in the whole corpus of Icelandic charters that a church might have been established by a group of people or even a commune. The six people named seem to be three couples and the special consideration they are accorded may suggest that they were instrumental in the establishment of the church or were responsible for its principal endowments. That there were many other people who had given alms to the church may also suggest that its upkeep was a communal interest. The church does not however seem to have been run communally because in the next clause the householder (*buande*) is required to light the church at night for a specified period, which suggests lay charge (*varðveizla*) of the church.[12] It is conceivable that the church property was considered to be in the control (*forráð*) of a group of people or the commune and that they delegated the charge (*varðveizla*) of the church to the secular householder of the church farm. The householder was then considered to have the same responsibilities as the *fundatores*, on the same principle

[12] Although 'patronage' might be used here, the terms charge and caretaker will be used throughout this discussion to avoid misleading connotations with canon-law distinctions, for reasons discussed in Ch. 3, s. 4.

as tenants of church-owners took over at least some of the responsibilities of church-charge (see below). Whatever arrangements there were at Álftamýri, it is clear from this clause that they were not of the same kind as at most private churches, where private control was justified on the basis that the owner, or his or her heir, was the principal donor (cf. *Grg 1a*, 20_{13-16}).

A fifth unusual feature is a clause where it is stated that the charter has now been declared in the law court (*DI* i. 372). As mentioned above, it was the intention of the legislators in the Old Christian law section that this should be done but this is only stated in four other charters and seems to be a sign of great antiquity (Vésteinsson forthcoming-*b*).

The exhortation at the end of the charter is unique: 'A priest and a deacon shall be resident at Álftamýri and should not fail to give morning praise and prayer for long; dress frequently for masses and take good care of the church good brothers, and do so for the sake of God' (*DI* i. 371–2).[13] This seems to be addressed mainly to the priest and deacon. But if it is they who are to take good care of the church that may suggest that the priest had more say in the running of the church than an ordinary *heimilisprestr*; the word *varðveita* (have charge of, keep safe, safeguard) in the context of churches is in charter language always used for the church-owner's responsibility for the church property or the maintenance of the church building.[14] It is however possible that here it has a more general meaning, for earlier in the charter the frequency and arrangement of masses to be sung at Álftamýri is referred to as *varðveizla;* (*DI* i. 371–2) *varþveitiþ vel kirkio* may therefore mean 'perform the rites diligently'. There are only two other instances of this usage known to me, the other dating from the fourteenth century when a priest's *varðveizla* of a church could well mean charge.[15]

Apart from reminding us that medieval priests were ordinary human beings who overslept and could not always be bothered to put on the robes when nobody was watching them in church, the uniqueness of this plea and the many unusual features of this charter indicate that there could be much more disparity in early charter-making than the bulk of the preserved material would suggest. It suggests that the vast majority of the pre-1300 charters were either made in the late thirteenth century when we know that episcopal scribes were

[13] The phrase *láta skömmum missa* + gen., is rare. *Skömmum* means 'not long' (cf. *FM* vi. 355_{18}; vii. 10611; Unger 1848, 4_{29}: Munch and Unger 1853: 71_{21}) and here this probably refers to not being absent from the church for long.

[14] *DI* i. 174, 217–18, 265, 275–6, 491–2; ii. 443–5; iv. 101–2, 180–3; *ÍF* xvii. 39_{2}, 41_{5-6}; cf. *Bsk* i. 157_{11}, 330_{26} (ferry). Also legal language, compare: 'But if the man who has charge of a church squanders its money . . .' (*Konungsbók*, *Grg 1a*, 15_{25}), with 'If he who owns a church squanders . . .' (*Staðarhólsbók*, *Grg II*, 19_{17}; *Grg III*, s.v. *kirkja*; also: *Grg 1a*, 8_{19} (= *Grg II*, 9_{13}), 18_{27}, 19_{1}; *Grg II*, 59_{17} (*varðveizlumaðr*)). In narrative texts: Unger 1871*b*: xxxiii_{14}; *Mork*, 438_{17}; *DI* v. 265_{8-9}; vii. 277_{17}; *SturlK* i. 224_{25}. Cf. *SturlK* ii. 216_{13}; *ÍF* v. 22_{1} (*varðveita bú*); *ÍF* iv. 6_{8} (*varðveita hof*); M. M. Lárusson 1961*e*: 378.

[15] *Grg III*, 42_{14}, 161_{22}, 322_{13}, 375_{9}: 'the priest who has charge of the church', all 14th-cent. or more recent MSS. The 13th-cent. MSS of this text have 'the priest who gives services at the church': *Grg 1b*, 216_{13}; *Grg II*, 59_{4}. And *Páls saga*, *Bsk* i. 140_{31} where a priest has charge of the chancel and clerics at Skálholt.

establishing conventions of charter-making, or were altered to conform with such conventions at some stage before they were copied into the existing manuscripts around 1600.

This charter also indicates that there is a possibility that there could be other forms of ownership of churches than that of single individuals. There is absolutely no other evidence pointing in this direction, and as the charter itself is far from unambiguous it can only be made to point to the possibility that there were other forms of ownership. It should, however, not be surprising that there were more differences in the forms of ownership than is suggested in the patchy and mostly late source material, especially as it is well known that many different forms of church ownership existed in the neighbouring countries. Lastly, the charters of Stafholt and Staðarhraun, while probably not wholly authentic twelfth-century documents (Vésteinsson forthcoming-*b*), do suggest that very substantial endowments were being made in the middle of the twelfth century.

On the whole, the scanty twelfth-century charter material does only a little to illuminate the process of establishment of ministries and the endowment of churches in the twelfth century. The inferences that can be drawn may be summed up as follows.

1. With the possible exception of Álftamýri, the charters indicate clearly that churches were privately owned and that control of ecclesiastical property was to all intents and purposes firmly in the hands of laymen. The bishops probably had the right to be consulted, and may sometimes have been able to use their powers of consecration to put pressure on church-owners. In the case of the charter of Húsafell, where Bishop Klængr is said to have granted certain burial rights, we cannot know whether he was in any position to deny burial to the church at Húsafell if he had been so inclined or whether he simply had to give his blessing to the church-owners' preferred arrangement.

2. The foundations for major *staðir* like Stafholt, Melar, and possibly Gaulverjabær were being laid as late as the second half of the twelfth century. The time range for each of these foundations is quite long, but Steini Þorvarðarson can hardly have made his endowment to Stafholt before 1120 and Magnús Þorláksson his to Melar not much before 1150. As both Melar and Stafholt had quite large ministries, this may either mean that these churches had been responsible for the cure of souls in their respective areas before they were endowed, or that ministerial boundaries were only being formed in the early or mid-twelfth century. The fate of the tithe area of Staðarhraun may support the latter alternative. In its earliest charter recording the endowments which were probably made in the 1120s the number of tithe-paying farms is said to be fourteen, but in an early or mid-fifteenth-century charter this number is down to six and a half (*DI* iv 593–4). Such reduction is unusual and as no major changes in the ecclesiastical landscape of the immediate area are known after

1200, it is more likely that the reduction of the tithe area took place in the twelfth century. That is, that the original endowment to Staðarhraun church was made before all the permanent ministries had formed in the region. This, it must be stressed, is not based on firm ground, and there are many other possible explanations for this difference in the size of tithe area.

3. The establishment of a *staðr* at Húsafell, probably in the 1170s or slightly later, and possibly at a similar date at Hítarnes, suggests that by that time stable ministerial boundaries had already formed. Both these rather well endowed churches had very small tithe areas,[16] and at Húsafell at least we know there was a church but no priest before the establishment of the *staðr* in or before 1178–93 (*HMS* i. 294–5).[17] This fits well the impression given by the narrative sources that most ministries had been established by the last two decades of the twelfth century, but also implies that the process was only just grinding to a halt at that time. There are no similar foundations or endowments known until the beginning of the fourteenth century.

4. The charter of Reykholt shows that the bulk of the landed property of this very rich church had already been donated to it before the beginning of the thirteenth century, but also that major donations had been made between the writing of the first clause in the 1180s and the second in 1202–23. Although reservations have to be expressed about the authenticity of the charters of Staðarhraun and Stafholt, they along with the charters of Melar, Húsafell, and Álftamýri indicate that the bulk of these churches' wealth was donated in the twelfth century, and the respective fourteenth-century charters show that additions in the intervening period were on a comparatively small scale.

5. Hítarnes, Staðarhraun, Stafholt, Húsafell, Reykholt, and Melar are all in the Borgarfjörður region, and although it is uncertain what relevance should be attached to this, it can hardly be a coincidence that all the datable early charters, along with a significant proportion of the undatable ones, are from this region. It does mean, however, that the inferences drawn above can only be taken to hold for this part of Iceland. Borgarfjörður was one of the regions where power consolidation happened late and it may be that ecclesiastical organization developed more slowly in such areas than elsewhere.

[16] There are no high medieval sources for the tithe areas of these churches but the late medieval evidence suggests that they were very small indeed. In a late 16th-cent. charter collection it is stated that the priest at Hítarnes pays his tithe to the church at Krossholt (*DI* xv. 614) and this suggests that the church at Hítarnes received no tithes at all. In 1560 the church at Krossholt had fallen into ruin and two farms were then transferred from its tithe area to Hítarnes's (*DI* xiii. 523). In 1442 the farm Reyðarfell which neighbours Húsafell on its western side belonged to the tithe area of Kalmannstunga, to the east of Húsafell (*DI* iv. 632), which suggests that the church at Húsafell received tithe only from the home-farm, and this was certainly the case in 1553–4 when a charter states explicitly that no farm belonged to the parish of the church at Húsafell (*DI* xii. 667). Reyðarfell was the property of the church at Húsafell and its tithes were transferred to Húsafell in 1504 (*DI* vii. 737) but it seems to have been abandoned shortly afterwards.

[17] This is a tale of a miracle that took place at Húsafell in the time of Brandr Þórarinsson but before there was a priest and before the feast of St Cecilia was legalized—which happened in 1179 (*Bsk* i. 106; *Sturl* 109).

We shall return to the charters in section 4 to consider their significance for changes in control over church property but let us first survey the Old Christian law section for its regulations on churches.

3. THE EVIDENCE OF LEGAL SOURCES

The Old Christian law section is the only legal source relevant to the discussion on early church foundations and the formation of ministries. Although earlier ideas on ecclesiastical organization in the twelfth and thirteenth centuries have to a large extent been based on this source, its value lies to a large extent in what it does *not* contain. While the laws indicate clearly the private nature of church ownership in Iceland, they are at the same time the product of considerable advances by the bishops towards tighter regulation over churches and church property.

On church building the rule is simply that churches should remain where they had been consecrated (*Grg Ia*, 12, 14; *Grg II*, 19; cf. *En tale*, 57). If a church has to be moved, it is to be moved with all its possessions, bones in the cemetery included, and only with the bishop's permission. The eventuality that a church may be abolished is however allowed for, as the property of a church from which the bones have been removed is to be transferred to the church to which the bones are moved (*Grg Ia*, 13; on reburial see above Ch. 1, s. 4). The property of the donors was protected even if the church was deprived of the right to have services given in it: 'Property is nowhere to be taken from a church even though services are no longer held there unless the bishop, the landowner and the donor or his heir permit it to be taken away, if they all agree, but otherwise in no circumstances' (*Grg Ia*, 20: trans. *LEI* i. 36).

It is likely that this was originally meant to protect the property of churches that were desecrated until they were reconsecrated, but the clause clearly gives landowners and donors the right to veto any transfers of one church's property to another if it did not suit them. It also follows from this that as a church from which the right to give services was taken cannot in any sense but architectural have been a church, a church's property could, for all practical purposes, revert to the donor if it was ruined or desecrated and not reconsecrated, built again, or moved elsewhere.

There is considerable regulation on maintenance and rebuilding of churches. If a new church has to be built, because an earlier one burnt down or was irreparably damaged, it

> is to be built where the bishop wishes, and it shall be as large as he wishes and it shall be called what he wishes [i.e. dedicated to which saint]. A landowner is required to have such a new church built on his farm, no matter who had the previous one built [within 12 months]. The landowner is so to endow the church that on that account the bishop is willing to consecrate the church. Then the bishop is to go there to consecrate the church. (*Grg Ia*, 14; also *Grg II*, 15_{17-24}: trans. *LEI* i. 31–2)

Here the bishops are given substantial powers which, it will be argued below, they did not acquire until around 1200. The bishops were required to visit every commune on their itineraries and be available to consecrate churches, chapels, and 'song-houses' (*Grg 1a*, 19_{11-14}) and in that context it is added in three manuscripts that 'if the bishop refuses to do what he is required to do in accordance with law, they may respond by withholding his tithes' (*Staðarhólsbók*, *Grg II*, 22: Trans. *LEI* i. 199).[18] This can hardly be understood as legislation—non-payment of tithe was of course illegal (*Grg 1b*, 209_2–211_{15}, 212_{20}–214_6)—this is simply a nod in the direction of reality. The conditions for consecrating a church were a matter of agreement between bishop and church-owner, and if there was disagreement the bishop was for all practical purposes in no position to enforce his will, as the examples in *Oddaverja þáttr* clearly indicate (*Bsk* i. 282–92) (see above, Ch. 3, s. 1).

On maintenance of churches the *Konungsbók* version has the simple rule that if a church is so dilapidated that services cannot be given in it, the landowner is to have it repaired within two weeks. If a tenant lives on the farm and he cannot reach the landowner he is to have it repaired and claim the costs from the landowner. The landowner is, however, not obliged to reimburse for more costs than were absolutely necessary, and the tenant then only gets God's thanks for his trouble (*Grg 1a*, 17_{2-14}).

The *Staðarhólsbók* version has the same text (*Grg II*, 18_{22}–19_7), but also adds a clause dealing with the same subject in a somewhat different way (*Grg II*, 19_{12}–20_{23}; also in AM 181 4to, *Grg III*, 317_{13}–318_{11}). This clause also covers the squandering of church property and the priest's board, issues already dealt with in clauses identical to the *Konungsbók* version (*Grg II*, 17_{17}–18_3 as in *Grg 1a*, 15_{20}–16_7; *Grg II*, 18_{14-22} as in *Grg 1a*, 16_{17}–17_2). The clause added in *Staðarhólsbók* also has regulations on the minimum service church-owners were required to buy, which are found nowhere else. This clause is extremely interesting, amongst other things because it is the only place in the Old Christian law section manuscripts where the expression 'the man who owns a church' (*Sa maðr er kirkio a*) is found. The usual expression is 'the man who has charge of a church' (*Sa maþr er kirkio varþveitir* (e.g. *Grg 1a*, 15_{12}, 18_{27}), *Sa maðr er varðveizlo kirkionnar a, varðveizlomaðr kirkio*), although expressions like 'the man who holds a church' (*Sa maðr er kirkio heldr*), 'the man who governs a church' (*sa maþr er kirkionni reþr* (e.g. *Grg 1a*, 18_{26})) and 'church-lord' (*kirkiu drottinn* (*Grg 1b*, $228_{12,\ 15-16,\ 20}$)) are also found (*Grg III*, s.v. *kirkja*). There is no doubt that 'charge' was for practical purposes the same as ownership; the difference was theoretical, but of course very important. Considering himself as being in charge of the church, being its caretaker, the church-owner acknowledged that he held the property as a vassal of God, and was as a consequence answerable to God and his servants for his management of it. That the concept

[18] *Skálholtsbók* has: 'If the bishop refuses *a man* what he . . . they *and their household men* may withhold . . .' (*Grg III*, 20; also AM 181 4to, *Grg III*, 324_{15}–325_2).

of church-owner is used in the additional clause in *Staðarhólsbók* may suggest either that its author was a realist, or, which is more likely, that the clause predates the distinction between church-owner and caretaker (see below, Ch. 3, s. 4). The clause is at any rate not contemporary with the main text of the Old Christian law section as it is preserved, because the greater part of its subject is found in different versions in the main text. It is therefore either earlier or later than the main text, and earlier must be considered more likely as the clause is only found in two of the eleven principal manuscripts, both of which contain several other clauses and sentences considered to be archaic (F. Jónsson 1920–4: ii. 895; M. M. Lárusson 1964*b*).

The author of this clause thought it was conceivable for a church to be owned by another person than the farm it stood on. He also envisaged that one man could own several churches, in which case he was to divide furnishings and property between them as he pleased if the bishop gave permission. It is added that services could be paid for with church property, with the bishop's permission, if the church-owner had nothing else (*Grg II*, 19_{19-22}). This practice is mentioned nowhere else, and seems to be in contradiction to the general rule that church property could not be alienated in any way, although it is possible that this refers to interest on church property. The main subject of the clause is maintenance of churches, and it contains the same procedures as prescribed in the main text. It adds, however, that if a church-owner does not come and repair a church, and the landowner pays for the repairs, the latter will thereby acquire the church. Similarly if the church-owner does not pay for services, but someone else does so, the latter acquires the church (*Grg II*, 20_{4-10}). The principle is clearly that, whoever maintains services and keeps a church in repair, has the right to own the church. The corresponding clause in the main text does not allow for this, and does not in fact consider the possibility that a church and the land it stood on could be owned by different people.

In the additional clause in *Staðarhólsbók* clear distinctions are made between church-owner and landowner on the one hand and the occupier of a church land (*sa er a lande byr, buande*) and church-owner on the other. The church-owner was to provide wax and pay for at least ten masses annually, whereas the occupier was to feed the priest and pay for at least three masses annually. In the main text it is not always transparent what relationship the 'occupier' had with the church although most often it seems equivalent to 'caretaker'; the occupier had for instance certain obligations resulting from the church being on his land: he was to feed men carrying corpses and it was he who was to bring lawsuits in case of non-payment of the church and priest's tithe (*Grg 1a*, 8_{14-18}; *Grg 1b*, 210_{18-21}, 217_{18-19}). It is often difficult or even impossible to ascertain whether meaningful distinctions are intended, for instance when the caretaker is to pay the priest his fee but the occupier is to feed him (*Grg 1b*, 210_{13-15}; *Grg 1a*, 16_{17}–17_{2}). It is tempting to interpret the distinction as meaningless, in the sense that irrespective of whether the occupier was a landowner or tenant he or she was considered to be the caretaker of the church. That makes practical sense, as it was simpler to make the tenant responsible for the church, and he or she may even have paid rent of the church's portion to the owner. The church-owner therefore only needed to be mentioned when he had to act in his capacity as landowner, for instance when major repairs were needed on pre-existing structures like the church, which the tenant must then be considered to have rented in a certain condition. The difference between the main text and the added clause in *Staðarhólsbók* may simply be that the former was a better piece of legislation which did away with unnecessary distinctions, and did not have room for naïve solutions like deciding ownership of churches on the grounds of contributions to service and repair. The problem of absentee church ownership was much more easily disposed of by changing the definitions; if a church could no longer be considered a property in the same sense as secular land, livestock, or utensils, but something which could only be in someone's care, the actual owner could transfer the care of a church in the same way as he or she transferred the care of a farm to a tenant. If the two different versions indicate something other than a refinement of legal definitions, it may be that church-owners had by the beginning of the thirteenth century improved their position from having to be involved in the running of their churches, even if they did not live close to them, to being able to rent them out, the financial benefits from owning a church no doubt being reflected in the rent figure.

The regulation in the additional clause in *Staðarhólsbók*, that the church-owner should provide wax for lighting the church also indicates that the expenses involved in owning a church decreased in the course of the twelfth and thirteenth centuries. By the mid-thirteenth century lighting-dues had been introduced, paid by all tithe payers to their church. The introduction of hay-dues before the beginning of the fourteenth century also indicates a comparable development; previously it had been the duty of the church-owner or caretaker to provide hay for the priest's horse (*Grg 1a*, 16_{23}). These developments, while no doubt serving the interest of church-owners in the short run, in the long run loosened the ties between church and church-owner and strengthened the ties between church and congregation, and probably made claims for ecclesiastical control over church property all the more acceptable.

In these developments the slow process of parish formation can be detected; originally it seems churches were considered like any other property, and if we take the clause in *Staðarhólsbók* literally, the minimum requirement was to pay for 13 masses annually and ask the priest 'who is nearest by' (*er þar er næst*) to celebrate legally prescribed offices (*synge lögtíþir*). The rather loose definition of the priest's whereabouts suggests that ministries were only loosely defined. A ministry was probably whatever area a priest happened to serve at any particular point in time. By the end of the twelfth century the concept of caretaker of a church had been established and a division of churches was in place whereby some churches had priests attached to them and others were annexed to them. It remains to consider in more detail the nature of the private ownership of churches and the question of why generous endowments seem to be restricted to the twelfth century and why they seem to cease in the thirteenth. These issues centre on the import of St Þorlákr's claims to ecclesiastical property: what sort of ecclesiastical control was he campaigning for and how unsuccessful was he?

4. PRIVATE CHURCES[19]

By the fourteenth century all parish churches owned some land, as did most dependent churches as well, and this was considered as a minimum insurance for the payment of the priest's fee.[20] Outside the western quarter it was a common arrangement for the poorest churches to own a share in the land sufficient to provide for the upkeep of a priest. In these cases the priest's fixed fee was understood as rent of this hypothetical parcel of land.[21] The concept *heimanfylgja* or dowry (as in the Latin *dos*) for donations to a church at its foundation is first accounted for in the thirteenth century (M. Stefánsson 1975: 74; e.g. in the B version of *Þorláks saga*, *Bsk* i. 287_{26}; New Christian law section, *NgL* v. 23_{18}) and, from the late twelfth century at least, the type and amount of property owned by a church was included among the conditions for its consecration.

Around 1183 a complex dispute developed between Bishop Þorlákr and the priest Högni Þormóðarson. It arose because of the marriage of Högni's daughter to a kinsman which the bishop opposed on grounds of consanguinity, but it happened that Högni had built a new church at his farm, Bær (S), which awaited consecration. St Þorlákr wanted Högni to donate the land at Bær itself to the church but Högni would only concede attached holdings (*útlönd*). The source discloses that the priest who sang at Bær had previously been paid only 12 ounce units (half the normal fee for an annex-church) which suggests that it had been an annex-church before Högni built his new church. The disagreement about the endowment of the church seems therefore to have arisen because Högni wanted to endow his church so that it could support a permanently resident priest. St Þorlákr had to give in, but his insistence may be evidence that the bishops normally tried to secure for churches a stake in the farm where they stood (*Bsk* i. 285, 287).[22] The source, *Oddaverja þáttr*, claims

[19] Stutz 1895, 1913; 1948; Schäferdiek 1986. On Iceland: Skovgaard-Petersen 1960; M. M. Lárusson 1968*d*; M. Stefánsson 1975: 72–81, 98–104.

[20] Consider the consecration charters of Ingjaldshvoll (S) (*DI* ii. 410–11), and Engey (S) (*DI* iii. 338–9).

[21] A good example is Bólstaðarhlíð in Langidalur (N): *ä prestskylld vpp j land. oc gialldi presti. iiij. merckr j leigu* (*DI* ii. 47). Another version is from Gnúpur in Gnúpverjahreppur (S): *a suo mikid j heimalanndi sem prestz skylld oc diäknna heyrir* (*DI* ii. 662–3).

[22] According to a 14th-cent. charter of Bær the church was served by two priests and a deacon and owned three nearby farms but no stake in the land of Bær (*DI* iii. 123–4).

that the value of the outlying holdings was the same as that of the land at Bær and that suggests that St Þorlákr's demand had its grounds in strategic rather than financial considerations. The question is whether his aims were those *Oddaverja þáttr* indicates: to make Bær a *staðr* which might make his claim to control the property more easily justifiable or easier to achieve (M. Stefánsson 1975: 102). As we shall see, the indications are that *Oddaverja þáttr* was composed in the late thirteenth century for propaganda purposes in the conflict between Bishop Árni Þorláksson and church-owners over control of church property. There is no particular reason to suspect that the account of the dispute is a fabrication, but the reasons behind it may not have had anything to do with the control of the property.

While it is not surprising that in the twelfth century the bishops were trying to ensure that churches were sufficiently endowed to secure their future and maintain ministries it is difficult to imagine that churches were from the outset thought capable of owning things. Like other peoples in Northern Europe who had little or no experience of Roman institutions or laws, the Icelanders were not at home with the idea that things could be owned by impersonal entities or that such phenomena could have a judicial existence. It is likely that the farmers who built churches in the beginning of the 11th century considered them to be like any other house in their possession, set apart only by their function. It is not apparent that the missionary bishops managed to convince church-owners to donate land to their churches; Bishop Hróðólfr who is supposed to have left three monks in Bær (*ÍF* i. 65) had at least not achieved much in the way of endowments if *Oddaverja þáttr* is to be believed.[23] Bishop Ísleifr (1056–80) seems to have served the church at Skálholt as his private property, his wife Dalla insisted on living on her part of the estate after his death (*Bysp* 1. 85) and Ari *fróði* states categorically that it was Bishop Gizurr (1082–1118) who donated the land at Skálholt to the church and established it as a cathedral (*ÍF* i. 22–3). It is among the next generation that we begin to get evidence of endowments of churches; according to his descendants it was Sæmundr *fróði* (d. 1133) who established the *staðr* at Oddi (S) (*ÍF* xvii. 37); the Vatnsfirðingar claimed that their forefather, Þórðr Þorvaldsson, who was among the greatest chieftains in the country in 1118, established the church at Vatnsfjörður (N) (*ÍF* xvii. 38–9; *ASB* xi. 53); and Þórðr Böðvarsson from Garðar (S) claimed that he had more right to inherit the *staðr* in Reykholt (S) because he was a grandson of Þórðr Magnússon than Magnús Pálsson who was in control and was the son of Þórðr's illegitimate nephew (see Figure 3), which suggests that the *staðr* was established by Þórðr's father, the priest Magnús Þórðarson, who was among the chieftains who were ordained in Bishop Gizurr's episcopacy (*Sturl* 211; *ASB* xi. 50). As we have seen, the charter material indicates that churches with large tithe areas were still being endowed in the middle of the twelfth century, whereas towards

[23] There is of course no way of showing that the missionary bishops did not manage to secure donations to churches.

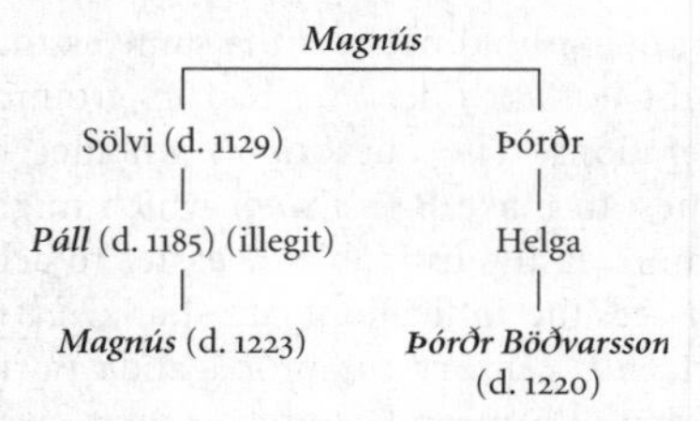

FIGURE 3. *Genealogical table showing the relationship between Magnús Pálsson and Þórðr Böðvarsson*

its end rich endowments are made to churches with small tithe areas, indicating that most churches with permanent ministries had been endowed by that time.

The fact that endowments were being made at all shows that by the beginning of the twelfth century the Icelanders had mastered the idea that churches could be judicial persons which could own property. Judging from the available evidence it was in that century that most Icelandic churches acquired the basis of their landed wealth. It is likely that the bishops were instrumental in persuading church-owners to endow their churches; it was the only way of ensuring permanency of pastoral care in any given area and can in no way have been painful for the donors. As a result of their endowments the donors could expect episcopal sanction of their tithe areas and the land they donated became exempt from tithe payments, which was probably a well-appreciated incentive. Apart from practical considerations it is likely that many endowments were made primarily for pious and/or charitable reasons;[24] such must surely have been the motives of Steini the priest with his immensely rich endowment of Stafholt (S) wherewith he secured the upkeep of two relatives (*DI* i. 179–80; *Bsk* i. 285); or Þorkell Geirason who donated his patrimony at Þykkvibær (S) to found a house of canons which he himself joined (*Bsk* i. 95–6, 106). A related concern was the upkeep of the poor; it was common that endowments were made on condition that a kinsman or kinswoman of the *fundator* be supported by the church and sometimes whole farms were donated to Christ for the sole purpose of maintaining the poor (*kristfé*) (Jónsson 1953; *Álitsgerð kirkjueignanefndar* 1984: 150–80; M. M. Lárusson 1958*g*, 1961*b*; J. Benediktsson 1970*a*, 1976*b*). In this issue self-interest and charity cannot be separated; the poor who benefited were not always particularly poor but retired householders who wanted to be financially independent of their heirs (e.g. *ÍF* xvii. 331; *DI* iii. 303–4), and if they were poor it was the poor whom the householder would otherwise have had to support. In the case of farms donated to Christ it was the commune which benefited as it was normally its officers who appointed the occupants (e.g. *DI* i. 199_{6-7}, 200_4, 203_{19}). As argued in Chapter 2, section 2, the maintenance of the poor was a

[24] On the right to donate property to churches without consulting heirs and its extension see Hamre 1958*a*; 1970; Sandvik 1965: 23–30; M M. Lárusson 1958*c*; J. Benediktsson 1970*a*.

major concern in Icelandic society and endowments of churches provided the means to invest in pensions and poor relief.

Of the benefactors mentioned above, Þorkell was without close relatives and the same seems to have been the case with Steini, but where there were heirs—especially where power was to be handed down—it is likely that endowments were made in order to consolidate and not to decrease a family's authority in its area. If prominent chieftains were endowing their churches richly in the beginning of the twelfth century and looked like doing well by it, it is reasonable to assume that the practice gathered a momentum of its own and that those who saw themselves as competing for power or aspired to increase their influence felt that they had to do the same as, or better than, their competitors. In Chapter 6 a hypothesis is proposed which explains the twelfth-century endowments of churches as a way of tying the idea of a family's authority in an area with a particular place, thereby making possession of the place and not the leadership qualities of the individual the precondition for power. For the present purposes it is enough to note that it is close to unthinkable that early or mid-twelfth-century chieftains would have donated their principal estates to their churches if they had thought they or their descendants would not have had full control over the property as before. It is also interesting that, whereas in Norway endowments of churches were divided in two, the *fabrica* (= *uppheldis góz*) or property allocated for the upkeep of the church building and the *mensa* (= *presttekja*) or property allocated to the maintenance of the priest, endowments to Icelandic churches were made without any such distinctions (Sandvik 1965: 30–67; Hamre 1959, 1963*b*; 1966). This meant that Icelandic church-owners had more discretion in their use of their church property than their Norwegian counterparts and that the Icelandic priests were much more firmly under the heel of church-owners than their Norwegian colleagues.

The problem of how church-owners viewed their ownership of their churches is confounded by problems of dating the relevant sources. *Oddaverja þáttr* in the B and C versions of *Þorláks saga* is the only source for St Þorlákr's claims to ecclesiastical control over church property[25] and the date and context of its composition is disputed. One alternative is that *Oddaverja þáttr* was composed as a part of the original version of *Þorláks saga*—in the first one or two decades of the thirteenth century—and that the A version is a shortened version of this original saga. If this is the case we would have to accept *Oddaverja þáttr*'s relation of St Þorlákr's challenge to the church-owners as the account of a contemporary. The other possibility is that *Oddaverja þáttr* was composed for propaganda purposes during Bishop Árni's conflict with church-owners in the late thirteenth century. In that case the piece becomes primarily a source for late thirteenth-century attitudes although a view would still have to be formed on the source for *Oddaverja þáttr*'s version of events. Apart from the

[25] There is a short account of St Þorlákr's claims in *Árna saga* (*ÍF* xvii. 20–1), but this is obviously related to *Oddaverja þáttr* and seems to be derived from it rather than the other way around.

uncertainty about the nature of St Þorlákr's claims, it is next to impossible to ascertain whether the laws and the pertinent charters pre- or postdate St Þorlákr's challenge. The laws survive only in mid or late thirteenth-century manuscripts and none of the few charters which are attributable to the twelfth century can be dated with enough precision to be useful milestones.

Let us first look at the dating of *Oddaverja þáttr.* The three versions of *Þorláks saga* have not been the subject of a detailed philological study and their relationship is therefore still ambiguous. There is however a consensus that the A version is oldest, written shortly after the translation of St Þorlákr's bones in 1199 and probably before Bishop Páll's death in 1211, and that it is at least in part closely related to a Latin Life written around 1200 of which fragments survive. The B version postdates the death of Sæmundr Jónsson in 1222 and the C version a miracle which took place in 1325 (Aðalbjarnarson 1958; Helgason 1950, 1976; Tómasson 1988*a*: 357–9; *ÍBS* i. 474–7). There are clear textual differences between the A and B versions and it has been suggested that the B version is a reworking of the A version (Böðvarsson 1968). But it has also been shown that the A version abridges the material found in the Latin fragments and the B version is much closer to the Latin text (J. Benediktsson 1969*a*: 103–4). The possibility therefore arises that the Latin Life—of which only fragments survive—contained the material which is now found in *Oddaverja þáttr* and the stylistic differences between the *þáttr* and the A version therefore arise because they are different adaptations. To a layman like the present author it seems, however, that the stylistic differences are too profound to be explained by different translators; while the A version is a tightly knit description of the course of the saint's life using exempla to illustrate the saintly qualities of Þorlákr and clearly modelled on European hagiographies (Astås 1994: 74), *Oddaverja þáttr* is a dramatic narrative in conventional saga style. One striking difference is that, whereas the A version is characterized by its many Bible quotations (Astås 1994), there are none in *Oddaverja þáttr* as far as I can see.

Even if *Oddaverja þáttr* fused more smoothly with the rest of the saga there would be reasons to be suspicious of its account of St Þorlákr's claim to church property. The first objection is that the saint's dramatic clashes with Jón Loptsson over the control of his churches and over his affair with Þorlákr's sister are not mentioned in any other source. While the silence of other sources is of course not conclusive evidence it is strange that, while St Þorlákr's forceful stance against Högni in Bær merited a deferential mention in *Prestssaga Guðmundar*, his alleged conflicts with Jón Loptsson—and hotter news can hardly be imagined if *Oddaverja þáttr* is to be believed—go unnoticed. Stranger still is that in the five archiepiscopal letters which survive from Þorlákr's episcopacy there is not a breath on control over church property but plenty on other reforming interests—which are, furthermore, attested independently as concerns of Þorlákr (see Ch. 4, s. 3).

The other main objection is to the significance of St Þorlákr's claims as they are portrayed by the *þáttr.* According to it St Þorlákr claimed that the bishops should have power (*vald*) over all *staðir*/churches and church property and when he was given power over Svínafell (A) he handed it back to the owner as a fief for the time being (*lén um stundar sakir*) and the owner of Rauðilækur (A) gave the control of his church (*kirkjuforráð*) to the bishop (*Bsk* i. 281). It is far from clear what sort of power over church property is involved here but from the terminology used it seems clear that the author did not consider that St Þorlákr's claims were essentially different from those put forward by Bishop Árni a century later. Modern scholars have also interpreted the claims as the same, thinking—like the author of *Oddaverja þáttr* no doubt did—that St Þorlákr claimed control over church property initially with some success but ultimately with abject failure and that the matter was not raised again until Bishop Árni took up the cause in 1270. While scholars agree that St Þorlákr and Bishop Árni had the same aim, they disagree about what their claim entailed; most Icelandic scholars approaching the subject from the better sourced times of Bishop Árni think that St Þorlákr was pushing for absolute control over church property (M. M. Lárusson 1968*d*: 465–6),[26] whereas foreign scholars tend to approach the subject from the point of view of twelfth-century canon law and think that both were trying to establish lay patronage of churches in place of lay ownership. Magnús Stefánsson (1975: 100) thinks that St Þorlákr's aim was to abolish heritable charge of church property and ultimately to gain absolute control over it. Conversely Inge Skovgaard-Petersen (1960: 258–60, 290), who has written the only monograph on the subject, interprets the saint's aim as to establish lay patronage in place of outright ownership.[27] In essence this meant that severe limitations were put on the caretaker's rights over the property while he or she nevertheless continued to control it.

There is no ambiguity about Bishop Árni's claim and he puts it clearly in his New Christian law section from 1275:

> The bishop shall control the churches and all their property . . . and tithes and all donations which men give legally to God and his saints to help their soul, because laymen can have no power over such things except as bishops ordain. The bishop shall appoint priests and clerics to churches as the charters determine. . . . Men shall build their churches to [the glory of] God but not for their own profit or any kind of dominion. (*NgL* v. 23)

There is no talk here of lay patronage, in the sense of acknowledging the right of the *fundatores* to oversee the management of their endowments. If laymen were given the power to manage church property it was entirely at the discretion of the bishop and not because the layman had any sort of right to the property in question. Nobody has suggested that it was this that St Þorlákr was claiming

[26] J. Jóhannesson 1956: 217 appreciates that St Þorlákr was only attempting to introduce *ius patronatus* but does not seem to realize that this meant only lay patronage and was a very different claim from Bishop Árni's (Jóhannesson 1956: 220).

[27] Björn Þorsteinsson 1978: 204 seems to realize the difference.

and as we shall see the church was in the late twelfth century content with much less direct control over ecclesiastical property.

To appreciate the meaning of St Þorlákr's claims it is necessary to look at the situation in Norway and see what sort of claims Archbishop Eysteinn was likely to ask St Þorlákr to promote. It appears that, following the establishment of the metropolitan see in Niðarós in 1153, the Norwegian kings formally gave up their right of selecting bishops and this is reiterated by King Magnús (1164–84) in his letter of privileges to the Norwegian church (*Lat.dok*, 63; *En tale*, 14–15; Kolsrud 1958: 186–202; Helle 1964: 27–32). It does not seem that the Norwegian church tried to exercise this privilege until Archbishop Eiríkr resurrected it in 1190 as the grounds for his claim to control over churches (Skånland 1969: 81–2).[28] What he claimed exactly is unclear and it has been argued that his demands were restricted to the most prominent churches in the bishopric of Niðarós and did not include the rest of the archdiocese (*Sv* 122–3; Bagge 1976*a*: 26–47). For our purposes it is sufficient to note that there are no signs of any dispute between King and Church in Norway over the control of churches, or over its other side, the investiture of ecclesiastical offices, until Archbishop Eiríkr clashed with King Sverrir in 1190, a decade *after* St Þorlákr is supposed to have made his attempt.[29]

The only possible source for the agenda of Archbishop Eysteinn in the matter of control over churches is the first canon in the so-called *Canones Nidarosiensis*. The date and purpose of this document has long been debated; the dating suggestions range from the early 1150s to the mid-1180s and it may be a synodal decree or a draft for such a decree never ratified or an excerpt from a more formal document (Gunnes 1971: 118–22; Sandaaker 1988). Few now believe that the *Canones* are earlier than 1163, when the papal legate Stephanus visited Norway (Bull 1915; Helle 1964: 36–44), and whatever the case may be about their *terminus ante quem* it is clear that they represent the agenda of the reforming church in Norway in the late twelfth century and they are our only guide to what Archbishop Eysteinn can possibly have asked St Þorlákr to implement in 1178.

The first canon is based entirely on Gratian's *Decretum* and can be summarized thus:

(i) requires lay patrons to see to it that the priest does not squander the church's property (from C. 16 q. 7 c. 31);
(ii) decrees that patrons cannot use the church's property as their own and they have to present the priest of their choice to the bishop before instating him (from C. 16 q. 7 c. 31);
(iii) decrees that if patrons become impoverished they can only be supported

[28] On King Sverrir's and Archbishop Eiríkr's struggle see Kolsrud 1958: 223–33; Helle 1964: 58–61; Gunnes 1971: 197–203; Lunden 1976: 81–100.

[29] In two of his letters to Archbishop Eysteinn Pope Alexander III (1159–81) forbids lay investiture (*Lat.dok* 79), but there is no evidence for any consequent actions.

by their endowment if it is a monastery or a chapter-church (from C. 16 q. 7 c. 30);

(iv) decrees that patrons shall manage church property with the bishop's consent, but if they contest his authority it is left to him whether he lets the matter rest or has the relics removed (from C. 16 q. 7 c. 34, 35);

(v) decrees that if heirs to a church dispute its control the bishop is to have the relics removed and the church closed until a priest is appointed with everyone's consent and the bishop's approval (from C. 16 q. 7 c. 34, 35) (*Lat.dok* 43; Skånland 1969: 67–73, 187–8).

These provisions are clearly in the spirit of *ius patronatus*, the doctrine of lay patronage which had been worked out by the canonist Rufinus and Pope Alexander III in the 1150s and 1160s (Addleshaw 1956: 17–18). The aim was to get church-owners to acknowledge that they did not own their churches outright but were only their patrons or caretakers on behalf of God. The patrons still had the *proprium ius* but their ability to exercise this right was limited to the *ius presentandi*, the advowson or the presenting of a priest to the bishop for approval (Skånland 1969: 75–6). The doctrine was of course worked out on the basis that, once appointed, the priest would control the stipend that came with his church and thus the direct influence of the patron would be done away with except when a new priest had to be appointed. As we shall see below, it did not work out like that in Iceland.

There is nothing in *Oddaverja þáttr* which allows us to ascertain whether it was these clauses that St Þorlákr attempted to implement, except the information, echoed in *Árna saga*, that when Sigurðr Ormsson in Svínafell had given in to his demands he gave the church there back to Sigurðr as a fief (*lén*) (*Bsk* i. 281; *ÍF* xvii. 20). *Oddaverja þáttr* claims that this was to be only a temporary arrangement while *Árna saga* sees it as the root of the 'custom whereby chieftains in Austfirðir appointed to the bishops' *staðir* up until [the time of] Bishop Árni' (*ÍF* xvii. 20–1). The simplest explanation is of course that the granting of the church as a fief by the bishop to the owner was the whole object of the exercise and that St Þorlákr never aimed to achieve more than a formal recognition by the church-owners that they held their churches of a higher authority.

If this was so it tells us that before St Þorlákr church ownership was absolute, but it also allows us to reconsider the significance of some of the charters as well as putting his achievements in a new light. The only two charters which can be dated to the second half of the twelfth century both contain clauses on the control of the property. The charter of Húsafell (S) gives the control of the *staðr* to its founder and his sons but if they were to leave or did not have heirs the bishop of Skálholt was to select a suitable man from their kin group. In his charter for the house of canons in Helgafell (D) the founder names two men whom he wants to succeed him as abbot, but in case that does not happen he wants them to control the property and take an abbot who should preferably be from his kin group, if at all possible, with the bishop's supervision (*DI* i. 217–18, 282: a translation of both texts is given in Ch. 3, s. 2). Similar provisions are found in one other charter, from Hítarnes (S) (*DI* i. 275–6).

Traditional scholarship would have it that it was this kind of inheritance of church property which St Þorlákr campaigned against (M. Stefánsson 1975: 100) but it will be argued here that it was this that he campaigned *for*. If church-owners had previously not recognized any infringement of their proprietorial rights the ultimate authority of the bishop ceded in these charters was a major achievement. The other concerns of the bishops expressed in the charters also suggest that making the control of church property compulsorily heritable was an improvement on the earlier situation.

The charter of Húsafell quoted above ends with an insurance clause: 'He who has charge of the church property is responsible for the church and all its equipment in case of fire or any kind of damage' (*DI* i. 217–18). This is the responsibility also asserted in the Old Christian law section that the landowner must rebuild a church which is damaged by fire or otherwise (*Grg 1a*, 13_{28}–14_{6}) and having it accepted must have been a major victory for the bishops. An almost identical clause to the one in the Húsafell charter is found in a charter of Saurbær in Hvalfjarðarströnd (S) (*DI* i. 265) and three other charters have an insurance clause where the responsibility is put on the householder (Skarð in Rangárvellir (S), DI I, 355; Bjarnarhöfn (S), *DI* ii. 257; Hjörsey in Mrar (S), *DI* i. 303–4). One of these, the charter of Hjörsey (S), is later than 1199 as the church is dedicated to St Þorlákr and it may be that allocating the charge of the church to the householder, who might be a tenant, is a relatively late development as was discussed in section 3 above. The significance of the insurance clauses in these three charters may be that the arrangements differed from the norm of the law in that it was the householder and not the landowner who was responsible, but in the cases of Húsafell and Saurbær, which seem to be somewhat earlier, the inclusion of an insurance clause suggests that an obligation to renew a church was not universally accepted and had to be formally affirmed. A related concern which is reflected in the *Canones Nidarosiensis* as well as the Old Christian law section is the squandering, or selling, of church property (*Grg 1a*, 15_{20}–16_{7}). This is also forbidden in the charter of Saurbær as well as in an ancient-looking charter from Ölfusvatn (S) (*DI* i. 265, 270). Like the insurance clauses these suggest that some church-owners reserved the right to sell off the property of their churches if it suited them. It is probable that church-owners normally intended to rebuild their churches in case of catastrophe and that they had no intention of alienating the property which they had donated, but as long as this was only a voluntary undertaking the system of pastoral care was always liable to be unstable on account of the occasional bankrupt or simply obdurate church-owner. It was therefore of great importance to the bishops if they could make the church-owners see that their charge was in fact as much a responsibility as a right. And it was only after achieving a widespread recognition among church-owners that they held their churches as fiefs that the bishops can possibly have had these responsibilities accepted as law. If it was St Þorlákr who introduced *ius patronatus* in Iceland the fruits of his labours are visible in the legislation on the relocation and rebuilding of churches, the squandering of church property, and the handling of fire in a church (*Grg 1a*, 12_{21}–14_{9}, 15_{20}–16_{17}).[30]

Oddaverja þáttr adds to the sense that St Þorlákr's claims were novel and revolutionary by making him meet fierce resistance and have to abandon his campaign after only a single season. *Oddaverja þáttr* and *Árna saga* agree that St Þorlákr had in his first summer as bishop in Iceland (1179) visited the eastern quarter and, after overcoming the resistance of the chieftain Sigurðr Ormsson in Svínafell (A) and his father Ormr in Rauðilækur (A), he acquired control over all churches east of Hjörleifshöfði (S) except Þvottá and Hallormsstaður (*Bsk* i. 280–2; *ÍF* xvii 20). Hjörleifshöfði seems to have been the eastern limit of the Oddaverjar's sphere of power at this time (cf. Þorláksson 1989*a*: 129–32). On his way back, *Oddaverja þáttr* explains, St Þorlákr encountered their chieftain Jón Loptsson at his estate in Höfðabrekka (S). Jón flatly refused to yield to St Þorlákr's demands and the saint had to give in. After this defeat we are told that all followed Jón's lead and, after Archbishop Eysteinn went into exile in England in 1180, St Þorlákr had no support to continue his campaign (*Bsk* i. 284).

This does not of course explain why St Þorlákr did not continue his struggle after Archbishop Eysteinn returned to Norway in 1183 and it certainly does not explain how the saint got his hands on Breiðabólstaður in Fljótshlíð (S) and why he gave it to his nephew, the Oddaverjar chieftain Ormr Jónsson, who, although a deacon, can hardly be considered as a man of the church (*Sturl* 172). The source for this, *Prestssaga Guðmundar*, calls Breiðabólstaður the best estate over which St Þorlákr had control, which may suggest that its author thought the saint had control over a number of places like that. In *Árna saga* there is furthermore the information that in the 1280s people thought that Holt in Önundarfjörður (N) had been under the control of the bishops in Skálholt since the days of St Þorlákr (*ÍF* xvii. 160, 169). Both Breiðabólstaður and Holt are in parts of the country where St Þorlákr is supposed to have had no success, if *Oddaverja þáttr* is to be believed; if we take the charters of Húsafell, Helgafell, Hítarnes, and Saurbær as evidence for the successful implementation of policies which can realistically be attributed to the period, it appears that St Þorlákr was in fact quite successful in all parts of his diocese.

The charter of Húsafell mentions that Bishop Klængr (1152–76) gave permission for burial and this suggests that the *staðr* was established in his period of office and the terms recorded in the charter are likely to have been agreed on at that occasion, while the charter itself may have been drawn up later. It is of course possible that Bishop Klængr's permission was unconnected with, and predated, the establishment of the *staðr* or that the terms were renegotiated at

[30] The clause in *Grg 1a*, 20_{13-16} probably represents an earlier version of the more detailed clause in *Grg 1a*, 15_{20}–16_{7}.

some later date, on which occasion the charter was drawn up. The possibility that the charter is from Bishop Klængr's time remains and both he and Bishop Brandr (1163–1201) may well have sought to introduce *ius patronatus*; Bishop Brandr was in Norway in the winter 1163–4 when Cardinal Stephanus was there and if the *Canones Nidarosiensis* were drawn up then he was certainly in a good position to acquaint himself with them. Bishop Brandr also claimed authority over church property, although his methods were somewhat more direct than St Þorlákr's. In 1190–95 Bishop Brandr removed the heirs of Eyjólfr in Vellir in Svarfaðardalur (N) from the *staðr* there on the grounds that they were incapable (*ekki til færir*), probably too young, and installed a caretaker who was apparently not related to Eyjólfr but was married to a relative of Bishop Brandr. Eyjólfr 'had received the *staðr* on the terms that it was heritable' (*Sturl* 174). The phrase used here, *taka handsölum,* is formal language for legal transfer and can in this context mean that Eyjólfr bought the *staðr* at Vellir with the previous owner renouncing any claim to the property on behalf of his heirs. It is equally likely, however, that the church had always been in Eyjólfr's family and that he had, like Sigurðr Ormsson in Svínafell (A) or Brandr Þórarinsson in Húsafell (S), received his church from the bishop as a fief with conditions similar to those expressed in the charters of Húsafell and Hítarnes. Both charters acknowledge the right of the bishop to judge if the caretaker was fit and it seems that Brandr was using some such clause as an excuse to install his man in this immensely rich *staðr*. It is not apparent whether Bishop Brandr installed his man because he wanted to eradicate familial influence over church property; it may just as well have been because he saw an opportunity to give a protégé a rich benefice. He certainly was not trying to consolidate the Church's position in the same sense as Bishop Árni would have understood it eighty years later; Brandr's protégé was a layman and after the sons of Eyjólfr made a rather desperate attempt to recover control of Vellir in 1200 (see Ch. 4, s. 2) Brandr appointed another layman who was to hold the *staðr* until his death, after which it was to revert to Eyjólfr's heirs (*Sturl* 175).[31] Brandr clearly acknowledged the heir's right to control the *staðr*; what was at stake was not a principle but the suitability of caretakers as Bishop Brandr saw it and that probably had more to do with Brandr's own political interests than the ability of the people in question to manage the *staðr*. It may be that shortly before his death Bishop Brandr also got control over another important *staðr*, Möðruvellir in Hörgárdalur. Þorgrímr *alikarl* had been householder there in 1198 (*Sturl* 156) but soon after he came back from his consecration journey, Bishop Guðmundr appointed Sigurðr Ormsson as caretaker of Möðruvellir, probably in 1205 (*Sturl* 214).

It is of course perfectly likely that both Bishops Klængr and Brandr were instructed by Archbishop Eysteinn to establish patronage instead of ownership

[31] Eyjólfr Valla-Brandsson, grandson of Eyjólfr, lived at Vellir in 1218 and 1237 (*Sturl* 257, 386), and later became abbot of Þverá (1254–93).

and that both pursued the policy. St Þorlákr may well have made a more concentrated effort in the first year of his episcopacy and it is likely that he met with resistance from the likes of Jón Loptsson. There were no doubt those who felt it too much a gamble to give up the theoretical ownership of their familial estates. The indications are, however, that this was not nearly as dramatic an affair as *Oddaverja þáttr* makes it out to be and that St Þorlákr was in fact quite successful in establishing *ius patronatus* in Iceland. That this achievement seemed unremarkable and was not even recognized as such a century later is not surprising; by then the concept that church-owners were only in charge of their churches and their property was so firmly established that absolute lay ownership had become unthinkable. Instead of being content to campaign for having its rights acknowledged the Church now sought to act on them and stamp out any secular influence over ecclesiastical property.

Arguments have been presented here suggesting that the writing of *Oddaverja þáttr* must be considerably removed in time from the events it describes. Its author clearly did not understand the difference between the claims of the Church in the late twelfth century and the claims for absolute control which were beginning to be aired in the middle of the thirteenth. The arguments that the *þáttr* was written as a propaganda piece in Bishop Árni's struggle against secular church-owners in the 1270s or 1280s must remain circumstantial, but its content and objective certainly fit such a context best. That *Oddaverja þáttr* portrays Jón Loptsson in particular as a figure of resentment may be because he was a famous chieftain whom late thirteenth-century audiences would have recognized, but it may also suggest that the *þáttr* was written in the 1270s when Bishop Árni's main opponents were Jón's descendants in Oddi.

So far we have argued that the bishops were in the late twelfth century trying to introduce *ius patronatus* and that the laws and the few available charters show that they were on the whole successful. The bishops' main incentive was probably more to get church-owners to recognize their responsibilities than to increase their own immediate influence over the churches. We must understand that, before church-owners recognized that they were answerable to a higher authority for their handling of their churches and their property, the system of pastoral care is likely to have been unstable if not chaotic. It was therefore a major victory to be able to ensure the permanence of the churches and the ministries by getting church-owners to accept that they had to rebuild and maintain their churches and that they were not allowed to alienate their property. If the Old Christian law section in *Konungsbók* was written in its present form between 1199 and 1217—the *post* and *ante quem*s found in the text itself—that suggests that *ius patronatus* had already by that time become the norm. There may still have been church-owners who had never formally recognized that they were only caretakers, but they were clearly sufficiently outnumbered by the others for the concepts of constancy of churches and inalienability of ecclesiastical property to be accepted as legal norm. The divergent forms of ownership are, on the other hand, reflected in the confused terminology for church-owners apparent in the law codes (see Ch. 3, s. 3).

As explained above, the doctrine of patronage was devised in Italy, where by becoming the patron of his church the owner's influence was limited to presenting a priest to the bishop. It did not work like this in Iceland. The reasons are complex but they have to do with the economic organization as well as the social position of priests. Iceland had a simple economy which did not produce enough surplus for structures which depended entirely on surplus consumption to develop quickly. This meant that before the thirteenth century every individual's social position was defined according to his or her function in the procurement of the necessities of life. Everyone belonged to a household and within a household there were only two tiers, the head and the members. There could be great differences within each tier as to respect and influence but this division remained the most important. The social and political history of the twelfth and thirteenth centuries is about the slow and painful development of a third tier, a small group of overlords and later royal officials who lived off plunder and/or taxes and dues. This development is mirrored within the Church; in the twelfth century priests were either householders themselves or members of households as district priests and this distinction was far more important for their social status than their ordination (see further in Ch. 5, s. 3). In the second half of the thirteenth century there began to appear priests who owed their status primarily to being the holders of benefices. These conditions, and the fact that endowments in Iceland were not specific as to their purpose as they were in Norway, where endowments were allocated either to the upkeep of the priest or the fabric of the church, meant that it was of paramount importance what kind of property a church was endowed with. The other important factor was that the economic organization was such that a smaller product-making unit than the household was not thinkable. An Italian church might own the yields from a strip of land which was only a part of the land a peasant farmed and would receive those yields. The poorest churches in Iceland on the other hand owned only livestock or rights like pasture. The yields from such property would not in themselves constitute either easily exchangeable commodities or the necessary foodstuffs to sustain an individual. The yields of such property had to be assimilated by the household, put to whatever use it had for them, and then transformed into different types of consumables according to the needs of the church or its priest. Thus the charter material suggests that churches which owned less than a unit of independently farmable land received income from their property as rent in whatever form the farm had available and the church might need at any one time. When this was the case it was the householder, the production manager, who decided what commodities could be spared for the church and the priest.

In this kind of system priests could not exist independently of the basic production unit, the household, and if they were not householders themselves they were in every aspect subordinate to their householder. It is for this reason that the term caretaker has been preferred here instead of patron; the patron owned only the advowson and was, in theory at least, not involved in the running of his or her church in other ways, while in Iceland a caretaker managed the church's property as an integral part of his household's economy and remained the priest's superior. The caretaker's influence was therefore not diminished even if he or she admitted to not being the absolute owner of the church's property. It is for this reason that the concept of *staðr* became so important in Iceland.

A *staðr* was a church which owned a large enough part of the estate where it was situated to support a household. In most cases this was the whole homestead (*heimaland*) where the church stood but when the farm was very large the church could be called a *staðr* even if it owned only a part (usually half).[32] The deciding criterion was that the church had to own the land on which it was situated; if the church owned no part of the land where it stood, and even if it owned a number of farms elsewhere, it was not a *staðr*. This suggests that there was a strong link between a church and the household for which it had originally been built;[33] it does not seem that a priest could take over the charge of a church, even if he was economically independent of the head of the household with which the church was associated, for instance by being himself the head of a household on one of the church's farms (an eventuality which is not attested in our period but is known in early modern times). The charge belonged to the head of the household where the church was situated and, as long as the church did not own all the land and livestock from which the household lived, the church and its property would be managed by the householder as an integral part of his household. Such a household was basically the private concern of its head and the interests of the church would always come second. It was only when the church owned all the land from which the household lived, when it was a *staðr*, and when its head became his or her own church's vassal, that pressure could be put upon the householder to put the church's interests first.

We can only speculate why church-owners in the early and mid-twelfth century commonly chose to donate the homestead and why others were less generous. It is likely that it had something to do with the relative wealth of the donors. One would presumably only donate the homestead to a church if he or she owned other assets which could be sold or given away. It is likely that a pious *fundator* like Steini in Stafholt donated everything they owned, but men of chieftainly rank like Sæmundr *fróði* in Oddi or Magnús Þórðarson in

[32] Like Staðarhóll in Saurbær (D) (*Sturl* 182); Staður in Reynines (N) (*Sturl* 743); *DI* ii. 300–2; Bakki in Hrútafjörður (N) (*DI* ii. 277–8); Hrafnagil in Eyjafjörður (N) (*ÍF* xvii. 389); Tjörn in Svarfaðardalur (N) (*DI* iii. 387; iv. 393; v. 259).

[33] Consider the clause in *Grágás* which allows a man who builds himself a church to refuse burial to others 'even if it is a burial church' until he himself, his wife, or children have been buried there. It is then added that if he allows anyone else to be buried there, he is henceforth obliged to accept all other corpses (*Grg II*, 8; *Grg III*, 302). Other evidence is not as clear but it seems that the attachment between family/household and its church was usually very strong.

Reykholt had the futures of sons and daughters to think about and no doubt kept a number of assets separate from the endowment. Even if the principle of inalienation had not been established as law, it is likely that endowments were made with the intent to keep them intact, whatever the practice then turned out to be.

In the late twelfth century we have St Þorlákr and the priest Högni in Bær disputing about the endowment of the church there; St Þorlákr insisted on the church getting the homestead at Bær while Högni was only prepared to donate attached holdings (*útlönd*). This has traditionally been interpreted as evidence that St Þorlákr intended to wrench control over Bær from Högni as soon as it had been established as a *staðr*, in the same way as Bishop Árni would enjoy doing a century later.[34] It has been argued here that it is anachronistic to attribute any such aims to St Þorlákr; there is nothing to suggest that he wanted to replace Högni as caretaker but he may have wanted to get a more direct influence over him, influence which he could only gain if Högni became a vassal of his own church. Another consideration St Þorlákr might have had was that, even if the attached holdings put together had the same value as the homestead, the latter was a far more important asset and a better guarantee for the perpetual good of the church and the ministry attached to it. While most of St Þorlákr's dealings with church-owners seem to have aimed to establish the hereditary caretaker-right of the founder's family, he did somehow himself obtain the advowson of the *staðr* at Breiðabólstaður in Fljótshlíð (S) and it has been mentioned that either Bishop Brandr or Bishop Guðmundr acquired the advowson of Möðruvellir in Hörgárdalur (N). *Oddaverja þáttr* mentions that St Þorlákr was unhappy with the appointment of Eyjólfr Þorgeirsson as caretaker of Stafholt in Borgarfjörður. The *fundator*, Steini the priest, had apparently not made arrangements for the control over the *staðr* after his day and the men of the region had installed Eyjólfr there without consulting the bishop. It is likely that the bishops claimed control over such *staðir*; they had no reason to tolerate an unregulated right of advowson, but when they appointed a caretaker they always seem to have been laymen (Ormr Jónsson in Breiðabólstaður (S); Sigurðr Ormsson in Möðruvellir (N)) and, whether it was the original intention or not, these *staðir* tended to become the hereditary possession of the family of the original caretaker (Breiðabólstaður in Fljótshlíð (S); Kirkjubær in Síða (S)).

It has been argued that, as a result of St Þorlákr's supposed campaign for control over church property, church-owners ceased to donate land to their churches in the thirteenth century (M. Stefánsson 1975: 102; Þorláksson 1982*b*: 87–8). It is certainly true that the available sources indicate that the endowments of *staðir* were slowing down in the late twelfth century (as s. 2 above) but it must be remembered that the evidence is patchy at best and mostly confined to one part of the country (Borgarfjörður). The let-up in endowments may to some extent be explained by the diminishing returns from such donations

[34] It is the interpretation of *Oddaverja þáttr* itself—also M. Stefánsson 1975: 102.

because of the increasing density of ministries. While Steini the priest seems to have secured a huge tithe area for his church with his generous endowment in the middle of the twelfth century, the *fundatores* of the *staðir* at Húsafell and Hítarnes only acquired very small tithe areas by their initiative. It is also not true that there was a complete cessation of endowments; Árni in Tjaldanes established a right to a ministry by a small endowment to his annex-church in the first half of the thirteenth century (*DI* i. 466); Jón the priest endowed his annex-church at Ingunnarstaðir with the whole homestead and gave the control to the bishop of Skálholt, which suggests that this happened towards the middle of the thirteenth century (*DI* i. 266); the chieftain priest Þorvaldr Gizurarson bought Viðey in 1224 and established a house of canons there (*Sturl* 288); farmer Þorbjörn donated half a farm to the church at Skarð so that an independent tithe area and ministry could be established at his church in Búðardalur in 1239–68 (*DI* ii. 117, 635–6, 650–1). Except for Viðey these are all small endowments. It is likely that the majority of churches which are known to have had ministries before the fourteenth century, but are not listed in the church inventory associated with Bishop Páll's counting of churches, are endowments of the thirteenth century.[35]

It appears then that although there were new endowments of churches in the thirteenth century they were modest compared to the endowments of the twelfth. The main reason seems to be that the pattern of ministries and tithe areas had become stable and there was therefore little room for large new foundations.

While new foundations got fewer and smaller for understandable reasons, it may be a sign of change that donations to already endowed churches seem to have all but dried up in the thirteenth century. This can be argued by comparing the twelfth century charters of Reykholt, Húsafell, and Stafholt with fourteenth century charters of the same churches. In all these cases the original endowments were very generous but there are little or no additional donations until the fourteenth century. There are three possible explanations for this. One is that, as all these churches are in the same region the cessation of donations may have something to do with economic and/or political conditions in Borgarfjörður. This would also hold if we added the charters of Staðarhraun, Hítarnes, and Saurbær in Hvalfjarðarströnd, which also show the same dearth

[35] The candidates are: Bessastaðir in Fljótsdalur (A) (*DI* i. 342, cf. *DI* iv. 209–12); Mýnes in Eiðaþinghá (A) (*DI* i. 249); Ljótarstaðir in Landeyjar (S) (*DI* i. 257, cf. *DI* ii. 685); Ey in Landeyjar (S) (*DI* i. 257, cf. *DI* iii. 263–4); Njarðvík (A) (*DI* ii. 65–6); Heynes in Akranes (S) (*DI* i. 417–18; ii. 403–4 cf. *DI* iii. 249–50); Stóriás in Hálsasveit 1258 (S) (*DI* i. 594); Langárfoss in Mýrar (S) (*DI* i. 276–7). Several of the churches listed in the inventory are not known to have had ministries in the 14th cent. or later and these are likely to have been endowed shortly before 1200: Svínadalur in Skaftártunga (S) (*DI* ii. 784); Hlíðarendi in Fljótshlíð (S) (*DI* ii. 686); Gegnishólar in Flói (S) (*DI* iv. 58); Laugarvatn in Laugardalur (S) (*DI* xv. 646); Hof in Kjalarnes (S) (*AM* 263 fol. p. 63); Eyri in Kjalarnes (S) (*DI* i. 402; ii. 404); Stóri Kroppur in Reykholtsdalur (S) (*AM* 263 fol. p. 69); Ásgarður in Hvammssveit (D) (*DI* ii. 633–4). Three churches which are listed in the inventory but seem to have recently acquired ministries in the 13th cent. which they retained are Akrar in Mýrar 1239–68 (S) (*DI* i. 596; ii. 113) Reykjavík in Seltjarnarnes (S) (*DI* iii. 340) and Setberg in Eyrarsveit (S)—*DI* II, 257.

of donations in the thirteenth century. Another explanation could be that, even if the owners of some of these churches had accepted that they were only caretakers, they did not translate the income of their churches (tithes, dues, burial-fees, minor donations) into land or livestock but into something else either to the benefit of the church (improvements on the building, more ornaments and vestments) or for their own personal profit. The main reason behind the increased wealth of churches in the late middle ages was not large donations but payments of debts accumulated by caretakers or benefice-holders to their churches. It was one of the main functions of the bishops to oversee the accounts of the churches regularly and see to it that the caretakers or benefice-holders paid up. The bishops only seem to have begun to do so consistently and meticulously around 1300 when they first began to assemble records on the property of the churches in a systematic manner (Vésteinsson 1994). Before this change in episcopal administration they can have had no systematic overview of the finances of the churches in their dioceses and therefore only very limited means of ensuring that the churches got what was due to them. While the caretaker system ensured that churches became permanent institutions and that their endowments were not alienated, it could not prevent caretakers from using the income of their churches for their own ends. Stopping this gap was of course one of the main aims of Bishop Árni's campaign for absolute control over churches in the late thirteenth century. The lack of supervision does not explain, however, why pious donations should have become more infrequent in the thirteenth century. Many church-owners may have felt that their forefathers who had made the original endowments had done so on behalf of the family in perpetuity and that as long as they took good care of the church and its property they shared in the good deed. Even if this was a factor—and there is no direct evidence supporting it—this cannot be made to hold for everyone wishing to secure good will in heaven.

The third possible explanation for the let-up in endowments is that it was a symptom of genuine political change. On the one hand, the conditions that stimulated endowments in the twelfth century may not have applied any longer in the thirteenth and, on the other, the *staðir* in particular may have become a too vulnerable type of property for it to be advantageous to establish them any more. This last possibility is the one favoured by earlier scholars, who saw the threat to come from the Church. It has, however, been suggested here that the Church was not interested in taking over control of the *staðir*, and furthermore that it would not have had the power to do so. There is on the contrary good evidence that increasingly aggressive secular politics began to threaten the possession of *staðir* around 1200.

It will be argued at more length in Chapter 6 that the building and endowment of churches with ministries in the late eleventh and early twelfth centuries was a symptom of power consolidation among a small number of families and that these account for a high number of the *staðir*. Also that in areas where overlordships had been established, a second tier of locally influential householders was responsible for the high number of small to middle-size endowments, usually not *staðir.* By the beginning of the thirteenth century there was no longer room to establish new power centres, as more and more power lay in the hands of fewer and fewer people. In those sorts of conditions it was not viable for families aspiring to power to attempt to start from scratch; it was much easier to take over already established *staðir.*

The *staðir* were a particularly vulnerable type of property which *ius patronatus* had made even more precarious. The idea of inalienability had probably appealed to the *fundatores* because it ensured that the estate would remain intact and undiminished in the hands of the family. As families were transitory phenomena this could become a danger to the owner when several generations had passed. An example of this is the *staðr* at Reykholt (S), which had probably been established by the priest and chieftain Magnús Þórðarson at the beginning of the twelfth century. His grandson Páll Sölvason was illegitimate and although this had not been a problem when he took over, or when his son Magnús took over from him in 1185, it became one shortly before 1200. For unknown reasons Magnús was not a very successful chieftain and this prompted the chieftain of the neighbouring Garðamenn, Þórðr Böðvarsson, to encroach on his authority. Þórðr argued that, as his mother was the granddaughter of the *fundator*, he had a greater right to inherit the *staðr* than Magnús who was the son of the illegitimate Páll (as above, *Sturl* 211). This demonstrates one kind of weakness: if the caretaker was politically weak there would always be relatives who could push equally or more valid claims. The second kind of weakness of the *staðir* is demonstrated in the sequel to this dispute. Snorri Sturluson took over the church-farm Borg in Mýrar (S) on the death of his father-in-law in 1202. He did, however, aspire to greater things and acquired the claim to Reykholt from Þórðr who was his uncle and had already given him half his *goðorð*. He also got the claims of two other descendants of the *fundator* and thus armed made Magnús in Reykholt an offer, probably of the type he could not refuse. The deal they struck was that Snorri was to take over but maintain Magnús and his wife and try to make men of his sons. 'He then became a great chieftain', says Sturla when Snorri had moved to Reykholt (*Sturl* 212). The second kind of vulnerability of the *staðir* was their attractiveness. Not only were they usually very large estates which were an ideal economic base for an energetic chieftain, but they were also normally centrally and strategically placed in their respective areas and the foci of local loyalties. The *staðir* were therefore obvious points to attack and their ambiguous ownership made them all the more easy to acquire.

It is therefore not surprising that chieftains did not think their money was spent wisely on endowing new *staðir.* Only the very strongest and best organized families managed to keep hold of their *staðir* throughout the twelfth and thirteenth centuries; the Oddaverjar and Svínfellingar are probably the only examples of continuous familial possession of the same *staðr* from the early twelfth to the late thirteenth century.[36] Most of the others had begun their rise later and from estates which were only partly owned by the local church. Of these the Sturlungar are particularly noteworthy for their predatory attitude to other people's *staðir*.

Apart from this point about the particular vulnerability of the *staðir*, the political turmoil which made them unsafe possessions also provides the excuse for other potential donors. While it has been shown here that endowments did not in fact cease completely in the thirteenth century, it is reasonable to assume that the endemic conflict of the years 1220–60 did not make favourable conditions for rich endowments. It may also be that towards the end of this period the increased force of the Church's demands on control over ecclesiastical property was beginning to be felt.

On the basis of *Oddaverja þáttr*'s tale of St Þorlákr's dramatic defeat at the hands of Jón Loptsson in 1180, traditional historiography has constructed a long hiatus in the Church's campaign for control over ecclesiastical property which came to an end only when Bishop Árni took up the cause in the 1270s. As we have seen there is no reason to accept *Oddaverja þáttr* on this point; St Þorlákr was only trying to implement *ius patronatus* and the indications are that he was both energetic and successful. There is also no reason to expect that his colleague at Hólar, Bishop Brandr, or his successors at Skálholt, Bishops Páll and Magnús, did not follow the same policy. Their loyalties may have lain closer to their families than St Þorlákr's had but they are nevertheless likely to have sought to increase the authority and power of their office and they may well have been ruthless in claiming the Church's rights as long as the victims were not kin or allies. In 1216–26 a verdict was given at the Alþing that the bishop of Skálholt should control the important and immensely wealthy *staðr* at Kirkjubær in Síða (S). A Benedictine nunnery had been established at Kirkjubær in 1186 but a new abbess was not appointed after the death of abbess Halldóra Eyjólfsdóttir in 1210. With the death in 1217 of Prioress Guðrún and in 1224 of the nuns Halldóra and Þuríðr—both daughters of the chieftain Gizurr Hallsson—the convent seems to have ceased to function (*IA* 125, 127, 184, 186).[37] The convent may have been a private establishment like Helgafell (D), founded with the provision that the bishop had ultimate responsibility for the property, if not the community. When the community ceased to function it was therefore natural for the bishop to seek a verdict on his right of control. Bishop Magnús (1216–37)—brother of the two nuns—must have been behind the verdict and this suggests that he did not let chances of acquiring control over ecclesiastical property go past him. He probably secured the continuation of Kirkjubær as a major ecclesiastical centre. In 1252 there were three priests at the *staðr* (*Sturl* 563)—but like St Þorlákr had done with Breiðabólstaður he handed the charge

[36] The Haukdælir are a special case because of their relationship with Skálholt, but of the family estate at Haukadalur (S) the church owned only one quarter (*DI* ii. 667–8).

[37] It is not known for a fact whether these three were at Kirkjubær. It makes most sense that they were, but they could in theory have been attached to one of the episcopal sees.

of the *staðr* to a prominent layman and seems to have sanctioned or at least acquiesced in the transfer of the charge to this man's son in 1235. When the son was outlawed from Síða in 1252 things had however changed and Abbot Brandr, acting as *officialis*, appointed a priest as benefice-holder (*Sturl* 566). Bishop Heinrekr of Hólar was, however, not as up to date; in 1253 he handed Möðruvellir in Hörgárdalur (N) to the chieftain Eyjólfr *ofsi* and Flugumýri to the chieftain Gizurr Þorvaldsson, in what were clearly political manœuvres (*Sturl* 570, 610, 628). The first datable sign of a harder line on control over ecclesiastical property is a foundation charter for the house of canons in Viðey (S). The house was the private foundation in 1226 of the Haukdælir chieftain Þorvaldr Gizurarson, who seems to have headed the community until his death in 1235. The charge was then handed to the priest Styrmir *fróði* Kárason (*DI* i. 513) who had been in the service of Snorri Sturluson and seems to have represented Snorri's interest in the *staðr* (cf. *Sturl* 288). Styrmir was called a prior and it was only following his death in 1245 that an abbot was appointed in 1247. It is most likely that the charter which gives the control of the *staðr* in Viðey to the abbot under the supervision of the bishop of Skálholt was composed when the first abbot was installed:

> The abbot shall control the *staðr* and the brothers and all the property of the *staðr* under the supervision of the bishop in Skálholt, but the men who have given donations to the *staðr* or their heirs shall not have any say and no control. The right of transfer and the control of the *staðr* shall be as the rule dictates and God's law provides, and not be subject to secular heredity. (*DI* i. 489–90)

The allusion is probably to the provisions Þorvaldr Gizurarson had either made or left unclear, no doubt with the support of his brother Bishop Magnús, and may also refer to established practices at other houses of canons (see below). The language of this charter is unequivocally that of the hard-line church policy of absolute control over church property. It strongly suggests that Bishop Sigvarðr (1238–68) was already advocating it in the 1240s but it seems that he was far more politic about it than his successor Árni Þorláksson. Three charters survive composed by or under the supervision of Bishop Sigvarðr and in none of those is there any mention of control (*DI* i. 592, 594, 596). None of the churches in question were *staðir* or particularly wealthy and it may be that Sigvarðr limited his claims to more important ecclesiastical centres. It is to his period in office and the first years of Bishop Árni's episcopacy that a small number of charters must belong which state that the control of the property is in the hands of the bishop.[38] Of these charters two suggest a more relaxed approach than Bishop Árni contented himself with, if his saga is to believed. A charter for Bakki in Hrútafjörður (N) states that the bishop shall control the property but the charge was given to father and son as long as

[38] Villingaholt in Flói (S) (*DI* ii. 62–3); Búrfell in Grímsnes (S) (*DI* ii. 63); Staður in Steingrímsfjörður (N) (*DI* ii. 261). The charters of Staðarhraun (S) and Bakki (S) with similar clauses are probably forgeries from this period (Vésteinsson forthcoming-*b*).

they were capable (*DI* i. 277–8). This was of course a relatively painless way for church-owners to give up their churches, especially after the bishops' claims were beginning to be generally recognized. In a charter for Ingunnarstaðir, which was only an annex-church but nevertheless endowed with the whole homestead and therefore technically a *staðr*, Jón the priest was allowed to serve there as long as he wished and receive maintenance from the church. It is then added that the bishop had the right to transfer the property and he alone controlled it and could sell it, spend it, or add to it (*DI* i. 266). It appears that pastor Jón was the donor and that he secured himself lifelong upkeep with his endowment. The uniquely phrased control-clause may suggest that the charter dates from the very early days of claims to absolute episcopal control, when what it meant still needed to be defined.

According to *Árna saga*, Bishop Árni had no sooner arrived in Iceland from his consecration journey in 1269 than he began to claim control over churches. In the autumn of 1269 and summer of 1270 he travelled far and wide in the southern and eastern quarters and got control over all but two churches in the latter and all the minor ones in the former (*ÍF* xvii. 17–20). It was only the owners of the wealthiest *staðir* who resisted Bishop Árni, influential men who had no intention of giving up their familial estates to the Church. These seem in many cases to have been owners of churches whose ancestors had never given an inch to episcopal demands. A struggle ensued which was to last for nearly thirty years. According to *Árna saga* the opposition to Bishop Árni came primarily from the new class of royal officials who were in most cases the old chieftains or their descendants and who based their new powers as much on their holdings in Iceland as on royal favour. The Treaty of Ögvaldsnes in 1297 was a crushing defeat for this class of church-owners; the Church got absolute control over all *staðir* which owned more than half of the homestead, that is, all the wealthiest and most important *staðir*. The Church was, however, not entirely victorious because the owners of lesser churches, churches which owned less than half of the homestead, retained their control (*DI* ii. 34–5). This compromise was as far as the Church ever got; a significant proportion of parish churches and all annex-churches and chapels remained private property and the bishops of the late middle ages were to encounter serious opposition when they attempted to increase their supervision of lesser churches (J. Jóhannesson 1958*a*: 122–36). The Treaty of Ögvaldsnes is evidence for the resilience of the private nature of church ownership in Iceland and it suggests that *Árna saga* probably exaggerates Bishop Árni's initial successes. While ensuring the continuing private ownership of minor churches, the treaty also marks the end of a power structure which began to develop with the introduction of the tithe two centuries earlier and the beginning of the domination of Icelandic society by the Church.

5. ORIGINS OF THE RELIGIOUS HOUSES[39]

Iceland is unusual in that religious houses do not figure at all in the conversion process. The first monasteries were only established after basic ecclesiastical structures, like fixed episcopal sees and the tithe, were in place, more than a century after the conversion. It is also unusual in that very little information is preserved about the religious houses or monastic life; even though a number of works are known by the hands of monks from Þingeyrar and the canons Styrmir *fróði* in Viðey, Gamli and Brandr Jónsson in Þykkvibær, they deal mostly with the outside world and give only a limited insight into monastic attitudes and none into the size or condition of these establishments. More than half of the nintey-five people known to have taken monastic orders before 1300 were either abbots or priors; twenty-eight were Benedictine monks and seven Benedictine nuns; thirteen canons and three indeterminate monastics, as well as three anchoresses and one anchorite.[40] For many of the abbots in particular we know nothing, but the names and the familial background of many of the monastic clergy are unclear, although they seem generally to have belonged to the upper echelons of society. What we can say about the religious houses is that they are conspicuously private in origin, that they were all very small and that their principal function was to be retirement homes for aristocrats.

In the fourteenth century the monks of Þingeyrar (N) were keen to connect the establishment of their monastery with the northern diocese's first bishop and saint, St Jón. They made a certain Þorkell *trandill*, who is mentioned in *Jóns saga* as a friend of St Jón and who died in Skálholt before 1121 (*Bsk* i. 172 (245)), the *fundator* of the *staðr*, 'with the designation that it should be a monastery', and claimed that St Jón consecrated the first church at Þingeyrar (*DI* iii. 494–5). This is explained in the context that the monastery had owned episcopal tithes from thirteen parishes which Bishop Jörundr (1267–1313) had taken from it and these, the monks claimed, had been given by St Jón because the original endowment had consisted of nothing more than the homestead at Þingeyrar.

Jóns saga also claims that St Jón laid the foundations to the church and *staðr* at Þingeyrar (*Bsk* i. 171). This story is supported by one annal which puts the establishment of the monastery at Þingeyrar to 1112 (*IA* 320). All the other annals however put it to 1133 or 1134 (*IA* 59, 113, 252, 321) and the list of abbots only begins at that date (*DI* iii. 28, 153, 311). This has led some modern scholars to think that between 1112 and 1133 there was a cell at Þingeyrar under the authority of a prior, but most think St Jón only contributed the intention and that nothing happened until Bishop Ketill consecrated Vilmundr Þórólfsson

[39] *HE* iv. 15 ff.; J. Jónsson 1887, 1914, J. Jóhannesson 1956: 227–36; M. M. Lárusson 1963*g*; M. Stefánsson 1975: 81–5.

[40] Excluding prehistoric hermits like Ásólfr *alskikk* (*ÍF* i. 62–5) or Guðrún Ósvífursdóttir in Helgafell (D) (*ÍF* v. 228), and Guðríður Þorbjarnardóttir in Glaumbær (N) or Staður in Reynines (N) (*ÍF* iv. 269). Cf. K. v. Maurer 1874*a*: 255–6; also Jesch 1985, 1987.

abbot in 1133 (M. M. Lárusson 1963g: 545; 1967c: 46; M. Stefánsson 1975: 82–3; J. Jóhannesson 1956: 228–9; Þorsteinsson 1953: 218–19; G. Þorsteinsson 1988: 90–1). We do not know if the story in *Jóns saga helga* was in Gunnlaugr Leifsson's original version, and even if it was it is likely that from an early date the monks at Þingeyrar were anxious to claim as respectable origins for their monastery as possible. Why they had to implicate Þorkell *trandill* in this is unclear— it may of course be that the story has some basis in reality. It is at any rate perfectly plausible that the *staðr* was established during St Jón's episcopacy (1106–21) but there is no reason to stretch the monastery any further back than 1133.

Abbot Vilmundr had been educated at Hólar in St Jón's school (*Bsk* i. 168 (241)) and this is usually taken as further evidence for St Jón's involvement in the establishment. There is another dimension to this as Vilmundr (d. 1148) appears to have been a local aristocrat; his father Þórólfr Sigmundarson was a chieftain in the northern quarter and the author of *Þorgils saga ok Hafliða* suggests that his authority was waning around 1120. The saga depicts him as the senior but yet less influential partner of Böðvarr Ásbjarnarson of the Ásbirningar from Skagafjörður (*Sturl* 31). Þórólfr's other, and probably elder, son Sigmundr was married to a daughter of Hafliði Másson in Breiðabólstaður in Vesturhóp (N) and this and the association with Böðvarr suggests that Þórólfr was a chieftain in the eastern half of Húnaþing (Ingvarsson 1986–7 iii. 355–9).[41] The establishment of the monastery at Þingeyrar may therefore have as much to do with the initiative of a local family of power as episcopal encouragement. Our sources are unfortunately not substantial enough to allow us to discern which was the greater influence. A possible second abbot of Þingeyrar, Nikulás Sæmundarson, is completely obscure and his place in the list of abbots may be due to a misunderstanding (*HE* iv. 30–1, cf. *DI* iii. 311 n. 2). The second or third abbot, Ásgrímr Vestliðason, died in 1161 and the author of *Ólafs saga Tryggvasonar*, Oddr Snorrason, lists him among his sources (*IA* 116; *Sturl* 106; *SÓT* 247; *HE* i. 212; iv. 31), which suggests that the literary activity for which Þingeyrar later became famous had started in Ásgrímr's abbacy. It is only with the third or fourth abbot Hreinn Styrmisson (d. 1171) that we enter better charted waters. Hreinn was of the Gilsbekkingar and the son of Styrmir Hreinsson who had been one of the greatest chieftains in the country in 1118. Like Vilmundr, Hreinn had received his education at Hólar under St Jón (*Bsk* i. 168 (241)) but the only thing we know about his activities before he succeeded Ásgrímr is that he had a daughter, Valdís, who was married to Magnús Þorláksson in Melar (S) (*Sturl* 92). Hreinn was married to Hallbera, daughter of Hrafn Úlfhéðinsson lawspeaker (1135–8) from Grenjaðarstaður (A) and therefore the brother-in-law of

[41] Þórólfr's grandson, Þórólfr Sigmundarson, lived at Möðrufell in Eyjafjörður (N) but he seems to have acquired that estate through his wife, a daughter of Þorsteinn *ranglátr* in Grund (N) (d. 1149); it had at least reverted to that family in the 13th cent. when Jón Eyjólfsson (son of Guðrún, daughter of Ólafr, in Saurbær in Eyjafjörður (N), son of Þorsteinn) lived there.

Abbot Hallr Hrafnsson of Þverá (d. 1190) (*ÍF* i. 278, 279). Hreinn was only abbot of Þingeyrar for a few years because in 1166 he became the abbot of a new foundation in Hítardalur (S) where his second cousin was the wife of the *fundator* Þorleifr *beiskaldi* (*IA* 117; *Sturl* 107).

Hreinn is an excellent example of a high-placed aristocrat who combined aristocratic family life with an ecclesiastical career. He is likely to have succeeded his father as chieftain of the Gilsbekkingar and must have been around 60 when he became abbot in the early 1160s; for him the abbacy may therefore have been a retirement from the world. His successor Karl Jónsson (d. 1213) is of unknown family but seems to have dedicated his life to the Church. He abdicated in 1181 and was succeeded by Kári Rúnólfsson, who may have been the son of the priest Rúnólfr, son of Bishop Ketill Þorsteinsson of Hólar (1122–45). When Kári died in 1187 Karl returned to Þingeyrar as its abbot and remained until he abdicated a second time in 1207 (*DI* iii. 28; *IA* 117, 118, 119, 124; *Sturl* 107, 117). It was during Karl's abbacy that the writers Oddr Snorrason and Gunnlaugr Leifsson were active. Karl was himself the author of the first part of *Sverris saga* and it seems that in this period the monastery was truly a centre of learning—a pupil of Gunnlaugr's is mentioned (*Bsk* i. 193)—as well as devotion: around 1200 an anchoress as well as a saintly anchorite are attached to the monastery (*Bsk* i. 365, 368, 454, 478). About Karl's successor Þórarinn Sveinsson nothing is known save the dates of accession (1207) and death (d. 1253) (*IA* 123, 133, 181, 191, 329; *Sturl* 628) whereas his successor, Vermundr Halldórsson (d. 1279), is known to have at least once been involved in mediation (*Sturl* 537).

The pattern at Þingeyrar is repeated at the other monasteries; incredibly little is known about the abbots and only about a third of them can be connected with known families. All those who can are however clearly of aristocratic birth and although all the monasteries seem to have been aristocratic foundations crammed with redundant and elderly aristocrats they also seem to have been quite independent of familial politics.

According to *Hungrvaka* Bishop Magnús Einarsson in Skálholt (1134–48) bought Vestmannaeyjar (S) off the south coast and intended to establish a monastery there, but this came to nothing when he died in the fire of Hítardalur in 1148 (*Bysp* 1. 102; Sigfússon 1955). It was therefore left to Bishop Björn Gilsson at Hólar (1147–62) to make the second foundation. In 1155 he founded a monastery on his ancestral estate Þverá (later Munkaþverá) in Eyjafjörður (N) (*IA* 115, 252, 322) (see Ch. 4, s. 1). Its first abbot was a distinguished prelate, Nikulás Bergsson (d. 1159), who had travelled all the way to Jerusalem and written a travel guide (*AÍ* i. 12–31; *HE* iv. 30–1; Hill 1983), but the second was Bishop Björn's brother and namesake (d. 1181) who was installed by his brother shortly before the bishop's death in 1162 (*Sturl* 106, 114; *IA* 118, 180).

The next monastery to be established was in Hítardalur (S); it may have been colonized from Þingeyrar as its abbot, Hreinn Styrmisson, came to head this new foundation. Hreinn was a second cousin of the wife of Þorleifr *beiskaldi*

(d. 1200), the chieftain and householder in Hítardalur, who we must presume was the founder of the monastery. After Hreinn's death in 1171 it is unclear what came of the foundation. An abbot called Hafliði Þorvaldsson (d. 1201), who was according to one fourteenth-century list of abbots an abbot of Flatey (N) (*DI* iii. 154),[42] is sometimes regarded as the second abbot of Hítardalur but this is far from certain. It is also customary to connect three unattached abbots in the early thirteenth century to this monastery on the grounds that they must have been consecrated to some specific monastery even if it did not function and they lived elsewhere (*DI* iii. 31; J. Jónsson 1887: 214–15). In fact the evidence for this monastic foundation is very insubstantial and it only adds up to a single abbot for a few years in the late 1160s. The fact that Þorleifr *beiskaldi* made this attempt is however important; it is a testimony to the importance major chieftains attached to patronizing ecclesiastical institutions in the middle of the twelfth century.

In 1168 the wealthy landowner Þorkell Geirason (d. 1187) in Þykkvibær in Álftaver (S) made a more successful attempt. According to *Þorláks saga* he had no close relatives and gave those who stood to inherit from him enough money so that he was free to donate the rest of his wealth to establish a house of canons on his estate. He asked St Þorlákr, who had been a district priest at nearby Kirkjubær in Síða for some years, to come and head the community (*Bsk* i. 95 (269); *ÍF* i. 322, 323). St Þorlákr having given his consent, the *staðr* was formally established with the counsel and supervision of Bishop Klængr and the men of the region (*Bsk* i. 95–6 (270)). Þorkell then became a canon in his establishment (*Bsk* i. 106).

There is no comparable description of the establishment of a community in Flatey (N) in 1172 (*IA* 117, 323). It was presumably a house of canons and is referred to as such when it was moved to Helgafell (D) in 1184 (*IA* 119; *Bsk* i. 428; also *IA* 254 and 180, 323, which date the establishment to 1185). Helgafell had been in the hands of important people up to 1181 (*Sturl* 89, 99) and it seems that the estate was bought for the house of canons rather than donated by the previous owner. A charter survives where an unnamed man resigns the control of the house to Guðmundr, Ólafr, and Eyjólfr—none of whom can be identified with certainty (*DI* i. 282: quoted in part in s. 2 above). The first abbot of Helgafell was Ögmundr Kálfsson and it is usually assumed that the charter was issued by him. Ögmundr drowned in 1188 (*IA* 120, 180, 254, 324; *Sturl* 120) which makes a probable time frame for the charter 1184–8. Abbot Ögmundr had been a candidate for the bishopric of Skálholt in 1174 (*Bsk* i. 98 (272)) and he may have been abbot of the establishment in Flatey from the outset. It is clear from the charter that its composer had personally owned the *staðr* at Helgafell and was handing it over to the trio on the condition that they run the community. He specified that he wanted his 'seat', the abbacy, to go to either

[42] As the monastery in Flatey was moved to Helgafell in 1186 and a place cannot be found for this Hafliði among its abbots this is not an unreasonable assumption. It is however only an assumption.

Ólafr or Guðmundr, but in case that did not come to pass he wanted them to control the finances (*hafa fjárráð*) and appoint an abbot, preferably from the issuer's kin if that was possible with the bishop's supervision.

Whether the composer was Ögmundr or not, it is clear that the first head of the community at Helgafell had owned the estate himself and that he felt that he could decide who succeeded him. While acknowledging that the bishop had a right to decide who did not become abbot it seems that the *fundator* could bequeath the *staðr* to whom he pleased and it is implied that a prospective abbot would not necessarily control the finances. We may presume that Guðmundr and Ólafr were kinsmen of the *fundator* and that the succession was not regulated because it was understood that they would appoint other kinsmen in their stead. What is interesting is the apparent division between the ownership of the *staðr* and the headship of the community. It suggests that in the twelfth and possibly early thirteenth century the houses of canons and possibly even the monasteries could be privately owned and that the abbots did not have full authority over the property. We are reminded of the charter of Viðey from 1226–47 which, it was argued above, is the earliest sign of the hard stance the Church took in the late thirteenth century on the control over ecclesiastical property. That charter stresses that the abbot has full control over the finances, that donors or their heirs have no right to control, and that the succession should be according to the Rule and not secular heredity (*DI* i. 489–90: the text is quoted above in s. 4). There are no other indications as to the ownership of religious houses but these two charters suggest that it is quite possible that the abbots had authority only over the brothers and the worship, while the *fundator* or his heirs continued to manage the property. These provisions also suggest that the arrangements at the houses of canons could be quite loose and this may account for a number of abbots who cannot be matched with any known monastery.[43]

In 1186 a convent was established at Kirkjubær in Síða (S) (*IA* 119, 254, 323). Kirkjubær had been a distinguished ecclesiastical centre under the aristocratic priest Bjarnhéðinn Sigurðarson in the middle of the twelfth century but after his death in 1173 it is not known who controlled it. In 1189 one Halldóra Eyjólfsdóttir was made abbess (*IA* 120, 180). She had presumably headed the community as prioress from the outset and it is possible that she owned the estate. In 1195 she asked Guðmundr Arason who was then a district priest in Vellir in Svarfaðardalur (N) to come to Kirkjubær and lead the community with her (*til forustu með henni*). Guðmundr sought the leave of both bishops to go to Kirkjubær and was granted permission, but changed his mind after his flock in Svarfaðardalur asked Bishop Brandr to prevent him from going (*Sturl* 173). It

[43] Like Abbot Arnis (*ÍF* i. 178); Þorsteinn Tumason (*Sturl* 114, possibly the same Abbot Þorsteinn (d. 1224) who is mentioned in *Bsk* i. 366 and *IA* 24, 64, 127, 187; Rúnólfr Sighvatsson (d. 1237) (*IA* 130, 188); and Lambkárr Þorgilsson (d. 1249). As mentioned above, 14th-cent. tradition marked the last three as 'unattached' abbots in Hítardalur (*DI* iii. 31), but this may only be an educated guess. Some of these abbots may have owed their titles to Bishop Guðmundr's sometimes unusual actions.

may be that leadership is an exaggeration and that Abbess Halldóra only wanted Guðmundr to be the convent church's priest. After the death in 1210 of Abbess Halldóra a new abbess was not appointed as far as can be seen and by 1250 there do not seem to have been any nuns left. As discussed in the previous chapter the bishop of Skálholt had a verdict declared in 1216–26 that he controlled the *staðr* at Kirkjubær and this also suggests that while Halldóra was abbess she was considered to be the owner.

Sometime around 1200 a monastery was established at Saurbær in Eyjafjörður (N). According to a fourteenth-century list of abbots a Þorkell Skúmsson (d. 1203) was the first abbot at Saurbær (*DI* iii. 31; also *Bsk* i. 147, 486; *IA* 122, 181, 324, 477; *ÍF* i. 283). In 1178–80, when Guðmundr Arason lived in Saurbær, the householder there was the chieftain Ólafr Þorsteinsson of the Grundarmenn (*Sturl* 109, also 50, 124, 126). According to an annal Ólafr was a canon on his death in 1204 (IA; 122) and this suggests that Saurbær was a house of canons. The second abbot at Saurbær was Eyjólfr Hallsson (d. 1212) from Grenjaðarstaður (A). Eyjólfr was a priest and a chieftain and was married to Ólafr Þorsteinsson's daughter (*Sturl* 50–1, 123–8, 154, 165). His father had been abbot of Þverá and Eyjólfr seems to have had a reputation as a priest as Guðmundr Arason had asked him in 1201 to put himself forward as a candidate for bishop of Hólar (*Sturl* 200). Eyjólfr was consecrated in 1206 (*IA* 122, 181; *IA* 62 has it in 1204) and it is simplest to interpret his elevation as an inheritance from his father-in-law. Another fourteenth-century list of abbots makes Þorsteinn Tumason the second abbot of Saurbær and places Eyjólfr in Flatey which is almost certainly a corruption (*DI* iii. 154). Þorsteinn was of the Ásbirningar, an illegitimate brother of Bishop Guðmundr's enemies Kolbeinn and Arnórr. His abbacy is not mentioned in the annals and it seems that the community had ceased to exist already by the 1220s.

Shortly before his death in 1197 the chieftain Jón Loptsson built a church and monastic buildings at Keldur in Rangárvellir (S) and intended to found a monastery. This did not come to pass, claims the source, *Oddaverja þáttr*, and according to it the buildings were dismantled after the death of Jón's son Sæmundr in 1222 (*Bsk* i. 293). A signet has however been found at Keldur bearing the inscription SIG: SUEINONIS: PRI: PAL. PAL has been read as *paludensis*, a translation of Keldur = 'bog', 'marsh', but it can also be read as Pálsson. The question is whether to read PRI as *prioris* or *presbyteri* (M. Þórðarson 1909*a*; M. Stefánsson 1975: 84). If the former is right it suggests that the monastery was established enough for Sveinn the prior to have a signet made, but it is clear that this community was not long-lived.

Keldur was not Jón's family estate but there were probably not many like him who owned additional estates where they could establish their private monasteries when they wanted to retire from the world. The last house of canons to be established in our period is however comparable. The chieftain Þorvaldr Gizurarson of the Haukdælir bought the island Viðey (S) in 1224 and established a house of canons there a year or two later (*Sturl* 288; *IA* 24, 64, 127,

186, 255, 326; *Bsk* i. 546). This was clearly a retirement plan and Þorvaldr seems to have headed the community until his death in 1235 (*IA* 129). It was only then that a prior was appointed (*DI* i. 513) and only following his death in 1245 (*IA* 131, 189, 328, 481) that an abbot was consecrated. It was probably on that occasion that the charter which we have already considered in some detail was composed. It was no doubt significant for the permanence of the house of canons in Viðey that Þorvaldr had the support of his brother, Bishop Magnús, who issued a letter exhorting farmers in the region to give what they could to the *staðr* in Viðey (*DI* i. 491–2). That does not seem to have had much effect and in 1226–9 it was decided at the Alþing that each farmer in a large area around Viðey should give one cheese to the *staðr* every autumn (*DI* i. 496). This seems to have secured the financial well-being of the house of canons in Viðey.

In the late thirteenth century the convent at Kirkjubær was re-established and a new one founded at Staður in Reynines (N), as well as a new house of canons at Möðruvellir in Hörgárdalur (N). It was the bishops who initiated these foundations and in that sense they were quite different from the earlier aristocratic foundations and are symptomatic of the changes in the Icelandic church with its new centralized administration.

We have seen here how all the early religious houses were founded by aristocrats. Even Bishop Björn's establishment of Þverá can be considered as such as it was on his family estate. It remains to ask why aristocrats did found religious houses and what function they had for aristocratic society as well as society at large.

It has been suggested that Þorleifr *beiskaldi*'s foundation in Hítardalur in 1166 was a pious reaction to the death of Bishop Magnús Einarsson and eighty-two others by fire in Hítardalur in 1148 (J. Jóhannesson 1956: 230; *Bysp* 1. 103–4; *IA* 20, 60, 114, 252, 321; *Sturl* 81). That may well have influenced Þorleifr but his initiative must be seen in the context of similar foundations in this period; the monastery at Þingeyrar had been established in 1133, followed by Þverá in 1155; Hítardalur came next in 1166, then a house of canons in Þykkvibær in 1168 and another in Flatey in 1172 and a nunnery in Kirkjubær in 1186. It seems that it was in vogue to establish religious houses in the mid and late twelfth century and it is simplest to interpret this as a natural inflation of the processes which prompted the endowments of *staðir* in the twelfth century; it is not a big step from an endowment like that of Steini the priest to the church in Stafholt (S), which was to have three priests, a deacon, and maintain two incapable persons of Steini's kin (*DI* i. 179–80) to that of Helgafell with five priests (*messu söngs menn*), a deacon and subdeacon (*DI* i. 282). The *messu söngs menn* (lit. 'mass singers') were the permanent canons, that is, those who served the church and were supported by the endowment. It was no doubt understood that in general canons would be supported by prebends donated by themselves—as is clear from the charter of Viðey (*DI* i. 489–90). These endowments were probably on a similar scale as regards the property donated, but the latter was more ambitious in that it created a community under an abbot and a rule which would be a greater good for the community and a greater monument to the *fundator*. By the mid-twelfth century when most of the large endowments of churches seem already to have taken place it may therefore have been that the only way to outdo other householders was to establish a religious house. It seems however that the main impetus was a pious one; Þorkell Geirason in Þykkvibær, Ólafr Þorsteinsson in Saurbær, Jón Loptsson in Keldur, and Þorvaldr Gizurarson in Viðey, all established and joined their religious houses towards the end of their lives, most after long careers as chieftains. They were probably more worried about their souls than their prestige in the world, but so of course were many others who simply joined other religious houses. There could be no greater sign of a chieftain's magnanimity and prestige than to establish his own religious house when he felt that he should retire from the world; the motive was shared by a much larger group but the ability was the privilege of the few. This is one of the situations where piety and prestige go hand in hand and the latter is acquired by showing the former.

Þorláks saga attributes the idea of founding the first house of canons at Þykkvibær to the *fundator* Þorkell Geirason, but the saint is supposed to have composed the rule. It is often surmised that, as St Þorlákr had studied in Paris, he might have been influenced by the Victorines (J. Jóhannesson 1956: 214; M. Stefánsson 1975: 83–4, 96; B. Þorsteinsson 1978: 139; Tómasson 1988*a*: 23; *ÍBS* i. 276). Such influence is commonly argued by Norwegian historians for the Archbishops Eysteinn and Eiríkr to provide a connection to the reform movement in Europe (Johnsen 1945*b*; Kolsrud 1958: 205–7; 1962: 41; Helle 1964: 37, 58, 168; Bagge 1984: 3–4)[44] but in the case of St Þorlákr this is only an assumption. The monasteries at Þingeyrar and Þverá presumably followed the Benedictine rule—there is no evidence that the Cistercians ever reached Iceland—and the houses of canons are likely to have followed some form of the Augustinian rule although nothing is in fact known about this until the fourteenth century (*IA* 210, 214, 352; see also Gallén 1956*c*: 281; 1956*e*: 454; M. M. Lárusson 1963*g*). Ascribing the rise and success of the canons regular in Iceland to an imported reform movement without any supporting evidence is dubious and unnecessary. It is entirely possible that St Þorlákr got acquainted with the Augustinian rule while he was abroad and brought the idea to Iceland, but there are many other ways by which the idea could be transmitted and it cannot in any case explain the more important problem of why houses of canons became so much more popular than Benedictine monasteries.

The most plausible explanation is that the houses of canons were easier to establish, more likely to succeed, and that less was risked if they failed. Or in other words: they required less start capital, were more likely to attract the high

[44] On Victorian influence on Nordic literature see Bekker-Nielsen 1968, 1976.

number of ordained aristocrats in the twelfth century, and could function as major churches even if no canons joined.

The first point is difficult to prove in Iceland because we know nothing of what was required of the monasteries as opposed to the houses of canons. It is, however, supported by analogy with other parts of Europe where the success of the Augustinian canons in the twelfth century is partly explainable by their cheapness compared with Benedictine foundations (Southern 1990: 245–7). The houses of canons in both Helgafell and Viðey were endowed to support five and three priests (*messu söngs menn*) respectively, as well as two deacons each (*DI* i. 282, 489–90). In both charters this is expressed as the minimum. In Helgafell this was the provision in case a house of canons did not become functional and in Viðey the provision is for three *messu söngs menn*, two deacons, and 'as many canons as there will be' (*DI* i. 489). Both charters indicate that the success of the house was conditional on canons joining who donated their own prebends and this may have been the difference between the houses of canons and Benedictine monasteries; the latter were probably not as flexible and needed a more secure financial footing to come into being.

The flexibility of the houses of canons as opposed to the Benedictine monasteries leads to the second and third points; the houses of canons were more likely to succeed because they were easier/cheaper to establish and, being institutions for priests, they may have had a greater appeal to the high number of ordained chieftains and wealthy householders in the twelfth century. The contrast between *messu söngs menn* and ordinary—self-financing—canons in the two charters suggests that the former were not considered sufficient to constitute a house of canons on their own. They were probably the priests ascribed to the church and the pastoral duties that came with it,[45] who could be counted among the canons if the house was successful but who could function independently if it did not. This meant that even if recruitment failed the foundation was still a valuable one which would support a major ecclesiastical centre.

The reasons for the establishment of religious houses seem therefore to have been the pious inclinations of aristocrats and their desire for salvation as much as prestige or local influence. The reason why houses of canons became more popular seems simply to have been that they were easier to establish. Religious houses did, however, also answer to a social need; the fact that people could just as well become monks, canons, and nuns at the episcopal sees as the religious houses[46] suggests this and there was clearly a number of people who wanted and could afford to devote their lives to God as well as a much larger group who for one reason or other needed to retire from the world.

The former group is probably under-represented in our sources; people who

[45] Helgafell at least had a large tithe area and several annex churches to service (*JJ* 161; *PP* 153, as *DI* ii. 672–3).

[46] As in *Grg II*, 97_{18}–98_{5}; *Grg III*, 43_{3-8}, and 145_{14-19}, where the clause is marked as an amendment.

joined religious houses at an early age and lived there all their lives are not likely to appear in the type of source that survives from the high middle ages in Iceland. It is also difficult to distinguish people like these from the latter group; some may have been installed in religious houses because they were for one reason or another of no use to their family or not likely to survive on their own in secular society. We do not know for instance why the scholar monks Oddr Snorrason and Gunnlaugr Leifsson joined the community at Þingeyrar; religious devotion is only one among several possible explanations. There is also fusion between the two groups in that many of the people who joined religious houses late in their lives had not had the opportunity earlier. This seems to have been the case with the anchoress Úlfrún in Þingeyrar who had had a son before she took the veil but took her seclusion so seriously that she would not let her son see her when he came to visit (*Bsk* i. 368; *Sturl* 208). The best representative of religious devotion is the anchoress Hildr who lived in a hut attached to the cathedral at Hólar from before St Jón's death in 1121 to her death in 1159. She had come to the see with her grandfather, the priest Hámundr, and had at an early age requested to be allowed to take the veil but had been refused. She then disappeared and made herself a shelter in a nearby uninhabited valley. After she had been found she was ordained as nun and later she instructed virtuous women as well as fostering a poor boy whom she taught to read the Psalter (*Bsk* i. 167 (239), 194–5, 203–7 (254–7); see Carlé 1985*a*).

The majority of known people in monastic orders were aristocrats retiring after active lives in the world. The first monk known to us is the chieftain Þorgils Oddason from Staðarhóll (D) who had clashed memorably with Hafliði Másson around 1120. In 1150 he handed his estate and chieftaincy over to his sons and became a monk at Þingeyrar, where he died the following spring (*Sturl* 56). When Bishop Ketill Þorsteinsson of Hólar died in 1145 his widow, Gróa daughter of Bishop Gizurr Ísleifsson, lived as a nun at Hólar where she died in the time of Bishop Klængr (1151–76) (*Bysp* 1. 92). Some families had close ties with particular monasteries; in 1204 Bishop Guðmundr asked the chieftain Sigurðr Ormsson (d. 1235) to go to Þverá and restore the buildings on the *staðr.* We are told that Sigurðr undertook this gladly because he loved the *staðr* dearly for his father, the chieftain Ormr Jónsson, had died as a monk there in 1191 and Ormr had been the nephew of Bishop Björn who established it. It was a further incentive that the present abbot, Ormr Skeggjason, was Sigurðr's relative, a nephew of old Ormr (*Sturl* 210). Sigurðr later became a monk himself, most likely at Þverá (*Sturl* 49). The fact that the Svínfellingar's core region was on the other side of the country from Þverá suggests that their involvement with the monastery had a personal rather than political significance. Another, more local, family which had close ties with Þverá was that of the chieftain Þorgeirr Hallason in Hvassafell in Eyjafjörður (N) and his sons. Þorgeirr had been among the greatest chieftains in the country in 1118 but shortly before his death in 1169 he became a monk at Þverá (*Bsk* i. 31; *IA* 117; *Sturl* 107). One of Þorgeirr's younger sons, Þórðr, was a monk at Þverá all his life it seems (*Sturl*

101) and Þorgeirr's son and successor as chieftain, Þorvarðr, also became a monk before his death in 1207, presumably at Þverá (*IA* 123, 182).

This pattern was to continue throughout the twelfth century and into the thirteenth but in the middle of that century the evidence for retiring aristocrats begins to get thin, partly because in this period the most prominent aristocrats with whom our sources tend to be concerned did not live very long. There are, however, examples like Klængr Teitsson of the Haukdælir (*ÍF* xvii. 142, 167) and Þorsteinn Hjálmsson from Breiðabólstaður in Vesturhóp (N) (*ÍF* xvii. 331), which show that the trend continued throughout the thirteenth century.

The third possible group of people who might have become attached to the religious houses and the sees in the twelfth and thirteenth centuries is boarders (*próventumenn*) or lay people of retirement age who wished to vacate their estates for their heirs but were not interested in taking religious vows. There are numerous examples of such people negotiating their corodies with religious houses in the fourteenth and fifteenth centuries, but none from the twelfth or thirteenth. That of course does not mean that the practice was not in place.

That the principal function of the religious houses was to be retirement homes is supported by their unobtrusiveness and independence. They were independent in the sense that no particular families can be shown to have dominated individual houses. The abbots of the same house came from different families and often from other parts of the country. Absolutely nothing is known of how they were selected, although it seems that the bishops of Skálholt had the final say about the abbots of the houses of canons in that diocese (*Bsk* i. 106; *DI* i. 282). As was pointed out above, it is possible that the abbots did not have financial control over their establishments and that this control remained in the hands of the *fundator* or his or her heirs. As long as it did, these patrons must have had a say in the appointment of abbots but it does not seem likely that this sort of arrangement survived long into the thirteenth century, as we should then expect to know more about it from indignant reformers.

Very little is known of how large the religious houses were; when Þorvaldr Gizurarson established the house of canons in Viðey there were five canons there (*Bsk* i. 546), in 1344 they were six (*IA* 352) while in 1403 there were thirteen canons in Þykkvibær and fourteen nuns in Kirkjubær (*IA* 286) and these seem to have been the sort of numbers common in the religious houses. By the middle of the thirteenth century some of the religious houses had become institutions of considerable strength and it is in them that increasing numbers of men like Brandr Jónsson and Eyjólfr Valla-Brandsson (see Ch. 5, s. 5), who had a clear sense of their identity as men of the church, were bred.

4
The Bishops

1. THE BISHOPS AND FAMILY POLITICS

With Ísleifr's son, Gizurr, becoming bishop in 1082, the domination of the Icelandic church by the Haukdælir was established. Bishop Gizurr seems to have succeeded his father without difficulty. *Hungrvaka* has a story about a priest called Guttormr Finnólfsson from Laugardalur (S) whom Ísleifr indicated as his successor and who was chosen at the Alþing in the absence of Gizurr. Gizurr had been abroad and returned to the country about the time of the Alþing. Knowing that a choice of an *electus* would be made he waited discreetly at his landing place until he got news that the priest had been chosen and then made his way to the assembly. But when the priest knew that Gizurr was there he announced that there was no chance he would undertake the responsibility as Gizurr was now available. The chieftains and people then turned to Gizurr and only after much pleading and promises of good behaviour did Gizurr agree to seek consecration (*Bysp* 1. 83–4).

The priest in this story is otherwise unknown and the story must be considered in its hagiographic context. Gizurr was in the eyes and pen of *Hungrvaka*'s author a true ecclesiastical hero, and in this story we get the motif of the reluctant hero expressed in terms of Christian modesty. It is also likely that the author or somebody before him felt slightly embarrassed by what might be claimed to be simple inheritance of an ecclesiastical office. Whatever the truth behind this story it does not allow us to think that bishops were selected by some kind of communal decision. In fact nothing can be known with certainty about the selection procedures until 1150. Down to that time there never seems to have been a second contestant, and the choice of *electus* seems to have been mostly in the hands of the preceding bishop, and, after 1106, in the hands of the bishop of the other see. The choice of successor can be shown always to have been influenced, to some degree at least, by familial and/or discipular relationships (cf. M. M. Lárusson. 1967*c*: 50–5).

Gizurr was, like his father, educated in Saxony (*Bysp* 1. 83)—*Jóns saga helga* adds that it was in Herford as well (*Bsk* i. 153, 219)—but all the later bishops, down to St Þorlákr, were educated in Iceland as far as can be established. Ari tells us that many chieftains and good men gave their sons to Ísleifr to be educated, and among these were St Jón, first bishop of Hólar, and Kollr who later became a bishop in Norway (*ÍF* i. 20). But unlike his father, Gizurr is not credited with any educational efforts. That responsibility was taken up by Gizurr's brother Teitr, priest in Haukadalur (S).

Teitr had been fostered by Hallr Þórarinsson *hinn mildi* in Haukadalur. Hallr was 94 when he died in 1089; he had been in Norway in his twenties and followed St Ólafr but came back to Iceland in 1025 to farm at Haukadalur (*ÍF* i. 20–1; xxvii. 420). Hallr was probably childless and Teitr seems to have inherited the land from him. Ari *fróði* was fostered by Hallr from the age of 7 and was at Haukadalur for fourteen years (*c.*1075–89), but he also says he was with Teitr at the age of 12 (*ÍF* i. 20–1), which suggests that Teitr and Hallr lived together at Haukadalur even after Teitr came of age. As opposed to Bishop Gizurr who neither had disciples nor sons who achieved anything,[1] Teitr had two bishops and Ari *fróði* among his disciples and his son, Hallr, became the family's chieftain and was a bishop elect when he died in 1150. We do not know the particulars of Þorlákr Rúnólfsson's (b. 1087, bishop of Skálholt 1118–33) and Björn Gilsson's (Bishop of Hólar 1147–62) relationship with Teitr. The source, *Jón saga helga*, only says that they were nurtured and educated by him (*Bsk* i. 153, 219). It seems however safe to assume that their pupilage was more akin to traditional fosterage rather than formal schooling (cf. Tómasson 1988*a*: 20–1).

Fosterage was a complex institution (M. M. Lárusson 1959*i*), but the aspect of it that matters in this context is that the foster child was seen to benefit from it both personally (i.e. became a better person) and politically (i.e. an alliance was forged). Whether money was exchanged is besides the point; known fosterers like Teitr, Sæmundr *fróði*, his son Eyjólfr, and others, can be safely assumed to have been of the financial standing that they were not taking on boys for the money. The benefits to them were rather political; taking on a boy meant alliance with his kin and when grown up he would be as a son to his foster father and brother to his foster siblings. This was especially significant if the foster child could be helped to positions like bishop or lawspeaker, which were politically important without involving familial wealth. The point was of course that the foster child did not inherit from the fosterer but could in all other aspects be expected to behave towards him and his family like a son. The principle of primogeniture being far from well established in Iceland in the twelfth century, younger sons of powerful chieftains could not be relied on to forsake their chance of inheritance for ecclesiastical posts which at best wielded limited powers. The powers of bishops, and later on abbots, were nevertheless important to chieftains and it was therefore ideal to have somebody as bishop who could make no financial claim but could be relied upon for support when needed. Whatever the practice, this attitude would explain why so many of the powerful chieftains in the twelfth century let it suffice to be priests and spent

[1] Gizurr had five sons, four of whom died before him, and about the fifth nothing more is known (*Bysp* 1. 89, 92). Gizurr's son Teitr was with him in Norway in 1083, and may have accompanied him on his consecration journey. Teitr Gizurarson was among the Icelandic chieftains who swore that Bishop Ísleifr had sworn that King Ólafr Haraldsson had given Icelanders certain rights in Norway (Grg *1b*, 197; J. Jóhannesson 1956: 141–2), which suggests that he had considerable status, but he seems to have died before he could establish a family of his own. Also *ÍF* iii. 334–42, where he is in Norway in 1093–1103 and lives only a short while after returning to Iceland.

their lives power-broking in their respective regions and why a large number of bishops were the sons of penniless men of little consequence but respectable ancestry.

Jón Jóhannesson (1956: 181) wondered why Sæmundr *fróði* never became bishop, considering that he was regarded as the most learned man in the country in his time, that he was influential both in the passing of the tithe law in 1097 and the writing of the Christian law section between 1122 and 1133, and that Ari regards him as an equal of the bishops by submitting his first draft of *Íslendingabók* also to him. We cannot of course know the details of the political issues which affected who became bishop and who did not, but the explanation that Sæmundr did not become bishop because he did not want to makes good sense—if he had, he could have been imperilling the position and continuity of his family, the Oddaverjar.

Bishop Gizurr was almost certainly not the eldest son of Bishop Ísleifr. Teitr died before him (d. 1110) and when Gizurr came home from Saxony there seems to have been no room for him in his family's region in the south, since he went to live at his wife's inheritance at Hof in Vopnafjörður (A), suggesting that his brothers Teitr and Þorvaldr had already acquired what wealth and power there was within their family. Gizurr was also a merchant and often sailed abroad (*Bysp* 1. 83), and thus in every way behaved like a youngest son busily trying to further his and his descendants' chances of power. From the point of view of the only son who outlived him, Gizurr seems to have forsaken these chances by becoming a bishop.

The choice of St Jón as bishop for the new northern diocese seems to have been made by his friends and relatives in the south. It seems unlikely that the men of the north preferred somebody with no connections in their regions. The initiative for the establishment of the see no doubt came from the north (*ÍF* i. 23), but in selecting the man to do the job Bishop Gizurr could not be bypassed. The Archbishop could not be expected to agree to consecrate a bishop to the new see against the wishes of the bishop whose bishopric was being diminished by more than a fourth.

St Jón was a disciple of Bishop Ísleifr, a fact which no doubt influenced his selection. He was also a third cousin of Teitr Ísleifsson's wife, a relationship which would have been recognized. But unlike many of the later bishops St Jón was a man of good position and if he was not a chieftain it can only have been because he was not interested in it. He was the great-grandson of a primary settler,[2] through a direct male line, and his mother was the daughter of one of the sons of Síðu-Hallr, a chieftain from the south-east who was the leader of the Christian side in 1000 and from whom at least six of the twelve Icelandic bishops in the Commonwealth period were descended. St Jón's estate and church, Breiðabólstaður in Fljótshlíð (S), was in the area of his

[2] Ásgeirr *kneif*: on him see Sigurðsson 1886: 504–5. The line is curiously short, and one or two generations may be missing (*ÍF* i. 340–2; *Bsk* i. 151, 216).

great-grandfather's land-claim and was, later at least, one of the richest and most important *staðir* in the country. The evidence is circumstantial but it suggests strongly that St Jón was a chieftain of his own family, whose absence from the area can hardly have been regretted by the neighbouring family of the Oddaverjar. It is not known into whose possession Breiðabólstaður came after St Jón moved to Hólar, but shortly before 1200 it was held by one of the Oddaverjar (*Sturl* 172).

Why St Jón felt free to leave his patrimony we cannot know; his being childless may partly explain that. He was 50 when he was consecrated, already married to his second wife, and may have given up all hope of an heir. Whatever the reason, any chance of a family of *Breiðbælingar ceased with St Jón becoming bishop in 1106.

Bishop Gizurr's successor at Skálholt, Þorlákr Rúnólfsson, was a very different type of man from St Jón. There is nothing to suggest that he had either wealth or power coming to him from his immediate family, whereas there is everything to suggest that he owned his career entirely to the Haukdælir. His ancestry was very respectable: he was descended from Ketilbjörn *gamli* like the Haukdælir and from Önundr *bíldr* like St Jón, and on his mother's side he was of the Reynistaðarmenn from the north (*Bysp* 1. 11; *ÍF* i. 73, 374). He was thus second cousin of his fellow student and later bishop at Hólar, Björn Gilsson.

More important though was that he was the great-nephew of Hallr Þórarinsson, which was probably what landed him in Haukadalur in the first place. Þorlákr is the best example of a protégé of the Haukdælir. Not only was he a disciple of Teitr Ísleifsson, but when Bishop Gizurr felt that his life was nearing its end, probably in 1117, he sent Þorlákr to Lund and had him consecrated to Skálholt,[3] thus taking no risks with the choice of successor. Þorlákr was only 32 when consecrated, and the author of *Hungrvaka* records that when he came to Denmark, people there thought that there could not be much to choose from in Iceland if this was the best the Icelanders could come up with (*Bysp* 1. 94). Why the author of *Hungrvaka* was far from impressed by Þorlákr is unknown—the author of *Þorgils saga ok Hafliða* depicts him quite differently—but the unusual circumstances of his consecration do suggest that Þorlákr was not the most obvious choice and, that for some unknown reason, the Haukdælir were desperate to secure him the see.

With Ketill Þorsteinsson succeeding St Jón to Hólar in 1122 and Bishop Þorlákr's death in 1133 the absolute domination of the Church by the Haukdælir came to an end. There are two separate developments that can be discerned. One is that, with Bishop Ketill of Hólar (1122–45), other influential families begin to take an active interest in choosing bishops, resulting in more than one candidate to choose from, and therefore some kind of selection at the Alþing

[3] Ari's words: *hann lét Gizurr vígja til stóls í Skálaholti at sér lifanda*. Þorlákr was consecrated 28 April 1118, thirty days before Bishop Gizurr died (*ÍF* i. 25). *Hungrvaka* says he was consecrated to Reykholt in Borgarfjörður (*Bysp* 1. 94).

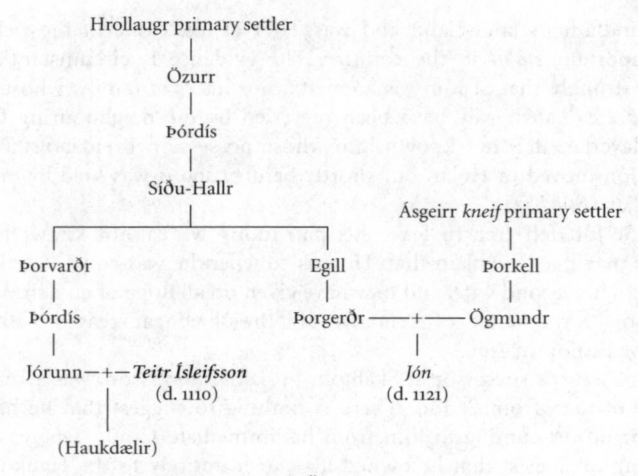

FIGURE 4. *St Jón Ögmundarson's lineage*

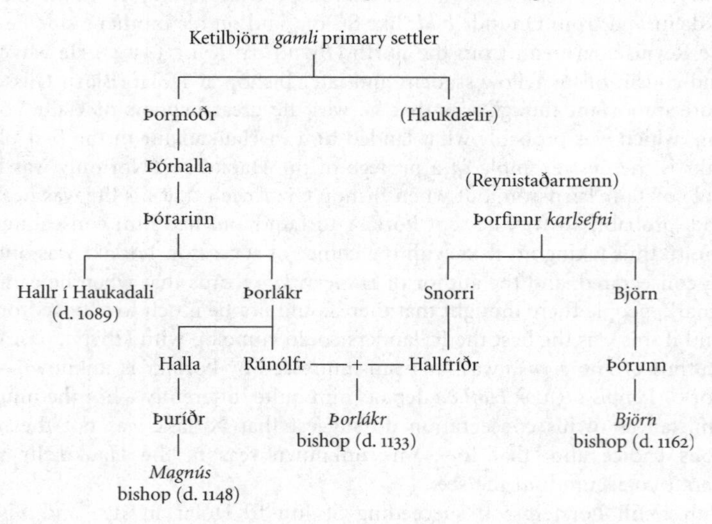

FIGURE 5. *Bishop Þorlákr Rúnólfsson's lineage*

from at least 1150. The other development was that the church establishment itself was slowly beginning to be able to exert its own influence. First in that, since there were two sees in the country, a bishop could not be elected to one of the sees without the consent and support of the bishop of the other. Secondly in that, as the inner structure of the Church slowly grew, careers began to be made within it, without the families having much influence.

Thus we have Ketill Þorsteinsson (b. 1074 d. 1145), a chieftain of the Möðruvellingar, one of the oldest and most respectable families in the north, succeeding St Jón as bishop of Hólar in 1122. Ketill was the last chieftain of his line (Ingvarsson 1986–7: iii. 520–4)[4] and also the last chieftain to become bishop (although both Páll Jónsson and Magnús Gizurarson had held *goðorð* neither were leaders of their respective families). Besides being related to more or less everybody of consequence in the country—he was for instance first cousin of Sæmundr *fróði* (*ÍF* i. 27, 229)—Ketill was married to Bishop Gizurr's daughter, which no doubt had some influence on his election.

Of Bishop Þorlákr's successor at Skálholt Magnús Einarsson we know very little in terms of connections. It is not known where he got his education, but he was Bishop Þorlákr's first cousin once removed, which is too close a relationship to be a coincidence. Bishop Magnús had splendid ancestry; like Þorlákr he was a distant relative of the Haukdælir and like St Jón he was a descendant of Síðu-Hallr, through a direct male line from Síðu-Hallr's eldest son, which may have constituted a family of power, although nothing is known about chieftaincies in the east in this period.[5] Magnús's stepmother, who loved him dearly according to *Hungrvaka* (*Bysp* 1. 99), was of the rising ecclesiastical family of the Reykhyltingar. Magnús then owed his episcopacy either to his parents' families or to Bishop Þorlákr (or all three), but there is nothing in particular to suggest influence from the Haukdælir although it is difficult to imagine that they were cold-shouldered in the selection process.

Bishop Ketill's successor at Hólar, Björn Gilsson (1147–62), is of uncertain ancestry. His mother was a granddaughter of Þorfinnr *karlsefni* in Staður in Reynines (*ÍF* iv. 236–7) and her father Björn or Þorbjörn seems to have been of considerable standing; his son Árni was a priest (*Bysp* 1. 97) and his other daughter was married to the chieftain Þorsteinn *ranglátr* at Grund in Eyjafjörður (N) (d. 1149) (*Sturl* 50). It has been suggested that Björn had another son in Snorri (d. 1151), father of Grímr in Hof in Höfðaströnd (N) (d. 1196) (*SturlR* ii. 35, *ættskrá*; Ingvarsson 1986–7: iii. 387–9, 396–400), and this would allow us to identify Bishop Björn's maternal family as minor chieftains in eastern Skagafjörður. Of Bishop Björn's paternal family we know that his sister, Þórný—mother of the chieftain Ormr Jónsson (*Bsk* i. 488)—was the daughter of a Gils Einarsson (*Sturl* 48). The suggestion that Gils Einarsson was the son of Einarr, son of Járnskeggi, son of Einarr *Þveræingr* (Dofri 1939: 390; Tobíasson

[4] Ketill is called *höfðingi* in *Kristni saga* (*ASB* xi. 51, 53), and as much can be inferred from the story about how he lost his eye (*Sturl* 42–3, *ÍF* x. 105). It is possible that his *goðorð* passed to his uncle's descendants if Ketill Guðmundsson and Þorvaldr *auðgi* were the sons of Guðmundr Guðmundsson, but this is nowhere stated, cf. *SturlR* 39, *ættskrá*. There is also a chance that his son, the priest and later monk Rúnólfr (d. 1186), was a chieftain since he is counted among many such in the priest list of 1143 (*DI* i. 186), and it may be him that is called 'göfugr prestr' in verse 43 of *Leiðarvísan* (*Skjald* i. 626; see F. Jónsson 1920–4: ii. 118, and de Vries 1964–7: ii. 61).

[5] Ingvarsson 1986–7: ii. 74–118 bravely attempts to reconstruct the owners of *goðorð* in this region and ascribes one to Bishop Magnús's father, Einarr Magnússon (pp. 83–5) but this must be considered optimistic.

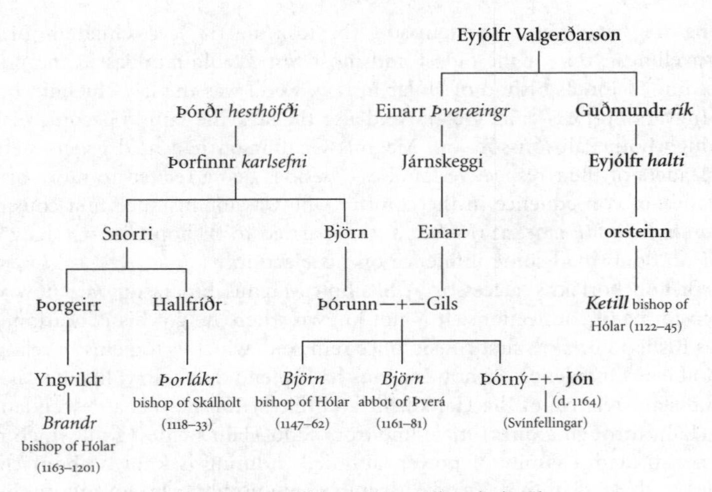

FIGURE 6. *Bishop Björn Gilsson's family*

1943: 173–4; Ingvarsson 1986–7: iii. 484–91), has the virtue of explaining why Björn established a monastery at Þverá (N), for it would then have been his ancestral estate. This link also places Björn firmly among the most powerful families of Eyjafjörður. Björn had been sent to Teitr Ísleifsson in Haukadalur for education (*Bsk* i. 153 (219)) and later he studied at Hólar under St Jón (*Bsk* i. 168 (241)). Björn may have remained at Hólar under Bishop Ketill and succeeded to the episcopacy with the support of his many powerful relatives and in-laws in the north and east. If he was not the eldest son of Gils and Þórunn he was apparently the oldest surviving one in 1155 when he established a monastery on his patrimony at Þverá. His family may not have owned a *goðorð* but they were nevertheless of high status as their connections show; Björn is listed among the high-born priests of 1143 (*DI* i. 186). As in St Jón's case, Bishop Björn's family came to an end as a political entity with his elevation to the see of Hólar and when he ordained his brother and namesake as abbot of Þverá in 1181 it seems that the *Þveræingar were finally absorbed into the Church.

Like Björn Gilsson, Klængr Þorsteinsson bishop of Skálholt 1152–76 was educated under St Jón at Hólar. His mother placed him there at the age of 12, around 1117 (*Bsk* i. 240 (only in B version)),[6] and he seems to have lived there without interruption until he became bishop of Skálholt in 1152 (*Bsk* i. 168, 240–1; *Bysp* 1. 106). Unlike Björn, but like his predecessors Magnús and Þorlákr at Skálholt, Klængr's family does not seem to have been influential although the

[6] Klængr was 47 when he was consecrated in 1152 so he was born *c.*1105 (*Bysp* 1. 113).

ancestry was respectable.[7] Klængr is listed among the high-born priests of the north in 1143—when he was probably a cathedral priest at Hólar—and the author of *Hungrvaka* calls him a northerner (*norðlenzkr maðr*) (*DI* i. 186; *Bysp* 1. 106). His family may well have been from the north but the identification is more probably connected with his long association with the see of Hólar. It was clearly Bishop Björn who brought about Klængr's elevation to the see of Skálholt. The Haukdælir had had their chance but their chieftain and *electus* Hallr Teitsson had died in Utrecht before receiving consecration. And, as *Hungrvaka* puts it, when news of his death reached Iceland Hallr's son and successor as chieftain, Gizurr, was abroad and 'it was the selection of everyone who was to decide, under the guidance of Björn bishop of Hólar' that Klængr should be *electus* (*Bysp* 1. 106). If the Haukdælir had not had complete control over the selection of Klængr, they did however adapt to this and it may not have been a chance only that when Klængr had been consecrated in 1152 he returned to Iceland in the company of Gizurr Hallsson (*Bysp* 1. 107). In 1175 when Klængr had become bedridden on account of old age Gizurr was in Skálholt to greet the incumbent, St Þorlákr (*Bsk* i. 99). It is likely that Gizurr was an ever-present influence on the see in the intervening years (cf. *Sturl* 73).

While Bishop Björn seems to have had a decisive role in selecting Klængr it is not apparent that Klængr controlled the appointment of Brandr Sæmundarson as *electus* to the see of Hólar in 1163. Brandr's career up to this time is unknown except that he was a priest and had been present at Bishop Björn's burial, which suggests that he had connections with the see before he became bishop (*Bysp* 1. 111; *Bsk* i. 207). On his father's side Brandr was of a side-branch of the Oddaverjar and Jón Loptsson accompanied him on his consecration journey to Norway in 1163–4, which suggests their influence on his appointment. Brandr's grandfather, Grímr, was probably the younger son of Loðmundr in Oddi. He married locally it seems, as his wife was the sister of Skeggi Brandsson in Skógar (S). Both Grímr's sons were however married to women from the north; Svertingr to Þórdís Guðmundardóttir of the Möðruvellingar, sister of Þorvaldr *auðgi* (d. 1161) and aunt of Guðmundr *dýri* (d. 1212) (*Sturl* 47). Sæmundr—possibly named after his older and more famous cousin in Oddi—was married to Yngvildr Þorgeirsdóttir of the Reynistaðarmenn. Yngvildr may have had a much older brother in Guðmundr Þorgeirsson, lawspeaker 1122–34, who was the father of Þuríðr, mother of Guðmundr *dýri*

[7] Klængr's ancestry is recorded in *Biskupa ættir* (*ÍF* xvii, 464–5). None of the names on his mother's side are identifiable nor on his paternal grandfather's. His paternal grandmother, however, was the daughter of Ari in Reykjanes (D) of the Reyknesingar and her mother was a granddaughter of Síðu-Hallr and Einarr *Þveræingr*. Klængr was therefore distantly related to Bishop Björn (third cousin once removed), a first cousin once removed of the chieftain Þorgils Oddason (d. 1150) and Guðmundr Arason was Klængr's second cousin once removed. Through his descent from Síðu-Hallr Klængr was distantly related to almost everyone of consequence in the country. He was, for instance, fourth cousin of both Jón Loptsson of the Oddaverjar and Gizurr Hallsson of the Haukdælir who were his great friends while he was bishop of Skálholt (*Bysp* 1. 109).

(d. 1212) and Þórðr Þórarinsson in Laufás (N). Guðmundr may also have been the father of Þorgeirr Guðmundarson, who is listed among the high-born priests of 1143 (*Sturl* 94; *DI* i. 186; Ingvarsson 1986–7: iii. 389–92). If these links are correct it seems that Yngvildr was much younger than her brother and she could easily have outlived her nephew the priest. This could explain why Bishop Brandr's son Þorgeirr became householder at Staður in Reynines (N), the Reynistaðarmenn's ancestral estate. Yngvildr may have inherited the estate from her brother or nephew; Þorgeirr Brandsson's name suggests close links with his cousin the priest. Bishop Brandr may therefore have been a man of considerable local importance in Skagafjörður with close familial connections with some of the most powerful people in the quarter. If he had inherited Staður in Reynines it is also likely that he inherited his family's chieftaincy, although it is not known whether the Reynistaðarmenn owned a *goðorð*. It is therefore a simplification to view Bishop Brandr only as a protégé of the Oddaverjar; it is probable that, like his predecessor, he was of a family of ancient but waning importance and was in a position to promote himself. Secondly he had powerful relatives both in the north and the west as well as in Rangárþing who doubtless considered him as their representative. Unlike Klængr and Björn, Bishop Brandr was a family man who not only took an active part in politics but seems to have used his position to further the interests of his family and its influence in Skagafjörður.

St Þorlákr, Klængr's successor at Skálholt, was a very different man from his colleague in Hólar. St Þorlákr was clearly a protégé of the Oddaverjar but he was also the first bishop to have a clear agenda of his own. He is the first bishop on whom we have relatively detailed information and his career prior to his becoming bishop is considered in detail in Chapter 5, section 4. Like many of his predecessors St Þorlákr was of a poor and insignificant family but respectable ancestry. The family was dissolved when Þorlákr was a child and he accompanied his mother and sister to Oddi. There he was fostered by the priest and chieftain Eyjólfr Sæmundarson (d. 1158) and it appears that his family developed quite close ties with the Oddaverjar; one of his sisters later became a concubine of Jón Loptsson. It must have been the Oddaverjar who paid for St Þorlákr's six-year studies in England and France. When he returned it is probable that they were the 'relatives' who wanted him to marry a widow in Háfur (S), a church-farm close to Oddi. Here, however, St Þorlákr showed that he had an independent turn of mind and refused to get married. Instead of becoming a householder in the Oddaverjar's core-region and starting a family of his own, St Þorlákr joined the household of the priest Bjarnhéðinn Sigurðarson in Kirkjubær (S) (d. 1173). Six years later a wealthy local landowner asked St Þorlákr to head a new house of canons which was to be established at Þykkvibær (S). Bishop Klængr and the men of the region are cited as the interested parties in the establishment of the house of canons at Þykkvibær (*Bsk* i. 96) and it is difficult to see that the Oddaverjar can have had much to do with it. St Þorlákr became prior in 1168 and abbot a few years later. In the early

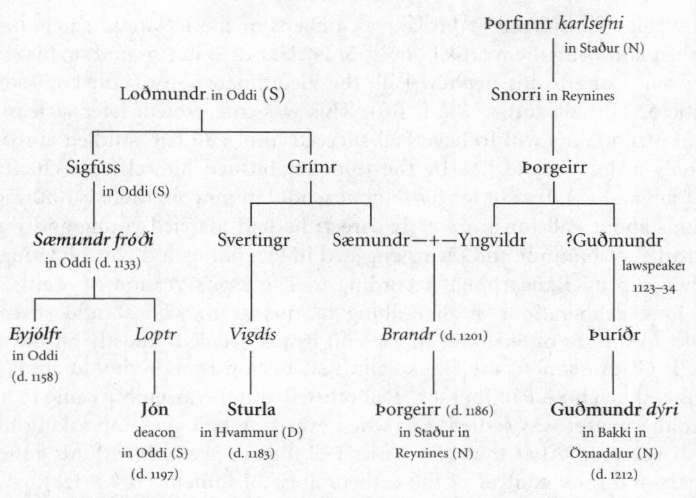

FIGURE 7. *Bishop Brandr Sæmundarson's family*

1170s Bishop Klængr was becoming increasingly frail and wrote to the archbishop asking for another bishop to be consecrated in his place. The archbishop wrote back and allowed another bishop to be selected and sent to him (*DI* i. 223). At the Alþing of 1174 three candidates were named: St Þorlákr, Ögmundr Kálfsson abbot, presumably of Flatey (N) (d. 1188), and Páll Sölvason priest and chieftain in Reykholt (S). Both our sources claim that in the end Bishop Klængr was asked to select one of these three and he chose St Þorlákr (*Bysp* 1. 112; *Bsk* i. 98–9). It was of course unusual that an outgoing bishop was alive to influence the selection of his successor but even if Klængr was allowed complete freedom in his choice it is likely that he was influenced by the political factions in his diocese. And even if St Þorlákr was appointed on merit only, the Oddaverjar clearly interpreted this as a nod in their direction; shortly before Easter 1175 when Bishop Klængr had become too infirm to manage his see St Þorlákr was sent for and on his way from Þykkvibær he was accompanied by Jón Loptsson 'who was then the greatest chieftain in Iceland' (*Bsk* i. 99). To greet them in Skálholt was the chieftain Gizurr Hallsson of the Haukdælir, who became resident at Skálholt towards the end of St Þorlákr's episcopacy (*Sturl* 172; *Bsk* i. 128–9; cf. *Bsk* i. 110–13). The Oddaverjar could not hope to oust the Haukdælir from Skálholt but they could hope to have more influence on the affairs of the diocese if it could be made to look as if Gizurr accepted St Þorlákr from Jón Loptsson.

Bishop Klængr died 28 February 1176 but St Þorlákr did not leave for Norway until the summer of 1177 on account of conflict between Norwegians and Icelanders. When he came to Norway it appears that King Magnús and his father Earl Erlingr opposed his consecration and this can only have been because they considered St Þorlákr as a client of the Icelandic chieftains who had been annoying them (*Bsk* i. 100).[8] St Þorlákr died in 1193 and on his sickbed had given a ring to his nephew Páll, the illegitimate son of Jón Loptsson and Ragnheiðr Þórhallsdóttir (*Bsk* i. 110). This was interpreted, later at least, as a sign of St Þorlákr's will to have Páll succeed him. Páll had studied abroad but was only a deacon and had by the 1190s established himself as a chieftain at Skarð in Land (S). Except for his stint at school in Lincoln there is nothing very religious about Páll Jónsson's early career; he had married young and was like his brothers Sæmundr and Ormr engaged in extending and consolidating their family's grip on Rangárþing. According to *Páls saga*'s version of events, there were long deliberations at the Alþing of 1194 as to who should succeed St Þorlákr in the see of Skálholt. In the end it was decided, 'mostly on the advice of Hallr Gizurarson' of the Haukdælir, that Bishop Brandr should appoint the *electus* and he chose Páll Jónsson. Páll refused and the assembly came to a close before the matter was settled. But when everyone had given up asking him he quickly accepted. After these dramatics Páll rode to Skálholt with his father and brothers and took control of the cathedral establishment (*Bsk* i. 128).[9]

Even if St Þorlákr was not the irritating reformer which *Oddaverja þáttr* makes him out to have been, a greater contrast to him than Páll Jónsson can hardly be imagined. His appointment no doubt reflects the power of the Oddaverjar in the last days of Jón Loptsson. It appears to have been achieved in peace and co-operation with the Haukdælir who had signalled their lack of preference by allowing Bishop Brandr to decide and by Gizurr Hallsson's continuing presence at Skálholt until his death in 1206 (*Bsk* i. 128–9). Gizurr and Jón seem to have got along well and it is likely that the appointments of St Þorlákr and Páll Jónsson reflect a deal between them whereby the Oddaverjar selected the man but the Haukdælir were allowed to influence him behind the scenes.

Gizurr Hallsson was again involved in bishop-making in 1201 but this time with negative results for him, and the collective chieftains of Iceland as it turned out. Bishop Brandr of Hólar had died 6 August 1201 and this time the Alþing in the following June could not be waited for. Instead, a meeting was convened at Vellir in Svarfaðardalur (N) on 1 September, attended by the abbots of Þingeyrar and Þverá, the chieftains of the north as well as Gizurr Hallsson. Two options were discussed: one was the popular miracle-working priest Guðmundr *góði*

[8] It is not clear what this dispute was about, although it is likely it had something to do with the priest Helgi Skaptason's dispute with Norwegian merchants in 1172 and 1175 (*Bsk* i. 418, 419; *IA* 118, 323, 476). This dispute is referred to in Archbishop Eysteinn's first letter to the Icelanders as conflict between the Icelanders and the Norwegian king (*DI* i. 223).

[9] It may be that it was Gizurr Hallsson and not his son who gave this advice. Páll Jónsson was not really the type for extreme modesty of this sort; as it seems highly unusual that people should leave the Alþing without resolving an important matter like selecting a bishop, it may be that *Páls saga*'s version of events is veiling a more bitter conflict in which the Oddaverjar had their way with some last-minute ploy. The modest candidate is of course a topos in hagiographic literature, cf. *HMS* i. 30, 387, 557. I am indebted to Svanhildur Óskarsdóttir for these references.

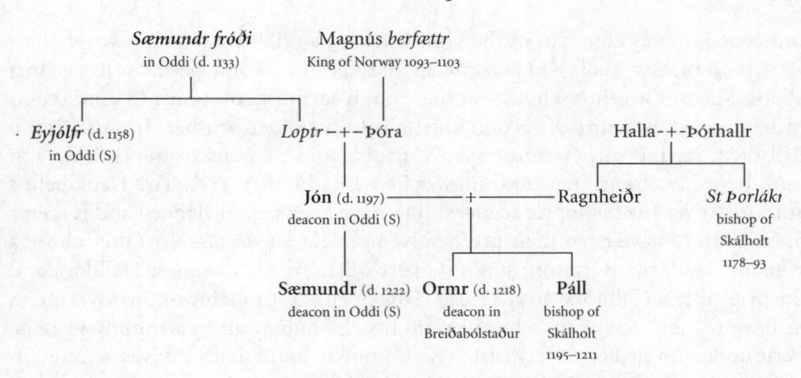

FIGURE 8. *St Þorlákr's relations with the Oddaverjar*

Arason and the other Gizurr Hallsson's son, the priest Magnús. Gizurr argued that his son was better connected and had more experience of financial responsibilities. The northern chieftains however insisted that the bishop should be a northerner and so Guðmundr *góði* was appointed. Guðmundr was himself not present and when he heard he had been appointed he refused and put up an unusually vigorous resistance. Another meeting was convened at Víðimýri (N) on 14 October and this time Kolbeinn Tumason managed to persuade Guðmundr. Having achieved his consent, Kolbeinn and Guðmundr's uncle, the ageing chieftain Þorvarðr Þorgeirsson (d. 1207), immediately rode to Hólar and Kolbeinn assumed control of the cathedral establishment (*Sturl* 202–3). It was however to take several more months before final consent was obtained from the powerful chieftains of the south (*Sturl* 206–7).

Like many bishops before him Guðmundr *góði* was of insignificant parentage but respectable ancestry. His grandfather was a chieftain in Eyjafjörður but the father was a younger son and Guðmundr was the illegitimate product of Ari's love affair with a married woman. When Ari died adventuring in Norway, Guðmundr's paternal kin nevertheless assumed responsibility for him and it was decided that his uncle, the priest Ingimundr, should take care of him and instruct him for the priesthood. Guðmundr had quite a spectacular career as a priest and miracle worker (discussed in more detail in Ch. 5, s. 4) and his popularity and apparent *naïveté* seems to have convinced Kolbeinn Tumason that he would be an ideal bishop. Kolbeinn's family, the Ásbirningar, controlled most of Skagafjörður by 1200 and it was a natural ambition for Kolbeinn to want to control the see in the same way as the Haukdælir controlled the see of Skálholt. If alliance with the politically waning family of Guðmundr could be made as well, and capital made of elevating an immensely popular figure, so much the better. It proved to be a miscalculation which Kolbeinn paid for with his life at the battle of Víðines in 1208, but the strategy is transparent.

Gizurr Hallsson died in 1206 and his son, the priest Þorvaldr in Hruni (S), succeeded him as chieftain of the family. Gizurr's other sons Magnús and Hallr were both priests. Hallr had become lawspeaker in 1203 and was later to become abbot. Magnús was householder at the church-farm Bræðratunga (S) and seems to have acted as a sort of second chieftain to his older brother. In 1211 Bishop Páll died, having earlier summoned Þorvaldr and Magnús to his bedside and told them how to arrange all things as he wished (*Bsk* i. 144). The Haukdælir's authority over the bishopric seems still to have been acknowledged and it seems once again to have been their prerogative to select an *electus*. Now they chose a nephew, one Teitr Bersason, son of Gizurr's illegitimate daughter Halldóra and the priest Bersi Halldórsson (d. 1204). This Bersi was probably of the Mýramenn in Borg (S) and seems to have given up his chieftaincy and patrimony to Bersi Vermundarson in Borg. Very little else is known about Teitr; he was selected in 1212, left for Norway with Þorvaldr Gizurarson a year later, and died abroad in 1214 (*IA* 124, 183, 325; *Sturl* 193, 227, 230). Magnús had moved to Skálholt in 1213, probably as soon as Teitr and Þorvaldr left for Norway, and taken over control of the see. News of Teitr's death arrived in Iceland and Magnús was selected in 1215 and consecrated in 1216 (*IA* 23, 63, 124, 184, 325; *Sturl* 255).

In 1237 both bishops, Guðmundr *góði* and Magnús, died. Both had had stormy episcopacies and were old and frail and arrangements had been made to appoint their successors even before they died. In 1235 Magnús Guðmundarson (d. 1240) had been selected as the next bishop of Skálholt and it was probably in the same year that the men of the north selected the priest Kygri-Björn Hjaltason (d. 1238) (*IA* 65; *Sturl* 382). They sailed together to Norway in 1236 but neither of them were consecrated. Kygri-Björn was a career-priest and scholar of some distinction (see Ch. 5, s. 5) who had been attached to the household of Sighvatr Sturluson in Eyjafjörður and had led the clerical opposition to Bishop Guðmundr. A fourteenth-century source implies that Kygri-Björn was rejected on grounds of illegitimacy (*Bsk* ii. 186). This may well be right (M. M. Lárusson 1967*c*: 56–7) although it is equally likely that the archbishop did not find him acceptable because he was a puppet of the Ásbirningar and Sturlungar and would allow them to continue to control the see of Hólar.

Kygri-Björn may have been an ambiguous choice but he was at least an eminent cleric, although his loyalties may have been open to question. The choice of Magnús Guðmundarson as *electus* to the bishopric of Skálholt on the other hand must indicate that the chieftains of the south were running out of ideas and loyal clerics. Magnús was a chieftain-priest—one of the last of his kind—son of Guðmundr *gríss* Ámundason (d. 1210), chieftain in Þingvellir (S). Magnús was a grandson of Jón Loptsson and therefore closely related to the Oddaverjar and a brother-in-law of both Þorvaldr Gizurarson of the Haukdælir (d. 1235) and Jón Sigmundarson of the Svínfellingar (d. 1212). Magnús had been in the alliance of chieftains who assembled an army and marched on Hólar in 1209 to teach Bishop Guðmundr his place, and in 1216 and 1217 he had struggled with Snorri Sturluson for supremacy over Kjalarnes (*Sturl* 220, 252, 253–4).

Apart from this, and being listed among other noteworthies in two charters and a donation to the house of canons in Viðey (S) (*DI* i. 395, 496, 507), Magnús does not figure in accounts; however these scraps strongly suggest that he was in every way a respectable chieftain who was being overshadowed by his more powerful neighbours in Árnesþing and Borgarfjörður. Magnús is unlikely to have been illegitimate and was not married, as far as can be seen; it is therefore difficult to see any reason for the archbishop to reject him other than that he was a chieftain (cf. M. M. Lárusson 1958*b*: 200).

The archbishop used the opportunity, after having rejected these not over-cautiously appointed bishops-elect, to consecrate Norwegians without consulting the Icelanders. Henceforth the selection of bishops in Iceland was in the hands of the archbishop and the chapter in Niðarós, an arrangement which was to have swift and weighty consequences for the development of the Icelandic church.

The sources usually talk of election (*kjør*; *kosning*) of the bishops before they were sent for consecration but whether the selection process had anything to do with the requirements of canon law, and whether distinction was made between *electio* and *postulatio,* cannot be said with any degree of certainty (cf. M. M. Lárusson 1967*c*: 53; Gallén 1956*f*: 612–15).[10] It is possible that in the twelfth century there was in place a procedure of elimination, whereby the men of each of the three quarters which made up the diocese of Skálholt proposed a candidate. This would appear from *Þorláks saga*'s information that in 1174 the choice boiled down to Abbot Þorlákr (eastern quarter), the priest Páll Sölvason (southern quarter), and Abbot Ögmundr (western quarter) (*Bsk* i. 98). The author of *Þorgils saga ok Hafliða* seems to be referring to an arrangement of this kind when he says of Guðmundr Brandsson from Hjarðarholt (D) that he was 'most often named, other than Klængr, when there were to be episcopal elections in the Western quarter' in 1151 (*Sturl* 32).

What we can say is that in the second half of the twelfth century some kind of public deliberations took place and that the reigning bishop always seems to have had the last word. Whether his word was decisive or whether it was just the formal confirmation of an already achieved consensus cannot be discerned; it probably varied. When Guðmundr *góði* had been appointed by the northerners in 1202, he wrote to Bishop Páll asking him to support or reject. Páll wrote to Sæmundr, his brother and chieftain of his family, and asked him what to do. Sæmundr replied:

> You know brother that Guðmundr *electus* has not been a great friend in our dispute with Sigurðr [Ormsson]. But he is greatly acclaimed by men and it is likely that he has been elected because it is God's will. I have heard that he is suitable for many reasons, on account of his benevolence and virtue and asceticism which is most important. But if there is more to it, then [by rejecting him] you lift the responsibility for their choice off

[10] For a thorough treatment of episcopal selection in Norway see Joys 1948.

the backs of the northerners. But it is my counsel that you give him your vote rather than reject him because it is uncertain who is more likely to please God than this one and it is best to bet on the favourite. It is uncertain that anyone can be found who is above criticism. The northerners acted on their own in their election so let them take the responsibility for the consequences. (*Sturl* 206)[11]

Páll then summoned Sigurðr Ormsson and the Haukdælir brothers and announced that he had been asked to decide and that he had decided to support Guðmundr. The chieftains seem to have indicated their assent and from this point the coast was clear for Guðmundr to become bishop.

Sæmundr indicates that he thought it was irregular that the northerners had made up their minds unilaterally, although he also makes it clear that he thought it was their problem to decide on their bishop. It is unlikely that Sæmundr was more than a child when the previous bishop of Hólar had been selected in 1163 so his opinion may have been based as much on his sense of political propriety as any knowledge of earlier practice. Sæmundr clearly had his reservations about Guðmundr *góði* but it is also apparent that he prized consensus more highly than fighting for optimal results for himself. The Oddaverjar were not, any more than the Haukdælir, in a position to force their choice upon the northerners once these had united and Sæmundr apparently saw no political mileage in making a dispute of the issue.

Whether they did it at the Alþing or not, it seems that apart from St Jón all the bishops of Hólar were selected by the northerners; Bishops Ketill, Björn, and Brandr were all of northern chieftain families, although Brandr's paternal family came from the south. It seems therefore always to have been *de facto* the decision of the northern chieftains to choose their bishop, although they may have showed deference to their southern counterparts, and the bishop of Skálholt, in allowing them to take part in the decision-making process.

As to the bishops of Skálholt, it is likely that the appointments of Ísleifr, Gizurr, and Þorlákr were entirely in the hands of the Haukdælir. It is possible that the appointment of Magnús Einarsson represents an attempt by other families, the Reykhyltingar and Síðumenn, to gain influence over the see but there are no indications that this was in conflict with the interests of the Haukdælir. It is likely, however, that as the twelfth century wore on the Haukdælir had to allow other families greater access to the bishops and the see; if this was a problem they seem to have solved it by making an alliance with the Oddaverjar. If Bishop Klængr was not the Haukdælir's preferred option they seem to have adapted to this and found that it was possible and in many ways advantageous to have someone else as bishop while retaining virtual control over the see by simply being always present. This may not have worked entirely satisfactorily in Bishop Klængr's episcopacy; towards the end of his life the see was in serious financial trouble and both *Hungrvaka* and *Þorláks saga* claim that in the autumn of 1174 no offerings reached the see (*Bysp* 1. 113; *Bsk* i. 99), which

[11] I am grateful to Peter Foote for help on this translation.

suggests that they were being withheld. Klængr had been extravagant in his spending of the see's revenues (*Bysp* 1. 107–8, 109–10) and it may be that the Haukdælir had not been able to control him, because as soon as he became infirm they intervened and froze all assets, in order to curb his spending. St Þorlákr seems to have owed his elevation in part to having a reputation as a prudent manager, but it is primarily a sign of an alliance between the Haukdælir and the Oddaverjar. These neighbouring families had come to dominate the southern flatlands by the second half of the twelfth century and it is possible that the more powerful Haukdælir had supported the Oddaverjar against their rivals in Rangárþing. Together they made up a formidable alliance which will have been near impossible to challenge. The Haukdælir thus retained their influence over the see but allowed the Oddaverjar to select the bishops. The political clout of the Oddaverjar diminished after Jón Loptsson's death in 1197 and this is reflected in the appointments of the Haukdælir Teitr Bersason and Magnús Gizurarson after Bishop Páll's death in 1211. There are, however, no indications that they were selected in the face of opposition from the Oddaverjar and it is in fact unlikely that by this date the Haukdælir could have appointed anyone without the Oddaverjar's help. The increasing competition and rise of other families to national importance is reflected in the selection in 1235 of Magnús Guðmundarson, a prestigious if peripheral chieftain, a perfect compromise between the Haukdælir and the Sturlungar.

There are interesting differences in the types of bishops selected for the two dioceses; all the northern bishops down to Guðmundr *góði* were of chieftainly rank, if they were not chieftains themselves, and only Bishop Björn was not a family man. This contrasts with the four bishops of Skálholt in the period 1122 to 1195 who were all—with the possible exception of Bishop Magnús—of insignificant parentage and did not have wives or legitimate children. Around 1200 this pattern was reversed; an ascetic was appointed to the see of Hólar in 1202 while chieftains with their own families ruled in Skálholt between 1195 and 1237.

It was argued at the beginning of this chapter that by the time of Bishop Gizurr the chieftains of the south no longer saw it as advantageous to be bishops themselves and preferred to have as bishops controllable protégés. This naturally implies that the Haukdælir had complete control over the see of Skálholt and were even able to retain this control when outsiders became bishops. In the last quarter of the twelfth century the Haukdælir had to acknowledge the influence of the Oddaverjar but they continued to hold all the reins by allying with their neighbours rather than competing with them, an arrangement no doubt advantageous to the rising Oddaverjar.

In the north on the other hand the fact that different chieftain-families had representatives at Hólar suggests that there was in Skagafjörður no single family with absolute control over the region such as the Haukdælir had in Árnesþing. The bishops of the north seem to have been selected because they were the best candidates from families who were influential but unlikely to use their control of the bishopric to menace others. Ketill Þorsteinsson was clearly a chieftain, and possibly his son too, although their branch of the Möðruvellingar did not reassert itself. Bishop Björn seems to have been the last of a family of waning power centred on the important estate Þverá (N); if Bishop Brandr was not a chieftain when he became bishop, he certainly seems to have done everything in his power to consolidate the position of his family, the Reynistaðarmenn. It was through no fault of his that the Reynistaðarmenn had become overshadowed by the Ásbirningar by 1200. It is traditionally accepted that the Ásbirningar reigned supreme in Skagafjörður for much of the twelfth century (J. Jóhannesson 1956: 279; G. Karlsson 1975: 34; J. V. Sigurðsson 1989: 51, 60–1), but while it is likely that they were among the most influential families in the region there is little reason to assign pre-eminence to them until the close of the twelfth century. Kolbeinn Tumason may have pretended that he had no preference (*Sturl* 202) but it is clear that the selection of Guðmundr *góði* reflects Kolbeinn's absolute control over Skagafjörður and prominence in the northern quarter (*Sturl* 195). Kolbeinn clearly thought that he would be able to have full control of the bishopric and the ascetic Guðmundr would be content to leave all worldly matters to him.

Kolbeinn's miscalculation on this score reflects a growing awareness at least among aristocratic clerics that the clergy had an identity and agenda of their own (see Ch. 5, s. 5); it may be that the opposite development in the diocese of Skálholt where chieftains occupied the see from 1195 reflects the southern chieftains' caution in this matter. The answer depends on the relevance we attach to the reforms of St Þorlákr and the problems they caused for the chieftains.

The reason why men like Páll Jónsson and Magnús Gizurarson became bishops may, however, be less conspiratorial. Although both were chieftains neither was the leader of his family. Both were younger sons—and Páll was illegitimate—who could not expect to supplant their brothers or promote their own sons as leaders of their families. It may therefore simply be a coincidence that men of this sort needed respectable posts in 1194 and 1215. Another possible factor is that the sees had been accumulating wealth throughout the twelfth century and it may be that by the close of that century the see of Skálholt had become so rich and controlled so much land that the chieftains of the southern flatlands did not care to take any chances with the management and therefore took it into their own hands. That this was a major concern is reflected in *Hungrvaka,* which stresses the importance of prudent management of episcopal finances, and in the chieftains' persecution of Bishop Guðmundr on account of his liberal attitude to money.

2. BISHOPS AND CHIEFTANS

For the early bishops of Skálholt down to the episcopacy of Klængr (1152–76) *Hungrvaka* is virtually our only source. In the context of the bishops' political power this source therefore requires special consideration. We have already seen how the author of *Hungrvaka* depicted Bishop Gizurr as the perfect bishop (Ch. 2, s. 1). Bishop Þorlákr Rúnólfsson (1118–33) cuts a very different figure. According to the annals, his episcopate saw a series of conflicts. This is reflected in *Hungrvaka*, where it says that 'Many chieftains were difficult to Bishop Þorlákr because of their disobedience, but some because of their unrighteousness and lawbreaking, but he managed everything as well as possible' (*Bysp* 1. 98). This is hardly flattering, and the author of *Hungrvaka* concentrates on other aspects of Þorlákr's episcopate, his teaching and financial prudence, the writing of the Christian law section which he instigated with Bishop Ketill of Hólar, but mainly his devoutness and humility, giving the impression that Þorlákr was not a very forceful personality (*Bysp* 1. 93–8). It is interesting that *Hungrvaka*'s description of Bishop Þorlákr in many ways resembles Gunnlaugr's description of St Jón, that is, they were both models of spiritual virtue rather than statesmen. The difference is that this was Gunnlaugr's ideal while the author of *Hungrvaka* is respectful but reserves his admiration for a very different kind of bishop.

Bishop Magnús Einarsson (1134–48) was a much more imposing character according to the author of *Hungrvaka*. He distinguished himself in conciliation even before he became bishop; he 'always reconciled all men where he was present at [court] cases, and spared neither his words nor his wealth'. After being consecrated in Denmark he was just off the ship when he made a dramatic entry at the Alþing: 'the court was in session and there was a disagreement concerning some case or other. Then a man came to the court and said that Bishop Magnús was riding to the assembly. But the men were so glad to hear this news that they all went home [i.e. to their booths] promptly.' The reader is left to assume that Magnús's presence was in itself enough for peace to be made: disputes simply evaporated wherever he went. This is emphasized even more strongly:

> It was soon apparent what an excellent man he was in his magnanimity and [good] management of his own and others' matters, in that he never spared wealth while he was bishop to reconcile those who had earlier been at odds, and gave all the time of his own [wealth] to make up the difference when terms could not be agreed on, and therefore no conflicts occurred between men while Magnús was bishop. (*Bysp* 1. 99–101)

It is significant that the other aspect of Magnús's episcopate which the author of *Hungrvaka* emphasizes is his attention to the financial health of the see and the grandeur of the cathedral. Among the assets Magnús secured for the see were Vestmannaeyjar, which, if not already by this time, were later one of Iceland's most important fishing stations. We are told that Magnús intended to found a monastery there but did not live to realize this intention (*Bysp* 1. 101–2).

Here we have what was to the author of *Hungrvaka* probably the ideal bishop. Bishop Magnús was not only committed to peace, he also had the means to make it. He sought to strengthen the see's financial position and enhance its prestige, in order that the Church's power to make and maintain the peace would be secured for coming generations. That this is what Bishop Magnús did is of course only the author's interpretation which we have no means of verifying. What is significant is that this is a role the author of *Hungrvaka* was keen to see the Church have. We cannot know how consciously or clearly the author of *Hungrvaka* and his contemporaries were thinking about this. For instance, there is no way of showing that the author of *Hungrvaka* wanted the Church to grow in power at the expense of the secular chieftains—he probably would not even have liked the idea. Although it may seem like a contradiction to us, the author of *Hungrvaka* wanted at the same time to preserve whatever it was he perceived as the existing order and to increase the power and prestige of the Church. To him that probably meant the strengthening of the existing order and not any call for supremacy by the Church.

Klængr Þorsteinsson (1152–76) is the last bishop treated in *Hungrvaka* and the description of his episcopate is clearly affected by its being much closer in time to the author. The description of Klængr's political involvement is much more realistic than those of his predecessors:

> Bishop Klængr was such a great advocate when he was asked for help, that he was a great chieftain both because of wisdom and rhetoric; he also had considerable knowledge of the laws of the country. Because of that, those chieftains who had the support of the bishop [always] won their cases. And there was not an arbitration on major issues for which Bishop Klængr was not selected (*Bysp* 1. 109)

The author goes on to say that his most trusted friends were the chieftains Jón Loptsson and Gizurr Hallsson, who were probably the two most powerful chieftains in Iceland in the latter half of the twelfth century. Here we have a very different type of conciliation; Bishop Klængr took sides. He used his skill and position to support some chieftains against others and we are not told what his motives were. We are not even told how Klængr's involvement affected the peace and we can only guess whether the author of *Hungrvaka* saw this as conciliation at all or only as a different type of conciliation from that of Bishops Gizurr and Magnús. The latter seems more likely though. The author is all admiration for Klængr's involvement in political conflict and this is the way he would have realistically wanted the bishops of his own day to behave. When it comes to the gritty details of everyday politics conciliation ceases to be a simple issue.

Hungrvaka's descriptions of conciliation under the bishops up to Klængr are probably based on little more than the author's vague perceptions of the extent of unrest in each period. Knowing that there was considerable unrest during

Bishop Þorlákr's episcopate—many conflicts are recorded in the annals[12]—he attributed to him modest success in peacekeeping. Knowing of little unrest during Bishop Magnús's episcopate—there is rather less sign of unrest in the annals[13]—the author interpreted that as the bishop's doing. With Bishops Klængr in Skálholt and Brandr Sæmundarson in Hólar (1163–1201), we begin to have other sources which give a more balanced picture of the bishops' involvement in politics.

In 1160 the friends of Sturla Þórðarson in Hvammur and Einarr Þorgilsson in Staðarhóll decided to try and put a stop to their conflict, which was getting increasingly vicious. They asked Bishop Klængr to arbitrate and in the end both Sturla and Einarr agreed to this. Sturla did however make the condition that Klængr swear a *fimmtardómseiðr*, the strongest form of oath (*Grg III*, s.v. *eiðr*), that his verdict was fair. After Klængr had given his verdict whereby Sturla only got a little more than Einarr and had sworn his oath Sturla remarked: 'I respect the bishop's oath like Easter mass and it is an honour for us. But most will call the payments small and the settlement unprofitable' (*Sturl* 63).

It may be that Klængr was asked to arbitrate because his being bishop was meant to guarantee his impartiality but it is clear that Sturla did not have much faith in this. He was no doubt justified: Klængr and Einarr were second cousins and Klængr may have had his affair with Einarr's sister by this time.[14] Ten years later Sturla and Einarr were still at loggerheads and this time the chieftains of the country split into two camps, the one supporting Einarr led by Bishop Klængr and the other supporting Sturla led by Bishop Brandr, his first cousin once removed. Here blood-relations seem to have decided alliance. This time all mediation failed and each prosecuted and convicted the other at the Alþing. Before the Alþing was adjourned it was however agreed that it was too dangerous to let matters stand thus and a settlement was reached whereby Bishop Klængr and Sturla's father-in-law Böðvarr Þórðarson in Garðar (S) were to arbitrate. True to form Sturla was unhappy about their verdict and the conflict continued unabated (*Sturl* 73–4).

This is all we know of Bishop Klængr's involvement in secular politics and although this is not much to build on it seems that the role Klængr was playing out was identical to the one in which we find extremely powerful chieftains like Jón Loptsson. Their role was defined by their exalted position, by being too powerful to be interested in gaining anything but prestige from other people's conflicts. It was clearly not unbecoming for the bishops to take sides according

[12] Conflicts of varying degrees are mentioned in 1118, 1120, 1123, 1124, 1125, 1127, 1128, and 1129—i.e. in eight years of Þorlákr's fifteen-year episcopate. Based on *Annales regii*, *IA* 112–13.

[13] Killings and one robbery are mentioned in 1136, 1138, 1140, 1143, and 1146—i.e. in five years of Magnús's fourteen-year episcopate. Based on *Annales regii*, *IA* 113–14.

[14] Two years earlier Klængr had supervised an ordeal where the chieftain Þorvarðr Þorgeirsson cleared himself of being the father of Yngvildr Þorgilsdóttir's child. Einarr, Yngvildr's brother, had brought the accusation and Klængr made him pay a compensation (*Sturl* 60–1). It is tempting to assume that Klængr and Yngvildr met on this occasion and that thenceforth Klængr supported Einarr, possibly in return for Einarr not making an issue of the bishop's affair.

to their familial relations but they were probably expected to advocate peaceful settlement and an end to conflicts within their party. In this they were no different from chieftains who had absolute control of their areas and did not need to pick quarrels with their neighbours in order to retain the support and respect of their own *þingmenn*.

The basis of the bishops' power was of course in reality different from that of the chieftains but it was natural for them to assume as their role-model the ideal chieftain. This idea of the bishop as the ideal chieftain is particularly transparent in *Hungrvaka* and *Páls saga* but we can also see it at work in the career of Bishop Brandr of Hólar who is the only twelfth-century bishop for whose involvement in politics we have relatively detailed descriptions.

After Bishop Brandr had aided Sturla in 1170 we hear nothing of his involvement in politics until 1180 when Sturla had finally got Einarr out of the way and had begun to encroach on chieftains in other regions. This time his adversary was the priest Páll Sölvason in Reykholt (S), whose wife was the sister of Bishop Brandr's wife. Páll's daughter was married to the northern chieftain Guðmundr *dýri* and Guðmundr and Brandr brought a large force to Páll's aid in the early spring of 1180 (*Sturl* 93). There was however no fighting and the dispute remained unsolved for another year. At the Alþing of 1181 Sturla learnt that Bishop Brandr had appealed to Jón Loptsson to support Páll with all his might. On hearing this Sturla gave in and publicly announced that he would reconcile himself to Jón's arbitration (*Sturl* 98).

In 1183 a conflict erupted in Húnaþing among the Húnröðlingar. The issues and personalities are obscure but Bishop Brandr and his son Þorgeirr came down heavily on the side of Þórðr Ívarsson in Þorkelshvoll (N) and brought a force to his aid in the summer of 1184 after he had successfully prosecuted his adversary Jón Húnröðarson. The intimidation was successful and the issue was submitted to Bishop Brandr's arbitration (*Sturl* 116). Brandr's son Þorgeirr had been married in 1179 to a daughter of the chieftain Þorvarðr Þorgeirsson and was a householder at Staður in Reynines (N) (*Sturl* 109, 116–17). He seems to have been establishing himself as a chieftain in Skagafjörður but he died in 1186 (*Sturl* 118).

In 1187 trouble arose in Fljót (N); a group of thugs pillaged in the area and were sheltered by the householder Björn Gestsson in Sandur in Ólafsfjörður (N). The chieftain of Fljót, the priest Jón Ketilsson (d. 1192), had an estate at Holt in Fljót but lived at Hólar. Two householders from Fljót sought him out there and asked him to help them out. Jón turned to Brandr for advice and the bishop told him that it was advisable to rid the countryside of sinister characters like Björn. Jón and his followers then went to Ólafsfjörður and killed Björn, incurring the wrath of his chieftain Önundr Þorkelsson as a result. A revenge killing ensued and Jón quickly found that he was no match for Önundr. Again he sought the advice of Bishop Brandr who told him to seek the help of the chieftain Guðmundr *dýri*. Guðmundr however refused to help Jón and, faced with a complete loss of honour, he gave his *goðorð* to Guðmundr (*Sturl* 129–30).

It is impossible to know whether Brandr had foreseen this outcome but considering his vested interests in the region and that Guðmundr *dýri* was Bishop Brandr's first cousin once removed it is likely that his involvement was coloured more by his own political interests rather than any ecclesiastical agenda.

In 1191 one Sumarliði, a major householder at the church-farm Tjörn in Svarfaðardalur (N), was killed by his neighbour's son. The killer got away and one of the men who aided him was the subdeacon Snorri Grímsson from Hof in Höfðaströnd (N) (d. 1208). Snorri's father, Grímr Snorrason (d. 1196), seems to have been a minor chieftain and they had asked Sumarliði for his sister's hand in marriage for Snorri. He had rejected their offer and Snorri seems to have been offended by this. Sumarliði was a *þingmaðr* and relative of Guðmundr *dýri* and he prosecuted Snorri for conspiracy to kill and aiding and abetting. According to *Guðmundar saga dýra* Snorri paid a heavy fine and was outlawed from Skagafjörður and went to Oddi (*Sturl* 135–7). This may have been a settlement because *Prestssaga Guðmundar Arasonar* claims that Bishop Brandr supported the prosecution of Snorri and had intended to make a panel declare that Snorri was guilty of conspiracy to kill and of aiding and abetting, but Guðmundr Arason and other supporters of Snorri persuaded Bishop Þorlákr to have a panel declare Snorri's innocence (Sturl, 172). Guðmundr *góði* was Snorri's first cousin and had been a district priest at his father's household at Hof in 1185–7. Snorri and Bishop Brandr may have been third cousins but Brandr seems to have once again chosen to support Guðmundr *dýri*. St Þorlákr's involvement in this affair is interesting; it is the only known instance where he influenced court proceedings but our sources are unfortunately not clear enough for us to appreciate what his motives were.

In 1197 when Guðmundr *dýri* had burnt Önundr Þorkelsson in his farmstead both bishops joined Jón Loptsson in seeking a settlement and in the end it was agreed that Jón was to arbitrate (*Sturl* 154). The following year when the truce had broken down and Guðmundr *dýri* and his adversaries led by Þorgrímr *alikarl* were poised to fight in Svarfaðardalur (N), Brandr came and urged them to break up their garrisons. He even persuaded Þorgrímr to leave the region altogether and violent conflict was thus avoided for the time being (*Sturl* 161). While this looks like a peacemaking mission it was hardly a coincidence that it was Guðmundr *dýri*'s enemy who had to give ground.

Shortly after 1190 Bishop Brandr had taken control of the church-farm Vellir in Svarfaðardalur (N). The owner had died and in the bishop's opinion his sons were not capable to take over. By the year 1200 the heirs thought they were old enough and asked the caretaker, whom Brandr had appointed, to give up the *staðr*. He refused and skirmishes ensued until the heirs enlisted the help of the chieftain Ögmundr *sneis*. Under his command they occupied the farmstead and prepared for battle by fortifying the churchyard. Bishop Brandr on the other side was not prepared to give up this important church-farm and assembled a force from as far afield as Húnaþing. This force marched on Vellir under the command of Brandr's grandson Kolbeinn Arnórsson and one Hafr Brandsson, who may have been the bishop's son. It did not come to any fighting, however, and in the end Brandr's army retreated and Guðmundr *dýri* intervened, removing the heirs from Vellir. He then made a deal with Brandr whereby a new caretaker was appointed and the heirs were promised control of Vellir after that man's death (*Sturl* 173–5).

It is questionable to what extent the accepted church law of the time was behind Brandr in this case; the *staðr* at Vellir was church property and seems to have come under the control of the bishops of Hólar. It seems more likely that the control had somehow passed to the bishop in this particular case, just as it could have passed to a secular chieftain, rather than that Brandr was fighting a battle over a newly introduced principle. His methods were anyway those of any well-connected chieftain, enlisting the help of friends and relatives to mount expeditions and ensuring success by intimidation and even force if needed. This kind of episcopal authority depended on the bishop being a part of the secular power structure, maintaining strong ties with a power base built on familial relations. Brandr's family may have owned a *goðorð*—it is likely to have been among those which Brandr's great-grandson Brandr Kolbeinsson owned (*Sturl* 531)—and it possessed one of the largest estates in the country at Staður in Reynines. It was as a major chieftain in Skagafjörður that Brandr became bishop. To what extent he was effective as a bishop is a difficult question; the visible consequences of his policies are mainly the dramatic rise of Guðmundr *dýri* as the dominant chieftain in Eyjafjörður and it may be that he delayed the rise of Kolbeinn Tumason as the dominant chieftain in Skagafjörður until after 1200. We lack the source material to evaluate Brandr's influence on the development of the Church but as his forceful stance in the matter of the control of Vellir suggests he promoted what he considered as its rights vigorously, if not in an entirely orthodox manner.

Bishop Brandr was no doubt the last of his kind. While Bishops Páll and Magnús of Skálholt were both chieftains they were probably better acquainted with ideas on the different stature and behaviour required of church dignitaries. Bishop Páll had not been averse to using his status as bishop to take an almost sinister part in his brother's humiliation of Sigurðr Ormsson chieftain of the Svínfellingar in 1200 (*Sturl* 189–90), but after Guðmundr *góði* became bishop of Hólar in 1203 and started to insist on every possible kind of liberty for the Church, it was no longer possible to be seen to side openly with the secular powers. *Páls saga*'s irritation on this score is the best evidence we have regarding the effect Guðmundr's ideas had on the *ancien régime* in the Icelandic Church. Although Bishop Guðmundr represents a watershed in the development of the church in Iceland, change had long been in the air; it is to the matter of reform of the Church we now turn.

3. REFORM AND REACTION

In 1153 a new archdiocese was created for Norway and the colonies in the Atlantic with a metropolitan in Niðarós. In the following decades the Norwegian church embarked upon a serious programme of reform, gaining a number of privileges from King Magnús Erlingsson (1164–84) but running into serious confrontation with King Sverrir (1185–1202) (Bagge 1981, 1989*a*; Bjørkvik 1970*a*; Bugge 1916*b*; Bull 1915; Gunnes 1970*a*, 1970*b*, 1971, 1974*a*; Helle 1964: 27–32; 1988; Holmsen 1965; Holtzmann 1938; Johnsen 1945*a*, 1951*a*, 1951*b*; 1967; Joys 1948: 136–89; Kolsrud 1937–40, 1940–3; 1958: 186–202; Skånland 1969). There is no sign of any of these currents reaching Iceland until the 1170s. Bishop Brandr was the first Icelandic bishop to be consecrated in Niðarós, in 1163, but there are no indications that the great reformer Archbishop Eysteinn Erlendsson (1161–88) used the opportunity to influence the new bishop of Hólar. It was not until Bishop Klængr had become burdened by old age in the early 1170s that the archbishop of Niðarós began to make his authority felt in Iceland. In response to Klængr's plea to be relieved of his duties Archbishop Eysteinn wrote a letter to the bishops of Iceland, all other dignitaries, and the whole people, most likely in 1173. He started by reminding the Icelanders of his authority—an indication that this was indeed the first time he had written to Iceland—and then went on to denounce those who killed or maimed clerics and those who led promiscuous lives. He ostracized clerics who had killed and forbade all clerics to involve themselves in litigation except on behalf of destitute relatives (*DI* i. 221–3). Promiscuity and the privileges of clerical status (*privilegium canonis*) as well as ecclesiastical jurisdiction over clerics (*privilegium fori*) were the issues on which the Church was to fight in the following decades (J. Jóhannesson 1956: 220–4; Grímsdóttir 1982; Rafnsson 1982*b*).

There is no doubt that St Þorlákr (1178–93) was the first Icelandic bishop to advocate the reform policies of the Norwegian archbishops. The question is which policies he emphasized. As I have already discussed (Ch. 3, s. 4), his claims to church property have been misunderstood. While he did call for a recognition of the Church's authority over ecclesiastical property by church-owners, this was a much less dramatic affair than the author of *Oddaverja þáttr* liked to imagine and was probably not as significant as St Þorlákr's main interests.

The A version of *Þorláks saga helga* is far from specific in its account of St Þorlákr's reforms. It speaks in general terms of the saint's efforts to keep his flock on the straight and narrow path, people's disobedience, and his discipline (*Bsk* i. 105–7). In similarly general terms it mentions his guidance to the clergy and how he favoured clerics who 'lived virtuously and preserved their holy orders as appropriate' and 'those who were less virtuous and preserved their holy orders carelessly he gently admonished to do better and change their ways' (*Bsk* i. 102). The only issues the saga identifies as special interests of St Þorlákr are marriage and adultery. He 'put great emphasis on holding those together who were joined in holy matrimony, and punished those severely who fell short with fines and penances' (*Bsk* i. 106) and 'broke up all those unions in his days which he knew to be illegally joined, whether greater or lesser men were involved' (*Bsk* i. 107). And on St Þorlákr's tactics we are informed that

> 'he was not entirely of one mind with some men and chieftains because he only sanctioned that which was proper in their actions. It was in his opinion a greater lapse of holy Christianity if noble men got away with grave things. He saw no reason to think that those who already had great good fortune from God in both wealth and prestige should have more indulgence for not refraining from disobedient acts. (*Bsk* i. 107)[15]

Phraseology of this sort is the stuff of hagiographies but it is significant that the author chose to highlight the reforming aspect of St Þorlákr's sanctity and that he draws attention to the saint's particular interest in enforcing church law on incest.

This general impression given by the A version of *Þorláks saga* is supported by other evidence. One of two letters Archbishop Eysteinn sent to Iceland after St Þorlákr became bishop, datable to 1179–88, seems to be written on request after St Þorlákr had managed to have some law accepted but feared that it would not survive the procedure whereby new laws only became permanent laws if they were announced at three consecutive Alþings (*Grg 1a*, 37).[16] The archbishop explains in his letter that he had received letters from Bishop Þorlákr where he reported that he had advocated 'God's commands' for the Icelanders as the archbishop had instructed him. The Icelanders had been positive and Þorlákr had expressed his optimism that God's glory was definitely on the increase in Iceland. There were, however, those who had grumbled over novelties replacing age-old custom and to these the archbishop pointed out that with that sort of attitude they would never have accepted Christianity in the first place. The thrust of the archbishop's argument is on the different nature of church law. St Þorlákr's 'novelties' seem to have been accepted like any other law and may have been in danger of not surviving the three-year trial period. The archbishop pointed out that church law was God's law and as a consequence not equivalent to ordinary secular law. It was therefore to be accepted without reservation and for perpetuity and was not to be subject to any trials by human beings (*DI* i. 259–60). It is not apparent that this important distinction made any headway among Icelandic legislators until the latter part of the thirteenth century.

The only laws St Þorlákr is known to have initiated are stricter rules on fasting and the inclusion of the feast days of St Ambrose, St Cecilia, and St Agnes in the calendar of the Icelandic church at the expense of two days in the week after Whitsun (*Sturl* 109; *Bsk* i. 106; *Grg 1b*, 250–1; *Grg III*, 79). The B version also

[15] I am indebted to Peter Foote for help with this translation.
[16] On this see *Grg III*, s.v. *nýmæli*; Kjartansson 1986*b*: 7–9.

claims he changed rules regarding confession but it is unlikely that these had the force of law (*Bsk* i. 277).

It was probably not this sort of legislation which the archbishop was referring to, although stricter fasting may of course have encountered opposition. In another, possibly earlier letter, datable to 1179–81 the archbishop specifically addressed the chieftains Jón Loptsson and Gizurr Hallsson and admonished them for the promiscuity which was condoned in Iceland. He accuses them of being involved in sinful unions and asks them how the populace can be persuaded to improve if the chieftains' example is so wicked. After briefly referring to the unacceptability of clerics bearing arms he appeals to the chieftains to support the discipline of the bishops over the masses. He asks them to see to it that an arrangement is made so that the bishops can impose fines for moral offences (*at sekter se settar til biskupa soknar vm kristne spell. þa hefer hann handa festing til hegningar*) (*DI* i. 262–4). Exactly which offences these were is not transparent, but the context suggests that the archbishop was referring to sexual and marital offences in particular, although his words may be interpreted as a claim to a separate jurisdiction in all matters which the Church considered within its domain.

It was a long time before the Church achieved that goal and there are no clear indications that St Þorlákr campaigned openly for a separate jurisdiction. There is, on the other hand, good evidence that he worked hard to establish the Church's authority over marital and sexual matters. According to an annalistic clause in *Prestssaga Guðmundar* St Þorlákr forbade in 1183 a marriage between Þórðr Böðvarsson from Garðar (S) and Snælaug Högnadóttir from Bær (S) because there were two impediments to their union. He forbade the union 'with such strength of God that he went to the Law rock with his clerics and took oaths that this union was contrary to the law of God. He then named witnesses and dissolved the marriage and excommunicated everyone who had been involved (*Sturl* 115–16).

Oddaverja þáttr contains a much fuller account of this dispute and adds that after a long struggle the couple and their kinsmen finally agreed to the dissolution of the marriage and were absolved by St Þorlákr (*Bsk* i. 284–8). *Oddaverja þáttr* has two further stories of St Þorlákr's chastisement of chieftains. Sveinn, son of Sturla in Hvammur, had taken as a concubine a relative of his wife and Jón Loptsson himself had as a concubine St Þorlákr's sister. It is not disclosed whether Sveinn ever relented but Jón gave in after a long and dramatic dispute (*Bsk* i. 288–93). It is likely that these stories are in essence true. Jón's relationship with St Þorlákr's sister is attested in other sources (*Sturl* 46) and Sveinn was clearly an indefatigable womanizer (*Sturl* 90, 109). It is, however, probably not a coincidence that the three stories represent the three main manifestations of promiscuity: incestuous marriage, illicit sexual union on account of affinity, and concubinage.

That promiscuity weighed heavily on St Þorlákr's mind appears furthermore from his penitential where sexual offences of every description figure prominently (*DI* i. 240–4; cf. *Bsk* i. 277).[17] He seems to have been campaigning for improved morals for most of his episcopacy; in one of two letters Archbishop Eiríkr Ívarsson (1189–1205) sent to Bishops Þorlákr and Brandr, datable to 1189–93, he sets out in considerable detail rules on bigamy, incest, fornication, affinity, divorce, defective spouses, betrothal and the woman's assent, elopement, and inability to consummate a marriage. In this letter the archbishop also repeats his predecessor's rules; forbidding clerics to bear arms and instructing them not to become involved in litigation on behalf of other than their needy relatives. He also told the bishops to chastise disobedient clerics with excommunication and, if that did not work, anathema. Just as the archbishop's long treatment of various aspects of promiscuity seems to answer questions the Icelandic bishops had posed to him, so this ruling on chastisement of clerics seems to be a response to a query. That suggests that the Icelandic bishops were also trying to assert their authority over their clergy.

The other letter Archbishop Eiríkr sent to Bishops Þorlákr and Brandr informs them of decisions taken at a synod held in May 1190 and reasserts earlier decrees on clerical immunity and the ban on bearing arms and involvement in litigation. In this letter the archbishop adds a new rule: it was henceforth forbidden to ordain men who were in positions of secular authority and held *goðorð* (*DI* i. 290–1).

The evidence assembled here suggests that St Þorlákr was an active promoter of the reform programme of the Norwegian archbishops in Iceland, but that he put particular emphasis on marital reform. There is no independent evidence that he campaigned against clerics bearing arms; *Sturlu saga*'s account that he advised the priest Páll Sölvason to take up arms and defend himself against his adversaries is probably not an accurate reflection of his stance on the issue (*Sturl* 97–8) and he may well have enjoined his clergy to put their arms aside. It is however perfectly clear that, if he did, success was not immediate and as we shall see in Chapter 5, section 5, clerics were actively involved in armed conflict well into the thirteenth century. The same is true of clerical involvement in litigation; as long as ordained chieftains existed, priests continued to be a common sight in the secular courts. As to the rule banning the holders of *goðorð* from being ordained it does not seem to have been broken much and excuses may have been found for priests like Ketill Þorláksson (d. 1273) of the Hítdælir, who probably owned a *goðorð*, although they may not have controlled it. As discussed in Chapter 5, section 1, there were other reasons why the ordinations of chieftains decreased in the second half of the twelfth century. The archbishop was outlawing a practice which was already becoming outdated.

While this first wave of reform was not immediately successful in establishing the clear distinctions between secular and ordained of which its protagonists dreamt, it did sow the seeds for the growing sense of a shared identity which

[17] An English translation of the bulk of the text is found in McNeill and Gamer 1938: 355–7. See further Rafnsson 1982*a*; 1982*b*; 1985*a*.

became apparent among high-born clerics in the first half of the thirteenth century (see Ch. 5, s. 5). St Þorlákr does, however, seem to have had a remarkable influence in the field of sexual and marital regulation. There is no reason to suppose that such regulation had not been enforced before his times or that there was an actual measurable change in people's behaviour as a result of his campaign against promiscuity. The difference his struggle made was to have the Church's authority over marital matters acknowledged.

The compilation of laws called *Grágás* represents Icelandic law as it was in the middle of the thirteenth century. These laws do not concede that the Church had a separate jurisdiction and according to them the bishops had very limited powers and were not given any policing capacity over matters dealt with in the Christian law section. In the Betrothal section however the bishops are given a range of powers in matters relating to consanguinity and, in particular, separation (*Grg 1a*, $224_{21, 26}$; *Grg 1b*, 39_{24}, $40_{11, 15}$, $41_{11, 14, 16, 27}$, $42_{2, 5–23}$, $43_{10–11, 24, 27}$, 44_{16}, $56_{4, 11–18}$, 59_{18}, 61_{1}; *Grg II*, 165_{22}, $173_{4, 6–8}$, $199_{19, 20}$, 200_{4}). There is nothing in the laws which suggests that the powers they give to the bishops were acknowledged in the days of St Þorlákr but the indications are that these laws are more recent than the late twelfth century and therefore represent the fruits of St Þorlákr's labours. A limited acknowledgement of the bishops' right to fines for moral offences is the proviso that when couples, who were related in the fifth degree on one side and the sixth on the other, paid the capital tithe to the law court for a permit to marry, the members of the court took 6 marks and the bishops received the surplus if there was any (*Grg 1b*, 60_{14}–61_{4}).[18] In cases of childbirth through incestuous or adulterous unions the bishop had an absolute right to a 3 mark fine, provided he had earlier forbidden the relationship in question (*Grg 1b*, $56_{6–19}$).[19] This important acknowledgement of the bishop's right to impose fines for sexual transgressions may well have been pushed through after Archbishop Eysteinn's instruction to the chieftains in 1179–81 to arrange for the bishops to be able to impose fines for moral offences (quoted above, *DI* i. 263).

The pivotal role the laws give to the bishops in divorce proceedings, as mediators and final arbiters, represents the greatest advance the bishops made in gaining influence over people's private lives. As *Þorláks saga* claims St Þorlákr put emphasis on supporting married couples and punishing divorcees (quoted above, *Bsk* i. 106) it may be that he managed to have the legislation changed in his day. But it could be argued on equally good grounds that the Betrothal section was not composed in the form we know it until the middle of

[18] The capital tithe was paid only once in a lifetime, either for a permit to wed a relative or for salvation. It was 10% of property value, while ordinary tithe was a 1% property tax. See K. v. Maurer 1874*c*.

[19] It may be these fines which the A version of *Þorláks saga* refers to when it claims that St Þorlákr never mixed the moneys which people paid for their transgressions together with other wealth but spent them on supporting married couples who were in danger of breaking up on account of poverty (*Bsk* i. 107).

the thirteenth century, as it refers to the bishop's representative (*umboðsmaðr*), a term which is not attested until 1255 (*Grg 1b*, 56_{12}; *Sturl* 714).[20]

Whatever the case, and this issue deserves a much closer scrutiny than has been attempted here, it is abundantly clear that St Þorlákr fought to establish the Church's authority over people's personal and familial affairs and that in the long run at least he was successful. It is a matter for another study but the indications are that St Þorlákr's was not really such an uphill struggle. The extremely detailed way in which the laws deal with people's personal lives is suggestive of a society with a strong tradition of external regulation of familial matters. It may therefore have been entirely natural that the Church should take over the policing of the family and only had to overcome resistance from a small group of aristocrats who had previously lived by different norms from ordinary people.

St Þorlákr's successor as bishop of Skálholt, Páll Jónsson, was no reformer. He did continue his uncle's policies of separating illicit unions (*Sturl* 178–9) but he probably interpreted this as holding only for insignificant people. Páll was himself the fruit of Jón Loptsson's illicit love affair with St Þorlákr's sister. His brother Sæmundr, the chieftain of the Oddaverjar, never married but had children by several concubines, one of whom was his second cousin (*Sturl* 46, 212–13). It is unlikely that Páll confronted his brother on this score and it is clear that aristocrats openly kept concubines into the middle of the thirteenth century without the Church raising more than token objections and that children of such unions did retain the privileges aristocratic birth bestowed on them.[21]

The political situation in Norway had changed when Páll went there for ordination in 1194. The new archbishop, Eiríkr Ívarsson, who had been elevated in 1189, was a much more aggressive man than his predecessor and he was soon at loggerheads with King Sverrir. Archbishop Eysteinn had supported the kingship of Magnús Erlingsson (1164–84) who was only of royal blood on his mother's side and had in turn secured important privileges for the Norwegian church (*DI i.* 226–30; Helle 1964: 36–44). When the Faeroese priest Sverrir, who claimed he was the son of King Sigurðr *munnr* (1136–55), started his guerrilla war for the control of Norway the Church stood firmly by the side of King Magnús and even after Sverrir had killed Magnús in 1184 and assumed control of the country it continued to oppose him. For most of his time as king, Sverrir (1185–1202) was not in firm control of his kingdom. Archbishop Eiríkr was active in his opposition to him and contrived to have Pope Celestine III excommunicate Sverrir in 1194; it was one of Innocent III's first tasks to place Sverrir's domain under interdict in 1198 (*Sv* 129 as in *Lat.dok* 102 and *Lat.dok* 118–22).

[20] The same term is also used of the caretaker of a monastery in between abbots in 1253 (*Sturl* 617).

[21] On concubinage in the 12th and 13th cents. see Magnúsdóttir 1988. She stresses the political advantages to chieftains of having a large number of children as one of the main reasons why this practice was so widespread in Iceland.

The origins of the disagreement between King Sverrir and the Norwegian church are complex but it became expressed as well-established bones of contention between Church and State. As a result of the Church's hostility, Sverrir became the champion of royal and secular control over ecclesiastical property and appointments, and he and his constituency began to look for and develop arguments against the reformers. A stance was created whereby the King and secular magnates were the defenders of the Church against an irresponsible and greedy clergy who were not to be trusted to handle property or appointments, the reason being that the clergy were not answerable to God for their worldly responsibilities as the secular authorities were.[22]

To what extent the dispute between King Sverrir and the Norwegian church had reverberations within the Icelandic clergy is unclear. Sverrir clearly had supporters in Iceland; Abbot Karl Jónsson of Þingeyrar travelled to Norway in 1185 and wrote the first part of Sverrir's biography (*ÍBS* i. 391–3), and Pope Innocent III saw reason to write specially to Bishops Brandr and Páll in 1198 and warn them against associating with Sverrir, 'the excommunicate and apostate enemy of God and his saints on account of his deeds' (*DI* i. 300). Whether the pope knew the bishops to be sympathetic to Sverrir's cause we cannot know, but the author of *Páls saga* was certainly proud on behalf of his hero when after Christmas 1194 he

> sought out the king with his retinue, and there was then a great number of the king's men with him; but the king received him as well as if it was his son or brother who had come to his side, and enhanced his honour and dignity as he would have asked himself or his friends. The thing was that he [Sverrir] was more capable than most men and had greater ability and did everything in his power, which was beneficial, so that the honour of them both might become greater. (*Bsk* i. 129)

After staying with Sverrir well into Lent, Páll sought out the exiled archbishop in Denmark and was consecrated in Lund. Páll then went back to Norway and again he met Sverrir 'and stayed with him until he returned to Iceland in the summer, and the [king] respected him the more in all aspects the longer he stayed with him and the better he knew him' (*Bsk* i. 130).

It is clear that Sverrir was popular in Iceland and that he got a good press among Icelandic writers—the author of *Páls saga* was an ardent admirer. He obviously did not feel that his hero's association with this excommunicate who had died unabsolved was anything to be ashamed of. Although there is little direct evidence for it, the indications are that Bishop Páll and his successor Magnús Gizurarson subscribed to Sverrir's view of the relationship between Church and secular power. We have seen how Páll referred an important decision like selecting a bishop-elect for Hólar to his brother Sæmundr, the chieftain of their family. Another example of his accommodating attitude to secular authority is that, when he went to Norway to be consecrated, his

[22] Sverrir's views are spelt out in a pamphlet issued in his defence after the excommunication of 1194, printed in *En tale*.

brother Sæmundr lent him money and received in return the right to collect the bishop's quarter of the tithe from a certain number of farmsteads around the familial estate in Oddi. The Oddaverjar were still collecting these tithes in 1273 when, disgusted by Bishop Árni's attempt to take them back, they appealed to the archbishop (*ÍF* xvii. 42). If not because of conviction or familial pressure, Bishops Páll and Magnús probably adopted Sverrir's view because of their total lack of common ground with Bishop Guðmundr *góði*.

Guðmundr *góði*'s father was killed in 1166 defending Earl Erlingr, father of King Magnús and regent of Norway (*Sturl* 104–5; *ÍF* xxviii. 409) and Guðmundr's family seems to have supported the cause of King Magnús and his successors in opposing King Sverrir.[23] Guðmundr had been put to study because he was illegitimate and had no inheritance coming to him and he owed his elevation to the see of Hólar entirely to his success as a popular and miracle-working priest. He had therefore every reason to come out on the side of the reformers. Matters were probably cooling somewhat when he came to Norway for consecration a year after King Sverrir's death but if he had not already committed himself to the reforming stance it is likely that Archbishop Eiríkr took care to instruct him (*Bsk* i. 485 n. 3).

Bishop Guðmundr (1203–37) is probably the most debated figure in Icelandic medieval history. Historians have felt that his influence was profound and the debate has raged about to what extent he was responsible for the increased authority of the Norwegian king (Magnús Jónsson 1921*b*, 1941; Helgason 1931; Kristjánsson 1937; Sigfússon 1937; Guðbrandur Jónsson 1940*b*; Nordal 1942: 318–20; Sigurbjörnsson 1951; B. Þorsteinsson 1951, 1953: 276–85; 1978: 147–52; J. Jóhannesson 1956: 236–53; M. M. Lárusson 1960*g*; John Simpson 1973; M. Stefánsson 1975: 119–36; Margeirsson 1985; Sigtryggsson 1986). That question is losing its momentum as the search for scapegoats falters but it remains that Guðmundr *góði* was a most curious man. When Guðmundr was chosen by Kolbeinn Tumason to be the next bishop of Hólar, it was his religious fervour and total lack of any statesmanlike qualities which made him a feasible candidate. Guðmundr had earlier shrunk from taking on any worldly responsibilities, as he did when he refused to take control over the *staðr* at Vellir (N) in 1196 (*Sturl* 173). Kolbeinn was therefore justified in thinking that Guðmundr would allow him to control the diocese's finances. It quickly transpired that, inept as he was, Guðmundr was nevertheless going to make full use of the powers which being bishop bestowed upon him.

The first sticking point was control over the everyday running of the see and the diocese's revenues. Prior to Guðmundr's appointment, men had always been chosen as bishops who could be trusted to manage the considerable wealth one diocese turned over. They could come in for criticism, as Bishop Klængr did for extravagance, but on the whole the chieftains had not interfered with them directly. The bishops on the other hand seem always to have tolerated the

[23] As in Ögmundr Þorvarðarson's appeal to King Jón *kuflungr* (*Sturl* 120).

fact that the chieftains monitored their management of the sees. There was, therefore, an understanding that the chieftains had a certain right to review the management of the dioceses and that in return for acknowledging this the bishops were in practice allowed to manage the affairs of their diocese on their own.

It was Kolbeinn Tumason who attempted an innovative arrangement by the appointment of an ascetic who, as such, was not supposed even to be interested in management. While Guðmundr *góði* probably had no great interest in financial matters he had no intention of being a puppet of Kolbeinn. He himself was probably in no doubt of his right and in the short periods when he was in control of the see he seems to have depleted the revenues without much consideration for the see's financial health. Guðmundr took an uncompromising stance on charity. This meant giving everyone who asked everything he had. He was therefore always surrounded by several hundreds of what householders would consider undesirable characters.

It was spending money on an uncontrollable crowd of beggars and vagabonds which really made the householders' blood run cold. Excessive expenditure was bad but encouraging sloth was positively horrific and Guðmundr's image became inextricably linked with the mob that followed him everywhere he went. As I discussed in Chapter 2, section 2, control of poverty was a fundamental concern of the householding class and Guðmundr's conduct was therefore not only irresponsible but directly menacing to the social order. Unlimited charity was, of course, not a priority of the reformers but Guðmundr's insistence on it played into the hands of those who saw themselves as defenders of the old order. They had long since pointed out that the so-called reformers were nothing but a group of greedy and irresponsible clergy taking advantage of the trust good men had placed in them (*En tale*, 2–3, 6–7).

After his defeat in the battle of Hólar in 1209 Bishop Guðmundr was never in real control of the finances of his diocese, although he often managed to command enough resources to maintain a large following on his wanderings. He never retracted any of his demands and, although his authority was largely ineffective in the last twenty-eight years of his thirty-four-year episcopacy, he was sufficiently influential to maintain his status as the leader of the reform movement in Iceland.

From the reformers' point of view Bishop Guðmundr was the worst agent they could hope for. His contribution to the reform was mainly an exercise in relentless obstinacy; he never really managed to fight for actual changes but was sufficiently menacing to stimulate a strong and coherent opposition to himself and the ideals he was seen to represent, both within the Church and among the secular magnates.

In his honeymoon period before the battle of Hólar in 1209 Bishop Guðmundr did try to assert his authority, in particular with regard to the Church's jurisdiction over its clerics. *Íslendinga saga* gives the particulars of two cases; both concerned clerics who were being prosecuted by Kolbeinn and who sought the aid of Bishop Guðmundr. In 1205 the priest Ásbjörn asked Guðmundr for protection from Kolbeinn who accused him of non-payment of debts. While the court was in session Guðmundr came and forbade them to try the priest. He was nevertheless tried and sentenced. As a result, Bishop Guðmundr banned Kolbeinn and those who had been involved in the litigation from religious services and took the priest under his protection. The priest's wife gave Kolbeinn money so that he would leave their farmstead alone. Later in the year Kolbeinn went to Hólar and laid a summons on Guðmundr's servants for association with his outlaw. Bishop Guðmundr excommunicated Kolbeinn instead. At this point their friends intervened and a settlement was reached whereby Kolbeinn agreed that Bishop Guðmundr would judge alone. The householders of the region promised to pay whatever fines Guðmundr imposed on Kolbeinn. At the following Alþing Bishop Guðmundr took counsel with Bishop Páll and his brother Sæmundr in Oddi and then pronounced a heavy fine on Kolbeinn. The fine was never paid in full because the bishop insisted that Kolbeinn should deliver the fine himself while Kolbeinn claimed that Guðmundr should collect from the householders who had promised to pay (*Sturl* 214).

In this first round Guðmundr had forced at least a partial acknowledgement of his jurisdiction but the war was far from over. In the summer of 1206 he excommunicated the chieftains Sigurðr Ormsson in Möðruvellir in Hörgárdalur (N) and Hallr Kleppjárnsson in Grund in Eyjafjörður (N) because they had forcibly taken a man from a monastery where he had sought refuge, beaten him up, and amputated a limb. Kolbeinn was soon known to have associated with Sigurðr and Hallr and the three put a trade-embargo on the see. By the autumn Sigurðr and Hallr gave in and agreed on Bishop Guðmundr's self-judgment. Kolbeinn was not involved in the settlement and before Christmas Bishop Guðmundr had excommunicated him again, this time for associating with excommunicates and for not paying the fines from the previous dispute. After Easter 1207 Kolbeinn came to Hólar and laid a summons on the members of the household for a variety of minor offences. The bishop again read his excommunication over Kolbeinn. In the spring Kolbeinn assembled his men and Þorvaldr Gizurarson of the Haukdælir came to his aid and together they prosecuted the bishop's men at the spring assembly in Hegranes (N). Again friends of both parties mediated and a settlement was reached whereby the archbishop should judge in the dispute, Kolbeinn should retract all his litigation, and Bishop Guðmundr should lift the excommunication.

Again Bishop Guðmundr was partially successful but the dispute never reached the archbishop. In the following year there seem to have been a series of minor disputes between Bishop Guðmundr and Kolbeinn's followers: 'The bishop habitually brought actions against Kolbeinn's men on various charges like tithe-cases, management of church property or the maintenance of their poor relatives. The householders reacted with displeasure and it seemed to them that the bishop would leave no one in peace' (*Sturl* 216).

It was Guðmundr's inability to select his targets tactfully which was soon to be his downfall. He seems to have quickly forfeited any sympathy he might have had among the local householders and without it he was easy prey for Kolbeinn. In 1208 Kolbeinn was pursuing an acolyte who had fathered a child. The mother's brothers wanted compensation and had handed the case over to Kolbeinn. The acolyte for his part sought the protection of Bishop Guðmundr. Guðmundr offered to pay compensation but Kolbeinn refused any settlement, claiming that the bishop broke every truce. The case then took a familiar course; Kolbeinn had the acolyte convicted at the spring assembly and Bishop Guðmundr excluded Kolbeinn and his accomplices from services. Kolbeinn together with Sigurðr Ormsson then confiscated the property of the acolyte and the bishop in turn excommunicated them both. At the following Alþing many people associated with Kolbeinn and Sigurðr and they convicted six of Bishop Guðmundr's household members for aiding their outlaw. Kolbeinn again assembled a host and was going to march on Hólar to confiscate the property of those he had convicted. This time Bishop Guðmundr and his men fled the see, but when he returned Kolbeinn had joined forces with his brother Arnórr, Sigurðr, and Hallr. The day after Guðmundr came to Hólar Kolbeinn attacked but was himself killed and his army put to flight (*Sturl* 214–19).

The following spring a coalition of most of the more prominent chieftains in the country marched on Hólar and dispersed Guðmundr's following and captured the bishop himself (*Sturl* 220–4). After this Bishop Guðmundr was never in a position to advance his claim to jurisdiction over clerics, or any other reforming claims for that matter.

The author of *Páls saga* was initially happy with Bishop Guðmundr because his abhorrent behaviour showed Bishop Páll in such a good light (*Bsk* i. 136), but when it came to describing their relationship he was clearly irritated by Bishop Guðmundr's conduct, which put Bishop Páll in an awkward position 'because the archbishop had sent him letters under his seal, telling him to support and assist the cause of Bishop Guðmundr as well as he could, but many of Bishop Páll's dearest friends, his relatives and in-laws supported Kolbeinn' (*Bsk* i. 141).

The author claims that, although Bishop Páll was horrified by Bishop Guðmundr's aggressive politics and liberal use of the weapon of excommunication, he tried all that he could to mediate; he dissuaded the chieftains from mounting an expedition against Guðmundr immediately after Kolbeinn's fall and sent his chaplain to Bishop Guðmundr to mediate a settlement. The stubborn Guðmundr had refused to budge an inch and accused Páll of siding with the chieftains. To the author of *Páls saga* the battle of Hólar was a divine judgement:

> But it soon became clear, which of them [Páll or Guðmundr] had been wiser in their strategy, because in that same year chieftains went to Hólar and ousted Bishop Guðmundr from his see and chased away a large number of villains who were found

there—outlaws, robbers and bandits—and killed some of them and this garrison of wickedness was thereby dissolved and from then on people's fortune improved. (*Bsk* i. 142)

It does not seem that Bishop Páll opposed the operation which removed Bishop Guðmundr from his see and he was no doubt relieved by its successful outcome because it allowed him to disassociate himself completely from Bishop Guðmundr.

Bishop Páll seems to have supported his colleague in his claim to jurisdiction over the priest Ásbjörn in 1206, although how active this support was we cannot know. It was Bishop Guðmundr himself who, by his uncompromising tactics, provided the excuse for Bishop Páll and his successor Magnús Gizurarson (1216–37) to distance themselves from him and his policies.

There can hardly be disagreement that Guðmundr *góði* was not a competent politician and the polarization he caused within the Icelandic church had more to do with his methods than his policies. Bishops Páll and Magnús were clearly no reformers and neither seems to have attempted to increase the influence of the Church in any way, but their defensive position was created and maintained by the aggression of Bishop Guðmundr and was not a continuation of an older order. In the twelfth century the bishops had been able to further the cause of the Church in relative harmony with the secular powers and even a slightly irritating St Þorlákr did not manage to cause noticeable apprehension. Páll Jónsson's appointment to Skálholt in 1194 may have been a sign of unease among the southern chieftains but it was only after Guðmundr *góði* became bishop that it became clear where the battle-lines lay.

The appointment of Magnús Gizurarson was clearly a reaction to Bishop Guðmundr. There can hardly be talk of a reactionary movement, however, because although it did help to create certain views on Church and society, his episcopacy is notable mainly for his inaction. The main consequence of Bishop Guðmundr's attempts at reform was that the development of episcopal power in Iceland was put on hold for thirty years or more. It was not until Norwegian bishops arrived at both sees in 1239 that real changes began to be implemented, but in the mean time the social status of priests had been through important changes, and it is to these we turn in Chapter 5.

5
The Priests

1. SHORTAGE OF PRIESTS IN THE TWELFTH CENTURY

In the Old Christian law section there is a clause which describes how a church-owner can take on young boys, have them educated and ordained as priests at his own expense, and they in turn are bound to serve his church for the rest of their lives, unless they educate another priest in their place. If such a priest ran away, consorting with him incurred the same penalties as consorting with an outlaw. If he became sick it was up to the employer whether he sustained the priest or handed him over to his relatives. When this type of priest died the church and its guardian were to inherit three hundreds (= three cows or more), and only if he owned more would his relatives inherit from him (*Grg 1a*, 17_{19}–19_{2}).[1] From this one could only describe the status of such Icelandic priests as unfree and servile.

While chieftain-priests are well attested in the non-legal sources, explicit mention is nowhere made in them of the servile type of priest (J. Jóhannesson 1956: 198–9; G. Karlsson 1975: 22; M. Stefánsson 1975: 80). That does not mean such servile priests did not exist. Our sources—that is, *Sturlunga saga* and the sagas of bishops—are not concerned with people of that calibre. Nevertheless it makes it awkward to build grand theories on this legal provision and considering that there are over 400 priests known to us in Iceland up to 1300, none of whom can be shown to have lived this kind of life, we cannot suggest that these servile priests were in any way characteristic of the conditions of Icelandic priests.

Depending on which view people take of slavery in Iceland in the high middle ages (Foote 1975, 1977*c*; Agnarsdóttir and Árnason 1983; Karras 1988) this clause can either be seen as a legal exercise aimed at creating a lowest rank of personal rights for clerics comparable to (the possibly equally fictional) secular slaves. Or it can be seen as a natural response by a legal expert to the perceived formation of a new class of people. It may be that church-owners were pressing for a cheap and efficient way of running their churches, perhaps when it was no longer in vogue for them to be priests themselves, or this may be indicative of the Church's concern over shortage of priests, a concern which it sought to alleviate by offering destitute youngsters this opportunity of a semi-respectable position, even if it meant that they gave away their freedom.

[1] The idea of servile priests is integrated into the legislation—*Grg 1a*, 78_{9-10}—which indicates that someone took the servile aspect quite seriously.

The last option deserves more consideration because it can be supported by other evidence for a persistent shortage of priests. Between 1148 and 1152, when the episcopal seat at Skálholt was empty there seems to have been such an acute shortage of priests in the diocese that Bishop Björn from Hólar ordained many priests at the Alþing, among them St Þorlákr, and he can only have been 19 at the time, and possibly younger (b. 1133) (*Bsk* i. 91). Both Magnús Stefánsson (1984: 296–302) and Arne Odd Johnsen (1979) have shown convincingly that as in many other places the canon law requirement that priests should not be ordained until they were 30 was not heeded in Iceland in the middle ages, whether it was known or not. The reason was probably economic; society or its ecclesiastical institutions could not afford to keep able-bodied young men in lower orders for years on end and not put them into service. Nevertheless those priests whose age of ordination is known had all reached 20 when they took their vows, and brilliant and promising as young Þorlákr undoubtedly was, ordaining teenagers and giving them a cure of souls can hardly have been regular practice, and can be seen as a sign of stress.

The author of *Þorláks saga* makes his hero fear ember days

> because he regarded it as a grave responsibility to ordain men, who sought ordination over great distances, and whom he considered ill-fit, both on account of their lack of learning and their other ways which were not to his liking, but he did not want to refuse them, partly because of their poverty and also for the sake of those men who had given them instruction or sent their tokens. (*Bsk* i. 107)[2]

We can assume that he had little choice in the matter: it was better to ordain unfit priests than none.

Among the troublemakers who gave cause for chieftains to dispute in Dalir in 1150 was Aðalríkr, son of a foreign priest called Gunnvarðr. Three of the priest's children are named with the comment that they were useful men who sold their labour in summer (*Sturl* 53). The priest's children clearly belonged to the lower end of the social scale, but Aðalríkr at least had powerful protectors because Oddi Þorgilsson from Staðarhóll took him under his protection and got him safely out of the country after he had killed a householder without provocation. The indications are that the priest Gunnvarðr was active in pastoral care in Iceland in the first half of the twelfth century, probably with the support of the Staðarhólsmenn, and possibly at Staðarhóll (D) itself. It is of course not possible to infer much from a single example but, considered in the context of other evidence for a shortage of priests in Iceland in the twelfth century, it seems likely that Gunnvarðr had gone, or been brought, to Iceland because of a lack of priests who could give service to the rapidly growing numbers of householders who wanted to provide a tithe-paying congregation with regular services. The social station of Gunnvarðr's children suggests that foreign priests

[2] Cf. *ÍBS* i. 271, where it is pointed out that this is a well known topos in hagiographic literature. Such observations, while undoubtedly correct, normally fail to appreciate that there must have been a reason why some topoi were included and not others.

were not likely to become economically independent or to be able to acquire social respectability for themselves or their kin.

From the time of his ordination as priest in 1185 until his election to the see of Hólar in 1201 Guðmundr Arason served no less than seven ministries in a relatively restricted area in the vicinity of Hólar.[3] Guðmundr was no doubt an unusually distinguished and sought-after cleric but that cannot have been the only reason why he seems to have had the choice of a range of ministries, all of them placed sufficiently close to Hólar for an ambitious cleric to keep himself involved and abreast of things. That so many ministries, some of them among the most exclusive in the country (notably Vellir in Svarfaðardalur (N) and Staður in Reynines (N)), were available to Guðmundr in the seventeen years of his priesthood suggests that in this area at least householding priests had become rare and that in most ministries pastoral care was in the hands of district priests. It also suggests that there was not a great number of district priests available, or at least not suitable district priests.

Like St Þorlákr his successor to the see of Skálholt, Bishop Páll (1195–1211), seems to have been concerned about a shortage of priests. The author of his saga tells us that Bishop Páll had the churches and priests in his diocese counted to know if he could allow his priests to go abroad without it affecting the services (*Bsk* i. 136). While some scholars have found this reason for Bishop Páll's inventory unnecessarily unexciting,[4] it is clear that the author was thoroughly acquainted with Bishop Páll's administration and it is therefore difficult to see why he should have chosen to be misleading on this point. Even if Icelandic priests were not going abroad in hordes it was a natural response to a shortage of priests to try first to prevent those who were already there from leaving their cures.

All this suggests that it would have been natural for the Church to try to make arrangements for a steady supply of priests, but why it chose to solve it by inventing servile priests or if this ever worked we cannot know. It does however say something about twelfth-century attitudes to economic and social freedom that at least somebody thought this was viable.

The evidence for a shortage of priests in the twelfth century presented here is far from conclusive, but there is absolutely no evidence to the contrary and it would be difficult to equate large numbers of priests with the evidence for the

[3] Hof in Höfðaströnd (N) 1185–7 (28 farmstead tithe area, *bændakirkja*); Miklibær in Óslandshlíð (N) 1187–9 (9 farmstead tithe area, *bændakirkja*); Viðvík (N) 1189–90 ([11] farmstead tithe area, *staðr*); Vellir in Svarfaðardalur (N) 1190–6 (30 farmstead tithe area, *staðr*); Ufsir in Svarfaðardalur (N) 1196–8 (15 farmstead tithe area, *bændakirkja*); Staður in Reynines (N) 1198–9 (14 farmstead tithe area, *staðr*); Víðimýri (N) 1199–1201 (12 farmstead tithe area, *bændakirkja*)—*Bsk* i. 430–66.

[4] Rafnsson 1993: 83–9 points out that the 17th-cent. MSS in which the inventory is preserved do not suggest that counting priests was its original function. He fails to appreciate that we do in fact not know what the original inventory looked like and while it can be argued convincingly that the preserved documents are ultimately derived from Bishop Páll's inventory there is nothing to suggest that they are a faithful rendering of it. Cf. Ó. Lárusson 1944: 131–2 who saw the need to count priests as a result of Icelandic priests flocking to richer ministries in Norway.

social make-up of the clergy in the late twelfth century. The fact that in the early and middle twelfth century many chieftains were ordained as priests or had their sons ordained would fit ill in a scenario where there was also a great number of priests of more humble origin. It is difficult to see why the chieftains should have wanted to become priests if it did not in some way give them a firmer grip on their followers/subordinates and an edge over their rivals. And it is unlikely that the chieftains could have achieved this if they were taking on roles which had already been played by some other class of people and with whom they would be in competition.

It makes much more sense to allow for a small number of missionary priests in the eleventh century, and possibly into the twelfth, who were then gradually superseded by ordained chieftains. It seems that permanent ministries only began to be established in significant numbers in the first decades of the twelfth century, as a result of the introduction of the tithe, and that these were dominated for a generation or two by chieftains or aristocratic householders. The success of the union between priesthood and chieftaincy will have prompted rich householders and others who aspired to power or influence to do the same, but when the immediate goal of the householders/chieftains to increase their influence or tighten their grip on their neighbours had been achieved they no longer needed to be seen to perform the services themselves and it began to suffice to be seen to provide these services. It is then that a demand for 'professional' priests will have arisen.

2. CHIEFTAIN-PRIESTS IN THE TWELFTH CENTURY

The discussion of the evidence for priests in the eleventh century in Chapter 1, section 3 revealed that, as far as our sources can tell us, there were very few priests in Iceland throughout the eleventh century. It is only in the last quarter of that century that a small number of aristocratic householders like Sæmundr *fróði* in Oddi (S), Jón Ögmundarson in Breiðabólstaður in Fljótshlíð (S) later bishop of Hólar, Teitr Ísleifsson in Haukadalur (S), Þórðr Sölvason in Reykholt (S), and Illugi Bjarnarson in Hólar (N) appear as priests. Some of these men were actively involved in establishing Christian institutions (Sæmundr and Jón) and others instructed young men for the priesthood (Sæmundr and Teitr). All of them seem to have been chieftains (see Ch. 1, s. 2; Ch. 1, s. 3; Ch. 4, s. 1) and all, except for Bishop Jón who does not seem to have had any children, had sons who became priests and chieftains.

In *Kristni saga* there are two lists of important men in the early twelfth century. One lists the thirteen greatest chieftains in the country at the time of Bishop Gizurr's death in 1118 (*Bsk* i. 30–1) and the other names ten chieftains as examples of the many respectable men who were 'learned and ordained as priests, even if they were chieftains' in the time of Bishop Gizurr (1082–1118) (*Bsk* i. 29). The latter list comes in the context of Bishop Gizurr's achievements: he had 'pacified the country so well that no major disputes broke out among chieftains and the carrying of arms all but ceased' (*Bsk* i. 29). The ordained chieftains are therefore being cited as evidence for the early Christian golden age which thirteenth-century scholarship had created out of Bishop Gizurr's episcopacy (see Ch. 2, s. 1).

There is little doubt that all these men were ordained—nine out of ten are known as priests from other sources[5]—and most if not all were chieftains,[6] but it is doubtful whether being ordained had already by this time become standard practice among chieftains. Only three of these priests can have been much more than middle aged in 1118;[7] most of the rest have death dates around 1150 (see Table 6), which suggests that for the most part this list represents the generation of chieftains born in 1080–90.[8]

The other list in *Kristni saga*, the list of thirteen major chieftains in 1118, supports this.[9] Only two of these great chieftains were priests themselves but nine of them had their sons ordained as priests and the descendants or successors of two more were also priests. Of these thirteen chieftains whose sons and grandsons dominated Icelandic politics in the twelfth century, only two had no descendants of note who became priests. The two are, however, important exceptions because their descendants, the Ásbirningar and the Sturlungar, became two of five families which dominated Icelandic politics in the thirteenth century. It seems, then, that while a few powerful families had decided to have their sons ordained shortly before or around 1100, it became almost a norm among chieftains after 1100.

[5] Sæmundr Sigfússon in *ÍF* i. 3; Hallr Teitsson in *DI* i. 185; Magnús Þórðarson in *Bsk* i. 76; Ari *fróði* in *Bsk* i. 145, 158, 231; Guðmundr Brandsson in *Bsk* i. 79, *Sturl* 8; Ingimundr Einarsson in *DI* i. 186; Ketill Guðmundsson in *DI* i. 186; Ketill Þorsteinsson in *Sturl* 35; Jón Þorvarðarson in *DI* i. 186. Símun Jörundarson is not known from any other source.

[6] It is not known if Símun Jörundarson, Guðmundr Brandsson, or Jón Þorvarðarson owned *goðorð*—the sons of the latter two did not, but they were nevertheless men of considerable significance.

[7] Sæmundr Sigfússon was born in 1056 (*IA* 108, 318, 470) and was therefore 64 in 1118—he may even have been ordained before Gizurr became bishop in 1082 as he is supposed to have come from abroad in 1076–8 (*IA* 110, 251, 471) and soon afterwards become a pastor at Oddi (*Bsk* i. 157, 229). Ari *fróði* was born in 1066–7 (*IA* 18, 58, 109, 318, 471) and was therefore 51 or 2 in 1118. Ketill Þorsteinsson was more than 70 when he died in 1145 (*Bsk* i. 77) so he must have been around 45 in 1118. Magnús Þórðarson may also have been elderly by 1118 as the author of *Þorgils saga ok Hafliða* makes his son Þórðr represent the family in the events of 1120 (*Sturl* 29) and his grandson Páll Sölvason was already of respectable age in 1143 and 1148 (*DI* i. 186; *Bsk* i. 79).

[8] On the life-expectancy of chieftains in Iceland see Ingvarsson 1986–7 i. 274–303.

[9] This list is a probably a 13th-cent. reconstruction rather than based on any 12th-cent. evidence—it is only just that these men were all contemporaries—one of them, Sigmundr Þorgilsson died on pilgrimage in 1118, while Þorgeirr Hallason can hardly have been much more than a teenager then as he died in 1169 (*IA* 117; *Bsk* i. 418). Just as it ends with this list *Kristni saga* has another at its beginning naming twenty-eight major chieftains in 983 (*Bsk* i. 4). Such lists are a common feature and clearly underlie much 13th-cent. historical scholarship. The author of *Þorgils saga ok Hafliða* has for instance had access to a similar list—he has nine chieftains in common with *Kristni saga*'s list and adds at least two *goðorðsmenn* and two lawspeakers (Þorsteinn *ranglátr* d. 1149, Þórólfr Sigmundarson and Finnr Hallsson (1139–45), Guðmundr Þorgeirsson (1123–34) respectively). The use of lists like these in 13th-cent. reconstructions of the past lacks full treatment—for an overview see Ingvarsson 1986–7 i. 214–62.

TABLE 6. *Ordained chieftains in the twelfth century*

Major chieftains in 1118	Ordained chieftains in 1080–1118	High-born priests in 1143	Descendants
Southern quarter			
	Sæmundr Sigfússon in Oddi (S) (d. 1133)	h.s. Eyjólfr in Oddi (d. 1158)	
		h.s. Loptr	h.s. Jón deacon and chieftain in Oddi (d. 1197) father (d. 1133) of Sæmundr deacon and chieftain at Oddi (d. 1222) and Páll bishop of Skálholt 1195–1211
Hallr Teitsson in Haukadalur (S) (d. 1150)	Hallr Teitsson	Hallr Teitsson	h.s. Gizurr deacon and chieftain and lawspeaker 1181–1202 (d. 1206) father of Hallr priest, lawspeaker 1203–9 and abbot of Helgafell (D) 1221–25 and Þykkvibær (S) 1225–30, Þorvaldr priest and chieftain (d. 1235) and Magnús bishop of Skálholt (1217–37)
Skúli Egilsson		h.s. Þórðrs h.s. Einarr?	h.s. Böðvarr chieftain in Garðar (S) (d. 1187) father of Þórðr priest and chieftain (d. 1220) and Guðný mother of Þórðr, Sighvatr, and Snorri chieftains of the Sturlungar
	Símun Jörundarson in Bær (S)		Descendants unknown, possibly father of Þórðr priest killed in 1128. In 1183 and 1196 Högni Þormóðarson 'the rich', a priest, was living at Bær, considered of poor family
	Magnús Þórðarson	h.g.s Páll Sölvason	h.s. Magnús priest and chieftain in Reykholt (S) (d. 1223)
Western quarter			
Styrmir Hreinsson		h.c. Ormr Koðránsson (d. 1179)	Son of Styrmir was Abbot Hreinn of Hítardalur (S) (d. 1171). Ormr's descendants are unknown but his brother was Hermundr chieftain in Kalmannstunga (S) (d. 1197) father of Ketill priest in Skálholt and abbot of Helgafell (D) 1217–20 and Hreinn priest
Halldórr Egilsson		h.s. Egill	h.g.s. Bersi Halldórsson priest (d. 1204), father of Teitr bishop elect (d. 1214)

	Ari *fróði* (d. 1148)	h.s. Þorgils in Staðarstaður (S) (d. 1170)	h.s. Ari chieftain in Staðarstaður (d. 1188). From him the chieftaincy passed to his son-in-law Þórðr Sturluson deacon (d. 1237)
	Guðmundr Brandsson in Hjarðarholt (D) (d. 1151)		h.s. Magnús priest in Hjarðarholt who gave the *staðr* to Sighvatr Sturluson in 1197
Þorgils Oddason in Staðarhóll (D) (d. 1151)		h.s. Oddi in Staðarhóll (d. 1151)	Oddi's younger brother Einarr chieftain (d. 1185)
	Ingimundr Einarsson in Reykhólar (D) (d. 1169)	Ingimundr Einarsson	Ingimundr's descendants are unknown. He gave his *goðorð* to Þorgils Oddason.
Þórðr Gilsson			h.s. Sturla chieftain in Hvammur (D) (d. 1183) father of Þórðr deacon and chieftain at Staðarstaður (d. 1237) father of Guttormr deacon (d. 1255) and Ólafr subdeacon, poet, and scholar at Stafholt (S) (d. 1259). None of the other chieftains of the Sturlungar were ordained although some like Snorri Sturluson (d. 1241) and Sturla Þórðarson (d. 1284) were learned
Þórðr Þorvaldsson in Vatnsfjörður (N)			h.s. Páll priest in Vatnsfjörður (drowned 1171) married daughter of Bishop Brandr. The chieftaincy passed to his brother Snorri (d. 1194)
Northern quarter			
Hafliði Másson at Breiðabólstaður (N) (d. 1130)			h.s.l. Ingimundr Illugason priest (d. 1150) father of Illugi in Breiðabólstaður
sons of Ásbjörn			None of the descendants of Ásbjörn, the Ásbirningar who ruled supreme in Skagafjörður by 1200, were ordained as far as is known
	Ketill Guðmundsson (d. 1158)	Ketill Guðmundsson	h.s. Jón priest and chieftain in Holt (N) (d. 1192) who gave his *goðorð* to his cousin Guðmundr *dýri*

TABLE 6. *Ordained chieftains in the 12th Century (continued)*

Major chieftains in 1118	Ordained chieftains in 1080–1118	High-born priests in 1143	Descendants
Ketill Þorsteinsson in Möðruvellir (N) (d. 1145)	Ketill Þorsteinsson	h.s. Rúnólfr (d. 1186)	Ketill was bishop of Hólar 1122–45. The son of Rúnólfr may have been Kári abbot of Þingeyrar (N) 1181–7 who was probably the father of Styrmir *fróði* scholar, lawspeaker 1210–14, 1232–5, and prior of Viðey (S) 1235–45. Ketill's nephews were Guðmundr and Rúnólfr, sons of Dálkr, both listed among the high-born priests of 1143 in the western quarter
Þorgeirr Hallason in Hvassafell (N) (d. 1169)			h.s. Ingimundr priest (d. 1189) fostered h.g.s. Guðmundr Arason bishop of Hólar 1203–37
	Jón Þorvarðarson (d. 1150)	Jón Þorvarðarson	h.s. (?) Örnólfr (d. 1197) father of Jón in Möðruvellir (N) (d. 1222) and Þorvarðr in Mikligarður (N), *stórbændr* if not chieftains
Eastern quarter			
Gizurr Einarsson	h.s. Oddr in Valþjófsstaður (A) (d. 1180)		h.s. Teitr deacon and chieftain in Hof in Vopnafjörður (A) (d. 1223)
Sigmundr Þorgilsson (d. 1118)			h.s. Jón chieftain in Svínafell (A) and brother-in-law of bishop Björn Gilsson (d. 1164), father of Ormr chieftain who became a monk at Þverá (N) (d. 1191) and grandfather of Ormr Skeggjason abbot of Þverá *c.*1191–1212. Ormr Jónsson's sons were Sigurðr chieftain at Svínafell and Möðruvellir in Hörgárdalur (N) later monk at Þverá (d. 1235) and Sigmundr priest and chieftain at Svínafell (d. 1198) father of Jón chieftain at Valþjófsstaður and Svínafell (d. 1212) father of Ormr chieftain at Svínafell (d. 1241) who was the most popular of ordained chieftains, and of Brandr bishop of Hólar 1263–4

h.c. his cousin; h.g.s. = his grandson; h.s. = his son; h.s.l. = his son-in-law—in all cases 'his' relates to the man named in the column immediately to the left.

Of the families or kin groups which are known to have held power in the twelfth century the Haukdælir in Árnesþing (Bishops Ísleifr and Gizurr, Teitr's son Ísleifr and his son Hallr) were first to become involved with the Church. Next were the Oddaverjar in Rangárþing (Sæmundr Sigfússon) and Reykhyltingar in Borgarfjörður (Þórðr Sölvason and his son Magnús). In the last quarter of the eleventh century these families were joined by the Snæfellingar (Ari *fróði*) in Snæfellsnes, the Fljótamenn in Fljót (Ketill Guðmundsson), and the Möðruvellingar in Eyjafjörður (Ketill Þorsteinsson). To this generation belongs also Vilmundr Þórólfsson, the first abbot of Þingeyrar (1133–48); he was the son of Þórólfr Sigmundarson who was according to *Þorgils saga ok Hafliða* a senior chieftain in the north (Húnaþing or Skagafjörður) whose power and influence was fading around 1120 (*Sturl* 31).[10]

About the same time, or shortly after, these families are joined by the Reyknesingar (D) (Ingimundr Einarsson and Guðmundr Brandsson: *ASB* xi. 50; *DI* i. 186; *Sturl* 8, 32; *Bsk* i. 418; *Bysp* 1. 105); a branch of the Möðruvellingar from Þverá (N) (Bishop Björn Gilsson d. 1162); a family from Mikligarður (N) (Jón Þorvarðarson (d. 1150): *ASB* xi. 50; *DI* i. 186; *IA* 114) and the Reynistaðarmenn (N) (Árni Björnsson: *Bysp* 1. 97). Eyjólfr Gunnvaldsson (d. 1142) from Grenjaðarstaður (A) (*Bsk* i. 242; *IA* 114) probably also represents a family of power as does Finnr Hallsson priest and lawspeaker 1139 (d. 1145) from Hofteigur in Jökuldalur (A) (*Sturl* 25; *DI* i. 185; *IA* 114, 321, 474), Skapti Þórarinsson from Mosfell in Mosfellssveit (S) (*DI* i. 186; *ÍF* ii. 299), and Brandr Úlfhéðinsson from Víðimýri (N) (d. 1159) (*Sturl* 55; *DI* i. 186; *IA* 116). It is also possible that Hámundr and Þorbjörn, sons of Tyrfingr, represent a family of power in Skagafjörður in this period (*ÍF* i. 372). The Staðarmenn in Steingrímsfjörður (N) may have an early representative in the Brandr Bergþórsson who hurt his hand while preparing the coffin for Jón Ögmundarson in 1121 (*Bsk* i. 176)[11] and the Húnröðlingar in Húnaþing are represented by Hafliði's nephew Sigurðr Bergþórsson, who was killed in the battle at Hvalir in Norway, 12 November 1139, and Hafliði's son-in-law Ingimundr Illugason at Breiðabólstaður (d. 1150) (*ÍF* xviii. 316; *ASB* xi. 55; *IA* 114).

Much of the evidence for these early twelfth century priests and their familial relations is circumstantial and uncertain and many of these families did not continue to hold power in their regions in the latter part of the twelfth century. It is only with the next generation (i.e. the sons of the chieftains of 1118) that the evidence becomes fuller and it seems that towards the middle of the twelfth century significant numbers, and even a majority, of chieftains and aristocratic householders were ordained. In this period it is not only the oldest sons of

[10] On Vilmundr: *Bsk* i. 168, 241; *IA* 114, 321; *DI* iii. 28, 153, 311. On his family *Sturl* 123.

[11] He may have been a grandfather of Brandr Bergþórsson, father of Jón priest at Staður in Reykjanes (D) and later Staður in Steingrímsfjörður (N) (d. 1211) *Bsk* i. 425; *Sturl* 47, 63–4, 113–15, 179, 893–4. Jón's father may have been the same as Skegg-Brandr, father of Halldóra (d. 1190), wife of Jón Loptsson in Oddi—*Sturl* 46.

chieftains who become priests but there is also a clear tendency for chieftains to marry their daughters to priests and sons of priests.

An important source in this context is the list of high-born priests from 1143 (*DI* i. 185–6).[12] It has the names of forty priests, ten from each quarter. Sixteen of them are not known from other sources[13] but the rest were either chieftains or aristocratic householders of local importance, which suggests that the same applies to those who are not known. The majority of the unknown priests are in the eastern quarter, for which there are far fewer sources than other parts of the country. As the criterion behind the list is pedigree and not political power it is of course possible that there were regional differences in the social importance of the priests. There may have been fewer chieftains among the priests of the eastern quarter than the western, for instance, reflecting either different tactics among the most powerful in the east or the possibility that the most powerful had already by this time become very few in the east. On the whole, however, it is likely that the list gives only the names of those who had put their high birth to good use and come to positions of influence. The fact that the list omits Ari *fróði*, who had still five years to live when it was compiled, but includes his son Þorgils also suggests that it reflects the current political situation; Ari was at least 75 years old in 1143 and had probably handed the chieftaincy to his son who was probably more than middle aged by this time (d. 1170). Whatever purpose the list had, or if it was only an intellectual exercise, the men it records were men who wielded real power—whether they owned *goðorð* or not—and it can confidently be taken as a confirmation of the strong indications from other sources that in the middle of the twelfth century the majority of chieftains were ordained. Forty must have been a sizeable proportion of priests in Iceland in the middle of the twelfth century. Bishop Páll Jónsson found that he needed 290 priests if all the churches in his diocese were to be served fully, which by implication means that around 1200 some 430 priests were needed in the country as a whole. If the number of priests was slowly increasing in the latter half of the twelfth century the list of high-born priests therefore has more than 10 per cent of priests in the country in 1143. It is with this 10 per cent of the clerical population that we will be concerned in the following. Information on clerics in the twelfth century is almost entirely restricted to the upper echelons of society, it is only in the thirteenth century that we meet priests who belong

[12] On this list see Arnórsson 1942: 49–51; Ingvarsson 1986–7 i. 214–19; Einarsdóttir 1964: 102–3; Ellehøj 1965: 58.

[13] Skeggi Fenkelsson; Svarthöfði Arnbjarnarson; Ögmundr Þorkelsson, from Breiðabólstaður in Fljótshlíð (S)?; Brandr Þorkelsson, from Helgafell (D)?; Þórðr Þorvaldsson, usually not regarded as the same as the chieftain of that name from Vatnsfjörður (Ingvarsson 1986–7: i. 217); Guðmundr Dálksson, usually regarded as the brother of Rúnólfr priest at Helgafell, nephews of Ketill Þorsteinsson, bishop of Hólar (Ingvarsson 1986–7: i. 217); Bersi Hallvarðsson; Bjarni Konálsson; Guðmundr Knútsson, in Svarfaðardalur? (Ingvarsson 1986–7: i. 218); Páll Bjarnason, is most probably the same as the chieftain who supported Sturla Þórðarson at the Alþing in 1159 (*Sturl* 62); Helgi Starkaðarson; Hjalti Arnsteinsson; Markús Marðarson, d. 1149? (*IA* 20, 60, 114); Teitr Kárason; Þorvarðr Jóansson; Þórarinn Þorvarðsson.

to the lower strata of society. As will be discussed below, there is reason to believe that there were always clerics of widely varying social standing but it is maintained here that in the twelfth century the priesthood was predominantly upper class.

This is suggested by the patterns of ordinations in some families in the west and north. The Staðarhólsmenn, Seldælir, Vatnsfirðingar, and Grundarmenn were not closely associated with the church in the twelfth century but all were prominent in political conflict in their respective areas and owned *goðorð*. The principal estates of all these families were church-farms, centrally located in each area, which later at least were among the most important churches in the country.[14] For three of these families it is known, and for the Grundarmenn it is reasonably certain, that in the early or middle part of the twelfth century the respective chieftains had their elder sons ordained as priests.

The chieftain Þorgils Oddason in Staðarhóll (D) sent his older son Oddi to be educated with Sæmundr *fróði* in Oddi (S); he then became a priest and was considered to have become learned. He died in the same epidemic as his father in 1151 (*Sturl* 51–2, 53–6; *DI* i. 186). Markús, the elder son of the Seldælir's chieftain Sveinbjörn Bárðarson in Eyri in Arnarfjörður (N), was put to study in childhood and became a priest but was mainly remembered for his super-human strength. He died in an avalanche, leaving the task of heading the family to his younger brother Hrafn (d. 1213), who was not even a *hostiarius*.[15] The Seldælir's main rivals for power in Vestfirðir were the Vatnsfirðingar. Þórðr Þorvaldsson who established the *staðr* in Vatnsfjörður (N) had his older son Páll ordained as priest, but after Páll had shown himself to be a promising bully—by fighting in the law court at the Alþing and abducting women—he drowned in 1171 and his brother Snorri inherited the family *goðorð* (*Sturl* 50, 88, 89–90, 106, 108; *IA* 117).

The chieftain Þorsteinn *ranglátr* at Grund in Eyjafjörður (N) (d. 1149) had many children through whom he made marriage alliances with a number of important families. His son, the priest Ketill, succeeded him at Grund but he does not seem to have been old when he died in 1173 because his son Þorlákr died as late as 1240 and Ketill's brother Ólafr who seems to have inherited the family *goðorð* died in 1204. The reason why Ketill seems to have been older than Ólafr is that it was he who inherited Grund from his father and his son Þorlákr seems to have lived there until 1199 when he was exiled from Eyjafjörður. Ólafr, who lived at Saurbær in Eyjafjörður (N), had the family's *goðorð* in 1187 and it may be that this was because Þorlákr was still only a teenager (*Sturl* 50, 108; *IA*

[14] None of these was a *staðr*, but all owned other lands and had more than one priest attached (*DI* ii. 452–3; iii. 79–80, 198 (iv. 145–6); iv. 133–5).

[15] *Hrafns saga Sveinbjarnarsonar hin sérstaka* asserts that Hrafn was 'well educated, but not ordained more than *krúnuvígsla*' (=*prima tonsura*) (*Sturl* 884). The *prima tonsura* 'marked admission to the clerical state before further progress through the seven orders . . . It imposed an obligation to read the canonical hours . . . keep a decent hair style and wear sober clothes.' (Helgadóttir 1987: 60 n. 2/29–30). As in *Messk* 108; *Lexicon für Theologie und Kirche* 10: 250–1.

61; *Sturl* 109, 124, 126; *IA* 122). In addition to these cases, there are numerous others where the relative age of chieftains' sons cannot be ascertained but where sons who were clearly intended to wield power were ordained: Sigmundr Ormsson of the Svínfellingar in Svínafell (A) (d. 1198) (*Sturl* 48–9; *IA* 121, 324; *Bsk* i. 437, 455); Kleppjárn Klængsson of the Hrafngilingar in Hrafnagil (N) (d. 1194) (*Sturl* 125, 126, 128, 138; *Bsk* i. 445); Jón Ketilsson of the Fljótamenn in Holt (N) (d. 1192) (*Sturl* 129–30; *Bsk* i. 439; *IA* 22, 61, 120, 180, 324); Halldórr Snorrason of the Melmenn (d. 1163) (*Sturl* 103; *IA* 116); Bersi Halldórsson of the Mýramenn (d. 1204) (*Sturl* 193; *Bsk* i. 489; *IA* 62, 112) and Bjarni Bjarnason of the Vallverjar (d. 1181) (*Sturl* 184; *ÍF* i. 291–3, 363–5; *IA* 118) are the most conspicuous examples in the generation after the priests on the list from 1143.

In most of these cases the families in question had not had other brothers ordained and in many of them there were no priests in the subsequent generations. As is clear from Figure 9 there was a sharp drop in the number of chieftain-priests around and after 1200 and chieftains began to let it suffice for them to be deacons or some other lesser order. It is notable that the families which had first become associated with the church, the Oddaverjar, Haukdælir, and the Reykhyltingar, were also those which kept the association longest. In these cases it had probably become a matter of family tradition by the beginning of the thirteenth century and it is unlikely that the likes of Þorvaldr Gizurarson were actively involved in the cure of souls.

In the latter half of the twelfth century when many chieftains were priests but had on the whole ceased to have their eldest sons or likely heirs ordained, several developments can be discerned.

1. From the late twelfth century onwards younger brothers and sons of sisters in powerful families begin to be ordained in significant numbers. Examples: Ólafr Þorvarðsson, Hallbjörn Jónsson, Vilhjálmr Sæmundarson (d. 1273) and his nephew Ísarr Pálsson of the Oddaverjar (*Sturl* 46; *Sturl* 212–13, 787; *IA* 139, 331;

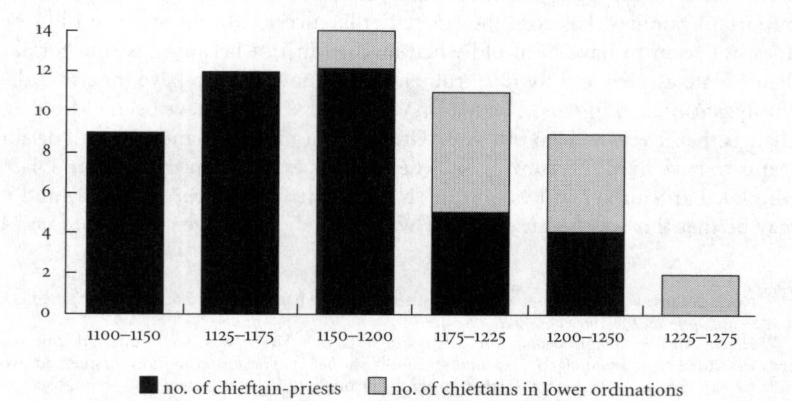

FIGURE 9. *The numbers of ordained chieftains by period, based on Table 7*

TABLE 7. *Ordained chieftains in Iceland 1100–1275*

Region	1100–1150	1125–1175	1150–1200	1175–1225	1200–1250	1225–1275
Rangárþing	Eyjófr Sæmundarson	Loptr Sæmundarson	Teitr Hauksson Bjarni Bjarnason *Jón Loptsson*	*Sæmundr Jónsson* *Ormr Jónsson* *Páll Jónsson*	Vilhjálmr Sæmundarson *Páll Sæmundarson* *Jón Ormsson*	
Árnesþing	Hallr Teitsson		*Gizurr Hallsson*	Þorvaldr Gizurarson Magnús Gizurarson	Magnús Hallsson *Klængr Þorvaldsson*	
Kjalarnes	Skapti Þórarinsson				Magnús Guðmundarson	
Borgarfjörður	Símun Jörundarson	Páll Sölvason Þóðr Skúlason Ormr Koðránsson	Bersi Vermundarson	Magnús Pálsson Þórðr Böðvarsson		*Egill Sömundarson*
Snæfellsnes and Dalir	Guðmundr Brandsson Ingimundr Einarsson Ari Þorgilsson	Oddi Þorgilsson Brandr Þorkelsson Þorgils Arason Rúnólfr Dálksson	Þorgils Snorrason	*Þórðr Sturluson*		
Vestfirðir			Markús Sveinbjarnarson Jón Brandsson Páll Þórðarson	*Hrafn Sveinbjarnarson*		
Húnaþing			Halldórr Snorrason			
Skagafjörður	Ketill Guðmundsson	Brandr Úlfhéðinsson Þorgeirr Guðmundarson	Jón Ketilsson		Jón Markússon	*Guttormr Kálfsson*
Eyjafjörður	Jón Þorvarðarson	Rúnólfr Ketilsson	Ketill Þorsteinsson Kleppjárn Klængsson		*Kálfr Guttormsson*	
Þingeyjarþing				Eyjólfr Hallsson		
Austurland		Oddr Gizurarson	Sigmundr Ormsson	*Teitr Oddsson*	*Ormr Jónsson*	

Note: Names of priests in roman type, names of deacons in italic type.

Sturl 428, 537); Teitr Þorvaldsson of the Haukdælir (d. 1259) (*Sturl* 193, 401, 455, 475; *IA* 134, 192, 330); Jón *krókr* Þorleifsson of the Sturlungar (d. 1229) (*Sturl* 325; *IA* 128); Abbot Þorsteinn Tumason of the Ásbirningar (*Sturl* 48, 114; *Bsk* i. 366; *IA* 64); Þórðr, son of Önundr Þorkelsson (*Sturl* 156); Ingimundr Þorgeirsson and his nephew Guðmundr Arason and Abbot Arnórr Helgason of the Kirkbæingar (*Sturl* 550; *DI* i. 395; *IA* 65, 131, 132, 190, 329, 482).

2. Some families which were beginning to lose out in the race for power began to concentrate on involvement with the Church. This applied to some extent to the Reykhyltingar[16] but more conspicuously to the Hítdælir,[17] Skarðverjar,[18] Staðarhólsmenn,[19] Seldælir in Selárdalur,[20] and Ámundaætt.[21] In the cases of the Skarðverjar and Reykhyltingar the leaders of both families had been priests for more than two generations around 1200 but in other families entering the priesthood was a thirteenth-century reaction to relative deterioration of these families' political authority.

3. In the late twelfth century examples begin to crop up of very rich men of

[16] With the priest Páll Sölvason (d. 1185) being the last powerful chieftain of the family. His son the priest Magnús (d. 1221) gave up Reykholt (S) to Snorri Sturluson on condition that he made men out of Magnús's sons, the priests Ari and Brandr (*Sturl* 211).

[17] The son of Þorlákr Ketilsson in Hítardalur (d. 1240) was the priest and lawspeaker Ketill (d. 1273).

[18] Þorgils the priest in Skarð (D) (d. 1201) gave his part of the family *goðorð* to Þórðr Sturluson in 1198 (*Sturl* 187). His son Haukr the priest (d. 1245) moved to Hagi in Barðaströnd (N) where he married a daughter of the priest and local leader Steinólfr Ljótsson (*Sturl* 240 (923)). Þorgils's brother was the priest Narfi (d. 1202) and it was his son the priest Snorri who became the leader of the family. Snorri's son was the priest Narfi (d. 1284) who married a daughter of the priest Ketill of the Hítdælir and lived at Kolbeinsstaðir (S). Through his son Snorri the lawman (d. 1332) at Skarð the Skarðverjar family was continued. The Skarðverjar were close allies of the Sturlungar in the 13th cent. and were among the few families in the century which retained their family estate and continued to wield influence in the late middle ages.

[19] With the death of Einarr Þorgilsson in 1185 the chieftaincy of the Staðarhólsmenn came to an end (Sigurðsson 1989: 68). Einarr's nephews, the priests Hallr (d. 1228) and Þorgils in Staðr in Reykjanes (D), represent the next generation of the family. Hallr's son the priest Páll, who married a daughter of the priest Sámr Símunarson in Narfeyri (D), was a local leader and ally of the Sturlungar. The son of Þorgils was the priest and abbot, Lambkárr (d. 1249) who was a career cleric in the first half of the 13th cent. His grandsons were the priests Aðalbrandr (d. 1286) and Þorvaldr (d. 1289) who figure in *Árna saga biskups* as a new breed of church dignitaries which was appearing in the late 13th cent. Þorvaldr was one of the first rural deans in Iceland.

[20] The Seldælir failed in their bid for supremacy in the Vestfirðir at the beginning of the 13th cent., and the descendants of the chieftain, Hrafn Sveinbjarnarson (d. 1211), did not wield local power. The gap left by Hrafn was filled by a side-branch of the family, the sons of his cousin Ragnheiðr Aronsdóttir, two of which—Eyvindr in Hagi (N) and Tómas in Selárdalur (N) (d. 1253)—were priests. Their sister was married to the priest Skúli Þorsteinsson in Staðarhraun (S). Eyvindr and Tómas were local leaders in the southern Vestfirðir in the middle of the 13th cent. and it was Tómas's descendants who headed the family in the late middle ages.

[21] The chieftain Guðmundr *gríss* in Þingvellir (S) (d. 1210) married his daughters to chieftains of the Svínfellingar and Haukdælir but these powerful in-laws do not seem to have been much help to the elder son, the priest Magnús (d. 1240). His temporal powers in Kjalarnes seem to have been waning in the 1210s when Snorri Sturluson made concerted efforts to undermine him. He was later selected to become bishop of Skálholt but was rejected by the archbishop. Magnús's younger brother Þorlákr lived most of his life in the east among the Svínfellingar (apparently his wife's kin) and two of their sons became priests—on of them was Bishop Árni (d. 1298). Among his nephews and nieces were one bishop, one abbess, and three priests.

non-aristocratic family who were ordained as priests and were attempting to better their social positions through marriage alliances. The best examples are Högni Þormóðarson in Bær (S) and Þórir Þorsteinsson in Deildartunga (S). Bersi Vermundarson in Borg (S) may be another.

4. In the early thirteenth century members of successful families tended to hold lower orders (deacons, subdeacons, acolytes). This is particularly true of the Oddaverjar, where it can be put down to family tradition, but in other families, which had had very little involvement with the Church, it also becomes common and may have been regarded as a sign of refinement.[22] Examples: Þórðr Sturluson and some of his sons of the Sturlungar; Snorri Markússon from Melar (S); Oddr Sveinbjarnarson from Álftanes (S); Snorri Grímsson from Hof in Höfðaströnd (N); Kálfr Guttormsson and his son Guttormr and Teitr Oddsson in Hof in Vopnafjörður (A) (see Table 7).

It seems, then, that from the late twelfth century the aristocracy began to distance itself from active involvement in pastoral duties. We do not of course know whether the likes of Sæmundr *fróði* or his pupil Oddi Þorgilsson actually had ministered to a flock and had sung masses regularly or if they had some completely different sense of what their pastoral duties involved. In this context it does not matter much; it is clear that in the early and mid-twelfth century aristocrats attached significance to being ordained and we can with confidence assert that this also meant that they found it expedient to be, or be seen, as patrons of the Church. As the aristocrats were followed into the priesthood by more modest householders, the exclusivity of the office diminished and the aristocrats began to distance themselves from pastoral duties (however they had been perceived). This may have coincided with increased episcopal supervision of the cure of souls in each area, which may have resulted in more onerous duties for the pastors and which consequently may have become less appealing for people who considered themselves to be of high rank. More clearly, however, the decrease in the number of ordained chieftains coincides with the increased consolidation of power which is evident nationally from the late twelfth century. This suggests that the pastoral office had aided a few generations of chieftains in developing the means of wielding institutionalized power but that once these means had become fairly secure in their hands they were able to stop being priests.

It is probably not a coincidence that the four examples enumerated above of older sons being ordained in aristocratic families, all come from areas where power consolidation took place relatively late or took longer to accomplish. It suggests that in this these chieftains were imitating their more successful peers in the southern flatlands whose success was, or at least appeared to be, inextricably linked with their intimate involvement with the Church.

Towards the end of the twelfth century the social make-up of the clergy looks

[22] It may also, as Helgi Þorláksson (1982*a*) has pointed out, have been considered as a protection against violence.

much more complex than it did in the beginning of that century. There are still a few chieftain priests, but many are householders of more modest, although it seems in most cases respectable, rank. The institutional expansion of the Church, with the monastic foundations of the mid and late twelfth century, was giving disinherited aristocrats a chance of saving themselves from obscurity as well as creating opportunities for promising young men of lower status to better their position. In addition a number of priests have appeared who were in service for the owners of churches and do not always seem to have been of very respectable parentage.

This picture is of course to a large extent conditioned by the nature of our sources. Detailed narrative accounts from which distinctions of social class and political influence can be gleaned are only available for the last three or four decades of the twelfth century. For the early twelfth century, on the other hand, the evidence is much more sparse and incomplete; it is mostly evidence written in the succeeding century and deals, as can be expected, almost exclusively with people occupying the highest rung in society's ladder. It is therefore perfectly possible that we are deceived by our sources and that the social make-up of the clergy was quite complex as early as the eleventh century. It is no good to shelter behind the silence of the sources and further below it will be argued that, while there probably always was an underclass of priests, it did not become socially significant until the latter half of the twelfth century.

It has been argued above that owning churches and being priests had helped chieftains around and after 1100 to overcome problems of consolidating and perpetuating power. It has also been shown how, as these chieftain families developed overlordships, others bowed out of that race in the late twelfth and early thirteenth century and concentrated instead on strengthening their local powers by being their subordinates' spiritual as well as political leaders. When it suited them these local magnates could use their ecclesiastical identities as an excuse not to take sides in political conflict and this had become, by the middle of the thirteenth century, a valuable asset. This no doubt contributed a great deal to an increasingly separate identity of the priesthood (discussed further below), and in general to the growth of a new set of social distinctions, where the powers of a magnate, his behaviour, and interests, became defined by the office he held.

In this we can see how the Church contributed to increasingly complex and compartmentalized power structures; it helped to create conditions with different tiers of magnates and helped them to define their roles in respect to each other. These issues will be discussed in more detail in Chapter 6.

3. THE STATUS OF PRIESTS ACCORDING TO THE OLD CHRISTIAN LAW SECTION

The Old Christian law section was first drafted in 1122–33 but the version surviving in *Konungsbók* (the slightly older of the two main manuscripts of *Grágás*) was probably arranged between 1199 and 1217, but not earlier. There is no knowing how much or what parts exactly of the surviving version originate in the earliest version, and it is therefore safest to regard the text as relevant to conditions around 1200.

Most history books that mention the Icelandic church in the Commonwealth period will stress two apparently contradictory indications about the status of the Icelandic priesthood. On the one hand reference is often made to the servile priests and on the other attention is drawn to the high status of priests, that priests owned churches and as often as not were chieftains as well. As discussed above, there is no direct evidence for the existence of servile priests and while householding priests certainly are a conspicuous and important feature of ecclesiastical organization in Iceland in the twelfth century and remained a strong influence throughout the thirteenth century, their class was in the course of the latter century beginning to be outnumbered by priests who did not own the church which they served and were not heads of the households they belonged to.

These latter are the *þingaprestar* or district priests who sold their services on the open market, and it is to this type of priest that the Old Christian law section devotes most space. The regulations concerning the district priest place him in the social group of skilled servants who were free to choose their employers but had to have a fixed abode come spring every year and were closely regulated as to the work they had to carry out and what pay they could demand (*Grg 1a*, 20_{18}–22_{10}, $132_{15–24}$; *Grg 1b*, $210_{10–25}$, $217_{2–16}$; *Grg II*, 24_5–26_{19}, 52_{14}–53_{11}, $58_{8–16}$, $60_{4–7}$; cf. *Grg 1a*, $130_{21–6}$. Þ. Jóhannesson 1933: 83–92, 106–20). The difference between them and ordinary servants was that they did not take orders for their daily routine and were paid in proportion to their service or manufacture. That is, shipbuilders were paid for the ship they built and priests for the mass they sung, while servants were paid fixed wages for specific periods. This type of priest is well attested in both *Sturlunga saga* and the sagas of bishops, and we may assume that the majority of priests in twelfth and thirteenth century Iceland belonged to this category. We do have more examples of priests who were householders or chieftains (118 against 59), but that is natural considering the nature of our sources.

A district priest had to have a legal abode (*Grg 1a*, $4_{12–19}$, $16_{17–20}$, $20_{18–27}$, $132_{15–24}$; *Grg 1b*, $217_{5–16}$; *Grg II*, $3_{4–8}$, $269_{8–16}$), but he did not seem to be required to live at a church-farm, although it seemed to be regarded as the norm (*Grg 1a*, $8_{19–20}$, $16_{9–11}$; *Grg II*, 7_{21}–8_1). He might have had to serve more than one church (*Grg 1a*, $16_{20–3}$, $21_{9–11}$; *Grg II*, $19_{24–5}$), but there are contradicting indications as to whether such a priest was hired by a single church-owner or several church-owners collectively (*Grg 1a*, 16_{17}–17_{2}, $20_{24–7}$, $132_{16–19}$ vs. *Grg 1b*, $217_{2–3,\ 9–16}$). The priest's duties to his flock are not regulated; the only requirement which is clearly spelt out is that the priest was always to be available to perform baptism, and could not leave his abode without the necessary implements to perform the rite (*Grg 1a*, 4_{11}–5_{4}; *Grg II*, 2_{17}–3_{12}, $7_{2–3}$). Priests seem also to have been obliged to perform funerals and bless bones that had been transferred between cemeteries (*Grg 1a*, $10_{7–16}$, $13_{12–13}$), but penalties are not mentioned in case of non-compliance as they are if a priest refused to baptize or was not available to do so. Priests were paid a separate, fixed fee for performing funerals, and in a case where the deceased was impoverished it is regulated that the funeral fee should be paid rather than the burial fee to the church-owner. This suggests that the funeral service was considered to be essential, if not mandatory, and that priests had a duty to perform it if asked to, although the law only mentions the limitations to a priest's claim to corpses from his ministry (*Grg 1a*, $9_{7–24}$, $10_{7–16}$). Hearing last confession is referred to but not as a duty (*Grg 1a*, $12_{8–13}$), and only oblique mention is made of visiting the sick (*Grg 1a*, 21). The Old Christian law section was of course a law of the land, regulating how laymen should conduct themselves as Christians and their relationship with priests and churches; it is not to be expected to be a manual of pastoral care. We can only assume that in Iceland the basic duties of a priest towards his flock were the same as elsewhere in medieval Christian Europe.

According to an additional clause in the *Staðarhólsbók* version of the section church-owners were obliged to pay for a minimum amount of services annually (*Grg II*, $19_{22–6}$; on this clause see further in Ch. 3, s. 3), but the tithe law seems to indicate that the church-owner should only buy so much service as the income from his tithe allowed him (*Grg 1b*, 210). The maximum of a priest's total annual income is regulated (*Grg 1a*, 20_{27}–21_{9}; *Grg 1b*, $217_{3–9}$: 12 marks), and one late manuscript gives the maximum annual fee for full service at a single church (*Grg III*, $24_{13–15}$: 4 marks). Another late manuscript also has a formula for the price of masses which were sung at other times than legally prescribed holy days (*Grg III*, $318_{11–12}$: 0.3 ells per mass). Priests were not to sing more than two masses daily, and were forbidden to sing nocturnal masses except on Christmas morning (*Grg 1a*, $21_{11–15}$).[23] The main worry of the legislators seems to have been that priests might sing masses ceaselessly and exact payments for all of them.

District priests had some say in the management of the church they served. The church-owner and priest were to decide together where graves should be taken in the cemetery. If the church-owner did not do so, the priest was allowed to bring fire into his church, light candles, and ring the bells or could appoint someone to do it for him. This meant that, if the church was damaged by fire or a bell was broken, the priest was not held responsible provided that a verdict

[23] St Þorlákr's penitential also has a prohibition against saying more than two masses daily (*DI* i. 244).

that he had treated his church as if it were his own property and had meant to take good care of it was proclaimed. Also if the church-owner did not bring a suit in case of non-payment of the church's and priest's quarters of the tithe, the priest was allowed to do so (*Grg 1a*, 8_{19-20}, 16_{9-15}; *Grg 1b*, 210_{21-3}). This suggests that by 1200 at least district priests, even if they only were attached to a church for a year, were considered to be more than just hired hands to perform certain services. Their spiritual position gave them a limited right to intervene in matters which were normally a function of ownership. Extremely limited as this right was, it is nevertheless significant and signals changing perceptions of the reasons behind a person's rights and responsibilities; it was beginning to be possible for a man to act in the capacity of an office.

The bishops decided which priests were allowed to sing mass, and could forbid priests from officiating. Detailed regulations follow on the rights of Icelandic priests who had been abroad and of foreign priests to officiate in Iceland (*Grg 1a*, 21_{30}–22_{10}). Intended to strengthen diocesan authority, these regulations also indicate that the bond between priest and bishop was thought of in similar terms as the bond between chieftain and householder; it was personal, and a bishop's commitments were not binding on his successor (cf. a bishop's right to change the size of tithe areas: *Grg 1b*, 214_{11-20}; *Grg III*, 14_{8-14}). A priest who had had a previous bishop's permission to officiate, but had gone abroad, had to get permission anew when he got back. While foreign priests had to have 'the writ and seal of the bishop, and the testimony of two men who were present at their ordination and who repeat the bishop's words saying that it is lawful for people to receive all priestly offices from them' (trans. *LEI* i. 38, *Grg 1a*, 22; cf. *Grg II*, 26_{16-19}).

This refers to the writ, seal, and words of the foreign bishop who ordained the priest and represents somewhat tighter regulations than those given in *Staðarhólsbók*, where the priest only had to produce the two witnesses if he did not have the seal. In *Staðarhólsbók* it is also added that the bishop must provide his priests with chrism and consecrate their vestments, but if they want to have wine or flour for the bread of the Eucharist they must pay him 3 ells annually (*Grg II*, 26_{1-4}; also in *Skálholtsbók*: *Grg III*, 23_{4-7}; *DI* ii. 518–19, 545, 557; ii. 792, 800, 805, 814, 816). If, as seems likely, the bishops governed the distribution of chrism, wine, and flour, that of course was a tangible way of refusing priests the means of officiating.[24]

The regulations on priests' obedience to the bishop were presumably meant to apply to all priests: 'Priests must be obedient to their bishop and show him their books and vestments. . . . A priest must not wear fashions forbidden by the bishop, and must have his moustache and beard cut off and be tonsured once a month, and obey the bishop in all things' (trans. *LEI* i. 37; *Grg 1a*, 21). This clause on obedience is based on a Norwegian model (*NgL* i. 310_{13}). It is not

[24] St Þorlákr's penitential requires that a priest does not say mass without 'wine and water, the host.' (*DI* i. 243).

the impression given by the saga literature that modesty of attire was an acceptable form of social differentiation for Icelandic aristocrats, whether secular or ordained (B. Þorsteinsson 1963: 472). Tonsure on the other hand may well have been; from 1234 we have the homely scene where the chieftain Kálfr Guttormsson who was an acolyte and his son Guttormr who was a deacon have just been shaved and tonsured when their enemies fall upon them (*Sturl* 356).[25] If chieftains in lower orders bothered to be shaved and tonsured regularly that indicates that they considered these symbols of their piety or religious obligations to be important, but it is doubtful if they could afford not to dress ostentatiously.

If a priest disobeyed the bishop he could be fined 3 marks. The bishop was to bring the suit at a special court of priests at the Alþing. He was to nominate twelve priests to sit as judges in the court and the case was to be prosecuted without oaths. The bishop formed a panel of three with two priests to give verdicts as a means of proof before the court (*Grg Ia*, 21_{21-30}; in *Staðarhólsbók* it is added that the court of priests was to be held in the church at Þingvellir: *Grg II*, 25_{18}). The court of priests seems to some extent to have been based on the model of a panel of twelve (*tólftarkviðr* or *tylptarkviðr*), an institution a chieftain could be called upon to form at any assembly, consisting of himself and eleven others from his *vorþing* region. It was a means of establishing proof, mainly used in cases involving a greater degree of public interest instead of a panel of neighbours (*búakviðr*) or a panel of five (*bjargkviðr*), and the verdict was decided by a simple majority. The verdict of such a panel could then be used as a means of proof in any court of law (*Grg Ia*, 22_{25}–23_{1}, 51_{2-15}, 65_{11-15}, 65_{32}–67_{28}, 123_{5-8}, 143_{11-17}, 157_{17-27}; *Grg III*, s.v. *kviðr*; *LEI* i. 253–4). The difference between a panel of twelve and a court of priests was that in the latter the verdict of guilty carried with it an automatic sentence: a fixed fine of 3 marks payable to the bishop. If the guilty priest did not pay his fine, he was to be prosecuted for a breach of judgment like anyone else in a secular court. It is not entirely clear how the court of priests functioned but it seems that the bishop himself was not among the twelve judges, but acted as plaintiff and produced the evidence from himself and two priests.

In *Staðarhólsbók* it is added that if 'a priest discloses anyone's confession without what his diocesan thinks legitimate excuse, the penalty is lesser outlawry. Nine of the priest's neighbours are to be called at the assembly' (trans. *LEI* i. 200; *Grg II*, 25; also in *Skálholtsbók* and AM 181 4to; *Grg III*, 24_{16-19}, 328_{2}). Lesser outlawry involved confiscation of property and a three year stay abroad (*Grg III*, 608–9). This is the same penalty and procedure described for if a priest refused to baptize a child (*Grg Ia*, 4_{14-16}). In cases when a priest did not take a legal abode, refused to give services, or charged more than the legally prescribed

[25] Kálfr did not own a *goðorð*, but was a *stórbóndi*. It is implied that Kálfr had a hunch that their days were numbered, and the tonsure may therefore be seen as having formed a part of their preparations for execution.

maximum for his services, there was a 3 mark fine (*Grg 1a*, 20_{23-7}, 21_{6-9}; *Grg II*, 19_{24-6}). In all these cases the suit was to be brought in secular courts as far as can be seen (*Grg 1a*, 36_{16-23}).

The Old Christian law section is primarily a manual for laymen on how to practise Christianity. It is devoted largely to practical problems like taking children to be baptized, corpses to be buried, and what chores could be performed in times of fasting. It regulates the rights and obligations of church-owners, but regarding priests and bishops it only contains rules which had a bearing on their relationship with laymen. The only exception is the clause on priests' obedience to their bishop and on the court of priests (*Grg 1a*, 21_{15-30}). It is not unthinkable that in the twelfth century the Church had some internal regulations like the episcopal statutes preserved from the thirteenth century onwards, although there is nothing to suggest it had. What it did have was a penitential from St Þorlákr's episcopacy (1178–93) where penances are prescribed both for secular sinners and priests who were negligent in their office (*DI* i. 240–4).[26]

Regarding priests the Old Christian law section is best seen as an attempt to reconcile the hierarchical ideology of the Church on the one hand and Icelandic social conditions on the other. In part priests are seen as subordinate to their bishop, receiving from him the means of their office, but mostly the interest lies in regulating them as free agents who performed specific services. There were no formal channels available to a layman who felt injured by a priest to complain to the bishop; he could only bring a civil law suit and hope that the bishop did not throw his weight behind the priest. The bishop was supposed to be able to make his priests obey him, but there is no sense that he was responsible for them. This relationship is very much akin to the *goði–þingmaðr* relationship. It was not enshrined in law but if a *goði* could not make his *þingmenn* obey him, he lost grounds for his power, and although, for the same reason, he had better stand by them, he was not obliged to do so. That the relationship between priest and bishop was, in the minds of the legislators at least, perceived of in similar terms as the relationship between *goði* and *þingmaðr* is further suggested by the apparently personal nature of ordination and the similarity between the court of priests and the panel of twelve.

As is indicated towards the end of the Old Christian law section, it was the bishops who made the first draft of it (*Grg 1a*, 36_{23-6}), and although it presumably had to be accepted, and was subject to alteration, by the law council, it is likely that subsequent changes were primarily initiated by the bishops. If it was they who saw themselves as chieftains and their priests as followers (*þingmannalið*), that does have implications for our view of the nature of the early Icelandic church (see further in Ch. 4, s. 2).

It is not surprising that there is no mention of priests owning churches or being householders or chieftains in the Old Christian law section; it is difficult

[26] Trans. in McNeill and Gamer 1938: 355–8. Further in Rafnsson 1982*a*; 1982*b*; 1985*a*.

to see what problems might arise from such a union which had to be regulated by law, that is, as long as private ownership of churches was not considered problematic. What is surprising is that there is very little sense of priests having a special status, rights, or privileges that had to be protected. As mentioned above, priests were considered to have a limited say in the running of the churches they served, and although significant for the definition of church property, this say was more a recognition of the priests' profession and a fallback in case the guardian of the church failed to do his duty. The concern of the legislators was not to establish the authority or rights of priests, but to protect laymen from them; the main worry was that priests might force church-owners to pay for an inordinate number of masses. The type of priest the legislators are primarily concerned with is the district priest and it is likely that the regulations reflect the unease of a farming society towards classes of people who were free to choose their employment and could demand high wages for their services. But these regulations also suggest that the district priests (not to speak of the servile priests, if they existed) were not the sort of men the bishops identified with. The company the bishops kept was that of ordained householders and chieftains, and the rights of such men were defined not by their ordination, but in secular terms of pedigree, wealth, and political influence. They did not need protection or special privileges on account of their ordination. This is reflected in the reception of the idea of *privilegium canonis* in Iceland. The privilege is mentioned in the earliest preserved archiepiscopal letter to Iceland from 1174 (*DI* i. 222), and consistently in such letters after that (Grímsdóttir 1982: 38–45). In St Þorlákr's penitential, however, the maiming of priests is mentioned almost in passing, among the maltreatment of all kinds of people punishable only by penance at the bishop's discretion (*DI* i. 243).[27] The impression that maiming or killing priests was not considered to be the worst problem is given by the series of archiepiscopal letters sent to Iceland between 1174 and 1190. In these the archbishops seem much more worried that priests carried weapons, maimed and killed laymen, took part in secular politics, and held secular offices (*DI* i. 222, 263, 288–9, 291).

The reforming archbishops Eysteinn Erlendsson (1161–88) and Eiríkr Ívarsson (1188–1205) were concerned with establishing the Church as an institution, and that could only be done by differentiating clearly between the secular and ecclesiastical spheres. That this was an uphill struggle not only in Norway, but also in Iceland, is clearly reflected in the tone of their letters, and by the fact that they did not have an advocate in Iceland until Bishop Guðmundr Arason (1203–37) came to the see of Hólar.[28] The resistance he met, and failure on all

[27] Killing of priests is not mentioned here, and Grímsdóttir 1982: 40 interprets that as an indication that it was considered to result in excommunication. Her interpretation that similar lenience is attested in a Norwegian synodal decree from 1189–90 (*DI* i. 233) is not acceptable as there a reference is being made to mitigating circumstances (cf. *DI* ii. 214; *NgL* v. 26_{7-9}).

[28] St Þorlákr can hardly be counted as such, as he, no doubt wisely, concentrated his efforts on sexual reform, see Ch. 4, s. 3.

counts, demonstrates that the Icelandic clergy were still not prepared to shed their secular identity.

It seems, then, that throughout the twelfth century and well into the thirteenth, Icelandic clergy were basically secular in their outlook. This suggests that the prevalence of chieftains and householders among priests indicated by our sources gives a more or less correct picture of this class. If the vast majority of priests had been men of low birth and little economic or political significance it is likely that their influence would have been felt sooner and that there would have been significant numbers to flock to Bishop Guðmundr *góði*'s side. As it was, in 1210–11 when Bishop Guðmundr had placed his see under interdict, 'priests did as they wanted in their services whatever the bishop said' (*Sturl* 225).[29]

4. PRIESTHOOD AND SOCIAL MOBILITY

In the above account I have almost exclusively been preoccupied with ordained chieftains and aristocratic householders. It is that sort of person who is most conspicuous in the sources for the earlier periods; they were endowing churches in the twelfth century and it is easy to understand how they could benefit politically from being priests.

It has been suggested that the sources do give a correct picture and that there were only very few Icelandic priests in the late eleventh century, and that these were of aristocratic birth. The number of ordained chieftains increased until the middle of the twelfth century but then dropped and we begin to find different kinds of people as priests. This is no doubt a simplification but, it is hoped, a useful one, especially regarding the long-term influence of the Church on the structure of Icelandic society.

There probably were from an early date Icelandic priests who were not householders, as well as householding priests who were not aristocratic. It may be, for instance, that the priest Þorkell who was householder in Hvammur (D) in the early twelfth century was not aristocratic. His lineage was probably unknown to the author of *Sturlu saga* as not even his patronymic is given, but he is called *góðr bóndi* (lit. 'householder of standing' = bonus vir?) which is not used of just anybody and the full name of his wife is given, which may suggest that the author intended the reader to recognize her. Þorkell had two sons, one of whom was also a priest, but although they were promising men they lost control over their finances after their father's death and had to sell the estate.[30]

[29] Cf. a clause earlier in the text which must be written by someone else: 'The Church there was then a poor and unhappy sight to behold. Some priests ceased singing masses because of fear of God, some continued because of fear of magnates, some because of their own will. The head-church, the mother, was sad and miserable and some of her daughters with her but some were in tears because of her sorrow. Each lived as he pleased but no one dared to reprimand or tell the truth.' (*Sturl* 224).

[30] They must have sold Hvammur sometime before Böðvarr sold it to Sturla Þórðarson in 1150 (*Sturl* 56).

The evidence for Þorkell's social status is ambiguous, as is that of the priest Erlendr Hallason who was a householder in neighbouring Ásgarður in *c*.1160. Erlendr was a *þingmaðr* of Einarr Þorgilsson and is called *gildr bóndi* (lit. 'worthy householder'). Erlendr was not a chieftain but he was clearly a prominent householder in his area since he often gave hospitality to his chieftain Einarr and initiated a quarrel with Einarr's chief rival, Sturla in Hvammur. Einarr's lineage is not known and it may well be that his parentage was not considered aristocratic; that we cannot know, but it is clear that he was a prominent householder in his area who determined to remain independent of Sturla. We can apply the same model to householding priests like Erlendr and possibly Þorkell as to the chieftains of the early twelfth century, only on a smaller scale. Becoming priests and owning churches was a way for ambitious householders of means, if not high birth, to assert their authority and prominence among their neighbours.

More spectacular are the examples of Högni *auðgi* Þormóðarson in Bær (S) and Þórir *auðgi* Þorsteinsson in Deildartunga (S) in the 1170s and 1180s. Both were of low birth, Högni was downright *ættsmár* (of insignificant family) (*Bsk* i. 284) while Þórir was told by his prospective father-in-law, the chieftain Páll Sölvason, that although Þórir was wealthy Páll would decide the terms of the marriage contract because Þórir was greatly inferior to them (*mun þykja mannamunr mikill*) (*Sturl* 90–1; *IA* 118). As their nicknames indicate, both were extremely wealthy and both sought to marry their children into chieftain families.

Högni was the better established of the two. He had married one daughter to a local magnate in Stafholt and another to a son of the chieftain at Garðar. It turned out that there was an impediment on account of affinity to the latter marriage, and Bishop Þorlákr (1178–93) made this a test case for his reform of marriage customs. It is a clear indicator of the aims and aspirations of Högni the priest that he put up fierce resistance to his bishop in defence of his marriage alliance and even went so far as to try to arrest the saint. He had also newly built a church at Bær when the dispute about his daughter's marriage broke out. The church there had not had a permanent ministry attached to it but it seems that Högni wanted to endow it adequately so it could support a priest or two.[31] He did not, however, want to donate the land of Bær itself—the core holding of the estate—but only satellite holdings.

Högni had to accept the annulment of the marriage but had his way with the endowment of his church. His agenda seems clear; he strove to consolidate Bær as a centre of his area by attaching a permanent ministry to the church there and he attempted to increase his influence and social standing through marriage alliances with chieftains in the region. As he had no sons his efforts did not result in an independent family of influence, but Bær became later in the thirteenth century one of the chief seats of Högni's descendants among the Garðamenn.

[31] In the 14th cent. there were two priests and a deacon at the church in Bær (*DI* iii. 123–4).

The information available to us regarding the priests Þórir and Högni is unusually rich in detail but their likes, householding priests who were not chieftains but clearly men of local influence—whether aristocrats or not—are the most common type of priest mentioned in our sources in the late twelfth and early thirteenth centuries. Often we know very little about these householding priests. In some cases their social standing is indicated by marriages; Sámr Símunarson at Narfeyri (D) for instance was married to a sister of the chieftain Hrafn Sveinbjarnarson and his daughter to the *stórbóndi* and priest Páll Hallsson of the Staðarhólsmenn, and this of course suggests that he was acceptable in respectable society (*Sturl* 49, 435, 457, 883; *DI* i. 464). The social status of others is suggested by their actions, like Árni priest in Skúmsstaðir (S) who invited Guðmundr Arason to stay with him in 1201 (*Sturl* 196). Sometimes no indications are available but there is only one example of a householding priest being described as impoverished (*Bsk* i. 348–9 (322–3)).

It goes without saying that, being householders, these priests already belonged to the upper strata of society. Where indications are available it seems that they were furthermore the affluent and locally influential householders. Some may have been aristocrats who did not have grand political aspirations and were content to be well respected locally, but it seems that a sizeable proportion of householding priests were men of non-aristocratic parentage who had in one way or other acquired wealth. The prejudice in Icelandic society against wealth accumulation, especially by non-aristocrats, is well known (Þorláksson 1991*b*: 178) and it seems likely that, by becoming priests, wealthy men of low birth sought social respectability. If we surmise that their aim was to have political influence in proportion to their economic strength, being priests served this aim in two ways; as it did for the chieftains it formalized and strengthened their relationship with, and influence over, their immediate neighbours and it may also have made them more acceptable company in polite circles.

It is usually not known whether householding priests owned the church and the land where they lived. It is usually assumed that they did and it seems that this was considered the norm. In several pre-fourteenth century charters of annex-churches it is allowed that a priest be permanently stationed at the church if he owns the land it stands on (*DI* i. 257(×2), 594; ii. 113; cf. *DI* i. 266, 276–7, 466). At the very least this suggests that it was considered normal, and possibly preferable, that priests should own the church they served and the land it stood on.

It seems, therefore, that the priesthood facilitated social mobility among the landowning classes, making it easier for men of non-aristocratic status to increase their influence and possibly even move their families up a rung on the social ladder. This helped bring about a change in the system of social distinctions, where family and lineage became less significant and the type of land owned, and office held, more important as definitions of an individual's social standing.

While being priests seems to have helped to nudge some householders up the social ladder and aided others in halting their slide down it, these were insignificant changes compared to the opportunities opened up by posts at the sees and the institution of the district priest.

Except for Tjörvi Böðvarsson who was the aide of Bishops Gizurr, Þorlákr, and Magnús of Skálholt and Bishop Jón's aide Hámundr Bjarnarson, Jón's cousin Hjalti, and his foreign teachers Gísli Finnason and Rikinni at Hólar (*Bysp* 1. 95–6, 104; *Bsk* i. 167–8 (239–40))—none of which can be related to any known family or lineage—St Þorlákr is our earliest example of a non-householding priest.

St Þorlákr's ancestry is known in considerable detail and this supports his saga's claim that his parents were 'of good family and noble ancestry' (*góðrar ættar ok göfugra manna fram í kyn*) but it is clear that his parents and grandparents were not prosperous and probably not influential either. His father had been a merchant before he became a householder but it seems that he was not successful and the family was dissolved when Þorlákr was still young and he and his mother went to Oddi where he was taught by the priest Eyjólfr Sæmundarson (*Bysp* 1. 12; *ÍF* xi. 65; *Bsk* i. 89–90). That suggests that his mother was at least well connected, although we do not of course know about the arrangements concerning her son's education. When he was ordained as priest—about the age of 19—he became a district priest in a small but profitable ministry and his saga claims that these revenues made it possible for him to go abroad and study for six years in Paris and Lincoln. That sounds unlikely; although the costs involved in travelling and staying abroad are difficult to appreciate, he must have had the backing of his earlier benefactors for such a prolonged, and it seems rare, expedition.[32] When he returned he was with his relatives and had healthy finances but it is not clear whether he had pastoral responsibilities. At the last minute he decided not to marry a widow who lived at the church-farm Háfur (S), the idea having been, it seems, that he would become a householding priest there. Instead he became a district priest at the major church-farm and later convent Kirkjubær in Síða (S) under the priest Bjarnhéðinn Sigurðarson, who was among the high-born of 1143. After six years at Kirkjubær he became prior of a new house of canons in Þykkvibær in Álftaver (S) from where he progressed to become bishop of Skálholt (*Bsk* i. 91–9, 101).

As his saga stresses, St Þorlákr was extremely thrifty and a good manager of his own and his see's finances. This was in clear contrast to his parents who had faced financial ruin in his childhood and while a study of his character will not be attempted here, interesting as it would be, it seems that he became from an early age bent on improving his social station. He probably would not have got far without the support of the Oddaverjar but his example shows how young men of impoverished family could, given the right circumstances, improve

[32] On the cost of education in the middle ages see M. M. Lárusson 1967*c*: 121–8.

dramatically on their social station through the priesthood. St Þorlákr is an example of a very successful priest but there were doubtless others who started off in similar circumstances as the saint but had less spectacular careers.

St Þorlákr may have been of good family but its fortunes were sinking and his success in life represents a dramatic improvement on his prospects at birth. It was the other way around with the priest Ingimundr Þorgeirsson, the uncle of Guðmundr Arason later bishop of Hólar. Ingimundr was the fourth son of the chieftain Þorgeirr Hallason and his ordination as priest can be seen as his opportunity to save himself from obscurity. Of his three elder brothers, the oldest one Einarr had died young it seems, Þorvarðr inherited the chieftaincy, while Þórðr spent his life as a monk at Þverá. Ingimundr's younger brother Ari was killed in the Norwegian civil wars in 1166 but had earlier fathered several children out of wedlock. One of these children was Guðmundr, and when news of his father's death reached Iceland it was decided that as he did not inherit from his father on account of being illegitimate Guðmundr should be made Ingimundr's charge and put to study (*Sturl* 101, 107). In 1201 when Guðmundr had been chosen as bishop of Hólar but was still resisting, his uncle the chieftain Þorvarðr told him to obey his command to accept the appointment. Þorvarðr claimed that, as the head of the family, he had had authority over Guðmundr's father and other relatives of theirs and insisted on Guðmundr's obedience. Guðmundr thought he should decide himself and replied: 'You did not offer me to inherit from my father and you have hitherto not sought to increase my honour except for having me beaten to study. It seems to me that you are more interested in getting me into trouble than esteem so I will not consent' (*Sturl* 201). This was probably intended by the author to be humorous, but there is also a clear sense that in chieftain families becoming a priest was in the second half of the twelfth century considered to be a way of sidelining younger sons and illegitimate offspring.

Ingimundr the priest seems to have been a rootless man, or he may simply have been difficult to get along with, because he lived in no less than nine places between 1168 and 1185. He began to keep house with his brother Þorvarðr but this arrangement only lasted for one year. He then moved to his brother-in-law where he stayed two years and from there he set up his own household first at Vaglir (N) for one year and then leasing Möðruvellir in Eyjafjörður (N) for another. When he lived at Möðruvellir he married Sigríðr Tumadóttir of the Ásbirningar, a very advantageous alliance, but the marriage did not work well so they moved to her father's in Ás in Hegranes (N). That did not work either and Ingimundr soon left and went to live at Grenjaðarstaður (A) where he presumably had pastoral responsibilities. He stayed there for four years and then became a co-householder at Staður in Kaldakinn (N) for two years. He made an abortive attempt to go abroad and lived in at least two places before he embarked for Norway again five years later. In Norway he held two benefices in four years before perishing in Greenland on his return trip to Iceland. *Prestssaga Guðmundar* makes much of Ingimundr and claims he was offered the chance to become bishop of Greenland when he was in Norway but had refused (*Sturl* 107–22). Ingimundr's career was singularly bumpy and he does not seem to have been one to grasp the opportunities when they appeared. His nephew Guðmundr, whom he had raised from the age of 6 or 7 and with whom he is said to have been strict because the boy resembled his kin in being uproarious and obstinate, took after his uncle and never stayed long in the same place.

Guðmundr followed his uncle around until he was 17. He was by then a deacon, and then spent two years in Saurbær in Eyjafjörður (N), possibly for further education. In 1180 he and Ingimundr attempted to leave for Norway but the ship was caught in a storm and they narrowly escaped with their lives, Guðmundr with a badly broken leg. He then stayed with kinsmen in the Vestfirðir and tried his hand at litigation, with pathetic results. Guðmundr stayed with Þorgeirr, son of Bishop Brandr of Hólar, at Staður in Reynines (N) in 1183–5. Þorgeirr was a promising magnate and brought Guðmundr's litigation to a conclusion, an act of friendship which seems to have deeply influenced Guðmundr. From the *Prestssaga* it seems almost as if Þorgeirr was the only person ever to be nice to Guðmundr.

Guðmundr was ordained priest in March 1185 and became a district priest at the church in Hof in Höfðaströnd (N), which was owned by his aunt and her husband, a minor chieftain. That same summer both Ingimundr and Þorgeirr left for Norway. On his return the following year Þorgeirr fell sick and died at sea and this, the *Prestssaga* claims, caused a dramatic change of character in Guðmundr. He had become gradually more serious and spiritually inclined after he had broken his leg in 1180 but now he turned into a complete ascetic. His religious devotion soon became almost fanatical and he began to earn himself a reputation as a miracle worker.[33] He took on clerics for teaching and also seems to have started early to spend all his revenue on charity. This, it seems, alarmed Bishop Brandr, who made him move to the less profitable ministry of Miklibær in Óslandshlíð (N) and sometime later demanded he hand over the books and vestments Ingimundr had given to him when he went to Norway. Bishop Brandr claimed that the see of Hólar was Ingimundr's inheritor (*Sturl* 118–19).[34]

Guðmundr's popularity kept growing however and he was only two years at Miklibær, then a year at Viðvík (N), and in 1190 he became district priest at the major church-farm Vellir in Svarfaðardalur (N). There he stayed six years but when he declined to accept the *staðr* at Vellir as a benefice, which would have meant he had to take financial responsibility for it, he moved to nearby Ufsir (N). About this time, in 1196, Guðmundr had become a national celebrity and started touring the country in the summertime, visiting the rich and famous

[33] On Guðmundr's religious views see Óskarsdóttir 1992.

[34] This must have been sometime after 1189 when Ingimundr disappeared—his body was not found until 1200 (*IA* 121, 181, 477). This was probably when Guðmundr was at Vellir (N).

and blessing and consecrating most things in his way. In 1198–9 he was back at Staður in Reynines (N), this time as a district priest in the household of the chieftain Kolbeinn Arnórsson, but the year after he moved to Víðimýri (N), to the household of the chieftain Kolbeinn Tumason head of the Ásbirningar and overlord of Skagafjörður. In 1201 when Bishop Brandr died Kolbeinn Tumason acted swiftly and had Guðmundr appointed as bishop-elect (*Sturl* 120, 122, 171–4, 176–80, 196–202).

Guðmundr's rise to fame was first and foremost due to his extraordinary character and religious fervour. As already recounted, he owed his elevation to the see of Hólar to a miscalculation on the part of Kolbeinn Tumason who seems to have thought that Guðmundr would be content with being religious and would leave real control in his hands. As it was, Bishop Guðmundr turned out to be every chieftain's worst nightmare.

It seems clear that Guðmundr occupied a rung below his uncle in the social ladder. Ingimundr was the legitimate son of a chieftain and does not seem to have been a district priest in any of his many homes. Sometimes it is said that he held house together with the resident householder and in his four-year stay at Grenjaðarstaður it can be assumed that he held a position of senior priest at the major church there.[35] Guðmundr on the other hand was illegitimate and fatherless and it does not seem that Ingimundr had trained him to accept financial responsibilities. His kinsmen intended him to become just a district priest and it was probably resentment because of this which lay behind Guðmundr's response to his uncle Þorvarðr in 1201. While Guðmundr was supposed to accept a slightly lower station in life than had belonged to his father, he was nevertheless extremely well connected through the marriage alliances of his numerous kinsmen. There was hardly a region in the north and west of the country where he did not have relatives, and this he exploited to his advantage.

Ingimundr Þorgeirsson became a priest because he was a chieftain's younger son and it kept him from falling further down the social ladder than he otherwise might have done. St Þorlákr and Guðmundr Arason, on the other hand, had meagre prospects at birth and for them the priesthood became a means to improve their station. These three men were all aristocrats and many of the earliest district priests known to us seem to have been of high birth. That seems to be the case with Gellir Höskuldsson at Snóksdalur (D) (*Sturl* 117, 249), Magnús Þórðarson at Mýrar (N) (*Sturl* 897–8), and Halldórr Hallvarðsson at Hof in Vopnafjörður (A) (*Sturl* 200). Others do, however, seem to have been of lower status. An example is Ljúfini the priest who may have been a priest at Staðarhóll (D) (*Sturl* 64), as was one Ívarr who was killed in a skirmish in 1170 (*Sturl* 72). At Sturla's household in Hvammur (D) there were

[35] In the 14th cent. there were three priests, a deacon, subdeacon, and two minor clerics attached to the church at Grenjaðarstaður (*DI* ii. 431–4). It was the most numerous staff at any parish-church in the country.

also district priests. The priest Ásbjörn was there in 1171 with his mother and sister who was the current concubine of Sturla's son Sveinn. Ásbjörn's brother had previously been a member of the household at Hvammur so it seems that the family had close ties with Sturla. Another priest called Oddr is mentioned in Hvammur on the same occasion and he took part in the battle in Sælingsdalsheiði (D) (*Sturl* 76, 80).

It is almost impossible to ascertain the status ascribed to men such as these. They often appear like any other domestic servants and do not seem to belong among respectable people but we cannot know whether they were menials in origin who were made priests by their householders, even as servile priests, or whether they were younger sons of householders who were starting out at the bottom. An example of the latter is the deacon Helgi Einarsson in Snóksdalur (D), son of Einarr Bjarnason, householder at the church-farm Kvennabrekka (D). Helgi took up arms in defence of his householder and was killed for it (*Sturl* 249–50). While possibly not an aristocrat, Helgi was clearly from a locally important family, but being part of the household at Snóksdalur decided his loyalties and actions.

It goes without saying that, just as we have success stories in St Þorlákr and Guðmundr Arason, there must have been many failures and misfits among the illegitimate and younger sons of aristocratic parentage. We may well ask what happened to the likes of Brandr and Ari, priest sons of Magnús Pálsson, erstwhile chieftain of the Reykhyltingar, after their father had surrendered his estate and his power to Snorri Sturluson (*Sturl* 211). They are never mentioned after their father's surrender and it is unlikely that they managed to do much better than becoming district priests. There were many casualties like these in the political turmoil of the late twelfth and early thirteenth centuries which no doubt accounted for a large part of the supply of district priests.

Whatever the social origin of district priests they were subject to the head of the household they belonged to. They were therefore not independent persons and membership of the household was for the majority of them probably a more significant parameter than their ordination. There are over sixty examples of domestic priests in the late twelfth and thirteenth centuries performing an array of tasks which have no relation to their pastoral duties, but are exactly like those of any other armed member of a household in dispute (see s. 5 below). These priests are messengers, spies, and bodyguards, they take part in war-parties and battles, and they kill. It does not seem that in executing these tasks these priests were particularly troubled by a sense that being ordained made them less qualified. It seems that their identity as members of a household or retinue, as the case might be, was more important than their ordination as priests. It is likely that only the extremely well connected like St Þorlákr and Guðmundr Arason could afford to adopt their own identity as churchmen. It is also likely that within the class of district priests there were considerable differences in social status. At the bottom of the range there were the likes of Ljúfini who was equally at home running after sheep as singing mass, representing a servile or near-servile rung of the social ladder. It is not necessary to think that Ljúfini was technically unfree as described by the legislation on servile priests, but there was probably a substantial part of the servants' class which in practice had very limited freedoms, and it is completely reasonable to assume that there were priests who belonged to this social group. It may be that the term household priest (*heimilisprestr*) applies to these most menial of priests as it seems to have a different shade of meaning from district priest (*þinga-prestr*). It is often found used for priests who seem to be permanently attached to the same household, and who can be considered as one of the servants of that household. The district priests were more independent. They seem to have been able to negotiate contracts with householders and occupy a similar position to specialized craftsmen (shipwrights, silver smiths, and such) who, on account of their rare and expensive talents, were not dependent on a single householder. It is likely that the difference between household and district priests was one of education, with the household priests just having enough training to be able to stumble through the obligatory services whereas the district priests were often men of considerable learning. The parish system, which was developing in the twelfth and thirteenth centuries, also reflected these differences, in that many cures coincided with single estates and their satellite holdings, where the parishioners would all be the tenants of the householder of the church-farm. The position of a priest in such a parish, would—whatever his social origins—be very different from a priest serving a cure which included two or more estates. That sort of priest—a district priest—would serve several households in their own chapels or annex-churches and while he would be associated primarily with the head of the household where he resided, he would still be much more independent than most other members of that household.[36]

In the twelfth century being a priest was first and foremost beneficial to chieftains and others of high rank. St Þorlákr and Guðmundr Arason were pioneers in forging an ecclesiastical identity for themselves and this was made possible only by their extraordinary connections. To most other priests their ordination was only an extra talent or skill which was useful to them in what we would consider a secular context. It is only in the mid thirteenth century that clear signs begin to appear that the Icelandic church was adopting a corporate identity and the clergy at large began to make clear distinctions between themselves and laymen.

5. THE SHAPING OF CLERICAL IDENTITY[37]

In 1196 the sons of Þórðr Þórarinsson in Laufás (N) left Ögmundr *sneis* for dead some distance from their farmstead. He had begged them to send him a priest to administer the last rites and they sent pastor Erpr from Laufás to administer

[36] On the parish system see Vésteinsson 1998*a*.
[37] Grímsdóttir 1982: 50–7; Þorláksson 1982*a*.

to the dying man. When Erpr came to the site of the skirmish Ögmundr was, however, away and lived long after (d. 1237) (*Sturl* 142).

Two years later the sons of Þórðr were on the defensive with the sons of Arnþrúðr against a revenge party led by Þorgrímr *alikarl* for their part in the burning of Önundr Þorkelsson in Langahlíð (N) in 1197. Þorgrímr and his men took their enemies by surprise in their beds in Laufás but promised Hákon, one of Þórðr's sons, safety (*grið*). When pastor Erpr came on the scene he urged Hákon to go to the church and save his life. Hákon said he had received guarantees of safety and was anyway not allowed to go to the church. Erpr thought that Þorgrímr's men would break their promise of safety and claimed that he would take the responsibility if Hákon saved his life and went to the church. It seems that Hákon, gentleman that he was, thought that having received a guarantee of safety he must honour it on his part by not betraying their trust. Erpr on the other hand took a more practical view and was prepared to take upon himself the loss of honour as it seemed less important to him than life. Hákon did not budge and was subsequently executed. Having failed to persuade the honour-conscious Hákon to save his life, Erpr the priest opened up the church and then administered the last rites to three of the sons of Arnþrúðr. One of them however managed to shake himself free of his captors and got into the church and thus saved his life, while Hákon's brother Hildibrandr, who also made a run for it, only managed to grasp a corner post and was torn away and executed.

One of Önundr's sons in the revenge party was the priest Vigfúss. He declared that it would be appropriate for him to execute Þorsteinn Arnþrúðarson, presumably for Þorsteinn's part in the killing of Vigfúss's brother Þorfinnr, but thought that being a priest made him unsuitable for the task (*Sturl* 158–9).

Erpr was clearly a household priest at Laufás and a member of Þórðr's household. His role in these episodes is very much what we would expect of a priest; he administers the last rites and concerns himself with the safety of one of his flock, but is otherwise not directly involved. He even attempted what seems an almost theological debate when he tried to persuade Hákon to value his life above his honour. Vigfúss Önundarson's reluctance to execute Þorsteinn on account of being a priest also strengthens the impression given that priests had by this date acquired an identity of their own which defined what sort of actions befitted them and distinguished them from laymen.

There is no doubt that priests did have a special status on account of their ordination from an early stage. According to *Sturlu saga*, Sturla Þórðarson and his son Sveinn had in the 1160s overpowered their neighbour and opponent the priest Erlendr Hallason in Ásgarður (D) and Sturla asked Sveinn to execute him. Sveinn, however, excused himself on account of Erlendr having baptized him and Erlendr therefore kept his head (*Sturl* 70). In 1181 Sturla was still harassing people who got in his way. He had entered a dispute between his in-laws the Garðamenn and the Reykhyltingar regarding the inheritance of Þórir in Deildartunga (S). The fortunes of the Reykhyltingar's chieftain, the priest Páll

Sölvason, were rapidly sinking when Jón Loptsson from Oddi decided to come to his aid. It was in his opinion not proper for powerful chieftains to pick fights with old and noble clergymen (*Sturl* 97). Páll also enlisted the support of his bishop, St Þorlákr. The saint said: 'Your dispute with Sturla does not seem fair to me; they are powerful and unscrupulous men but you are a venerable clergyman. I would like you to be on your guard and carry arms and defend yourself if it comes to that because you never know with men like these' (*Sturl* 97–8). It is added that Páll often forgot his weapons when he walked away from church and that this showed that he was not used to bearing arms.

It is likely that these attitudes reflect the author's world-view rather than being accurate reports of Jón Loptsson's and St Þorlákr's reactions. Their replies are better understood as a part of the author's depiction of Sturla as a ruffian and vulgar oaf compared to respectable people like Páll Sölvason and Jón Loptsson (Foote 1984*a*: 9–30). However that does not change the fact that these were considered by the author to be realistic attitudes which must therefore have been current in the first two decades of the thirteenth century when the saga was written (*ÍSB* i. 316).

It is perfectly likely that from an early stage priests were expected to behave in certain ways and concern themselves with some matters more than others. That certain positive qualities were associated with the priesthood is suggested by its appeal to the chieftains in the twelfth century but it is difficult to discern which qualities these were. Intelligence, responsibility, and pacifism are likely options but whether they were associated with all priests or only those of high birth is doubtful. The evidence is that in the twelfth and early thirteenth century there was no very sharp dividing line between priests and laymen and the priesthood as a whole did not have a corporate identity.

There were those, like St Þorlákr and Guðmundr Arason, who identified their fortunes with the Church's and the number of such men was on the increase in the beginning of the thirteenth century. For the majority of priests, however, whether they were householders or district priests, their secular identity continued to be more important to them than that of the priesthood. Out of 186 identifiable priests in the twelfth and thirteenth centuries of whose actions some account is preserved, only twenty-three appear performing tasks related to their office. In most of these cases the priests are called on to administer extreme unction and it is true that there are many more accounts of extreme unction being administered without the priest involved being mentioned or identified. It is also true that our source material is not concerned with the daily chores of priests and we should therefore not expect detailed or numerous accounts of officiating priests. What is remarkable is the high number of priests who are on record doing very secular deeds; some of which we would consider completely incompatible with a priest's office. There are nineteen examples of priests taking part in battles and a further eight of priests joining war-parties. Five priests are known to have killed but, as we shall discuss below, more lost their lives violently. In all there are fifty examples of priests being a principal party to a dispute—most of these were chieftains or major householders—and fifty-three examples of priests supporting others in disputes: giving advice, seeking help on behalf of others, giving shelter and food, and raising war-parties. Most of these were householders. Furthermore there are sixty-five examples of priests in dependent roles in disputes. These were either householders who followed their chieftains into battle or did them some service or members of chieftains' retinues who are found in a variety of roles, ranging from quite violent ones like taking part in battles to more peaceful, but sometimes dangerous, ones like being spies and messengers. Not included in the latter group are those priests who are found in chieftains' retinues entirely in their capacity as priests. These sometimes appear as advisers but more often as army chaplains. Except for this last group, which becomes visible in the first half of the thirteenth century, the actions of these priests do not in any way differentiate them from other men. In fact it is often by chance only that we happen to know that somebody was a priest; the narrative sources are not consistent in giving such information and often it is only found in the annals or obituaries.[38] There is hardly any discernible relationship between ordination and behaviour which would allow us to identify more than a handful of priests as such if the sources did not contain the information. Just as becoming priests did not change the interests or conduct of chieftains, it does not seem to have affected greatly the behaviour patterns of householders and ordained servants.

The priest Páll Sölvason may have assumed a peaceful demeanour and abandoned his arms for symbols of his priesthood but this did not stop him from being a chieftain who could not budge an inch when it came to claims on a wealthy inheritance. In his dispute with the Garðamenn and Sturla in Hvammur over the inheritance of Þórir in Deildartunga Páll was just as obstinate as any other chieftain who could not afford a loss of face. And while he may not have carried arms it is unlikely, whatever St Þorlákr's advice, that he did not have under his command men who did. Being the politically weaker party in the dispute it would however not have been worth the risk for him to resort to violence; his high birth and the respectability of his office stood him in good stead when it came to recruiting support among mightier chieftains, who took sides, it seems, on the basis of the social acceptability of the contestants rather than any strategic considerations. That at least is the interpretation of the author of *Sturlu saga* and that is why Páll's priestly qualities are stressed as a contrast to Sturla in Hvammur's more aggressive and hard-hearted disposition. Had Páll been in a more favourable position it is unlikely that he would have let his ordination get in the way of vanquishing his adversaries in whatever manner was politically expedient.

In a similar way it is unlikely that the priest Erpr in Laufás (N) could have declined to undertake a mission like the one the priest Ljúfini in Staðarhóll (D) did for his householder and chieftain Einarr Þorgilsson in the 1160s. Ljúfini was

[38] And these sources are not entirely consistent in giving information on people's ordinations either so there is a possibility that many more of the men mentioned in *Sturlunga saga* were priests.

sent to replace the sheep of Einarr Ingibjargarson with those of his householder in island pastures which Einarr Þorgilsson claimed he had rights to. Ljúfini performed his task with such zeal that when an elderly tenant of Einarr Ingibjargarson's refused to lend him a boat to transport the sheep the priest struck the householder with an axe (*Sturl* 64). There is no reason to expect that Ljúfini was any more wicked than Erpr or that his pastoral duties were performed with any less zeal. Nor is there reason to expect that Erpr would have declined to take up arms to defend his household had he been given the opportunity. He can hardly have been much different from the priest Þorkell Bergþórsson who defended himself bravely in the battle of Hólar in 1209 against the enemies of Bishop Guðmundr Arason (*Sturl* 222–3). Or the priest Skeggi who attacked Norwegian merchants after they had killed the chieftain Ormr Jónsson and his son Jón in Vestmannaeyjar (S) in 1218, and was killed as a result, or the priest Héðinn who was killed in his own churchyard with his chieftain Björn Þorvaldsson in the battle at Breiðabólstaður (S) in 1221 (*Sturl* 255, 267–8). Skeggi may have been the father of Héðinn (*PP* 59).

For these priests their membership of a household was more important in shaping their loyalties, and hence behaviour, than their ordination. What they did not have and what Icelandic priesthood in general lacked until the middle of the thirteenth century was a common identity supported by the authority of the bishops. The reason lay partly in the social order which made it difficult for the bishops to identify with their priests as a homogeneous group with common interests, but ultimately it lay in the economic foundations of the Church. As long as most ecclesiastical property was essentially under secular control priests continued to place their loyalties according to the ownership of the land which sustained them, rather than in an institution which could do little to protect them. This situation began to be reversed in the middle of the twelfth century, particularly with the foundation of the monasteries; these created a small body of men who could be in no doubt that their loyalties lay with God and the institution he had provided for their upkeep. It did however take a long time before the growth of the Church as an institution began to affect the majority of priests, that is, those who had pastoral responsibilities. It may be that we can detect a sign of change in the behaviour of the priest Jón Halldórsson in the burning of Flugumýri (N) in 1253. He seems to have been the household priest at Flugumýri and when the houses had been set on fire and Eyjólfr *ofsi* and his men were charging the wedding party room by room, he did not have arms but did his bit by encouraging the defenders and throwing clothes on the weapons of the attackers (*Sturl* 636). It seems clear from this that pastor Jón did not own weapons, but whether he would have taken to arms had there been some available we cannot know. It may be that pastor Jón showed incredible restraint in not trying to do bodily harm to the attackers in what must have been an extremely harrowing situation.

In this context it is worth looking at the statistics for the number of ordained men who were killed or executed in the twelfth and thirteenth centuries as they seem to be genuinely reflective of social change (see Figure 10).

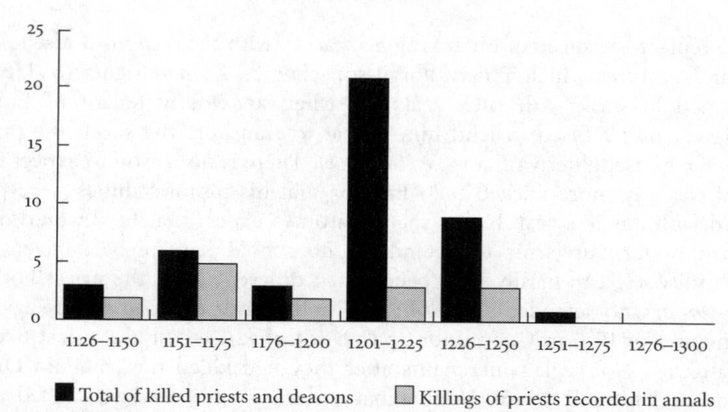

FIGURE 10. *Numbers of killed priests in all sources compared to those mentioned in annals*

The high number of total recorded killings of priests in 1201–50 is due to the detailed nature of the sources dealing with this period. But it is also a reflection of the warfare and violence in Icelandic society which characterized this period in particular. It is interesting to compare these figures with the number of killed priests recorded in the annals because it is to be expected that in them the same criteria would be applied in the selection of entries in all periods. The annals should therefore give a less biased picture of the development of priests' involvement in violent conflict. The figures extracted from the annals suggest that there may have been an outburst of violent conflict in 1151–75 or, more accurately, that in this period there were particularly many men involved in conflict, and who were important enough to be mentioned in annal entries, who were priests. The figures also suggest that violence was a permanent feature of conflict in all periods down to 1250. Large-scale warfare ceased around 1260, but no clerics are known to have taken part in battles after 1244, and no priest after 1232.[39] This seems to indicate changes in the status of priests, especially since large-scale warfare was limited to the period 1238–59 and clerics seem to have had little part in it, in sharp contrast with earlier periods when clerics appear on every scene with sword in hand.

I have already discussed how the Church gradually gained greater control over ecclesiastical property (Ch. 3, s. 4) and how the leadership of the Church began in the late twelfth century to put pressure on clerics to distance themselves from secular affairs and create a separate social class of churchmen (Ch. 4, s. 3). In what follows I will look at how these changes are reflected in the social conditions of clerics in the thirteenth century. After a discussion on signs of increased specialization of ordained men in service, the emphasis on conciliation as a

[39] That is, excepting priests like pastor Jón at Flugumýri (N), who were caught up in violent conflict through no intention of their own.

special calling of churchmen will be considered. Finally the introduction of the idea of clerical celibacy will be treated.

Professional skills: Scribes and Counsellors

In section 3, above, it was argued that the law considered a priest as a kind of skilled person who was qualified to perform certain tasks but was not in other ways different from other people. Much in the same way as a shipwright would be expected to spend his day in the shipyard building a ship and could be called upon to repair a damaged ship, so the priest would be expected to spend the day in church singing mass and reciting the hours, and could be called upon to baptize, visit the sick, administer extreme unction, and recite funeral rites. Over supper priest and shipwright might have a special status in the household on account of their craft, but they would nevertheless be subject to the head of the household and would take orders from him or her.

This interpretation fits well the available evidence for the status of district priests in the second half of the twelfth century. In the first half of the thirteenth century a new dimension is added to the career opportunities of priests as a result of the increasingly complex administrative needs of chieftains. It is likely that great and distinguished chieftains relied on clerics to write letters in the twelfth century but it does not seem from the conduct of rank-and-file chieftains like Sturla in Hvammur that exchange of letters was a mode of communications which came naturally to them. It was probably only in the circle of literate chieftains that letters circulated and the indications are that this circle was still very small in the twelfth century. Political conflict in the twelfth century was also more relaxed than it became in the thirteenth century, and was rarely carried out over long distances, so chieftains could still settle their affairs in person.

By 1200 this was changing. In winter 1200–1 the deacon Lambkárr Þorgilsson (d. 1249) who had recently joined Guðmundr Arason's retinue had taken care of all letter making for Kolbeinn Tumason when he was at home in Víðimýri, but when Kolbeinn took over the household at Hólar following Bishop Brandr's death in August 1201 Lambkárr was shunned as a scribe in favour of the priest Kygri-Björn (*Sturl* 203). There was clearly professional rivalry between Lambkárr and Kygri-Björn as the author of *Prestssaga* Guðmundar Arasonar—who may have been Lambkárr himself or someone very sympathetic to him—proceeds to vilify Kygri-Björn who 'immediately became cool towards the bishop-elect [i.e. Guðmundr] because he felt he was not regarded highly enough by him. Thus it was at once predicted which later transpired with Björn because this jealousy grew in him and increased as it lasted longer' (*Sturl* 203).

The men of the northern diocese elected Kygri-Björn as their bishop in 1236 but he died in 1237 or 1238 without having been consecrated (*Sturl* 382–3; *IA* 130,

188, 327).[40] Kygri-Björn seems to have been resident at Hólar in 1201 and had probably been Bishop Brandr's scribe, so Kolbeinn's preference for him over the less experienced Lambkárr was probably justified. Kygri-Björn seems to have stayed with Kolbeinn's household after he moved from Hólar and some time after Kolbeinn's death in 1208 Kygri-Björn went abroad and was in Rome in 1214 shortly before the Lateran council. He came back to Iceland in 1224 (*Sturl* 289)[41] and seems to have been attached to the household of Sighvatr Sturluson in Grund in Eyjafjörður (N) (*Bsk* ii. 92, 147). As alluded to by the author of *Prestssaga*, Kygri-Björn was considered the leader of the clerical opposition to Bishop Guðmundr (*Bsk* ii. 186). He is an early example of a career priest who did not rise quietly to prominence within a bishop's household, like some of the twelfth century bishops had done, but by making his clerical skills available to chieftains. We do not know enough about Kygri-Björn's position *vis-à-vis* the chieftains Kolbeinn and Sighvatr to appreciate to what extent he was his own man. His trips abroad and his authorship of *Maríu saga* suggest that, if he was a chieftain's client, he was at least a highly regarded and pampered one.

Forty years after deacon Lambkárr's humiliating experiences at Hólar he appears again, this time with the title of abbot and attached to Sturla Þórðarson's household in Staðarhóll (D). Kolbeinn *ungi* had arrested Sturla in the aftermath of Snorri Sturluson's killing and taken him to Flugumýri (N). Lambkárr went there with a message from the priest Páll Hallsson in Narfeyri (D) and other followers of Sturla that they would become the friends of Kolbeinn if he let Sturla go free. It was then agreed that Sturla acknowledged Kolbeinn's overlordship. Lambkárr was with him when he swore the oath to Kolbeinn. It is not clear whether Lambkárr swore as well, although it seems likely from the context. Lambkárr did not accompany Sturla back to the west but came a while later with the task of supervising the oath-takings of the men of Fellsströnd, Skarðsströnd, and Saurbær on Kolbeinn's behalf (*Sturl* 455, 457).

Lambkárr's title of abbot seems to have been honorary; there are at least no indications that he was associated with any monastery. If his was the abbacy of Hítardalur (S), the monastery there was with little doubt long defunct at this time (see Ch. 3, s. 5). It is equally likely that he owed his title to Bishop Guðmundr who may have appointed a trusted follower like Lambkárr as an anti-abbot to one of the monasteries in the north or simply invented the distinction as a reward for dutiful service. It is at least clear that Lambkárr was an adherent of Sturla by the 1240s but was, on account of his clerical status, also neutral enough to be a credible messenger. And rather than having to talk

[40] Kygri-Björn died on his way back from Rome, which may suggest that the archbishop had raised objections to his suitability and that he had sought papal dispensation. Abbot Arngrímr claims that he was illegitimate (*Bsk* ii. 186; see Ch. 4, s. 2).

[41] That homecoming could of course have been after a second trip abroad. Kygri-Björn witnessed a charter of Kirkjubær (S) in 1216–26 (*DI* i. 395) and as most of the witnesses were local men it suggests that at the time he lived in the south, possibly attached to the house of canons in Þykkvibær (S).

his own followers into submission to Kolbeinn it was less humiliating for Sturla to let the more detached Lambkárr do the work. From Kolbeinn's point of view it was also advantageous to make a respectable cleric supervise the oath-takings; while secular chieftains were loath to break their oaths, they did break them if they felt it was politically justified, but churchmen on the other hand were not likely to become oathbreakers. Sturla never openly challenged Kolbeinn *ungi* but he supported his enemies and Kolbeinn cannot have realistically hoped to get more out of Sturla's submission. But through Lambkárr he could reach Sturla's followers and important allies in the west and this, he could realistically hope, could have made a difference at least in so far as it made it more difficult for Sturla to rally his followers against Kolbeinn.

It is in capacities like these that we meet several clerics in the first half of the thirteenth century attached to the households of great chieftains. They were no ordinary district priests whose main tasks were singing masses and visiting the sick. They were often men of good family, like Lambkárr, and of considerable learning and erudition, like Styrmir Kárason, who commanded respect in their own right. It was this quality which made them valuable to their chieftains; they were not only useful as scribes and counsellors but their high social status and ecclesiastical credentials made them extremely useful in negotiations and every kind of contact with other chieftains. Chieftains normally had good reason not to trust each other, but they could agree to trust in a respectable cleric acting as proxy for his chieftain. An extreme example of deep-felt mistrust being overridden by confidence in clerical handshakes is when in 1228 a truce was established between Sturla Sighvatsson and his uncle and bitter enemy Snorri Sturluson. They had agreed on a meeting but Snorri did not turn up, sending instead his priest Styrmir Kárason and his chief ally the chieftain Þorleifr in Garðar. Sturla did not trust this arrangement and refused to shake hands with them but made one of his men shake hands with Þorleifr and his priest Torfi Guðmundsson shake the hand of Styrmir Kárason (*Sturl* 308–9).

Of priests of this type Torfi Guðmundsson is the best example, on account of the relatively detailed accounts of his role in Sturla's service. Torfi is first mentioned in 1223 when Sturla was making friends with Þorvaldr *Vatnsfirðingr*. The two met in Saurbær (D) and held their discussion in the company of Torfi the priest and Snorri Narfason, the priest from Skarð (D). The talks went well and they promised each other mutual support. To seal their alliance both of them handed their *goðorð* to Torfi and had him ride to the Alþing and thus represent both of them as one (*Sturl* 286). In 1227 when Sturla was home at Sauðafell Torfi was approached there by a group of men who had killed a follower of Sturla's cousin Dufgus in Hjarðarholt (D) and wounded Dufgus himself. Torfi persuaded Sturla to mediate on their behalf in order to secure the support of the attacker's in-laws in Fellsströnd (D). A settlement was reached whereby Sturla and his uncle Þórðr Sturluson who then lived in Hvammur arbitrated (*Sturl* 299). Uncle and nephew, however, did not hold the peace for long: Þórðr ignored Sturla in his plans for the governance of the region and

Sturla expressed his anger by attacking Þórðr's household in Hvammur. A complete stalemate ensued, complicated by a dispute between Sturla and Bishop Guðmundr who was then in the region. The following winter Torfi the priest went back and forth between Sturla and Þórðr attempting to mediate a settlement and before Lent they agreed to talk (*Sturl* 303). These were busy times for Torfi as Sturla's enemies were in no short supply. In the summer of 1228 Þorvaldur *Vatnsfirðingr*, Sturla's one-time ally, was with Snorri Sturluson in Reykholt and Sturla sent Torfi to him to ask him to mediate between him and Snorri (*Sturl* 305). Þorvaldr did nothing, but there followed the truce where Torfi shook hands with Styrmir Kárason. In the spring of 1230 Torfi was again with Sturla, this time at a peace meeting in Skálanes (N) between Sturla and the sons of Þorvaldr *Vatnsfirðingr* (*Sturl* 327). In 1232 Torfi headed the household in Hjarðarholt; a reward it seems for his loyal service. The sons of Þorvaldr came to him there and he immediately sent word to Sturla but he also offered to mediate on their behalf. They refused, trusting in an earlier truce, and rode on the following day to be intercepted and executed by Sturla after a brief skirmish (*Sturl* 335). Torfi is not heard of after this. In 1242 the sons of Dufgus lived in Hjarðarholt (*Sturl* 461–2) and he may have been dead by then.

It is clear that Torfi belonged to a very different league from Sturla's other priests—Sveinn Þorvaldsson who was wounded in his bed in Sauðafell in 1228 when the sons of Þorvaldr Vatnsfirðingr attacked Sturla's household, or Þorkell who was in Sturla's party when he finally finished them off in Hundadalur (D) in 1232 (*Sturl* 312, 314, 337, 339). Torfi was probably a full-time counsellor of Sturla's, an indispensable agent in the increasingly complex existence of a thirteenth century chieftain. Of others like him we have already met Lambkárr Þorgilsson in Sturla Þórðarson's household and Styrmir Kárason (d. 1245) in Snorri Sturluson's household.[42] Halldórr Oddsson seems to have had this function in the household of Þórðr Sturluson in Staðarstaður (S) (*Sturl* 185–6, 320; *DI* ii. 165) and Ísarr Pálsson in that of Kolbeinn *ungi* and later Brandr Kolbeinsson (*Sturl* 355, 428, 537). Torfi is the only one of these priests whose family is unknown; the others were all of aristocratic descent: Lambkárr was of the Staðarhólsmenn (*Bsk* i. 460–1, 464), Ísarr of the Oddaverjar (*Sturl* 428), and Styrmir is believed to have been the son of Kári abbot of Þingeyrar 1181–87, son of Rúnólfr the priest, son of Bishop Ketill Þorsteinsson, and thus of the Möðruvellingar (H. Þorsteinsson 1912: 126–48; *ÍF* i. p. civ). Although Torfi's family is not known it seems almost inconceivable that a man not of aristocratic birth could have acted as a *goðorðsmaðr* at the Alþing, and we are therefore justified in assuming that he belonged to the same social group as the others.

Halldórr Oddsson was the son of Oddr Jósepsson, householder in Búðardalur (D), who was of respectable if not aristocratic family and one of Sturla in

[42] On Styrmir: *Sturl* 308–9, 328–9, 430; *IA* 131, 189, 328, 481; *DI* i. 496, 513; *DI* ii. 85; *ÍF* i. 397; *ÍF* xiii. 97; *Flat* ii. 67, 68, 118, 533; iii. 237; H. Þorsteinsson 1912: 126–48; Jóhannesson 1941: 88–9, 137–40; *ÍF* xiii. pp. xliv–lxvii; Nordal 1914: 69–72; L. Lönnroth 1968.

Hvammur's more important followers (*Sturl* 69–76). It is interesting that in this case the relationship between a householding father and his chieftain is maintained in the second generation between priest and chieftain. It is likely that Sturla in Hvammur had offered Oddr to foster his son—Sighvatr Sturluson calls Halldórr his *fóstbróðir* (*Sturl* 320)— and Halldórr may have been a younger son who did not stand to inherit his father's farmstead. If it was the Sturlungar who had him educated and ordained, as seems likely, it would be an important insight into their approach to being chieftains. Instead of copying successful families like the Haukdælir and Oddaverjar and becoming priests themselves, they nurtured young men from families loyal to them and made them their priests. This was of course a similar approach to that which the Haukdælir had long before adopted towards the episcopacy; as soon as it became more cumbersome than profitable for a chieftain to be a bishop a safe and dependable protégé like Þorlákr Rúnólfsson had to be found (Ch. 4, s. 1.)

It is with a division of labour of this kind that the early thirteenth century chieftains managed to expand their powers and consolidate their hold over larger areas than had previously been possible. Instead of working alone or in father-and-son or brother-and-brother teams, which had invariably proved troublesome, short-lived, and ineffective, the foundations for administrative structures were being laid by the resident counsellor-priests. From the point of view of the chieftains it was ideal to have at their side men who could perform a variety of managerial tasks as well as representing them with other chieftains but who did not have ambitions to become chieftains themselves. It is their different ambitions which made these priests useful to the chieftains and in order to keep being useful these priests had to stress their separate identity as churchmen.

This class of priest was probably never large, there were probably no more than a dozen in the first half of the thirteenth century, but it was nevertheless a significant addition to the very small nucleus of clerics at the episcopal sees and monasteries who had adopted an ecclesiastical identity. It was a significant addition because these were high-born and, more importantly, very visible priests who were in a position to influence the views of both aristocracy and clergy of what a priest should be like. It is in their roles as intermediaries and mediators that the new clerical identity is crystallized. Their success in mediation depended on their being able to make both sides in a dispute trust them and this no doubt depended to a degree on their personalities but also on their professional capacity as priests. It was a useful shortcut for everyone involved; instead of having to establish the benevolence and neutrality of a mediator through experience it was expected of a priest that he was endowed with these qualities. Finding strength in their capacity as mediators it is not surprising that men of the Church began to stress that conciliation was a special calling of theirs, and that this in turn strengthened the institutional image of the Church and the shared identity of its clergy.

Conciliation: The Case of Abbot Brandr Jónsson

As we have seen, there were by the end of the twelfth century notions in place that priests should preferably not be involved in conflict. In the cases of Páll Sölvason in Reykholt and Vigfúss Önundarson, however, this only stretched as far as hindering them from wielding weapons, it did not prevent them from taking part in disputes or ordering others to commit violent acts. Páll and Vigfúss were both aristocrats and it was rare in the thirteenth century that men of that calibre, even if they took part in battles, carried out the actual killings or executions themselves.[43] It may be a sign of ecclesiastical influence on aristocratic behaviour that thirteenth-century chieftains preferred not to soil their hands with blood even if they were not ordained. And it is probably no coincidence that it was often those chieftains who were not ordained and came from families who had had little involvement with the Church who found the strongest need to stress publicly their religious fervour and respect for the Church. Kolbeinn Tumason is remembered equally for his highhandedness with Bishop Guðmundr and his treatment of the see of Hólar as his own property as for the simple gracefulness of his religious poetry (*Skjald* ii. 45–9; Paasche 1948: 153–6; W. Lange 1958: 84). Another such chieftain was Þórðr *kakali* who before instigating a particularly violent phase in the civil wars publicly announced his resolve not to seize men who had sought sanctuary in churches whatever offences he held against them (*Sturl* 498, also 496).

The reluctance of Páll and Vigfúss to inflict bodily harm in person is therefore primarily a sign of the refining influence the Church had had on the upper classes; as we have seen, less prestigious priests continued to kill, maim, and be killed well into the thirteenth century. There were, however, powerful pressures in place trying to distance the Church as a whole from every kind of secular conflict and others which would stress its role as a peacemaker. As I discussed in Chapter 4, section 3 the Icelandic bishops received a series of letters from the archbishops of Niðarós in the last quarter of the twelfth century in which the basic theme was to exhort clerics to distance themselves from secular conflict and to establish the immunity of priests. No immediate change set in as a result of these letters but they no doubt had an influence which began to be felt in the thirteenth century. The ideals which these letters propagated were those of the reforming papacy belatedly arriving in Scandinavia. These ideals do form the ideological background of reformers like Bishop Guðmundr *góði* and were no doubt the standard against which well-educated priests in chieftains' retinues measured themselves.

Complete withdrawal from the bloody world of secular strife did not however become an ideal for the main current of opinion within the Icelandic church in the thirteenth century. The authors of *Hungrvaka* and *Þorgils saga ok*

[43] Sometimes a chieftain's sword-thrust may have had a symbolic or ritual significance, as when Þorvarðr Þórarinsson cut the already captured and bleeding Þorgils *skarði* with his sword and then ordered one of his men to behead Þorgils (*Sturl* 736). He could of course just have been fumbling.

Hafliða both emphasized pacification as an ideal of the church. For the author of *Hungrvaka*, writing in the first one or two decades of the thirteenth century, the ideal bishop was able to enforce peace but this was more along the lines of forcing a resolution by taking sides in a dispute rather than through successful mediation. This ideal bishop was a sort of optimal chieftain: extremely benevolent and extremely powerful, a Jón Loptsson in a mitre. The author of *Þorgils saga ok Hafliða*, writing towards the middle of the thirteenth century, was also concerned with peace but in his world the clergy were preferably not involved in the conflict itself but intervened successfully on behalf of fairness and good sense. By the 1240s no chieftain could pretend he aimed primarily to contain violence and uphold the peace—a view late twelfth-century chieftains like Jón Loptsson had managed to promote of themselves—on the contrary it had become abundantly clear to everyone that chieftains were the principal source of violence in society. This of course affected the attitude of the Church which, instead of trying to live up to a no doubt completely illusory ideal of a chieftain's government, began to define its own agenda and field of operations. It began to influence the course of events not through direct participation but by occupying the third side to every conflict, the sensible and peaceful one.

The official leadership of the Icelandic church did not take the lead in this field until after the deaths of Bishops Guðmundr and Magnús in 1237. Although Bishop Guðmundr would probably have embraced the ideal of pacification in theory, his own combative stance against the chieftains and many of his own priests hardly made him a champion of peace. Bishop Magnús on the other hand seems to have been a diligent administrator (*Bsk* i. 507; *IA* 125, 184; *Bsk* i. 545; *IA* 382; *Grg 1a*, 36–7; *DI* i. 423–63) and often mediated and arbitrated in disputes (*Sturl* 254, 264, 284, 296, 349, 359–61, 382) but his position as a married chieftain and brother of one of the most powerful chieftains in the country made him an unlikely rallying point for those who would stress their ecclesiastical identity. In the last ten years of his episcopacy Magnús's position seems to have been precarious; he narrowly escaped being deposed in 1226 and a replacement was elected even before his death (*IA* 127, 479, 480, 129, 256, 130; *Sturl* 382).

It is, however, in the 1230s that signs of change begin to emerge. In 1232 a priest called Knútr was in Bishop Guðmundr's retinue. Knútr's valet had wounded Jón Birnuson, another of Bishop Guðmundr's followers, and after he had recovered Jón took the first opportunity and killed Knútr. It is explained that Knútr always carried weapons because he was unruly and had been deprived of his priesthood (*ódæll ok embættislauss*).[44] In 1242 one Snorri Þórálfsson arrived in Iceland in the retinue of Þórðr *kakali*. He had been a priest and had followed Bishop Guðmundr but 'was then a layman' (*var þá leikmaðr*) because he had been

[44] *Sturl* 323. Knútr was a very uncommon name in Iceland and it may be that this Knútr belonged to the same family as Guðmundr Knútsson who was among the high-born priests in the northern quarter in 1143 (*DI* i. 186; *NID* 688–9; *NIDs* 565). *Embætti* here probably refers to holy orders rather than an ecclesiastical appointment (cf. *Bsk* i. 285_{13}—which is not unambiguous either—and *DI* ii. 441–3; iv. 454–5; *IA* 269–71).

involved in the killing of Knútr the priest in 1232 (*Sturl* 457).[45] Snorri had become a follower of Þórðr *kakali* as early as 1235 (*Sturl* 372) but whether he had lost his ordination then is uncertain. The killing of Knútr represents the final collapse of order in Bishop Guðmundr's retinue and he was soon afterwards interred at Hólar and the following dispersed. Bishop Guðmundr seems to have tried to maintain discipline among his followers, as Knútr's expulsion from office suggests, but whether it was Guðmundr who had disciplined Snorri and whether it was the same kind of punishment is unclear. It is clear that Snorri was no longer a priest in 1242, whereas Knútr may have kept his title and only been banned from officiating, and it is possible that Snorri's harsher punishment was a result of him having to answer to ecclesiastical authorities in Norway during his stay there with Þórðr *kakali* in 1238–42.

It was of course only through being seen to keep tight discipline on its clergy that the Church could claim to be a harbinger of peace. With the arrival of two Norwegian bishops in Iceland in 1239 the Icelandic church finally acquired a leadership which could work towards shaping its corporate identity. Two fields of operations can be identified: on the one hand, a wedge was driven between the clergy and secular society by insisting on clerical celibacy and, on the other, stress was laid on the institutional interest of the Church in peace and a more practicable political system. Clerical celibacy will be considered in a later section but let us here look more closely at the Church's involvement with politics and its emphasis on pacification in the 1240s to 1260s.

Bishop Bótólfr of Hólar (1238–46) does not seem to have been a great achiever. He was an Augustinian canon from Helgisetur near Niðarós, to where he returned in 1243 leaving only memories of his lack of clout (*Sturl* 430; *IA* 131, 189, 256, 328; *Bsk* ii. 186–7). Both his colleague at Skálholt, Bishop Sigvarðr Þéttmarsson (1238–68), and his successor at Hólar, Bishop Heinrekr Kársson (1247–60), were on the other hand energetic administrators. Heinrekr in particular was an active power-broker, supporting whichever chieftain who looked like furthering the cause of King Hákon. Bishop Sigvarðr's political aims are less clear; he did take sides but was much less confrontational than Bishop Heinrekr and was more often involved in mediation and arbitration. Sigvarðr had been an abbot of the Benedictine monastery at Selja in Norway and seems to have been selected on account of his ecclesiastical credentials. Heinrekr seems to have owed his appointment to the trust King Hákon placed in him, although he was not simply a tool of King Hákon's; his commitment to the Church is evidenced by his insistence on clerical celibacy and he no doubt justified his involvement in secular politics on the grounds that the interests of the Church were best served if effective political authority was established in the country.

While neither Heinrekr nor Sigvarðr were particularly angelic figures they cut a sharp contrast to their predecessors in that they commanded great respect and

[45] It is possible that Snorri Þórálfsson was the same priest as the Snorri who was castrated along with Knútr in Grímsey in 1222 (*Sturl* 277).

were for instance able to use excommunication effectively in politics. The difference was that the Norwegian bishops were in no doubt about their role and affiliations; they were there to protect and advance the interests of the Church and they seem to have had a much clearer view of what constituted the Church and set it apart from the rest of society. It was their attitude and sense of direction rather than their actual efforts which became an important example for the increasing numbers of Icelandic clergy who were adopting an ecclesiastical identity.

As we have seen, a small but influential number of clerics were in the beginning of the thirteenth century building careers on their special status as priests. To such priests bishops who would underline the separateness of the clergy and special concerns of the Church were no doubt welcome. The presence of such bishops no doubt also helped householding priests to distance themselves from secular strife in the 1250s when the stakes had been raised too high for anyone but the most powerful. Several householding priests, who had previously been actively supportive of one chieftain or other or even had aspirations to power themselves, began to channel their political involvement towards mediation in the 1250s. The evidence for this sort of change of allegiance is not however plentiful or unambiguous; there were many other developments affecting political involvement in the 1240s and 1250s and in general political conflict was increasingly becoming the speciality of a handful of overlords and their men at arms. Local leaders—who were as often as not priests—had in the 1230s and early 1240s seen their fortunes linked with those of their overlords and followed them diligently, but by the early 1250s it was becoming clear that the overlords' control was extremely fragile and that the local leaders often did better to stay out of harm's way and look after their home-patch. Four out of the five noteworthies who came to mediate between Hrafn Oddsson on one side and Þorgils *skarði* and Sturla Þórðarson on the other at the fortification in Sauðafell (D) in 1257 were householding priests. But whether this tells us that many local leaders were still priests at this late point or that householding priests were the only local leaders who dared involve themselves because their clerical status would protect them from having to take sides is a difficult question. On the one hand, it is clear that Ketill Þorláksson in Kolbeinsstaðir (S), Guðmundr Ólafsson in Miklaholt (S), Páll Hallsson in Langidalur (D) (formerly in Narfeyri (D)), and Snorri Þórðarson in Staðarfell (D) made up the majority of prominent leaders in the west at the time and, while householding priests were becoming rare nationally at this time, it may be either a coincidence or a regional peculiarity that all these were priests. On the other hand their neutral position is suggested by the fact that, following the truce and subsequent discussions between Þorgils, Sturla, and Hrafn, it was decided that Páll, Snorri, and the priest Snorri Narfason from Skarð (D) would arbitrate on behalf of Sturla and Þorgils and that Guðmundr, the priest Þorkell from Síðumúli (S) and a layman on behalf of Hrafn (*Sturl* 728–9). This does suggest that, while these priests were seen to belong to different sides of the conflict, they were at the same time considered trustworthy by both parties; that they saw their role as dampening rather than fuelling conflict and that their role and perceived trustworthiness was a consequence of their being priests.

Much clearer and more consistent evidence for ecclesiastical emphasis on pacification comes to us through the activities of Brandr Jónsson, abbot of Þykkvibær (S) 1247–63 and bishop of Hólar 1263–4. Unlike householding priests, whose position was always influenced by their ties with the land, the monastic clergy, and the abbots in particular, had both the room to manœuvre and the incentive to put themselves up as intermediaries and peacemakers. Monastics and monastic life go largely unnoticed in our sources until the middle of the thirteenth century when several abbots begin to appear at peace meetings and try to avert battles. Of these Brandr Jónsson was the most prominent and we are blessed with relatively detailed accounts of his involvement in politics which make it possible to examine his—and by inference the Church's—attitude towards political conflict.

Brandr was of the Svínfellingar (Þórhallsson 1923; Bull 1925), the only son of his father's second marriage to Halldóra Arnórsdóttir of the Ásbirningar. His older legitimate half-brother Ormr (d. 1241) succeeded their father as the family's chieftain in Svínafell (A) and the illegitimate half-brother Þórarinn (d. 1239) inherited the family's newly acquired chieftaincies in Austfirðir. From the time of Brandr's youth his family ruled the whole eastern quarter and it remained throughout the thirteenth century one of the most constant powers in Icelandic politics. Through his mother and aunt Ásdís Sigmundardóttir, wife of Arnórr Tumason (d. 1221), Brandr was closely related to the Ásbirningar of Skagafjörður. Brandr therefore belonged to the most prestigious and powerful circle of people in the country. To posterity he is best known for his literary achievements; he translated both *Alexandreis* by Galterus de Castilone and *Gyðinga saga*, a compilation of Old Testament stories, and parts of the biblical translations in *Stjórn* have also been attributed to him (K. Wolf 1995: pp. lxxxiii–lxxxvii, 219; Storm 1886; Widding 1960*b*; Sveinsson 1961; Kirby 1986: 60–73; K. Wolf 1988, 1990).

Brandr was born sometime after 1202 when his father was still married to his first wife and at which time the illegitimate Þórarinn was born (*Sturl* 209). He was therefore somewhat younger than his two brothers and was probably earmarked for an ecclesiastical career at an early stage. His return to Iceland in 1232 was considered to be such a significant event that it is recorded in one of the annals (*IA* 129). It is likely that he was returning from studies abroad but why his homecoming was attributed such significance is difficult to say. Nothing is heard of Brandr after his return until 1238 when he and his brother-in-law Ögmundr Helgason advised Brandr's brother Ormr to release Gizurr Þorvaldsson who had been betrayed by his enemy Sturla Sighvatsson and entrusted to Ormr's keeping. Ögmundr and Brandr seem to have met Ormr and his captive, and Gizurr's friends who had come to ask for his release, at the church-farm Skarð in Meðalland (S), but although the source is unclear it does not seem that either Ögmundr or Brandr lived there. Ögmundr's father Digr-Helgi (d. 1235) had lived at Kirkjubær (S), which had been a convent for a period around 1200 and was a *staðr* under the control of the bishops of Skálholt (*DI* i. 394–5). Ögmundr inherited control of Kirkjubær from his father and it is possible that Brandr served the church there, heading the small community of priests attached to this major ecclesiastical centre.[46]

The advice Brandr and Ögmundr gave Ormr seems to have been to cease his alliance with Sturla, a decision of potentially momentous significance. Instead of leaving the country as Sturla had intended, Gizurr mustered his forces after Ormr freed him, and together with his ally Kolbeinn *ungi*, put a stop to Sturla's power, killing him and his father at the battle of Örlygsstaðir later in the same year. Ormr did not accompany Sturla to the battle, thus saving his family from becoming entangled in the bitter conflict that followed. Had he supported Sturla the outcome of the battle might have been quite different, but it is likely that Brandr and Ögmundr had pointed out to him that there was no way he could support Sturla against both Gizurr and Kolbeinn *ungi*, seeing that both were his first cousins[47] and even if familial considerations did not weigh much (although they probably did) they will have advised him that he did not have much to gain from his support of Sturla and that combined Gizurr and Kolbeinn were probably a far stronger force than the divided Sturlungar.

Four years later Gizurr and Kolbeinn were well on their way to exterminating the Sturlungar. In 1241 Gizurr had Sturla's uncle Snorri Sturluson killed and the following year saw Snorri's son Órækja on the defensive. Gizurr's ally Kolbeinn *ungi*—whose sister was married to Órækja—sent his brother-in-law Böðvarr Þórðarson in Bær (S), who was also Órækja's cousin and a traditional ally of the Sturlungar, to offer Órækja peace talks. Despite warnings from Böðvarr, Órækja decided to attend but asked that Bishop Sigvarðr and Brandr Jónsson also be present (*Sturl* 451). Kolbeinn obliged him and both Brandr and Sigvarðr attended the meeting at the bridge over Hvítá (S). Brandr and Sigvarðr acted as intermediaries, taking messages to and fro over the bridge and negotiating a settlement. Órækja agreed that the complex dispute would be submitted to the arbitration of Bishop Sigvarðr and Kolbeinn *ungi* and asked that they would either meet to shake hands in the middle of the bridge or that Brandr and Sigvarðr would carry the handshakes between them. Gizurr refused to meet on the bridge and the bishop and Brandr asked Órækja to cross over to Gizurr's side. Órækja did and was immediately arrested by Gizurr and Kolbeinn. Realizing that Órækja had been deceived, Bishop Sigvarðr and Brandr became furious with Gizurr, accusing him of having betrayed them (*Sturl* 452–3). In this account in *Íslendinga saga* Brandr is called abbot, a title he did not receive until 1247. There is however no suggestion that Brandr was not present, because

[46] In 1252 there were three priests living at Kirkjubær (*Sturl* 563) and no doubt there were others of lesser orders.

[47] Ormr's mother was Þóra the elder, sister of Gizurr's mother Þóra the younger.

the author, Sturla Þórðarson, was himself at the meeting and was captured there along with Órækja.[48] That Brandr—still a priest—was requested to attend these peace talks suggests that he had at an early stage begun to earn a reputation as an ecclesiastic dignitary in whom both sides could place their trust. It is of course possible that Órækja requested that Brandr be present because he was a first cousin of Kolbeinn *ungi* and would therefore deter his cousin from breaking faith. Órækja seems, however, to have trusted Kolbeinn completely, so the other explanation, that Brandr was already by this time considered as a priest who would stick his neck out for peace, is more likely.

Three years after the betrayal at Hvítá bridge fortunes had again turned; Sturla Sighvatsson's younger brother Þórðr *kakali* was on the offensive and a disease was killing Kolbeinn *ungi*. Brandr accompanied Gizurr from the south to be at Kolbeinn's bedside when he divided his dominions and advised that Brandr's first cousin Brandr Kolbeinsson (also Kolbeinn's first cousin) should succeed to Kolbeinn's dominion in Skagafjörður and Húnaþing (*Sturl* 531). It is unlikely that maternal cousins were normally called upon to give counsel on family matters like these and, although Brandr would not have been invited if he had not been close kin, his presence will have been requested because of his status as a church dignitary.

In 1247 Brandr became abbot of the house of canons in Þykkvibær (S). Þykkvibær was in the heartland of the Svínfellingar's domain and his appointment can therefore be seen as a strengthening of their hold over the region. His brother Ormr had died in 1241 and left the chieftaincy to his young son Sæmundr. Sæmundr was probably only a teenager when his father died—his younger brother Guðmundr was only 7 years of age in 1241—and their aunt's husband Ögmundr Helgason in Kirkjubær soon became influential in the region. In 1248 Sæmundr began to assert his authority and there followed a bitter struggle which ended when Ögmundr had the two brothers executed in 1252.[49] Brandr tried to mediate between his nephews and his brother-in-law at every stage of the dispute but although he gets a splendid compliment from the author—'as always abbot Brandr was regarded as having achieved the best results' (*Sturl* 553)—he was eventually unsuccessful. Both parties betrayed his confidence; Sæmundr prosecuted Ögmundr when Brandr had publicly made him agree not to and Ögmundr had the brothers killed when a truce had been established by Brandr. Executing the brothers was a desperate act which Ögmundr did not expect to profit from; he appointed Abbot Brandr and another brother-in-law, Skeggi Njálsson in Skógar, to decide the penalties and compensations. He heeded their verdict and was outlawed from the region.

While Brandr was unsuccessful in making his in-laws and relatives keep the peace in their own backyard—and his reputation may have been dented as a

[48] The text here also refers to 'the bishops' which suggests that Brandr's later offices as abbot and bishop had got the compiler or a scribe confused: *SturlR* i. 572–3 (n. 1 to ch. 157); *SturlK* i. 568 nn. 3, 4.

[49] This conflict is the subject of *Svínfellinga saga* (*Sturl* 550–66).

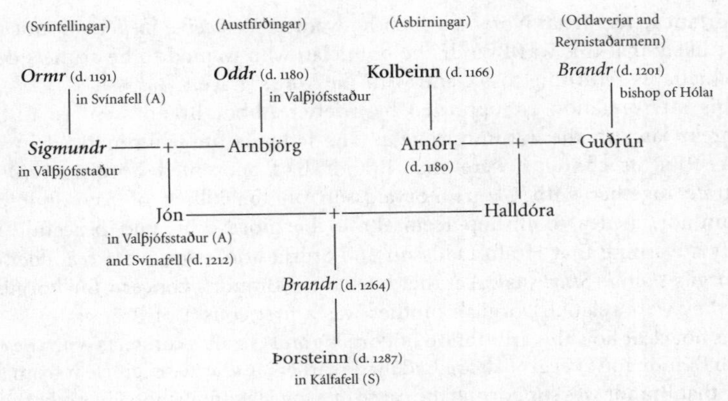

FIGURE 11. *Abbot Brandr Jónsson's family*

Other relatives of Abbot Brandr
Brothers: **Ormr** in Svínafell (A) (d. 1241); **Þórarinn** in Valþjófsstaður (A) (d. 1239)
Brothers-in-law: Ögmundr Helgason in Kirkjubær (S); Skeggi Njálsson in Skógar (S) (d. 1262)
Nephews: **Sæmundr Ormsson** in Svínafell (A) (d. 1252); **Ormr Ormsson** (d. 1270); **Oddr Þórarinsson** (d. 1255) **Þorvarðr Þórarinsson** in Hof (A), Grund in Eyjafjörður (N), Oddi (S), Keldur (S), Arnarbæli in Ölfus (S) (d. 1296)
Uncle: Kolbeinn *kaldaljós* in Staður in Reynines (N), Hólar (N) (s. 1246)
First cousins: **Kolbeinn *ungi*** in Ás in Hegranes (N), Viðimýri (N), Flugumýri (N) (d. 1245): **Brandr Kolbeinsson** in Staður in Reynines (N) (d. 1246)
Great-uncles: **Sigurðr Ormsson** in Svínafell (A) and Möðruvellir in Hörgárdalur (N) (d. 1235); **Teitr Oddsson** in Hof (A) (d. 1223); **Tumi Kolbeinsson** in Ás in Hegranes (N) (d. 1184); **Þorgeirr Brandsson** in Staður in Reynines (N) (d. 1186)

result—the outcome was probably that his influence in the region increased. By this time Brandr had become *officialis* in the diocese of Skálholt while Bishop Sigvarðr was in Norway (1250–4) and it is symptomatic of the changing climate that after Ögmundr left Kirkjubær—a *staðr* which had been formally under the control of the bishops of Skálholt—Brandr appointed an otherwise unknown priest to head the household at Kirkjubær (*Sturl* 566).[50]

In his capacity as a bishop's representative Brandr came to meet Gizurr Þorvaldsson, Þorgils *skarði*, and Finnbjörn Helgason (Ögmundr's brother) at Gásir (N) in the summer of 1252 and was among the guests when Gizurr married Gróa Álfsdóttir in the autumn (*Sturl* 568). Gróa and Gizurr had been living together at least since 1238 (*Sturl* 422) but there had apparently been an impediment to their marriage. It seems that Gizurr had acquired an exemption from the archbishop and Brandr's attendance at the wedding seems to have symbolized the consent of the Icelandic clergy. The fact that Brandr rode all the way to Gásir to meet Gizurr may only mean that he was expecting

[50] The priest's name was Arnórr *skull*. The name was common among the Ásbirningar—Brandr's maternal kin—and a brother of Ögmundr in Kirkjubær was Arnórr abbot of Viðey 1247–9. The name is otherwise not common (*NID* 53; *NIDs* 37–8) and this suggests that Brandr had selected someone either related to himself or to the previous householders in Kirkjubær. This Arnórr was soon superseded by Grímr Hólmsteinsson (*IF* xvii. 6).

important letters from Norway which he wanted to receive in person, but it is more likely that this was Brandr the politician who wanted to be at the side of the chieftains returning to Iceland with the king's grace.

This interpretation is supported by a letter Abbot Brandr sent to Bishop Heinrekr later in the autumn of 1252. The letter is only summarized in our source but its contents were that Brandr had appointed Þorgils *skarði* to arbitrate together with Gizurr Þorvaldsson on the killing of Sæmundr and Guðmundr, a plea to Bishop Heinrekr to be more calm and peaceful, and finally a warning that Hrafn Oddsson and Sturla Þórðarson were real enemies of Þorgils *skarði* (*Sturl* 592). Another reason for Brandr's concern for Þorgils is that they were related. Þorgils's mother was a first cousin of Brandr.

It is not clear how this arbitration of Þorgils's and Gizurr's connects with the one which Brandr and Skeggi Njálsson had made earlier.[51] Otherwise it is clear from this letter that Brandr was supporting the cause of King Hákon; Bishop Heinrekr seems to have had an uncompromising and confrontational character and Brandr will have been warning him that overbearing behaviour might damage both his plans of ecclesiastical reforms and their common political cause. Hrafn Oddsson and Sturla Þórðarson had been left to look after Þórðr *kakali*'s domain when he left for Norway in 1250 and were not at all happy with the new arrangements where Gizurr, Finnbjörn, and Þorgils accepted parts of Þórðr's domain from the king. In particular they objected to Þorgils's appointment to Borgarfjörður which came under their sphere of influence. As Brandr saw reason to warn Þorgils of his uncle Sturla's lack of friendship and Hrafn's enmity, this suggests that Brandr together with Bishop Heinrekr actively supported the new royal appointees, and Brandr's ride north to Gásir therefore becomes perfectly understandable.

In January 1253 Bishop Heinrekr suddenly turned soft and arranged a peace meeting between himself—on Þorgils's behalf—and Sturla and Hrafn. The meeting was set in Borgarfjörður and Bishop Heinrekr sent word to Skálholt to Brandr to attend. Brandr arrived when the talks had started and the author describes their joyful reunion. Brandr seems to have taken the lead in the discussions and exhorted Hrafn and Sturla to give up Borgarfjörður to which Þorgils had been appointed by the king but they refused and the talks ended in confusion. Afterwards bishop and abbot rode together to Reykholt where they sang mass together and Brandr preached the sermon. In it Brandr discussed Bishop Heinrekr's excommunication of Sturla and Hrafn. Brandr gave his support to the excommunication but explained that they would be absolved if they agreed to a reasonable settlement (i.e. gave up Borgarfjörður) (*Sturl* 611–14).

Soon after this Þorgils left Hólar where he had been staying with Bishop Heinrekr and accepted Abbot Brandr's invitation to come and stay in Skálholt. Þorgils stayed there until May 1253 when he—despite Brandr's warnings—left for his patrimony in Snæfellsnes. On leaving Brandr gave him an ox and a quilt. In the mean time Brandr had attended a peace meeting concerning the killings

[51] On this confusion see *SturlR* ii. p. xlv.

of Sæmundr and Guðmundr but it is not known what happened there and Þorgils was not present to arbitrate (*Sturl* 614–16).

When Þorgils had established himself at Staðarstaður (S) he raided the household of the deacon Halldórr Vilmundarson at Ytri Rauðimelur (S), who was an informant of Hrafn's. Halldórr complained to Guðmundr, who was in charge of the house of canons at Helgafell which had not had an abbot since 1244.[52] Guðmundr sent one of his canons to Þorgils asking him to return the loot and threatened to excommunicate him and others who consumed the meat; the resident priest at Staðarstaður had refused to eat the meat of the livestock stolen from Halldórr and so had other clerics as soon as the deed was done. Þorgils refused to return the loot and Halldórr then turned to Hrafn for help. Hrafn took Halldórr and his household under his wing and promised to take care of the matter. It does not seem, however, that he was very active because Halldórr left for Kolbeinsstaðir (S) where he sought the advice of Ketill the priest and his son-in-law Narfi Snorrason. They advised him to seek out Abbot Brandr and enlist his help. Brandr was not entirely sympathetic to Halldórr but nevertheless wrote a letter to Þorgils asking him to return the loot. Brandr also sent word to Ketill the priest in Kolbeinsstaðir to accompany Halldórr to Staðarstaður. Þorgils now agreed to return the loot but insisted on deciding alone on the dispute between them. Ketill seems to have mediated successfully because in the end Þorgils gave Halldórr clerical vestments and Halldórr gave Þorgils an ox and three wethers and they parted friends (*Sturl* 617–18).

Later the same year Þorgils made an assault in Borgarfjörður and executed Valgarðr, son of Þorkell, priest in Síðumúli (S). When he had returned home to Staðarstaður Brandr sent him word that he should go to Bishop Heinrekr at Hólar to get absolution; it seems that Brandr did not think himself qualified to absolve such a crime (*Sturl* 645).

The following autumn things were beginning to look more promising; Sturla and Þorgils had sealed their friendship and Sturla had promised to marry his daughter to Gizurr's son. At a peace meeting at Breiðabólstaður in Vesturhóp (N), Hrafn and Gizurr agreed to appoint Abbot Brandr as an arbitrator in their dispute while Gizurr and Sturla decided to settle their dispute between themselves, appointing Hrafn as arbitrator where they failed to agree (*Sturl* 628).

Things turned sour again with the burning of the wedding party at Flugumýri (N) in October 1253. Bishop Sigvarðr returned to Iceland in 1254 and now we hear nothing of Abbot Brandr until July 1255 when he attended a meeting between Þorgils *skarði*, Brandr's nephew Þorvarðr Þórarinsson, and Sturla Þórðarson in Borgarfjörður. Þorvarðr had come to ask Þorgils to join him in seeking revenge for the killing of his brother Oddr in January of the same year. Oddr, who was trying to establish himself as overlord of Skagafjörður, had abducted Bishop Heinrekr and held him captive for a few days in 1254 and was

[52] It is possible that this Guðmundr was the same priest as Guðmundr Ólafsson in Miklaholt (S) (*Sturl* 6, 481, 716–18, 728–9; *IA* 133, 330).

as a result killed by Hrafn Oddsson and Eyjólfr *ofsi*, the bishop's closest allies. Brandr had at first been unhappy with Þorgils for having rattled swords at Bær a fortnight earlier. Böðvarr in Bær (S) was married to Herdís Arnórsdóttir, a cousin of Brandr's. The abbot was, however, reassured it seems and when Þorgils asked his advice on Þorvarðr's boon he replied that he would not encourage anyone to wage war on other regions:

But you and Þorvarðr should not think that I am not vexed because of the killing of my relative Oddr where he was put away in rubble like a fox or a thief but it is forbidden for me to have any part in plans of vengeance or any kinds of violence. But it is better for you not to be alone if you think it is likely that you will not be inactive. (*Sturl* 687)

Þorgils then said that he would like to have Skagafjörður and Húnaþing if he joined Þorvarðr and they got any sort of result. Brandr retorted: 'I can much better suffer you Þorgils to enjoy Skagafjörður, our birthright, rather than those who now hold it. But I do not want to encourage you to go because I do not think it is for the taking' (*Sturl* 687).

And the author of *Þorgils saga* continues:

The abbot then sprang to his feet and asked that God's will be done. Some men said then that he became excited because he was red as blood and said this when he walked away:

It is hard that we should endure that our noble relatives are left unatoned on account of farmers' sons and so would my brother Ormr think if he lived. (*Sturl* 687–8)

Brandr having made his dramatic exit Þorgils and Þorvarðr came to an agreement and decided to attack Hrafn and Eyjólfr *ofsi*. When Brandr was told of the deal he had cooled somewhat and said now that he would not support it and strongly advised them not to go: 'Many innocent men will be harmed in this expedition so it is improper that I give my consent and it may be that I am so incensed with some men that I will not be able to pick all my words as carefully as I should if I say much about it' (*Sturl* 688–9).

Þorvarðr and Þorgils nevertheless shook hands and parted the same day. Brandr intended to meet Þorgils again the following day but missed him. On realizing that he would not meet Þorgils, Brandr said to Þorgils's brother-in-law Þórðr *Hítnesingr*:

I will not ride any further [to seek Þorgils] because I can see how this will develop. At our meeting yesterday evening I thought this expedition was a folly. But that which is preordained always comes to pass and there is hope that it will not be totally irresponsible. But it seems to me that your party is small and badly equipped but nevertheless not unsightly and not visibly fey. Bear my relative Þorgils my greetings and implore him to do as little wrong as possible to innocent men. It is important to me what news I get of him and I will be very worried about this expedition until I hear how you fare. You, in-law, I ask to follow Þorgils diligently and urge him to do good. I pray that God will be your weapon and shield and Archbishop Thomas your protector. But do not trust in Þorvarðr's honour because I am not of one mind about how the partnership of Þorgils and Þorvarðr will end and suspect that Þorvarðr will break the pact. (*Sturl* 689–90)

Þórðr *Hítnesingr*—whose wife was a daughter of Brandr's first cousin Sigríðr and therefore his in-law—was probably himself the author of *Þorgils saga skarða* so there cannot be a better source for these speeches, although they have no doubt been polished by the author. It appears that Brandr wanted Þorgils to succeed to Skagafjörður, no doubt because in Þórðr *kakali*'s absence Þorgils was the only chieftain descended from the Ásbirningar and Brandr seems to have considered it important that the region stayed in the hands of the family. Gizurr Þorvaldsson had been appointed to Skagafjörður by the king and he had put Oddr there in his place when he left for Norway in 1254. As Gizurr was not there to take care of things it was arguably up to Oddr's friends and relatives to avenge him and rid Skagafjörður of his killers. Although Bishop Heinrekr had decided that the king's cause was best served by Oddr's killers Hrafn and Eyjólfr *ofsi*—and Brandr seems to have been following that line late in the summer of 1254 when he refused to speak to Oddr at a wedding (*Sturl* 656)—their killing of Oddr was demonstrably an attack on the king. Although open support of the enemies of Bishop Heinrekr would have been awkward for Brandr, it is clear that the situation was very advantageous to him; an alliance between Þorgils and Þorvarðr meant that there was a good chance that Oddr would be avenged, that an Ásbirningr would again rule Skagafjörður, and that all this could be accomplished in the name of the king. As it was, Brandr could not have got a better result in the short run; Þorgils and Þorvarðr were victorious at the battle at Þveráreyrar 19 July 1255 and killed Eyjólfr *ofsi*. Soon afterwards Þorgils became overlord of Skagafjörður and made peace with both Bishop Heinrekr and Hrafn Oddsson. Brandr's warning of Þorvarðr's deceitful nature is probably made up in the light of later developments; two years later Þorvarðr surprised Þorgils at Hrafnagil (N) and had him executed. As that was a rather foolish act in terms of political expediency—in many ways reminiscent of Oddr's capture of Bishop Heinrekr—it may be that Brandr simply knew that his nephews were not the brightest of men and he may well have shared his reservations about his nephew's character with Þórðr.

Regarding Brandr's behaviour, it is possible that he simply lost his temper on the evening of the meeting and was then genuinely retracting his first words, words which could only be interpreted as advice to wage war on Hrafn and Eyjólfr *ofsi*, and therefore indirectly on Bishop Heinrekr. It may, however, have been a cunning show to satisfy Brandr's thirst for revenge and his desire to see a kinsman once more ruling Skagafjörður without staining his ecclesiastical image. What is interesting is the lengths to which he went to preserve this image. In his shoes most would probably not have hesitated in being openly supportive; Brandr was the only surviving male of his generation of the Svínfellingar, as well as one of only three surviving males of the Ásbirningar.[53]

[53] Þórðr *kakali* (son of Halldóra Tumadóttir, Brandr's mother's first cousin) was in Norway and died in 1256. The other one was Brandr's first cousin Páll Kolbeinsson in Staður in Reynines (N). He was still alive in 1259 (*Sturl* 743).

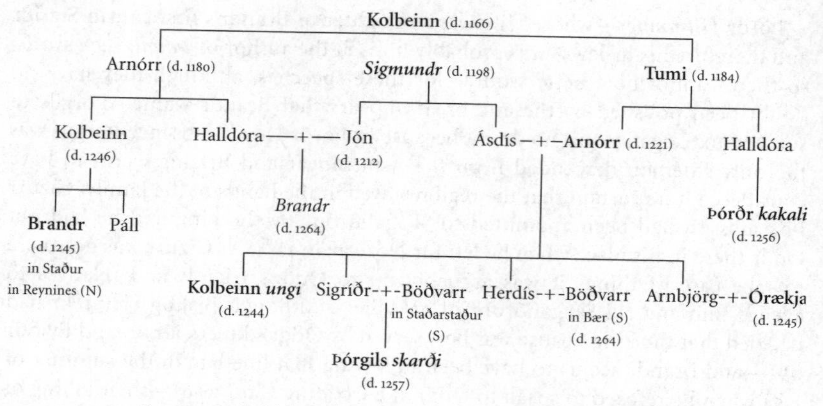

FIGURE 12. *Bishop Brandr's relations with the Ásbirningar*

It is clear that he took his membership of the Ásbirningar seriously, claiming Skagafjörður as his birthright (*ættleifð*, lit. ancestral bequest). That Brandr chose to emphasize his ecclesiastical identity speaks volumes about the changing social conditions of high-placed clergy.

In 1252 Aron Hjörleifsson returned to Iceland having spent years in exile in Norway and made peace with the sons of Sigmundr *snagi* whom he had killed in 1225. According to the fourteenth century *Arons saga* this peace was made in 1254 and the settlement arbitrated by Bishop Heinrekr and Abbot Brandr (*SturlR* ii. 269, 278). According to *Þorgils saga skarða*, however, it was King Hákon who made peace between Aron and Sigmundr's son Erlingr and the two of them returned together to Iceland in 1252 (*Sturl* 627). The two accounts are not incompatible; Erlingr and Aron could have made their peace in Norway and Heinrekr and Brandr then arbitrated between him and Sigmundr's other sons. There is no evidence to corroborate *Arons saga*'s claim that Sigmundr had had more than one son and it is possible that the author made this up, although his motive in so doing is not transparent.

Around Easter 1258 Sturla Þórðarson and Þorgils *skarði*'s brother Sighvatr were hunting for Þorvarðr Þórarinsson in Eyjafjörður because he had killed Þorgils the previous autumn. Þorvarðr slipped away into Þingeyjarþing and sent a priest to ask for a settlement. They agreed and a meeting was held at Gásir (N) in the presence of Abbot Eyjólfr Valla-Brandsson of Þverá. A deal was made whereby a panel of judges was to adjudicate on the matter. The panel was to be made up of equal numbers from each side but Abbot Brandr was to preside. This panel never convened and Þorvarðr was prosecuted and convicted at the Alþing of 1259 (*Sturl* 741–2, 743).

In 1262 Brandr was at the Alþing in the company of Bishop Sigvarðr and witnessed Hrafn Oddsson and Gizurr Þorvaldsson—now earl of Iceland—shake hands on their reconciliation (*Sturl* 751, 758). This same summer Archbishop

Einarr sent a message to Iceland and summoned Brandr to Norway. He stayed with the archbishop over the winter and in Lent the chapter at Niðarós agreed that Brandr should be consecrated bishop of Hólar. He was consecrated 9 March 1263 and returned to Iceland in the same year (*Sturl* 759; *ÍF* xvii. 8). Both *Árna saga* and *Íslendinga saga* agree that it was Archbishop Einarr who summoned Brandr to Norway, but one of the annals, *Høyers annáll*, claims that Brandr was chosen in 1262 apparently before he left for Norway (*IA* 67). It is impossible to verify this claim and safer to trust the agreement of all the other sources.

Brandr was bishop for only a little more than a year. He died on 26 May 1264. His influence did however last much longer; the great reforming bishops Árni Þorláksson in Skálholt (1269–98) and Jörundr Þorsteinsson in Hólar (1267–1313) had been his pupils at Þykkvibær, as had Árni's deputy, Abbot Rúnólfr Sigmundarson in Þykkvibær (1264–1307) (*ÍF* xvii. 7). It was in the episcopacies of Árni and Jörundr that the Church won control over most church property and can truly be said to have become an independent institution.

Brandr left more than successful pupils; he had a son called Þorsteinn who was a householder at the church-farm Kálfafell in Fljótshverfi (S) in Árni Þorláksson's youth (*ÍF* xvii. 6),[54] no doubt as a result of his father's influence in the region. Sæmundr Ormsson (d. 1252) had lived at Kálfafell before he moved to Svínafell which suggests that it was owned by the family and also that it was a particularly important estate where leaders of the men of Fljótshverfi would live.

It is clear that Brandr quickly earned a reputation as a model cleric. The author of *Svínfellinga saga*—written shortly before 1300 (*SturlR* ii. p. xlvi; *ÍSB* i. 315)—describes him as an 'excellent chieftain, good cleric, wise and popular, influential and benevolent. In that time [*c.*1247] he had the best fortune of all those who were then in Iceland' (*Sturl* 550). We have also seen how the same author described Brandr as always having achieved the best results in public affairs. Not only was Brandr eminently respectable but he also managed to project an image of himself as a conciliator. His excellent pedigree was no doubt a precondition for his success but his dedication to his ecclesiastical identity was the basis for his becoming a required presence at almost every peace meeting. Brandr was not always neutral and he clearly had his own agenda and views, but he never allowed such considerations to take over. The drama of his agitation at the meeting of Þorgils and Þorvarðr in 1254 arises from the sympathy the audience must surely have for this benevolent and respectable cleric who is allowed no outlet for his frustration over the killing of a kinsman and over ancestral territory in the hands of enemies. It was the restrictions clerics imposed on their behaviour which made them special and which made high clerics able to intervene in conflict with safety and a chance of success.

The clergy did not of course have a monopoly on conciliation. There were in all periods laymen who were successfully involved in mediation and were

[54] Árni was born in 1237 and this was probably in the years after 1256.

sought after as arbitrators. The difference between the two and the reason clerics began to have the advantage over secular conciliators in the thirteenth century was that whereas the latter depended on their personality, skill, and reputation the clerics were ready-made, so to speak, on account of their ordination. As the thirteenth century wore on it slowly became established that clerics were, in the nature of their ordination, benevolent and trustworthy. Even if they as individuals were not particularly trustworthy it became seen as a function of their ordination to be so.

Clerical Celibacy

It is a historiographical misconception of long standing that clerical celibacy really never was properly accepted in Iceland (Gunnes 1982: 20; cf. Jochens 1980: 382–3, 388–9; Stefánsson 1978: 147–8). The facts in the matter are unusually clear and have been so at least since Jón Jóhannesson dealt with the issue (1956: 256–8). There are absolutely no indications that anyone agitated for clerical celibacy in Iceland until the 1240s, and then it was as a direct result of increased efforts by the Archbishop of Niðarbs to eradicate clerical marriage in line with the teaching of the Roman church from 1237 onwards (Gallén 1957*d*). That policy seems to have been pursued forcefully and successfully so that deacons and subdeacons had become the primary targets by the 1260s and 1270s. Marriage is forbidden to clerics in the New Christian law section of 1275 (*NgL* v. 38) and there are no indications that priests at least got married after that date. As elsewhere, clerics had concubines and fathered children but that does not mean that the policy was not successful. While in theory the ideal of sexual abstinence was the basis of the policy of clerical celibacy, its effective aim was to cut the formal ties between priest and his land and his family. Such ties were of course never completely severed, but by the second half of the thirteenth century they had become of secondary importance to the majority of priests. Their inability to marry set them apart from secular society and made them more dependent on the institutions of the Church.

There are signs of embarrassment in *Jóns saga helga* about St Jón's marriages. Stephan Kuttner (1975) has shown that the saga's claim that St Jón went to Rome before his consecration to get dispensation on account of his marriages (*Bsk* i. 160–1 (232–3)) is anachronistic and could at the earliest fit conditions around 1200. Gunnlaugr Leifsson wrote the first version of the saga in the first years of the thirteenth century and the embarrassment may well have been his. If it was him it does not mean that he believed in celibacy for all clergy; as a monastic no doubt familiar with foreign hagiographic material he will have considered that his saint would have better prospects if he had settled his marriage affairs with the pope. Both principal versions of the saga have this account but as they are both of fourteenth century date it cannot be precluded that the trip to Rome, or the reason for it, was an addition to Gunnlaugr's original account.

As far as is known not all bishops of the twelfth century were married. Þorlákr Rúnólfsson of Skálholt (1118–33); Magnús Einarsson of Skálholt (1134–48), and Björn Gilsson of Hólar (1147–62) are not known to have been married and no descendants of theirs have been identified. It is known that Klængr Þorsteinsson of Skálholt was not married but he had a daughter by his second cousin, the twelfth century's *femme fatale,* Yngvildr Þorgilsdóttir (*Sturl* 51, 57, 60–1, 101, 182, Arnórsson 1949–53: 177–8). St Þorlákr likewise was not married and in his case at least it can be ascribed to his monastic ideals; having gone to woo a respectable widow, he had a dream where he was told that another and more elevated bride was intended for him. Shortly afterwards he became abbot of Þykkvibær. The author of *Þorláks saga* introduces his account of the wooing: 'But God's Christendom has for a long time prospered and become stronger and the predicament of clerics increased, on account of decrees, because in that time it was not of great concern to the superiors if priests got married to widows, but now it is forbidden' (*Bsk* i. 93 (267–8)).

Þorláks saga is considered to be written early in the thirteenth century (*ÍSB* i. 474) and this is evidence that the so-called *Canones Nidarosiensis* were taken to hold for Iceland. In canon 6 priests are forbidden to marry women who have been married earlier. In the *Canones* only canons in cathedral chapters are forbidden to marry and/or keep concubines, whereas priests are instructed not to divorce their wives. The furthest the *Canones* go towards clerical celibacy is to require married clerics who are ordained as priests to take a vow of abstinence (*Lat.dok* 46–8). While the dating of the composition of the *Canones* in the form in which they have survived is disputed (see Ch. 3, s. 4) it is likely that they were derived in essence from Cardinal Nicholas Breakspear's (Pope Hadrian IV) visit to Norway in 1152–3 and his establishment of the archdiocese of Niðarós (see Kolsrud 1940–3; 1958: 198–200; Johnsen 1945*a*; 1951*a*; 1967; Skånland 1968). The *Canones* therefore reflect what a reforming prelate could realistically hope to achieve in the far north at that time. Nicholas is accredited with having forbidden *bigamam in clero* and it is likely that the *Canones* are an elaboration of this edict (*Lat.dok* 94–6. Gunnes 1982: 23–4). Although *Þorláks saga* is evidence that these regulations were known there are no other indications that emphasis was laid on their enforcement either in Norway or Iceland.

There is at any rate not a breath on marital restrictions of the clergy in any of the letters of the archbishops in the late twelfth century. Nor does it appear that St Þorlákr—concerned as he was with marital reform in general—campaigned for marital reform among his clergy. Nor does Guðmundr Arason, who was himself no doubt celibate, seem to have advocated any such thing; in fact he is supposed to have found a wife for one of the priests he himself had ordained (*Bsk* i. 589–90). It does not seem to have been a problem for Bishop Páll Jónsson of Skálholt (1195–1211) or his successor Magnús Gizurarson (1216–37) that they were married. In *Páls saga* Páll's wife Herdís is complimented for her brilliant management of the bishop's household:

Bishop Páll had been one winter at Skálholt when Herdís, his wife, came there to manage the household and she was such a pillar of strength to him and the see that there was no one like her while he was bishop. Such was her energy and supervision that she had only been a few winters there when there was everywhere plenty of the things needed and no things had to be requested for the household even if there were 100 people to feed and 70 or 80 belonging to the household. (*Bsk* i. 131–2)

This author writing in the second decade of the thirteenth century (*ÍBS* i. 348) was clearly in no doubt about the beneficial aspects of bishops being married. It seems to have been about this time or shortly afterwards that elements in the Norwegian church began to call for the introduction of clerical celibacy. Their progress will however have been obstructed by the frequent changes in occupancy of the archiepiscopacy. It was not until a synod was held in 1236 that the issue surfaced. At this synod the priests claimed that Cardinal Nicholas had permitted clerical marriage but could not produce any evidence to support this. They were of course right in a sense; if the *Canones* are his edicts he condoned clerical marriage by not forbidding it outright. Archbishop Sigurðr, who seems to have raised the matter, obtained a papal letter in 1237 where Pope Gregory IX instructs him to see to it that his clerics do not marry (*DI* i. 518). From then on clerical celibacy was official church policy in the archdiocese of Niðarós.[55]

Bishop Sigvarðr of Skálholt (1238–68), Bishop Heinrekr of Hólar (1247–60), and Bishop Brandr Jónsson of Hólar (1263–4) all campaigned against clerical marriages (*ÍF* xvii. 10, 44). In 1252 Bishop Heinrekr became furious when he learnt that the priest Gunnlaugr Hallfreðarson, who was Þorgils *skarði*'s brother-in-law and in the latter's company at Hólar, was married. Heinrekr forbade Gunnlaugr to attend church but relented when Þorgils asked his forbearance (*Sturl* 606). We do not know much about the bishops' progress but it appears to have been satisfactory. When Árni Þorláksson was *officialis* in Hólar between Bishop Brandr's death in 1264 and Bishop Jörundr's return in 1267 he successfully prevented the marriage of a wealthy deacon who had the endorsement of Earl Gizurr (*ÍF* xvii. 9–11). In 1273 when Árni had himself become bishop he turned on the subdeacon Egill Sölmundarson householder in Reykholt (S) and chieftain of the Sturlungar (d. 1297). Egill, who must have been past middle age at this time, had been married in the episcopacy of Bishop Sigvarðr, despite the bishop's denunciation. Egill and his wife had several children and were not at all happy to have their marriage annulled but Árni persisted, threatening excommunication and anathema and in the end they relented and the wife was married to another man (*ÍF* xvii. 44–5).

It is likely that Bishop Árni targeted important men like Egill and the deacon to set an example, but the fact that these were men in lower orders, who were possibly not even active as clerics at all, suggests that the fight to make priests celibate was to all intents and purposes over by this time. It is difficult to

[55] On its acceptance in Norway see Gunnes 1982: 24–5.

corroborate this with other evidence but there are no examples of clerics who came of age in or after 1240 being married and this suggests that the shift to clerical celibacy was relatively swift in Iceland.

By 1300 clerical marriage had become the stuff of myth. The fourteenth century middle version of *Guðmundar saga biskups* contains two stories of priests ordained by Bishop Guðmundr. Both got married 'but then there came here the edict that no priest should have a wife and that those who were married previously should divorce their wives or lose their office, and then their children would be called legitimate' (*Bsk* i. 597). Bishop Guðmundr had prophesied as much and he had also told both these priests that neither would lose their office on account of their marriages. In the case of Narfi Snorrason (d. 1284) in Kolbeinsstaðir (S) he sought out the archbishop and got a dispensation from him and continued to live with his wife and never lost his office. Or that at least was what Narfi's son Þorlákr (d. 1303) told the author of the version (*Bsk* i. 596–7). In the case of the incredibly long-lived Einarr *klerkr* Ásbjarnarson in Einarsstaðir (A) (b. 1190 d. 1305!), his keeping of both wife and office was simply a miracle due to Bishop Guðmundr (*Bsk* i. 589–90). That the marriages of priests had become material for miracle stories around 1300 suggests that they were then a thing of the past.

6
The Church and the Increase in Social Complexity

In the early and mid-twelfth century a great number of chieftains were priests and all owned churches. It is argued here that owning churches and being priests helped chieftains to consolidate their powers. By providing services for their neighbours and receiving tithes from them they forged strong ties with the householders who lived closest to them and by richly endowing their churches they advertised their magnanimity and authority. Most importantly, however, the churches made it possible for the chieftain families to link their claim to power to their property so that the possession of a church-farm was what decided who wielded power. This was probably the stepping-stone needed for the development of complex power structures to begin.

By the first decade of the thirteenth century a handful of families had acquired or were in the process of acquiring all the *goðorð* in the country. This did not mean that these overlords had much direct control over anything but their home-patch; it meant that a large number of local leaders and *stórbændr* had forfeited their right of representation at the Alþing and instead acknowledged the right of these overlords to lead in national politics. The local leaders had probably not grown weaker as a result of the power consolidation, except in relative terms. It seems that the *stórbændr* in Skagafjörður in the 1250s had much tighter control of their areas and a better organization than the *goðorðsmenn* in Dalir had had in the 1170s. The *stórbændr* had only lost out in the power struggle in the sense that they now acknowledged that there was a tier above them occupied by the chieftains to whom they owed allegiance.

There were therefore many families around 1200 who were losing the political initiative but nevertheless had firm control over their respective areas—a much firmer grip than their fathers or grandfathers had had. In the west, where the most detailed evidence is available, a number of families which had wielded power in the twelfth century disappeared around 1200—the Reykhyltingar; Gilsbekkingar; Mýramenn; Snæfellingar—and in other parts of the country, the Reynistaðarmenn and the Austfirðingar. Others who lost their *goðorð*—like the Garðamenn, Hítdælir, Skarðverjar, and Staðarhólsmenn[1]—continued to control their areas and were indispensable supporters of the chieftains in the struggles of the mid-thirteenth century. Furthermore these families managed,

[1] It is nowhere stated that the Hítdælir or Staðarhólsmenn gave away their *goðorð*, but neither are they mentioned as holding them after 1200. It may be that they never gave them away but 'lent' them to the Sturlungar who then had actual control over them.

unlike the five great chieftain families, to keep hold of their principal estates and rise to prominence again after the union with Norway in 1262–4. A similar pattern can be discerned in a few families which first appear around or shortly before 1200 and whose relationship with local power earlier in the twelfth century is therefore unclear. The Melamenn, the men of Staðarfell, Rauðsendingar, Seldælir in Selárdalur, and Staðarmenn in Steingrímsfjörður all became quite prominent in their respective areas in the thirteenth century.

What is notable about these families who did not play national politics but continued to govern their respective areas is that in most of them the heads were priests. In this they differed from the chieftain families the heads of which, as we have seen, for the most part, ceased becoming priests before the end of the twelfth century. This suggests that the local leaders had different aspirations from the chieftains. While regional and even national overlordship had become the aim of most of the *goðorð*-owning families by the beginning of the thirteenth century, it seems that the local leaders reacted to the changing political situation by concentrating their efforts on consolidating their local power and improving their government. Many of them being priests is a clear indication that local power was their primary consideration.

The power spheres of these families were in many cases quite small, often not comprising more than a single commune and in some cases a single ministry. In the cases of the men of Staðarfell, the Skarðverjar, and Rauðsendingar, the respective spheres of power included only one commune which was also more or less coterminous with the ministry. These were among the largest ministries in the country in the fourteenth century and there may have been a connection between that and the fact that the churches had been owned by powerful families in the thirteenth century. The Staðarmenn in Steingrímsfjörður probably had a larger sphere of power than a single commune, and the ministry belonging to their church was enormous before the establishment of the church at Kaldaðarnes in 1317. The power spheres of the Hítdælir and Garðamenn were probably also considerably larger than a single commune or ministry, although the ministries of Garðar and Kolbeinsstaðir, which was the Hítdælir's principal estate after 1221, were also extremely large.

By being priests the heads of the Garðamenn, Hítdælir, the men of Staðarfell, the Skarðverjar, the Seldælir in Selárdalur, and the Staðarmenn in Steingrímsfjörður nurtured a strong and personal relationship with the flocks in their large ministries and this no doubt was an important element in strengthening their influence over their areas. Being priests gave them special status as magnates, which became increasingly important as the thirteenth century wore on. It is particularly striking that in the 1250s when the political conflict in the country was beginning to seem unsolvable and unwinnable, many of the heads of the families named above who had previously actively supported one chieftain or another began to take a more neutral stance and act as mediators and arbitrators between the warring overlords. At this point it seems that many of these men had chosen to adopt an ecclesiastical identity instead of a secular one; they begin to conform to patterns of behaviour fitting ecclesiastical dignitaries. In the political turmoil of the 1250s this was probably, first and foremost, a welcome way for the heads of these families to distance themselves from political alliances and ties which were becoming increasingly uncomfortable. They had already begun to discard the old way of making politics, where power was measured in brute economic and military strength, and had adopted the new one where appointment to an office became the basis for power. It is no coincidence that families like the Hítdælir and the Skarðverjar became extremely successful in the new secular administration after 1262–4; it was families like them which had the resources and refinement to compete for offices at the Norwegian court and the economic and political organization back home to be able to accomplish their tasks and hold on to their offices.

As there seems to be a connection between the size of ministry and the type of power associated with the family owning the church in the twelfth and thirteenth centuries it is worth looking closer at the patterns which are revealed by studying ministry sizes. The geographical and economic data is mostly of fourteenth-century date and the following discussion centres on the ministries of Dalir (D) where such data is particularly plentiful.

There were twelve ministries in the region of Dalir in the early fourteenth century. Their size varied considerably both in area and number of farmsteads. The two smallest had only three and eight farmsteads (Búðardalur and Sælingsdalstunga respectively) while the three largest had over twenty farmsteads (Hjarðarholt, Staðarfell, and Skarð). Most of the ministries, however, had eleven to fifteen farmsteads, which corresponds to the modal range of ministry sizes in the western quarter. It is difficult to compare ministry sizes in different regions, because charters are not available for every church and many of them do not mention ministry size. The tables represent an attempt, based on available fourteenth-century charter evidence.[2] It seems from the figures given in Table 8 that for some reason churches with large ministries are less represented in the charter material (or that their charters have a greater tendency not to disclose ministry size), but this does not alter the overall impression that in the regions surrounding the episcopal sees[3] most ministries tend to be very small (one to five), with a few very large ministries (twenty plus) in between. In other regions very small ministries are rare, while the majority are middle-sized (six to fifteen) or large.

[2] For the northern quarter the charter collection of Bishop Auðun from 1318 was used (*DI* ii. 428–85), and where this fails the charters of Bishop Pétur Nikulásson from 1394 (*DI* iii. 512–90). For the others: *DI* i. 174, 180, 255–6, 266, 269, 272, 275, 304, 406, 408, 413, 418–20, 522, 594–7; ii. 62–4, 66, 113, 257, 260–1, 378, 397, 403, 577, 616–17, 633, 637, 651, 662–70, 679–92, 695–8, 736, 741–2, 769–71, 774–9, 782–3, 785, 832–3; iii. 69, 78–82, 85–92, 100–5, 107–11, 115, 124–6, 193–7, 237, 239–44, 256, 260–3, 267, 270, 301, 305–6, 324, 330–1, 403–4; iv. 39–236. The number of churches in Skálholt diocese is based on Bishop Páll Jónsson's list of churches from around 1200 with additions (*DI* xii. 3–15). The record of tax-paying farmers from 1311 is in *DI* iv. 9–10.

[3] Especially in Rangárþing, Árnesþing, and Kjalarnesþing in the south. The same tendency can be observed in Skagafjörður in the north but it is not as marked as in the south.

TABLE 8. *Mean ministry sizes in Iceland in the fourteenth century*

	Expected mean	Observed mean	Modal range	Based on % of churches
Northern quarter	10.55	10.97	6–10	85%
Western quarter	14.66	13.96	11–15	71%
Dalir		14.10	11–15	100%
Southern quarter	9.60	8.47	1–5	49%
Eastern quarter	11.06	8.30	6–10	51%
Iceland	11.24	10.77	6–10	66%

Notes: Ministry size is expressed as the number of farmsteads from which tithes were paid to the church. The expected mean is found by dividing the number of tax paying householders in each quarter in 1311 by the total number of churches in each quarter.

TABLE 9. *Distribution of ministry sizes in Iceland in the fourteenth century*

Number of farmsteads	1–5	6–10	11–15	16–20	21–25	26–30	31–35	36+
Northern quarter	12	37	27	9	4	4		
Western quarter	9	10	17	7	1	4	2	1
Dalir	1	3	5	1	1	1		
Southern quarter	21	14	9	3	1	2	1	
Eastern quarter	10	11	4	1			1	
Iceland	52	72	57	20	6	10	4	1

Note: This shows the number of churches in each quarter by modal range of ministry size in the 14th cent. Based on charters of 66% of the churches.

It has been argued here that church organization is most likely to have developed first, and most rapidly, in the largest continuous areas of settlement, that is on the southern plains and the river valleys of the north. It must have been because of this that the episcopal sees were placed precisely in these regions. The establishment of the sees must have further accelerated the development of church organization, and the strongest impact is most likely to be found in the regions surrounding the sees. That this results, among other things, in small ministries can be explained. There is nothing to suggest that the farmsteads of the southern plains or the northern valleys produced higher tithes on average than farmsteads elsewhere, nor were individual churches in these regions particularly rich, especially not on the southern plain, where small ministries were most common. That this is a matter of priests rather than church buildings is clear; there is no significant difference in the ratio between farmsteads and church buildings (i.e. any consecrated building, whether church, annex-church, or chapel) between the different regions of the country. The difference is that, on the southern plain and in Húnaþing, Skagafjörður, and Eyjafjörður, more of the churches had ministries. There were fewer priests per capita in the east and west, they had larger ministries and were paid better for the chapel-mass, 3 ells instead of 2 ells in the north and south.

The reason for the difference in ministry size between regions probably lies in demand for priests. Scholars agree that power consolidation first began on the southern plain and in Skagafjörður. The Haukdælir seem to have already acquired all powers in Árnesþing in the eleventh century, and by the late twelfth the Oddaverjar controlled Rangárþing and the Ásbirningar Skagafjörður. In other areas power structures continued to be more fragmentary until after 1200 (J. V. Sigurðsson 1989: 54–61). In a relatively densely populated region like Árnesþing where the Haukdælir owned all the *goðorð* and therefore presumably had complete control, the contention for power must have been on a different scale and of a different nature than for instance in the smaller region of Dalir where there were at least two families owning *goðorð* and nobody was an undisputed leader of the region. In the latter region there was a small number of wealthy householders who could realistically contend for regional powers and representation at the Alþing. These were the men who would gain politically by building churches and providing the services of a priest to their neighbours and followers. Their goal was regional dominance and national importance. Whereas in Árnesþing the same kind of powers that were still a matter of contention in Dalir were already in the hands of the Haukdælir family and we can therefore expect a lower tier of affluent householders who could expect to win local prominence and influence with the Haukdælir by providing pastoral care for their neighbours.

The difference in ministry size between regions may therefore be a result of regional differences in political and social complexity in the period the ministry system was taking form. According to this explanation large ministries were predominant in regions with only one tier of authority but small ministries in regions with two tiers—because the second tier accommodated a proportionately larger number of householders to whom it was politically advantageous to seek influence by providing pastoral care.

This explanation is only useful as a generalization, and there were no doubt other factors which influenced developments in particular cases. This line of argument is useful, not only to explain developments on a national scale but also at local level. Dalir was a politically fragmented region in the twelfth century, and this appears to have resulted in fairly large ministries. The differences in size within the region can be explained on similar premises. In the three large ministries of Skarð, Staðarfell, and Hjarðarholt, the church is situated in the centre of large, continuous, and relatively sparsely settled areas, each corresponding to a modern commune, Skarð and Staðarfell each in a coastal area and Hjarðarholt in the mouth of the large and broad valley of Laxárdalur overlooking the coastal lowlands of the eastern side of Hvammsfjörður. Not counting the ministry of Búðardalur, the other eight smaller ministries are in more confined landscapes, valleys with a higher density of settlement. In these ministries the church is situated towards one end of its area, but as close to the centre of the geographical zone as was possible. Thus we have two churches in Saurbær (a single modern commune), Hvoll and Staðarhóll each in a small valley branching off from the main lowland area, both closer to the geographical centre of the area than the centre of their respective ministries. In Hvammssveit, also a single modern commune, there were three churches with ministries around 1200, Hvammur, Sælingsdalstunga, and Ásgarður—the last one was later to lose its ministry—all within a short distance of each other. In Suðurdalir the situation is slightly more complex. The ministry of Vatnshorn is a geographically well-defined area, a narrow valley with a large lake at its opening creating a natural boundary; and so is the ministry of Snóksdalur, clearly divided from Miðdalir by a mountain ridge. Each area corresponds to a single modern commune, but the churches are in both cases situated at the extreme edge of the ministries, as close as possible to the central lowlands of Miðdalir. In Miðdalir (a single modern commune) there were two churches, Sauðafell and Kvennabrekka, close to each other and both overlooking the lowlands.

In his study of the prominence of Sauðafell as a seat of secular power in the thirteenth century, Helgi Þorláksson (1991*a*) has convincingly argued that the principal reason for its importance was because of its location on the crossroads of much-used routes. In this and his other main study on communications and power consolidation, Helgi Þorláksson (1989*a*) has mainly been concerned with showing how the strategic location of chieftains' power bases was an important element in state formation, and in Dalir in particular he emphasizes the military advantages of controlling crossroads and frequented routes. There is no arguing against the fact that in the early and mid-thirteenth century turmoil, strategic location could be of paramount importance for a chieftain's power struggle. It is arguable that in more peaceful times, the same applied, albeit on a different scale.

The principal land route from the Vestfirðir peninsula to Borgarfjörður and beyond lay through Dalir. Coming by way of Gilsfjörður in the north the route lay through Saurbær, passed Hvoll on its way up to the mountain pass in Svínadalur, came down again on the southern side to pass Sælingsdalstunga and Ásgarður, continued along the coast of the eastern side of Hvammsfjörður, past Hjarðarholt, and on the plains between Haukadalsá and Miðá, west of Sauðafell and Kvennabrekka, it crossed the other main route through Dalir, an east–west route between the northern quarter and Snæfellsnes, coming through Haukadalsskarð in the east, through Haukadalur, over a low ridge by Kvennabrekka, over Tunguá past Sauðafell, and thence westward past Snóksdalur. The north–south route continued from the crossroads south through Miðdalir and to Borgarfjörður by way of Brattabrekka (see Map 2).[4]

It is hardly a coincidence that the churches with smaller ministries are more or less lined up on these principal routes. A contributory factor may have been the religious desire to aid travellers, a concern expressed in many early charters, but that sentiment also had a more mundane side to it. A church with pastoral

[4] Based on the research of Þorláksson 1991*a*: 99–101, 105, and the maps of the Danish High Command (Generalstabens Topografiske kort), Copenhagen 1911–14.

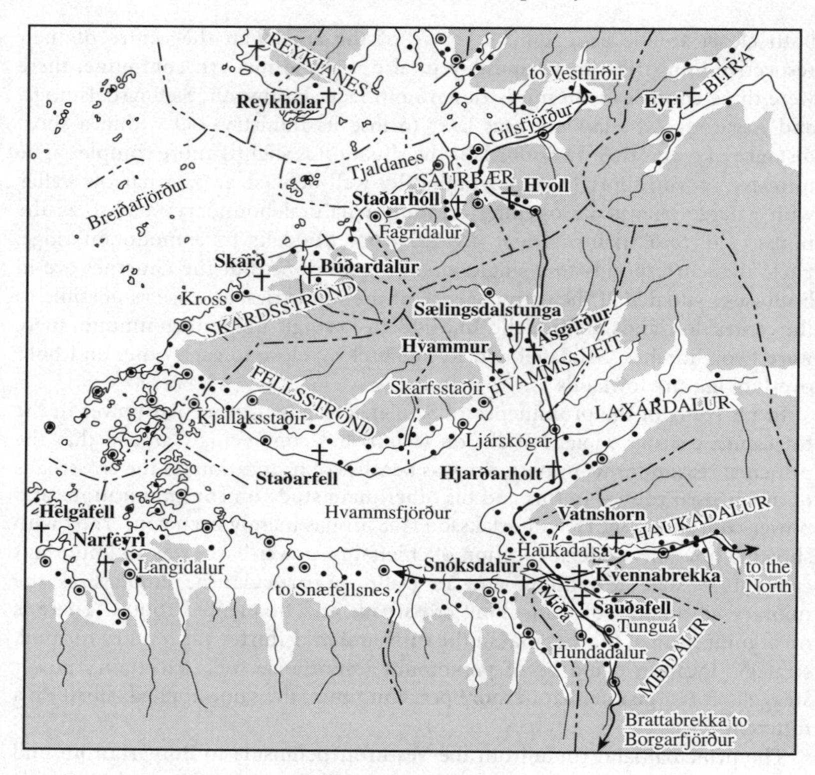

MAP 2. *Dalir: places mentioned in the text and principal routes through the region*

responsibilities was not only a centre of local devotion and gatherings; if it could attract people from other regions passing by, it also had the potential of becoming a centre where people would come and get news of foreign parts and even do some trading. The church's and its owner's reputation could reach other regions, but more importantly it would grow in his own backyard as a consequence of accommodating travellers.

Being situated on a much-used route may therefore be viewed as a resource for a householder aspiring to, or wanting to consolidate, local power. In areas of relatively dense settlement, this resource can have been tapped into by wealthy householders motivated to increase their influence. Density of settlement is the decisive factor here, because the benefits of attracting local people depended on their being able to attend the church frequently and in reasonable numbers. On this basis we can formulate the hypothesis that there are more churches with smaller ministries in densely settled areas, through which frequently used routes lay, than elsewhere. In Dalir at least this holds true.

The combined ministries of Hvoll and Staðarhóll had some twenty-four farmsteads in them, the ministries of Hvammur and Sælingsdalstunga had thirteen before the enlargement of the former in 1308 (*DI* iii. 8–9) and Sauðafell and Kvennabrekka had twenty-seven farmsteads together. The reason why single large ministries did not form in these three areas, must be connected with the potential for wealthy householders to increase their influence by providing pastoral care, created by the circumstances of dense settlement and proximity to regional highways.

The model of change presented here assumes that before the introduction of Christianity there were no mechanisms in place which allowed individuals or families to wield power over territory and the people contained within it, except through ownership of land.[5] As far as can be seen, lordship based on extensive landholding did not develop in Iceland, nor did lordship based on military superiority. It was only with the churches and the subsequent division of the country into tithe areas and ministries that the basis for sustainable territorial power was created. While this was the leverage needed for a few families to become overlords it effected an increase and not a decrease in the total number of men wielding power. Instead of a relatively limited number of chieftains with non-territorial powers there developed in the twelfth century an even smaller group of territorial overlords who were able to exercise power over large areas and even whole quarters through their authority over a much larger number of local leaders. It was these local leaders who survived the upheavals of the thirteenth century to become the gentry of the late middle ages.

In the late 1230s the Norwegian archbishops took up the issue of clerical celibacy and it became an effective policy in Iceland in the 1240s to 1270s. It is in this period that in both countries the Church really begins to assert itself as an independent institution. Clerical celibacy was being pursued in the same period as the Church was strengthening its image as conciliator and both aspects relate to its aim of separation from secular society. This was not, however, an original aim of the native clergy, but an adopted one. The reasons why it was adopted

[5] This is a different question from the geographically fragmented power of *goðar* in the late 12th and early 13th cent. The fact that a *goði* might have *þingmenn* in other areas intermixed with *þingmenn* of other *goðar* does not mean that the latter did not have core territories inside which they were all-powerful; it only means that the *þingmaðr* was, or wanted to be, independent of their local *goði*.

and why clerics began to impose restrictions on their behaviour in the thirteenth century are complex.

A precondition was the increasing amount of property under direct control of churchmen. Another factor was that by the late twelfth century most high-born clerics—those who became bishops and abbots—were younger and illegitimate sons with no other prospect of advancement in the world. It was to their benefit to identify with the Church and to strengthen it as an institution, both by ensuring that more property came under its control and by extending its formal powers. A third important factor was the development of secular politics. As overlords became increasingly powerful and their numbers decreased their actions became better aimed and their retinues began to consist of professional retainers. In short, politics became a specialized full-time occupation of a small number of people. To these it was advantageous to have at their disposal clerics with particular skills and well-defined qualities which could be used in certain situations. It was also advantageous to this new type of lord to have access to the Church's muscle in conciliation. To aristocratic families the Church was also useful because it offered opportunities for their surplus sons who might otherwise become a nuisance and pose a threat to their older brothers. Each of these factors was a function of another and together they created the conditions for an institutional church.

BIBLIOGRAPHY

The alphabetical order including the Icelandic and Scandinavian characters is:
aábcdðeéfghiíjklmnoópqrstuúüvxyzþæöøäå

Aakjær, Svend (1927). 'Om det olddanske Herred og Sogn', *Festskrift til Kristian Erslev den 28. Decebr. 1927 fra danske Historikere*, ed. P. Nørlund (Copenhagen), 1–30.

Addleshaw, Georg W. O. (1956). *Rectors, Vicars and Patrons in Twelfth and Early Thirteenth Century Canon Law*, (St Anthony's Hall Publications, 9; York).

—— (1957). *The Early Parochial System and the Divine Office* (Alcuin Club Prayer Book Revision Pamphlets, 15; London).

—— (1970*a*). *The Beginnings of the Parochial System*, 3rd edn. (St Anthony's Hall Publications, 3; York).

—— (1970*b*). *The Development of the Parochial System from Charlemange (768–814) to Urban II (1088–1099)*, 2nd edn. (St Anthony's Hall Publications, 6; York).

Aðalbjarnarson, Bjarni (1937). *Om de norske kongers sagaer* (Skrifter utgitt av Det Norske Videnskaps-Akademi i Oslo II. Hist.-Filos. Klass, 1936/4; Oslo).

—— (1958). *Bemerkninger om de eldste bispesagaer* (*SI* 17; Reykjavík).

Aðalsteinsson, Jón Hnefill (1971). *Kristnitakan á Íslandi* (Reykjavík).

—— (1978). *Under the Cloak: The Acceptance of Christianity in Iceland with Particular Reference to the Religious Attitudes Prevailing at the Time* (Acta Universitatis Uppsalensis, Studia Ethnologica Upsalensia, 4; Stockholm).

—— (1985). 'Blót og þing: Trúarlegt og félagslegt hlutverk goða á tíundu öld', *Skirnir*, 159: 123–42.

Afmælisrit Björns Sigfússonar (Reykjavík, 1975).

Afmælisrit Jóns Helgasonar 30. júní 1969 (Reykjavík, 1969).

Agnarsdóttir, Anna, and Árnason, Ragnar (1983). 'Þrælahald á þjóðveldisöld', *Saga*, 21: 5–26.

Ahrens, Claus, ed. (1981). *Frühe Holzkirchen im nördlichen Europa* (Veröffentlichung des Helms-Museums, 39; Hamburg).

Andersen, Per Sveaas (1969). *Nytt fra norsk middelalder*, i. *Vikingtid og rikssamling* (Norsk Lektorforlags faglig-pedagogiske skrifter, 9; Oslo).

—— (1977). *Samlingen av Norge og kristningen av landet 800–1130* (Handbok i Norges historie, 2; Bergen).

—— (1989). 'The Orkney Church of the Twelfth and Thirteenth Centuries: A Stepdaughter of the Norwegian Church?', *Collegium Medievale*, 2/1: 6–25.

Andersson, Hans, and Anglert, Mats, eds. (1989). *By, huvudgård och kyrka: Studier i Ystadsområdets medeltid* (Lund Studies in Medieval Archaeology, 5; Stockholm).

Andersson, Karin (1982). 'Aspekter på den medeltida kyrkobyggnaden', *Bebyggelsehistorisk tidskrift*, 3: 159–70.

Andersson, Theodore M. (1964). *The Problem of Icelandic Saga Origins: A Historical Survey* (New Haven, Conn.).

—— (1967). *The Icelandic Family Saga: An Analytical Reading* (Harvard Studies in Comparative Literature, 28; Cambridge, Mass.).

Andersson, Theodore M. (1975). 'The Emergence of Vernacular Literature in Iceland', *Mosaic*, 8: 161–9.

—— (1977). 'The Conversion of Norway According to Oddr Snorrason and Snorri Sturluson', *MS* 10: 83–95.

—— (1993). 'Snorri Sturluson and the Saga School at Munkaþverá', in A. Wolf (ed.), *Snorri Sturluson: Kolloquium anläßlich der 750. Wiederkehr seines Todestages* (Tübingen), 9–25.

—— and Miller, William I. (1989). *Law and Literature in Medieval Iceland: Ljósvetninga Saga and Valla-Ljóts Saga* (Stanford, Calif.).

Andersson, Thorsten (1988). 'Den medeltida sockenbildningen från språklig synpunkt', *KVHAA årsbok 1988*: 65–82.

—— and Sandred, K. I., eds. (1978). *The Vikings: Proceedings of the Symposium of the Faculty of Arts of Uppsala University June 6–7, 1977* (Uppsala).

Anglert, Marit (1984). 'Vem försvarade vad? Några reflexioner kring de så kallade försvarskykorna', *Meta*, 84/3–4: 19–38.

Anglert, Mats (1984). 'Kapell—vad är det?', *Meta*, 84/3–4: 11–18.

—— (1986). 'Medeltida kapell i Skåne—en första sammanställning', *Medeltiden och arkeologin* (Lund), 117–29.

—— (1989). 'Den kyrkliga organisationen under äldre medeltid', in H. Andersson and A. Anglert (eds.), *By, huvudgård och kyrka* (Stockholm), 221–42.

Arneborg, Jette (1991). 'The Roman Church in Norse Greenland', *Acta Archaeologica*, 61: 142–50.

Arnórsdóttir, Agnes S. (1986). 'Viðhorf til kvenna í Grágás, *Sagnir*, 7: 23–30.

—— (1991). 'Þankar um konur og stjórnmál á þjóðveldisöld', *Yfir Íslandsála*, (Reykjavík), 7–19.

—— (1995). *Konur og vígamenn: Staða kynjanna á Íslandi á 12. og 13. öld* (Sagnfræðirannsóknir, Studia historica, 12; Reykjavík).

Arnórsson, Einar (1930*a*). 'Alþingi árið 930', *Skírnir*, 104: 6–48.

—— (1930*b*). 'Alþingi árið 1000', *Skírnir*, 104: 68–106.

—— (1930*c*). 'Alþingi árið 1262', *Skírnir*, 104: 116–34.

—— (1941). 'Kristnitökusagan árið 1000', *Skírnir*, 115: 79–118.

—— (1942). *Ari fróði* (Reykjavík).

—— (1944–8): 'Sifjaspell lögsögumanns í Hungurvöku', *Blanda*, 8: 225–52.

—— (1945). *Réttarsaga Alþingis* (Reykjavík).

—— (1949–53): 'Hjúskapur Þorvalds Gizurarsonar og Jóru Klængsdóttur', *Saga*, 1: 177–89.

—— (1950). *Árnesþing á landnáms- og söguöld* (Reykjavík).

—— (1954–8). 'Suðurgöngur Íslendinga í fornöld', *Saga*, 2: 1–45.

Astås, Reidar (1994). 'Om bibelanvendelse i *Þorláks saga byskups*', *Alvíssmál*, 3: 73–96.

Axelsdóttir, Björk (1984). 'Þingeyraklaustur á miðöldum', *Húnavaka*, 24: 73–87.

Ágústsson, Hörður (1972). 'Stavkirke. Island', *KHL* xvii. 101–4.

—— (1981). 'Isländischer Kirchenbau bis 1550', in C. Ahrens (ed.), *Frühe Holzkirchen im nördlichen Europa* (Hamburg), 343–7.

—— (1988). 'Minnisgrein um kirkjugrunnsleifar á Stóruborg', *Árbók 1987*: 41–3.

—— (1990). *Skálholt: Kirkjur* (Staðir og kirkjur, 1. Skálholt; Reykjavík).

Álitsgerð kirkjueignanefndar (Reykjavik, 1984), i.

Árnadóttir, Lilja (1982). 'Fundin mannabein í Neðranesi', *Árbók 1981*: 48–50.

Árnason, Jón (1954–61): *Íslenzkar þjóðsögur og ævintýri*, i–vi (Reykjavík).

Baetke, Walter (1935). 'Die Isländersaga als Quellen der Missionsgeschichte', *Deutscher evangelischer Missionskalendar für das Jahr 1935*, 10: 34–8.
—— (1951). *Christliches Lehngut in der Saga-religion* (Berichte über die Verhandlungen der Sächsischen Akademie der Wissenschaften zu Leipzig. Phil.-hist. Klasse, 98/6; Berlin).
Bagge, Sverre (1975). 'Samkongedømme og enekongedømme', *HT* 54: 239–73.
—— (1976*a*). *Den kongelige kapellgeistlighet 1150–1319* (Bergen).
—— (1976*b*). 'Sættargjerden i Tønsberg', *KHL* xxi: 326–30.
—— (1981). 'Kirkens jurisdiksjon i kristenrettssaker før 1277', *HT* 60: 133–59.
—— (1984). 'Nordic Students at Foreign Universities until 1660', *Scandinavian Journal of History*, 9: 1–29.
—— (1986*a*). 'Borgerkrig og statsudvikling i Norge i middelalderen', *HT* 65: 145–97.
—— (1986*b*). 'The Formation of the State and Concepts of Society in Thirteenth Century Norway', in E. Vestergaard (ed.), *Continuity and Changes* (Odense), 43–59.
—— (1989*a*). 'Theodoricus Monachus: Clerical Historiography in Twelfth Century Norway', *Scandinavian Journal of History*, 14: 113–33.
—— (1989*b*). 'Det politiske menneske og det førstatlige samfunn', *HT* 68: 227–47.
—— (1991). 'Propaganda, Ideology and Political Power in Old Norse and European Historiography: A Comparative View', in J.-P. Genet (ed.), *L'Historiographie médiévale en Europe* (Paris), 199–208.
Bartlett, Robert (1986). *Trial by Fire and Water: The Medieval Judicial Ordeal* (Oxford).
Bauman, Richard (1986). 'Performance and Honor in Thirteenth-Century Iceland', *Journal of American Folklore*, 99: 131–50.
Beckmann, Natanael (1912*a*). 'Annalstudier', *Studier i nordisk filologi*, 3/4: 1–12.
—— (1912*b*). 'Quellen und Quellenwert der isländischen Annalen', in *Xenia Lideniana; Festskrift tillägnad professor Evald Lidén på hans femtioårsdag den 3 oktober 1912* (Stockholm), 16–39.
—— (1914–16). 'Inledning', *AÍ* ii, pp i–cxciv.
—— (1915). 'Vetenskapligt liv på Island under 1100 och 1200-talen', *Maal og Minne 1915*: 193–212.
Bede (1896). *Historia ecclesiastica gentis Anglorum*, ed. C. Plummer (Baedae opera historica, 1; Oxford).
Bekker-Nielsen, Hans (1960). 'Hvornaar blev Ísleifr Gizurarson bispeviet?', *Opuscula*, 1 (BA 20): 335–8.
—— (1961). 'A Note on Two Icelandic Saints', *Germanic Review*, 36: 108–9.
—— (1962). 'On a Handlist of Saint's Lives in Old Norse', *Medieval Studies*, 24: 323–34.
—— (1968). 'The Victorines and their Influence on Old Norse Literature', in B. Niclasen (ed.), *The Fifth Viking Congress* (Tórshaun), 32–36.
—— (1970). 'Skotakollr', *Fróðskaparrit*, 18: 145–50.
—— (1972). 'Hungrvaka and the Medieval Icelandic Audience', *Studi germanici*, 10/1: 95–8.
—— (1976). 'Viktorinsk indflydelse', *KHL* xx. 61–3.
—— (1985). 'Hungrvaka', *DMA* 6: 351–2.
—— (1986). 'Church and Schoolroom—and Early Icelandic Literature', in R. Simek *et al.* (eds.), Sagnaskemmtun (Vienna), 13–18.
—— (1992). 'Et par ord om de ældste norrøne helgensagaer', in F. Hødnebø *et al.* (eds.), *Eyvindarbók* (Oslo), 29–33.
—— and Widding, Ole (1969). 'Religiøs prosalitteratur: Norge og Island', *KHL* xiv: 42–4.

Bekker-Nielsen, Hans, Olsen, Thorkil D., and Widding, Ole (1965). *Norrøn fortællekunst: Kapitler af den norsk-islandske middelaladerlitteraturs historie* (Copenhagen).
Benediktsson, Bogi (1881–1932). *Sýslumannaæfir*, i–v (Reykjavík).
Benediktsson, Gunnar (1961). *Sagnameistarinn Sturla* (Reykjavík).
—— (1967). *Skyggnst umhverfis Snorra: Nokkrar ritgerðir um Snorra Sturluson, vandamenn hans og vini* (Reykjavík).
—— (1976). *Rýnt í fornar rúnir: Ritgerðir í sambandi við frásagnir fornra rita íslenzkra* (Hafnarfjörður).
Benediktsson, Hreinn (1962). 'Islandsk språk', *KHL* vii. 486–93.
—— (1965). *Early Icelandic Script as Illustrated in Vernacular Texts from the Twelfth and Thirteenth Centuries* (Íslenzk handrit, Series in folio, 2; Reykjavík).
—— ed. (1972). *The First Grammatical Treatise* (University of Iceland Publications in Linguistics, 1; Reykjavík).
Benediktsson, Jakob, ed. (1958*a*). *Skarðsárbók: Landnámabók Björns Jónssonar á Skarðsá* (*RHÍ* 1; Reykjavík).
—— ed. (1958*b*). *Sturlunga saga: Manuscript No. 122A Fol. in the Arnamagnæan Collection* (*EIM* 1; Copenhagen).
—— (1961). 'Hauksbók', *KHL* vi. 250–1.
—— (1964*a*). 'Kors: Island', *KHL* ix. 181–2.
—— (1964*b*). 'Kristdigte', *KHL* ix. 292–4.
—— (1965*a*). 'Latin: Island', *KHL* x. 342–3.
—— (1965*b*). 'Lorica', *KHL* x. 695–6.
—— (1968). 'Pilegrim, Island', *KHL* xiii. 305–6.
—— (1969*a*). 'Brot úr Þorlákslesi', *Afmælisrit Jóns Helgasonar*, 98–108.
—— (1969*b*). 'Landnámabók: Some Remarks on its Value as a Historical Source', *Saga-Book*, 17: 275–92.
—— (1969*c*). 'Religiøs digtning', *KHL* xiv. 37–40.
—— (1969*d*). 'Romansk stil: Island', *KHL* xiv. 390–1.
—— (1969*e*). 'Rågång: Island', *KHL* xiv. 566–7.
—— (1970*a*). 'Sjelegave: Island', *KHL* xv. 312.
—— (1970*b*). 'Skatter: Island', *KHL* xv. 435–6.
—— (1970*c*). 'Skole: Island', *KHL* xv. 640.
—— (1971). 'Sogn: Island', *KHL* xvi. 380–1.
—— (1972*a*). 'Statuter: Island', *KHL* xvii. 70–1.
—— (1972*b*). 'Studieresor: Island', *KHL* xvii. 341–2.
—— (1972*c*). 'Sturlunga saga', *KHL* xvii. 355–9.
—— (1972*d*). 'Sturlu saga', *KHL* xvii. 359–60.
—— (1972*e*). 'Synode: Island', *KHL* xvii. 641–3.
—— (1974*a*). 'Landnám og upphaf allsherjarríkis', *Saga Íslands*, 1: 155–96.
—— (1974*b*). 'Markmið Landnámabókar: Nýjar rannsóknir', *Skírnir*, 148: 207–15.
—— (1974*c*). 'Ting: Island', *KHL* xviii. 359–60.
—— (1975). 'Úlfljótslög', *KHL* xix. 274–5.
—— (1976*a*). 'Visitation: Island', *KHL* xx. 193.
—— (1976*b*). 'Votivgåvor: Island', *KHL* xx. 257.
—— (1976*c*). 'Þorgils saga ok Hafliða', *KHL* xx. 384–5.
—— (1976*d*). 'Þorgils saga skarða', *KHL* xx. 385.
—— (1976*e*). 'Þorlákr helgi Þórhallsson', *KHL* xx. 385–8.
—— (1976*f*). 'Årböcker: Island', *KHL* xx. 435–7.

—— (1976*g*). 'Økonom: Island', *KHL* xx. 647–8.

—— (1978). 'Some Problems in the History of the Settlement of Iceland', in T. Andersson and K. I. Sandred (eds.), *The Vikings* (Uppsala), 161–5.

Bergling, Ragnar (1965). 'Kyrkstad', *KHL* x. 19–21.

Birkeland, K. B. (1913). *Under bispestav og kongespir: Kirkepolitiske brytninger og religiøse steder i Norge i middelalderen* (Christiania).

Birkeli, Fridtjov (1982). *Hva vet vi om kristningen av Norge? Utforskningen av norsk kristendoms- og kirkehistorie fra 900- til 1200-tallet* (Oslo).

Biskupasögur Jóns prófasts Halldórssonar (Sögurit, 2/1; Reykjavík, 1903).

Bjarnason, Þorkell (1898). *Um Þorlák Þórhallsson biskup helga* (Reykjavík).

Bjarnason, Þorvaldur, ed. (1878). *Leifar fornra kristinna fræða íslenzkra* (Copenhagen).

Björnsson, Árni (1963). *Jól á Íslandi* (Sögurit, 31; Reykjavík).

—— (1990). 'Tímatal', *ÍÞ* vii. 53–101.

Björnsson, Lýður B. (1968). 'Guðshús í Barðastrandarsýslu', *Ársrit Sögufélags Ísfirðinga*, 12: 7–56.

—— (1970). 'Guðshús í Vestur-Ísafjarðarsýslu', *Ársrit Sögufélags Ísfirðinga*, 14: 7–36.

—— (1971). 'Guðshús í Norður-Ísafjarðarsýslu', *Ársrit Sögufélags Ísfirðinga*, 15: 7–40.

—— (1972*a*). *Saga sveitarstjórna*, i (Reykjavík).

—— (1972*b*). 'Guðshús í Strandasýslu', *Ársrit Sögufélags Ísfirðinga*, 16: 7–39.

—— (1975). 'Nokkrir viðaukar við greinaflokkinn Guðshús á Vestfjörðum', *Ársrit Sögufélags Ísfirðinga*, 18: 118–19.

—— (1978). 'Eigi skal höggva', *Skírnir*, 152: 162–5.

Bjørkvik, Hallvard (1961). 'Gästning. Norge', *KHL* vi. 11–17.

—— (1965). 'Leidang', *KHL* x. 432–42.

—— (1969). 'Reide', *KHL* xiv. 9–11.

—— (1970*a*). 'Dei kongelege kapella: Framvokster og økonomisk grunnlag', *Bergens historiske forening. Skrifter*, 69/70: 45–82.

—— (1970*b*). 'Skatter: Noreg', *KHL* xv. 424–35.

Blaaberg, Claus (1992). *Sognedannelsen i dansk middelalder* (Hørsholm).

Blair, John (1985). 'Secular Minster Churches in Domesday Book', in P. H. Sawyer (ed.), *Domesday Book: A Reassessment* (London), 104–42.

—— (1987). 'Local Churches in Domesday Book and Before', in J. C. Holt (ed.), *Domesday Studies: Papers read at the Novocentenary Conference of the Royal Historical Society and the Institute of British Geographers Winchester, 1986* (Woodbridge), 265–78.

—— (1988*a*). 'Introduction: From Minster to Parish Church', in Blair (ed.), *Minsters and Parish Churches* (Oxford), 1–19.

—— ed. (1988*b*). *Minsters and Parish Churches: The Local Church in Transition, 950–1200* (Oxford Committee for Archaeology, Monograph 17; Oxford).

—— and Sharpe, R., eds. (1992). *Pastoral Care before the Parish* (Studies in the Early History of Britain; Leicester).

Blom, Grethe Authén (1960). 'Geistlighetens handel', *KHL* v. 232–4.

—— (1967). *Kongemakt og priviligier i Norge inntil 1387* (Oslo).

—— (1983). *Magnus Eriksson og Island: Til belysning av periferi og sentrum i nordisk 1300-talls historie* (Det kongelige norske videnskabernes selskabs Skrifter, 1983/2; Oslo).

Blöndal, Sigfús (1931). 'Goden Snorri Thorgrimsson. Et 900–Aars Minde', *Aarbog udgivet af dansk-islandsk samfund*, 4: 68–87.

Boden, F. (1903). 'Die isländischen Häuptlinge', *Zeitschrift der Savigny-Stiftung für Rechtsgeschichte*, 24, *Germanistische Abteilung*: 148–209.

Boden, F. (1905). *Die isländische Regierungsgewalt in der freistaatlichen Zeit* (Breslau).
Bolin, Sture (1934). *Ledung och frälse: Studier och orientering över danska samfundsförhållanden under äldre medeltiden* (Lund).
—— (1960). 'Gesta Hammaburgensis ecclesiae pontificum', *KHL* v. 283–9.
Bolvig, Axel (1992*a*). 'Hvem blev kirkerne bygget til?', *Siden Saxo*, 9/4: 7–9.
—— (1992*b*). *Kirkekunstens storhedstid: Om kirker og kunst i Danmark i romansk tid* (Copenhagen).
Bonnier, Ann Catherine (1983). 'Kyrkor och städer', *Meta*, 82/4: 2–11.
—— (1991). 'Gamla Uppsala—från hednatempel till sockenkyrka', in O. Ferm (ed.), *Kyrka och socken i medeltidens Sverigs* (Stockholm), 81–111.
Boyd, Catherine E. (1952). *Tithes and Parishes in Medieval Italy: The Historical Roots of a Modern Problem* (Ithaca, NY).
Boyer, Régis (1975). 'Paganism and Literature: The So-Called "Pagan Survivals" in the samtíðarsögur', *Gripla*, 1: 135–67.
Bragason, Úlfar (1981). 'Frásagnarmynstur í Þorgils sögu skarða', *Skírnir*, 155: 161–70.
—— (1986). 'Hetjudauði Sturlu Sighvatssonar', *Skírnir*, 160: 64–78.
—— (1988). 'The Structure and Meaning of Hrafns saga Sveinbjarnarsonar', *SS* 267–92.
—— (1989). '"Hart er í heimi, hórdómur mikill" Lesið í Sturlungu', *Skírnir*, 163: 54–71.
—— (1990). 'Sturlunga saga: Atburðir og frásögn', *Skáldskaparmál*, 1: 73–88.
—— (1992). 'Sturlunga saga: Textar og rannsóknir', *Skáldskaparmál*, 2: 176–206.
—— (1993). 'Um ættartölur í Sturlungu', *TMM* 54: 27–35.
—— (1994). 'Um samsetningu Þórðar sögu kakala', in G. Sigurðsson *et al.* (eds.), *Sagnaþing helgað Jónasi Kritjánssyni sjötugum 10. apríl 1994* (Reykjavík), 815–22.
Breengaard, C. B. (1982). *Muren om Israels Hus: Regnum og Sacerdotium i Danmark 1050–1170* (Copenhagen).
Breisch, Agneta (1994). *Frid och fredlöshet: Sociala band och utanförskap på Island under äldre medeltid* (Studia historica Upsaliensia, 174; Uppsala).
Breiteig, B. (1966). 'Elucidarius og kong Sverre', *Maal og Minne 1966*: 22–34.
—— (1967). *Studier i 'En tale mot biskopene'* (Det kongelige norske Videnskabers Selskabs Skrifter 1966, 1; Trondhjem).
Briem, Ólafur (1985). *Heiðinn siður á Íslandi*, 2nd edn. (Reykjavík).
Briem, Páll (1885). 'Um Grágás', *THÍB* 6: 133–226.
—— (1889). 'Nokkur orð um stjórnskipun Íslands í fornöld', *Andvari*, 15: 120–54.
Brink, Stefan (1990). *Sockenbildning och sockennamn: Studier i äldre territoriell indelning i Norden* (Acta Academiae Regiae Gustavi Adolphi, 57; Studier till en svensk ortnamnsatlas, 14; Uppsala).
—— (1992). 'Kultkontinuitet från bosättningshistorisk utgångspunkt', in B. Nilsson (ed.), *Kontinuitet i kult och tro från vikingatid till medeltid* (Uppsala), 105–27.
Brím, Eggert Ó. (1892). 'Athuganir og leiðréttingar við Sturlunga sögu', *ANF* 8: 323–67.
—— (1899). Athuganir við fornættir nokkrar, er koma fyrir í Sturlungasögu', *StSÍ* 3: 511–67.
Brooke, Christopher N. L. (1956). 'Gregorian Reform in Action: Clerical Marriage in England 1050–1200', *Cambridge Historical Journal*, 12: 1–21.
—— (1982). 'Rural Ecclesiastical Institutions in England: The Search for their Origins', *Cristianizzazione ed organizzazione ecclesiastica* (Spoleto), ii. 685–711.
Brown, Ursula (1946–53): 'The Saga of Hrómund Gripsson and Þorgilssaga', *Saga-Book*, 13: 51–77.
—— (1952). 'A Note on the Manuscripts of Sturlunga Saga', *Acta Philologica Scandinavica*, 22: 33–40.

Brundage, James A. (1987). *Law, Sex, and Christian Society in Medieval Europe* (Chicago).

Buckhurst, H. T. McM. (1928–36): 'Sæmundr inn fróði in Icelandic Folklore', *Saga-Book*, 11: 84–92.

Bugge, Alexander (1916*a*). *Tidsrummet 1103–1319* (Norges historie fremstillet for det norske folk, 2/2), Christiania).

—— (1916*b*). 'Kirke og stat i Norge 1152–64', *HT* 24: 160–212.

Bull, Edvard (1912). *Folk og kirke i middelalderen: Studier til Norges historie* (Christiania).

—— (1915). *Den pavelige legat Stephanus i Norge (1163)* (Skrifter utgit av Videnskapsselskapet i Christiania II. Hist.-filos. klasse, 1915/2; Christiania).

—— (1920). 'Studier over Norges administrative inddeling i middelalderen', *HT* 25: 257–82.

—— (1923). 'Arne Thorlaksson', *NBL* i. 234–7.

—— (1925). 'Brand Jonsson', *NBL* ii. 133–4.

—— (1931). *Fra omkring 1000 til 1280* (Det norske folks liv og historie gjennem tidene, 2; Oslo).

Bullough, D. A. (1983). 'Burial, Community and Belief in the Early Medieval West', in P. Wormald, D. Bullough, and R. Collins (eds.), *Ideal and Reality in Frankish and Anglo-Saxon Society: Studies Presented to J. M. Wallace-Hadrill* (Oxford), 177–201.

Byggðir Borgarfjarðar (1989). ii. *Borgarfjarðarsýsla og Akranes* (n.pl.).

Byock, Jesse L. (1982). *Feud in the Icelandic Saga* (Berkeley, Calif.).

—— (1984*a*). 'Dispute Resolution in the Sagas', *Gripla*, 6: 86–100.

—— (1984*b*). 'Saga Form, Oral Prehistory and the Icelandic Social Context', *New Literary History*, 16: 153–73.

—— (1985*a*). 'Cultural Continuity, the Church, and the Concept of Independent Ages in Medieval Iceland', *Skandinavistik*, 15/1: 1–14.

—— (1985*b*). 'The Power and Wealth of the Icelandic Church: Some Talking Points', *Sixth International Saga Conference* (Copenhagen) i. 89–101.

—— (1986*a*). 'The Age of the Sturlungs', in E. Vestergaard (ed.), *Continuity and Change* (Odense), 27–42.

—— (1986*b*). 'Governmental Order in Early Medieval Iceland', *Viator*, 17: 19–34.

—— (1986*c*). 'Milliganga: Félagslegar rætur Íslendingasagna', *TMM*, 7: 96–104.

—— (1988). 'Valdatafl og vinfengi', *Skírnir*, 162: 127–37.

—— (1989). 'Inheritance and Ambition in *Eyrbyggja saga*', in J. Tucker (ed.), *Sagas of the Icelanders: A Book of Essays* (New York), 185–205.

—— (1990). *Medieval Iceland: Society, Sagas and Power* (Berkeley, Calif.).

—— (1992). 'History and the Sagas: The Effect of Nationalism', in G. Pálsson (ed.), *From Sagas to Society*, 43–59.

Böðvarsson, Jón (1968). 'Munur eldri og yngri gerðar Þorláks sögu', *Saga*, 6: 81–94.

Bøgh, Anders, Sørensen, Jørgen Würtz, and Tvede-Jensen, Lars, eds. (1988). *Til kamp for friheden: Sociale Oprør i Nordisk Middelalder* (Ålborg).

Cant, Ronald G. (1984*a*). 'Norse Influence in the Organisation of the Medieval Church in the Western Isles', *Northern Studies*, 21: 1–14.

—— (1984*b*). 'Settlement, Society and Church Organisation in the Northern Isles', in A. Fenton and H. Pálsson (eds.), *Northern and Western Isles in the Viking World* (Edinburgh), 169–79.

Carlé, Birte (1985*a*). 'Enboersken Hildr: En norrøn jomfru-fortælling', *Sixth International Saga Conference* (Copenhagen), i. 103–10.

Carlé, Birte (1985*b*). 'En jartægn fra biskop Jóns saga', *Sixth International Saga Conference* (Copenhagen), i. 111–14.

Cederschiöld, Gustaf (1887). 'Studier öfver isländska kyrkomåldagar från fristatstiden', *Aarböger 1887*: 1–72.

Chaney, William A. (1963). 'Anglo-Saxon Church Dues: A Study in Historical Continuity', *Church History*, 32: 268–77.

—— (1970). *The Cult of Kingship in Anglo-Saxon England: The Transition from Paganism to Christianity* (Berkeley, Calif.).

Charles-Edwards, T. M. (1992). 'The Pastoral Role of the Church in the Early Irish Laws', in J. Blair and R. Sharpe (eds.), *Pastoral Care before the Parish* (Leicester), 63–80.

Christensen, Aksel E. (1968). *Kongemagt og Aristokrati: Epoker i middelalderlig dansk statsopfattelse indtil unionstiden*, 2nd edn. (Copenhagen).

Christensen, C.A. (1965). 'Leidang: Danmark', *KHL* x. 443–50.

Christiansen, Eric (1992). *The Works of Sven Aggesen: Twelfth Century Danish Historian* (Viking Society for Northern Research Text Series, 9; London).

Christie, Håkon (1960). 'Försvarskyrka: Norge', *KHL* v. 145.

—— (1963). 'Kapel: Norge', *KHL* viii. 254–5.

—— (1976). 'Votivkirke', *KHL* xx. 258.

—— (1983). 'Den förste generasjon av kirker i Norge', *Hikuin*, 9: 93–100.

Ciklamini, Marlene (1978). *Snorri Sturluson* (Twayne's World Authors Series, 493; Boston, Mass.).

—— (1983). 'Biographical Reflections in *Íslendinga saga*: A Mirror of Personal Values', *SS* 55: 205–21.

—— (1984). 'Veiled Meaning and Narrative Modes in *Sturlu þáttr*', *ANF* 99: 139–50.

—— (1988*a*). 'The Christian Champion in *Íslendinga saga*: Eyjólfr Kársson and Aron Hjörleifsson', *Euphorion*, 82: 226–37.

—— (1988*b*). 'Sturla Sighvatsson's Chieftaincy: A Moral Probe', in G. A. Grímsdóttir and J. Kristjánsson (eds.), *Sturlustefna* (Reykjavík), 1988: 222–41.

Cinthio, Erik (1964). 'Kyrka', *KHL* ix. 607–12.

Clanchy, Michael T. (1993). *From Memory to Written Record: England 1066–1307*, 2nd edn. (Oxford).

Clover, Carol J. (1974). 'Scene in Saga Composition', *ANF* 89: 57–83.

—— (1982). *The Medieval Saga* (Ithaca, NY).

Clover, Carol J., and Lindow, John, eds. (1985). *Old Norse-Icelandic Literature: A Critical Guide* (Islandica, 45; Ithaca, NY).

Constable, Giles (1964). *Monastic Tithes from their Origins to the Twelfth Century* (Cambridge).

—— (1982). 'Monasteries, Rural Churches and the Cura Animarum in the Early Middle Ages', *Cristianizzazione ed organizzazione ecclesiastica* (Spoleto), i. 349–89.

La Conversione al Christianesimo nell'Euuropa dell'Alto Medioevo (Settimane di Studio del centro Italiano di studi sull'alto medioevo, 14; Spoleto, 1967).

Cormack, Margaret (1994). *The Saints of Iceland: Their Veneration from the Conversion to 1400* (Subsidia Hagiographica, 78; Brussels).

Cramer, Peter (1994). *Baptism and Change in the Early Middle Ages, c.200–c.1150* (Cambridge).

Crawford, Barbara E. (1987). *Scandinavian Scotland* (Studies in the Early History of Britain, Scotland in the Early Middle Ages, 2; Leicester).

—— ed. (1988). *St Magnus Cathedral and Orkney's Twelfth Century Renaissance* (Aberdeen).

Cristianizzazione ed organizzazione (1982). *Cristianizzazione ed organizzazione ecclesiastica della campagne nell'alto medioevo: Espansione e resistanze. 10–16 aprile 1980*, i–ii (Settimane di Studio del centro Italiano di studi sull'alto medioevo, 28; Spoleto).

Dahlerup, Troels (1958*a*). 'Diakon, Subdiakon', *KHL* iii. 52–3.

—— (1958*b*). 'Eleemosyne', *KHL* iii. 583–6.

—— (1974). 'Tiend. Danmark', *KHL* xviii. 291–5.

—— (1981). 'Om tienden', *Fortid og Nutid*, 24: 3–14.

Davíðsson, Jóhannes (1959). 'Bænhús og undirgangur í það á Álfadal', *Árbók 1959*: 127–8.

Davies, Wendy (1978). *An Early Welsh Microcosm: Studies in the Llandaff Charters* (London).

Dofri, Steinn (1921). *Bútar úr Ættasögu Íslendinga frá fyrri öldum (Rannsóknir eldri og yngri ætta)* (Winnipeg).

—— (1939). 'Rannsóknir eldri ætta, til skýringa ýmsra óljósra atriða í miðaldasögu Íslendinga', *Blanda*, 6: 371–91.

—— (1940). 'Rannsóknir eldri ætta til skýringar ýmissa óljósra atriða í miðaldasögu Íslendinga II. Ætt og uppruni lögmannsins mikla á Urðum', *Blanda*, 7: 73–89.

—— (1941). 'Rannsóknir eldri ætta til skýringa ýmissa óljósra atriða í miðaldasögu Íslendinga III. Nokkrir ættfeður og frændur Ögmundar biskups Pálssonar', *Blanda*, 7: 193–236.

—— (1943). 'Rannsóknir eldri ætta til skýringar ýmissa óljósra atriða í miðaldasögu Íslendinga. IV. Nokkrar nýfundnar karlkvíslir Mýramannaættar, sem rekja má til núlifandi manna', *Blanda*, 7: 362–72.

—— (1948). 'Rannsóknir eldri ætta til skýringar ýmissa óljósra atriða í sögu Íslendinga á fyrri öldum. V. Víg Ljósvetninga 1221 o.fl', *Blanda*, 8: 377–88.

Dommasnes, Liv Helga (1991). 'Arkeologi og religion', in G. Steinsland *et al.* (eds.), *Nordisk hedendom Et symposium* (Odense), 47–64.

Dronke, Ursula (1971). 'Classical Influence on Early Norse Literature', in R. R. Bolgar (ed.), *Classical Influences on European Culture AD 500–1500* (Cambridge), 143–50.

—— *et al.*, eds. (1981). *Specvlvm norroenvm: Norse Studies in Memory of Gabriel Turville-Petre* (Odense).

Durrenberger, E. Paul (1988*a*). 'Stratification without a State: The Collapse of the Icelandic Commonwealth', *Ethnos*, 3–4: 239–65.

—— (1988*b*). 'Chiefly Consumption in Commonwealth Iceland', *Northern Studies*, 25: 108–20.

—— (1989). 'Anthropological Perspectives on the Commonwealth Period', in Durrenberger and G. Pálsson (eds.), *The Anthropology of Iceland* (Iowa City), 228–46.

—— (1990). 'Text and Transactions in Commonwealth Iceland', *Ethnos*, 55: 74–91.

—— (1991). 'The Icelandic Family Sagas as Totemic Artefacts', in R. Samson (ed.), *Social Approaches to Viking Studies* (Glasgow), 11–17.

—— (1992*a*). *The Dynamics of Medieval Iceland: Political Economy and Literature* (Iowa).

—— (1992*b*). 'Law and Literature in Medieval Iceland', *Ethnos*, 57: 31–47.

Durrenberger, E. Paul, and Pálsson, Gísli, eds. (1989). *The Anthropology of Iceland* (Iowa City).

Düwel, K. (1978). 'Die Bekehrung auf Island: Vorgeschichte und Verlauf', *Kirchengeschichte als Missionsgeschichte*, 2. *Die Kirche des frühen Mittelalters*, 1. Halbband, ed. K. Schäferdiek (Munich), 249–75.

Edda Snorra Sturlusonar (1880–7). *Edda Snorronis Sturlæi*, iii (Copenhagen).
Eggen, E. (1968). *The Sequences of the Archbishoric of Nidarós* (BA 21; Copenhagen).
Egilsdóttir, Ásdís, ed. (1989). *Þorláks saga* (Reykjavík).
—— (1992). 'Eru biskupasögur til?', *Skáldskaparmál*, 2: 207–20.
—— (1994). 'Mannfræði Höllu biskupsmóður', in G. Sigurðsson *et al.* (eds.), *Sanaþing helgað Jónasi Kritánssyni sjötugum 10. april 1994* (Reykjavík).
Einarsdóttir, Ólafia (1964). *Studier i kronologisk metode i tidlig islandsk historieskrivning* (Bibliotheca historica Lundensis, 13; Stockholm).
—— (1967). 'Árið 1000', *Skírnir*, 141: 128–38.
—— (1968). 'Om de to håndskrifter af Sturlunga saga, 1. Króksfjarðarbók og Reykjarfjarðarbók', *ANF* 83: 44–80.
Einarsson, Bjarni ed. (1955). *Munnmælasögur 17. aldar* (Íslenzk rit síðari alda, 6; (Reykjavík).
—— (1961). *Skáldasögur. Um uppruna og eðli ástaskáldsagnanna fornu* (Reykjavík).
—— (1962). 'Íslendingadrápa', *KHL* vii. 495–6.
—— (1974*a*). 'Kolbeinn Tumason og Hómilíubókin', *Maukastella færð Jónasi Kristjánssyni fimmtugum 10. apríl 1974* (Reykjavík), 10–11.
—— (1974*b*). 'On the Status of Free Men in Society and Saga', *MS* 7: 45–55.
—— (1976). 'Hörð höfuðbein', *Minjar og menntir, afmælisrit helgað Kristjáni Eldjárn, Reykjavík* (Reykjavík), 47–54.
Einarsson, Bjarni F. (1994). *The Settlement of Iceland: A Critical Approach. Granastaðir and the Ecological Heritage* (GOTARC, Series B, Gothenburg Archaeological Theses, 4), Gothenburg).
Einarsson, Sigurbjörn, Kvaran, Guðrún, and Ingólfsson, Gunnlaugur, eds. (1993). *Íslensk hómilíubók: Fornar stólræður* (Reykjavík).
Einarsson, Stefán (1994). 'Sauðanessókn', *Þingeyjasýslur: Sýslu- og sóknalýsingar hins íslenska bókmenntafélags 1839–1844* (Reykjavík), 275–302.
Ekbom, Carl Axel (1979). *Ledung och tidig jordtaxering i Danmark: Studier i Nordens äldsta administrativa indelning* (Skrifter utg. av Institutet för rättshistorisk forskning, Serien I, Rättshistorisk bibliotek, 28; Stockholm).
Eldjárn, Kristján (1943). 'Skálarústin í Klaufanesi og nokkrar aðrar svarfdælskar fornleifar', *Árbók 1941–42*: 17–33.
—— (1953). 'Kort oversigt over gravskikke på Island i oldtid og middelalder', *Dansk ligbrændingsforenings beretning for 1953*: 63–85.
—— (1956). *Kuml og haugfé úr heiðnum sið á Íslandi* (Akureyri).
—— (1957). 'Kapelluhraun og Kapellulág', *Árbók 1955–56*: 5–34.
—— (1960*a*). 'Grav og gravskik, Island', *KHL* v. 445–7.
—— (1960*b*). 'Gård, Island', *KHL* v. 632–5.
—— (1964). 'Fornkristnar grafir á Jarðbrú í Svarfaðardal', *Árbók 1963*: 96–9.
—— (1967). 'Níð um Laurentíus biskup Kálfsson', *Árbók 1966*: 118–23.
—— (1974). 'Kirkjurúst á Krossi á Skarðsströnd', *Árbók 1973*: 142–4.
—— (1984). 'Graves and Grave Goods: Survey and Evaluation', in A. Fenton and H. Pálsson (eds.), *Northern and Western Isles in the Viking World* (Edinburgh), 2–11.
Eldjárn, Kristján ed. (1958). *Þriðji Víkingafundur: Third Viking Congress. Reykjavík 1956* (Fylgirit, Árbók 1958; Reykjavík).
—— and Ágústsson, Hörður (1992). *Skálholt. Skrúði og áhöld* (Staðir og kirkjur, 1. Skálholt; Reykjavík).
—— and Gunnarsson, Þorsteinn (1993). *Um Hóladómkirkju* (n.pl.).

—— Christie, Håkon, and Steffensen, Jón (1988). *Skálholt: Fornleifarannsóknir 1954–1958* (Staðir og kirkjur, 1. Skálholt; Reykjavík).

Ellehøj, Svend (1965). *Studier over den ældste norrøne historieskrivning* (BA 26; Copenhagen).

Espólín, Jón (1821–55): *Íslands Árbækur í sögu-formi*, i–xii (Copenhagen).

Feine, Hans Erich (1950). 'Ursprung, Wesen und Bedeutung des Eigenkirchentums', *Mitteilungen des Instituts für österreichische Geschichtesforschung*, 58: 195–208.

—— (1964). 'Kirche und Gemeindebildung', *Vorträge und Forschungen*, 7: 53–77.

—— (1972). *Kirchliche Rechtsgeschichte*, 5th edn. (Cologne and Graz).

Fenger, Ole (1977). *Romerret i Norden* (Copenhagen).

—— (1987). 'Om kildeværdien af normative tekster', in Hastrup and Sørensen (eds.), *Tradition og historieskrivning: Kilderne til Nordens ældste historie* (Århus), 39–51.

Fenton, Alexander, and Hermann Pálsson, eds. (1984). *Northern and Western Isles in the Viking World: Survival, Continuity and Change* (Edinburgh).

Ferm, Olle, ed. (1991). *Kyrka och socken i medeltidens Sverige* (Studier till Det medeltida Sverige. 5; (Stockholm).

—— and Rahmqvist, Sigurd (1985). 'Stormannakyrkor i Uppland under äldre medeltid', in R. Sandberg (ed.), *Studier i äldre historia tillägnade Herman Schück 5/4 1985* (Stockholm), 67–83.

—— Tengér, Göran, eds. (1987). *Tanke och tro: Aspekter på medeltidens tankevärld och fromhetsliv* (Studier till Det medeltida Sverige, 3; Stockholm).

Festskrift til Ludvig Holm-Olsen på hans 70-årsdag den 9. juni 1984 (Øvre Ervik, 1984).

Fett, Harry (1910). *En islandsk tegnebog fra middelalderen* (Christiania).

Fidjestøl, Bjarne (1984). 'Arnórr Þórðarson: Skald of the Orkney Jarls', in A. Fenton and H. Pálsson (eds.), *Northern and Western Isles in the Viking World* (Edinburgh), 239–57.

—— (1991). 'Skaldediktninga og trusskiftet: Med tanker om litterær form som historisk kjelde', in G. Steinsland *et al.* (eds.), *Nordisk hedendom. Et symposium* (Odense), 111–31.

Finnbogason, Guðmundur (1930). 'Alþingi árið 1117', *Skírnir*, 104: 107–15.

Finsen, Vilhjálmur (1873). 'Om de islandske love i fristatstiden', *Aarbøger 1873*: 101–250.

—— (1888). *Om den oprindelige ordning af nogle af den islandske fristats institutioner*, (Det kongelige danske videnskabers selskabs skrifter, 6: 2/1; Copenhagen).

Foote, Peter G. (1961). 'Bishop Jörundr Þorsteinsson and the Relics of Guðmundr inn góði Arason', *Studia Centenalia in honorem memoriae Benedikt S. Þórarinsson* (Reykjavík), 98–114.

—— ed. (1963). *Lives of Saints. Perg. Fol. Nr. 2 Royal Library Stockholm* (*EIM* 4; Copenhagen).

—— (1975). 'Træl. Alment, Norge og Island', *KHL* xix. 13–19.

—— (1977*a*). 'Oral and Literary Tradition in Early Scandinavian Law: Aspects of a Problem', *Oral Tradition. Literary Tradition. A Symposium* (Odense), 47–55.

—— (1977*b*). 'Some Lines in Lögréttuþáttr', in E. G. Pétursson and J. Kristjánsson (eds.), *Sjötíu ritgerðir helgaðar Jakobi Benediktssyni 20. júlí 1977*, i. (Reykjavík), 198–207.

—— (1977*c*). 'Þrælahald á Íslandi. Heimildakönnun og athugasemdir', *Saga*, 15: 41–74.

—— (1978). 'Bischofssaga (Byskupa sogur)', *RGA* 3: 40–3.

—— (1984*a*). *Aurvandilstá. Norse Studies*, ed. M. Barnes, H. Bekker-Nielsen, and G. W. Weber (Odense).

—— (1984*b*). 'Things in Early Norse Verse', *Festskrift til Ludvig Holm-Olsen* (Øvre Ervik, 1984), 74–83.

—— (1987). 'Reflections on *Landabrigðisþáttr* and *Rekaþáttr* in *Grágás*', Hastrup and

Sørensen (eds.), *Tradition og historieskrivning: Kilderne til Nordens ældste histoire* (Århus), 53–64.

Foote, Peter G. (1992). 'Beyond All Reasonable Doubt?' in F. Hødnebø *et al.* (eds.), *Eyvindarbók* (Oslo), 63–70.

—— (1994). 'The B version of *Jóns saga helga*: Two Benedictine Associations?', in G. Sigurðsson *et al.* (eds.), *Sagnaþing helgað Jónasi Kristjánssyni sjötugum 10. apríl 1994* (Reykjavík), 181–7.

Frank, Roberta (1973). 'Marriage in Twelfth- and Thirteenth Century Iceland', *Viator: Medieval and Renaissance Studies*, 4: 473–84.

Friðriksson, Adolf (1994*a*). *Sagas and Popular Antiquarianism in Icelandic Archaeology* (Aldershot).

—— (1994*b*). 'Sturlungaminjar', *Samtíðarsögur* (Níunda alþjóðlega fornsagnaþingið; Akureyri), 1–15.

—— and Vésteinsson, Orri (1989). 'Skýrsla um uppgröft á Hellu á Árskógsströnd 1. og 2. september 1989' (unpublished excavation report, National Museum of Iceland, Reykjavík).

—— (1992). 'Dómhringa saga: Grein um fornleifaskýringar', *Saga*, 30: 7–79.

—— (1994). *Fornleifaskráning i Eyjafirði I. Fornleifar í Eyjatjarðarsveit norðan Hrafaagils og Þverár* (Akureyi).

—— (1995). *Fornleifaskráning í Eyjafirði*, ii. Fornleifar á Staðarbyggð norðan Munka-þverár (Akureyri).

—— (1997). 'Hofstaðir Revisited', *Norwegian Archaeological Review*, 30/2: 102–13.

—— (forthcoming). 'Creating a Past. A Historiography of the Settlement of Iceland', in J. Barrett (ed.), *Culture Contact, Continuity and Collapse: The Archaeology of North Atlantic Colonization, A.D. 800–1800*.

Friðriksson, Sturla (1987). 'Þróun lífríkis Íslands og nytjar af því', *ÍÞ* i. 149–94.

Fuhrmann, H. (1967). 'Provincia constat duodecim episcopatibus', *Studia Gratiana*, 11: 389–404.

Fæhn, Helge, ed. (1962). *Manuale Norvegicum (Presta handbók)* (Libri liturgici provinciae Nidarosiensis medii aevi, 1; Oslo).

Gallén, Jarl (1956*a*). 'Abbot', *KHL* i. 3–5.

—— (1956*b*). 'Akolyt', *KHL* i. 65.

—— (1956*c*). 'Augustinkorherrar', *KHL* i. 280–3.

—— (1956*d*). 'Augustinregeln', *KHL* i. 283–4.

—— (1956*e*). 'Benediktinorden', *KHL* i. 451–5.

—— (1956*f*). 'Biskop', *KHL* i. 610–19.

—— (1957*a*). 'Botsakrament', *KHL* ii. 181–8.

—— (1957*b*). 'Buden', *KHL* ii. 335–8.

—— (1957*c*). 'Bön', *KHL* ii. 500–5.

—— (1957*d*). 'Celibat', *KHL* ii. 545–8.

—— and Skyum-Nielsen, Niels (1965). 'Libertas ecclesiae', *KHL* x. 530–3.

Georgsson, Ágúst Ó., ed. (1990). *Fornleifaskrá: Skrá um friðlýstar fornleifar* (Reykjavík).

Gestsdóttir, Hildur, and Vésteinsson, Orri (1998). *Beinafundur við Glerá í Kræklingahlíð* (Reykjavík).

Gestsson, Gísli (1977). 'Alen: Island', *KHL* xxi. 82–3.

—— and Árnadóttir, Lilja (1987). 'Kúabót í Álftaveri', *Árbók 1986*: 7–101.

Gissel, S. *et al.*, eds. (1981). *Desertion and Land Colonization in the Nordic Countries c. 1300–1600* (Stockholm).

Gíslason, Gísli (1944). *Íslenzkt stjórnarfar síðustu öld þjóðveldisins* (Reykjavík).
Gíslason, Jónas (1985). 'Lengi er von á einum: áður óprentað páfabréf um Skálholt komið í leitirnar', *Saga*, 23: 187–94.
Gíslason, Tryggvi (1968). 'Áhrif kristninnar á íslenzkan orðaforða að fornu', *Mímir*, 12: 5–17.
Gjerløw, Lilli (1980). *Liturgica Islandica*, i–ii (BA 35–6; Copenhagen).
—— ed. (1968). *Ordo Nidarosiensis Ecclesiae. Orðubók* (Libri liturgici provinciae Nidarosiensis medii aevi, 1; Oslo).
—— (1979). *Antiphonarium Nidarosiensis Ecclesiae* (Libri liturgici provinciae Nidarosiensis medii aevi, 3; Oslo).
Glendinning, Robert J. (1969). 'Arons saga and Íslendinga saga: A Problem in Parallel Transmission', *SS* 41: 41–51.
'Greinargerð félagsmálaráðuneytisins um kristfjárjarðir og aðrar sambærilegar jarðeignir' (1984). *Álitsgerð kirkjueignanefndar* (Fylgiskjal, 9; Reykjavík).
Gren, Leif (1989). 'Platon mitt i byn: Kyrksocknens uppkomst från monumentologisk synpunkt', *Mänsklighet genom millenier: En vänbok till Åke Hyenstrand* (Stockholm), 63–71.
Grimm, Jakob (1875–78). *Deutsche Mythologie*, 4th edn. (Berlin).
Grímsdóttir, Guðrún Ása (1982). 'Um afskipti erkibiskupa af íslenzkum málefnum á 12. og 13. öld', *Saga*, 20: 28–62.
—— (1988). 'Sturla Þórðarson', in Grímsdóttir and J. Kristjánsson (eds.), *Sturlustefna* (Reykjavík), 9–36.
—— (1994). 'Árna saga biskups og Björn á Skarðsá', in G. Sigurðsson *et al.* (eds.), *Sagnaþing helgað Jónasi Kritjánssyni sjötugum 10. apríl 1994* (Reykjavík), 243–56.
—— and Kristjánsson, Jónas, eds. (1988). *Sturlustefna: Ráðstefna haldin á sjö alda ártíð Sturlu Þórðarsonar sagnaritara 1984* (*RSÁ* 32; Reykjavík).
Gräslund, Anne-Sofie (1985). 'Den tidiga missionen i arkeologisk belysning—problem och synpunkter', *Tor*, 20: 291–313.
—— (1991). 'Arkeologi som källa for religionsvetenskapen: Några reflektioner om hur gravmaterialet från vikingatiden kan användas', in G. Steinsland *et al.* (eds.), *Nordisk hedendom Et symposium* (Odense), 141–8.
—— (1992). 'Kultkontinuitet—myt eller verklighet? Om arkeologins möjligheter att belysa problemet', in B. Nilsson (ed.), *Kontinuitet i kult och tro från vikingatid till medeltid* (Uppsala), 129–50.
Gschwantler, Otto (1976). 'Bekehrung und Bekehrungsgeschichte. IV. Der Norden', *RGA* 2: 193–205.
Guðmundsson, Ásmundur (1943). 'Ísleifur Gissurarson', *Samtíð og saga*, 2: 78–99.
Guðmundsson, Barði (1936*a*). 'Goðorðaskipun og löggoðaættir', *Skírnir*, 110: 49–58.
—— (1936*b*). 'Tímatal annála um viðburði sögualdar', *Andvari*, 61: 32–44.
—— (1937). 'Goðorð forn og ný', *Skírnir*, 111: 56–83.
—— (1938). 'Uppruni Landnámabókar', *Skírnir*, 112: 5–22.
—— (1953). *Ljósvetninga saga og Saurbæingar* (Reykjavík).
—— (1959). *Uppruni Íslendinga* (Reykjavík).
Guðmundsson, Finnbogi (1984). 'Gripið niður í Íslendingasögu Sturlu Þórðarsonar', *Andvari*, 109: 62–89.
Guðmundsson, Gunnar (1978). 'Grafir á Höfða og Brekku', *Ársrit Sögufélags Ísfirðinga*, 21: 92–4.
—— (1982). 'Bænhúsið á Bakka í Dýrafirði', *Ársrit Sögufélags Ísfirðinga*, 25: 46.

Guðmundsson, Gunnar F. (1993*a*). *Jarðabréf frá 16. og 17. öld. Útdrættir* (Reykjavík).
—— (1993*b*). 'Rómaskattur og páfatíund', *Ný saga*, 6: 4–15.
—— (1993*c*). 'The Four Saints of Iceland', *St. Ansgar's Bulletin*, 87: 2–3.
Guðmundsson, Halldór (1990). 'Skáldsöguvitund í Íslendingasögum', *Skáldskaparmál*, 1: 62–72.
Guðmundsson, Helgi (1967). *Um Kjalnesinga sögu* (*SI* 26; Reykjavík).
Guðmundsson, Jón (1896–1902): 'Um ættir og slekti', *StSÍ* iii. 701–28.
Guðmundsson, Vigfús (1931). *Saga Oddastaðar* (Reykjavík).
Guðnason, Bjarni (1977). 'Theodoricus og íslenskir sagnaritarar', in E. G. Pétursson and J. Kristjánsson (eds.), *Sjötíu ritgerðir helgaðar Jakobi Benediktssyni 20. júlí 1977* (Reykjavík), 107–120.
Guðnason, Einar (1963). 'Rúðólfur biskup í Bæ', *Kirkjuritið*, 29: 351–9.
Gunnes, Erik (1970*a*). 'Kirkelig jurisdiksjon i Norge 1153–1277', *HT* 49: 121–60.
—— (1970*b*). 'Erkebiskop Øystein som lovgiver', *Lumen*, 39: 127–49.
—— (1971). *Kongens ære: Kongemakt og kirke i 'En tale mot biskopene'* (Oslo).
—— (1974*a*). 'Erkebiskop Öysten og Frostatingsloven', *HT* 53: 109–21.
—— (1974*b*). 'Tale mot biskopene, En', *KHL* xviii: 98–102.
—— (1974*c*). 'Tonsur', *KHL* xviii: 467–8.
—— (1976*a*). *Rikssamling og kristning 800–1177*, (Norges historie, 2; Oslo).
—— (1976*b*). 'Visitation: Norge', *KHL* xx. 191–3.
—— (1982). 'Prester og deier—sølibatet i norsk middelalder', in S. Imsen and G. Sandvik (eds.), *Hamraspor* (Oslo), 1982: 20–44.
—— (1987). 'Klosterlivet i Norge. Tilblivelse—økonomi—avvikling', *Foreningen til Norske Fortidsminnesmerkers Bevaring, Årbok 1987*: 49–84.
Gurevich, Aaron J. (1968). 'Wealth and Gift-Bestowal among the Ancient Scandinavians', *Scandinavica*, 7: 126–38.
—— (1969). 'Space and Time in the Weltmodell of the Old Scandinavian Peoples', *MS* 2: 42–53.
—— (1971). 'Saga and History: The "Historical Conception" of Snorri Sturluson', *MS* 4: 42–53.
—— (1977). 'De frie bønder i det føydale Norge', *Frihet og føydalisme: Fra sovjetisk forskning i norsk middelalderhistorie. Utdrag fra en avhandling av A. Ja. Gurevitsj* (Oslo).
—— (1987). 'Semantics of the Medieval Community: "Farmstead", "Land", "World" (Scandinavian Example)', *Les Communautés rurales. Cinquième partie: Europe occidentale et Amérique synthèse générale* (Recueils de la Société Jean Bodin pour l'historie comparative des institutions, 44; Paris, 525–40.
—— (1990). 'Free Norwegian Peasantry', *HT* 69: 275–84.
—— (1992). 'From Saga to Personality: Sverris Saga', in G. Pálsson (ed.), *From Sagas to Society* (Enfield Lock), 77–87.
Gustafson, Evald (1963). 'Kirkegård, Alm. og Danmark', *KHL* viii. 391–5.
Hafström, Gerhard (1949*a*). *Ledung och marklandsindelning* (Uppsala).
—— (1949*b*). 'Sockenindelningens ursprung', *Historiska studier tillägnad Nils Ahnlund 23/8/1949* (Stockholm), 51–67.
—— (1965). 'Leidang: Sverige', *KHL* x. 450–6.
Hagnell, Eva (1938). *Are frode och hans författarskap* (Lund).
Hallan, Nils (1972). 'Snorri fólgsnarjarl', *Skírnir*, 146: 159–76.
Hallberg, Peter (1969). 'Jóns saga helga', *Afmælisrit Jóns Helgasonar (Reykjavík)*, 59–79.
—— (1976). '"Medieval Man" and Saga Studies', *MS* 9: 164–6.

—— (1983). 'Sturlunga saga—en isländsk tidsspegel', *Scripta Islandica*, 34: 3–28.

Halldórsson, Ólafur, ed. (1904). *Jónsbók: Kong Magnus Hakonsons Lovbog for Island vedtaget paa Altinget 1281* (Copenhagen).

Halldórsson, Ólafur (1963). 'Úr sögu skinnbóka', *Skírnir*, 137: 83–105.

—— (1966). *Helgafellsbækur fornar* (*SI* 24; Reykjavík).

—— (1979). 'Sagnaritun Snorra Sturlusonar', G. Karlsson and H. Þorláksson (eds.), *Snorri, átta alda minning* (Reykjavík), 113–38.

—— (1981). 'The Conversion of Greenland in Written Sources', in H. Bekker-Nielsen *et al.* (eds.), *Proceedings of the Eighth Viking Congress. Århus 24–31 August 1977* (Odense), 203–16.

—— (1990*a*). 'Bókagerð. Skrifaðar bækur', *ÍÞ* 6: 57–89.

—— (1990*b*). 'Lidt om kilderne til Den store saga om Olav Tryggvason', *Selskab for Nordisk filologi: Årsberetning 1987–1989*: 46–57.

Hallgrímsson, Jónas (1989). *Ritverk*, i–v (Reykjavík).

Hamilton, Bernard (1986). *Religion in the Medieval West* (London).

Hamre, Lars (1958*a*). 'Donasjon', *KHL* iii. 224–9.

—— (1958*b*). 'Eleemosyne: Norge', *KHL* iii. 586–8.

—— (1959). 'Fabrica', *KHL* iv. 115–20.

—— (1963*a*). 'Jurisdiktion, Noreg', *KHL* viii. 37–41.

—— (1963*b*). 'Kirkeværger, Noreg', *KHL* viii. 412–15.

—— (1963*c*). 'Kollegiatkapitel, Noreg', *KHL* viii. 626–7.

—— (1966). 'Mensa, Noreg', *KHL* xi. 531–4.

—— (1970). 'Sjelegave', *KHL* xv. 310–12.

—— (1971). 'Sogn: Noreg', *KHL* xvi. 377–80.

—— (1974). 'Tiend: Noreg', *KHL* xviii. 280–87.

Handbuch der Kirchengeschichte (Freiburg, 1973).

Hansen, Jørgen Q. (1966). 'Regnum et sacerdotium: Forholdet mellem stat og kirke i Danmark 1157–1170', *Middelalderstudier tilegnede Aksel E. Christensen på tresårsdagen 11. september 1966* (Copenhagen), 57–76.

Hansson, Ólafur (1966). *Gissur jarl* (Reykjavík).

Haraldsdóttir, Kolbrún (1986). 'Átti Sturla Þórðarson þátt í tilurð Grettis sögu?', *Equus Troianus sive Trjóuhestur tyggjaður Jonnu Louis-Jensen 21. október 1986* (Reykjavík), 44–51.

Haraldsson, Jón Thor (1980). 'Hugdetta um Solveigu Sæmundardóttur', *Saga*, 18: 287–8.

—— (1988). *Ósigur Oddaverja* (Ritsafn Sagnfræðistofnunar, 22; Reykjavík).

Harðarson, Gunnar (1987). 'Enn um Íslendingabók', *TMM* 48: 374–7.

Hartridge, R. A. R. (1930). *A History of Vicarages in the Middle Ages* (Cambridge).

Hasle, Annette (1967). *Hrafns saga Sveinbjarnarsonar* (EAB 25; Copenhagen).

Hastrup, Kirsten, and Sørensen, Preben Meulengracht, eds. (1987). *Tradition og historieskrivning: Kilderne til Nordens ældste historie* (Acta Jutlandica, 63/2, Humanistisk Serie, 61; Århus).

Haugen, Einar, ed. (1972). *First Grammatical Treatise*, 2nd edn. (London).

Hauksdóttir, Sólveig (1974). 'Snorri Sturluson og konungsvaldið', *Mímir*, 21/13: 5–11.

Hauksson, Magnús (1985). 'Einar Hafliðason: húnvetnskur kirkjuhöfðingi og rithöfundur á 13. öld', *Húnavaka*, 25: 165–72.

Helgadóttir, Guðrún P. (1981). 'Laukagarðr', in U. Dronke *et al.* (eds.), *Specvlvm norroenvm* (Odense), 171–84.

—— (1984). 'Hrafn Sveinbjarnarson á Eyri: Erindi flutt á Hrafnseyri 17. júní 1983', *Ársrit Sögufélags Ísfirðinga*, 27: 69–77.

—— ed. (1987). *Hrafns saga Sveinbjarnarsonar* (Oxford).

Helgason, Jón, 1866–1942 (1923). 'Den islandske kirkes kaar under katolicismen', *Norvegia sacra*, 3: 6–29.

—— (1925*a*). *Islands kirke fra dens grundlæggelse til reformationen* (Copenhagen).

—— (1925*b*). 'Jon Ögmundsson den hellige, biskop i Holar', *Norvegia sacra*, 5: 1–34.

—— (1937). 'Die Kirche in Island', *Ekklesia. Eine Samlung von Selbstdarstellungen der christlichen Kirchen*, ii. *Die Skandinavischen Länder* (Leipzig), 411–39.

Helgason, Jón, 1899–1986 ed. (1950). *Byskupa sogur: MS perg. fol. no. 5 in the Royal Library of Stockholm* (*CCI* xix; Copenhagen).

—— (1960). 'Et sted i Hungrvaka', *Opuscula*, 1 (*BA* 20): 352–3.

—— (1976). 'Þorláks saga helga', *KHL* xx. 388–91.

—— (1977). 'Tólf annálagreinar frá myrkum árum', in E. G. Pétursson and J. Kristjánsson (eds.), *Sjötíu ritgerðir helgaðar Jakobi Benediktssyni 20. júlí 1977* (Reykjavík), 399–418.

—— (1980). 'Athuganir Árna Magnússonar um fornsögur', *Gripla*, 4: 33–64.

Helgason, Magnús (1931). 'Guðmundur biskup Arason', *Kvöldræður í Kennaraskólanum 1909–1929* (Reykjavík), 168–98.

Helgason, Ögmundur (1969). 'Smáræði um Gissur jarl dauðan', *Skagfirðingabók*, 4: 122–3.

Hellberg, Staffan (1986). 'Tysk eller Engelsk Mission? Om de tidiga kristna låneorden', *Maal og Minne 1986*: 42–9.

Helle, Knut (1964). *Norge blir en stat 1130–1319*, 2nd edn. (Handbok i Norges historie, 3; Bergen).

—— (1972). *Konge og gode menn i norsk riksstyring ca. 1150–1319* (Bergen).

—— (1981). 'Norway in the High Middle Ages: Recent Views on the Structure of Society', *Scandinavian Journal of History*, 6: 161–89.

—— (1988). 'The Organisation of the Twelfth-Century Church in Norway', in B. E. Crawford (ed.), *St Magnus Cathedral* (Aberdeen), 46–55.

Heller, Rolf (1958). *Die literarische Darstellung der Frau in den Isländersagas* (Saga. Untersuchungen zur nordischen Literatur- und Sprachgeschichte, 2; Halle).

—— (1961). 'Laxdæla saga und Sturlunga saga', *ANF* 76: 112–33.

—— (1964). 'Studien zur Svínfellinga saga', *ANF* 79: 105–16.

—— (1966*a*). 'Aron Hjörleifssohn und Gísli Surssohn', *ANF* 81: 57–63.

—— (1966*b*). 'Þóra, frilla Þórðar Sturlusonar', *ANF* 81: 39–56.

—— (1968). '"Flagð þat, er þeir kölluðu Selkollu"', *ANF* 83: 35–43.

—— (1977). 'Hrafns saga Sveinbjarnarsonar und Isländersagas', *ANF* 92: 98–105.

—— (1978). 'Sturla Þórðarson und die Isländersagas: Überlegungen zu einer wichtigen Frage in der Sagaforschung', *ANF* 93: 138–44.

—— (1984). 'Die Gebeine des Goden Snorri: Beobachtungen zu Eyrbyggja und Laxdœla saga', *ANF* 99: 95–106.

Hermanns-Auðardóttir, Margrét (1995). 'Skýrsla til Rannsóknarráðs Íslands um fornleifarannsóknir að Gásum og víðar á Norðurlandi eystra', report on file, Icelandic Research Council, Reykjavík.

Hermannsson, Halldór (1929). *Icelandic Manuscripts* (Islandica, 19; Ithaca, NY).

—— (1930). *The Book of Icelanders (Íslendingabók)* (Islandica, 20; Ithaca, NY).

—— (1932). *Sæmund Sigfússon and the Oddaverjar* (Islandica, 22; Ithaca, NY).

—— (1943). 'Goðorð í Rangárþingi', *Skírnir*, 117: 21–31.

—— (1948). 'Ari Þorgilsson fróði', *Skírnir*, 122: 5–29.

Hertzberg, Ebbe C.H. (1898). *Om Eiendomsretten til det norske Kirkegods* (Christiania).

Heusler, Andreas (1911). *Das Strafrecht der Isländersagas* (Leipzig).

—— (1912). *Zum isländischen Fehdewesen in der Sturlungenzeit* (Abhandlungen der könglich-preussischen Akademie der Wissenschaften, Phil.-hist. Klasse, 4; (Berlin).

Hill, Joyce (1983). 'From Rome to Jerusalem: An Icelandic Itinerary of the Mid-Twelfth Century', *Harvard Theological Review 1983*: 175–203.

—— (1993). 'Pilgrimage and Prestige in the Icelandic Sagas', *Saga Book*, 23: 433–53.

Hjálmarsson, Angantr H., and Kristjánsson, Pálmi (1957). *Örnefni í Saurbæjarhreppi* (n.pl.).

Hofmann, Dietrich (1984). 'Die Vision des Oddr Snorrason', *Festskrift til Ludvig Holm-Olsen* (Øvre Ervik), 142–51.

—— (1994). 'Zur Geschichte der Clemenskirche auf den Vestmannaeyjar', in G. Sigurðsson *et al.* (eds.), *Sagnaþing helgað Jónasi Kritjánssyni sjötugum 10. apríl 1994* (Reykjavík), 433–44.

Holm, Poul (1988). 'De skånsk-hallandske bondeoprør 1180–82', in A. Bøgh *et al.* (eds.), *Til kamp for friheden* (Ålborg), 72–89.

Holmsen, Andreas (1949). *Norges historie fra de eldste tider til 1660* (Oslo).

—— (1965). 'Erkebiskop Eystein og tronefølgeloven av 1163', *HT* 44: 225–66.

—— (1976). *Nye studier i gammel historie* (Oslo).

—— (1982). 'Integreringen av innlandsdistrikterne i det gammelnorske riket', in S. Imsen and G. Sandvik (eds.), *Hamraspor* (Oslo), 9–19.

Holtsmark, Anne ed. (1938). *A Book of Miracles: MS No. 645 4to of the Arna-Magnæan Collection in the University Library of Copenhagen* (*CCI* xii; Copenhagen).

—— (1960). 'Grammatisk literatur om modersmålet', *KHL* v. 414–19.

Holtzmann, Walther (1938). 'Krone und Kirche in Norwegen in 12. Jahrhundert (Englische Analekten III)', *Deutsches Archiv für Geschichte des Mittelalters*, 2: 341–400.

Hrafnsson, Þórir (1986). 'Óstýrilátur og heimtufrekur glanni? Hugleiðingar um Órækju Snorrason', *Sagnir*, 7: 18–22.

Hugason, Hjalti (1988). 'Kristnir trúarhættir', *ÍÞ* v. 75–339.

Hødnebø, Finn, Jorgensen, Jon H., Mundal, Else, Rindal, Magnus, and Ólason, Vésteinn, eds. (1992). *Eyvindarbók: Festskrift til Eyvind Fjeld Halvorsen 4. mai 1992* (Oslo).

Imsen, Steinar, and Sandvik, Gudmund, eds. (1982). *Hamraspor. Eit festskrift til Lars Hamre. 1912–23. januar–1982* (Oslo).

Indrebø, Gustav (1935). *Fjordung: Granskingar i eldre norsk organisasjons-soge* (Bergens museums årbok. Historisk-antikvarisk rekke, 1; Bergen).

Ingvarsson, Lúðvík (1970). *Refsingar á Íslandi á þjóðveldistímanum* (Reykjavík).

—— (1972). 'Straff: Island', *KHL* xvii: 266–75.

—— (1986–7): *Goðorð og goðorðsmenn*, i–iii (Egilsstaðir).

ÍSLEIF gagnagrunnur um íslenskar fornleifar (Site and monument record, Institute of Archaeology, Reykjavík).

Íslenzkir annálar 1400–1800 (1922–98). i–vii (Reykavík).

Jacobsen, Bent Chr. (1977). 'Om lovebogernes kristendomsbalk og indledningskapitlerne i de yngre kristenretter', *Opuscula*, 2/2 (BA 25): 77–88.

Jacobsen, Henrik (1986). 'En statistik over de eksisterende middelalderkirker i Danmark', *Medeltiden och arkeologin* (Lund), 145–55.

Jacoby, M. (1986). *Germanisches Recht und Rechtssprache zwischen Mittelalter und Neuzeit unter besonderer Berückschitigung des skandinavischen Rechts: Gegenthese zu J. Grimm und zu romantischer Auffassung in 20. Jahrhundert* (Lexemdistribution und Lexemverhalten in Textsorten und Dialekten innerhalb historischer Sprachstufen, 1; Bern).

Jakobsen, Alfred (1986). 'Om forfatteren av Sturlu saga', *Scripta Islandica*, 37: 3–11.

Jakobsson, Ármann (1994). 'Nokkur orð um hugmyndir Íslendinga um konungsvald fyrir 1262', *Samtíðarsögur* (Níunda alþjóðlega fornsagnaþingið; Akureyri), 31–42.

Jeppesen, Jens, and Madsen, Hans Jørgen (1991). 'Storgård og kirke i Liseberg', in P. Mortensen and B. M. Rasmussen (eds.), *Høvdingesamfund og kongemagt* (Århus), 269–75.

Jesch, Judith (1985). 'Some Early Christians in Landnámabók', *Sixth International Saga Conference* (Copenhagen), i. 513–29.

—— (1987). 'Early Christians in Icelandic History: A Case Study', *Nottingham Medieval Studies*, 31: 17–36.

Jochens, Jenny M. (1980). 'The Church and Sexuality in Medieval Iceland', *Journal of Medieval History*, 6/4: 377–92.

—— (1985). 'The Impact of Christianity on Sexuality and Marriage in the King's Sagas', *The Sixth International Saga Conference* (Copenhagen), i. 531–50.

—— (1986). 'Consent in Marriage: Old Norse Law, Life, and Literature', *SS* 58: 142–76.

Johnsen, Arne Odd (1939). *Om Theodoricus og hans Historia de antiquitate regum Norwagensium* (Avhandlingar utg. av Det Norske Videnskabs-Akademi i Oslo II. Hist.-Filos. Klasse, 1939/3; Oslo).

—— (1945*a*). *Studier vedrørende kardinal Nicolaus Brekspears legasjon til Norden* (Oslo).

—— (1945*b*). 'Om St. Victorsklostret og nordmennene', *HT* 33: 405–32.

—— (1949). 'Om Hallvardslegenden og ordalieforbudet', *HT* 35: 133–54.

—— (1951*a*). 'Kongen og patronatsrettslige bestemmelsene av 1153', *Norsk teologisk tidskrift*, 52: 1–37.

—— (1951*b*). *Om erkebiskop Eysteins eksil 1180–1183* (Det kongelige Norske Videnskabers Selskabs Skrifter, 1950/5; Trondhjem).

—— (1967). *On the Background for the Establishment of the Norwegian Church Province: Some New Viewpoints* (Avhandlingar utgitt af Det Norske Videnskabs-Akademi i Oslo II. Hist.-Filos. Klasse. Ny Serie, 11; Oslo).

—— (1968). 'Biskop Bjarnhard og kirkeforholdene i Norge under Harald Hardråde og Olav Kyrre', in P. Juvkam (ed.), *Bjørgvin bispestol: Frå Selja til Bjørgvin* (Bergen), 11–26.

—— (1969). 'Torlak Torhallsson', *NBL* xvi. 532–6.

—— (1972). 'Subsidium pallii', *KHL* xvii: 410–19.

—— (1979). 'The Age of Ordination of the Priesthood in the North Atlantic Islands in the Twelfth Century', *Saga Book*, 20: 24–30.

Johnson, E. N. (1934). 'Adalbert of Hamburg-Bremen', *Speculum*, 9: 147–79.

Jonae, Arngrimi (1951). *Opera latine conscripta*, ii, ed. Jakob Benediktsson (BA 10; Copenhagen).

Jones, G. (1952). 'History and Fiction in the Sagas of the Icelanders', *Saga Book*, 13: 285–306.

Joys, Charles (1948). *Biskop og konge. Bispevalg i Norge 1000–1350* (Oslo).

Jóhannesson, Jón (1941). *Gerðir Landnámabókar* (Reykjavík).

—— (1948). 'Hirð Hákonar gamla á Íslandi', *Samtíð og saga*, 4: 116–36.

—— (1952). 'Tímatal Gerlands í íslenzkum ritum frá þjóðveldisöld', *Skírnir*, 126: 76–93.

—— (1954). 'Sannfræði og uppruni Landnámu', *Saga*, 2: 217–29.

—— (1956). *Íslendinga saga*, i. *Þjóðveldisöld* (Reykjavík).

—— (1958*a*). *Íslendinga saga*, ii. *Fyrirlestrar og ritgerðir um tímabilið 1262–1550* (Reykjavík).

—— (1958*b*). 'Upphaf Skálholts og hinir fyrstu Skálhyltingar', in S. Víkingur (ed.), *Skálholtshátíðin 1956* (Hafnarfjörður), 131–8.

Jóhannesson, Þorkell (1933). *Die Stellung der freien Arbeiter in Island bis zur Mitte des 16. Jahrhunderts* (Reykjavík and Copenhagen).

—— (1965). 'Atvinnuhagir á Íslandi fram um siðaskipti', *Lýðir og Landshagir*, i. (Reykjavík), 38–67.

Jónsson, Brynjólfur (1918). *Lýsing Vestmannaeyjar sóknar* (Copenhagen).

Jónsson, Brynjúlfur (1893). 'Nokkur bæjanöfn í Landnámu í ofnaverðri Hvítársíðu og Hálsasveit', *Árbók 1893*: 74–80.

—— (1902). 'Kirkjutóft á Esjubergi', *Árbók 1902*: 33–5.

—— (1907*a*). 'Rannsókn í Vestmannaeyjum sumarið 1906', *Árbók 1907*: 3–15.

—— (1907*b*). 'Fornleifar í Landssveit', *Árbók 1907*: 26–8.

Jónsson, Finnur (1901). 'Kristnitakan á Íslandi', *Eimreiðin* 7: 1–16.

—— ed. (1916). *Eirspennill—AM 47 fol—Nóregs konunga sogur, Magnús góði—Hákon gamli* (Christiania).

—— (1919). 'Sturlunga-prologen', *ANF* 35: 297–302.

—— (1920–4). *Den oldnorske og oldislandske litteraturs historie*, i–iii, 2nd edn. (Copenhagen).

—— ed. (1930). *Árni Magnússons levned og skrifter*, i–ii (Copenhagen).

Jónsson, Guðbrandur (1919–29). *Dómkirkjan á Hólum í Hjaltadal: Lýsing íslenzkra miðaldakirkna* (StSÍ V/6; Reykjavík).

—— (1934). 'Löghelgur og rúmhelgur', *Skírnir*, 108: 209–10.

—— (1940*a*). 'Almenn kirkjubæn, martyrologium og messudagakver á Íslandi fyrir siðaskiptin', *Afmælisrit helgað Einari Arnórssyni sextugum* 24. febrúar 1940 (Reykjavík), 103–25.

—— (1940*b*). 'Guðmundur biskup góði', *Að utan og sunnan* (Ísafjörður), 152–68.

—— (1953). 'Um Kristfé, Kristfjárjarðir, sælubú og sælugjafir', *Alþingistíðindi* 1952 A. *Þingskjöl með málaskrá* (Reykjavík), 608–30.

Jónsson, Guðni (1960). 'Genealogier', *KHL* v. 247–9.

Jónsson, Janus (1887). 'Um klaustrin á Íslandi', *THÍB* 8: 174–265.

—— (1893). 'Saga latínuskóla á Íslandi' *THÍB* 14: 1–97.

—— (1914). 'Sturla Þórðarson. Sjö alda afmæli', *Almanak hins íslenzka Þjóðvinafélags*, 40: 69–79.

Jónsson, Magnús (1914). 'Áhrif klaustranna á Íslandi', *Skírnir*, 88: 283–98.

—— (1921*a*). 'Athugasemdir um kristnitökuna á Íslandi árið 1000', *Eimreiðin*, 27: 329–41.

—— (1921*b*). 'Guðmundur biskup góði', *Eimreiðin* 27: 172–92.

—— (1939). *Ásbirningar* (Skagfirzk fræði 1; Reykjavík).

—— (1940). *Guðmundar saga dýra: Nokkrar athuganir um uppruna hennar og samsetning, SI* 8; (Reykjavík).

—— (1941). 'Guðmundur biskup góði', *Samtíð og saga*, 1: 115–34.

—— (1944). 'Hvar var stakkgarðurinn þar sem Vatnsfirðingar voru drepnir?', *Skírnir*, 118: 198–206.

—— (1948*a*). *Ríki Skagfirðinga: Frá Haugsnesfundi til dauða Gizurar jarls* (Skagfirzk fræði, 7; Reykjavík).

—— (1948*b*). 'Þar reis at undir króki', *Skírnir*, 122: 152–4.

—— (1958). 'Skrúðganga Skálholtsbiskupa', in S. Víkingur (ed.), *Skálholtshátíðin 1956* (Hafnarfjörður), 139–44.

Jónsson, Margeir (1941). *Frá miðöldum í Skagafirði* (Skagfirzk fræði, 3; Reykjavík).

Jungmann, J. A. (1962). *Pastoral Liturgy* (London).

Jørgensen, A. D. (1874–6). *Den nordiske kirkes grundlæggelse og føste udvikling*, i. (Copenhagen).

Jørgensen, Bent (1980). *Stednavne og administrationshistorie* (Navnestudier udgivet af Insititut for Navneforskning, 20; Copenhagen).

Jørgensen, Stig (1987). *Danmarks kongemakt og dens fødsel* (Århus).

Kaalund, Kristian (1877). *Bidrag til en Historisk-Topografisk beskrivelse av Island*, i–ii (Copenhagen).

—— (1901). 'Om håndskriftene af Sturlunga saga og dennes enkelte bestandelse', *Aarbøger* 1901: 259–300.

—— ed. (1905). *Palæografisk atlas. Oldnorsk-islandsk afdeling* (Copenhagen).

Kahle, B. (1901). 'Das Christentum in der altwestnordischen Dichtung', *ANF* 17: 1–40, 97–160.

Karlsson, Gunnar (1972). 'Goðar og bændur', *Saga*, 10: 5–57.

—— (1975). 'Frá þjóðveldi til konungsríkis', *Saga Íslands*, ii. 1–54.

—— (1977). 'Goðar and Höfðingjar in Medieval Iceland', *Saga-Book*, 19: 358–70.

—— (1979). 'Stjórnmálamaðurinn Snorri', in Karlsson and H. Þorláksson (eds.), *Snorri, átta alda minning* (Reykjavík), 23–51.

—— (1980*a*). 'Völd og auður á 13. öld', *Saga*, 18: 5–30.

—— (1980*b*). 'Icelandic Nationalism and the Inspiration of History', in R. Mitchinson (ed.), *The Roots of Nationalism* (Edinburgh), 77–89.

—— (1983). 'Um valdakerfi 13. aldar og aðferðir sagnfræðinga', *Saga*, 21: 270–5.

—— (1984). 'Saga í þágu samtíðar eða Síðbúinn ritdómur um Íslenska menningu Sigurðar Nordal', *TMM* 45: 19–27.

—— (1985*a*). 'Dyggðir og lestir í þjóðfélagi Íslendingasagna', *TMM* 46: 9–19.

—— (1985*b*). 'The Ethics of the Icelandic Saga Authors and their Contemporaries: A Comment on Hermann Pálsson's Theories on the Subject', *Sixth International Saga Conference* (Copenhagen), i. 381–99.

—— (1988). 'Siðamat Íslendingasögu', in G. Grímsdóttir and J. Kristjánsson (eds.), *Sturlustefna* (Reykjavík), 204–21.

—— (1992). 'Ritunartími Staðarhólsbókar', *Sólfhvarfasumbl samanborið handa Þorleifi Haukssyni fimmtugum 21. desember 1991* (Reykjavík), 40–2.

—— (1994). 'Nafngreindar höfðingjaættir í Sturlungu', in G. Sigurðsson *et al.* (eds.), *Sagnaþing helgað Jónasi Kritjánssyni sjötugum 10 apríl 1994* (Reykjavík), 307–16.

—— and Þorláksson, Helgi, eds. (1979). *Snorri, átta alda minning* (Reykjavík).

Karlsson, Stefán, ed. (1963). *Islandske originaldiplomer indtil 1450*, i–ii (EAA 7; Copenhagen).

—— (1964). 'Aldur Hauksbókar', *Fróðskaparrit*, 13: 114–21.

—— ed. (1967). *Sagas of Icelandic Bishops: Fragments of Eight Manuscripts* (*EIM* 7; Copenhagen).

—— (1969). 'Fróðleiksgreinar frá 12. öld', *Afmælisrit Jóns Helgasonar*, (Reykjavík), 328–49.

—— (1970). 'Ritun Reykjarfjarðarbókar. Excursus: Bókagerð bænda', *Opuscula*, 4 (BA 30): 120–40.

—— (1974). 'Testamente: Island', *KHL* xviii. 231–3.

—— (1977). 'Misskilin orð og misrituð í Guðmundar sögum', *Gripla*, 2: 121–31.

—— (1978). 'Kringum Kringlu', *Árbók Landsbókasafns* 1976: 3–23.

—— (1980). 'Hákon gamli og Skúli hertogi í Flateyjarbók', *Árbók* 1979: 149–54.

—— (1984). 'Textaspjöll í Prestssögu og draugmerking orðs', *Gripla*, 6: 297–301.

—— (1985). 'Guðmundar sögur biskups: Authorial Viewpoints and Methods', *Sixth International Saga Conference* (Copenhagen), ii: 983–1005.

—— (1986*a*). '*Bóklausir menn*: A Note on Two Versions of Guðmundar saga', in R. Simek *et al.* (eds.), *Sagnaskemmtun* (Vienna), 277–86.

—— (1986*b*). 'Kirkjudagsmál', *Merki krossins*, 1: 1–8.

—— (1988). 'Alfræði Sturlu Þórðarsonar', in G. A. Grímsdóttir and J. Kristjánsson (eds.), *Sturlustefna* (Reykjavík), 37–60.

Karras, R. M. (1988). *Slavery and Society in Medieval Scandinavia* (New Haven, Conn.).

Kealey, Edward J. (1985). 'Hospitals and Poor Relief, Western European', *DMA* 6: 292–7.

Ker, William P. (1906). *Sturla the Historian* (The Romanes Lecture 1906: Oxford).

—— (1907). 'The Life of Bishop Gudmund Arason', *Saga-Book*, 5: 86–103.

—— (1908). *Epic and Romance: Essays on Medieval Literature* (London).

Keyser, Rudolf (1847). *Nordmændenes Religionsforfatning i Hedendommen* (Christiania).

—— (1856–8). *Den norske Kirkes Historie under Katolicismen* (Christiania).

Kirby, Ian J. (1986). *Bible Translation in Old Norse* (Université de Lausanne, publications de la faculté des lettre, 27; Geneva).

Kjartansson, Helgi Skúli (1986*a*). 'Hverju jók Ari við Íslendingabók?', *TMM* 47: 385–6.

—— (1986*b*). *Lagauppsaga lögsögumanns* (Félag áhugamanna um réttarsögu. Erindi og greinar, 23; Reykjavík).

—— (1989). *Fjöldi goðorða samkvæmt Grágás: Erindi flutt á málstefnu Stofnunar Sigurðar Nordals 24.–26. júlí 1988* (Félag áhugamanna um réttarsögu. Erindi og greinar, 26; Reykjavík).

—— (1994). 'De te fabula . . . —Samtíð Sturlunga í spegli Laxdælu', in G. Sigurðsson (eds.), *Sagnaþing helgað Jónasi Kritjánssyni sjötugum 10 apríl 1994* (Reykjavík), 377–88.

Knirk, James, ed. (1987). *Proceedings of the Tenth Viking Congress, Larkollen, Norway 1985: Festskrift for Charlotte Blindheim on her 70th Birthday July 6th 1987* (Universitetets Oldsaksamlings Skrifter. Ny rekke, 9; Oslo).

Koch, Hal (1969). *Kongemakt og Kirke 1060–1241*, 2nd edn. (Danmarks historie, 3; Copenhagen).

—— (1972). *Danmarks Kirke i den begyndende Højmiddelalder*, 2nd edn. (Copenhagen).

Kolsrud, Oluf (1913*a*). *Den norske kirkes erkebiskoper og biskoper indtil reformationen* (DN 17B; Christiania).

—— (1913*b*). 'Kirke og folk i middelalderen', *Norsk Teologisk Tidskrift*, 14: 35–59, 131–56.

—— (1929). 'Tiende' *KLN iv.* 570–7.

—— (1937–40). 'Kong Magnus Erlingssons kronings-eid 1163: Nye dokument til norsk historie millom 1152 og 1194 I', *HT* 31: 453–9.

—— (1940–3). 'Kardinal-legaten Nicolaus av Albano i Noreg 1152: Nye dokument til norsk historie millom 1152 og 1194 II', *HT* 33: 485–512.

—— (1958). *Norges kyrkjesoga*, i. *Mellomalderen* (Oslo).

—— (1962). *Presteutdaningi i Noreg* (Norvegia Sacra, 21; Oslo).

Koppenberg, Peter (1980). *Hagiographische Studien zu den Biskupa sögur: Unter besonderen Berücksichtung der Jóns saga helga* (Bochum).

Kratz, Henry (1994). 'Þórlákr's Miracles', *Samtíðarsögur* (Níunda alþjóðlega fornsagnaþingið; Akureyri), 480–94.

Kristinsdóttir, Guðrún (1988). 'Kuml og beinafundur á Ansturlandi', *Árbók 1987*, 89–97.

Kristinsson, Axel (1986). 'Hverjir tóku þátt í hernaði Sturlungaaldar?' *Sagnir*, 7: 6–15.

Kristjánsson, Benjamín (1937). 'Guðmundur biskup góði Arason. Sjö alda minning flutt að Hólum 29. ág. 1937', *Kirkjuritið*, 3: 346–71.

—— (1947). 'Menntun presta á Íslandi fram að siðaskiptum', *Kirkjuritið*, 13: 2–31, 140–73, 233–58.

Kristjánsson, Benjamín (1955). 'Þrenningarhátíð á Munkaþverá', *Kirkjuritið*, 21: 345–56.
—— (1958). 'Skálholtsskóli', in S. Víkingur (ed.), *Skálholtshátíðin 1956* (Hafnarfjörður), 195–259.
Kristjánsson, Jónas (1975). 'Bókmenntasaga', *Saga Íslands*, 2: 147–258.
—— (1980). 'Annálar og Íslendingasögur', *Gripla*, 4: 295–319.
—— (1981). 'Learned Style or Saga Style?', in U. Dronke *et al.* (eds.), *Specvlvm norroenvm* (Odense), 260–92.
—— (1988). *Eddas and Sagas: Iceland's Medieval Literature*, trans. P. Foote (Reykjavík).
Krogh, Knud J. (1975). 'Seks Kirkjur heima á Sandi', *Mondul*, 2: 21–54.
—— (1983*a*). 'Gård og Kirke: Samhørighed mellem gård og kirke belyst gennem arkæologiske undersøgelser på Færøerne og i Grønland', *Hikuin*, 9: 231–44.
Kuhn, Hans (1942). 'Das nordgermanische Heidentum in den ersten christlichen Jahrhunderten', *Zeitschrift für deutsches Altertum und deutsche Literatur*, 79: 133–66.
—— (1971*a*). *Das alte Island* (Düsseldorf).
—— (1971*b*). 'Das älteste Christentums Islands', *Zeitschrift für deutsches Altertum und deutsche Literatur*, 100: 4–40.
Kuttner, Stephan (1975). 'St. Jón of Hólar: Canon Law and Hagiography in Medieval Iceland', *Analecta Cracoviensia*, 7: 367–75.
Köhne, Roland (1972). 'Bischof Ísleifr Gizurarson, ein berühmter Schüler des Stifts Herford: Kirkliche Verbindungen zwischen Deutschland und Island im 11. Jahrhundert', *67. Jahrsbericht des Historischen Vereins der Grafschaft Ravensberg Jg. 1970*: 1–38.
—— (1974). 'Herford und Island', *Island: Deutsch-isländisches Jahrbuch*, 7: 21–3.
—— (1987). 'Wirklichkeit und Fiktion in den mittelalterlichen Nachrichten über Isleif Gizurarson', *Skandinavistik*, 17/1: 24–30.
Laasonen, P. ed. (1975). *Investigatio memoriae patrum: Libellus in honorem Kauko Pirinen die 10 ianuari A.D. 1975* (Finska kyrkohistoriska samfundets handlingar, 93; Helsinki).
Lagerlöf, Erland (1983). 'Medeltida träkyrkor i Sverige: En översikt', *Hikuin*, 9: 125–42.
Lange, Gudrun (1989). *Die Anfänge der isländisch-norwegischen Geschichtsschreibung*, (*SI* 47; Reykjavík).
Lange, Wolfgang (1958). *Studien zur christlichen Dichtung der Nordgermanen 1000–1200* (Palaestra, 222; Göttingen).
Lárusson, Björn (1961). 'Valuation and Distribution of Landed Property in Iceland', *Economy and History*, 4: 34–64.
—— (1967). *The Old Icelandic Land Registers* (Lund).
Lárusson, Magnús Már (1951). 'Fornt helgidagaboð (AM 696, 4to, fragm XXIX)', *Skírnir*, 125: 199–206.
—— (1952). Review of Messk, *Skírnir*, 126: 239–43.
—— (1954). 'Dómkirkjan í Skálholti', *Samtíð og saga*, 6: 41–67.
—— (1956*a*). 'Alminding: Island', *KHL* i. 102–3.
—— (1956*b*). 'Altare: Island', *KHL* i. 114–15.
—— (1956*c*). 'Árna saga biskups', *KHL* i. 251.
—— (1956*d*). 'Arons saga', *KHL* i. 251.
—— (1956*e*). 'Belysning: Island', *KHL* i. 448–50.
—— (1956*f*). 'Beneficium: Island', *KHL* i. 457–8.
—— (1956*g*). 'Biskupa sögur', *KHL* i. 630–1.
—— (1957*a*). 'Bonde: Island', *KHL* ii. 95–7.
—— (1957*b*). 'Bro: Island', *KHL* ii. 254–5.
—— (1957*c*). 'Bulla: Island', *KHL* ii. 362.

—— (1957*d*). 'Busetnad. Island: Bebyggelse', *KHL* ii. 373–4.
—— (1958*a*). 'Íslenzkar mælieiningar', *Skírnir*, 132: 208–45.
—— (1958*b*). 'Domkapitel: Island', *KHL* iii. 198–201.
—— (1958*c*). 'Donasjon: Island', *KHL* iii. 233.
—— (1958*d*). 'Dåp: Island', *KHL* iii. 420–2.
—— (1958*e*). 'Dødebøger: Island', *KHL* iii. 426–7.
—— (1958*f*). 'Einar Hafliðason', *KHL* iii. 529–30.
—— (1958*g*). 'Eleemosyne: Island', *KHL* iii. 588–9.
—— (1958*h*). 'Embedesindtægter: Island', *KHL* iii. 612–15.
—— (1959*a*). 'Um hina ermsku biskupa', *Skírnir*, 133: 81–94.
—— (1959*b*). 'Eremit', *KHL* iv. 6–7.
—— (1959*c*). 'Fabrica: Island', *KHL* iv. 120–2.
—— (1959*d*). 'Fasta: Island', *KHL* iv. 190–1.
—— (1959*e*). 'Ferje: Island', *KHL* iv. 225–6.
—— (1959*f*). 'Festgrader: Island', *KHL* iv. 243.
—— (1959*g*). 'Festum chori o. festum fori: Island', *KHL* iv. 244.
—— (1959*h*). 'Fjerding: Island', *KHL* iv. 381–2.
—— (1959*i*). 'Fostring', *KHL* iv. 544–5.
—— (1959*j*). 'Framfærsla', *KHL* iv. 556–8.
—— (1959*k*). 'Fredskys', *KHL* iv. 608–10.
—— ed. (1960–3). 'Bréf Magnúsar Gizurarsonar Skálholtsbiskups í Niðarósi 1232 um tygilsstyrk', *Saga*, 3: 288–90.
—— (1960*a*). 'On the So-Called "Armenian" Bishops', *SI* 18: 23–38.
—— (1960*b*). 'Doktorsvörn', *Íslenzk tunga*, 2: 83–118.
—— (1960*c*). 'Fylgð', *KHL* v. 37–8
—— (1960*d*). 'Geistlighetens handel: Island', *KHL* v. 234–7.
—— (1960*e*). 'Generalvikarie: Island', *KHL* v. 252.
—— (1960*f*). 'Gilde: Island', *KHL* v. 313.
—— (1960*g*). 'Guðmundr inn góði Arason', *KHL* v. 538–42.
—— (1960*h*). 'Gudsdom: Island', *KHL* v. 553–5.
—— (1960–3a): 'Um tygilsstyrkinn í íslenzkum heimildum', *Saga*, 3: 281–7.
—— (1960–3b): 'Sct. Magnus orcadensis comes', *Saga*, 3: 470–503.
—— (1961*a*). 'Auðun rauði og Hólakirkja', *Árbók 1960*: 5–18.
—— (1961*b*). 'Gästning: Island', *KHL* vi. 17–19.
—— (1961*c*). 'Hegn: Island', *KHL* vi. 291–2.
—— (1961*d*). 'Helgener: Island', *KHL* vi. 333–6.
—— (1961*e*). 'Helige Ande: Island', *KHL* vi. 376–9.
—— (1961*f*). 'Herred: Island', *KHL* vi. 494–5.
—— (1961*g*). 'Hovedgård: Island', *KHL* vi. 707–10.
—— (1962*a*). 'Hreppr', *KHL* vii. 17–22.
—— (1962*b*). 'Hundrað', *KHL* vii. 83–7.
—— (1962*c*). 'Hungrvaka', *KHL* vii. 88–9.
—— (1962*d*). 'Husbonde: Island', *KHL* vii. 103–4.
—— (1962*e*). 'Incest: Island', *KHL* vii. 374–6.
—— (1962*f*). 'Indulgensbrev: Island', *KHL* vii. 397.
—— (1962*g*). 'Investitur [Island]', *KHL* vii. 457–8.
—— (1962*h*). 'Jóns saga helga', *KHL* vii. 617–18.
—— (1962*i*). 'Jóns þáttr biskups Halldórssonar', *KHL* vii. 618.

Lárusson, Magnús Már (1962*j*). 'Jordejendom: Island', *KHL* vii. 671–7.
—— (1963*a*). 'Jurisdiktion: Island', *KHL* viii. 42–3.
—— (1963*b*). 'Kalendarium II: Island', *KHL* viii. 106–9.
—— (1963*c*). 'Kapel: Island', *KHL* viii. 255.
—— (1963*d*). 'Katedralskole: Island', *KHL* viii. 353–4.
—— (1963*e*). 'Katekes och katekisation: Island', *KHL* viii. 358–60.
—— (1963*f*). 'Kirkegård: Island', *KHL* viii. 399–402.
—— (1963*g*). 'Kloster: Island', *KHL* viii. 544–46.
—— (1963*h*). 'Kommunion: Island', *KHL* viii: 676–8.
—— (1964*a*). 'Kostplan: Island', *KHL* ix. 237–8.
—— (1964*b*). 'Kristenrettar: Island', *KHL* ix. 304–6.
—— (1964*c*). 'Kristfé', *KHL* ix. 306.
—— (1964*d*). 'Kristni saga', *KHL* ix. 356.
—— (1964*e*). 'Kyrka: Island', *KHL* ix. 636–9.
—— (1964*f*). 'Kyrkans finanser: Island', *KHL* ix. 667–9.
—— (1964*g*). 'Kyrkmässa: Island', *KHL* ix. 679–80.
—— (1965*a*). 'The Church in Iceland I. Its History', in L. S. Hunter (ed.), *Scandinavian Churches: A Picture of the Development and Life of the Churches of Denmark, Finland, Iceland, Norway and Sweden* (London), 104–11.
—— (1965*b*). 'Kyrkostraff: Island', *KHL* x. 13–15.
—— (1965*c*). 'Kyrkotukt: Island', *KHL* x. 16–17.
—— (1965*d*). 'Kyrktagningen: Island', *KHL* x. 25.
—— (1965*e*). 'Landskyld: Island', *KHL* x. 282.
—— (1965*f*). 'Laurentius saga', *KHL* x. 354–5.
—— (1965*g*). 'Leje', *KHL* x. 470–1.
—— (1965*h*). 'Liturgiska funktionärer: Island', *KHL* x. 616–17.
—— (1966*a*). 'Lögberg', *KHL* xi. 135.
—— (1966*b*). 'Máldagi', *KHL* xi. 264–6.
—— (1966*c*). 'Mantal: Island', *KHL* xi. 342.
—— (1966*d*). 'Matgjafir', *KHL* xi. 500–2.
—— (1967*a*). 'Gizur Ísleifsson', *Kirkjuritið*, 33: 350–69.
—— (1967*b*). 'Þrístirnið á norðurlöndum', *Skírnir*, 141: 28–33.
—— (1967*c*). *Fróðleiksþættir og sögubrot* (Reykjavík).
—— (1967*d*). 'Ocker: Island', *KHL* xii. 492
—— (1967*e*). 'Odelsrett', *KHL* xii. 499–502.
—— (1967*f*). 'Offer: Island', *KHL* xii. 527–8.
—— (1967*g*). 'Official: Island', *KHL* xii. 539.
—— (1968*a*). 'Ossuarium: Island', *KHL* xiii. 49–50.
—— (1968*b*). 'Oäkta barn: Island', *KHL* xiii. 74–6.
—— (1968*c*). 'Páls saga biskups', *KHL* xiii. 90–1.
—— (1968*d*). 'Privatkirke', *KHL* xiii. 462–7.
—— (1968*e*). 'Próventa', *KHL* xiii. 517–18.
—— (1968*f*). 'Registrum: Island', *KHL* xiii. 714–15.
—— (1969). 'Ränta: Island', *KHL* xiv. 591–2.
—— (1970). 'Á höfuðbólum landsins', *Saga*, 9: 40–90.
Lárusson, Ólafur (1923). *Grágás og lögbækurnar* (Árbók Háskóla Íslands 1922, Fylgirit; Reykjavík).
—— (1936). 'Befolkning i oldtiden', *Nordisk kultur*, 1: 121–37.

—— (1939). 'Ortnamn: Island', *Nordisk kultur*, 5: 60–75.

—— (1944). *Byggð og saga* (Reykjavík).

—— (1951). 'Maríufiskur', *Maal og Minne 1951*: 34–41.

—— (1958*a*). *Lög og saga* (Reykjavík).

—— (1958*b*). 'On Grágás: The Oldest Ielandic Code of Law', in K. Eldjárn (ed.), *Þriðji Víkingafundur* (Reykjavík), 77–89.

—— (1960*a*). 'Grágás', *KHL* v. 410–12.

—— (1960*b*). 'Gårdsnavne, Island', *KHL* v. 642–5.

—— (1961). 'Hafliðaskrá', *KHL* vi. 42–3.

Lexicon für Theologie und Kirche (1957–65). 2nd edn., i–x, ed. J. Höfer and K. Rahner (Freiburg).

Lidén, Hans-Emil (1964). 'Kyrka, Norge', *KHL* ix. 624–36.

—— (1969). 'From Pagan Sanctuary to Christian Church: The Excavation of Mære Church in Trøndelag', *Norwegian Archaeological Review*, 2: 1–32.

Lindow, John, Lönnroth, Lars, and Weber, Gerd Wolfgang, eds. (1986). *Structure and Meaning in Old Norse Literature: New Approaches to Textual Analysis and Literary Criticism* (Odense).

Líndal, Sigurður (1964). 'Utanríkisstefna Íslendinga á 13. öld og aðdragandi sáttmálans 1262–64', *Úlfljótur*, 17: 5–36).

—— (1969). 'Sendiför Úlfljóts: Ásamt nokkrum athugasemdum um landnám Ingólfs Arnarsonar', *Skírnir*, 143: 5–26.

—— (1974*a*). 'Ísland og umheimurinn', *Saga Íslands*, 1: 199–223.

—— (1974*b*). 'Upphaf kristni og kirkju', *Saga Íslands*, 1: 227–88.

—— (1976). 'Ætt. Island', *KHL* xx. 591–4.

—— (1982). 'Lögfesting Jónsbókar', *Tímarit lögfræðinga*, 32: 182–95.

—— (1984). 'Lög og lagasetning í íslenzka þjóðveldinu', *Skírnir*, 158: 121–8.

—— (1992). 'Löggjafarvald og dómsvald í íslenzka þjóðveldinu', *Skírnir*, 166: 171–8.

Loth, Agnete, ed. (1960). *Membrana Regia Deperdita* (EAA 5; Copenhagen).

—— (1984). *Den gamle jærtegnebog om biskop Thorlak* (Odense).

—— (1989). *To islandske bispekrøniker: Fortælling om Isleif. Hungervækker* (Odense).

Louis-Jensen, Jonna (1977). *Kongesagastudier: Kompilationen Hulda-Hrokkinskinna* (BA 32; Copenhagen).

Lund, Niels, and Hørby, Kai (1980). *Samfundet i vikingetid og middelalder 800–1500* (Dansk socialhistorie, 2; Copenhagen).

Lund, Niels, ed. (1993). *Norden og Europa i vikingetid og tidlig middelalder* (Copenhagen).

Lunden, Kåre (1976). *Norge under Sverreætten 1177–1319* (Norges historie, 3; Oslo).

Lönnroth, Erik (1940). *Statsmakt och statsfinans i det medeltida Sverige: Studier över skatteväsen och länsförvaltning* (Göteborgs högskolans årsskrift, 46, 1940 3; Göteborg).

—— (1966). 'Government in Medieval Scandinavia', *Gouvernés et gouvernants*, iii. *Bas moyen âge et temps modernes (I)* (Recueils de la Société Jean Bodin pour l'historie comparative des institutions, 24; Brussels), 453–60.

—— (1981). 'Olav den Heilige als nordeuropäische Erscheinung', *St. Olav, sein Zeit und sein Kult* (Acta Visbyensia, 6. Visbysymposiet för historiska vetenskaper 1979; Visby), 9–16.

—— (1982). 'Administration och samhälle i 1000-talets Sverige', *Bebyggelsehistorisk tidskrift*, 4: 10–23.

Lönnroth, Lars (1963). 'Studier i Olaf Tryggvasons saga', *Samlaren*, 84: 54–94.

Lönnroth, Lars (1964). 'Tesen om de två kulturerna: Kristiska studier i den isländska sagaskrivningens sociala förutsätningar', *Scripta Islandica,* 15: 1–97.
—— (1965). *European Sources of Icelandic Saga-Writing: An Essay Based on Previous Studies* (Stockholm).
—— (1968). 'Styrmir's Hand in the Obituary of Viðey', *MS* 1: 85–100.
—— (1969*a*). 'Det litterära porträttet i latinsk historiografi och isländsk saga-skrivning en komparativ studie', *Acta Philologica Scandinavica,* 27: 68–117.
—— (1969*b*). 'The Noble Heathen: A Theme in the Sagas', *SS* 41: 1–29.
—— (1975). 'The Concept of Genre in Saga Literature', *SS* 47: 419–26.
McCreesh, Bernadine (1978–9). 'Structural Patterns in the Eyrbyggja Saga and Other Sagas of the Conversion', *MS* 11: 271–80.
McNeill, John T., and Gamer, Helena M. (1938). *Medieval Handbooks of Penance: A Translation of the Principal* Libri Poenitentiales *and Selections from Related Documents* (New York).
Magerøy, Hallvard (1959). 'Guðmundr góði og Guðmundr ríki: Eit motivsamband', *Maal og Minne 1959*: 22–34.
—— (1965). *Norsk-islandske problem* (Omstridde spørsmål i Nordens historie, 3; Oslo).
—— (1966). 'Sturla Tordsson', *NBL* xv. 188–201.
—— (1971). 'Har Sturla Þórðarson skrivi Laxdæla saga?', *Maal og Minne*: 4–33.
—— ed. (1981). *Bandamanna saga* (Oslo).
Magnúsdóttir, Auður G. (1988). 'Ástir og völd: Frillulífi á Íslandi á þjóðveldisöld', *Ný Saga,* 2: 4–12.
Magnússon, Árni (1921–3): 'Um klaustrin', *Blanda,* 2: 33–47.
Magnússon, Ásgeir Blöndal (1989). *Íslensk orðsifjabók* (Reykjavík).
Magnússon, Eiríkr (1906). 'The Last of the Icelandic Commonwealth', *Saga-Book,* 5: 308–40.
—— (1908). 'The Last of the Icelandic Commonwealth', *Saga-Book,* 6: 90–122.
Magnússon, Þór (1972). 'Staursetning', *Árbók 1971*: 108–12.
—— (1983). 'Skýrsla um Þjóðminjasafnið 1981', *Árbók 1982*: 188–99.
—— (1985). 'Skýrsla um Þjóðminjasafnið 1984', *Árbók 1984*: 193–213.
Margeirsson, Jón (1985). 'Ágreiningsefni Kolbeins Tumasonar og Guðmundar Arasonar', *Skagfirðingabók,* 14: 121–44.
Marwick, H. (1931). 'Orkney Farm-Name Studies', *Proceedings of the Orkney Antiquarian Society,* 9: 25–34.
Maurer, Friedrich, ed. (1964). *Die religiösen Dichtungen des 11. und 12. Jahrhunderts,* i. (Tübingen).
Maurer, Konrad von (1852). *Die Entstehung des isländischen Staats und seiner Verfassung* (Munich).
—— (1855–6). *Die Bekehrung des Norwegischen Stammes zum Christentum in ihrem geschichtlichen Verlaufe quellenmäßigt geschildert,* p. i–ii. (repr. Osnabrück, 1965).
—— (1869). 'Graagaas', *Allgemeine Encyklopädie der Wissenschaften und Künste,* i/77. 1–36.
—— (1870*a*). 'Über das Alter einiger isländischer Rechtsbücher', *Germania,* 15: 1–17.
—— (1870*b*). 'Über Ari Thorgilsson und sein Isländerbuch', *Germania,* 15: 291–321.
—— (1874*a*). *Island, von seiner ersten Entdeckung bis zum Untergange des Freistaats* (Munich).
—— (1874*b*). 'Das Gottesurtheil im altnordische Rechte', *Germania,* 19: 139–48.
—— (1874*c*). *Ueber den Hauptzehnt einiger nordgermanischer Rechte* (Abhandlungen der köngl. bayer. Akademie der Wissenschaften, 1/13/2; Munich).

—— (1881). 'Ueber die norwegisch-isländischen gagnföstur', *Sitzungsberichte der köngl. bayer. Akademie der Wissenschaften. Philosopisch-philologische Classe*, 2: 225–68.

—— (1887). 'Die Rechtsrichtung des älteren isländischen Rechtes', *Festgabe für Planck* (Munich), 117–49.

—— (1891). 'Über Ari fróði und seine Schriften', *Germania*, 36: 61–96.

—— (1892). 'Das Bekenntniss des christlichen Glaubens in den Gesetzbüchern aus der Zeit des Königs Magnús lagabœtir', *Sitzungsberichte der köngl. bayer. Akademie der Wissenschaften. Philosopisch-philologische Classe*, 4: 537–81.

—— (1895). 'Nogle bemærkninger til Norges kirkehistorie', *HT* 13: 1–113.

—— (1899). 'Yfirlit yfir lagasögu Íslands', trans. Eggert Briem, *Lögfræðingur*, 3: 1–48 (Trans. of the chapter on Iceland in Maurer's *Udsigt over de nordgermanske Retskilders Historie*, Christiania, 1878).

—— (1907–38). *Vorelesungen über altnordische Rechtsgeschichte*, i–v. (Leipzig).

Medeltiden och arkeologin. (1986). *Festskrift till Erik Cinthio* (Lund Studies in Medieval Archaeology, 1; Lund).

Melsteð, Bogi Th. (1899). 'Utanstefnur og erindisrekar útlendra þjóðhöfðingja á fyrri hluta Sturlungaaldar: 1200 til 1239', *THÍB* 20: 102–55.

—— (1900). 'Utanstefnur og erindrekar útlendra þjóðhöfðingja á Sturlungaöldinni: Síðari hlutinn 1239 til 1264', *THÍB* 21: 57–131.

—— (1903–30). *Íslendinga saga*, i–iii (Copenhagen).

Miller, William I. (1986). 'Gift, Sale, Payment, Raid: Case Studies in the Negotiation and Classification of Exchange in Medieval Iceland', *Speculum* 61: 18–50.

—— (1988*a*). 'Beating up on Women and Old Men and Other Enormities: A Social Historical Inquiry into Literary Sources', *Mercer Law Review*, 39: 753–66.

—— (1988*b*). 'Ordeal in Iceland', *SS* 60: 189–212.

—— (1990). *Bloodtaking and Peacemaking: Feud, Law and Society in Saga Iceland* (Chicago).

Morris, Colin (1989). *The Papal Monarchy: The Western Church from 1050* to *1250* (Oxford History of the Christian Church; Oxford).

Mortensen, Peder, and Rasmussen, Birgit M., eds. (1991). *Høvdingesamfund og kongemagt* (Fra Stamme til Stat i Danmark 2—Jysk Arkæologisk Selskabs Skrifter, 22 2; Århus).

Munch, Gerd Stamsø (1987). 'Borg in Lofoten: A Chieftain's Farm in Arctic Norway', in J. Knirk (ed.) *Proceedings of the Tenth Viking Congress* (Oslo), 149–70.

—— (1991). 'Hus og hall: En høvdinggård på Borg i Lofoten', in G. Steinsland *et al.* (eds.), *Nordisk hedendom Et symposium* (Odense), 321–33.

Munch, P. A. (1852–8). *Det norske folks historie*, i–iv (Christiania).

—— and Unger, C. R., eds. (1853). *Saga Olafs konungs ens helga* (Christiania).

Mundal, Else (1984). 'Íslendingabók, ættar tala og konunga ævi', *Festskrift til Ludvig Holm-Olsen*, 255–71.

—— (1990). 'Kristninga av Noreg og Island reflektert gjennom samtidig skaldedikting', *Collegium Medievale*, 3 2: 145–62.

—— (1994). '*Íslendingabók* vurdert som bispestolskrønike', *Alvíssmál*, 3: 63–72.

Mundt, Marina (1969). *Sturla Þórðarson und die Laxdæla saga* (Bergen).

Müller, Inger Helene Vibe (1990). 'From the Battle for Power to the Battle for Souls: The Basis for Parochial Division, and its Consequences', *Collegium Medievale*, 3: 137–44.

—— (1991). 'Fra ættefellesskap til sognefellesskap: Om overgangen fra hedensk til kristen gravskikk', in G. Steinsland *et al.* (eds.), *Nordisk Hedendom Et symposium* (Odense), 359–72.

Müller-Ville, M. (1984). 'Opferplätze der Wikingerzeit', *Frühmittelalterliche Studien*, 18: 187–221.

Niclasen, Bjarni, ed. (1968). *The Fifth Viking Congress: Tórshavn 1965* (Tórshavn).

Nielsen, Leif Chr. (1991). 'Hedenskab og kristendom; Religionsskiftet afspejlet i vikingetidens grave', in P. Mortensen and B. M. Rasmussen (eds.) *Høvdingesamfund og kongemagt* (Århus), 245–67.

Nilsson, Bertil (1987). 'Död och begravning: Begravningsskicket i Norden', in O. Ferm and G. Tengér (eds.) *Tanke och tro* (Stockholm), 133–50.

—— (1989). *De sepultris: Grevrätten i Corpus iuris canonici och i medeltida nordisk lagstiftning* (Bibliotheca theologiae practicae, 44; Stockholm).

—— ed. (1992). *Kontinuitet i kult och tro från vikingatid till medeltid* (Projektet Sveriges kristnande, Publikationer, 1; Uppsala).

Nordal, Guðrún (1992). '*Sturlunga saga* and the Context of Saga Writing', in J. Hines and D. Slay (eds.), *Introductory Essays on* Egils saga *and* Njáls saga (London).

Nordal, Sigurður (1914). *Om Olaf den helliges saga* (Copenhagen).

—— (1916). 'Snorri Sturluson: Brot úr mannlýsingu', *Skírnir*, 90: 225–55.

—— (1920). *Snorri Sturluson* (Reykjavík).

—— (1928). 'Þangbrandur á Mýrdalssandi', *Festskrift til Finnur Jónsson 29. maj 1929* (Copenhagen).

—— (1938). *Sturla Þórðarson og Grettis saga* (*SI* 4; Reykjavík).

—— (1941). 'Snorri Sturluson. Nokkurar hugleiðingar á 700. ártíð hans', *Skírnir*, 115: 5–33.

—— (1942). *Íslenzk menning*, i. *Arfur Íslendinga* (Reykjavík).

—— (1957). *The Historical Element in the Icelandic Family Sagas* (W. P. Ker Memorial Lecture, 15; Glasgow).

—— (1968). *Um íslenzkar fornsögur*, trans. Árni Björnsson (Reykjavík; original Danish edn., 'Sagalitteraturen', *Nordisk Kultur*, 7B (Copenhagen, 1953), 180–273).

Nyborg, Ebbe (1979). 'Enkeltmænd og fællesskaber i organiseringen af det romanske sognekirkebyggeri', in R. Egevang (ed.), *Strejflys over Danmarks bygningskultur. Festskrift til Harald Langberg* (Copenhagen), 37–64.

—— (1985). 'Den tidlige sognekirke-inkorporation: En studie i pave Innocens III.s lovgivning og dens anvendelse i 1200-tallets Danmark', *Festskrift til Troels Dahlerup på 60–årsdagen den 3. december 1985* (Arusia—Historiske Skrifter, 5; Århus), 17–35.

—— (1986). 'Kirke—sognedannelse—bebyggelse: Nogle overvejelser med udgangspunkt i et bebyggelsesprojekt for Ribeområdet', *Hikuin*, 12: 17–44.

Nylander, Ivar (1953). *Das kirchliche Benefizialwesen Schwedens während des Mittelalters: Die Periode der Landschaftsrechte* (Skrifter utg. av Institutet för rättshistorisk forskning. Serien I, Rättshistorisk bibliotek, 4; Lund).

—— (1968). 'Patronatsrätt', *KHL* xiii. 136–8.

Olavius, Ólafur (1964–5): *Ferðabók: landshagir í norðvestur-, norður-, og norðaustursýslum Íslands 1775–1777*, i–ii (Reykjavík).

Olgeirsson, Einar (1954). *Ættasamfélag og ríkisvald í þjóðveldi Íslendinga* (Reykjavík).

Olmer, Emil (1902). *Boksamlingar på Island 1179–1490 enligt diplom* (Göteborg).

Olsen, Magnus (1937*a*). 'Skálholts kirkedager i 12. århundre', *Festskrift til Francis Bull på 50 årsdagen* (Oslo), 194–200.

—— (1937*b*). 'Visen om Ambhofði', *Maal og Minne 1937*: 145–54.

—— (1963). 'Fyrsta málfræðiritgerðin: Um útskýringu hennar og höfundinn', *Þættir um líf og ljóð norrænna manna í fornöld* (Reykjavík), 261–97.

Olsen, Olav (1966). *Hørg, hov og kirke: Historiske og arkæologiske vikingetidsstudier* (Aarbøger, 1965; Copenhagen).
—— (1969). 'Die alte Gesellschaft und die neue Kirche', *Kirche und Gesellschaft im Osteeraum und im Norden vor der Mitte des 13. Jahrhunderts* (Acta Visbyensia, 3. Visby-symposiet för historiska vetenskaper 1967; Visby), 43–54.
—— (1981). 'Der lange Weg des Nordens zum Christentum', in G. Ahrens (ed.) *Frühe Holzkirchen im nördlichen Europa* (Hamburg), 257–61.
Oppermann, C. J. A. (1937). *The English Missionaries in Sweden and Finland* (London.)
Oppolzer, Theodor R. von (1962). *Canon of Eclipses*, trans. Owen Gingerich (New York).
Ottósson, Róbert A. (1959). *Sancti Thorlaci episcopi officia rythmica et proprium missæ* (BA, suppl. 3; Copenhagen).
Owen, Dorothy M. (1971). *Church and Society in Medieval Lincolnshire* (Lincoln).
Ólafsson, Guðmundur (1984). 'Forn grafreitur á Hofi í Hjaltadal', *Árbók 1983*: 117–33.
Ólafsson, Ragnar (1969). 'Hvaðan var Dalla kona Ísleifs biskups?' *Saga*, 7: 137–9.
Ólason, Páll E. (1944). *Sextánda öld. Höfuðþættir* (Saga Íslendinga, 4; Reykjavík).
Ólason, Vésteinn (1973). 'Concentration of Power in Thirteenth Century Iceland and its Reflection in Some Íslendingasögur', *Alþjóðlegt fornsagnaþing. Reykjavík 2.–8. ágúst 1973. Fyrirlestrar*, ii. hefti (Reykjavík, 16 pp.).
—— (1976). 'Nýmæli í íslenskum bókmenntum á miðöldum', *Skírnir*, 150: 68–87.
—— (1984). 'Íslensk sagnalist—erlendur lærdómur: Þróun og sérkenni íslenskra fornsagna í ljósi nýrra rannsókna', *TMM* 45: 174–89.
—— (1987). 'Norrøn litteratur som historisk kildemateriale', *Kilderne til den tidlige middelalders historie: Rapporter til den XX Nordiske Historikerkongres, Reykjavík 1987* (Reykjavík), 30–47.
Ólsen, Björn M. (1881). 'Ávellingagoðorð', *THÍB* 2: 1–31.
—— (1885). 'Om forholdet mellem de to bearbeidelser af Ares Islændingebog', *Aarbøger 1885*: 341–71.
—— (1889). 'Ari Þorgilsson hinn fróði', *THÍB* 10: 214–40.
—— (1893). 'Om Are Frode', *Aarbøger 1893*: 207–352.
—— (1900). *Um kristnitökuna árið 1000 og tildrög hennar* (Reykjavík).
—— (1902). 'Um Sturlungu', *StSÍ* iii: 193–510.
—— (1908). 'Um upphaf konungsvalds á Íslandi', *Andvari*, 33: 18–88.
—— (1909). 'Enn um upphaf konungsvalds á Íslandi', *Andvari*, 34: 1–81.
—— (1910). *Om den såkaldte Sturlunga-prolog og dens formodede vidnesbyrd om de islandske slægtsagaers alder* (Christiania Videnskabs-Selskabs Forhandlinger for 1910/6; Christiania).
—— (1915). 'Um skattbændatal 1311 og manntal á Íslandi fram að þeim tíma', *StSÍ* iv. 295–384.
Óskarsdóttir, Svanhildur (1992). 'Að kenna og rita tíða á millum: Um trúarviðhorf Guðmundar Arasonar', *Skáldskaparmál*, 2: 229–38.
Paasche, Fredrik (1922). *Snorre Sturlason og Sturlungene* (Christiania).
—— (1936). 'Jörund Thorsteinsson', *NBL* vii. 171–2.
—— (1948). *Hedenskap og kristendom* (Oslo).
—— (1949). 'Olav Tordsson Hvitaskald', *NBL* x, 392–3.
Pálsson, Árni (1931). 'Sambúð húsbænda og hjúa á lýðveldistímanum', *Skírnir*, 143: 216–35.
—— (1947). 'Snorri Sturluson og Íslendingasaga', *Á víð og dreif. Ritgerðir* (Reykjavík), 110–90.

Pálsson, Gísli, ed. (1992). *From Sagas to Society: Comparative approaches to Early Iceland* (Enfield Lock).
Pálsson, Hermann (1959). 'Um bókagerð síra Þórarins á Völlum', *Skírnir*, 133: 18–24.
—— (1961). 'Ari fróði og forsaga Íslendinga', *TMM* 22: 213–20.
—— (1960–3): 'Athugasemd um Arons sögu', *Saga*, 3: 299–303.
—— (1962). *Sagnaskemmtun Íslendinga* (Reykjavík).
—— (1965*a*). *Eftir Þjóðveldið: Heimildir annála um íslenska sögu 1263–98* (Reykjavík).
—— (1965*b*). 'Fyrsta málfræðiritgerðin og upphaf íslenskrar sagnaritunar', *Skírnir*, 139: 159–77.
—— (1965*c*). 'Upphaf Íslandsbyggðar', *Skírnir*, 139: 52–64.
—— (1967). *Helgafell: Saga höfuðbóls og klausturs* (Snæfellsnes, 2; Reykjavík).
—— (1970). *Tólfta öldin: Þættir um menn og málefni* (Reykjavík).
—— (1983). 'Eftir Njálsbrennu', *Andvari*, 108: 47–50.
—— (1985). 'The Transition from Paganism to Christianity in Early Icelandic Literature', *Sixth International Saga Conference* (Copenhagen), i. 483–97.
Perkins, Richard (1978). *Flóamanna saga, Gaulverjabær and Haukr Erlendsson* (*SI* 36; Reykjavík).
Pétursson, Einar G. (1977). 'Geirmundar þáttur heljarskinns og Sturlubók', *Bjarnígull sendur Bjarna Einarssyni sextugum* (Reykjavík), 10–12.
—— (1986). 'Efling kirkjuvaldsins og ritun Landnámu', *Skírnir*, 160: 193–222.
Pétursson, Einar G., and Kristjánsson, Jónas, eds. (1977). *Sjötíu ritgerðir helgaðar Jakobi Benediktssyni 20. júlí 1977*, i–ii. (Reykjavík).
Piebenga, G. A. (1982). 'Fridrek, den eerste buitenlandse zendelin op IJsland (Een bronnenstudie)', *Amsterdamer Beiträge zur älteren Germanistik*, 17: 129–44.
—— (1984). 'Fridrek, den første utenlandske misjonæren på Island: En undersøkelse av påliteligheten i de islandske tekstene som beretter om ham', *ANF* 99: 79–94.
Pierce, G. O. (1984). 'The Evidence of Place-Names', *Glamorgan County History*, ii. *Early Glamorgan*, ed. H. N. Savory (Cardiff), 456–92.
Pjeturs, Helgi (1906). 'Úr trúarsögu Forn-Íslendinga', *Skírnir*, 80: 50–71.
Pirinen, Kauko (1959). 'Fattigvärd', *KHL* iv. 201–8.
Pizarro, Joaquín M. (1985). 'Conversion Narratives: Form and Utility', *Sixth International Saga Conference* (Copenhagen), ii. 813–32.
Porter, John (1970–1). 'Some Aspects of Arons saga Hjörleifssonar', *Saga-Book*, 18: 136–66.
Rafnsson, Sveinbjörn (1971). 'Kirkja frá síðmiðöldum að Varmá', *Árbók 1970*: 31–49.
—— (1974). *Studier i Landnámabók: Kritiska bidrag till den isländska fristatstidens historia* (Bibliotheca historica Lundensis, 33; Lund).
—— (1975). 'Saga Íslands i–ii' [Review], *Skírnir*, 149: 210–12.
—— (1977*a*). 'Grágás og Digesta Iustiniani', *Sjötíu ritgerðir*, ii. 720–32.
—— (1977*b*). 'Um kristniboðsþættina', *Gripla*, 2: 19–31.
—— (1979*a*). 'Skjalabók Helgafellsklausturs. Registrum Helgafellense', *Saga*, 17: 165–86.
—— (1979*b*). 'Um kristnitökufrásögn Ara prests Þorgilssonar', *Skírnir*, 153: 167–74.
—— (1982*a*). 'Skriftaboð Þorláks biskups', *Gripla*, 5: 77–114.
—— (1982*b*). 'Þorláksskriftir og hjúskapur á 12. og 13. öld', *Saga*, 20: 114–29.
—— (1985*a*). 'The Penitential of St Þorlákur in its Icelandic Context', *Bulletin of Medieval Canon Law*, 15: 19–30.
—— (1985*b*). 'Um Staðarhólsmál Sturlu Þórðarsonar: Nokkrar athuganir á valdsmennsku um hans daga', *Skírnir*, 159: 143–59.

—— (1990*a*). *Byggðaleifar í Hrafnkelsdal og á Brúardölum* (Rit Hins íslenzka fornleifafélags, 1; Reykjavík).

—— (1990*b*). 'Forn hrossareiðalög og heimildir þeirra: Drög til greiningar réttarheimilda Grágásar', *Saga*, 28: 131–48.

—— (1993). *Páll Jónsson Skálholtsbiskup: Nokkrar athuganir á sögu hans og kirkjustjórn* (Ritsafn Sagnfræðistofnunar, 33; Reykjavík).

Regesta Norvegica (Oslo, 1978–).

Reykjaholts-máldagi. (1885). *Det originale pergaments-dokument over Reykjaholt kirkegods og -inventarium i 12. og 13. årh., litografisk gengivet, samt udførlig fortolket og oplyst* (Copenhagen).

Rindal, Magnus (1974). 'Tiggar. Noreg og Island', *KHL* xviii. 302–5.

—— (1975). 'Úmagi. Island og Noreg', *KHL* xix. 286–9.

Ringler, Richard (1972). 'The Saga of Men of Svínafell: An Episode from the Age of the Sturlungs', in J. M. Weinstock (ed.), *Saga og språk: Studies in Language and Literature. In Honour of Lee M. Hollander's Ninetieth Birthday, November 8, 1970* (Austin, Tex.), 9–30.

Roesdahl, Else (1991). 'Nordisk førkristen religion: Om kilder og metoder', in G. Steinsland *et al.* (eds.), *Nordisk hedendom Et symposium* (Odense), 293–301.

Roussel, Aage (1943). 'Utgrävda gårdar 1939: Stöng', in M. Stenberger (ed.) *Forntida gårdar i Island* (Copenhagen), 72–98.

—— (1944). *Farms and Churches in the Medieval Norse Settlements of Greenland* (Meddelelser om Grønland 89/1; Copenhagen).

Róbertsdóttir, Hrefna (1986). 'Helmingarfélög hjóna á miðöldum', *Sagnir*, 7: 31–40.

Saga og kirkja. (1988). *Afmælisrit Magnúsar Más Lárussonar* (Reykjavík).

Salvesen, Astrid (1955). 'En tale mot biskopene og Corpus Iuris Canonici', *HT* 37: 204–24.

Samson, Ross (1992). 'Goðar: Democrats or Despots?' in G. Pálsson (ed.), *From Sagas to Society* 167–88.

Samson, Ross, ed. (1991). *Social Approaches to Viking Studies* (Glasgow).

Samsonarson, Jón M. (1954–8): 'Var Gissur Þorvaldsson jarl yfir öllu Íslandi?', *Saga*, 2: 326–65.

Sandaaker, Odd (1988). 'Canones Nidarosiensis—intermesso eller opptakt?', *HT* 67: 2–38.

Sandnes, Jørn (1967). 'Trøndelags eldste politiske historie', *HT* 46: 1–20.

Sandvik, Gudmund (1965). *Prestegard og prestelönn: Studiar kring problemet eigedomsretten til dei norske prestegardene* (Oslo).

Sawyer, Birgit (1987). 'Scandinavian Conversion Histories', in B. Sawyer *et al.* (eds.) *The Christianization of Scandinavia* (Alingsås).

—— Sawyer, Peter, and Wood, Ian, eds. (1987). *The Christianization of Scandinavia: Report of a Symposium held at Kungälv, Sweden 4–9 August 1985* (Alingsås).

Sawyer, Peter H. (1986). 'The Christianisation of Scandinavia', in T. Kisbye and E. Roesdahl (eds.), *Beretning fra femte tværfaglige vikingesymposium* (Højbjerg and Århus), 23–37.

—— (1987). 'The Process of Scandinavian Christianization in the Tenth and Eleventh Centuries', in B. Sawyer *et al.* (eds.), *The Christianization of Scandinavia*, 68–87.

—— (1988). 'Dioceses and Parishes in Twelfth-Century Scandinavia', in B. E. Crawford (ed.), *St Magnus Cathedral* (Aberdeen), 36–45.

Sawyer, Peter H., ed. (1976). *Medieval Settlement: Continuity and Change* (London).

—— (1979). *English Medieval Settlement* (London).

Saxo Grammaticus (1931). *Gesta Danorum*, i–ii. ed. J. Olrik and H. Ræder (Copenhagen).

Schimmelpfennig, B. (1979). 'Ex fornicatione nati: Studies on the Position of Priests'

Sons from the Twelfth to the Fourteenth Century', *Studies in Medieval and Renaissance History*, NS 2: 1–50.

Schmeidler, B., Trillmich, W., and Buchner, R. eds. (1973). *Quellen des 9. und 11. Jahrhunderts zur Geschichte der Hamburgischen Kirche und des Reiches* (Darmstadt).

Schottmann, Hans (1981). 'Christentum der Bekehrungszeit. 14. Die altnordische Literatur', *RGA* 4: 563–77.

Schroeter, J. F. (1923). *Spezieller Kanon der Zentralen Sonnen- und Mondfinsternisse, welche innerhalb des Zeitraums von 600 bis 1800 n. Chr. in Europa sichtbar Waren* (Christiania).

Schück, Herman (1974). 'Tiend: Sverige', *KHL* xviii. 295–9.

Schönfeld, E. Dagobert (1902). *Der isländische Bauernhof und sein Betrieb zur Sagazeit nach den Quellen dargestellt* (Quellen und Forschungen zur Sprach- und Culturgeschichte der germanischen Völker, 91; Strassburg).

Schäferdiek, K. (1986). 'Eigenkirche', *RGA* 6: 559–661.

Seegrün, W. (1967). *Das Papsttum und Skandinavien bis zur Vollendung der nordischen Kirchenorganization (1164)* (Quellen und Forschungen zur Geschichte Schleswig-Holstein, 51; Neumünster).

Seggewiß, Hermann-Josef (1978). *Goði und Hofðingi: Die literarische Darstellung und Funktion von Gode und Häuptling in den Isländersagas* (Europäische Hochschulschriften Reihe 1. Deutsche Literatur und Germanistik, 259; Frankfurt am Main).

Seip, Jens Arup (1937–40): 'Ennu en kristenrett fra gammelnorsk tid', *HT* 31: 573–627.

—— (1942). *Sættargjerden i Tunsberg og kirkens jurisdiksjon* (Oslo).

—— (1963). 'Jærtegnsamlinger', *KHL* viii. 65–8.

Semmler, Josef (1982). 'Mission und Pfarrorganisation in den rheinischen, mosel- und maasländischen Bistümern. (5.–10. Jahrhundert)', *Cristianizzazione ed organizzazione ecclesiastica* (Spoleto), ii. 813–88.

Sharpe, Richard (1984). 'Some Problems Concerning the Organisation of the Church in Early Medieval Ireland', *Peritia*, 3: 230–70.

—— (1992). 'Churches and Communities in Early Medieval Ireland: Towards a Pastoral Model', in J. Blair and R. Sharpe (eds.) *Pastoral Care before the Parish* (Leicester), 81–109.

Sheehan, Michael M. (1988). 'Theory and Practice: Marriage of the Unfree and Poor in Medieval Society', *Medieval Studies*, 50: 457–87.

Sigfússon, Björn (1934). 'Veldi Guðmundar ríka', *Skírnir*, 108: 191–8.

—— (1937). '"Hefn þú nú drottinn!" Sjö alda dánarminning 1237—16. mars—1937', *Nýtt land*, 2: 56–61.

—— (1942*a*). 'Hlutur húsfreyju á Sturlungaöld', *Eimreiðin*, 48: 305–15.

—— (1942*b*). 'Víkingsrausn og Kristfé', *Samtíðin*, 12/1: 14–17.

—— (1944). *Um Íslendingabók* (Reykjavík).

—— (1955). 'Vestmannaeyjaklaustur', *Blik*, 16: 73–5.

—— (1960*a*). 'Full goðrð og forn og heimildir frá 12. öld', *Saga*, 3: 48–75.

—— (1960*b*). 'Guðmundar saga biskups Arasonar', *KHL* v. 542–3.

—— (1960*c*). 'Guðmundar saga dýra', *KHL* v. 543–4.

—— (1962*a*). 'Hrafns saga Sveinbjarnarsonar', *KHL* vii. 16–17.

—— (1962*b*). 'Íslendingabók', *KHL* vii. 493–5.

—— (1964). 'Millilanda-samningur Íslendinga frá Ólafi digra til Hákonar gamla', *Saga*, 4: 87–120.

Sigtryggsson, Erlingur (1986). 'Einn óþarfasti maður í sögu vorri? Deilur Guðmundar Arasonar og veraldarhöfðingja', *Sagnir*, 7: 12–15.

Sigurbjörnsson, Flosi (1951). 'Guðmundur biskup Arason hinn góði og hrun íslenzka þjóðveldisins 1262–'64', *Á góðu dægri. Afmæliskveðja til Sigurðar Nordals 14. september 1951 frá yngstu nemendum hans* (Reykjavík), 76–82.

Sigurðardóttir, Anna (1983). 'Ret er at en kvinde lærer ham at döbe et barn. Om dåb, konfirmation og fadderskab i Island i middelalderen', *Förändringar i kvinnors villkor under medeltiden* (Ritsafn Sagnfræðistofnunar, 9), ed. S. Aðalsteinsdóttir and H. Þorláksson (Reykjavík), 41–54.

Sigurðsson, Gísli (1994). 'Bók í stað lögsögumanns—Valdabarátta kirkju og veraldlegra höfðingja?' in G. Sigurðsson *et al.* (eds.), *Sagnaþing helgað Jónasi Kritjánssyni sjötugum 10 apríl 1994* (Reykjavík), 207–32.

—— Kvaran, Guðrún, and Steingrímsson, Sigurgeir, eds. (1994). *Sagnaþing helgað Jónasi Kritjánssyni sjötugum 10. apríl 1994* (Reykjavík).

Sigurðsson, Jón (1860). 'Lögsögumannatal og lögmanna á Íslandi með skríngargreinum og fylgiskjölum', *StSÍ* ii. 1–250.

Sigurðsson, Jón Viðar (1989). *Frá goðorðum til ríkja. Þróun goðavalds á 12. og 13. öld* (Sagnfræðirannsóknir. Studia historica, 10; Reykjavík).

—— (1991). 'Börn og gamalmenni á þjóðveldisöld', *Yfir Íslandsála* (Reykjavík), 111–30.

Sigurðsson, Páll, 1808–73 (1865). 'Bæjarfundrinn undir Eyjafjöllum', *Þjóðólfur 17*, 16–17: 67–68; 17/18–19: 77–8.

—— (1886). Um for örnefni, goðorðaskipan og Fronmenjar í Rangárþingi', StSÍ ii: 498–557.

Sigurðsson, Páll, b. 1944 (1967). 'Um fyrsta millirikjasamning Íslendinga og tildrög hans', *Úlfljótur*, 20: 110–38.

—— (1971). *Brot úr réttarsögu*, (Reykjavík).

Sigurðsson, Pétur (1928). 'Um Haukdælaþátt', *Festskrift til Finnur Jónsson 29. Maj 1928* (Copenhagen), 84–94.

—— (1933–5): 'Um Íslendinga sögu Sturlu Þórðarsonar', *StSÍ* ii/2: 1–179.

—— (1940). 'Föðurætt Hauks lögmanns Erlendssonar', *Afmælisrit helgað Einari Arnórssyni sextugum 24. febrúar 1940* (Reykjavík), 157–65.

Sigurfinnsson, Sigurður (1913). 'Gömul örnefni í Vestmannaeyjum', *Árbók 1913*: 3–16.

Sigurjónsson, Arnór (1970). 'Kveikurinn að fornri sagnaritun íslenzkri', *Saga*, 8: 5–42.

—— (1973). 'Jarðamat og jarðeignir á Vestfjörðum', *Saga*, 11: 74–115.

—— (1975). '*Vestfirðingasaga 1390–1450* (Reykjavík).

—— (1976). 'Um uppruna Íslendingasagna og Íslendingaþátta', *Andvari*, 101: 98–113.

Simek, Rudolf, Kristjánsson, Jónas, and Bekker-Nielsen, Hans (1986). *Sagnaskemmtun: Studies in Honour of Hermann Pálsson on his 65th Birthday, 26th May 1986* (Philologica Germanica, 8; Vienna).

Simon, John (1976). 'Snorri Sturlason: His Life and Times', *Parergon: Bulletin of the Australian and New Zealand Association for Medieval and Renaissance Studies*, 15: 3–15.

Simpson, Jaqueline (1957–61): 'Advocacy and Art in Guðmundarsaga dýra', *Saga-Book*, 15: 327–45.

—— (1960). 'Samfellan í Guðmundarsögu dýra', *Skírnir*, 134: 152–76.

Simpson, John (1973). 'Guðmundr Arason: A Clerical Challenge to Icelandic Society', *Alþjóðlegt fornsagnaþing. Reykjavík 2.–8. ágúst 1973. Fyrirlestrar* ii. hefti (Reykjavík, 30 pp.).

The Sixth International Saga Conference 28.7.–2.8.1985:. Workshop Papers, i–ii (Copenhagen, 1985).

Skovgaard-Petersen, Inge (1960). 'Islandsk egenkirkevæsen', *Scandia*, 26: 230–96.

Skre, Dagfinn (1988). *Gård og kirke, bygd og sogn: Organiseringsmodeller og organiseringsenheter i midelalderens kirkebygging i Sør-Gudbrandsdalen* (Riksantikvarens rapporter, 16; Øvre-Ervik).

—— (1995). 'Kirken før sognet: Den tidligste kirkeordningen i Norge', in H.-E. Lidén (ed.), *Møtet mellom hedendom og kristendom i Norge* (Oslo), 170–233.

Skúlason, Sveinn (1856). 'Æfi Sturlu lögmanns Þórðarsonar og stutt yfirlit þess er gjörðist um hans daga', *StSÍ* i. 503–639.

Skyum-Nielsen, Niels (1961). 'Gästning. Danmark', *KHL* vi. 6–11.

—— (1963). *Kirkekampen i Danmark 1241–1290: Jakob Erlandsen, samtid og eftertid* (Copenhagen).

—— (1971). *Kvinde og slave* (Danmarkshistorie uden retouche, 3; Copenhagen).

Skånland, Vegard (1968). 'Provinsialkonsil', *KHL* xiii. 527–9.

—— (1969). *Det eldste norske provinsilastatutt* (Oslo).

Skårup, Povl (1979). 'Aris frodes dødliste for året 1118', *Opuscula*, 6 (BA 30): 18–23.

Smedberg, Gunnar (1973). *Nordens första kyrkor: En kyrkorättslig studie* (Bibliotheca theologiae practicae, 32; Lund).

—— (1980). 'Ärkestiftets uppkomst och indelning', *Uppsala stifts herdaminne*, 1 1, ed. R. Norrman (Uppsala), 18–22.

—— (1981). 'Nordisches kontra kanonisches Recht', *St. Olav, seine Zeit und sein Kult* (Acta Visbyensia, 6. Visbysymposiet för historiska vetenskaper 1979; Visby), 235–9.

—— (1982). 'Stift, kontrakt och socken', *Bebyggelsehistorisk tidskrift*, 4: 42–51.

Snæsdóttir, Mjöll (1988). 'Kirkjugarður að Stóruborg undir Eyjafjöllum', *Árbók 1987*: 5–40.

—— Friðriksson, Adolf, and Lucas, Gavin (1991). 'Athugun á beinafundi að Urriðavatni í Fellum N-Múlasýslu 1991', (report on file, National Museum of Iceland, Reykjavík).

Southern, Richard W. (1990). *Western Society and the Church in the Middle Ages* (The Penguin History of the Church, 2; Harmondsworth).

Stardal, Egill Jónsson (1967). *Jón Loftsson, samtíð hans og synir* (Menn í öndvegi, 2; Reykjavík).

Steblin-Kamenskij, M. I. (1973). *The Saga Mind*, trans. K. H. Ober (Odense).

Stefánsson, Halldór (1945). 'Þáttur um Maríu- og Péturslömb', *Blanda*, 8: 161–80.

Stefánsson, Jón (1898). 'Leiði Guðrúnar Ósvífursdóttur', *Árbók 1898*: 39–40.

—— (1946–53): 'Rúðólf of Bæ and Rudolf of Rouen', *Saga Book*, 13: 174–82.

Stefánsson, Magnús (1974). 'Tiend: Island', *KHL* xviii. 287–91.

—— (1975). 'Kirkjuvald eflist', *Saga Íslands*, 2: 57–144.

—— (1978). 'Frá goðakirkju til biskupakirkju', *Saga Íslands*, 3: 111–257.

—— (1984). 'Kong Sverre—prest og sønn av Sigurd Munn?', *Festskrift til Ludvig Holm-Olsen* (Øvre Ervik), 287–307.

—— (1988). 'Drottinsvik Sturlu Þórðarsonar', in G. A. Grímsdóttir and J. Kristjánsson (eds.), *Sturlustefna* (Reykjavík), 147–83.

Steffensen, Jón (1946). 'Rannsóknir á kirkjugarðinum í Haffjarðarey sumarið 1945', *Skírnir*, 120: 144–62.

—— (1954–8): 'Líkamsvöxtur og lífsafkoma Íslendinga', *Saga*, 2: 280–308.

—— (1966). 'Aspects of Life in Iceland in the Heathen Period', *Saga Book*, 17: 177–205.

—— (1967). 'Ákvæði kristinna laga þáttar um beinafærslu', *Árbók 1966*: 71–8.

—— (1968). 'Population: Island', *KHL* xiii. 390–2.

Steinsland, Gro (1990). 'The Change of Religion in the Nordic Countries: A Confrontation between Two Living Religions', *Collegium Medievale*, 3/2: 123–35.

—— Drobin, Ulf, Pentikäinen, Juha, and Meulengracht Sørensen, Preben, eds. (1991). *Nordisk hedendom. Et symposium* (Odense).

Steinsson, Heimir (1985). 'Skálholt—södra, östra och västra Islands kyrkliga centrum', *Gardar: Årsbok för Samfundet Sverige-Island i Lund-Malmö*, 16–17: 54–60.

Stein-Wilkeshuis, Martina (1976). 'The Judicial Position of Children in Old Icelandic Society', *Recueils de la Société Jean Bodin*, 36: 363–79.

—— (1982). 'The Rights to Social Welfare in Early Medieval Iceland', *Journal of Medieval History*, 8: 343–52.

—— (1986). 'Laws in Medieval Iceland', *Journal of Medieval History*, 12: 37–53.

—— (1987). 'Common Land Tenure in Medieval Iceland', *Recueils de la Société Jean Bodin*, 44: 575–85.

Stenberger, Martin, ed. (1943). *Forntida gårdar i Island* (Copenhagen).

Stevenson, J., ed. (1988). *Chronicon monasterii de Abingdon*, p. i–ii (London).

Stiesdal, Hans (1980). 'Gård og Kirke', *Aarbøger 1980*: 166–72.

Storm, Gustav (1886). 'De norsk-islandske bibeloversættelser fra 13de og 14de aarhundrede og biskop Brandr Jónsson', *ANF* 3: 244–56.

Strömbäck, Dag (1975). *The Conversion of Iceland: A Survey*, trans. P. Foote (Viking Society for Northern Research, Text Series, 6; London).

—— (1976). 'Visionsdiktning', *KHL* xx. 171–86.

Stutz, Ulrich (1895). *Geschichte des kirchlichen Benefizialwesens von seinem Anfängen bis auf die Zeit Alexanders III* (Berlin).

—— (1913). 'Eigenkirche—Eigenkloster', *Realencyklopädie für Protestantische Theologie und Kirche*, xxiii (Leipzig).

—— (1948). 'The Proprietary Church as an Element of Medieval Germanic Ecclesiastical Law', in G. Barraclough (ed. and trans.), *Medieval Germany 911–1250: Essays by German Historians* (Oxford), ii. 35–70.

Ståhle, Carp (1965). 'Lagspråk', *KHL* x. 167–77.

Suvanto, Seppo (1961). 'Gästning: Sverige', *KHL* vi. 1–6.

Sveinbjarnardóttir, Guðrún (1992). *Farm Abandonment in Medieval and Post-Medieval Iceland: An Interdisciplinary Study* (Oxbow Monograph, 17; Oxford).

Sveinbjörnsson, Þórður, ed. (1847). *Hin forna lögbók Islendinga sem nefnist Járnsíða eðr Hákonarbók* (Copenhagen).

Sveinsson, Einar Ólafur (1936*a*). 'Jarteiknir', *Skírnir*, 110: 23–48.

—— (1936*b*). 'Nafngiftir Oddaverja', *Bidrag till nordisk filologi tillägnade Emil Olson. Den 9 juni 1936* (Lund), 190–6.

—— (1937*a*). 'The Icelandic Family Saga and the Period in which their Authors Lived', *Acta Philologica Scandinavica*, 12: 71–90.

—— (1937*b*). *Sagnaritun Oddaverja. Nokkrar athuganir* (*SI* 1; Reykjavík).

—— (1940). *Sturlungaöld* (Reykjavík).

—— (1942). 'Íslenzk sálmaþyíðing frá 13. öld. Heilags anda vísur', *Skírnir*, 116: 140–50.

—— (1944). 'Lestrarkunnátta Íslendinga í fornöld', *Skírnir*, 118: 173–97.

—— (1947). 'Byggð á Mýrdalssandi', *Skírnir*, 121: 185–210.

—— (1948). 'Á ártíð Ara fróða', *Skírnir*, 122: 30–49.

—— (1956). 'Snorri Sturluson', *Við uppspretturnar: Greinasafn* (Reykjavík), 53–260.

—— (1958). *Dating the Icelandic Sagas: An Essay in Method* (Viking Society for Northern Research. Text Series, 3; trans. G. Turville-Petre; London).

—— (1961). 'Athugasemdir við Alexanderssögu og Gyðingasögu', *Skírnir*, 135: 237–47.

Sveitir og jarðir í Múlaþingi i–v. (Egilsstaðir, 1991–5).

Sverdrup, G. (1942). *Da Norge ble kristnet: En religionssosiologisk studie* (Oslo).

Sæmundsson, Jóhannes Ó. (1978). *Örnefni í Eyjafjarðarsýslu* i/1 *Árskógshreppur* (Akureyri).

Sørensen, Preben Meulengracht (1974). 'Sagan um Ingólf og Hjörleif: Athugasemdir um söguskoðun Íslendinga á seinni hluta þjóðveldisaldar', *Skírnir*, 148: 20–40.

—— (1977). *Saga og samfund: En indføring i oldislandsk litteratur* (Copenhagen).

—— (1988). 'Historiefortælleren Sturla Þórðarson', in J. A. Grímsdóttir and J. Kristjánsson (eds.) *Sturlustefna* (Reykjavík), 112–26.

—— (1991*a*). 'Håkon den Gode og guderne: Nogle bemærkninger om religion og centralmagt', in P. Mortensen and B. M. Rasmussen (eds.) *Høvdingesamfund og kongemagt* (Århus), 235–44.

—— (1991*b*). 'Næsten alle sagaer var skrevet. En kommentar til den såkaldte Sturlunga-prolog', in F. Hødnebø *et al.* (eds.), *Eyvindarbók* (Oslo), 333–46.

—— (1992). 'Some Methodological Considerations in Connection with the Study of the Sagas', in Gísli Pálsson (ed.) *From Sagas to Society* (Enfield Lock), 27–41.

—— (1993). *Fortælling og ære. Studier i islændingasagaerne* (Århus).

Taranger, Absalon (1890). *Den angelsaksiske kirkes indflydelse paa den norske*, i. (Christiania).

Teitsson, Björn (1976). 'Ödekyrka: Island', *KHL* xx. 633–4.

—— and Stefánsson, Magnús (1972). 'Um rannsóknir á íslenzkri byggðarsögu tímabilsins fyrir 1700', *Saga*, 10: 134–78.

Tellenbach, Gerd (1993). *The Church in Western Europe from the Tenth to the Early Twelfth Century* (Cambridge).

Thomas, R. George (1950). 'The Sturlunga Age as an Age of Saga-Writing', *Germanic Review*, 25: 50–66.

Thoroddsen, Þorvaldur (1892–1904): *Landfræðisaga Íslands: Hugmyndir manna um Ísland, náttúruskoðun þess og rannsóknir, fyrr og síðar* i–ii. (Reykjavík).

—— (1908–22): *Lýsing Íslands.* i–iiv. (Copenhagen).

—— (1913–15): *Ferðabók: Skýrslur um rannsóknir á Íslandi 1882–1898* (Reykjavík).

Tierney, Brian (1959). *Medieval Poor Law: A Sketch of Canonical Theory and its Application in England* (Berkeley, Calif.).

Tobiassen, T. (1964). 'Tronfølgelov og priviligiebrev: En studie i kongedømmets ideologi under Magnus Erlingsson', *HT* 43: 181–273.

Tobíasson, Brynleifur (1943). *Heim að Hólum* (Skagfirzk fræði, 4–5; Reykjavík).

Tomasson, Richard F. (1980). *Iceland: The First New Society* (Minneapolis).

Tómasson, Sverrir (1975). 'Tækileg vitni', *Afmælisrit Björns Sigfússonar (Reykjavík)*, 251–87.

—— (1982). 'Ambhofði kom norðan', *Gripla*, 5: 257–64.

—— (1983). 'Helgisögur, mælskufræði og forn frásagnarlist', *Skírnir*, 157: 130–62.

—— (1988*a*). *Formálar íslenskra sagnaritara á miðöldum: Rannsókn bókmenntahefðar*, (*RSÁ* 33; Reykjavík).

—— (1988*b*). 'Fyrsta málfræðiritgerðin og íslensk menntun á 12. öld', *Tímarit Háskóla Íslands*: 71–8.

Tómasson, Þórður (1966). 'Kona Sæmundar fróða', *Goðasteinn* 5/2: 71.

—— (1983). 'Þrír þættir: Vaxspjald og vaxstíll frá Stóruborg, Hólmfríðarkapella á Eyvindarmúla, Katrín helga og Katrínarsel', *Árbók 1982*: 103–13.

Tranter, Stephen N. (1987). *Sturlunga Saga. The Rôle of the Creative Compiler* (European University Studies 1, German Language and Literature 941; Frankfurt am Main).

Turville-Petre, Gabriel (1942). 'Notes on the Intellectual History of the Icelanders', *History*, NS 27: 111–23.

—— (1953). *Origins of Icelandic Literature* (Oxford).

—— (1960). 'Introduction', *Víga-Glúms Saga*, ed. G. Turville-Petre, 2nd edn. (Oxford), pp. ix–lvi.

Turville-Petre, Joan (1978–81): 'The Genealogist and History: Ari to Snorri,' *Saga-Book*, 20: 7–23.

Tuulse, Armin (1960). 'Försvarskyrka', *KHL* v. 141–3.

Tölfræðihandbók 1984 (Hagskýrslur Íslands 2/82; Reykjavík, 1984).

Unger, C. R., ed. (1848). *Alexanderssaga* (Christiania).

—— (1871*a*). *Codex Frisianus: En samling af norske konge-sagaer* (Christiania).

—— (1871*b*). *Mariu saga: Legender on jomfru Maria og hendes jartegn* (Christiania).

Vestergaard, Elisabeth, ed. (1986). *Continuity and Change: Political Institutions and Literature in the Middle Ages* (Proceedings of the Tenth International Symposium Organized by the Center for the Study of Vernacular Literature in the Middle Ages; Odense).

Vestergaard, Torben A. (1988). 'The System of Kinship in Early Norwegian Law', *MS* 160–93.

Vésteinsson, Orri (1994). 'Skjalagerð og sagnaritun', *Samtíðarsögur*, (Níunda alþjóðlega fornsagnaþingið; Akureyri), 626–37.

—— (1996). *Menningarminjar í Borgarfirði norðan Skarðsheiðar: Svæðisskráning* (Reykjavík).

—— (1997). 'Kirkja og kirkjugarður í Nesi við Seltjörn', *Árbók 1995*: 99–122.

—— (1998*a*). 'Íslenska sóknaskipulagið og samband heimila á miðöldum', *Íslenska söguþingið 28.–31. maí 1997, Ráðstefnurit* (Reykjavík), i. 147–66.

—— (1998*b*). 'Patterns of Settlement in Iceland. A Study in Pre-History', *Saga-Book*, 25, 1–29.

—— (1998*c*). *Fornleifarannsókn í Neðra Ási í Hjaltadal* (Reykjavík).

—— (forthcoming-*a*): *Sókn og þing: Athuganir á félagsmótun á Íslandi á miðöldum.*

—— (forthcoming-*b*): 'Um upphaf íslenskra kirkjumáldaga'.

—— and Friðriksson, Adolf (1994). *Fornleifaskráning í Eyjafirði*, i. *Fornleifar í Eyjafjarðarsveit norðan Hrafnagils og Þverár* (Akureyri).

—— and Gunnarsdóttir, Sædís (1997). *Menningarminjar í Vesturbyggð. Svæðisskráning* (Reykjavík).

Vigfússon, Guðbrandur (1878). 'Prolegomena', *Sturlunga saga* (Oxford), i. pp. xv–ccxiv.

Vigfússon, Sigurður (1881). 'Rannsókn á blóthúsinu að Þyrli og fleira í Hvalfirði og um Kjalarnes', *Árbók 1880–81*: 65–78.

—— (1882). 'Rannsókn í Breiðafjarðardölum og í Þórsnesþingi og um hina nyrðri strönd', *Árbók 1882*: 60–105.

Vilhjálmsson, Vilhjálmur Ö. (1989). 'Stöng og Þjórsárdalur-bosættelsens ophør', *Hikuin*, 15: 75–102.

—— (1996). 'Gård og kirke på Stöng i Þjórsárdalur: Reflektioner på den tidligste kirkeordning og kirkeret på Island', in J. F. Krøger and H.-R. Naley (eds.), *Nordsjøen: Handel, religion og politikk. Karmøyseminaret 1994 og 1995* (Stavanger), 119–39.

Vilhjálmsson, Þorsteinn (1990). 'Raunvísindi á miðöldum', *ÍÞ* vii 1–50.

—— (1993). 'Time-Reckoning in Iceland before Literacy', in C. L. N. Ruggler (ed.), *Archaeoastronomy in the 1990s* (Loughborough), 69–76.

Vilmundarson, Þórhallur (1971). '-stad. Island', *KHL* xvi. 378–84.

—— (1976). 'Um klausturnöfn', *Árbók 1975*: 79–84.

—— (1977). 'Ólafur chaim', *Skírnir*, 151: 133–62.

Víkingur, Sveinn, ed. (1958). *Skálholtshátíðin 1956. Minning níu alda biskupsdóms á Íslandi* (Hafnarfjörður).

—— (1970). *Getið í eyður sögunnar* (Reykjavík).

Vlasto, A. P. (1970). *The Entry of the Slavs into Christendom* (Cambridge).

Vogt, Walther H. (1913). 'Charakteristikien aus der Sturlungasaga', *Zeitschrift für deutsches Altertum und deutsche Literatur*, 56: 376–409.

Vries, Jan de (1964–7). *Altnordische Literaturgeschichte*, i–ii. 2nd edn., (Berlin).

Wallem, Fredrik B. (1909). 'De islandske kirkers udstyr i middelalderen', *Foreningen til norske fortidsmindesmærkers bevaring, Aarsberetningen 1909*: 1–65.

—— (1910). 'De islandske kirkers udstyr i middelalderen', *Foreningen til norske fortidsmindesmærkers bevaring, Aarsberetningen 1910*: 1–64.

Warmind, Morten (1993). 'Religionsmøde og trosskifte', in N. Lund (ed.) *Norden og Europa: vikingetid og middelalder* (Copenhagen), 163–78.

Weber, Gerd W. (1986). 'Siðaskipti: Das religionsgeschichtliche Modell Snorri Sturlusons in Edda und Heimskringla', in R. Simek *et al.* (eds.), *Sagnaskemmtun* (Vienna), 309–29.

—— (1987). 'Intellegere Historiam: Typological Perspectives of Nordic Prehistory (in Snorri, Saxo, Widukind and others)', in K. Hastrup and P. M. Sørensen (eds.), *Tradition og historieskrivning. Kilderne til Nordens ældste historie*, (Acta Jutlandica, 63 2, Humanistisk Serie, 61; Århus), 95–141.

Whaley, Diana (1994). 'Miracles in the Biskupa sögur: Icelandic Variations on an International Theme', *Samtíðarsögur* (Níunda alþjóðlega fornsagnaþingið; Akureyri), 847–62.

Widding, Ole (1960*a*). 'Nogle problemer omkring sagaen om Gudmund den gode', *Maal og Minne 1960*: 13–26.

—— (1960*b*). 'Það finnur hver sem um er hugað', *Skírnir*, 134: 61–73.

—— Bekker-Nielsen, Hans, and Shook, L. K. (1963). 'The Lives of the Saints in Old Norse Prose: A Handlist', *Medieval Studies*, 25: 294–337.

Wienberg, Jes (1993). *Den gotiske labyrint. Middelalderen og kirkerne i Danmark* (Lund Studies in Medieval Archaeology, 11; Stockholm).

Winterer, H. (1966). 'Zur Priesterehe in Spanien bis zum Ausgang des Mittelalters', *Zeitschrift der Savigny-Stiftung für Rechtsgeschichte, kanonistische Abteilung*, 52: 370–83.

Wisén, T. ed. (1972). *Hómiliu-bók: Isländska homilier från tolfte århundradet* (Lund).

Wolf, Alois (1959). 'Olaf Tryggvason und die Christianisierung des Nordens', *Innsbrucker Beiträge zur Kulturwissenschaft*, 6: 9–32.

—— (1993). *Snorri Sturluson: Kolloquium anläßlich der 750. Wiederkehr seines Todestages* (Tübingen).

Wolf, Kirsten (1988). 'Gyðinga saga, Alexanders saga, and Bishop Brandr Jónsson', *SS* 60: 371–400.

—— (1990). 'Brandr Jónsson and Stjórn', *SS* 62: 163–88.

—— (1995). *Gyðinga saga* (*RSÁ* 42; Reykjavík).

Wood, Ian (1986). 'Christians and Pagans in Ninth-Century Scandinavia', in B. Sawyer *et al.* (eds.), *The Christianization of Scandinavia* (Alingsås), 36–67.

Wood, Ian, and Loud, G. A., eds. (1991). *Church and Chronicle in the Middle Ages* (London).

Wood, Ian, and Lund, Niels, eds. (1991). *People and Places in Northern Europe 500–1600: Essays in Honour of Peter Hayes Sawyer* (Woodbridge).

Würth, Stephanie (1994). 'Thomas Becket: Ein literarisches und politisches Modell für die islandische Kirche im 13. Jahrhundert', *Samtíðarsögur* (Níunda alþjóðlega fornsagnaþingið; Akureyri), 878–91.

Wåhlin, Birgitte (1988). 'Oprøret mod Knud den Hellige i 1086: Brydninger under stats- og klassedannelsen i Danmark', in A. Bøgh *et al.* (eds.) *Til kamp for friheden* (Ålborg), 46–71.

Yfir Íslandsála. (1991) *Afmælisrit til heiðurs Magnúsi Stefánssyni sextugum 25. desember 1991* (Reykjavík).

Zöega, Guðný, Snæsdóttir, Mjöll, Vésteinsson, Orri, and Gunnarsdóttir, Sædís (1997). *Fornleifaskráning í Fellahreppi* (Reykjavík).

Þorkelsson, Jóhannes (1916). 'Skýrsla um fund fornrar kirkjurústar og grafreits á Syðra-Fjalli haustið 1915', *Árbók 1915*: 43–5.

Þorkelsson, Jón (1921–3): 'Kirkjustaðir í Austur-Skaptafellsþingi', *Blanda*, 2: 247–68.

Þorkelsson, Þorkell (1930). 'Alþingi árið 955', *Skírnir*, 104: 49–67.

Þorláksson, Helgi (1979*a*). 'Snorri Sturluson og Oddaverjar', in G. Karlsson and H. Þorláksson (eds.), *Snorri, átta alda minning* (Reykjavík), 53–88.

—— (1979*b*). 'Stórbændur gegn goðum. Hugleiðingar um goðavald, konungsvald og sjálfræðishug bænda um miðbik 13. aldar', in B. Jónsson, E. Laxness, and H. Þorleifsson (eds.), *Söguslóðir. Afmælisrit helgað Ólafi Hanssyni sjötugum 18. september 1979* (Reykjavík), 227–50.

—— (1981). 'Arbeidskvinnens, särlig veverskens, ökonomiske stilling på Island i middelalderen', in H. Gunneng and B. Strand (eds.), *Kvinnans ekonomiska ställning under nordisk medeltid. Uppsatser framlagda vid ett kvinnohistoriskt symposium i Kungälv 8.–12. oktober 1979* (Lindome), 50–65.

—— (1982*a*). 'Rómarvald og kirkjugoðar', *Skírnir*, 156: 51–67.

—— (1982*b*). 'Stéttir, auður og völd á 12. og 13. öld', *Saga*, 20: 63–113.

—— (1983). 'Helgi Þorláksson svarar', *Saga*, 21: 275–9.

—— (1988*a*). 'Stéttakúgun eða samfylking bænda? Um söguskoðun Björns Þorsteinssonar', *Saga og Kirkja* (Reykjavík), 183–91.

—— (1988*b*). 'Var Sturla Þórðarson þjóðfrelsishetja?' in G. A. Grímsdóttir and I. Kristjánsson (eds.), *Sturlustefna* (Reykjavík), 127–46.

—— (1989*a*). *Gamlar götur og goðavald: Um fornar leiðir og völd Oddaverja í Rangárþingi* (Ritsafn Sagnfræðistofnunar, 25; Reykjavík).

—— (1989*b*). 'Mannfræði og saga', *Skírnir*, 163: 231–48.

—— (1991*a*). 'Sauðafell: Um leiðir og völd í Dölum við lok þjóðveldis', *Yfir Íslandsála* (Reykjavík), 95–109.

—— (1991*b*). *Vaðmál og verðlag. Vaðmál í utanlandsviðskiptum og búskap Íslendinga á 13. og 14. öld* (Reykjavík).

—— (1992*a*). 'Snorri goði og Snorri Sturluson', *Skírnir*, 166: 295–320.

—— (1992*b*). 'Social Ideas and the Concept of Profit in Thirteenth Century Iceland', in G. Pálsson (ed.) *From Sagas to Society* 231–45.

—— (1994). 'Þjóðleið hjá Brekku og Bakka. Um leiðir og völd í Öxnadal við lok þjóðveldis', *Samtíðarsögur* (Níunda alþjóðlega fornsagnaþingið; Akureyri), 335–49.

Þorsteinsson, Björn (1951). 'Guðmundur biskup góði', *Þjóðviljinn* (15 and 19 Aug. 1951).

—— (1953). *Íslenzka þjóðveldið* (Reykjavík).

—— (1956). *Íslenzka skattlandið* (Reykjavík).

—— (1961*a*). 'Historieskrivning', *KHL* vi. 597–602.

—— (1961*b*). 'Ísland og Noregskonungur', *Þjóðviljinn* (31 May 1961).

—— (1963). 'Klede: Island', *KHL* viii. 471–4.

Þorsteinsson, Björn (1966). *Ný Íslandssaga* (Reykjavík).
—— (1967). 'Gissur jarl og Snorri Sturluson', *Morgunblaðið* (7 Jan. 1967).
—— (1974). 'Tollr', *KHL* xviii. 452–4.
—— (1975). 'Tyende: Island', *KHL* xix. 110–12.
—— (1976). 'Vinhandel: Island', *KHL* xx. 130–1.
—— (1978). *Íslensk miðaldasaga* (Reykjavík).
—— (1983). 'Af íslenskum diplomötum og leyniþjónustumönnum.—Um íslensk utanríkismál fyrir 1100', *Sagnir*, 4: 37–46.
—— (1985). *Island* (Politikens Danmarks historie; Copenhagen).
—— (1986). 'Róttækasta samfélagsbreyting á Íslandi fyrir 1800', *Lesbók Morgunblaðsins*, 17: 12–13.
—— and Jónsson, Bergsteinn (1991). *Íslands saga til okkar daga* (Reykjavík).
Þorsteinsson, Guðmundur (1988). 'Þankabrot úr Þingeyraklaustri', *Saga og Kirkja*, (Reykjavík), 87–102.
Þorsteinsson, Hannes (1912). 'Nokkrar athuganir um íslenzkar bókmenntir á 12. og 13. öld', *Skírnir*, 86: 126–48.
Þórarinsson, Sigurður (1944). *Tefrokronologiska studier på Island* (Geografiska Annalen, 26; Copenhagen).
—— (1956). 'Ísland þjóðveldistímans og menning í ljósi landfræðilegra staðreynda', *Skírnir*, 130: 236–48.
—— (1957). 'Hérað milli sanda og eyðing þess', *Andvari*, 82: 35–47.
—— (1958). 'Iceland in the Saga Period: Some Geographical Aspects', in K. Eldjárn (ed.) *Þriðji Vikingafundur* (Reykjavík), 13–24.
—— (1961). 'Population Changes in Iceland', *Geographical Review*, 51/4: 519–33.
—— (1974). 'Sambúð lands og lýðs í ellefu aldir', *Saga Íslands*, i. 29–97.
Þórðarson, Björn (1949–53). 'Móðir Jóru biskupsdóttur', *Saga*, i.: 289–346.
—— (1950). *Síðasti goðinn* (Reykjavík).
—— (1955). 'Magnús Gizurarson Skálholtsbiskup', *Andvari*, 80: 33–63.
Þórðarson, Matthías (1909*a*). 'Klaustrið á Keldum', *Árbók 1909*: 32.
—— (1909*b*). 'Smávegis. Um nokkra staði og fornmenjar, er höf. athugaði á skrásetningarferð um Borgarfjarðar- og Mýrasýslu í júlímánuði 1909', *Árbók 1909*: 40–9.
—— (1913). 'Vestmannaeyjar. Nokkrar athugasemdir um söguatriði, örnefni, kirkjur o. fl. þar', *Árbók 1913*: 17–63.
—— (1922). *Fornleifar á Þingvelli. Búðir, lögrjetta og lögberg* (Reykjavík).
—— (1924). 'Smávegis. Um nokkra staði og fornminjar, er höf. hefir athugað á skrásetningarferðum sínum', *Árbók 1924*: 42–58.
—— (1934). 'Islands kirkebygninger og kyrkeinventar i middelalderen', *Nordisk kultur*, 23: 288–316.
—— (1943). 'Utgrävda gårdar 1939. Skeljastaðir', in M. Stenberger (ed.) *Forntida gårdar i Island* (Copenhagen), 121–36.
Þórhallsson, Tryggvi (1923). 'Brandr Jónsson biskup á Hólum', *Skírnir*, 97: 46–64.
—— (1936). 'Ómagahald, matgjafir o.fl', *Skírnir*, 110: 123–32.

LIST OF TERMS

alin, pl. álnir: Ell. A measure, 47.7 cm or 55.6 cm. As a length of homespun, the basic medium of exchange, the a. was a currency unit; one *hundrað* equalled 120 á. (M. M. Lárusson 1958*a*; Gestsson 1977).

annex-church: *See* útkirkja.

Alþing: *See alþingi.*

alþingi/Alþing: The general assembly convened at Þingvellir (S) at the end of June every year and lasted for two weeks. It was the venue for the law court (*lögrétta*), the legislative council, and the quarter courts and the fifth courts, the court of final instance (*LEI* 1–9; Finsen 1873, 1888; Maurer 1874*a*, esp. 160–86; Arnórsson 1945; Ó. Lárusson 1958*a*: 55–60; Miller 1990: 17–23).

annals: 10 principal a. survive from medieval Iceland. They are all based on the same source(s) for Icelandic events up to the 1270s and 1280s when the writing of the different a. commenced (*IA*, pp. i–lxxxiv; Beckmann 1912*a*, 1912*b*; Jónsson 1920–4 ii: 780–2, iii. 68–76; B. Guðmundsson 1936*b*; H. Pálsson 1965*a*, 1970: 32–43; Einarsdóttir 1964; *ÁB*, pp. lxii–lxxx; S. Karlsson 1969, 1988; J. Benediktsson 1976*f*; J. Helgason 1977; J. Kristjánsson 1980).

aristocrat: Although Old Icelandic had no corresponding term there was a clear sense that some people were by birth better than others. There was not a clearly defined class of nobility but distinctions were nevertheless made between families which determined their status. This is expressed with a range of terms like *göfugr* (=noble), *kynborinn* (=high-born), *stórmenni* (=distinguished person/people), *góðrar ættar* (=of good family/lineage) (Sørensen 1993: 173–6).

assembly-tax: *See þingfararkaupsbóndi.*

Árna saga biskups: The Biography of Bishop Árni Þorláksson of Skálholt (1269–98). Written around or after 1300 it stops short in its account in 1290 (M. M. Lárusson 1956*c*; *ÁB*, pp. lxii–cvii; Grímsdóttir 1994).

bóndi, pl. bændr: Householder. A b. (man or woman) was (in theory) in total control over his or her household, which in the majority of cases was made up of a married couple, their children, servants, and dependent relatives. Although a farmstead could be shared by more than one household, each household was an independent economic unit with its own field, meadows, pastures, and livestock. The b. was responsible for his or her household members in all outside dealings and was the only member of the household who had political rights (women b. only through a male intermediary), although grown-up sons of b. sometimes managed to be politically active without heading a household of their own. Invariably this was a short-lived arrangement. B. who owned a minimum property (*þingfararkaupsbændur*) paid the assembly-tax to those b. who accompanied their chieftain to the Alþing. Those who did not own this minimum (*þurfamenn*) qualified for support from the commune (Þ. Jóhannesson 1933: esp. 121–51; Pálsson 1931; M. M. Lárusson 1957*a*, 1962*d*, 1962*j*; Miller 1990: 111–37; Sørensen 1993: 152–61).

burial-church: *See* graptarkirkja.

bændakirkja: *See staðr.*

bænhús, pl. bænhús: Chapel. In a relative sense the term can be used of any small dependent church—in other records than charters, esp. episcopal statues, b. is regularly used as the alternative to parish church (*sóknarkirkja*) (*DI* ii. 188, 639, 795, 801). In the charter material the term does however seem to have a better defined meaning, at least to the extent that it always refers to churches of lesser status than a half-church. As opposed to annex-churches, the number of masses in b. seems to have been fixed for every year (12 masses p. a. is most common) probably because feasts were normally not celebrated in them. There are a few exceptions from the rule that feast days were not celebrated in chapels, e.g. *DI* ii. 409–10, 360. There are also indications that there could be a special kind of mass or service which was observed in b., distinct from, and probably less substantial than, that observed in full-churches and half-churches. The concept *bænhússöngr* (=chapel-song) used in a few charters as a definition of the service required at b. might refer to the type and not amount of service (*DI* ii. 635–6, 668). The term *bænhúsdagar* (=chapel-days) is also found as a different form of service to ordinary masses (*DI* ii. 63–4), suggesting that a special (reduced?) form of service was given in b. In one early charter two out of three b. had a service of 12 requiem masses (*DI* iii. 1) which would seem the most suitable type of service for these small buildings, which can hardly have been attended by more than the household of the farm where they stood. Presumably the primary function of b. was to be a place of prayer for the members of the household, and there may have been b. where priests never gave services. Direct influence over neighbours, such as owners of annex-churches could plan on, was unlikely, as b. received no tithes or dues and were serviced too infrequently for any relationships of dependency to have formed. If a b. was mainly a symbol of the wealth and piety of the family which owned it, there can hardly have been much reason to pay for public 'ordinary' masses in them. A more personal type of service, like singing requiem masses for deceased members of the household and the family's ancestors, seems a more likely option.

There were some 900–1,000 b. in Iceland in the 14th and 15th cents. and the indications are that they originated—like the churches—in the 11th cent. in the first Christian family graveyards (see Ch. 1, s. 6). The b. were then those churches whose owners either failed or did not attempt to receive a share of the tithe and did not develop permanent ministries in the course of the 12th cent.

caretaker: *See varðveizla.*

charge of church: *See varðveizla.*

charter: *See máldagi.*

chieftain: Used in this work in the wide sense of anyone with authority over men or territory. It includes men called *goði*, *höfðingi*, *stórhöfðingi*, and *stórbóndi*. The ownership of a *goðorð* is not considered to be a requirement for the status of c. There were people who owned *goðorð* (*goðorðsmenn*) who did not have any visible authority to go with it, and there were men of considerable influence who did not own *goðorð*. In the 13th cent. some c. were overlords (*stórhöfðingjar*). These usually owned or controlled more than one *goðorð* and their authority was acknowledged by a number of local leaders (*stórbændr*). The local leaders were often in firm control over their respective areas but the territorial range of their influence was limited.

The term *goði* is used in *Grágás* in the same sense as *goðorðsmaður* but in narrative sources it appears mainly as an appellation of certain chieftains. Why some chieftains earned the distinction and others did not is unclear.

Commonwealth: The term preferred here for the constitutional entity which existed in Iceland from the 10th cent. to 1262–4, when it became a domain of the Norwegian king. The term Free state which is also sometimes used in this context has the benefit of drawing attention to the main defining feature of this entity, namely that it was not a part of any other state. It is, however, more misleading than c. as it implies some sort of statehood.

commune: *See hreppr.*

control of church: *See forráð.*

district: Used of subdivision of region. A d. sometimes corresponds to the area of one *hreppr*, although often it is larger.

ell: *See alin.*

eyrir, pl. aurar: Ounce unit. Unit of measurement, 27 and 32.5 grams. 8 a. equalled 1 mark. As a currency unit the e. could equal 3–6 ells (M. M. Lárusson 1958*a*).

family, = ***ætt*****, pl.** ***ættir*****:** Family was significant in three ways: as lineage, as kin, and as the basic social/economic and sometimes political unit.

Lineage was important for social status. A lack of respectable ancestry was a serious drawback for people of wealth who aspired to influence and social respectability (like Högni in Bær (S) and Þórir in Deildartunga (S) (*Bsk* i. 284; *Sturl* 90–1)) whereas those who had important ancestors stood a good chance of bettering their position even if they lacked funds (e.g. St Þorlákr).

A person's kin could extend to fifth cousins according to *Grágás* but, following the Contemporary Sagas, in practice only second cousins were recognized as kin (A. S. Arnórsdóttir 1995). The kin also included the in-laws. As each individual's kin-group was particular to him or her and their siblings such groups did not constitute social groups capable of acting in unison or of recognizing common interests. The importance of the kin was primarily as a framework for the maintenance of paupers and as an accessible group of people who were likely to be well disposed towards a kinsman in need of economic, political, or even military support. Ties of kinship did not necessarily however decide allegiances and kinsmen are often found on opposing sides in conflict.

The primary importance of the f., and the sense in which the term is mainly used in this work, is as the basic social and political unit. This was always a fluid grouping and could connect more than one household. The f. included a father and a mother and at least the son or daughter who took over the f. farmstead. At any one time the numbers in this group could be swelled by grown sons and sons-in-law who sometimes headed their own households but acted in unison with each other and their father towards others. The coherence of this sort of group varied according to circumstance; in Rangárþing the sons and grandsons of Sæmundr Jónsson (d. 1222) appear as more or less a single political group and this was probably because their power over their region depended on their co-operation and unity. Brothers often made up teams in politics (the sons of Hrafn Sveinbjarnarson, the sons of Jón Brandsson in Staður in Steingrímsfjörður (N), the sons of Dufgus, etc.) but the f. was only continued through that one of them who came to possess the f. estate or wielded most power. If more than one brother managed to establish himself as a householder they might act in concert while they lived but the nephews would not necessarily do so and each of these would begin to constitute a f. of his own (Líndal 1976; Sørensen 1977: 30–7, 1993: 165–86; Miller 1990: 139–78).

forráð (pl.), also forræði: Control. In the case of churches this term is used of the right of the caretaker to govern his church. Cf. *varðveizla.*

goði: *See* chieftain.

goðorð, pl. goðorð: Chieftaincy. A g. was an inheritable and purchasable unit of power. Women and minors could own g. but could not act in them. According to *Grágás* there were 39 g. in Iceland, 12 in the northern quarter and 9 in each of the others. In theory each spring assembly was held for a region of three g. The owner of a g., a *goðorðsmaðr,* was entitled to a seat in the law court at the Alþing. *Grágás* gives detailed information as to the duties of people who owned g. at the Alþing, but it has little to say about the responsibilities or rights of *goðorðsmenn* when they were at home. It has proved impossible to identify the 39 g. or their owners at any particular point in time (Ingvarsson 1986–7 is the most serious attempt). In the 12th and 13th cents. it is clear that far fewer people wielded power in Iceland and some of them owned more than one g. The traditional interpretation of the nature of g. is to understand it as a unit of real power, i.e. that a g. automatically bestowed authority and political responsibility on its owner. It is furthermore normally assumed that the system was set up in 930 and that the lack of *goðorðsmenn* in the 12th and 13th cents. represents a decline of the system. The suggestion that g. was in fact only a licence to take a seat in the law court makes much more sense (Kjartansson 1989). That would explain the lack of congruence between the g. system as described in *Grágás* and the realities of power politics apparent in the Contemporary Sagas. *See also* chieftain.

goðorðsmaður, pl. -menn: Owner of a *goðorð. See goðorð* and chieftain.

graptarkirkja, pl. -kirkjur: Burial-church. The term itself suggests that there could be churches which did not have burial rights, and some of the contexts it appears in indicate that it was used as a definition of high-ranking churches. The term was coined some time in the early 12th cent., suggesting that at that time there were churches which did not have the right to burial, and that this right was in some way significant for the status of a church. It is however also clear that churches which did not have resident priests or full services could have burial rights. By the end of the 12th cent. the term is being used of churches with high status, churches on which chapels were dependent and churches where public events could take place. Some time in the 13th cent. the term lost ground, probably because the term *sóknarkirkja* (parish church) became a more accurate description of the emerging group of churches which had permanently resident priests and defined areas of jurisdiction. The continued use of the term in the 14th and 15th cents. was probably because the word already existed in the language and could be used to describe any church with a cemetery, and possibly because of the influence of Norwegian church rank terminology.

Grágás: The laws of the Icelandic Commonwealth, abolished in 1271. Preserved in two principal MSS, *Konungsbók* from *c.*1250 and *Staðarhólsbók* from the 1270s. The two MSS accord to a large extent but considerable differences suggest that they are not closely related. The laws were first codified in 1117–18 and fragments survive from the 12th cent. suggesting that the 13th-cent. codices are not substantially different from the 12th-cent. laws. The law codes are divided into sections, the first of which is the Old Christian law section, first assembled in 1122–33 but surviving in a form written between 1199 and 1217 (Maurer 1864; *Grg II*, pp. i–xxxv; *Grg III*, pp. iii–lvi; Briem 1885; Ó. Lárusson 1958*b*, 1960*a*, 1961; M. M. Lárusson 1964*b*; Ståhle 1965; *LEI* i. 15; Jacoby 1986: 210–23; J. Kristjánsson 1988: 118–19; G. Karlsson 1992).

hay-due: *See heytollr.*

heimaprestr: *See heimilisprestr.*

heimilisprestr, pl. -prestar: A priest attached to a household and its church. *See þingaprestur.*

heytollr, pl. -tollar: Hay-due. Paid by each household to the priest for his travels inside his ministry (*DI* i. 596). Legislation on h. is ill-preserved (*DI* ii. 292; iii. 469–70) and it is not clear when it was introduced. Like the lighting-due it appears first in the mid-13th cent. and was well established when *Auðunarmáldagar* were compiled in 1318. H. are regularily mentioned in the northern charters, while charters from the southern diocese hardly ever mention them. The only examples are all from a small region at the north eastern end of Faxaflói (Akrar, Krossholt, and Miklaholt (S) (*DI* i. 596; ii. 113; iii. 82, 86; iv. 189–90). Rather than meaning that h. were not paid in the southern diocese this may have to do with different attitudes to bookkeeping at the two sees. Although h. were supposed to go directly to the priest, in reality they were collected by the householder of the farm where the priest resided, who instead gave the priest a horse and fodder for the necessary travels (as in *DI* iii. 538–40 see also Cederschiöld 1887: 46–7; Bjorn Þorsteinsson 1974: 454).

home field = tún, pl. tún: The fenced field for hay-making around the farmhouses. The h. was normally the only improved (not ploughed) part of the farm and it produced the best hay, reserved for the milch-cows. Hay of lesser quality from meadows was given to other cattle and sheep (Thoroddsen 1908–22: iii. 90–102; Schönfeld 1902: 2–6). The h.-fence was a symbolic barrier around the household, frequently mentioned in *Grágás.*

homestead = heimaland: A central holding of a larger property. The term implies an estate divided into a central holding and outlying holdings (*útlönd*). The term became fossilized in charter language as a definition of the property where the church was situated.

householder: *See bóndi.*

hreppr, pl. hreppar: Commune. An association of at least 20 householders in a geographically continuous area. The h. organized certain common interests, e.g. compensation for fire damage, but its main function was to administer poor relief. See Ch. 2, s. 2.

hundrað, pl. hundruð: Hundred. Currency unit. 1 h. = 120 ells. By the 14th cent. the cow value became fixed at 1 h. (Þorláksson 1991*b*: 132–43). The value of land was measured in h. (M. M. Lárusson 1958*a*, 1962*b*).

hundred: *See hundrað.*

Hungrvaka: A chronicle of the bishops of Skálholt from the beginning to Bishop Klængr's death in 1176. Written in the first two decades of the 13th cent., probably by the same author as *Páls saga* (*IBS* i. 345–48; Arnórsson 1944–8; J. Helgason 1960; M. M. Lárusson 1962*c*; Bekker-Nielsen 1972, 1985; *Bsk* i. pp. xxv–xxvii).

höfðingi: *See* chieftain.

incapable person: *See ómagi.*

Íslendingabók: A short history of Iceland from the settlement to the 1120s. Written by the priest Ari *fróði* Þorgilsson in 1122–33. An earlier and longer version does not survive (K. v. Maurer 1870*b*, 1891; Ólsen 1885, 1889, 1893; Hagnell 1938: 87–113; Arnórsson 1942: 27–30; Sigfússon 1944, 1962*b*; Hermannsson 1948; H. Pálsson 1961; Ellehøj 1965; G. Turville-Petre 1953: 92–102; *ÍF* i. viii–xvii; Tómasson 1975; Mundal 1984, 1994; Kjartansson 1986*a*; Harðarson 1987; *ÍBS* i. 293).

Íslendinga saga: The central text of the Sturlunga compilation written by Sturla Þórðarson in 1264–84. Chronicles political conflict in Iceland from the 1180s to 1264 (Ólsen 1902: 385–437; P. Sigurðsson 1933–5; *SturlR* ii. pp. xxxiv–xli; G. Benediktsson 1961; J. Benediktsson 1972*c*: 357–9; Grímsdóttir 1988; *ÍBS* i. 324–6).

Jóns saga helga: The life of St Jón (b. 1052) first bishop of Hólar (1106–21). Survives in three vernacular versions which are all based on a Latin Life written by Gunnlaugr Leifsson, monk at Þingeyrar (d. 1219) (M. M. Lárusson 1962*h*: 617–18; Tómasson 1988*a*: 339–43; Foote 1978: 41).

kirkjuprestr, pl. -prestar: Church-priest. The term is used both of the servile priests described only in *Grágás* (see Ch. 5, s. 1) and of priests who served in the church at major *staðir*, as opposed to the *þingaprestr* who served the annex-churches and ministered to the congregation.

kirkjusókn: *See sókn.*

Konungsbók: *See* Grágás.

Kristni saga: A chronicle of the conversion of the Icelanders. It describes the early mission, the conversion itself at great length, and the subsequent history of the Icelandic church up to the death of St Jón in 1121. Based largely on *Íslendingabók*, but also *Jóns saga helga* and possibly *Hungrvaka.* Written after 1247, possibly by Sturla Þórðarson (*ÍBS* i. 306–8; *Bsk* i. pp. xi–xix; *Hauksbók*, lxv–lxxiv; Jóhannesson 1941: 70–1).

law court: *See alþingi.*

Law rock: *See Lögberg.*

lawman: *See lögmaðr.*

lawspeaker: *See lögsögumaðr.*

lighting-due: *See ljóstollr.*

ljóstollr, pl. -tollar, also lýsistollr: Lighting-due. L. was paid by each household to church-owners for provision of candles and other lighting of the church (*NgL* v. 35–6; *Grg III* 144_{20-5}, 191_{13-18}; *DI* iv. 450–1, also *DI* i. 594, 596, 597—Finnur Jónsson translates l. as *pensio in candelas* (*HE* ii. 95) and *pensio in lumina* (*HE* ii. 223). L. had been introduced by the middle of the 13th cent. but a clause in *Grágás* which requires that the church-owner pay for the wax himself (*Grg* ii. 19_{22-3}) suggests that the l. was a recent invention in the mid-13th cent.

local leader = stórbóndi: In the 13th cent. there appear in the sources chieftains who did not own *goðorð* and directly or indirectly acknowledged the authority of an overlord. Local leaders normally did not hold sway over larger areas than a single commune. *See also* chieftain.

Lögberg: Law rock. The place at the Alþing in Þingvellir (S) from where the lawspeaker directed proceedings and where public announcements and speeches were made (*Grg* iii. s.v. lögberg; M. M. Lárusson 1966*a*; M. Þórðarson 1922: 80–94).

lögbýli, pl. lögbýli: Independent farmstead. A political and geographical rather than a strictly agricultural unit. More than one householder could own and farm a l., and parts could be rented out as crofts or cottages (B. Lárusson 1967: 29–31), but in the Middle Ages land was bought and sold in units of l. which tended to have fixed value assessments.

lögmaðr, pl. -menn: Lawman. Head of the Icelandic judiciary after 1271, presided over the law court at the Alþing. Sturla Þórðarson was l. for the whole of Iceland in 1271–7 but after that there were two l., one for the southern and eastern quarters and one for the western and northern quarters (Jóhannesson 1958*a*: 82–4).

lögsögumaðr, pl. -menn: Lawspeaker. President of the Alþing to 1271. Elected by the law court the l. was charged with knowing the law and directing the proceedings at the assembly. L. were normally of chieftainly rank and were the only paid functionaries of the Commonwealth (J. Jóhannesson 1956: 66–8; Kjartansson 1986*b*; J. Sigurðsson 1860).

mark: *See mörk.*

máldagi, pl. máldagar: Charter. A particular type of document recording the property belonging to a church and the conditions of the endowment. The term originally meant 'contract'. The majority of m. survive in charter collections from the 14th cent. or later, but some 130 can be dated to the 12th and 13th cents. (Cederschiöld 1887; Skovgaard-Petersen 1960: 236–43; Smedberg 1973: 15, 112; Rafnsson 1974: 153–5; Nilsson 1989: 29–30; Vésteinsson 1994, forthcoming-*b*).

ministry: *See þing.*

mörk, pl. merkur: Unit of measurement, 214–17 or 257–60 grams. As a unit of currency one m. equalled 8 ounce units (M. M. Lárusson 1958*a*).

New Christian law section: A new Christian law, replacing the Old Christian law section of *Grágás*, introduced by Bishop Árni Þorláksson for the diocese of Skálholt in 1275 but not accepted for the diocese of Hólar until 1354 (*DI* iii. 98–9).

officialis: A priest or monk who governed a diocese in the absence of a bishop. The term is not attested until 1340 (M. M. Lárusson 1967*g*).

Old Christian law section: *See Grágás.*

ounce unit: *See eyrir.*

overlord = stórhöfðingi: In the 13th cent. there appear chieftains whose authority was acknowledged by local leaders and who could hold sway over a whole region or parts of the country. *See also* chieftain.

ómagi, pl. ómagar: Incapable person. Any person, child or grown-up, who was not capable of sustaining him- or herself and was therefore put in the charge of the nearest relative capable of providing maintenance. See Ch. 2, s. 2.

parish: *See þing* and tithe area.

pauper: *See þurfamaðr.*

Páls saga: Biography of Bishop Páll Jónsson in Skálholt (1195–1211). Written by a contemporary of Páll shortly after his death in 1211, possibly by the same author as *Hungrvaka* (M. M. Lárusson 1968*c*; *ÍBS* i. 348–50; Rafnsson 1993: 9–44).

Prestssaga Guðmundar Arasonar: An account of the early life of Guðmundr Arason, from his birth in 1161 to 1203 when he became bishop of Hólar. Part of the Sturlunga compilation but it survives also as a part of several versions of a compilation called

Guðmundar saga biskups. Written in the middle of the 13th cent. by someone close to the bishop who had been present at some of the events described (*SturlR* ii. pp. xxvii–xx; Sigfússon 1960*b*; S. Karlsson 1984, 1985; *GSB* i. pp. xxviii, cxliv–cliii; *Bsk* i. pp. lviii–lx; Ólsen 1902: 224–6).

prestskyld: In charter language, the minimum property a church had to own to maintain a priest.

quarter = fjórðungr: The division of Iceland into four quarters was well established by the beginning of the 12th cent. According to Ari the division dates back to the 960s when it was made as a part of judicial reform. New courts were created, one for each quarter, where cases that were not resolved at the regional spring assemblies could be resolved and where parties from different spring-assembly regions could meet for litigation (M. M. Lárusson 1967*g*) The quarter courts convened at the Alþing and represented the hub of its judicial activity (Ó. Lárusson 1958*a*: 100–18; M. M. Lárusson 1959*h*).

region: Used here in a loose sense of a large geographically defined area, which normally corresponds to a single spring-assembly area. The court system divided the country into 13 spring-assembly areas, three in every quarter, except the north where there were four. In theory there were three *goðorð* in each spring-assembly area.

skiptitíund: Tithe payable on property which amounted to more than 100 ounce units was divided in four, between bishop, priest, church, and the poor. Tithe payable on less property was not divided but went exclusively to poor relief. See Ch. 2, s. 2.

sókn, pl. sóknir: Parish. S. originally meant 'movement towards' but relating to churches its meaning of 'attendance' is the cognate object of the verb *sækja*, meaning 'go to', 'attend' as in *sækja tíðir/messu/kirkju* = attend/go to mass/church (*OGNS* s.v. *sókn*, A. B. Magnússon 1989: s.v. *sókn*, *sækja*; Jørgensen 1980: 34; Brink 1990: 68–74). It is as the object of the verb *sækja* that s. occurs in the 12th and 13th cents., normally in compounds like *kirkjusókn* = church attendance, or *tíðasókn* = service attendance, with no definite reference to territory, whereas by the 14th cent. s. and the compound *kirkjus*, had acquired a clear territorial sense and were used of the same kind of area as *þing* (*ÍF* xvii. 169_3 is the earliest example of this use of the term). The parish system, a network of churches with certain territorial rights (to tithes, dues, baptism, burial, etc.), took a long time to develop in Iceland and churches were still acquring territorial rights in the late middle ages (Vésteinsson 1998*b*). *See* tithe area and parish.

sóknarkirkja, pl. -kirkjur: Parish church. There was no specific term used for full-churches which had priests attached to them. In the charters they are simply called *kirkja* or church, while the term s. is used in episcopal statutes and secular legislation and seems sometimes to denote this kind of church. That usage, however, was probably based on Norwegian church rank terminology, which was distinct from the Icelandic one. Until the 14th cent. the Icelandic understanding of the term is more likely to have been 'a church which is attended from a certain area', i.e. any church where services were given and which had a defined congregation. The Norwegian understanding, 'a principal church of a parish', became accepted in Iceland by the 15th cent. in step with the consolidation of the parish system.

spring assembly: *See vorþing.*

Staðamál: The dispute over the control over *staðir* initiated by Bishop Árni Þorláksson (1269–98) and concluded by the Treaty of Ögvaldsnes in 1297. Traditionally St Þorlákr's claims to church property have also been termed S. and considered the first round of two.

Staðarhólsbók: *See Grágás.*

staðr, pl. staðir: Benefice. In the Treaty of Ögvaldsnes in 1297 a distinction was made between churches which owned more than half of the *heimaland*, the farmstead where they were situated and those which owned less. The former came under direct control of the bishops, while the latter continued to be under lay control. In late medieval documentation a clear distinction is made between s.—benefices appointed by the bishops or archbishops—and *bændakirkja*, literally 'farmers' church', where the priests were employed by the secular owner of the church. A s. was normally on good farmland, owned much additional property and rights, and was central to ecclesiastical organization in its area. Many were seats of ecclesiastical dignitaries and sometimes powerful secular allies of the bishops. The *bændakirkjur*, on the other hand, were more humble institutions, normally much less wealthy and the priests who served them were nearer the bottom of the ecclesiastical hierarchy.

These distinctions are important in the late Middle Ages but in the 12th and 13th cents. the term s. was used to refer to any church which owned a sizeable property as well as monasteries and the episcopal sees. The use of the term was flexible but it seems always to refer to churches which owned more than one farmstead and at least half the *heimaland*. Churches which only owned a *prestskyld* were not s.

The original meaning of s. is 'place, location' and it is interesting that in Brittany the Latin form *locus* is used in the same way for ecclesiastical institutions and in Wales it is found as a place-name element denoting a monastery (Davies 1978: 36; Pierce 1984: 487).

stórbóndi: *See* local leader and chieftain.

tithe area: The farmsteads whose households paid tithe to a particular church. Annex-churches normally had their own t. although such areas often included only the household of the farmer who owned the annex-church.

útkirkja, pl. kirkjur: Annex-church. Any church which did not have a resident priest and which had more services than a chapel. Ú. are divided into types according to the amount of service given, often expressed in terms of full-, half- or quarter-service (*alkirkja, hálfkirkja, fjórðungskirkja*).

varðveizla: Charge. The responsibility which the caretaker of a church took for it. The responsibility amounted to an undertaking to rebuild the church if it was destroyed or when it became too dilapidated for services to be given in it and a promise not to alienate or squander the church's property. The term is a symptom of the introduction of *ius patronatus* in Iceland in the last quarter of the 12th cent. *See also forráð* and Ch. 3, s. 4.

vorþing, pl. vorþing: Spring assembly. Assemblies held in May for each region. In theory one spring assembly was convened by three *goðorðsmenn* and attended by their followers/householders of the region. The main task of spring assemblies was to settle disputes which arose within the region but they could also pass legislation on matters such as prices. Spring assemblies figure prominently in some of the Sagas of Icelanders but by the 13th cent. some of them had been abolished and others do not seem to have been a regular feature of political or judicial life.

þing (pl.): Ministry. The area and churches within it served by a single priest. A þ.

normally consisted of the tithe area of the church of the farmstead where the priest was resident and commonly one or more smaller tithe areas of annex-churches.

þingaprestr, pl. -prestar: District priest. A priest hired on annual contracts to serve a church and its annex-churches. See Ch. 5, ss. 3 and 4. The term can also be used of the priest who serves the ministry as opposed to the (senior) *kirkjuprestr*, whose duties were only at the church to which both were attached.

þingfararkaupsbóndi, pl. -bændr: Assembly-tax-paying householder. Assembly-tax was payable by all householders who owned a minimum property requirement. Þ. took turns in following their chieftain to the Alþing and those who stayed at home paid the tax for the travel expenses of those who undertook the journey (*Grg III*, s.v. *þingfararkaup*).

Þorgils saga ok Hafliða: The first of the sagas of the Sturlunga compilation, it describes a dispute between two chieftains in western Iceland in 1117–21. Written in the 13th cent., possibly around 1240 (*SturlR* ii. pp. xxii–xxv; Brown 1952: pp. ix–lxii; J. Benediktsson 1976*c*; *ÍBS* i. 321–2).

Þorgils saga skarða: Biography of the chieftain Þorgils *skarði* Böðvarsson (1226–58), survives as a part of the Sturlunga compilation, but it is not original to it, and a fragment of a separate version shows that the saga has been cut drastically by the compiler. Written by Þorgils's contemporary, possibly his brother-in-law, Þórðr *Hítnesingr* (*SturlR* ii. pp. xlvi–xlviii; J. Benediktsson 1976*c*; Bragason 1981).

Þorláks saga helga: The Life of St Þorlákr (b. 1133), bishop of Skálholt (1178–93). Survives in three versions (see Ch. 3, s. 4). Miracles of St Þorlákr were recorded in 1199 and survive in an early manuscript. A Latin Life was composed *c.*1200 and a vernacular version before the death of Bishop Páll in 1211 (J. Benediktsson 1969*a*; J. Helgason 1976; Egilsdóttir 1989; *ÍBS* i. 473–4).

þurfamaðr, pl. -menn: Pauper. A householder who received support from other householders in his commune. A quarter of the tithe was collected by the commune and distributed by its officers for this purpose. See Ch. 2, s. 2.

Maps

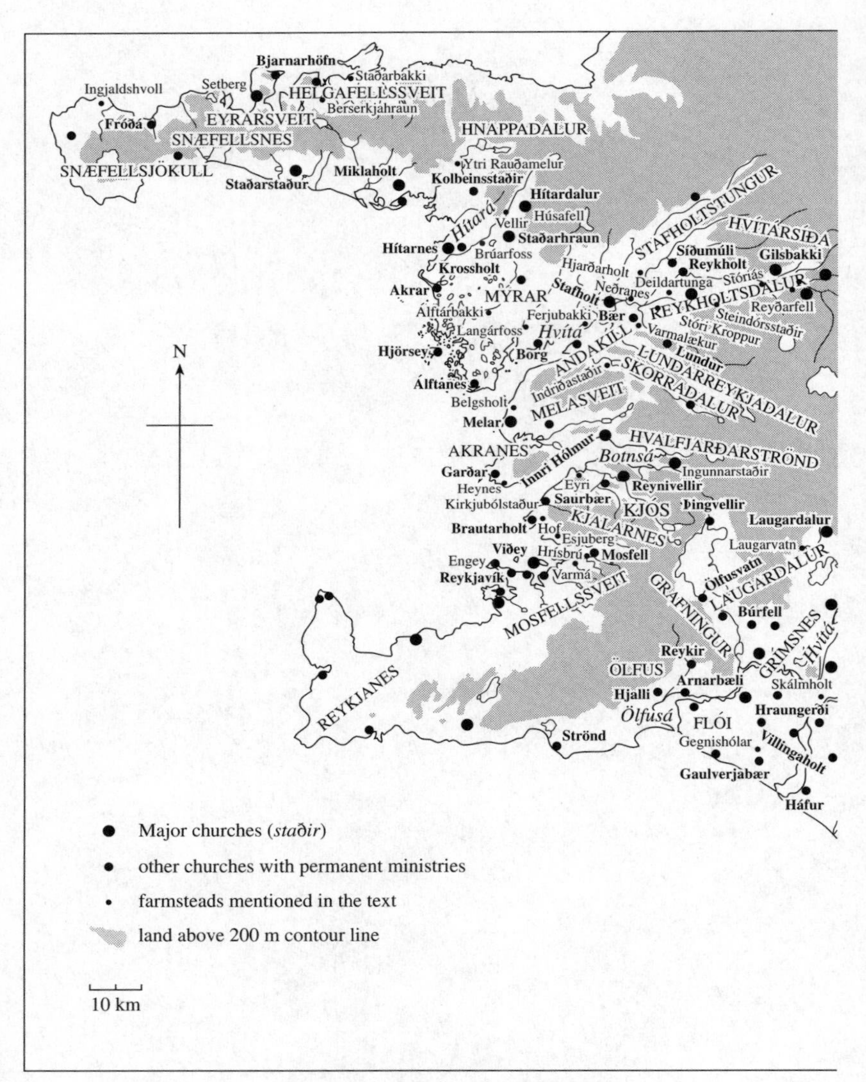

MAP 3. *The South and South-West*

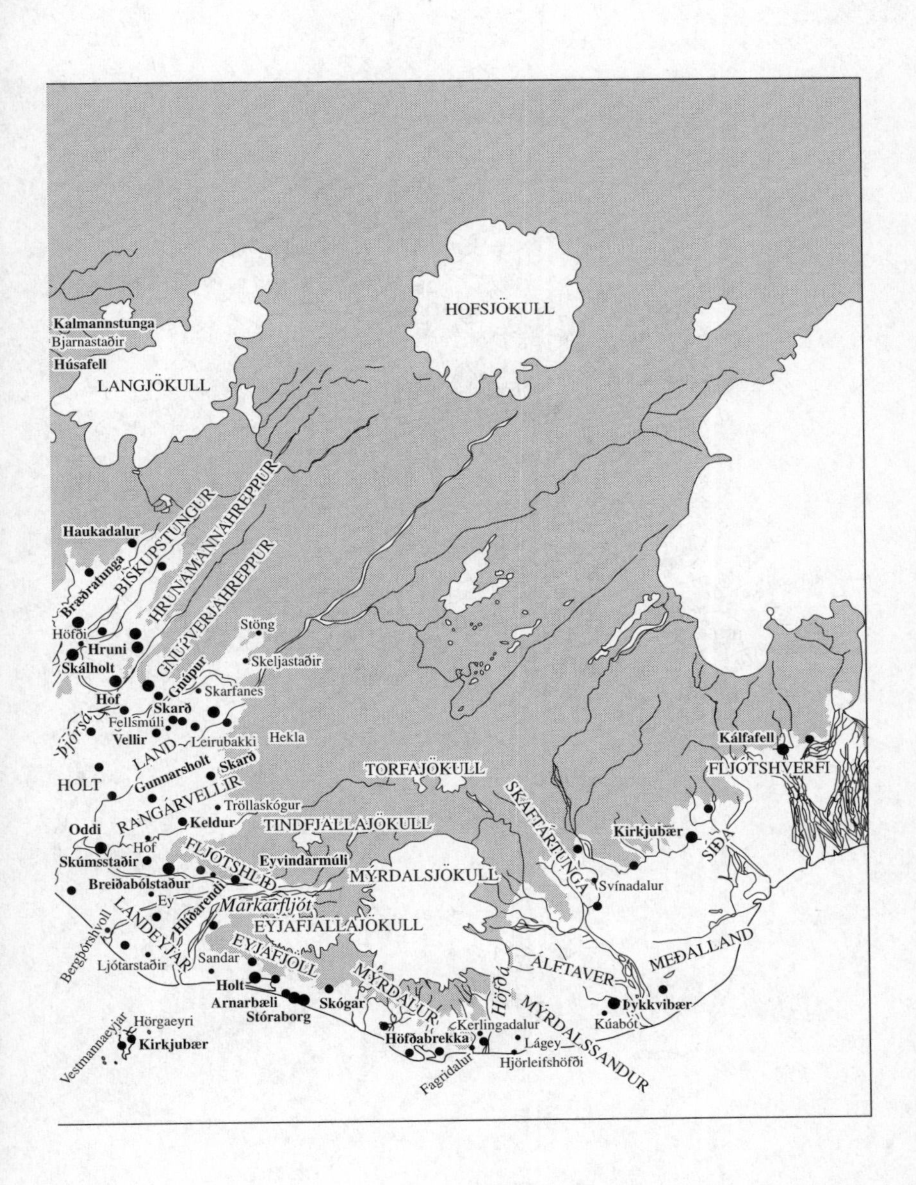
HOFSJÖKULL
Kalmannstunga
Bjarnastaðir
Húsafell
LANGJÖKULL
HRUNAMANNAHREPPUR
BISKUPSTUNGUR
GNÚPVERJAHREPPUR
Haukadalur
Bræðratunga
Höfði
Hruni
Skálholt
Stöng
Skeljastaðir
Gnúpur
Skarfanes
Hof
Skarð
Fellsmúli
Vellir
Þjórsá
LAND
Leirubakki
Hekla
HOLT
Gunnarsholt
Skarð
RANGÁRVELLIR
Tröllaskógur
Oddi
Keldur
Hof
Skúmsstaðir
FLJÓTSHLÍÐ
Eyvindarmúli
Breiðabólstaður
Ey
Markarfljót
Hlíðarendi
LANDEYJAR
Bergþórshvoll
Ljótarstaðir
Sandar
EYJAFJÖLL
Holt
Arnarbæli
Stóraborg
Skógar
Hörgaeyri
Kirkjubær
Vestmannaeyjar
TORFAJÖKULL
TINDFJALLAJÖKULL
MÝRDALSJÖKULL
EYJAFJALLAJÖKULL
MÝRDALUR
Höfðabrekka
Kerlingadalur
Lágey
Fagridalur
Hjörleifshöfði
Höfðá
MÝRDALSSANDUR
SKAFTÁRTUNGA
Svínadalur
ÁLFTAVER
Þykkvibær
Kúabót
MEÐALLAND
Kirkjubær
SÍÐA
Kálfafell
FLJÓTSHVERFI

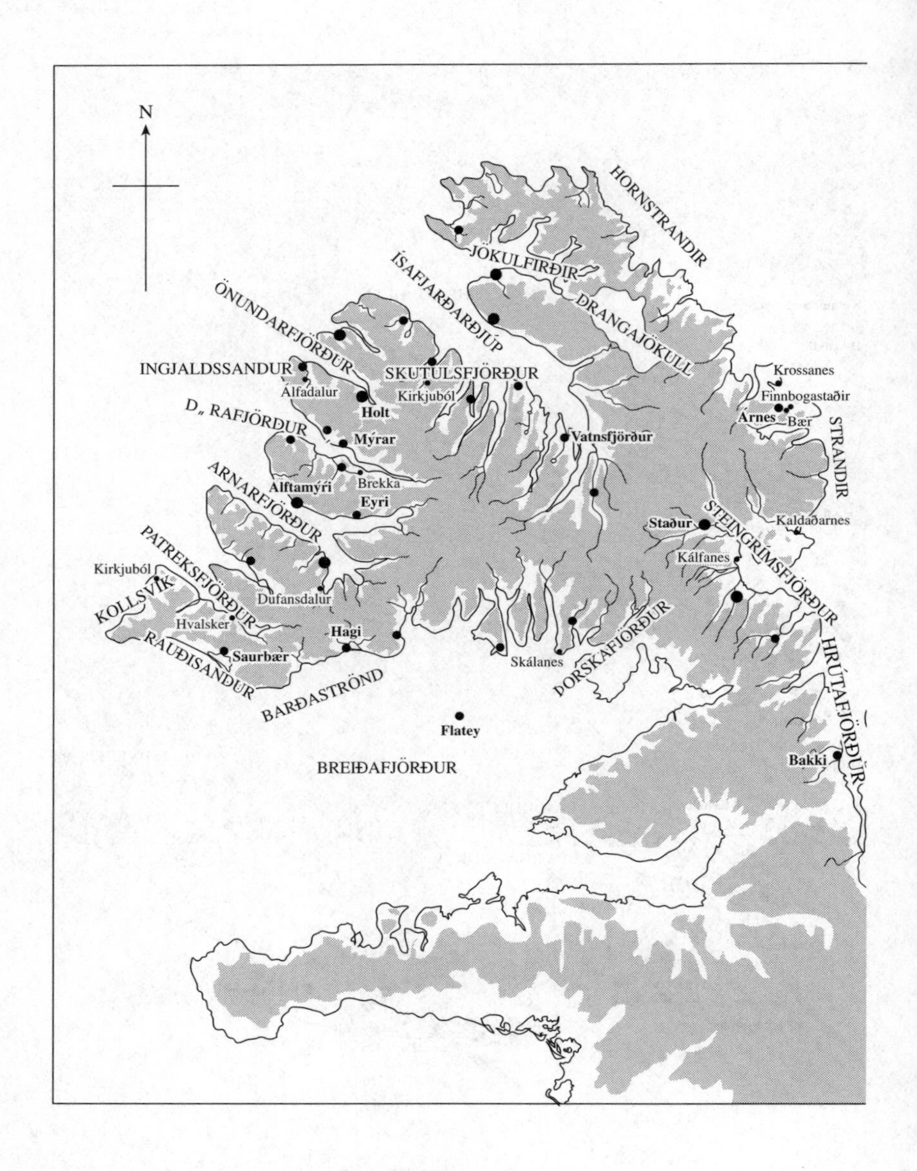

MAP 4. *The North and North-West*

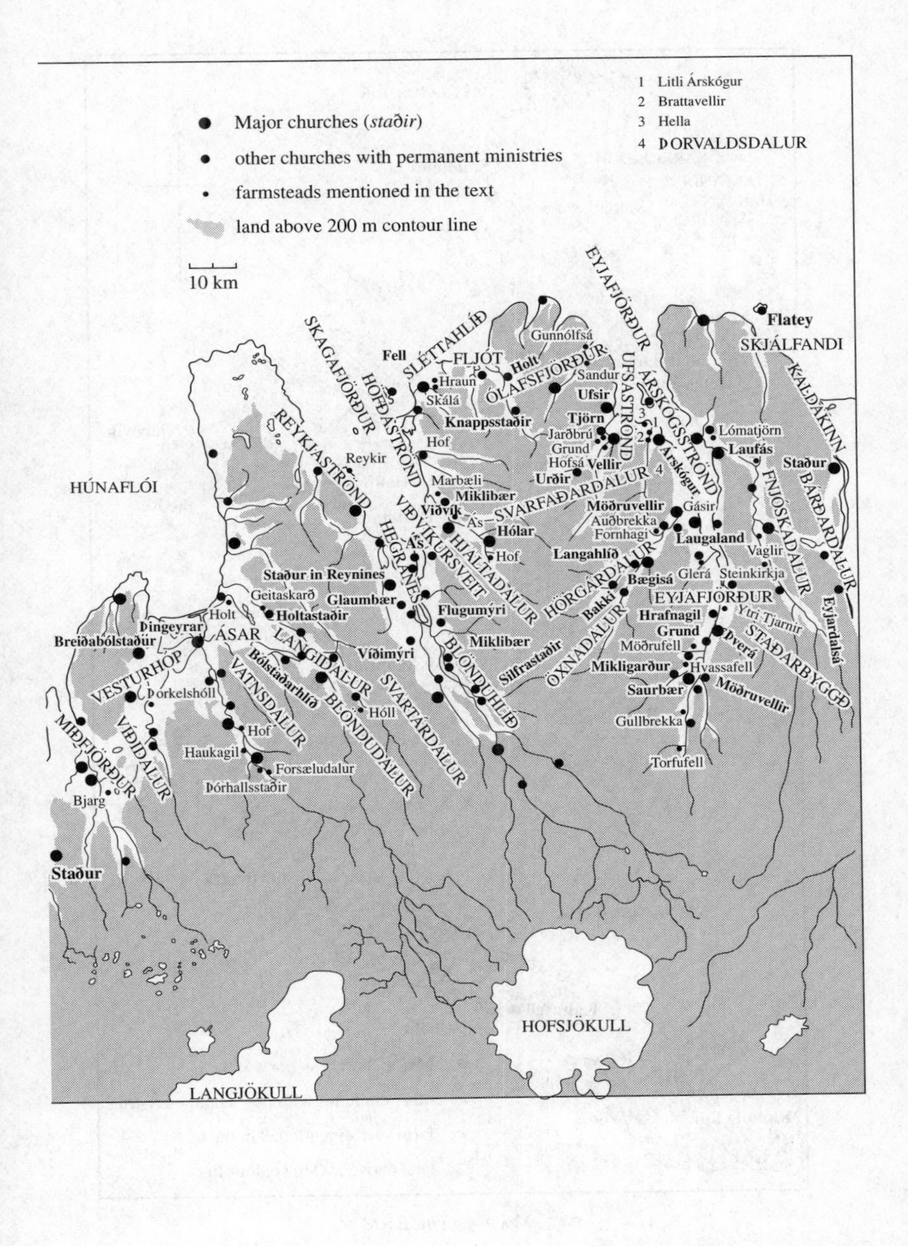
1 Litli Árskógur
2 Brattavellir
3 Hella
4 ÞORVALDSDALUR
Major churches (*staðir*)
other churches with permanent ministries
farmsteads mentioned in the text
land above 200 m contour line
10 km
EYJAFJÖRÐUR
SKAGAFJÖRÐUR
SLÉTTAHLÍÐ
Fell
FLJÓT
Holt
Gunnólfsá
ÓLAFSFJÖRÐUR
Sandur
Hraun
Skálá
Knappsstaðir
Ufsir
Tjörn
Jarðbrú
Grund
Hofsá
Vellir
Urðir
UFSASTRÖND
ÁRSKÓGSSTRÖND
Árskógur
Flatey
SKJÁLFANDI
KALDAKINN
Lómatjörn
Laufás
Staður
FNJÓSKADALUR
BÁRÐARDALUR
HÖFÐASTRÖND
REYKJASTRÖND
Reykir
Hof
Marbæli
Miklibær
Viðvík
Ás
SVARFAÐARDALUR
Möðruvellir
Gásir
Auðbrekka
Fornhagi
Laugaland
Vaglir
HÚNAFLÓI
VIÐVÍKURSVEIT
HEGRANES
HJALTADALUR
Hólar
Langahlíð
Staður in Reynines
Glerá
Steinkirkja
Geitaskarð
Glaumbær
HÖRGÁRDALUR
Bægisá
EYJAFJÖRÐUR
Holt
Holtastaðir
Flugumýri
Bakki
Hrafnagil
Ytri Tjarnir
Þingeyrar
ÁSAR
Grund
STAÐARBYGGÐ
Breiðabólstaður
LANGIDALUR
Miklibær
Víðimýri
Silfrastaðir
Möðrufell
Þverá
Eyjardalsá
VESTURHÓP
Bólstaðarhlíð
VATNSDALUR
BLÖNDUHLÍÐ
ÖXNADALUR
Mikligarður
Hvassafell
Saurbær
Möðruvellir
Þorkelshóll
Hóll
SVARTÁRDALUR
BLÖNDUDALUR
Gullbrekka
MIÐFJÖRÐUR
VÍÐIDALUR
Hof
Haukagil
Forsæludalur
Torfufell
Þórhallsstaðir
Bjarg
Staður
HOFSJÖKULL
LANGJÖKULL

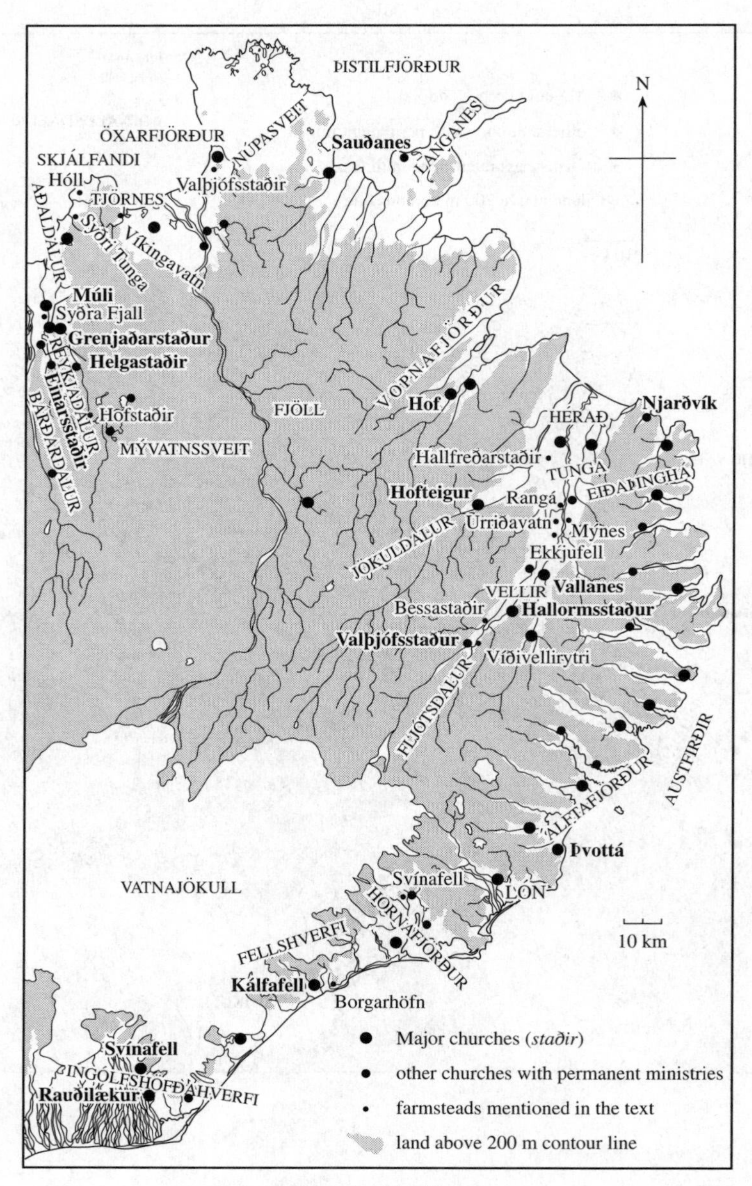

MAP 5. *The East*

INDEX

The alphabetical order of the Icelandic and Scandinavian characters is aábcdðeéfghiíjklmnoópqrstuúüvwxyzþæöøäå
Icelanders and medieval people are ordered by first name.